International Federation of Library Associations and Institutions
Fédération Internationale des Associations de Bibliothécaires et des Bibliothèques
Internationaler Verband der bibliothekarischen Vereine und Institutionen
Международная Федерация Библиотечных Ассоциаций и Учреждений
Federación Internacional de Asociaciones de Bibliotecarios y Bibliotecas

IFLA Universal Bibliographic Control
and International MARC Programme
Deutsche Bibliothek, Frankfurt am Main

UBCIM Publications – New Series Vol 18

An Annotated Guide
to Current National Bibliographies

2nd completely revised edition

by Barbara L. Bell

K · G · Saur   München 1998

UBCIM Publications
New Series

Edited by Marie-France Plassard

Die Deutsche Bibliothek – CIP-Einheitsaufnahme

Bell, Barbara L. : An annotated guide to current national bibliographies /
by Barbara L. Bell. [International Federation of Library Associations and
Institutions, IFLA Universal Bibliographic Control and International
MARC Programme, Deutsche Bibliothek, Frankfurt am Main]. – 2 nd,
completely rev. ed. – München : Saur, 1998
  (UBCIM publications ; N.S., Vol. 18)
  ISBN 3-598-11376-5

© 1998 by International Federation of Library Associations
and Institutions, The Hague, Netherlands
Alle Rechte vorbehalten / All Rights Strictly Reserved
K.G. Saur Verlag GmbH & Co.KG, München 1998
Part of Reed Elsevier

Printed in the Federal Republic of Germany

Druck / Printed by Strauss Offsetdruck GmbH, Mörlenbach
Binden / Bound by Buchbinderei Schaumann, Darmstadt
ISBN 3-598-11376-5

THE *NEW* ANNOTATED GUIDE
TO CURRENT NATIONAL BIBLIOGRAPHIES

TABLE OF CONTENTS

***ANALYTIC TABLE OF CONTENTS FOR CURRENT
NATIONAL BIBLIOGRAPHIES AND COUNTRY ENTRIES
(Alphabetically Arranged)**

A Δ beside an individual country in this analytic table indicates that there is
no separate entry listed, but it is covered in one of the **Regional
Bibliographies** [e.g., Bahamas Δ (see **The CARICOM Bibliography**),
Netherlands Antilles Δ (see **Bibliografía Actual del Caribe**), Solomon
Islands Δ (see **South Pacific Bibliography**)] or it is within the scope of
another country [e.g.,Greenland Δ (see **Denmark**)].

Individual Countries:

Regional Bibliographies:

LIST OF ABBREVIATIONS AND ACRONYMS

Most abbreviations are self explanatory in the country entries. Listed below are the most frequently used and more universal abbreviations.

AACR	Anglo-American Cataloguing Rules
AACR2	Anglo-American Cataloguing Rules, 2d edition
AACR2R	Anglo-American Cataloguing Rules, 2d edition, revised
AACR67	Anglo-American Cataloguing Rules, l967 edition
AFNOR	Association Française de Normalisation
ALA	American Library Association
AL,B	Accessions List, Brazil
AL,EA	Accessions List, Eastern Africa
AL,ESA	Accessions List, Eastern and Southern Africa
AL,ME	Accessions List, Middle East
AL,SA	Accessions List, South Asia
AL,SEA	Accessions List, Southeast Asia
ALECSO	Arab League Educational, Cultural and Scientific Organization
ASCOBIC	African Standing Committee on Bibliographic Control
ASEAN	Association of South East Asian Nations
BBK	Bibliotechno-bibliograficheskaia klassifikatsiia
BSTW	Bibliographical Services Throughout the World
CARICOM	Caribbean Community
CDU	Classification décimale universalle
CERLAL	Centro Regional para el Fomento del Libro en América Latina y el Caribe
CIP	Cataloguing-in-Publication
COM	Computer output on microform
COMLA	Commonwealth Library Association
CONSER	Conservation of Serials (North American Project)
DDC	Dewey Decimal Classification

DBMS	Data Base Management System
FOBID	Federation of Organizations of the Library, Information and Documentation
GIP	General Information Programme (Unesco)
HLAS	Handbook of Latin American Studies
HMSO	Her Majesty's Stationery Office
ICNB	International Conference on National Bibliographies, Paris, 1977
IFLA	International Federation of Library Associations and Institutions
IGO	International Governmental Organization
ISBD	International Standard Bibliographic Description
ISBD(CM)	International Standard Bibliographic Description (Cartographic Materials)
ISBD(G)	International Standard Bibliographic Description (General)
ISBD(M)	International Standard Bibliographic Description (Monographs)
ISBD(NBM)	International Standard Bibliographic Description (Non-Book Materials)
ISBD(PM)	International Standard Bibliographic Description (Printed Music)
ISBD(S)	International Standard Bibliographic Description (Serials)
ISBN	International Standard Book Number
ISDS	International Serials Data System
ISO	International Organization for Standardization
ISSN	International Standard Serial Number
LC	Library of Congress Classification Number
LCCN	Library of Congress Control Number or Library of Congress Card Number
LC/MARC	Library of Congress Machine-Readable Cataloguing
LCSH	Library of Congress Subject Headings
MARC	Machine-Readable Cataloguing
MARC2	Machine-Readable Cataloguing, 2d edition
MLA	Modern Language Association
MLC	Minimal Level Cataloguing
MUMS	Multiple Use MARC System of Library of Congress Information System
NOTIS	Northwestern Online Total Integrated System Data Base
NST	New Serial Titles
NUC	National Union Catalogue (Library of Congress)
NZBN	New Zealand Bibliographic Network
OCLC	Online Computer Library Center Data Base, Dublin, Ohio
OECD	Organization for Economic Coordination and Development
OIOC	Oriental and India Office Collections, British Library
QIPL,ESA	Quarterly Index to Periodical Literature, Eastern and Southern Africa
PRECIS	Preserved Context Indexing System
PGI	General Information Programme
RAK	Regeln für die alphabetische Katalogisierung

SALALM	Section on Acquisition of Latin American Library Materials
SEAPRINT	Southeast Asian Imprints
SCOLMA	Standing Conference on Library Materials on Africa
sn	Serial number; used with LCCN
SOAS	School of Oriental and African Studies, University of London
UBC	Universal Bibliographic Control
UDC	Universal Decimal Classification
UNIMARC	Universal MARC format
Unesco	United Nations Educational, Scientific and Cultural Organization
UNISIST	Intergovernmental Program for Cooperation in the field of Scientific and Technological Information

ACKNOWLEDGEMENTS

As with the first edition this *New Annotated Guide* stands in tribute to many libraries, librarians and library staff around the world. Somewhere, someone seemed ready to help and provide another piece of crucial information to complete what sometimes appeared to be an unsolvable puzzle. Many of those individuals who graciously assisted with information are acknowledged as verifiers, in the Notes and Comments sections, and in footnotes of the current national bibliographies discussed.

As the Introduction makes clear, this *New* edition has many changes due to major geo-political changes in our globe over the past decade and to advances in communications technology. For this edition I also had the advantage of attending numerous IFLA conferences from Brighton to Paris, Stockholm, Istanbul, Moscow, Barcelona, New Delhi, Beijing, and Copenhagen, and serving as a member of The Standing Committee on Bibliographies. My colleagues in IFLA have been a source of professional growth and joy for me. Correspondence with libraries and librarians around the world was vastly facilitated by fax, the Internet and e-mail. This put me in personal contact with librarians throughout the world and kept me current with many developments in the world of national bibliographies as they were occurring. This direct contact with librarians around the world is a new dimension in the preparation of this edition and one I value greatly.

It is important to mention my year, 1994, in The Republic of Namibia, where, as an American Library Association Library Fellow, I helped The National Library of Namibia establish their first national bibliography. The first *Namibia National Bibliography*, covering from 1990 (their year of Independence) through 1992, was officially launched in April of 1997. I wish to thank Johan Loubser, Director of the National Library, Louise Hansmann, editor of the *Namibia National Bibliography*, Robert Doyle, former director of the ALA Library Fellows program, and Helen Picard, former Public Affairs Officer of the USIS office in Windhoek, Namibia. This experience gave me the unusual opportunity not only to "describe" national bibliographies but to be a part of the creation of a new one.

Librarians across the United States have been extremely helpful in sharing their knowledge about a particular title, and in sending Interlibrary loans or photocopies. The University of Florida Latin American Collection Library was particularly responsive.

Colleagues at The College of Wooster and in its Libraries were always ready to help. Margaret Powell and Jennifer McMullen have been supportive friends throughout this process. Heidi Haverkamp, a senior at The College of Wooster, has helped enormously in the technical production and editing of this book over the past 16 months.

It is very difficult to start naming persons who have contributed to the *New Guide*, but I will acknowledge those libraries where major research was carried out and where numerous area specialists were generous with their time. The libraries were: The Library of Congress, The British Library, University of London SOAS Library, The University Library, Cambridge, Rhodes House Library, Oxford, The University of Edinburgh, The National Library of Scotland, The National Library of Wales, Princeton University Library, Saint Johns University, Collegeville, Minnesota, The University of Minnesota, The University of Wisconsin (Madison), The University of Illinois

(Urbana-Champaign), Indiana University, The University of Michigan, Biblioteksjänst AB Library, Lund, Sweden, and The College of Wooster.

Several area specialists went that "extra mile" in correspondence and conversations to provide me with information. I want to acknowledge the assistance of the African and Middle East Division, Library of Congress, with special thanks to George Selim and Lee Avdoyan. Librarians in other libraries were Helen Sullivan, David Hirsch, Dan Hazen, and Carl Horn. Many others are thanked specifically in footnotes.

I wish to thank the many people who assisted with translations. They are individually mentioned in respective Notes and Comments and in footnotes. Of particular help were colleagues and international students at The College of Wooster and in the town of Wooster. We are enriched at the College to have international students from many countries. Many work in the Libraries and eagerly helped with translations, making a seemingly impenetrable text become clear.

Another kind of translating dealt with computers. We have talented staff and students at the College with computer skills who could decode computer files from many countries into a legible file which made sense. Kim Strollo, User Services, Academic Computing, was very helpful in working through tough areas.

I thank Dorothy Anderson again for her revised Foreword. She has been my mentor in this field, and for her confidence I am grateful.

The College of Wooster has supported my work through a Library Research leave the summer of 1997, and through grants for research and library visits from their Henry Luce III Fund for Distinguished Scholars. They have also been generous in supporting my work with IFLA.

Last, I want to especially thank my family for supporting me once again through this project. Without the support of my husband, Richard, this revision would not have come to fruition. For his ability to understand and listen, and to willingly take on some of my other responsibilities temporarily, I am grateful.

Overall, I value having undertaken this project for the contacts I have made throughout the world and the appreciation I have gained about the countries and cultures of this world. I look forward to continued association with IFLA and to further involvement with the world of current national bibliographies!

Wooster, Ohio   Barbara L. Bell
October 10, 1997

FOREWORD

by
Dorothy Anderson

In the past twenty years the importance of national bibliographic control as one aspect of an overall plan for a country's library development has been recognized and vigorously promoted: that is, establishing within a country the means and the legislation whereby its publications are identified, recorded and preserved. National bibliographic control is not a new concept, although only recently accorded the distinction of its own label, and can be identified as early as the seventeenth century. For example, legal deposit, the basis of national bibliographic control, under which publishers are required by law to deposit copies of new publications, was established in Denmark as long ago as 1697. Since then in many countries, as a consequence of planning and legislation, collections of national publications have been established and recorded. More recently among the newer countries there has been recognition of the value of national bibliographic control, especially where there has been the need to distinguish or create a cultural, literary and even historical awareness. Knowing what is published within a country, conserving and recording those publications, is one way of providing an image to the outside world of what the country is like and where it is going.

The idea of a regular publication which lists new publications -- a national bibliography -- is also not new, and the national bibliographies of some European countries are made up of more than one hundred annual volumes. It was not until 1958, however, that there was an examination of the purposes of the national bibliography with recommendations for its organizational base. The 1958 Symposium on National Libraries in Europe, in considering the history and functions of the traditional old established national library, envisaged a future more active role, maintaining that the national library should be a focal point in national library development, even perhaps at the center of a national library service.

With the impact of the international programme of Universal Bibliographic Control (UBC) in the early 1970's, the aims and responsibilities of the national library in advancing national bibliographic control were further defined. In part this came about in recognition of the fact that in some countries a national library did not exist, or at least not under that title; or two or more existed carrying out different functions. The further analysis which followed concentrated on responsibilities and functions rather than on organizations, with the recognition -- or recommendation -- that within every country there should be an organization, (which could be part of a national library, or attached to a national library, or a separate body), which would be responsible for the range of activities basic to national bibliographic control and with its primary objective the production of the national bibliography. Such an organization, whatever its title and administrative structure, would be presumed to be acting as a country's "national bibliographic agency".

In the documents relating to the UBC programme the responsibilities of the national bibliographic agency were set out in detail: preparing the authoritative and comprehensive bibliographic records for new publications issued in the country in accordance with accepted international bibliographic standards; and publishing those records with the shortest possible delay in a national bibliography which appears regularly. In this way each national bibliography would serve as an acquisition tool and its records could be used and re-used in other countries. In the first stages of advancing the UBC programme, attention was paid equally to developing the required international bibliographic standards for making the records and to establishing standards for the national bibliography. The consequences of this impetus can be seen in the recommendations of the 1977 International Congress on National Bibliographies, with its agreed framework for the national bibliographic agency.

What also emerged during this period of developing UBC were the importance of the national bibliography within a country and the necessarily active role that a national bibliographic agency played in supporting national library development plans; and also as a natural corollary the energetic and imaginative work undertaken by the staff of such agencies. In preparing the bibliographic records for the national bibliography, the agency could be required to move into areas of historical and geographical as well as bibliographical research: in finding out about national authors past and present, in establishing national name patterns, in identifying historical or geographical details relating to the country. Such research became essential if an authority file of national authors were to be established, if worldwide classification schemes were to be adapted for national use. In many countries the national bibliographic agency has been in the forefront in bibliographic development: in initiating new cataloguing codes; in introducing new forms of technology; in organizing seminars and training schemes. From the agency thereafter there could be the overall involvement with libraries, library associations, and other professionals concerned with book development, publishing and bibliographic recording.

Worldwide there is now acceptance of the importance of the national bibliography and also of the necessity that it be prepared in accordance with international bibliographic standards and practices, irrespective of whether the national publishing output is 300 items a year or 3,000 or 30,000. At the same time there is the ready recognition that the production of national bibliographies of such differing sizes will require differing technology in reproduction.

Since the 1977 International Congress a number of new national bibliographies have appeared and some of the old established bibliographies have changed their content and style of production in accordance with the demands of users, publishers, new technology and the Congress recommendations. Information about the new and the revised national bibliographies has been available piece meal, in articles, publicity leaflets, conference papers, and in the actual products -- the printed issues or magnetic tapes or microfiche of the various national bibliographies. But there has been no survey of the overall picture of change and development. Directories of national bibliographies that have been published have been limited in scope -- to Third World countries and to those of the British Commonwealth. From this point of view it is very satisfactory to have in this *Annotated Guide* a worldwide account of what national bibliographies are being produced and in what form. It is accepted, of course, that the *Annotated Guide* cannot be complete and that its contents will be out of date for some entries in some details as soon as it is published. Indeed, if the *Annotated Guide* were not to become out of date, this would present a sad picture of national bibliographic control, with the implications that the situation was static and that there could be no further developments.

Publishing and book production, however, can never be static, and it is natural and inevitable that there should be continuing developments in national bibliographic control -- in its conception, limits, and means of enforcement and maintenance. It would seem at present that change and development are more prevalent than keeping to the traditional ways. On the other hand, there have been the enormous technological changes in the ways in which bibliographic records can be produced, so that the national bibliography in machine readable form or on microfiche is taken for granted in some countries. With automation has come an increased interest from publishers, more particularly in the market potential of the record in the national bibliography that appears pre-publication, that is, the Cataloguing-in-Publication (CIP) record. At the same time there has been a very large increase in the number of publications which are being produced, with the extra strain upon the resources of the national bibliographic agency to produce records efficiently and speedily, making use of CIP both as a necessity for speed and as an advantage from the point of view of publishers and acquisition librarians. New forms of publications are being produced by traditional book publishers, and traditional style books are appearing under the imprint of new style publishers using new technology. The national bibliographic agency, as well as coping with quantity, is being forced to examine what should be recorded, what is meant by "national publications", and to re-examine legal deposit stipulations to see whether definitions encompass the new style publications. There is the very practical difficulty of trying to define and distinguish publications in an area where technological developments are advancing faster than the terminology that describes them.

In some countries with a larger publishing output the national bibliographic agencies are having to re-assess traditional policies of freely available access to and transfer of bibliographic records, and to look at the possibilities of a more restrictive policy, on the basis that information is not free and that the records produced in one country cannot be expected to be in use worldwide without some charge granted to the producing agency. At the same time, in other parts of the world, the introduction of a microcomputer and a microfiche reader have made it possible for a national bibliographic agency to have access to international databases and to plan the establishment and maintenance of something as basic to national bibliographic control as a union catalogue of national serials.

The *Annotated Guide* provides a survey of national bibliographic control as it exists today, in so far as the successful production of a national bibliography presumes that there is an active bibliographic agency preparing and producing the records. Indeed, one of the more pleasing aspects of the *Annotated Guide* is that each entry, in setting out details of the national bibliography, is also providing a framework of information about library development, about the activities of the bibliographic agency, and about the overall pattern of national bibliographic control within the country.

As often noted in the *Annotated Guide*, a most unsatisfactory aspect of many current bibliographies is that of lateness in production. In today's terms the national bibliography should be serving the dual purposes of recording for posterity a country's publications and of acting as an acquisition tool, providing information within the country and to the outside world of what is published and how those publications can be obtained. It is apparent from examination of entries in the *Annotated Guide* that in too many countries the tasks of preparing the national records and of producing those records in a printed form have imposed too great an effort on resources of staff and possibly of technology. It appears that the national bibliography in some countries is still being produced as "an historical record rather than as an acquisition tool". It was in recognition of the difficulties of producing the national bibliography that the 1977 International Congress in its deliberations insisted that the physical appearance of printed issues of the national bibliography was not important; the objectives were on standards for contents and layout, not whether the physical issues were printed as the end product of computer technology or were typed and duplicated. It would seem, from this point of view, that there is still much to be done in advocating the importance of the national bibliography in building up the UBC network of contributing national component parts which inform on what has been published now and today worldwide. The compilation and publication of the *Annotated Guide* may perhaps encourage this particular aspect of national bibliographic control. In any case it is a valuable contribution to international access to information, which is the objective of the programme of UBC.

London, 1986

It would have been impossible when the *Foreword* to the first edition of *An Annotated Guide* was written, to anticipate all that has happened in the past eleven years, more especially the dramas of political and geographical changes, and the rapidity of technological advances, with the consequent acceptance of an information world of global immediacy. In 1986 computers and information technology were, for a large proportion of the public, specialized worlds which other people dealt with. Now the Internet has become a familiar and recognizable concept, and though we may not ourselves be users of high technology, we know of "surfing the web," we see web site addresses on the television, have friends who believe that we too should be users of e-mail. The demand for global information has expanded, and the suppliers of that information have multiplied in number, in kind and in depth. Indeed, information available appears to have outstripped our needs and our individual ability to manage it.

Is a national bibliography as relevant as it was twenty years ago when the International Congress on National Bibliographies set out its recommendations? The development of national libraries and national bibliographies has never been a high priority with governmental planning agencies. But providing information is. In the search for information in the world of Internet and with the many information suppliers of today what is the role of the national bibliography?

It remains constant: the definitions provided in the 1986 edition of *An Annotated Guide* and in the 1974 text of *Universal Bibliographic Control* still apply: the national bibliographic agency undertakes the preparation and production of the records of national publications. Today the differences are the increased range of physical and non-physical forms in which those "publications" may be available, and the varied production solutions provided by high technology. But just as the first purpose of national bibliographic control remains the same, so do its basic problems whatever the technology: finding out what has been published, obtaining the publications, and producing records of those publications without delay, with the basic requirements for the national bibliographic agency of resources of manpower and equipment. For many countries those resources are now inadequate.

The *Foreword* to the first edition presented the problems and suggested some of the solutions currently available. Most of these are still at hand, but one solution, addressed at the problem of timeliness, that of Cataloguing-in-Publication seems to have disappeared. There is, however, evidence of closer working relationships between bibliographic agencies and publishers, which could enhance the speed of the production of the record without CIP. It is in the way in which the bibliographic records are produced where divergences have multiplied and with those variations the increased difficulties in planning for or in expediting the exchange of compatible records. Are there ways in which the records from the high technology world can be made available for the use of libraries in countries where librarians do not sit in front of screens, and see no possibility of doing so in the future?

In 1983 in a paper presented at the IFLA Conference I presented a scenario of a world of "information rich" and "information poor," with the danger that the information pertaining to some countries could well become the property of others, then of necessity requiring to be bought back by the original source, which might not have funding available for purchase. Today's scenario is no better: according to the latest report from UNCTAD (United Nations Conference on Trade and Development), the inequality between developing countries has increased, with the very poorest countries in the world falling further and further behind; as a consequence, the gap between the "information rich" and "information poor" is widening. What practical solutions can be offered to those countries where the production of a national bibliography does not seem a high priority or even relevant?

It is pleasing to note, however, that the advantages of our new high technology world have made the preparations for this new edition the easier: to be able to send and check entries through e-mail, Internet and fax presents a life of bliss for all compilers of co-operative editing ventures -- as well as ensuring that the information contained in those entries is that much more up-to-date. It is to be hoped that the new edition will prove a valuable source tool for librarians and researchers and will enhance the basic concept of UBC: that each country as a component part of the "UBC web" accepts responsibility for recording its own publications.

Bath   `Dorothy Anderson
September 1997

In preparing the *Foreword* the following sources have been consulted:

Anderson, Dorothy P. "Universal Bibliographic Control." In *Encyclopedia of Library and Information Science*, vol. 37, suppl. 2, pp. 366-401. Edited by Allen Kent. New York and Basel: Marcel Dekker, Inc., 1984. Also published by the IFLA International Office for UBC, London, as Occasional Paper No. 10, 1982. (ISBN 0-903043-36-6).

Anderson, Dorothy P. "Waiting for Technology: An Overview of Bibliographic Services in the Third World." In: *IFLA Journal* 9 (no. 4 1983): 285-295.

Guidelines for the National Bibliographic Agency and the National Bibliography. Prepared by IFLA International Office for UBC. Paris: Unesco, [1979]. (PGI/79/WS/18).

International Cataloguing-in-Publication Meeting (Ottawa. 1982). *Proceedings*. Edited by the IFLA International Office for UBC. London: IFLA International for UBC, 1983. (ISBN 0-903043-39-4).

International Cataloguing and Bibliographic Control: various issues and articles from Vol. 17 (1988) -- Vol. 26 (1997). (Vol. 17, no. 1, p. 2, includes a review of the first edition of *An Annotated Guide*.)

National Libraries. Edited by Maurice B. Line and Joyce Line. Aslib Reader Series, vol. 1. London: Aslib, 1979. (ISBN 0-85142-116-4). This is a collection of articles on national libraries and includes papers and recommendations of the 1958 Symposium on National Libraries in Europe.

The Independent (London) 18 September 1997: analysis and discussion of UNCTAD's Trade and Development Report 1997.

THE *NEW* ANNOTATED GUIDE
TO CURRENT NATIONAL BIBLIOGRAPHIES

INTRODUCTION

WHAT IS A CURRENT NATIONAL BIBLIOGRAPHY?

A current national bibliography is a mirror that reflects the culture of a country. By looking at the current national bibliography one is able to learn about the uniqueness of a country. The emphasis on agriculture and technology, the make-up of its society through its various language publications, particular customs and ceremonies important in the life of the nation, the importance of education, literature and science, prominent literary authors of the time and political, social and religious trends within a country are all discernible. A current national bibliography should reflect the interests and unique characteristics of a country much as a mirror reflects the uniqueness of an individual.

Not only does a current national bibliography express the character and culture of a nation, but it also serves to present the history of the nation as it records its publishing output. By looking at current national bibliographies from years past, one is able to interpret literary, social, political, and technological emphases as well as cultural trends that are of historical importance to the life of the nation.

A current national bibliography also serves as a window to the country as it is distributed to other countries throughout the world. Through a nation's current national bibliography librarians, researchers, scholars, government officials, and the public become aware of titles published within a country or about a country. For librarians and bibliographers it can serve as an acquisition tool for collection development or as a verification aid. For researchers and scholars, it can identify new publications in their field. For governments and the general public, it can help identify changes in policies and politics and keep one abreast of current developments in a nation.

If a current national bibliography is to reflect effectively a nation's culture, it is important that it convey its information in a clear, timely fashion. A current national bibliography that is published several years after the time period covered, or is late in its distribution to other countries, can not serve as an effective acquisition tool, nor can it keep a user up-to-date on the current publishing life of a nation. Many titles cited in belated current national bibliographies may no longer be available for purchase because of the limited number of copies that were published.

In 1977, the International Congress on National Bibliographies (ICNB), held in Paris, established guidelines and recommendations for national bibliographies. These were created to help countries develop and shape an effective information tool and set standards that all nations might find useful. As one can imagine it was an impossible task to meet each nation's particular needs and create guidelines that would suit each situation. The ICNB set out to establish three levels of standards that would help nations create or strive toward an effective channel of information through its current national bibliography. A country could choose which level was best suited for them.

Appended to this book are the recommendations for national bibliographies drawn up at the International Congress.

In summary, in the country entries of this *New Annotated Guide*, 181 countries are listed of which there are 133 individual current national bibliographies or suitable substitutes, 12 regional bibliographies, Accessions Lists, or suitable substitutes. For 47 countries listed, no current national bibliographies could be traced, although often alternative sources for bibliographic information are given. 46 additional country names are listed in the analytical table of contents which are covered only in regional bibliographies or under other country entries. These are mostly small island countries of the South Pacific and Caribbean.

A WORLD OF CHANGES

This *New Annotated Guide* appears on the eve of a second International Conference on National Bibliographic Services to be held in Copenhagen, Denmark, in November 1998. In the twenty years since the Paris congress the world of national bibliographies has changed rapidly and since 1986 when the first *Annotated Guide* was published the *geo-political map* of the world has dramatically changed. These changes have affected this new volume significantly. For example, out of the disintegration of the Soviet Union has come both the Russian Federation and about fifteen newly independent countries including the Baltic states. The former Yugoslavia is currently divided into five parts. Czechoslovakia has officially divided into two parts. On the other hand, the two Germanys have united, as have North and South Yemen. At least 28 new countries have been created since 1986. With these geographic changes come changes both in a country's name and in its ethnic focus. Sometimes, unrest and instability continue to exist as new governments establish priorities and set new agendas. All of these geo-political changes directly affect the frequency, title, and scope of a national bibliography if not its very existence.

This is also a decade of phenomenal growth in *automation* which has spawned a variety of spin-off products and new formats. These changes make possible the development of new products and new access capabilities for those countries which are fortunate to have advanced technology to sustain them. The exchange of bibliographic information across geographic borders is occurring more rapidly as national and international networks are being created to facilitate access of information in ways not imagined ten (or even five) years ago. At the 1977 International Congress on National Bibliographies (Paris) recommendations were focused on printed bibliographies, with automated products only an "afterthought." CD-ROMs and the Internet were not household names as we know them today. In 1998 at the International Conference on National Bibliographic Services (Copenhagen) we will be focusing for the first time on recommendations for automated national bibliographic products as well as for printed sources. At present, there are six countries which offer their national bibliography only in electronic format: Australia, Malaysia, Mexico, Portugal, Singapore, and the United States.

A third effect on national bibliographies has been *global economic change*. Rapid market changes and the attempts of developing countries to catch up with such changes alter priorities. Some countries struggling to establish and maintain a new economic direction are also facing severe drought, famine, or civil war -- or have unstable electrical and communications infrastructures. These countries will not have the publication of a current national bibliography as a top priority. There are more pressing problems and priorities.

Even with (and perhaps in spite of) the three factors mentioned above, there have been some encouraging trends in national bibliographies within the last twelve years.

With the dissolution of the USSR and the former Yugoslavia, for example, national bibliographies are more clearly reflecting the specific ethnicities of their citizenries. Book publishing in the language of the country is encouraged, and an effort is made to include all titles published in the country. For example, where only about 30% of selected Georgian books were published in the USSR's *Knizhnaíã letopis*, now all of the books published in Georgia are listed, with a majority of them published in the Georgian language. The Latvian national bibliography reflects the heritage of its culture and language, as do those of Kazakhstan, Slovenia, and Croatia. Language, culture, social problems, trends in education, political persuasions are all recorded by the publishing output of the "new" countries. It is possible to see a more complete and authentic image of the country through its own publications, most of which are now written in languages not commonly encouraged under a previous regime. The national bibliography is often understood as a symbol of nationhood as Namibia's prime minister stated in his preface to the new *Namibia National Bibliography*, launched in April 1997.

National bibliographies are being affected by automation in several ways. In some cases the data for the national bibliography are already part of an existing database, or it may be that the national bibliography is now available only in CD-ROM format, or that it is available in several formats.

Since the first edition of *An Annotated Guide* countries have made many improvements in their national bibliographies to meet the recommendations of the *ICNB* 1977. Several countries have added features such as indexes, introductions, and classification schemes where none existed in national bibliographies produced before the mid-1980s. Some previously mimeographed national bibliographies are now attractively produced using desk-top publishing software and printers.

Accessibility to information is literally at our fingertips. Several national libraries maintain Internet sites which allow us to enter their national bibliography databases directly. Electronic services have organized information for users to retrieve (such as Australia has done); CD-ROM products provide multi-approaches which make it possible to gather quickly and efficiently needed information; and telneting, and surfing the net allow us to access distant databases of national bibliographic information almost instantaneously.

There are now more countries which have entered into cooperative arrangements with publishers, booksellers, and national libraries/national bibliographic agencies. Working together to set standards and procedures for the common good and towards "cooperative" goals is beneficial to all. Denmark, Great Britain, the Netherlands, Austria, and Italy are excellent examples where this kind of cooperation has improved the product and its timeliness as well as facilitating its distribution to meet the needs of publishers, booksellers, the public, and libraries. All of these many changes are reflected throughout the entries in this *New Annotated Guide*.

WHAT'S NEW IN THE NEW GUIDE?

The methodology for the first edition was to locate and examine the national bibliographies and analytically describe these titles. The primary support group was the subject or area specialist in libraries I visited. For this *New* edition, I wanted to include additional information (such as OCLC numbers, automation, formats, etc.), update information (e.g., new legal deposit laws, new enhancements in the national bibliography), add new countries, and include future plans within a country's bibliographic world. To do this, I needed once more to examine the most current national bibliography available from each country. In addition, I sent newly drafted entries to national libraries of countries and asked that the director or the appropriate person verify that the information was accurate. In a cover letter I also asked questions to clarify specific problem areas, to verify the most recent legal deposit law, and to find out what changes were planned for the national bibliography in the near future. Although 14 libraries did not respond, most did and the responses have been gratifying and very helpful. The national libraries are grateful for interest in their national bibliography, are pleased to be included, and have provided additional bibliographic information. This approach provided them with a chance to explain, for example, that the bibliography was late for two years while the bibliography was being automated. With each national library's additional review and input this second edition is more comprehensive and its contents have been enhanced. Furthermore, it has verified my work at the source.

I am including many new national bibliography titles which were not in the first edition -- a few of these are China, Bahrain, Tokelau, Uganda, Nicaragua, Cyprus, United Arab Emirates, Democratic Republic of Congo, and Greece (although some of these had substitutes or different titles described in the first edition). The majority of new titles to the second edition are from the break-up of the former USSR. These are newly described in this book since I did not include titles which covered a division or specific region within a country in the first edition. Anyone who is a specialist in Slavic Studies can appreciate the complexity of this investigation! When I began my investigations there were no guides to lead me to appropriate titles; now I have an information network created. I hope this will be a useful compilation for those doing research in this area and in acquisitions. As far as I am aware, no current title exists with this new information.

In addition, some countries in other parts of the world have established independence and have begun new national bibliographies, such as Namibia with its independence in 1990. Several countries had a title change in the national bibliography because of political changes, e.g., the Czech Republic, Bulgaria, Hungary, Belarus, Romania, and Lithuania. Some of them changed titles as I was working on them!

In the second edition, improvements are noted as national bibliographies comply with ICNB recommendations. Some examples are that Madagascar and Venezuela has now added the ISSN; Albania and Bulgaria are now organized by UDC and not by 20-plus subject classes, and have added enhancements such as ISSN; Austria and Cuba have changed to internationally accepted classification schemes. Bangladesh has assigned individual numbers to books rather than classifying by groups, and has improved its indexing, as has Turkey; Iran has DDC and LC numbers listed; Syria has added a periodicals section since 1985, Luxembourg has added an audio-visual section; and Uruguay added an abbreviations list and an introduction, to name a few.

Some countries, such as Singapore, Norway, and Sweden, have new legal deposit laws which cover materials in new formats.

While these new titles and developments are encouraging, there are some exemplary national bibliographies which are in hiatus or are now defunct. Some countries have seen no activity in the last ten years. In corresponding with librarians in the country, most are optimistic that when times are better politically or economically, they will again be able to continue the title. One example is Fiji which had a national bibliography following ICNB recommendations. Their publications are included in the regional South Pacific Bibliography, but it is sad to see *FNB* in hiatus. Several countries in Africa, the Caribbean, in Latin America, and elsewhere have seen no recent bibliographic activity--e.g., Bénin, Ecuador, Dominican Republic, Honduras, and Guyana. One hesitates to close the entry. As one subject bibliographer stated: "I could say that the title is now deceased but I wouldn't be surprised if it turned up on my desk next week." If there has been activity since the last edition, even if now ceased, the title has been included with explanatory notes. Puerto Rico and Laos are examples. In Laos' case, there may be a happy outcome. As will be seen in the section on Regional Bibliographies, activity is in severe decline, especially with the recent discontinuation of The Library of Congress *Accessions Lists*.

As mentioned earlier, automation has had an impact on national bibliographic services and the format of the national bibliography. It is a rare country which has not seen some changes in this area; if not in the last ten years, it may be coming in the near future. For the most part, automation has improved the quality, timeliness, and access to bibliographic information. New features enhance the national bibliography, including indexes where there were none, or MARC records in a classified listing which replaces a pre-AACR2 bibliographic format listed in an alphabetical sequence. Not all automated changes can be accommodated or accessed easily, particularly in Third World countries. It will be interesting to see if countries who have their national bibliography only available in CD-ROM format will see an increase or decrease in the use of the title. In my own research, I had a problem locating research libraries that now carry the CD-ROM version of a title which previously came in paper or microfiche. Libraries were unaware that the continuation of the paper title was in a CD-ROM format. The subscription to a national bibliography on CD-ROM usually costs a great deal more than the paper, and access is available only to those who have the equipment and technology. Libraries without CD-ROM readers do not have access to the CD-ROM information. Here the inequalities between the information-rich and information-poor countries have created a widening gap.

A GLANCE AT THE FUTURE

A number of common problems remain much the same as with the first edition. While some countries have used automation to increase the frequency and timeliness of their national bibliography, there are still countries for which the *frequency of publication* is not as often as the ICNB recommendations suggests or as often as the country has stated in their introduction. *Legal deposit legislation* may not be as effective as needed, and does not include enforcement clauses. *Distribution* continues to be a problem in some countries, especially distribution to other countries. Titles may go out-of-print before libraries know of its existence. I have become increasingly aware that area specialists, particularly for Latin America and Africa, can not rely solely on national bibliographies for acquisitions. They have had to find publisher contacts and catalogues, and reliable, timely bibliographic sources, wherever possible, to purchase titles from developing countries before a print run is depleted. All of these problems are usually directly tied to the economy and the current political atmosphere of a country.

Throughout my research and revisions, it is clear that national bibliographies are held to be important within the country. The British library community affirmed this in a recent seminar on the future of the national bibliography held at the British Library in London in June 1997. The national bibliography serves as a cooperative tool in cataloguing within libraries of that country, as an acquisitions tool, and as an historical record for libraries in and out of the country. Political and economic developments continue to have a decisive influence on a national bibliography. Legal deposit legislation has been upgraded in a number of countries to include non-print materials and enforcement clauses and has worked to establish cooperative efforts between publishers and national bibliographic agents.

It is essential that global sharing of resources be maintained and enhanced to achieve greater universal bibliographic control. The international library community should work toward cooperative means to realize this end. They must strive to weave a web of world-wide bibliographic information, "spun" from internationally standardized bibliographic records created by national bibliographic agencies. Such a world-wide web -- a UBC web -- could link countries and cultures, affording greater glimpses at local and national developments. Hopeful developments in weaving this web can be seen, for example, in OCLC's commitment to international issues. It has enabled Slovenia, Czech Republic and Australia to join the Library of Congress and the British Library in adding their bibliographic records to the OCLC database. These and other moves by utility information providers are costly ones and depend on an advanced level of automation, but they are nevertheless exciting. Continued assistance to developing countries by international organizations, utility information providers, and more affluent governments can help developing countries get their records into an internationally accepted form (as a current national bibliography is) and enable them to become another strand in the UBC web.

Many countries have met the recommendations drawn up in 1977 for mostly printed national bibliographies. It will be interesting to see what recommendations will be forthcoming from the International Conference on National Bibliographic Services (Copenhagen, 1998) that will include recommendations for new automated products and services.

A continuing joy comes in knowing how many dedicated librarians, scholars, book and data enthusiasts world-wide want to share their resources; that however large or small a nation may be, there is a pride of place reflected in their national bibliography and that a sense of equality in partnership is encompassed in their work.

HOW TO USE THIS ANNOTATED GUIDE

This *New Annotated Guide* is as "user friendly" as possible. It is also as inclusive and comprehensive of current national bibliographies as this vast and rapidly changing field allows. The energies of thousands of dedicated bibliographers throughout the world should not be hidden. This *New Annotated Guide* tries to gather that energy into a single source in order to promote greater communication between nations and cultures of the world, to assist the flow of information, and to encourage development toward standardization of current national bibliographies. To these ends, the information for each current national bibliography is organized under a systematic format that includes the following areas: Title, Compiler, Scope and Coverage, Contents, Cataloguing Rules and Classification Schemes Used, Entry Information, Arrangement, Indexes, Notes and Comments, Automation, Format and Services Available, Latest Issue Examined/Currency, Current Legal Deposit Laws, Available From, Selected Articles, and Verifier.

If it were determined that no current national bibliography exists for a country after research and consultations with area specialists, the author felt that this information should be conveyed rather than omitted. In these cases, any helpful alternatives or substitutes that have been useful for bibliographers or specialists, especially because of a lack of a current national bibliography, may also be included.

If the current national bibliography ceased since 1986, that information is given in the entry. However, if there was no activity in the intervening years, the national bibliography was closed unless the National Library said it was "in hiatus."

Name of Country: The authority list used to establish country names was *Names of States*. - London : IFLA, UBC, 1979. The shortened English name was selected with few exceptions. If a name was not included because of recent geographic changes, the current *Statesman's Yearbook* was used.

Title: The title was established by examining the volume. Verification of the title, years covered, place of publication, publisher, date of publication, frequency, brief notes (e.g., cover title or continues notes), DDC number, LC classification number, ISSN number or LCCN was accomplished by looking at the piece and/or by using OCLC, research libraries online catalogue, or *NST*. The title section information is formatted in the spirit of AACR2, consistently omitting the responsible agency element since this information is given as a publisher or under the heading of Compiler. In most cases the recent title is given, with the history of changes recorded in the Notes and Comments section. Frequency notes are given chronologically with current information first.

Compiler: The responsible body listed in the bibliography is given. In cases where this has changed over the years, the latest information is used.

Scope and Coverage: The scope of the current national bibliography is succinctly described. Elements mentioned are the official title (with title abbreviation to be used throughout the entry), the inclusion of the national and/or international imprints (whether the title is limited to imprints from a country or also includes entries about a country published elsewhere), time period covered and whether based on legal deposit legislation. Other significant information defining scope is given as necessary.

Types of publications included within the coverage of the title are listed in the next paragraph and are as inclusive as possible based on observation or as otherwise footnoted.

If an introduction stated specific exclusions or omissions, this information is given in a separate paragraph.

Contents: The parts of the bibliography as observed in the volumes checked are given in the order that they appear in the current national bibliography. In cases where contents vary, the latest issue checked is the one used to supply the information. If contents have varied substantially and it was possible to look at earlier volumes, contents of the volumes are given preceded by the date.

Cataloguing Rules and Classification Schemes Used: The cataloguing rules stated in the preliminary information and/or additional materials consulted are given. If this information is found elsewhere, it is footnoted.

The classification scheme used in the current national bibliography for the bibliographic entries is stated.

Entry Information: Elements of the bibliographic entry as related in the current national bibliography are listed. Care is taken to use the terminology provided in the preliminary pages of the bibliography. When this is not provided, information is derived from other sources such as letters from verifiers. If a substantial change has been made in current issues and earlier copies were available for observation, the changes are noted.

When entry information varies in sections other than the main bibliography section (a separate periodicals section, for example) this information is also analyzed.

Arrangement: The organization of the bibliographic section is stated.

Indexes: Various indexes are described. The number given to refer the user to the bibliographic entry is identified (e.g., classification number, entry number or page number). Information gathered on cumulative indexes or frequency of indexes is given when known.

Notes and Comments: This section is probably the most varied and extensive section in each country's entry. Specific or special information pertaining to the current national bibliography, historical information, information gathered from periodical articles read about the country's bibliography or points elaborated in the introduction of the current national bibliography, information provided through conversations, correspondence with librarians within the country or area specialists or librarians working on the national bibliography are all included here. Former titles and other titles that supplement the current national bibliography may be given, as well as CIP information or observation of change may be mentioned. In this section the author may also make some suggestions for improvement in meeting the recommendations of the ICNB where those seem appropriate. If a country is within the scope of a regional bibliography, it is mentioned here.

Latest Issue Examined/Currency: When possible, the currency of the bibliographic entries is noted. For some Asian and Middle Eastern countries it was not always possible to gather that information because of a different calendar or because of using another script where dates were not easily discernible.

Notation is given of the latest issue examined for information, the date of examination, and when it was published. The research for this *New Annotated Guide* has taken over two years, and while the temptation was great to constantly "update" on each research trip, it was impossible to do this and move ahead. At the time of examination the information was current. Information supplied from libraries also updates my information.

Automation: The hardware and software used to produce the bibliography is identified when possible through information in the national library, in literature, or by correspondence with the National Library in the country. The date the bibliography became automated is given if available. This section is new to this edition.

Format and Services Available: This is also a new section. Since one of the rapid changes is occurring in automation, the availability of information in various formats and services is necessary. Many national bibliographies are issued in printed form or in a variety of choices. A few countries only issue information electronically. Up-to-date information is from correspondence with the National Library.

Current Legal Deposit Laws: The most current legal deposit law as stated in the current national bibliography is given. If it was not located there, the

International Guide to Legal Deposit was used. If taken from a source other than the bibliography, the source is footnoted. Original research to discover a "new law in preparation" was not undertaken as part of this volume, although an effort was made to determine the status of some "pending" proposals by writing the National Library.

Available From: The subscription address is supplied. The address listed in the current national bibliography is given whenever possible. If this is not available, the address of the National Library as found in the *World of Learning* is given. *Ulriches International Periodicals Directory* was consulted for publishers' addresses when necessary. Some countries listed distributors; this information is provided when available.

Selected Articles: Articles of particular value for their informational content are listed in this section. Most, but not all, articles are listed in the bibliography.

Verifier: This is a new section. With permission I used the name of the person responding to my inquiry. Most countries responded. After several letters to some countries not responding, the statement "No rely received" is given.

Finally, with respect to the use of this *Annotated Guide*, the nature and purpose of the "Table of Contents" should be mentioned. The detailed "Table of Contents" serves as both a table of contents to the entire volume and as an index to the country entries section. Countries discussed in other entries (e.g., Greenland within the Denmark entry) are listed in the analytical table for easy identification. Countries only cited in regional bibliographies are also cross-listed in the analytical table (e.g., many South Pacific island countries are covered in the *South Pacific Bibliography*).

A BIBLIOGRAPHY ON CURRENT NATIONAL BIBLIOGRAPHIES

This *New Annotated Guide to Current National Bibliographies* has an extensive, though selective, bibliography. It has been significantly updated from the 1986 *Guide*. The selected bibliography includes books, articles and conference papers dealing with a variety of aspects of current national bibliographies as well as more general discussions of related topics such as Universal Bibliographic Control, and the documents of the International Congress of National Bibliographies held in Paris in 1977.

Part One lists general guides and source materials on national bibliographies which cover several countries or cross geographical regions. Part Two includes general sources by geographical regions: Africa, Central Asia, Eastern Europe and the Russian Federation, Latin America and the Caribbean, the Near and Middle East, North America, Oceania, South Asia and Southeast Asia, and Western Europe, with specific countries listed alphabetically under their respective geographical regions.

CONCLUDING REMARKS

It is hoped that this *New Annotated Guide* has a mirror-like quality, capturing bibliographic images as they are reflected from current national bibliographies around the world. A reader may find all of this information and its organization a bit overwhelming. The whole area of worldwide bibliographic control is somewhat labyrinthian. This *New Annotated Guide*, however, with all of its information is quite simple and straightforward. It cannot claim to be either complete or definitive. The information given is current but the nature and function of current national bibliographies are subject to change to reflect new developments and interests, new governmental policies, changing technologies and the changing culture of countries. This *New Annotated Guide* enhances the first Guide as a "base line" book, pulling together diverse and disparate materials and making them available to a worldwide audience. It is the author's hope that this book will encourage continued work in the field while making its own constructive contribution toward Universal Bibliographic Control.

CURRENT NATIONAL BIBLIOGRAPHIES

or SUITABLE SUBSTITUTES

AFGHANISTAN

No current national bibliography has been traced for Afghanistan. Due to the war during the last decade, distribution of publications has not been possible.[1]

Accessions List, Afghanistan (volumes 1-2; 1978-1979) merged with *Accessions List, India*; *Accessions List, Pakistan*, *Accessions List, Bangladesh* and *Accessions List, Sri Lanka* to become *AL,SA*. Afghanistan is included within the scope of *AL,SA* (ISSN 0271-6445).

Another source of information which may be the closest substitute available for a current national bibliography is *Kitab*. - vol. 1- . Kabul : The State Committee for Culture. Department of Culture. Division of Public Libraries, 1977- . Quarterly. Types of publications included are books, selected serials, and publications of the National Library (Pushtu), Islamabad, Pakistan. Publications omitted, according to Ibrahim Pourhadi, Iran and Central Asia Area Specialist, African and Middle East Division, Library of Congress, are official publications and newspapers. In 1982, *Kitab* issued a report in place of issue number 2 entitled "The Historic Course of Development of Libraries in Afghanistan" by Gh. F. Neelabe Raheemi.

Although the following title is not on-going, it may be of help in identifying national imprints for the time period covered: M. Ibrahim Stwodah. (*Kitābshināsī-i millī-i Afghānistān, mawẓū'l-i tawṣīfī, 26 Saratān 1352 tā imruz*). 1977. (Kabul University Library series; 11). Added title page: *Afghanistan's National Bibliography (Annotated), July 17, 1973 - August 17, 1977*. This is in Persian; prefatory material is in English. (LC: 77-938109).

CURRENT LEGAL DEPOSIT LAWS: According to *BSTW, 1975-1979* (p. 71) Afghanistan has legal deposit. No citation was given for the law in *International Guide to Legal Deposit*, *BSTW, 1975-1979* or in Pomassl's *Survey of Existing Legal Deposit Laws*.

VERIFIER: Ibrahim Pourhadi, Iran and Central Asia Area Specialist, African and Middle East Division, Library of Congress.

ALBANIA

TITLE: *Bibliografia kombëtare e librit që botohet në Republikën e Shqipërisë* [National bibliography of books published in the Republic of Albania]. - No. 1 (1991)-   . - Tiranë : Biblioteka Kombëtare, Sektori i Bibliografisë, 1991-   .
Quarterly.
Continues *Bibliografia kombëtare e librit që botohet në RPS të Shqipërisë*.
DDC: not found; LC: not found; LCCN: not found; OCLC: 34092580
ISSN not found

---

[1] In a 7 January 1997 telephone conversation, Mr. I. Pourhadi confirmed that the Library of Congress has not received publications from Afghanistan in the last ten years. Mr. James Armstrong, Library of Congress Field Director located in Islamabad, Pakistan, stated in a recent visit to the Library of Congress that he is hopeful publications soon will be available from Afghanistan.

COMPILER: Sektori i Bibliografisë, Biblioteka Kombëtare [Sector of Bibliography, National Library].

SCOPE AND COVERAGE: *Bibliografia kombëtare e librit që botohet në Republikën e Shqipërisë (BKL)* lists the non-periodical publishing output of Albania which is deposited at the National Library according to legal deposit legislation.

Types of publications include books, pamphlets, almanacs, official and government publications, theses and dissertations, maps and atlases, musical scores, translations, standards and patents, artistic prints, calendars, conference proceedings.

Omitted from *BKL* are periodicals, periodical articles and newspaper articles which are included in *Bibliografia kombëtare e Republikës së Socialiste të Shqipërisë. Artikujt e periodikut shqiptar* [Articles of the Albanian Press]. Also omitted are audio-visual materials.

CONTENTS: Classified bibliography, indexes, cumulative index (fourth issue), table of UDC scheme, table of contents, announcement (paragraph on scope and arrangement written in Albanian, French, English and Russian), colophon.

CATALOGUING RULES AND CLASSIFICATION SCHEMES USED: From 1980 AACR2 is followed..

The classification scheme used is UDC.

ENTRY INFORMATION: UDC number directly relating to UDC subject heading, consecutive entry number, author, title, place of publication, publisher, date, pagination, illustrations, size, series statement, notes including price, e.g., L 15.; "pa c." means "pa cmim" [no price], number of books printed, e.g., Tir. 6.000; "pa tir." means "pa tirazh" [no run], internal number in lower left corner; additional UDC numbers in lower right corner describe secondary subjects of the work and may or may not relate to the UDC subject heading used in the entry.

ARRANGEMENT: Arranged by UDC numbers under the UDC general headings. Earlier issues were arranged by 31 alphabetical subjects.

INDEXES: From 1992, there are five indexes, all alphabetically arranged: index of authors, index of translators, title index, index of individuals, and index of publishers. The fourth issue includes cumulated indexes for the year.

NOTES AND COMMENTS: Albania's government was transformed from a communist dictatorship to a democratic government during 1991 and 1992. With this new government came a name change. Because the name of the country is in the first part of the national bibliography title, there have been many title changes throughout the history of the national bibliography. A brief review of these title changes are listed below for the two series of the national bibliography.

BKL, analyzed above, continues *Bibliografia kombëtare e librit që botohet në RPS të Shqipërisë* [National bibliography of books published in the PSR of Albania]. - Viti 27, 1 (Jan.-Mar. 1986)-1990. - Tiranë : Biblioteka Kombëtare, Sektori i Bibliografisë, 1986-1990. Quarterly.

(LCCN:90-641453; LC: Z2854.A5B53; OCLC: 14634739). This title continues *Bibliografia kombëtare e Republikës Popullore Socialiste të Shqipërisë. Libri shqip* [National bibliography of the People's Socialist Republic of Albania. Albanian Books]. - Viti 18, nr. 1 (Jan.-Mar. 1977) -1985. - Tiranë : Biblioteka Kombëtare, 1977-1985. Quarterly (LCCN: sn 80-11287; OCLC: 4404391; ISSN 0250-5053). This title continues *Bibliografia kombëtare e Republikës Popullore të Shqipërisë. Libri shqip* [National bibliography of the People's Republic of Albania. Albanian book]. - 1960-1976. - Tiranë : Botim i Bibliotekës Kombëtare, 1960-1976. Quarterly (LCCN: 72-212749//r90; LC: Z2854.A5B53; OCLC: 2038579; ISSN 0523-1841).[1] This continues *Bibliografia e Republikës Popullore të Shqipërisë. Vepra origjinale dhe përkthime të vitit 19[ ]* [Bibliography of the People's Republic of Albania. Original works and translations of the year 19[ ]]. - Tiranë, 1959-1960. Annual. The first issue of *BKL* was published in 1959 and covers the publications of 1958. Because the volumes for 1958 and 1959 did not circulate, by error, 1960 was considered the first year of the first issue of *BKL*.[2]

Bibliografia kombëtare e Republikës së Socialiste të Shqipërisë. Artikujt e periodikut shqiptar [Articles of the Albanian Press]. - Viti 31, 2 (Shkurt [Feb.] 1991)-   . - Tiranë : Biblioteka Kombëtare, 1991-   . Monthly (LCCN: 72-212748//r962; DDC: 079.4956; LC: Z6956.A5B53; OCLC: 2036024; ISSN 0523-1833) is the current title which lists periodical and newspaper articles. The text is in Albanian, and summaries appear in English, French and Russian. The last issue of each year includes the cumulative index for that year. This title continues, with its numbering, *Bibliografia kombëtare e Republikës Popullore Socialiste të Shqipërisë. Artikujt e periodikut shqiptar.* - 1986-Jan. 1991. - Tiranë : Biblioteka Kombëtare, 1986-1991. Monthly. (same OCLC as above). From 1977-1985, the title was *Bibliografia kombëtare e Republikës Popullore të Socialiste të Shqipërisë. Artikujt e periodikut shqip*, and from 1965-1976 the title was *Bibliografia kombëtare e Republikës Popullore të Shqipërishe. Artikujt e periodikut shqip.* This continues *Bibliografia e periodikut të Republikës Popullore të Shqipërisë.* - Tiranë : Biblioteka Kombëtare, 1961-1964 (OCLC: 6004115; ISSN 0523-1752). Common titles in all languages vary.

No symbol is used to designate government publications.

Although a brief statement concerning the scope of *BKL* is given at the end of the issue in Albanian, French, English, and Russian, it would be helpful to have a more comprehensive introduction that would include an analyzed entry and a list of abbreviations and symbols used in the bibliography.

PROMPTNESS RECEIVED/CURRENCY: Entries are for the period covered. The latest issue examined in November 1996 from Indiana University was number 3/4, 1992, published in 1993.[3]

AUTOMATION: not automated.

---

[1] Mrs. Basha, Director of the National Library, indicated in a 23 January 1997 letter to the author the dates for this title begin with no. 1, 1965, rather than the 1960 date given in the OCLC record.

[2] Information about the 1958 and 1959 volumes are in Mrs. Basha's letter to the author.

[3] This was the latest published as of Mrs. Basha's letter to the author. Later issues are in process.

FORMAT AND SERVICES AVAILABLE: printed.

CURRENT LEGAL DEPOSIT LAWS: In 1992 the Parliament obligates all publishers to execute the law on legal deposit copy giving five free copies of each publication printed to the National Library and to the public library of the district or the City Hall in which they carry on their activity within one month from retreating from the typography.[1]

AVAILABLE FROM: Bibliotekës Kombëtare, Tiranë.

VERIFIER: Mrs. Nermin Basha, Director of the National Library.

ALGERIA

TITLE: *al-Bībliyūghrāfiyā al-Jazā'irīyah.* - Oct. 1963-   . - al-Jazā'ir : al-Maktabah al-Waṭanīyah [Bibliothèque Nationale], 1964-   .
Semiannual (1968-   ); irregular (1963-1967).
Added title page: *Bibliographie de l'Algérie.*
In Arabic and French.
Some numbers issued in combined form.
DDC: not found; LC: Z3681.B5; LCCN: ne 65-1914/NE; OCLC: 2495577
ISSN not found

COMPILER: Legal deposit section of Bibliothèque Nationale.

SCOPE AND COVERAGE: The *al-Bībliyūghrāfiyā al-Jazā'irīyah. = Bibliographie de l'Algérie* (*BA*) lists materials published in Algeria and received on legal deposit by the Bibliothèque Nationale during the year covered.

Types of publications included in *BA* are books, serials, official and government publications, theses and dissertations, maps and atlases, annual reports, IGO publications when published in Algeria, ephemera such as postage stamps, etc.

Excluded from coverage are publications about Algeria or by Algerians published elsewhere, and audio-visual materials.

CONTENTS: *BA* is a bilingual publication. Contents for the French and the Arabic sections are: table of contents, introduction (including the list of classes), list of abbreviations, bibliography, indexes.

CATALOGUING RULES AND CLASSIFICATION SCHEMES USED: Since 1977, *BA* has used ISBD(M) and ISBD(S) for entries in French, with modifications for the Arabic entries.

Classification follows the UDC system.

---

[1] Information in 21 February 1997 letter to the author from Mrs. Nermin Basha.

ENTRY INFORMATION: Consecutive entry number, author, title, place of publication, publisher, date, pagination, illustrations, size, series statement, occasional notes. Price is given in lower left corner when known, as well as the legal deposit number, e.g., D.L. 289-92. The shelf-mark of the Bibliothèque Nationale, e.g., 558.115, is given in the lower right corner.

Periodicals are marked with an asterisk (*) and placed at the head of the division in which they belong. Information includes entry number, title, beginning date if known, responsible agency, place of publication, publisher, date of issue received, size, occasional notes, frequency in lower left corner, shelf-mark number in lower right corner.

ARRANGEMENT: The main bibliography is arranged by the UDC system. Within each division, periodical titles are listed in alphabetical order by title at the beginning of each classification section. Books and other materials are in alphabetical order by main entry within the class. Entry numbers are consecutive throughout each language section.

INDEXES: Author index, collaborator index, corporate author index, title index. Numbers refer user to the entry number.

NOTES AND COMMENTS: The first issue for 1963 was a classification list of periodicals received on deposit by the Bibliothèque Nationale.

There is no annual cumulation for the *BA*. Therefore, it is necessary to check each issue when searching for a particular title. If it were possible to cumulate the indexes for the year it would eliminate having to search each issue.

L'Edition en Algérie depuis l'indépendance: 1962-1980. (Bibliographies et Catalogues: 6) Alger : S.N. ANEP, 1980 is a cumulation of the semiannual issues during the period covered and was published in 1980 by the Bibliothèque Nationale.[1] (LCCN: 84-198202/NE/r87; LC: Z3681.N37 1980; OCLC: 12133677).

The only *BA* issue which uses an asterisk (*) to designate official publications is number 2 of 1964. Otherwise, one may identify many government and official publications by using the corporate index.

In some issues there are specialized supplements or appendices which help to locate information not readily accessible. These supplements are not included in any regular pattern. For example, the volume covering 1 July 1965 to 31 December 1965 includes an appendix of "thèses et diplômes d'études supérieures", and the volume which covers the second part of 1967 includes a cumulative index of periodicals from July 1962 to July 1967.

Lists of the Bibliothèque Nationale publications available are included in *BA* through 1982.

LATEST ISSUE EXAMINED/CURRENCY: The latest volume examined was number 58, the first part for 1992 published in 1993. There is an improvement on currency of imprint dates since the 1980s when more than half the entries were for years earlier than those covered in the issue. For current numbers, a high percentage of entries are for the period covered. In checking

---

[1] *BSTW, Supplement 1980*, p. 3.

the legal deposit number it is clear that these titles were received during the year covered; the hold up seems to be between the time of publication and the deposition of the material.

AUTOMATION: MINISIS on an HP 300/42 computer.[1]

FORMAT AND SERVICES AVAILABLE: printed.

CURRENT LEGAL DEPOSIT LAWS: Décret No. 56978, 27.09.1956.

AVAILABLE FROM: For exchange or subscription: Bibliothèque Nationale, Service des échanges et de diffusion des publications, 1, Avenue Frantz Fanon, 16000 Alger.

SELECTED ARTICLES: Attia, Ridha. "National Bibliographies in the Maghreb: A Survey of their Contents and Perspective." Paper presented at the 50th IFLA General Conference, Nairobi, Kenya, 19-24 August 1984 (55-BIB-1-E).

VERIFIER: No reply received.

ANDORRA

No current national bibliography was traced for Andorra.

ANGOLA

No current national bibliography has been traced for Angola. *BB* has been in hiatus for the last 20 years.[2]

Boletim Bibliográfico. - no. 1- . Luanda : Instituto de Angola, 1963?- . (LCCN (090): Z3891.A59; OCLC: 1723882; ISSN 0020-3742) has not been published for the last twenty years due to several factors, not the least of which was civil war. The Biblioteca Nacional de Angola has plans to continue this title in the near future. When in publication, this duplicated monthly publication listed works published in Angola and deposited at the Instituto de Angola on legal deposit during the period covered. It also included some publications from abroad deposited at the Institut, e.g., Library of Congress *Quarterly Journal. Boletim Bibliográfico (BB)* is in the Portuguese language, the official language of Angola, although titles in other languages (mostly English) are included occasionally. Types of publications included within the scope of *BB* are

---

[1] Rehman, Sajjad. "National Infrastructure of Library and Information Services in Arab Countries." *Library Review* 40 (no. 1 1991):26.

[2] Mrs. Alexandra M. Aparício, Director, National Library of Angola, in a 14 May 1997 letter to the author indicates that the National Library intends to publish the national bibliography after the registration of those publications not received on legal deposit.

books, pamphlets, periodicals, and periodical articles. Contents include title page, bibliography of titles received which is divided by books and pamphlets, and periodicals. Entry information for books includes title, publisher (when known), place of publication (when known), date (when known), agency responsible if separate from publisher. Entry information for periodicals is as follows: title, place of publication, number, date. For some issues, contents of the periodical are analyzed listing author and title information of the articles. Most of the entries in *BB* are periodical articles; in the issue analyzed, over ninety percent is devoted to periodical articles. The bibliography is alphabetically arranged by title in both the book and periodical sections. No index is included.

Monthly issues of the *BB* were received at the British Library Lending Library, Boston Spa, England, three to four months after the period of time covered. Entries in the March 1974 issue range from 1971-1973. In the October issue, the majority of periodicals analyzed were from 1974. Fifty percent of the books listed were from 1974, with the range extending back to 1972. The latest issue examined was October 1974 at the Library of Congress, received 7 February 1977.

Catálogo do depósito legal. - 1995- . -Luanda : Ministério da Cultura, Biblioteca Nacional de Angola, 1995-   lists new publications and periodicals received on legal deposit by the National Library of Angola. The *Catálogo* is divided into two parts. The first part lists new publications by publisher. The second part presents periodicals. Then works published by the Instituto Nacional de Estatística, and Legislação are listed. The imprint dates listed throughout the *Catálogo* cover 1977-1995. There is a table of contents at the back of the publication. This is a well-presented publication which is partially sponsored by the Portuguese Embassy in Angola, Instituto de Cooperação Portugues, and Instituto CAMÕES. This catalogue is an attempt to list the lacunae that has accumulated from not publishing the national bibliography for the last 20 years. In preparation for the renewed publication of the national bibliography, the library is working with the book trade to follow the legal deposit law.

CURRENT LEGAL DEPOSIT LAWS: Despacho no. 3/79, dated 19 January 1979.[1]

VERIFIER: Mrs. Alexandria M. Aparicio, Director, Biblioteca Nacional de Angola.

ARGENTINA

No current national bibliography has been traced for Argentina.

A helpful source of current titles published in Argentina is *Libros Argentinos. ISBN*. - Buenos Aires : Cámera Argentina del Libro, 1984-   . Annual (LCCN: 87-641257; OCLC: 10635398). The latest volume examined covers 1992, and lists more than 7,000 titles. Contents for this volume are prologue, what is ISBN, composition of ISBN, the ISBN in our country, structure of the catalogue, alphabetical index of publishers, numerical index of publishers' prefixes in

---

[1] Information is given in *Catálogo do depósito legal,* Biblioteca Nacional de Angola (1995), p. 7 and in a 14 May 1997 letter from Mrs. Aparício. The Library is preparing a new project-law of legal deposit which should make legal deposit more efficient.

alphabetical order, list of authors/publishers in alphabetical order, subject tables, list of abbreviations, bibliographic information organized by DDC subjects, alphabetical index of authors and anonymous works, alphabetical index of titles. Bibliographic information follows AACR2 with some modifications, including title, author, translator, place of publication, publisher, pagination, size, series, and ISBN. From 1984-1991 this title was updated bimonthly by *Libros de edición argentina*, or *LEA*. (LCCN: 86-647785; OCLC: 13200426).[1]

Libros Argentinos is also now available as *CD-ROM Libros Argentinos*. This quarterly includes information for all books published in Argentina since 1982 to date which are still in print. Searches can be made by title, author, publisher, edition, subject, price, as well as other criteria. The classification system used is the DDC. An online user's manual is available. System requirements include a PC 386 SX or higher processor, 1 MB of available hard disk space, 2 MB RAM, CD-ROM drive, Windows 3.1 or later.

Libros argentinos: información en diskettes. Buenos Aires : Cámara Argentina del Libro is also available on 3.5 or 5.25 diskettes.[2]

Although *Boletín bibliográfico nacional* (*BBN*). - Jan./June 1937-1956?. - Buenos Aires : Biblioteca Nacional, 1937- 1963? is not considered a current source of national bibliographic information, it is important to include. *BBN* has had changes of title and publisher and has had an irregular publication schedule during its existence. Title variances include the following: *Boletín bibliográfico nacional*, nos. 27-33, 1952-1963 covering 1950-1956; *Boletín bibliográfico argentino*, nos. 1-26, 1937-1951 covering 1937-1949. Different publishers are Biblioteca Nacional, 1953-   ; Dirección General de Cultura, 1950-1953; Junta Nacional de Intelectuales, 1947-1949 and Comisión Nacional de Cooperación, 1937-1946.

BBN lists titles published in Argentina and deposited at the Biblioteca Nacional according to the legal deposit laws. It also includes translations of foreign books of indigenous interest, foreign books published in Argentina, and, on occasion, special bibliographic articles. Types of publications listed in *BBN* are books, translations of foreign works of indigenous interest, foreign works published in Argentina. Deposited at the Biblioteca Nacional but not included in *BBN* are non-book materials and academic papers.[3] Contents include a preface, table of contents, subject listing, classified bibliography, index. Entry information includes the classification number at the beginning of each subject area, consecutive entry number at the beginning of each listing, author, title, sub-title, edition, translator, place of publication, publisher, pagination, illustrations. Classification scheme of the bibliography follows UDC. Bibliographic entries are arranged by the 100 primary numbers of the UDC scheme, then arranged alphabetically by the main entry. The general index includes authors, collaborators, translators, pseudonyms, etc. in one alphabetical sequence. The numbers used refer the reader to the entry numbers in the classified bibliography. The volume for 1950-1951 includes a ten year index covering 1942-1951.

---

1 The section for Argentina (pp. 97ff.) in *Information Sources in Official Publications*, 1997 states that after a brief hiatus, the Cámera de Libros' *Boletin bibliografico bimestral* replaced *LEA* and continues to list publications of the book trade.

2 *Bibliography of Latin America and Caribbean Bibliographies. Annual Report 1994-1995*, nos. 88, 89.

3 G. Pomassl, *Survey of Existing Legal Deposit Laws*, p. 16.

No symbols are used to designate government publications in *BBN*. One may look in the index under Argentina or the name of the province and then look for the agency responsible for publication of the work.

From 1959-1971, the best source of Argentina's current national bibliography is *Bibliografía Argentina de Artes y Letras*. - No.1-51/52. - Buenos Aires: Fondo Nacional de las Artes, 1959-1971. This selective, classified bibliography gathers titles from a variety of sources, and includes periodical articles. Subjects covered are nonscientific, emphasizing the arts and literature. Full bibliographic information is given and is arranged by UDC.

Since 1 January 1971, the Registro Nacional de la Propriedad Intelectual (Copyright Office) has been sending the *Boletín Oficial de la República Argentina* daily lists of books, pamphlets, official publications, periodicals, theses, maps, musical scores, films, sound recordings, etc. which have been deposited for copyright purposes. Publications are arranged by accession numbers. The *Boletín Oficial* thus lists books, pamphlets, official and government publications, serial publications. The rest is listed in a separate section.[1]

Argentine publications are included within the scope of *Fichero Bibliográfico Hispanoamericano*. - 1961-1992. (ISSN 0015-0592). Frequency, place of publication and publisher have varied. This is a classified list of current Spanish trade publications printed in Spain and Latin America.

CURRENT LEGAL DEPOSIT LAWS: Article 57 of Law 11723 of 23 September 1933 as amended in Decree 3079 of 1957.[2]

ARMENIA

TITLE: *Hai Tpagrutian Taregir = Letopis' Armīanskoi Pechati* [Annals of Armenian books]. - 1995-   .
Monthly.
Continues: *Tpagrutian taregir = Letopis' Pechati* [Annals of books].
DDC: not found; LC: not found; LCCN: not found; OCLC: not found
ISSN not found (No ISSN or ISBN in Armenia).

COMPILER: Hayastani Azgayin Grapalat = Armenian National Book Chamber.

SCOPE AND COVERAGE: *Hai Tpagrutian Taregir = Letopis' Armīanskoi Pechati* (*HTT*) includes the publishing output of Armenia which is deposited at the Armenian National Book Chamber according to legal deposit laws.

Types of publications include books and pamphlets.

---

[1] *BSTW, 1975-1979*, p. 76-77.
[2] *International Guide to Legal Deposit*, p. 66.

Dissertations, music, reproduced art, periodical articles, newspaper articles, are covered in other parts of the national bibliography identified under the Notes and Comments section.

CONTENTS: Preface, abbreviations, classified bibliography, indexes, DDC subject heading index (once a year).

CATALOGUING RULES AND CLASSIFICATION SCHEMES USED: Bibliographic description is based on "Bibliograficheskoe opisanie dokumenta" GOST 7.1-84, Moscow, 1984.

The classification scheme used is DDC.

ENTRY INFORMATION: Author, title, place of publication, publisher, date, pagination, illustrations, size, series statement, number of copies printed. Russian language materials are described in Russian. After the collapse of the Soviet Union the ISBN is not included.

ARRANGEMENT: Arrangement is by DDC subject headings.

INDEXES: Author index, geography index.

NOTES AND COMMENTS: Before Armenia's independence, *Tpagrutian Taregir = Letopis' pechati* was considered a regional bibliography and Armenia was within the scope of *Knizhnaia letopis'* (USSR). Armenia gained its independence in September 1991. From 1990-1994 no national bibliography was published. The Armenian National Book Chamber has the issues prepared for these years and is planning to publish them in the near future. *HTT* continues *Tpagrutian Taregir = Letopis' pechati 1972-1990*. This title continued *Grk'i taregir = Knizhnaia letopis'* [Annals of books]. - Erevan : Petakan Grapalat, 1936-1971. (LCCN: 91-645096; OCLC: 23543157), which continues *Tpagrut'yan taregir = Letopis' pechati*. - Yerevan : Hratarakut'yun Hayastani Grapalati, 1925-1935. (LCCN: 91-645095; OCLC: 23534544).[1]

HTT is only one part of the national bibliography. Other parts are as follows.

Lragrayin hodvatsneri taregir = Letopis' gazetnykh statei [Annals of newspaper articles]. - Erevan : Knizhnaia palata. Monthly (LCCN: 88-645293//r93; OCLC: 18563950). Began in 1949.

Amsagrayin hodvac'neri taregir = Letopis' zhurnalnykh statei [Annals of periodical articles]. Monthly.

Spiurk'ahai mamuli taregir = Letopis' zarubezhnoi armianskoi pechati [Annals of articles from periodical press of Armenian diaspora]. Monthly.

---

[1] The author thanks Lee Avdoyan, Near East Section, African and Middle East Division, Library of Congress for putting the author in touch with Nerses Hayrapetian, Deputy Director of the National Library of Armenia. Over a period of 10 months, Nerses kept the author informed by e-mail about the current status of the national bibliography and supplied information about the current national bibliography in Armenia as it became available. The author is indebted to him. In the 1925-1935 record of *Tpagrut'yan taregir*, information for the Russian title which Nerses Hayrapetian supplied is different from the OCLC record which reads *Knizhnaia letopis' S.S.R. Armenii*.

Hayastane ashkhari mamulum = Armenia v mirovoĭ presse [Armenia in the world press]. Monthly.

Grakhosutiunneri taregir = Letopis' retsenziĭ. [Annals of reviews]. Biannual.

Kerparvesti taregir = Letopis' izoizdaniĭ. [Annals of reproduced art]. Annual.

Notaneri taregir = Notnaĩa letopis'. [Annals of music]. Annual.

Seghmagreri taregir = Letopis' avtoreferatov dissertatsiĭ. [Annals of authors' abstracts of dissertations]. Annual.

An index of articles and speeches is titled *Lragrayin hodvac'neri taregir & Amsagrayin hodvac'neri taregir. Hodvatsneri ev grakhosut'yunneri taregir = Letopis' stateĭ i retsenziĭ.* - Erevan : Matenagitutyune, 1972-1990. Monthly (ISSN: 0136-0779; OCLC: 30528740).

LATEST ISSUE EXAMINED/CURRENCY: The latest issue examined is 1996, no. 3 which was sent to the author from Armenia.

Imprint dates cover 1996.

AUTOMATION: not automated.

FORMAT AND SERVICES AVAILABLE: printed.

CURRENT LEGAL DEPOSIT LAWS: A legal deposit law exists, but information was not available. According to the Director of the Armenian National Book Chamber, Mr. Bekmezyan, no legal deposit law exists at present.[1]

AVAILABLE FROM: National Library of Armenia, 72, Terian Street, Yerevan, 375009; Armenia National Book Chamber, 21, Gevorg Kochar Street, Yerevan 9, 375009.

VERIFIER: Nerses Hayrapetian, Deputy Director of the National Library of Armenia.

AUSTRALIA

TITLE: *Australian national bibliography.* - Jan. 1961- Dec. 1996. - Canberra : National Library of Australia, 1961-1996.
Frequency varies.
Data available online from January 1997 as *Recent Australian Publications* (see Notes and Comments section).
Continues *Books published in Australia.*

---

[1] The author is indebted to Ms. Bella Avakian, reference librarian, American University of Armenia, who met with Mr. Bekmezyan to get the legal deposit information.

Cumulations are published on microfiche for the periods Jan.-April, Jan.-Aug., and Jan.-Dec. for 1980-Dec. 1996.
DDC: 015.94; LC: Z4015.A96; LCCN: 63-33739//r88, sf89-93211 (mf); OCLC: 1518850, 7562229 (mf)
ISSN 0004-9816

COMPILER: National Library of Australia.

SCOPE AND COVERAGE: The *Australian National Bibliography* (*ANB*) includes titles published in Australia and its territories within the current and preceding two years acquired and/or received on deposit at the National Library under the legal deposit legislation. It also includes overseas publications by Australians or with Australian subject content. "Until 1975, Papua New Guinea publications were also listed."[1]

Types of publication included are books, pamphlets, government publications, microforms published in Australia, new serial titles and those issued with changes in bibliographical details, printed music, atlases in book form, sound recordings (if issued in a multi-media package), translations, theses (if published), and kits when they contain a significant print component.

Omitted from *ANB* are reprints of editions by the same publisher, pamphlets under five pages unless they form part of a series, confidential or restricted access publications, published material of limited distribution, publications printed but not published in Australia, free promotional material, novelty or toy books, preprints and offprints of journal articles, conference papers, occasional speeches, course notes and texts, examination papers, unpublished material, individual acts, bills and ordinances since 1971, Australian standards, patents, theses (unless published), prints, posters, ephemera, industrial awards, determinations and transcripts of evidence. Since 1987, kits and audio-visual materials are not included in *ANB*.[2]

CONTENTS: Preface, including an analyzed entry, outline of DDC scheme, classified sequence, author/title/series index, periodicals list, subject index.

Microfiche: There is no preface, introduction or DDC outline. Entries are listed in the classified sequence, author/title/series index, periodicals list, and subject index.

CATALOGUING RULES AND CLASSIFICATION SCHEMES USED: AACR2 and its revisions as interpreted in the LC's *Cataloging Service Bulletin* is used in cataloguing entries for *ANB*. *LCSH* in microform and its updates published in the *LC Subject Headings Weekly Lists*, and *ANB*-approved subject headings are followed.

The classification scheme is the DDC, updated by *DC&*. In the literature section, Australian authors are identified with an "A" in front of the classification, New Zealand authors have an "NZ", and New Guinea authors have an "NG", e.g., A820, NG820.809287, NZ823.2.

---

[1] "Australia," *Commonwealth National Bibliographies*, 2d ed., rev. London: Commonwealth Secretariat, 1983. p. 4.
[2] Pam Gatenby, Graham Still and Mary Witsenhuysen. "The Australian Scene 3. Current and Retrospective National Bibliography." *ICBC* 17 (no. 3 July/Sept. 1988):36.

ENTRY INFORMATION: Classified sequence: DDC number, subject heading for the classification number, author, title, edition, place of publication, publisher, year, pagination, illustrations, size, series, notes including ISBN or ISSN, subscription information or price, tracings. Contributed cataloguing notes contain the National Union Catalogue of Monographs (NUCOM) symbol of the originating library and the phrase "contributed cataloguing." The classified sequence has the most complete information.

ISBD(S) information is given for the serials entries, e.g., title, place of publication, publisher, beginning and/or cessation date, frequency, subscription information or price, notes including ISSN, tracings.

ARRANGEMENT: The classified sequence is arranged by the DDC scheme. From 1961-1966, the bibliography was arranged alphabetically by the main entry; from 1967-1971, the bibliography was arranged alphabetically by the main entry, added entries, references, and subject headings.

Author/title/series index: entries are alphabetical.

Periodicals List: entries are listed by main entry, which could be author, title, or uniform title.

Subject index: entries are arranged alphabetically under the LC subject headings.

INDEXES: Author/title/series index, subject index. Both indexes use the classification number to refer the user to the bibliographical entry. The author/title/series index supplies the author, title, place of publication, publisher, year, classification number, ISBN, price. Pagination, size, and illustration information are not given. The subject index entries are bold-faced and give the title and classification number of the entry.

NOTES AND COMMENTS: The December 1996 monthly paper issue and the January-December 1996 microfiche cumulation are the last issues to be published. *Recent Australian Publications*, the name of files generated from the Australian Bibliographic Network, will make available those current records with Australian imprints. In a 19 October 1996 letter subscribers are given information about the *ANB* Supersearch which is to be used at present to retrieve records. Subscribers can execute this search but are warned that this search is very time consuming and expensive. The National Library will continue to execute this search with results (appproximately 2500 records) organized in DDC order with some subject categories and will make the results available each month in ftp files on the Library's ftp server. The text will be in ASCII format. Some entries will not have DDC numbers (approximately 300 records); these titles would have been eliminated in *ANB*, but are now available in a separate file listed by main entry. Libraries can scan these files for selection purposes at no charge. They will remain on the ftp server for three months. Users are warned that these records will not be edited in any way. Missing from the ftp files will be those entries for Australian authors published overseas, or overseas imprints with Australian content. Persons can request information about the availability of ftp files and the file address by sending an e-mail message to the National Library.[1]

---

[1] Information is taken from a 19 October 1996 letter addressed to subscribers from Sandra Henderson, Manager, National Bibliographic Publications. Additional information is available in a circular of 29 August 1996.

In this age one can understand to a point factors that led to this decision. It is expensive to produce a national bibliography. One concern, however, is how countries that do not have the communication technical capability to ftp files can be made aware of Australian publications. One would guess that this was not an easy decision for the National Library of Australia to make. Subscriptions to the printed version of *ANB* were steadily declining; the National Library believed that the availability of the data online affected the paper subscriptions.[1]

ANB continues *Books published in Australia* (1946-1960, monthly; OCLC: 18207483) and continues in part *Annual Catalogue of Australian publications* (1936-1960, annual; OCLC: 171165), and *Australian government publications*.

Government publications are listed in both the *ANB* and in *Australian Government Publications* [microform]. - Sept. 1988-   . - Canberra : National Library of Australia, 1988-   . Quarterly (LCCN: 90-643601; ISSN 0067-1878). The title is arranged in two sequences: author/title, and subject listing. Listed are all official and government publications "with the following exceptions: single issues of statutory rules, notice papers, journals, votes and proceedings, non-book materials, and single issues of acts, bills and ordinances of the Commonwealth territories and states. The *Australian Government Publications* which was published from 1961-1987 (OCLC: 1553270; LCCN: 63-36632//r902) supersedes the library's earlier publication with the same title which was issued monthly from 1952-1960. (OCLC: 1835404; LCCN: sc86-1021). Before 1971, the acts, bills and ordinances were included in *ANB*.

Government publications are not specially marked in the bibliography. By checking the author/title listing under Australia and then the issuing agency one may identify many of the government publications included in the current bibliography.

The National Library issues a number of bibliographies that complement *ANB* including *Australian Films* (ISSN 0045-0048), *Australian Maps* (ISSN 0045-0677), and *Australian Government Publications* (ISSN 0067-1878).[2]

Maps and atlases were included in the *ANB* from 1961-1967. In 1968, *Australian Maps* began publication. Since this time, except for atlases in book forms which are still listed in *ANB*, all forms of cartography are listed in this quarterly publication with annual cumulations. (ISSN 0045-0677; OCLC: 5320896).

Films were listed in *ANB* for the period 1961-1967. Currently, films are listed in *Australian Films* only. (ISSN 0045-0448; OCLC: 6039614).

Periodicals listed in *ANB* are brought together in the author/title/series index under the heading "Periodicals."

---

[1] Information about the online information possibly affecting the paper subscriptions of *ANB* was included in a 14 August 1997 e-mail message to the author from Sandra Henderson, Manager, National Bibliographic Publications, National Library of Australia.

[2] For further analysis of *Australian Films*, *Australian Maps*, Australian Public Affairs Information Service and *Australian Government Publications* see *Commonwealth National Bibliographies*, pp. 6-11.

Periodical literature is not included in *ANB* but is covered by several indexes, the largest of which are the *Australian Public Affairs Information Service* (ISSN 0727-8926) and the *Australian Science Index* (LCCN: sn86-15537).

The *Australian National Bibliography 1901-1950*. - Canberra : National Library of Australia, 1988. (LCCN:93-245219; OCLC: 28995678) fills a gap in Australian's bibliographic coverage between the years covered by *Bibliography of Australia 1784-1900* and the beginning of the National Library's comprehensive coverage by the *Annual Catalogue of Australian Publications* in 1951. The early years of the *Annual Catalogue*, 1936-1945, were not comprehensive in coverage.[1]

The "Directory of Australian Publishers" was not included in the paper or microfiche edition last examined. In earlier issues, this includes publishers, societies and institutions who have works listed in the current *ANB*. The number listed on the right in brackets is the publisher's ISBN prefix. Addresses of small publishers may be given in the entry information rather than in this list.

The National Library has participated in CIP since May 1973. Entries prepared in advance of publication are distinguished by "Cataloguing-in-publication entry" in the notes field. The final entry is then prepared upon receipt of the published item. A note "Revised entry" is included in these entries and also in entries to which major corrections have been made. CIP entries do not appear in the annual cumulation.

The *Australian National Bibliography 1961-1971* is available on microfiche, as a complete set, thus making available these out-of-print volumes.[2]

Entries included in the January - December 1996 microfiche cumulation include English, Chinese, and Alyawarra languages.

South Pacific Bibliography includes materials on the indigenous people of Australia.

LATEST ISSUE EXAMINED/CURRENCY: The November 1995 issue was the most recent printed issue examined at the University Library, Cambridge, England in June 1997. The January - December 1996 was the latest microfiche cumulation examined.

Entries are for the current year, extending back no later than two years as stated in the scope.

AUTOMATION: Beginning in January 1997, bibliographic information is available only in electronic form.

FORMAT AND SERVICES AVAILABLE: print and microfiche cumulations through 1996, online, ftp. From January 1997, ftp files.

CURRENT LEGAL DEPOSIT LAWS: Copyright Act of 1968.

---

[1] Gatenby, p. 36.

[2] "National Library of Australia," *GIP-UNISIST Newsletter* 11(nos. 3/4 1983):44.

AVAILABLE FROM: Sales and Subscription Unit, National Library of Australia, Canberra A.C.T. 2600.

SELECTED ARTICLES: Ellis, A. "Australian National Bibliography (ANB)." *International Library Review* 7 (1975):235-244.

Gatenby, Pam, Still, Graham, and Witsenhuysen, Mary. "The Australian Scene 3. Current and Retrospective National Bibliography." *ICBC* 17 (no. 3 July/Sept. 1988):35-38.

Kenny, J. "Australian Bibliographical Services." *International Library Review* 7 (1975):227-2339.

VERIFIER: Sandra Henderson, Manager, National Bibliographic Publications, National Library of Australia.

AUSTRIA

TITLE: *Österreichische Bibliographie. Reihe A, Verzeichnis der österreichischen Neuerscheinungen* [Austrian bibliography. Series A. Index of Austrian new publications]. - Nr. 1/2 (Jan. 1987)- . - Wien : Österreichische Nationalbibliothek, 1987- .
Semi-monthly, with 3 quarterly indexes and annual index.
Continues *Oesterreichische Bibliographie; Verzeichnis der österreichischen Neuerscheinungen.*
Issues for 1992- have title: *Österreichische Bibliographie. Reihe A, Verzeichnis der österreichischen Neuerscheinungen.*
DDC: 015.436/034; LC: Z2105.O33; LCCN: 89-647402//r92; OCLC: 16470193
ISSN 1023-1862

COMPILER: Österreichische Nationalbibliothek [Austrian National Library].

SCOPE AND COVERAGE: *Österreichische Bibliographie. Reihe A, Verzeichnis der österreichischen Neuerscheinungen.* (OB.A) lists the publishing output of Austria which is deposited at the Österreichische Nationalbibliothek according to legal deposit legislation.

Types of publications included in *OB.A* are books, pamphlets, periodicals (new, changes in title, or cessation), official and government publications, "other university publications" such as curriculums, research papers; maps, atlases, IGO publications, conference proceedings, translations, newspapers, and calendars.

Music scores are included in a special edition of Series A for music practice.

Not included in *OB.A* are slides (which are included in *Filmographie*, an annual included in *Filmkunst.* - Wien : Österreichische Gesellschaft für Filmwissenschaft, 1960-), films, film-strips, musical recordings (which are listed in *Deutsche Nationalbibliographie. Reihe T*), and microforms.

CONTENTS: Subject groups (functioning as a table of contents without page numbers), instructions for use, explanation of an entry, classified bibliography, author, title, and keyword index.

CATALOGUING RULES AND CLASSIFICATION SCHEMES USED: *Regeln für die alphabetische Katalogisierung in wissenschaftlichen Bibliotheken: (RAK-WB). - 2. - Berlin : Dt. Bibliotheksinst., 1993* is used, and *RAK-AV, RAK-Karten.* Deviations from these standards are made in accordance with specific bibliographic and other rulings of the Central Editorial Office of the Austrian Library Association. The title entries in the special edition *Praktische Musik* [Music Practice] are arranged/catalogued according to *RAK-Musik (Sonderregeln für Musikalien und Musiktonträger).*

No classification is used but publications are arranged by twenty-five subject groups.

ENTRY INFORMATION: Consecutive entry number, author, title, place of publication, publisher, date, pagination, size, series statement, notes including ISBN, price.

ARRANGEMENT: The bibliography is arranged in twenty-four subject categories, plus one additional heading for "corrections and ceased publications for a total of twenty-five.

INDEXES: Author, title and keyword index in each issue. Numbers refer to the entry number. Quarterly index called *Vierteljahresregister*; annual index called *Jahresregister*. The annual index has an author, title, keyword index and a subject index. Numbers refer to the issue number and entry number, e.g., 8, 153. The indexes also includes corporate headings; it is possible to locate IAEA publications in the yearly subject index under the corporate heading "International Atomic Energy Agency."

NOTES AND COMMENTS: *OB.A* is part of the reorganization of the national bibliography. As mentioned earlier, since 1987 *OB* is divided into: Series A. Index of new Austrian publications, and Index of new Austrian publications. Special edition Music Practice; Series B. Index of Austrian theses and dissertations; Series C. Selected bibliography of new foreign publications on Austrian themes. These titles continue *Oesterreichische Bibliographie. - Wein :* Verein des österr. Buch-Kunst-, Musikalien-, Zeitungs-und Zeitschriftenhándler, 1945-1986. Biweekly, 1949-1986 (LCCN: 51-21472//r922; OCLC: 1695545, ISSN 0029-8913). Arrangement was by 25 alphabetical subject groups, with publications available for sale and not for sale separated by a line within the subject categories. Excluded since 1960 are music scores which are included in the annual *OB. Sonderheft - praktische Musik.*

Bibliographic citations and information for the new series is as follows.

OB. Verzeichnis der österreichischen Neuerscheinungen. Sonderheft praktische Musik. - 1992- . Annual. (ISSN 1023-1870). The main difference in the reorganization of this title is the reordering of the subject categories from 40 to 22. The subject groups are included under the divisions of instrumental music, vocal music, and dramatic music. Some of these divisions are subdivided, e.g., Instrumental music has several subdivisions, such as Orchestral music (which is further divided into 6 subgroups), Keyboard instruments, and Electronic music. This title continues *OB. Sonderheft– praktische Musik.* (LCCN: 89-647312).

OB. Reihe B. Verzeichnis der österreichischen Hochschulschriften [Index of Austrian theses and dissertations]. - 1987, 1- . Quarterly (LCCN: 88-650409; LC: Z5055.A79; OCLC: 18329591; ISSN 1023-1900). Series B lists only theses, dissertations, and inaugural dissertations listed in the *OB*, Reihe B which are not included in *OB.A*. Title entries are arranged by the 24 subject groups of Reihe A. Indexes include author, title and keyword for each issue, and an annual index.

OB. Reihe C. Neuere ausländische Austriaca. Auswahibibliographie [Selected bibliography of new foreign publications on Austrian themes]. - 1983- . Annual (LCCN: 92-640263; LC: Z2116.O46; OCLC: 25962043; ISSN: 1023-1900). Foreign publications with an Austrian theme are included in Series C. It also covers publications of Austrian writers published abroad. Title entries are arranged by the 24 subject groups of Reihe A. Indexes include author, title and keyword for each issue, and a language index. Series C will cease with the report year 1991. The *Reihe G. Fremdsprachige Germanica und Übersetzungen deutschsprachiger Werke* (Series G. Germanica of the Deutsche Bibliothek, Frankfurt) will continue with the translated publications of German-speaking authors.[1]

Improvements in the *OB* have come with the reorganization. Current issues have a user's guide which explains rules followed, what is included and excluded in the scope and contents. An analyzed sample entry has also been added, and an explanation about publishers' addresses--all suggested by the ICNB recommendations. Earlier issues before 1987 did not include these in each issue. In the issues examined there is no abbreviations list which would be a useful addition.

No symbols are used to designate government publications.

OB. [Series A, Index of new Austrian publications]. Special edition Journals, Series A, was abandoned after its first issue (1993). Journals are included within *OB.A*.

Oesterreichische Musikbibliographie: Verzeichnis der österreichischen Neuerscheinungen auf dem Gebiete der Musik. - vol. 1- . - Wien : Oesterreichische Nationalbibliothek, 1949- include writings on music, musical scores. Title and subject index.

The *OB* does not have a CIP program. However, since 1978, Austrian publishers supply CIP information to *Deutsche Bibliographie. Neuerscheinungen Sofortdienst* (CIP).[2]

LATEST ISSUE EXAMINED/CURRENCY: The latest issue examined at the University Library, Cambridge in June 1997 was no. 10, 15 May 1997. This timeliness for a national bibliography is commendable. Entries included imprints from 1995 to 1997. *OB.A* includes titles from earlier years as well as titles published during the current year.

---

[1] Information about the cessation of Series C is included in a 9 July 1997 e-mail message from Wolf Lang, Editor, *OB*.
[2] *BSTW, 1975-1979*, p. 89.

AUTOMATION: *OB* is automated. Data are exported from the Austrian scientific-library-network 'BIBOS' to a database publishing system developed by DI Hellmut Ortner. This Macintosh-based application prepares camera-ready layouts automatically.[1]

FORMAT AND SERVICES AVAILABLE: printed, CD-ROM (titled Verbund-CD; updated every six months), Internet via the WWW-gateway 'bib-o-pac' which gives access to the OPAC of the Austrian scientific-library-network; www-address: http://bibopac.univie.ac.at/

'BIBOS' access is also possible via telnet: tn3270://opac.univie.ac.at

OB information is available in 'bib-o-pac' without retail prices, publishers' addresses, and format.[2]

CURRENT LEGAL DEPOSIT LAWS: Mediengesetz idF der Mediengesetz–Novelle [Media law–new] 1992: §43 (1) and §43(2).[3]

AVAILABLE FROM: Oesterreichische Nationalbibliothek, A-1015, Wien, Josefsplatz I.

SELECTED ARTICLES: Schonberger, V. "50 Jahre Österreichische Bibliographie." *Biblios* 45(1 1996):159-169.

VERIFIER: Wolf Lang, Redaktion d. *Österreichischen Bibliographie*

AZERBAIJAN

TITLE: *Azǎrbaĭjan mǎtbuat salnamǎsi.* - . - Baku : Palata-Kitab Palatasy, 1926- .
Monthly.
Began in 1926.
"Azarbaĭjan SSR dòvlǎt bibliografiĭa organy."
Added title page: *Letopis' pechati Azerbaĭdzhana*
DDC: not found; LC: Z3411.A96; LCCN 88-645301; OCLC: 5662945
ISSN 0572-2918

COMPILER: Azǎrbaĭjan SSR Nazirlǎr Sovetinin Dòvlǎt Nǎshriĭĭat, Poligrafiĭa vǎ Kitab Tijarati Ishlari Komitasi, Azǎrbaĭjan Dòvlǎt Kitab Palatasy.

SCOPE AND COVERAGE: *Azǎrbaĭjan mǎtbuat salnamǎsi.* (*AMS*) includes the publishing output of Azarbaijan, which is deposited at the national library according to legal deposit laws.

---

[1] Lang e-mail message.
[2] Lang e-mail message.
[3] "Benützungshinweise," *OB.A* 1997, no. 10. p. 3

Types of publications include books, pamphlets, music, journals, newspapers, technical documentation, Azerbaijan material.

CONTENTS: Subject bibliography by format with indexes in following order: books, music, journals, newspapers, technical documentation, Azerbaijan material; general indexes. All formats may not be in each issue.

CATALOGUING RULES AND CLASSIFICATION SCHEMES USED: ISBD is followed.

No classification scheme is used but materials are grouped by broad subject categories with the categories having numbers 1-50 assigned, e.g., 1 is Marx, Lenin, 26 is metallurgy.

ENTRY INFORMATION: Consecutive entry number, author, title, place of publication, publisher, date, pagination, illustrations, size, series statement, notes including price, number of copies printed; in square brackets is the legal deposit number, e.g., [83-633].

ARRANGEMENT: By format (books, music, journals, newspapers, technical documentation, Azerbaijan material) arrangement is by 50 broad subject categories; these divisions are subdivided, e.g., 49.5.

INDEXES: For each format, appropriate indexes are given, e.g., books: name main entry index, title main entry index; journals: title index. Numbers refer back to the entry number in the bibliography. Supplemental indexes for earlier numbers in previous issues are at the back. A general index at the back gives the order of the formats in the issue by their entry numbers.

At the back of the monthly issues, a subject listing of the classes is listed in tabular format and the page number for books, journals, and newspapers for each class is given.

NOTES AND COMMENTS: Before the breakup of the USSR, publications of Azerbaijan were recorded in *Knizhnaiā letopis'* and *Azărbaĭjan mătbuat salnamăsi.*. Since Azerbaijan established its independence, the primary record of Azerbaijan's publishing output is recorded in *AMS*.

According to Mr. I. Pourhadi, Library of Congress area specialist in Central Asia, the Library of Congress does not have up-to-date holdings for Azerbaijan because the United States has had no relations with Azerbaijan in recent years. When that embargo is lifted he expects to resume current holdings.

The text is written in Azerbaijani or Russian.

Two other titles which may be helpful are: *Azerbaĭdzhan v pechati SSSR / Ministerstvo kul'tury Azerbaĭdzhanskoĭ SSR, Azerbaĭdzhanskaiā Gosudarstvennaiā respublikanskaiā biblioteka im. M.F. Akhundova, Otdel kraevedeniiā i natsional'noĭ bibliografii.* - Baku : Biblioteka. Annual (LCCN: 84-642067) and *Birillik Azărbaĭjan kitabiĭaty / Azărbaĭjan SSR Dövlăt Năshriĭat, Poligrafiĭa vă Kitab Tijarăti Ishieri Komitasy [vă] Azărbaĭjan Dövlăt Kitab Palatsy.* - Baku : Azărbaĭjan Dövlăt Kitab Palatasy. Quarterly (LCCN: sn85-21534; OCLC: 7261987).

LATEST ISSUE EXAMINED/CURRENCY: The latest issue examined is for 1983, no. 5; it was published in 1988, and received at the Library of Congress 9 November 1989.

It would be helpful to have a more timely publication so that it could serve libraries as an acquisitions source. This is the latest that the author could locate at Indiana University and at the Library of Congress; this is due to relations between the U.S. and Azerbaijan.

Imprint dates cover 1982 and 1983.

AUTOMATION: not automated.

FORMAT AND SERVICES AVAILABLE: printed.

CURRENT LEGAL DEPOSIT LAWS: No information available.

AVAILABLE FROM: Azārbaĭjan Dȯvlăt Kitab Palatasy [Azarbaijan Book Chamber], Baku.

VERIFIER: Christopher Murphy, Central Asia Area Specialist, Library of Congress.

BAHRAIN

TITLE: *al-Bībliyūghrāfiyā al-waṭanīyah li-Dawlat al-Baḥrayn* [National Bibliography of Bahrain]: raṣd lil-in-tāj al-fikrī fī dawlat al-Baḥrayn ḥatt, a nihāyat 'ām.... - 1990-   . - al-Manāmah : Wizārat al-Tarbiyah wa-al-Ta'līm, Idārat al-Maktubāt al-'Āmmah [Ministry of Education, Department of Public Libraries], 1991-   .
Irregular.
DDC: not found; LC: Z3028.B34B53; LCCN: sn97-17695; OCLC: 37002677
ISSN not found

COMPILER: Prepared by Mansoor Mohammed Sarhan, Director of the Department of Public Libraries, and by Ribhi Mustafa Aliyyan, Department of Library Science, Bahrain University.

SCOPE AND COVERAGE: *al-Bībliyūghrāfiyā al-waṭanīyah li-Dawlat al-Baḥrayn* (*BW*) includes the publishing output of Bahrain, publications about Bahrain and those written by Bahrani nationals outside the country which are deposited at the Department of Public Libraries. Any reference to legal deposit legislation is not mentioned in the bibliography.

Types of publications include books, pamphlets, serials, official and government publications, theses and dissertations.

CONTENTS: Introduction and explanation of the bibliographic project which includes coverage, importance of the bibliography, sources of information, information offered, and how *BW* is organized; dedication, classified bibliography, index.

CATALOGUING RULES AND CLASSIFICATION SCHEMES USED: ISBD is followed.

The classification scheme used is DDC.

ENTRY INFORMATION: Title, author, place of publication, publisher, date, pagination, illustrations, size, series statement, and notes.

ARRANGEMENT: The bibliography is divided into three sections: books written by personal authors, books written by the government and non-government organizations, and masters' theses and doctoral dissertations written in Bahrain and in other countries. Within these divisions, arrangement is alphabetical.

INDEXES: Title index. The number refers the user to the main bibliography.

NOTES AND COMMENTS: It is gratifying to see this new national bibliography. *BW* is not widely available in research libraries in the US or Great Britain. It would seem that libraries who support Middle East studies should have this in their holdings. Researchers would benefit from this valuable source.

Arab Bulletin of Publications (OCLC: 2239670) and *AL, ME* (Vol. 1-31, no. 6, 1963-1993; ISSN 0041-7769) include Bahrain within their scopes.

LATEST ISSUE EXAMINED/CURRENCY: The latest issue examined in July 1997 from the UCLA Library is for 1991/1992/1993 published in 1994.

Imprint dates include the period covered.

AUTOMATION: not automated

FORMAT AND SERVICES AVAILABLE: printed.

CURRENT LEGAL DEPOSIT LAWS: A legal deposit exists.

AVAILABLE FROM: Department of Public Libraries, P.O. Box 43, Manama Bahrain.

VERIFIER: Mansoor Mohammed Sarhan, Director, Department of Public Libraries.

BANGLADESH

TITLE: *Bāṃlādeśa jātīẏa granthapañjī = Bangladesh national bibliography.* - vol. 1- , 1972- . - Dhākā : Bāṃlādeśa Ārakāibhs o Granthāgāra Paridaptara, Śikshā, Saṃskṛti, o Krīṛā Mantranālaẏa, Gaṇaprajātantrī Bāṃlādeśa Sarakāra. 1974- .
Annual.
DDC: not found; LC: Z3186.B36; DS393.4; LCCN: 84-644107SA; OCLC : 7687014
ISSN not found

COMPILER: Directorate of Archives and Libraries, National Library of Bangladesh.

SCOPE AND COVERAGE: *Bāṃlādeśa jātīẏa granthapañjī = Bangladesh National Bibliography* (BNB) lists the publishing output of Bangladesh which is deposited at the National

Library according to the copyright legislation. These are supplemented by purchased books not received from the publishers under the copyright act. Both Bengali and English books are listed.

Types of publications included in *BNB* are books, official and government publications, periodicals and newspapers (first issues only).

Excluded are notebooks and "made-easy textbooks written for students," pamphlets, brochures, National Assembly debates and commentary, reprints, maps, periodicals and newspapers (except for first numbers).

CONTENTS: English: title page or statement of purpose, foreword, abbreviations list, DDC outline, classified bibliography section, index (author/title/subject), list of publishers.

The Bengali part includes the same information.

CATALOGUING RULES AND CLASSIFICATION SCHEMES USED: AACR, with modification for Hindu and Muslim names.

The classification scheme used is DDC (20th), modified for Bengali literature and geography.

ENTRY INFORMATION: Classification number, author (with dates if known), title, editor, place of publication, publisher, date, pagination, illustrations, size, price, series, notes. Accession number, not in consecutive order, is listed in the lower right corner in parentheses, e.g., (6741).

ARRANGEMENT: *BNB* is divided into Bengali books and English books published in Bangladesh. Each of these parts is divided into two sections: the classified bibliography and the index. The bibliographies are alphabetically arranged by DDC subjects.

INDEXES: Author index, title index. In the author index, the user is referred to the classification number in the classified bibliography; the title index refers the reader to the author index section, e.g., "See, Bangladesh Academy for Rural Development."

Earlier volumes had an author/title/subject index in one alphabetical sequence.

The list of publishers includes the full addresses of those publishers whose books are incorporated in this issue of *BNB*.

NOTES AND COMMENTS: The *BNB* is divided into two parts. Approximately two-thirds of the entries are listed in the Bengali bibliography section, and one-third in the English section.

Improvements in the current national bibliography have been noted. One in particular is that each entry has its own classification number; earlier volumes listed titles under subject groupings. Another is the increased number of government publications that appear in *BNB*. This is an elusive but valuable source of information and it is important to have them recorded in the national bibliography. No symbol designates official publications in *BNB* but by looking in the author index under the government agency, one is able to locate them.

AL,SA includes Bangladesh within its scope.

LATEST ISSUE EXAMINED/CURRENCY: The majority of entries in the 1991 issue were from the period covered. The latest volume examined is for 1991 at the University of Wisconsin Madison library. As of July 1996, 1991 was the latest issue published; 1992 and 1993/1994 (combined) issues are at the printers.[1]

The *BNB* is attempting to close the gap between the coverage dates and the publication date. The 1981/1982, 1983/84, 1990, and 1991 have all been published in the 1990s. 1991 was published in 1994; this is an improvement from earlier years. It is hoped that the gap can continue to diminish so that the national bibliography may be used as a selection tool by other libraries.

AUTOMATION: not automated.

FORMAT AND SERVICES AVAILABLE: printed.

CURRENT LEGAL DEPOSIT LAWS: Copyright (Amendment) Act, 1974 (LIV of 1974); Press Act of 1975.[2]

AVAILABLE FROM: Bangladesh National Library, Sher-e-Bangla Nagar (Agargaon), Dhaka-1207.

VERIFIER: Syed Shahidul Karim, Editor, *Bangladesh National Bibliography*.

BARBADOS

TITLE: *National bibliography of Barbados.* -1975-   . - Bridgetown : National Library Service, 1975-   .
Annual (1994-   ); twice a year, the second being an annual cumulation (1982-1993); quarterly, with the last quarterly issue included in the annual cumulative issue (1975-1981).
Prior to 1983, published by the Public Library, Bridgetown.
DDC: 015.72981; LC (090): Z1502.B35N38; LCCN: sn84-11339; OCLC: 3838928
ISSN 0256-7709

COMPILER: National Library Service.

SCOPE AND COVERAGE: *The National Bibliography of Barbados* (*NBB*) lists all new works published in Barbados, as well as those works of Barbadian authorship published abroad, which have been received by the National Library Service under the legal deposit act.

The aim is complete coverage and includes monographs, first issues of new serials and subsequent title changes, government publications and legislative publications, annual reports,

---

[1] Information taken from a letter dated 24 July 1996 to the author by Syed Shahidul Karim, Editor, *Bangladesh National Bibliography*.
[2] *International Guide to Legal Deposit*, p. 68.

and works published abroad by Barbadian authors, theses and dissertations, maps and plans, and pamphlets.

Excluded are periodicals (except as noted above), periodical articles, musical scores, films, filmstrips, slides, and recordings.

CONTENTS: Preface, list of abbreviations and terms, outline of DDC scheme, classified subject section, author/title index, subject index, list of publishers/printers, statutory instruments, acts of [year covered], bills of [year covered], parliamentary debates.

CATALOGUING RULES AND CLASSIFICATION SCHEMES USED: In the preparation of entries, AACR2 is used for the cataloguing headings; for the body of the entries, ISBD(M) and ISBD(S) are used.

Entries have been classified using the DDC (20th ed.).[1]

ENTRY INFORMATION: "Classified Subject Section": DDC number, author, title, edition, place of publication, publisher, series statement, date, pagination, illustrations, size, notes including format, binding, price if known, ISBN when available, subject headings, *NBB* serial number, e.g., BB 90-28, in lower right position.

"Statutory Instruments" and "Acts": number, short title, and *Official Gazette* number, date, pagination.

"Bills": short title, number, date in *Official Gazette*, pagination.

"Debates": date, number, date in *Official Gazette*, pagination.

Foreign imprints are indicated by an asterisk (*).

ARRANGEMENT: The Classified Subject Section, the main part of *NBB* is arranged by DDC and supplies the most complete bibliographic description for the entries.

"Statutory Instruments" and "Acts" are numerically arranged.

"Bills" and "Debates" information is arranged in chronological order.

INDEXES: The Author and Title Index is alphabetically arranged. Names of editors, compilers, translators and illustrators are also included. In the index each entry includes an author, title, *NBB* serial number and the DDC number which refers the reader to the full bibliographic entry in the Classified Subject Section.

The Subject Index is alphabetically arranged by headings from the *UNBIS Thesaurus* English edition 1985 (United Nations); it incorporates the *Macrothesaurus for Information Processing in*

---

[1] Edition information from a letter dated 9 February 1996 to the author from Ms. L. Y. Herbert (Senior Librarian) responding for Director of National Library Service J. Blackman.

the field of Economic and Social Development, (Organisation for Economic Co-operation and Develolpment) used in the Caribbean, and other thesauri produced by the UN.[1]

Legislative material is in chronological order. In the 1990-1994 revised special edition (1995) there is a heading for the acts. Then the bills, amendments and statutory instruments relating to that act are interfiled, each section in chronological order. Also included in this special edition are the index of descriptors, names and places; list of House of Assembly Debates, List of Senate Debates, members of the Parliament, and a subject index.

The indexing has improved from earlier years when there was only an author/title/series index, with no subject index, or legislative material indexes. The first subject index appeared in 1986.

NOTES AND COMMENTS: The *NNB* has had several improvements in the last ten to twelve years that have made it easier to use. The most noticeable changes are providing better access through the indexes, adding subject headings to entries, and moving from a cyclostyled to a desktop publishing product.

The 1983 *NNB* was the first issue to use a word processing programme.

The 1986-1990 cumulation of the *NNB* represents a revised and updated version of the bibliography database. The most significant change occurs with the subject terms; except where an occasional record needed to be updated, other information was not changed.

The years 1991-1993 have been published in a cumulated edition.

Government and official publications are not specially designated by a symbol. However, by looking under Barbados in the author index, one can locate many of the government publications.

The legislative lists included in *NBB* can be particularly useful since this information is elusive to people overseas.

Barbados is included within the scope of *CARICOM Bibliography* (ISSN 0254-9646) which was published from 1977-1986.

The publishers' and printers' list includes those whose books appear in the *NBB*.

ICNB recommendations 5, 6, 8-11, 13 are met.

LATEST ISSUE EXAMINED/CURRENCY: The most current volumes of *NBB* examined were the five-year special revised edition for the years 1986-1990, published in 1993, and the *Special edition Parliamentary Debates* with subject index, 1990-1994, published in 1995. The annual cumulations were available in the library consulted seven months to a year after the year covered.

The majority of entries listed in each volume were for the year covered.

---

[1] Information taken from the Subject Index 1986-1990 special edition, vol. 1, p. 327.

AUTOMATION: Currently, *NNB* is published by a desktop publishing programme called Biblio Special Library Application for Inmagic. Inmagic records are converted to Unesco's CDS/ISIS although other word processing software is used for preparation of the publication.[1]

FORMAT AND SERVICES AVAILABLE: printed; available on CARIBBEAN ONLINE: a Regional Database.[2]

CURRENT LEGAL DEPOSIT LAWS: The Registration of Newspapers Act of 20 February 1900, Sect. 9 (1); The Copyright Act of 1915 and its amendments 1956, 1965; The Publications (Legal Deposit) Act, 1982.[3]

AVAILABLE FROM: National Library Service, Culloden Farm, Culloden Road, Bridgetown.

VERIFIER: Lolita Y. Herbert, Senior Librarian, National Library Service

BELARUS

TITLE: *Letapis druku Belarusi* [Chronicle of Belarus publications] / Ministėrstva infarmatsyi Rėspubliki Belarus', Dzi͡arz͡haŭnai͡a kniz͡hnai͡a palata Respubliki Belarus'. - 1992, no.1- . - Minsk : Palata, 1992-   .
Monthly.
Continues *Letapis druku Belaruskaĭ SSR.*
DDC: 015.4765L5671; LC: Z2514.W5L4; LCCN: sn93-33214; OCLC: 27951636
ISSN 0130-9218

COMPILER: National Book Chamber of Belarus.

SCOPE AND COVERAGE: *Letapis druku Belarusi* (*LDB*) includes the publishing output of Belarus which is deposited at the National Book Chamber of Belarus according to legal deposit laws.

Types of publications include books, pamphlets, periodical publications, government publications, list of journal and newspaper articles (for issues before 1995, no. 1), technical documentation, critical reviews, musical scores.[4]

Omitted from *LDB* are list of journal and newspaper articles (from 1995 onwards).

CONTENTS: Title page, classified bibliography under six basic groups (Book Chronicle, Chronicle of normative-technical, technical documents, and issues of special purpose;

---

[1] Information is from "Introduction," *NNB* 1986-1990, viii, and Herbert's letter.

[2] Herbert letter.

[3] Information from "Barbados," *General Information Programme - UNISIST Newsletter* 10 (supplement to no. 1, 1982):6, and *International Guide to Legal Deposit*, Part 2, p. 68.

[4] The author thanks Maxim Goloubev, student at The College of Wooster, for translating information for this entry.

Chronicle of critical reviews, chronicle of notes (musical), Chronicle of fine arts, and Belarus and other countries' publishing about Belarus), indexes, statistical tables by subject and formats, etc.

CATALOGUING RULES AND CLASSIFICATION SCHEMES USED: International standards are followed.

The classification scheme used is the UDC.

ENTRY INFORMATION: Classification number given at head of section, consecutive entry number, title, responsibility statement, place of publication, publisher, date, pagination, illustrations, size, series statement, notes including bibliographies, number of copies printed, UDC number in lower right corner.

ARRANGEMENT: The six basic groups (Book Chronicle, Chronicle of normative-technical, technical documents, and issues of special purpose; Chronicle of critical reviews, chronicle of notes (musical), Chronicle of fine arts, and Belarus and other countries' publishing about Belarus) are each arranged according to the UDC categories, and alphabetically arranged under the subject categories.

INDEXES: Names index, geographic index, titles of periodical issues and continuing issues index which is divided into journals and newspapers, languages index.

At the end of the index section are tables which shows the total entries included in the bibliography by subject and by type of publication.

NOTES AND COMMENTS: Before the breakup of the USSR, publications of Belarus' were recorded in *Knizhnaiia letopis* and *Letapis druku Belaruskaĭ SSR.* Since Belarus' established its independence, the primary record of Belarus' publishing output is recorded in *LDB.*

As mentioned above, *LDB* continues *Letapis' druku Belaruskaĭ SSR* / Dzi̇a̐rzhaŭny kamitėt Belaruskaĭ SSR pa druku, Dzi̇a̐rzhaŭnai̇a̐ knizhnai̇a̐ palata BSSR, Minsk : Palata, 1932-1991. It was suspended from 1944-1946. (LCCN: sn91-28606; LC number: Z2154.W5L4; OCLC: 2467694; ISSN 0139-9218). This title continued *Letapis druku Belaruskaha SSR. . -* Mensk : Vyd-ne Belaruskaĭ dzi̇a̐rzhaunaĭ bibliotėki, 1927-1929. (LC: Z2154.W5L4; LCCN: sn91-28606; OCLC: 24676954; ISSN 0130-9218). Three parts were published; part 1 was never published.

LDB has gone through some changes in format and coverage from 1993-1996. This entry description is based on 1996, no. 7. The two titles below were separated from *LDB.*

Letapis druku Belarusi. Letapis chasopisnykh artykulaŭ [Chronicle of Belarus publications. Chronicle of journal articles]. - 1 (1995)-   . - Minsk : Palata, 1995-   . Monthly (LC: Z2519.5.L47; LCCN: sn96-32002; OCLC: 34636351; ISSN 0130-9218). The compiler is Natsyi̇a̐nal'nai̇a̐ kni̇zhnai̇a̐ palata Belarusi [National Book Chamber of Belarus]. This title continues *Letapis druku Belarusi* and includes a listing of journals in Belarus and indexes the journal articles.

Letapis druku Belarusi. Letapis hazetnykh artykulaŭ [Chronicle of Belarus publications. Chronicle of newspaper articles]. - 1 (1995)-   . - Minsk : Palata, 1995-   . Monthly (LC: Z2519.5.L47; LCCN: sn96-32002; OCLC: 34636351; ISSN 0130-9218). The compiler is Natsyi͡anal'nai͡a kniz͡hnai͡a palata Belarusi [National Book Chamber of Belarus]. This title is separated from *Letapis druku Belarusi* and includes a listing of newspapers in Belarus and indexes the newspaper articles.

Knihi Belarusi. 1991-   . - Minsk : Ministerstva infarmedtysi respubliki Belarus, Natsyi͡anal'nai͡a kniz͡hnai͡a palata Belarusi, 1992-   . Annual (LCCN: 95-642134; LC: Z2154.B94K58; OCLC: 28663362; ISSN 0235-3393). This title continues *Knihi Belaruskaĭ SSR.* - 1956/1960-1990. Annual, with quinquennial cumulations. (LCCN: 88-656501//r953; LC: Z2514.B94K58; OCLC: 17332316; ISSN 0235-3393).

Another publication which is helpful in locating current publications is *Novyi͡a knihi Belarusi* [New Belarus Books] / Dzi͡arz͡haunai͡a bibli͡atėka Belarus [National Library of Belarus].. - 1992, 1-   . - Minsk : Dzi͡arz͡haunai͡a bibli͡atėka Belarus', 1992-   . Monthly (LCCN: sn92-27882; DDC: 015.4765N859; LC: Z2514.B94N98; OCLC: 26336239; ISSN 0134-7284). This title continues *Novyia Knihi BSSR.* - Minsk : Dzi͡arz͡haunai͡a bibli͡atėka BSSR imi͡a U. I. Lenina, 1960?-1991. (LCCN: 92-641702; LC: Z2519.5.N68; OCLC: 24371318; ISSN 0134-7284). *Novyi͡a knihi Belarusi* includes information about new books published in Belarus. This title functions as a recommendation bibliography which reviews the latest publications and presents lists of recommended releases.[1] The latest copy examined in June 1996 at the University of Illinois Library Urbana is no. 11, 1995. Imprint dates were from the period covered.

LATEST ISSUE EXAMINED/CURRENCY: The latest copy examined is July 1996 from the Library of Congress. Imprint dates were from the period covered.

AUTOMATION: Software used in producing the national bibliography is developed by the National Book Chamber of Belarus.

FORMAT AND SERVICES AVAILABLE: printed.

CURRENT LEGAL DEPOSIT LAWS: not known.

AVAILABLE FROM: National Book Chamber of Belarus, Kharuz͡hai͡a st. 31, 220123 Minsk. In the United States, the *Letopis' druku Belarusi* and *Novyi͡a knihi Belarusi* are available from East View Publications, 3020 Harbor Lane North, Minneapolis, MN 55447.

VERIFIER: Alexander Solodkov, formerly with the National Library. No reply received from the National Book Chamber of Belarus.

---

[1] Information in a 28 August 1997 e-mail to the author from Director G. Oleinik, National Library of Belarus.

BELGIUM

TITLE: *Bibliographie de Belgique = Belgische Bibliografie.* - année 1, no. 1 (Jan. 1875)- . - Bruxelles : Bibliothèque Royal Albert 1er, 1875 - .
Monthly, with annual cumulation of bibliographies and indexes (1982-).
Publisher varies.
Frequency varies.
Continues *Bibliographie de la Belgique* (1838-1868) by C. Muquardt.
DDC: 015.493; LC: Z2405.B58; LCCN: 07-30368//r945; OCLC: 1532712
ISSN 0006-1336

COMPILER: Bibliothèque Royal Albert 1er.

SCOPE AND COVERAGE: *Bibliographie de Belgique = Belgische Bibliografie (BB)* lists the publishing output of Belgium that is deposited at the Bibliothèque Royal Albert 1er according to the legal deposit legislation, books by Belgian authors published abroad, and books relating to Belgium published abroad as acquired by the Royal Library.

Types of publications included are books, pamphlets and brochures (of more than five pages), periodicals (new, cessations and changes), official and government publications, theses and dissertations (if printed), maps and atlases (in separate supplement), limited editions, first issues of annual reports, IGO publications published in Belgium, offprints, music (in separate supplement), translations, publications in series (in separate supplement).

Excluded from *BB* are periodical articles.

CONTENTS: [Introduction] (in French and Dutch), list of subjects (in French and Dutch), classified bibliography, author index, corporate authors index, title index, subject index (in French and Dutch), publishers' list.

CATALOGUING RULES AND CLASSIFICATION SCHEMES USED: Bibliographical descriptions are according to ISBD standards since January 1974. For numbers in series, description is based on the first number seen.

No classification is used; organization is based on 32 classes following Unesco's recommendation.

ENTRY INFORMATION: Consecutive entry number, author, title, place of publication, publisher, date, pagination, size, series, notes including ISBN and price if known, placement number of the title in the Bibliothèque Albert 1er in the lower left corner, e.g. BB A 1994 3.975.

The word [sic] is used with an ISBN if this number is incorrect; in earlier years an asterisk (*) in front of an ISBN meant the same.

ARRANGEMENT: Entries are alphabetically arranged within 32 subject groups recommended by Unesco.

INDEXES: Author index (personal, cooperate); title index; subject index in French and Flemish. Numbers refer to the entry number of the bibliographic entry. ndexes cumulate annually.

INOTES AND COMMENTS: The scope, arrangement and indexes of *BB* have changed over the years. This description is primarily based on the current bibliography.
BB issues three supplements: publications in series; maps and atlases; musical works or works relating to music; the citations follow.

Bibliographie de Belgique. Supplément 1, Périodiques nouveaux et séries nouvelles = Belgische bibliografie. Supplement 1, Nieuwe tijdschriften en reeksen. - Bruxelles : Bibliothèque royale Albert Ier, 1982- . Annual (LCCN: sc85-4464; LC (090): Z2405.B471; OCLC: 11281080; ISSN 0006-1336).

Bibliographie de Belgique. Supplément 2, Cartes et atlas = Belgische bibliografie. Supplement 2, Kaarten en atlassen. - Bruxelles : Bibliothèque royale Albert Ier, 1982- . Annual (LCCN: sc85-4465; LC (090): Z2405.B472; OCLC: 11282243; ISSN 0006-1336).

Bibliographie de Belgique. Supplément 3, Musique = Belgische bibliografie. Supplement 3, Musiek. - Bruxelles : Bibliothèque royale Albert Ier, 1982- . Annual. The bibliography is arranged alphabetically by the main entry. Indexes include personal author, collective author, title, and subject (Dutch and French). A publishers' list is given. (LCCN: sc85-4466; LC (090): Z2405.B473; OCLC: 11282277; ISSN 0006-1336). Automation has made it possible to capture 30 years of music listed in *BB* in four cumulation volumes: 1966-1975, 1976-1980, 1981-1990, and 1991-1995.

Since 1982 an annual cumulation is available: *Bibliographie de Belgique. Liste annuelle des publications belges = Belgische Bibliografie. Jaarlijkse lijst van belgische werken.* - Bruxelles : Bibliothèque royale Albert Ier, 1982- . Annual (LCCN: sc85-23041; LC (090): Z2405.B581; OCLC: 12436862; ISSN 0006-1336).

In 1984 *Aangekondigde publikaties = Publications annoncées.* - Brusselles : Koninklijke Bibliotheek, 1984- . Semimonthly (LCCN: 88-648575; LC: Z2405.A26; OCLC: 10969686). This lists CIP information for books before publication. When they are published these books are listed in *BB*.

From 1959-1974, the books by foreigners are listed in *Fascicule spécial*, "Liste annuelle des publications d'auteurs belges à l'étranger et des publications étrangères relatives à l'etranger et des publications étrangères relatives à la Belgique..." with separate indexes.[1]

Periodicals were included in a separate part through 1926.[2]

Volumes 47-57 (1921-1930) of *BB* are called "nouv. sér."

---

[1] *GRB* AA582, p. 63.
[2] Ibid.

BB includes official publications without any symbol. There appears to be no separate official publications bibliography for Belgium.

In the early years of *BB*, the scope included periodical articles. However, at present, periodical articles are included in *Bulletin des Sommaires des Périodiques de Belgique*. - Bruxelles : Association Belge de Documentation, 1951- . Irregular. The first number beginning with the 1951 issue explained that the "*Bulletin* had been begun in 1899 by the International Office ofBibliography and for a time published as a part of the *BB*, but that it had been suspended several times, last in 1946."[1]

LATEST ISSUE EXAMINED/CURRENCY: Entries include imprints from the period covered and from earlier years. On a sample page from December 1984, two entries were for 1984, three entries for 1983, one entry for 1982, four entries for 1980 and one entry for 1979.

The latest monthly issue of *BB* examined is number 11 for November 1994, received by the University of Minnesota 20 March 1995. The latest annual cumulation examined is for 1995. The latest issue of *BB. Supplément 3, Musique* examined at Rhodes House Library, Oxford is the cumulated 1991-1995. The latest *Publications announcees* examined is no. 2/3 1993.

AUTOMATION: *BB* has been automated since 198?.

FORMAT AND SERVICES AVAILABLE: printed.

CURRENT LEGAL DEPOSIT LAWS: Loi du 8 Avril 1965 .[2]

AVAILABLE FROM: Bibliothèque Royal Albert 1er, 4 Blvd. de l'Empereur, 1000 Brussels.

VERIFIER: No reply received.

BELIZE

No current national bibliography has been traced for Belize.[3]

A Bibliography of Books on Belize in the National Collection. 4th ed. - Belize City: Central Library, Bliss Institute, 1977, and its first supplement dated 1979 (OCLC: 6994654) list in classified arrangement the material on Belize and works written by Belizeans. DDC numbers are used and separate author and title indexes are supplied.

---

[1] *Current National Bibliographies*, p. 44.

[2] ["Introduction"], *BB*, November 1994, p. [i]

[3] The author was unable to verify the statement in Carol Collins' article "The Production of Current National Bibliographies in the Commonwealth Caribbean," *International Cataloguing* 6 (April/June 1977):22 which states that the "national bibliography of Belize is to be published quarterly, instead of previous intermittent publication." Latin American specialists were consulted at the British Library, London and the Senate House Library, University of London.

CURRENT LEGAL DEPOSIT LAWS: Belize Archives Act 1984; National Library Service Ordinance,1960.[1]

BÉNIN

TITLE: *Bibliographie du Bénin*. - 1976/77- . - Porto-Novo : Bibliothèque Nationale, 1978- . Irregular.
DDC: 015.669/3; LC Z3686.B52, DT541.A2; LCCN: 79-640809//r85; OCLC: 5035074
ISSN not found (not available)

COMPILER: Bibliothèque Nationale.

SCOPE AND COVERAGE: The *Bibliographie du Bénin* (*BDB*) includes national imprints, in both print and oral form, that are deposited at the Bibliothèque Nationale in accordance with the legal deposit ordinance. It also includes library purchases and gifts and materials on Bénin published elsewhere.

Types of publications in *BDB* are monographs, official and government publications. Books written by Bénin citizens and published abroad regardless of the subject are also within the scope. The scope has changed with regard to articles which were included in the first issue but are not included in the fourth issue(1989-1995).

Excluded are periodicals, maps and atlases, sound recordings and disks; they should be published in further separate volumes of the bibliography.[2]

CONTENTS: Volume 1 and 2: Table of contents, introduction, list of abbreviations, list of periodicals indexed, classification schedule, bibliography: section 1, books; section 2, periodical articles; section 3, official publications; section 4, other documents; index. Volume 4: foreword, introduction, classified bibliography, indexes.

CATALOGUING RULES AND CLASSIFICATION SCHEMES USED: Works are catalogued following ISBD.

BDB uses the main classes of the DDC system for classification.

ENTRY INFORMATION: Entry number, author, title, edition, place of publication, publisher, date, pagination, illustrations, size, series, ISBN, binding information.

ARRANGEMENT: Volume 1 and 2: Within the bibliography, sections 1 to 3 are arranged by the broad divisions of UDC, then alphabetically arranged by main entry. Section 4 is alphabetically arranged, as is the periodical list. Volume 4 is arranged by the main classes of the DDC, then alphabetically by author or title.

---

[1] *International Guide to Legal Deposit*, p. 68.
[2] Information in a 25 August 1997 fax to the author from Aubin Odah, Bibliothèque Nationale du Benin.

INDEXES: *BDB* uses a dictionary index which includes author and title. The number refers the reader to the consecutive entry number. No. 4: 1989-1995 has author index, corporate bodies index, title index, subject index.[1]

NOTES AND COMMENTS: The first volume of *BDB*, published in French, has eighty-six entries and follows many of the ICNB recommendations. The fourth volume has 121 entries. It is stated in the introduction of the first volume that articles included are about Bénin from publications edited in Bénin or foreign countries which are received at the Bibliothèque Nationale with the exception of "journaux". This leaves out articles in Bénin or elsewhere written by Bénin citizens about subjects other than Bénin, thus eliminating a part of the "national imprint" of value to a country with a small publishing output. In the first volume the information for the list of periodicals indexed only gave the titles. Complete bibliographic information should be given. A list of publishers and addresses is also missing. Since this is elusive information for foreigners who want to order books listed in *BDB*, it would be helpful to include this information at the source. Volume 4 does not include articles.

The introduction for volume one states that *BDB* would be published every three months. Because of the small number of publications deposited at the Bibliothèque Nationale this has not been possible. One hopes that *BDB* will become more frequent as legal deposit materials are deposited with regularity.

ISSN and ISBN are soon to be established at the Bibliothèque Nationale. It is hoped that this will be an incentive to increase legal deposit which is not observed by all publishers.[2]

Publications in English, French, and Yoruba are recorded in *BDB*.

The years covered in *BDB* are as follows: vol. (also called no.) 1: 1976/1977, vol. 2: 1978/1983, vol. 3: 1984/1988, vol. 4: 1989/1995.

LATEST ISSUE EXAMINED/CURRENCY: The 1976/77 volume was published in 1978 and was received by the Library of Congress in October 1978. Number 2, published in 1984, was received by the Library of Congress 14 May 1985. Numbers 3 and 4 have been received by the Library of Congress, but they were not available for examination. This is the last volume examined. No more current issues were located in visits to Indiana University, University of Michigan, Library of Congress, British Library, SOAS, and telephone inquiries to Northwestern University, and the University of Florida during 1996 and 1997.

The entries that were checked for currency were for the period covered by the volume, or had no date.

AUTOMATION: BDS is published automatically in ISBD format, starting with issue 4. The software used is CDS/ISIS (from Unesco), on a stand alone PC (Pentium 66).

FORMAT AND SERVICES AVAILABLE: printed.

---

[1] Information for no. 4, 1989-1995 in Odah's fax. This was not examined by the author.
[2] Ibid.

CURRENT LEGAL DEPOSIT LAWS: Ordinance number 75-79 of 28 November 1975 established legal deposit at the Bibliothèque Nationale. It became effective 1 January 1976.

AVAILABLE FROM: Bibliothèque Nationale, B.P. 401, Porto-Novo.

VERIFIER: Aubin Odah, Bibliothèque Nationale, Porto-Novo.

BERMUDA

TITLE: *Bermuda national bibliography*. - 1983-   . [Hamilton] : Bermuda Library, Technical Services, 1984-   .
Quarterly, with annual cumulation.
DDC: 016.97299 (quarterly, annual);   LC: Z1591.B46b (quarterly), Z1591.B46a (annual);   LCCN: 86-645455 (quarterly), 85-644493//r89 (annual);   OCLC: 14758615 (quarterly), 12537205 (annual)
ISSN 0255-0067

COMPILER: Technical Services, Bermuda Library.

SCOPE AND COVERAGE: *Bermuda National Bibliography* (*BNB*) includes works about Bermuda and Bermudians, and other subjects published in Bermuda or abroad, written by Bermudians, resident and expatriate.

Types of publications included within the scope of *BNB* are books, pamphlets, first issues, title changes and cessations of periodical publications, newspapers, annual reports, government publications (published and unpublished), maps and three-dimensional artifacts.

The 1983 first annual issue includes the full listing of local annual reports, newspapers, and periodicals received on a regular basis by the Bermuda Library.

CONTENTS: [Introduction] which includes scope and coverage, and information about the current legal deposit law in Bermuda, table of contents, explanation of entries, abbreviations, outline of the DDC system, classified bibliography (books, pamphlets, maps and printed sheets, audio-visual materials, and periodical publications, author/title/series index.

CATALOGUING RULES AND CLASSIFICATION SCHEMES USED: *BNB* follows AACR2 for its cataloguing.

The classification scheme used is DDC (20th ed.).

ENTRY INFORMATION: DDC number, author, title, place of publication, publisher, date, pagination, illustrations, size, notes (including ISBN if known, price, etc.), subject headings, and added entries.

ARRANGEMENT: The classified bibliography is arranged by the DDC scheme.

INDEXES: Author/title/series index, arranged in one alphabetical sequence.

NOTES AND COMMENTS: The first issue of *BNB* is offered free in celebration of 375 years of continuous settlement in Bermuda. The issue covering 1983 was issued as an annual only, and lists all local annual reports, newspapers and other periodicals received on a regular basis at the Bermuda Library, regardless of beginning dates.

BNB is conceived and compiled in accordance with ICNB 1977. The double-column arrangement, and the use of bold type sets off DDC headings and main entry information making the bibliography easy to use and pleasing to the eye.

Government publications are not designated by any symbol; however, it is relatively easy to locate them by browsing through the classified bibliography, or by looking in the index under Bermuda.

LATEST ISSUE EXAMINED/CURRENCY: The latest issue examined is the annual issue for 1995 sent to the author by the Bermuda Library in November 1996. Imprints include dates ranging from 1922 through 1995, with 41 percent of the entries from 1995, 26 percent from 1994.

AUTOMATION: The *BNB* is produced with Microsoft Word for Windows 95 Version 7 on a Compaq Prolinea 5133, 133MHz Pentium computer and an HP LaserJet IIID printer. One copy of the annual edition is printed at the Library and sent to a commercial printer to be reproduced and bound.

FORMAT AND SERVICES AVAILABLE: printed.

CURRENT LEGAL DEPOSIT LAWS: Printed Publications Act, 1971. [1]

AVAILABLE FROM: Head Librarian, The Bermuda Library, 13 Queen Street, Hamilton HM 11.

SELECTED ARTICLES: "UBC News." *International Cataloguing* 13 (no. 4, 1984):38-39.

VERIFIER: Mrs. Patrice Carvell, Technical Services Librarian, Bermuda Library.

BHUTÁN

No current national bibliography has been traced for Bhután.

AL,SA includes Bhután within its scope.

---

[1] [Introduction], *BNB*, 1991.

BOLIVIA

TITLE: *Bio-bibliografía boliviana.* - 1975-   . La Paz and Cochabamba : Editorial Los Amigos del Libro, 1975-   .
Continues *Bibliografía Boliviana* (1962-1974).
Annual.
DDC: not found; LC: Z1641.B5; LCCN: 79-648775; OCLC: 3020266
ISSN not found, ISBN 84-8370-195-2 (1995); ISSN 0067-6578 (*Bibliografía boliviana*)

COMPILER: Werner Guttentag Tichauer, M. Rita Arze Ramirez (vol. 34).
SCOPE AND COVERAGE: *Bio-bibliografía Boliviana* (*BB*) is a listing of books published in Bolivia and/or by Bolivians with occasional notes on the author or on the volume. Some issues provide information on books about Bolivia published abroad. *BB* is not considered an official national bibliography but includes many of the elements that one expects to find in a national bibliography. It is not directly connected with Biblioteca y Archivo Nacional de Bolivia, the Repositorio Nacional, La Paz or the legal deposit system.

Types of publications included in *BB* are books, pamphlets, periodicals (since 1976), official and government publications, theses and dissertations, maps, translations of Bolivian authors, foreign language publications (including periodicals which have articles by Bolivian authors).

CONTENTS: Based on volume for 1995: introduction, bibliography for 1995, indexes for 1995, supplement for 1962-1994; indexes for supplement; bibliographies of "revistas especializadas" [*De Cerca, Nueva Sociedad, Temas en la Crisis, Opiniones y Análisis*]; additions and corrections to *Bibliografia Boliviana* (1659-1908), abbreviations used, general index [functioning as a table of contents].

Based on volume for 1992: "Testimonio de un siglo" in honor of Stefan Zweig, "Una aventura compartida" discusses an overview of *BB* from volume 1-31, bibliography for 1992, title index, subject index, publishers' list, name index, supplement of *BB* 1962-1991, title index, subject index, publishers' index, name index, bibliography of books registered in the legal deposit (1992), bibliography of articles on Bolivia and Bolivian authors published en *Nueva Sociedad*, *Temas en la Crisis* bibliography, *Contrapunto* bibliography, *De Cerca* bibliography, "Opinions and Analysis" bibliography, abbreviations, general index.

CATALOGUING RULES AND CLASSIFICATION SCHEMES USED: AACR rules are followed in giving bibliographic information.

The classification scheme used is DDC.

ENTRY INFORMATION: Entry number, author, title, place of publication, publisher, date, size, pagination, occasional remarks about author and brief analysis of contents of the work, ISBN if known. No book price information is given. All of the above information is not in every entry. Numbers correspond to the system at Libreria - Editorial Los Amigos del Libro.

Some entries in the bibliography section appear to be identification of an author. Name and brief information of the author is given.

ARRANGEMENT: The main bibliography is arranged by author or main entry.

INDEXES: Indexes for 1995: title index; publishers' index; subject index; names index for the main bio-bibliography. The same indexes are repeated for the bio-bibliographic supplement. Numbers used in the indexes refer to the entry numbers in the main bibliography. Author approach is through the main bibliography.

Various volumes have cumulative indexes, e.g., the volume for 1981 has author, title and "onomástico" indexes for the period 1962-1981; 1979 has a cumulative index of subjects from 1962-1979.

NOTES AND COMMENTS: *BB* is not considered an official national bibliography. It is not sponsored by the National Library (Biblioteca y Archivo Nacional de Bolivia), or the Repositorio Nacional in La Paz and is not based on the legal deposit legislation that exists in Bolivia. *BB* is the work of an individual who is the head of the publishing firm Editorial Los Amigos del Libro. Through his efforts, Bolivia has a bibliography which appears on a regular basis and lists current works by and about Bolivia and Bolivians. Supplements appear on specific subjects, or are a continuing list of titles which extend and expand the bibliography's scope.

Each year a supplement to *BB* is published that includes titles from 1962 to the past year which have not been listed previously. The volume for 1992 includes the supplement for 1962-1991, 1981 includes a supplement to *BB* for the years 1962-1980. The volume for 1978 includes a supplement of titles for 1962-1977, and "Bibliografía Biográfica Boliviana" by Jose Roberta Arze. These supplements continue the entry number of the volume in which the title should have been originally included. It is necessary to check current volumes for a title if it is not found in the volume for the year in which it was published. This means that each volume needs to be checked when looking for a particular title.

The introduction usually includes information about the publishing world in Bolivia.

Major works included may have a reproduction of the table of contents included as part of the information given about the title.

CIP is not practiced in Bolivia.

LATEST ISSUE EXAMINED/CURRENCY: *BB* experiences a two to three year lag from the period of time covered to the time it is received by libraries. The latest volume examined was the 1995 volume, published in 1996.

Most entries have an imprint of 1995, with the exception of the supplement which includes imprints for earlier years.

AUTOMATION: Automation is planned for 1997.

FORMAT AND SERVICES AVAILABLE: printed.

CURRENT LEGAL DEPOSIT LAWS: Decreto Supremo No. 08617 of 8 January 1909 established the legal deposit office; this has been amended several times, the latest being Decreto Supremo No. 16762 of 11 July 1979.[1]

AVAILABLE FROM: Editorial Los Amigos del Libro, Cochabamba, Casilla 450, or Editorial Los Amigos del Libro, La Paz, Casilla 4415.

VERIFIER: Werner Guttentag T., compiler.

BOSNIA and HERCEGOVINA

TITLE: *Bibliografija bosanskohercegovačke knjige za* [ ] *godinu* [Bibliography of Bosnia/ Hercegovina books]. - Sarajevo : Narodna i univerzitetska biblioteka Bosne i Hercegovine [National and University Library of Bosnia and Hercegovina], 1977-1990.
Annual.
UDC: 015 (497.15); LC: Z2957.B68B5; LCCN: 80-646321; OCLC: 6594825
ISSN 0352-0951

COMPILER: National and University Library of Bosnia and Hercegovina.

SCOPE AND COVERAGE: *Bibliografija bosanskohercegovačke knjige* (*BBK*) includes books published in Bosnia and Hercegovina which are received by the National and University Library according to legal deposit legislation.[2]

Types of publications include books, pamphlets, atlases, music material, and catalogues.

Omitted from *BBK* are periodical publications which are included in another part of the national bibliography.

CONTENTS: Preface, abbreviations, classified bibliography, indexes, UDC subject heading index, list of indexes.

CATALOGUING RULES AND CLASSIFICATION SCHEMES USED: Bibliographic description follows ISBD(M) and *Pravilnik i prirucnik za izradu abecednih kataloga*, I i II, 1970-1986 [Laws and rules for catalogue entries] by Eve Verone.

The classification scheme used is the UDC.

ENTRY INFORMATION: At the head of each subject group is the general UDC subject heading and UDC number, author, title, place of publication, publisher, date, pagination, illustrations, size, series statement, notes including number of copies printed. The UDC number and an internal number (0000163433) are at the bottom left; the classification number used in

---

[1] *BSTW, Supplement 1981-1982*, p. 73.
[2] Nacionalna i Univerzitetska Biblioteka Bosne i Hercegovine. "Bibliografija monografskih publikacija 1992-1994," p. 4 (typescript).

the library is at the lower right, along with the consecutive national bibliography number, e.g., BiHK84-19.

ARRANGEMENT: Arrangement is alphabetical within UDC subject groups.

INDEXES: Author index, title index, subject index, series index, alphabetical list of UDC subject headings.

NOTES AND COMMENTS: The 1990s have been a period of turmoil for Bosnia and Herzegovina. The former Yugoslavian republics of Slovenia, Croatia, Macedonia, Yugoslavia, and Bosnia and Herzegovina are now independent. Some of the former republics had a regional bibliography which has now become their national bibliography. These bibliographies are analyzed separately under each nation's name.

The current title which records serial publications is *Bibliografija serijskih publikacija Bosne i Hercegovine.* - 1997-   . - Sarajevo : Biblioteka, 1997-   . ISSN has not been assigned. Although this was not stated by the Library, one assumes that this title continues *Bibliografija bosanskohercegovačke serijskih publikacija za ... godinu* [Bibliography of Bosnia and Hercegovina serial publications for the year ...] / Narodna i univerzitetska biblioteka Bosne i Hercegovine. 1984-199?. - Sarajevo : Biblioteka, 1986-199?. Annual (LCCN: sn87-40172; LC: Z2957.B68P73; OCLC: 16770108; ISSN 03352-0846). This title is a directory of periodicals and newspapers in Bosnia. It continues *Bibliografija bosanskohercegovackih časopisa i novina i bibliografija bosanskohercegovačke godišnjaka i periodičnik zbornika za ... godinu / Narodna i univerzitetska biblioteka Bosne i Hercegovine.* - Sarajevo : Biblioteks, 1980-1983. (LCCN: 86-650962//r93; LC: Z2957.B68P73; PN5355.Y8; OCLC: 13221218; ISSN 0352-0846). This continues *Pregled bosanskohercegovačke časopisa i novina za ... godinu / Narodna i univerzitetska biblioteka Bosne i Hercegovine.* - Sarajevo : Biblioteka, 1978-1979? (LCCN: 82-641257; OCLC: 8249891).

LATEST ISSUE EXAMINED/CURRENCY: The latest issue of *BBK* examined is for 1984, published in 1990. Because of the unrest, no issues have been published since this issue; it is in hiatus. *BBK* is expected to resume when life is more settled in Bosnia and Hercegovina. The analyzed title below is an attempt to fill the gap. Although the Library does not state this, one assumes that the title below may be a continuation of *Bibliografija bosanskohercegovačke knjige za [ ] godinu.*

Imprint dates are from the year covered.

AUTOMATION: not automated.

FORMAT AND SERVICES AVAILABLE: printed

AVAILABLE FROM: National and University Library of Bosnia and Herzegovina, Mak Dizdar 2, 71000 Sarajevo.

§

TITLE: *Bibliografija monografskih publikacija* [Bibliography of monographic publications]. - 1992/1994-   . -   Sarajevo : Nacionalna i Univerzitetska Biblioteka Bosne i Hercegovine, 1995- .
Annual, with first issue covering more than one year.
On cover: Popis ratnih izdanja [List of wartime publications]
An effort to revive the legal deposit coverage of *Bibliografija bosanskohercegovačke knjige*.
Description based on 1992/1994 issue.
Also appears in the journal *Bosniaca*.
DDC: not found; LC: not found; LCCN: not found; OCLC: not found
ISSN not found

COMPILER: Pripremljeno u Odjeljenju za bibliografiju, Nacionalna i Univerzitetska Biblioteka Bosne i Hercegovine [Prepared in the Section for Bibliography, National and University Library, Bosnia and Hercegovina].

SCOPE AND COVERAGE: *Bibliografija monografskih publikacija* (*BMP*) includes the publishing output of Bosnia and Hercegovina, which is deposited at the temporary national library according to legal deposit laws.

Types of publications include books, pamphlets, official and government publications.

Serials are omitted from *BMP*.

CONTENTS: Introduction (written in English and Croatian), bibliography, rebuilding of the National and University Library plans (in English).

CATALOGUING RULES AND CLASSIFICATION SCHEMES USED: ISBD is followed.

No classification scheme is used.

ENTRY INFORMATION: Author, title, place of publication, publisher, date, pagination, illustrations, size, series statement.

ARRANGEMENT: The bibliography is alphabetically arranged according to the main entry.

INDEXES: No index.

NOTES AND COMMENTS: On the night of 25-26 August 1992 the National and University Library of Bosnia and Hercegovina in Sarajevo was destroyed as the result of military bombardment. Temporarily the National Library is functioning from part of the university library and will move to an army barracks government building after the barracks have been remodeled for library use. The political and economic situations continue to be difficult.[1]

---

[1] Information about the current library situation in Bosnia and Hercegovina was given to the author in a 27 November 1996 telephone conversation with Library of Congress European Division specialist Predrag Pajic. He traveled to Bosnia and Hercegovina in October 1996.

As mentioned above, the Library has not stated that this current title continues *Bibliografija bosanskohercegovačke knjige za* [ ] *godinu*. However, *BMP* is the title which will continue to be published by the National and University Library of Bosnia and Hercegovina.[1]

Bosniaca is a new journal published semiannually by the National and University Library to inform people about the history and bibliography of Bosnia.[2] The first issue of this journal will include the *BMP* bibliography of 400 *Bosniaca* titles presented to the National and University Library during the 1992-1994 period. This bibliography has been prepared in an effort to record publishing during this period. The Library realizes that it is not complete "due to war, communication blockade, occupation of some parts of the country" as well as new publishers who do not have an understanding of legal deposit regulations. It is the hope of the National and University Library that in the future it will be possible to make the bibliography more complete than it is now.[3]

GIP/Unesco helped in the publication of this bibliography.[4]

Since the war, pamphlets listing 50 to 60 titles– mostly textbooks and translations from the Arabic, into French, Italian, etc.– include books which have been published as "war editions." These listings are about Bosnia, not by Bosnians.[5]

LATEST ISSUE EXAMINED/CURRENCY: The latest issue examined covers the 1992-1994 period, and was published in November 1995. All except three of the 400 imprints were from the period covered.

AUTOMATION: Not at present. Acquisition of bibliographic software "is contemplated after moving into barrack premises."[6]

FORMAT AND SERVICES AVAILABLE: printed.

CURRENT LEGAL DEPOSIT LAWS: Zakon o bibliteckoj djelatnosti Bosne i Herzegovine (*Official Gazette* No. 37, 2. Oct. 1995) Zakon o dostavljanu štampanih stvari odredenim organižacijama uruzenog rada ('Službeni list SR Bosnia i Hercegovina' br. 10/78).[7]

---

[1] In a 2 July 1997 letter to the author from Dr. Enes Kujundzic, Director.

[2] This title was mentioned in Jane Perlez's "Sarajevo Journal: A Library is in Ruins, but with a Will to Live," *New York Times* (12 August 1996):A4:1-5.

[3] "Bibliografija monografskih publikacija 1992-1994," p. 4. The author is indebted to Janet Crayne, Slavic Librarian, University Library, University of Michigan for information about this bibliography before its publication in *Bosniaca*.

[4] Statement at the end of the publication (p. 47): *Izdavanje ove publikacije pomagao je General Information Programme Unesco*.

[5] Information from Mr. Pajic.

[6] Quotation is taken from a 5 June 1997 letter to the author from Dr. Kujundzic, Director. Temporary headquarters for the library will be in former military barracks.

[7] Information about the current legal deposit law was given in letter to the author from Dr. Kujundzic.

AVAILABLE FROM: National and University Library of Bosnia and Herzegovina, Mak Dizdar 2, 71000 Sarajevo.

SELECTED ARTICLES: Kujundzic, Enes. *Prilog bibliografiji bibliografija Bosne i Herzegovine* / Prepared by Dr. E. Kujundzic, et al. – Sarajevo : NUB BiH, 1994.

VERIFIER: Dr. Enes Kujundzic, Director, National and University Library of Bosnia and Herzegovina.

BOTSWANA

TITLE: *The National bibliography of Botswana.* - 1969-   . - Gaborone : Botswana National Library Service, 1969-   .
Three numbers a year with the last issue cumulative for the year (1970-1981; 1983-   ); annual (1982); semiannual (1969).
DDC: 015.681/1; LC: Z3559.N38; LCCN: 74-13910; OCLC: 1588720
ISSN 0027-8777

COMPILER: Botswana National Library Service.

SCOPE AND COVERAGE: *The National Bibliography of Botswana* (*NABOB*) records all publications issued in the Republic of Botswana and deposited at the National Library under the legal deposit act. Beginning with volume 15 (1983) selected publications published elsewhere on Botswana or by Batswana are included. Many of the foreign publications included are deposited at the National Library Service under the *Anthropological Research Act* which requires researchers to deposit copies of their research reports at the National Library and in several other places.[1] Publications are from the period covered and other titles published and deposited in the last two years which have not been listed previously.

Beginning with the 1995 issues, publications received at the University of Botswana Library (the second depository library) are within the scope of *NABOB* even if these publications have not been received by the National Library Service.[2]

Types of publications included are monographs and serials (first issues and subsequent name changes) published in Botswana, including government publications, conference proceedings, theses and/or dissertations (presented at the University of Botswana and other universities whose subject content is or includes Botswana), audio-visual materials (not included in the current legal deposit law, so publishers are not obligated to deposit titles), maps and atlases. Volume 14 (1982) and earlier volumes include serials appearing less than six times a year with a note about serial cessations. Beginning with volume 15 (1983), only new periodical titles and subsequent name changes are listed, and coverage was broadened to include conference proceedings, theses or dissertations whose subject content is or includes Botswana; overseas

---

[1] Information about deposits relating to the *Anthropological Research Act* was included in a letter from G.K. Mulinda to the author dated 5 January 1996.
[2] Mulinda letter.

publications (monographs, monographic series) by Botswana or with Botswana subject content which was not included previously. These foreign publications come in all formats, including periodical articles.

Omitted from *NABOB* are periodical articles (except when received through the *Anthropological Research Act*), and ephemera.

CONTENTS: Table of contents, editorial, subscription rates, list of abbreviations and acronyms, guide to main classes of DDC scheme, classified subject sequence, index, list of local publishers (which now includes the publisher prefixes for those participating in the ISBN scheme), list of local bookshops.

CATALOGUING RULES AND CLASSIFICATION SCHEMES USED: *NABOB* is catalogued according to AACR2, adopted with volume 15, number 1.

The classification scheme used is DDC (20th ed.)

ENTRY INFORMATION: DDC number and classification headings, author, title, place of publication, publisher, date, pagination; illustrations, size, series, ISBN (when available, appear beginning with issues for 1989).

From volume 10, number 3 (1978) the cumulative issues use an "N" in the left-hand margin before entries to indicate new entries for the September-December period.

An asterisk (*) indicates all works of foreign origin.

ARRANGEMENT: The classified subject section, the main part of *NABOB*, is arranged by DDC.

INDEXES: Although the first issue covering 1969 had no index, subsequent issues do. One alphabetical index includes author, joint author, editor, title, issuing body, series. The access number used is the DDC number which refers the user to the classified subject section.

Beginning with the 1995 issues, the index is separated into author and title sequences.[1]

NOTES AND COMMENTS: The scope of the first volume (1969) was limited strictly to works published within the country. With volume 15 (1983) *NABOB* widened its scope to include foreign publications about Botswana or by Batswana. Previously, to include works about Botswana published in other languages in other countries was not possible because of the limited staffing positions at the National Library. Including local language publications in *NABOB* adheres to ICNB recommendation 6.

NABOB does not list titles in Setswana and other local languages issued annually in the Republic of South Africa since these are recorded in the *South African National Bibliography*.

---

[1] Ibid.

All priced government publications are available from the Government Printer's Bookshop, Private Bag 0081, Gaborone. National Institute of Research publications are available from the Botswana Book Centre, P.O. Box 91, Gaborone. All other publications, including unpriced government publications, are available from their respective publishers.

Government publications are not designated by any symbol. By looking under Botswana and the corporate author in the index, one can identify many of the government publications included. The consistent underlining of government departments in the classified subject section also aids in identifying government publications. Approximately half of the entries in *NABOB* seem to be government related.

The *AL,ESA* and *QIPL,ESA* include Botswana within their scopes.

During September 1969 many place names in Botswana changed, e.g., Gaberones became Gaborone; Lobatsi became Lobatse.

CIP is not used in *NABOB*, nor is there an agency to assign ISSN at present.

LATEST ISSUE EXAMINED/CURRENCY: Issues of *NABOB* were available for use in libraries consulted approximately one to two years after the period covered. Although this is better than many national bibliographies, the distribution is not as timely as is needed to order titles from it. Many times titles listed in *NABOB* are published in small quantities and are out-of-print shortly after publication. The lists of publishers and bookshops are helpful for those wanting to use this for acquisitions. According to Ms. Mulindwa, delays are caused by staff shortages and the manual production of the bibliography. It is expected that timeliness will improve when the automation production begins.

In a small sampling taken from the 1993 (vol. 25, no. 2) bibliography, 19 of 25 entries were 1993 imprints, 5 were 1992 imprints, and one was from 1990. This is timely coverage. If distribution could be improved, it would aid the collection development and acquisitions use.

The latest issue examined in November 1994 was volume 25, no. 2 (1993) at the University of Edinburgh Library; it was received October 1994.

AUTOMATION: *NABOB* is not automated through the 1994 issues. However, plans to automate are in process and the 1995 issues will be the first to be produced by automated means.[1]

FORMATS AND SERVICES AVAILABLE: printed.

CURRENT LEGAL DEPOSIT LAWS: "Deposit and Preservation of Copies of Books," Section 10 of the Botswana National Library Services Act, 1967.[2]

AVAILABLE FROM: For subscription or exchange: Botswana National Library Service, Private Bag 0036, Gaborone.

---

[1] Ibid.

[2] In the 5 January 1996 letter, Ms. Mulinda stated that plans are underway to revise the existing legal deposit law.

Cable: BONALIBS.

VERIFIER: Gertrude K. Mulindwa, Editor, *National Bibliography of Botswana.*

BRAZIL

TITLE: *Bibliografia brasileira.* - vol. 1, no. 1/2- , 1983- . - Rio de Janeiro : Biblioteca Nacional, 1984- .
Trimestral.
Available on CD-ROM since 1996.
Supersedes *Boletim bibliográfico da Biblioteca Nacional.*
DDC: 015.81; LC.: Z1671.B52; LCCN: 85-647938 (paper), sn94-31918 (microfiche); OCLC: 11764972 (paper), 29906465 (microfiche)
ISSN 0102-3144

COMPILER: Biblioteca Nacional.

SCOPE AND COVERAGE: *Bibliografia Brasileira* (*BB*) lists all titles published in Brazil and deposited at the Biblioteca Nacional according to the legal deposit law.

Types of publications in *BB* include books, pamphlets, official and government publications, theses, reprints, translations, IGO publications if received through legal deposit.

Since vol. 6, no. 4 1988 *BB* does not include new titles of periodicals.

CONTENTS: Legal deposit law, table of contents, DDC scheme, bibliography, indexes.

CATALOGUING RULES AND CLASSIFICATION SCHEMES USED: The Portuguese edition of AACR2 is used for cataloguing purposes.

The classification scheme used in *BB* is the DDC.

ENTRY INFORMATION: Printed issues through no. 2 1995: author, title, edition statement, place of publication, publisher, date, pagination, illustration, size, notes including ISBN, analytics. The complete classification number is in the lower left corner; the consecutive entry number is located in the lower right corner. No price information is given.

Since 1996, *BB* is part of the Brazilian National Library Database. See Notes and Comments.

ARRANGEMENT: Printed issues through no. 2 1995: arranged by DDC and then alphabetically by main entry within each heading. Periodicals are alphabetically arranged by title in the "anexo."

Since 1996, *BB* is part of the Brazilian National Library Database. See Notes and Comments.

INDEXES: Author index, title index, subject index. The number refers to the entry number in the main bibliography.

The range of indexes available in *BB* is an improvement over *Boletim Bibliográfico da Biblioteca Nacional* which had only an author index in the 1982 issues examined.

NOTES AND COMMENTS: The last number of *BB* to be published by photo-composition is vol. 13, no. 2 1995. Since then, the *BB* has been included as part of the Brazilian National Library Database, available in CD-ROM, first published in 1996. This includes all publications received by the Fundação Biblioteca Nacional through legal deposit, exchanges and donations since 1982 until June 1995. The second edition will be available before the end of 1997 and will be a cumulative edition of records produced through March 1997. This is planned to be an annual publication.[1]

From 1886-1888, the *Boletim das Aquisições Mais Importantes* was issued by the Biblioteca Nacional. This list was based on titles received under the legal deposit laws. It was not until 1918 when the *Boletim Bibliográfico da Biblioteca Nacional* (*BBBN*) was first published that a current national bibliography was attempted (OCLC: 1164181). The *BBBN* has had a history of starts and stops. This was suspended from 1922-1930, 1932-1937, and was covered retrospectively in 1939.[2] Another suspension included the years 1939-1944; the volume for 1945 was published in 1947. The new series began in 1951 through 1967 under the title *Boletim bibliográfico*. (OCLC: 7478838). It is continued by *Boletim bibliográfico da Biblioteca Nacional* 1973-1982. (OCLC: 12649108). According to I. Zimmerman "It is with its limitations, one of the best national bibliographies published in Latin America."[3]

In latter volumes of *BBBN* official and government publications are not designated by a symbol in the bibliographic listing, although for a ten year period from 1959-1969, an asterisk (*) was used to designate these publications. One may find these titles by looking under Brazil and the issuing agency in the index and checking the entry number given in the main bibliography, or by looking under the appropriate subject classification and then checking for the main entry of Brazil, and the issuing agency.

An introduction that explains the scope, contents and rules followed in *BB* is a feature that would be beneficial to its users, and comply with ICNB nos. 9 and 10. At present, there is no introductory material designed to aid the user.

Government publications are not designated by any symbol.

Bibliografia de Publicações Oficiais Brasileiras. - Vol. 1- . , 1975/1977-   . - Coordenação de Biblioteca, Seção de Recebimento e Controle de Publicações Nacionais, 1981-   . (ISSN 0100-

---

[1] Information about the CD-ROM is included in an 6 August 1997 fax to the author from C.A. Sepúlveda, Chief of Cabinet for the Presidency, Fundação Biblioteca Nacional. Information describing *BB* accurately describes the electronic format except for the contents and arrangement..

[2] Laurence Hallewell, "Development of National Bibliography in Brazil," *Libri* 23 (no. 4):293.

[3] I. Zimmerman, *Current National Bibliographies of Latin America*, p. 30.

722X; OCLC: 7938190) lists official publications in Brazil in a comprehensive manner, and is a good source for keeping up-to-date regarding official and government publications.

The *AL,BU*(ISSN 1041-1763) and its *Annual List of Serials* (ISSN 1042-1734) include Brazil within its scope until 1992 when it ceased. These titles continue *Accessions List, Brazil* (ISSN 0095-795X), and its *Annual List of Serials* (ISSN 0146-1060). The earlier titles cover the years 1975-1988. Although not intended to include all titles published in Brazil during a given year, this publication, listing acquisitions purchased by the Library of Congress, was a much more timely publication than the *BBBN* was in the past and could be relied upon to list many titles currently published in Brazil.

The Instituto do Livro has been responsible for *Bibliografia Brasileira*, an earlier title by the same name, publishing the first volume in 1941 covering the year 1938. It has been published monthly since November 1969, and "was interrupted in 1973 as a result of a settlement between the directors of both institutions, the Instituto and the National Library."[1]

There have been attempts by other publishers to cover the gaps in the national bibliography. For a history of these endeavors, see Laurence Hallewell, "Development of National Bibliography in Brazil," *Libri* 23 (no.4):291-197; I. Zimmerman, *Current Bibliographies of Latin America*, pp. 29-35 and Paulo da Terra Caldeira and Maria de Lourdes Borges de Carvalho, "O Problema Editorial da Bibliografia Brasileira Corrente," *Revista Brasileira de Biblioteconomia e Documentaçao* 13 (no.3/4):210-216, especially the chart on p. 212.

LATEST ISSUE EXAMINED/CURRENCY: Brazil is producing a more timely current national bibliography in its title *BB* than with *Boletim Bibliográfico da Biblioteca Nacional* (*BBBN*).

The latest issue examined in August 1997 is no. 2 for 1995 at Bibliotekstjänst AB Library, Lund, Sweden.

The majority of entries were for the period covered and the immediate preceding year.

AUTOMATION: Since 1976, *BBBN* has been produced by computer using CALCO (Catalogaçao Legível por Computador). Currently through volume 12, no. 2 (1995) *BB* was published by computer using the Sistema BIBLIODATA. It was then photo-composed. In 1995 the National Library introduced a Brazilian software called ORTODOCS, distributed by Pottron Informática to produce its bibliographic database which is published in CD-ROM format, linked with ORTODOCS OPAC module.[2]

FORMAT AND SERVICES AVAILABLE: printed (through vol. 13, no. 2 1995), magnetic tape, microfiche, CD-ROM. Plans to have the database accessible via the Internet are almost complete.

CURRENT LEGAL DEPOSIT LAWS: Decree No. 1.825 de 20 de Dezembro 1907.[3]

---

1 G. Pomassl, *Survey of Existing Legal Deposit Laws*, p. 21.
2 Information about ORTODOCS is from Sepúlveda's fax to the author.
3 *BB*, verso of title page, no.2, 1995.

Excerpts from the 1907 legal deposit law are given at the beginning of the main bibliography.

AVAILABLE FROM: Biblioteca Nacional, Av. Rio Branco, 219-39, 20040-008-Rio de Janeiro.

SELECTED ARTICLES: Caldeira, Paulo da Terra and Carvalho, Maria de Lourdes Borges de. "O Problema Editorial da Bibliografia Brasileira Corrente." *Revista Brasileira de Biblioteconomia e Documentacao* 13 (no. 3/4, 1980):210-216.

Hallewell, Laurence. "Development of National Bibliography in Brazil." *Libri* 23 (no.4):291-297.

Zimmerman, Irene. "Brazil." *Current National Bibliographies of Latin America.* Gainesville, University of Florida Center for Latin American Studies, 1971. pp. 29-35.

VERIFIER: Prof. Eduardo Portella, President, Fundação Biblioteca Nacional, Carlos A. Sepúlveda, Chief of Cabinet for the Presidency, Fundação Biblioteca Nacional.

BRUNEI

No current national bibliography has been traced for Brunei.

AL,SEA includes Brunei within its scope. Brunei also is included within the scope of *ISDS-SEA Bulletin.* - Bangkok : ISSN Regional Centre for Southeast Asia, 1980-   (ISSN 0125-4111).

BULGARIA

TITLE: *Natsionalna bibliografiiă na Republika Bŭlgariă.* - 1991-   . - Sofiă : Narodna Biblioteka 'St. St. Kiril i Metodiĭ', 1991 -   .
Continues *Natsionalna bibliografiă na NR Bŭlgariă.*
Divided into 8 series, of which *Bŭlgarski knigopis: Knigi, notni, graficheski i kartografski izdaniiă* (Series 1) is annotated below. See Notes and Comments section for information about other series.
Fortnightly.
DDC: 015.4977; LC: Z2893.N37; LCCN: sn92-15209; OCLC: 25597529
ISSN 0323-9616. Annual: ISSN 0323-9713

COMPILER: Narodna Biblioteka 'St. St. Kiril i Metodiĭ'.

SCOPE AND COVERAGE: *Natsionalna bibliografiiă na Republika Bŭlgariă* (NBB) lists the full publishing output of Bulgaria which is deposited in the National Library. Series 1 is described as follows.

material, children's picture books, musical scores (individual and collections), maps, atlases and plans, new Bulgarian periodical publications, title changes and jubilee numbers, and IGO publications if published in Bulgaria.[1]

Omitted from the graphic arts section are posters, illustrated calendars and postcards. Omitted from the cartographic section are contoured maps for schools. Omitted from the periodicals section are on-going periodicals which are covered in Series 4.

CONTENTS: Classified bibliography by UDC subject headings, separate sections for music, graphics, cartography and periodicals, additional editions, series; index; classification scheme at the end of the first issue of each year.

CATALOGUING RULES AND CLASSIFICATION SCHEMES USED: Bibliographical descriptions follow national (BDS) and ISBD standards. New standards for the description of sheet music and cartographic materials and periodicals began in 1984.

The classification scheme used is a Bulgarian adaptation of UDC.

ENTRY INFORMATION: Author, title, place of publication, publisher, date, pagination, illustration statement, size, series, UDC number, notes including information on ISBN, print run, price, bibliographies, etc.; subject headings, consecutive register number in lower left corner.

ARRANGEMENT: Series 1: arranged by broad UDC headings.

INDEXES: Alphabetical index including authors, collective authors and titles. The annual index includes publications in foreign languages, publications translated from a foreign language, index to publishers, series index, geographical index, subject index.

NOTES AND COMMENTS: The total publishing output of Bulgaria is covered by *NBB* in the following eight series. Only series 1 has been annotated by the author. Each of the series titles currently begin with the general title *Natsionalna bibliografiia na Republika Bŭlgariia* as from the date stated. From 1974-1990 the series titles begin with general title *Natsionalna bibliografiia na NR Bŭlgariia*. Other than this general title change, the series' names did not otherwise change. Information on all the series follows. The last sentence in the bibliographic information for each series states the coverage date from the beginning of the series.

Series 1. *Bŭlgarski knigopis: Knigi, notni, graficheski i kartografski izdaniia.* [Bulgarian Bibliography: Books, Music, Prints, Maps]. Sofiia. : Narodna Biblioteka 'St. St. Kiril i Metodiĭ', 1991- . Fortnightly, with annual cumulation (ISSN 0323-9616). Continues *Bŭlgarski knigopis: Knigi, notni, graficheski i kartografski izdaniia.* Sofiia : Narodna Biblioteka 'Kiril i Metodiĭ', 1974-1990 (ISSN 0323-9616), which supersedes in part *Bŭlgarski knigopis*. Sofiia, Biblioteka, 1945-1973 (OCLC: 8268372). This title was formed by the union of *Bŭlgarski knigopis za ...g. Tom. I. Knigi* (OCLC: 1755178), and *Bŭlgarski knigopis za...g. Tom.II, Spisaniizdaniia i vestnitsi* (OCLC: 17555343), and continues the numbering. Publisher varies: 1964- , Narodna Biblioteka 'Kiril i Metodiĭ'; 1953-1963, Bŭlgarski Bibliografski Institut; 1897-1952, Narodna

---

[1] The author thanks Luboslav Tzanev and Stefan Tzvetkov, students at The College of Wooster, for their help in translating information for this entry.

vestnitŝi (OCLC: 17555343), and continues the numbering. Publisher varies: 1964- , Narodna Biblioteka 'Kiril i Metodiĭ'; 1953-1963, Bŭlgarski Bibliografski Institut; 1897-1952, Narodna Biblioteka 'Kiril i Metodiĭ'. Frequency varies: fortnightly (1969-); monthly (1949-1968); quarterly (1945-1948); annual (1897-1944). Coverage since 1897.

Bŭlgarski knigopis: Knigi, notni, graficheski i kartografski izdaniiâ. Obsht Godishen Ukazatel. [Annual cumulation]. Sofiiâ : Narodna Biblioteka 'St. St. Kiril i Metodiĭ', 1990- . Annual. (ISSN 0323-9713). Continues *Bŭlgarski knigopis: Knigi, notni, graficheski i kartografski izdaniiâ. Obsht Godishen Ukazatel.* 1969-1989. Sofiiâ : Narodna Biblioteka 'Kiril i Metodiĭ', 1970-1989. Annual (ISSN 0323-9713). Coverage since 1969.

Series 2. *Bŭlgarski knigopis: Sluzhebni izdaniiâ i disertatŝii.* [Bulgarian Bibliography: Official Publications and Dissertations]. 1990- . Sofiiâ : Narodna Biblioteka 'St. St. Kiril i Metodiĭ', 1990- . Monthly, with separately issued annual index. (LCCN: sn92-15207; OCLC: 25598897; ISSN 0323-9667). Continues *Bŭlgarski Knigopis: Sluzhebni izdaniiâ i disertatŝii.* *1974-1990.* Sofiiâ : Narodna Biblioteka 'Kiril i Metodiĭ', 1974-1990 (OCLC: 2256189; ISSN 0323-9667). Monthly, with annual indexes for *Sluzhbeni izdaniiâ*, and with annual cumulations for dissertations with title *Bŭlgarski disertatŝii.* Supersedes in part *Bŭlgarski Knigopis.* Sofiiâ, Biblioteka, 1945-1973 (OCLC: 8268372). This title was formed by the union of *Bŭlgarski knigopis za ...g. Tom. I. Knigi* (OCLC: 1755178), and *Bŭlgarski knigopis za...g. Tom.II, Spisaniiâ i vestnitŝi* (OCLC: 17555343), and continues the numbering. Frequency, publisher varies. Coverage since 1962.

Series 3. *Bŭlgarski gramofonni plochi. Godishen ukazatel.* [Bulgarian Records. Annual Index]. Sofiiâ : Narodna Biblioteka 'St. St. Kiril i Metodiĭ', 1990- . Annual (OCLC: 28613783; ISSN 0323-9365). Continues *Bŭlgarski gramofonni plochi. Godishen ukazatel.* *1972-1990.* Sofiiâ : Narodna Biblioteka 'Kiril i Metodiĭ', 1974-1990. Annual (OCLC: 13566329; ISSN 0323-9365). Coverage since 1972.

Series 4. *Bŭlgarski periodichen pechat: vestnitŝi, spisaniiâ, biuletini i periodichni sbornitŝi.* [Bulgarian Periodicals, Newspapers, Journals, Bulletins and Periodical Collections]. Sofiiâ : Narodna Biblioteka 'Kiril i Metodiĭ', 1988- . [Since 1990, Narodna Biblioteka 'St. St. Kiril i Metodiĭ'.] Annual (OCLC: 28613721; ISSN 0323-9764). Continues *Seriia 4, 1972-1987.* Sofiiâ : Narodna Biblioteka 'Kiril i Metodiĭ'. Annual (OCLC: 6283551; ISSN 0323-9764). Supersedes *Bŭlgarski periodichen pechat, 1965-1971.* Sofiiâ : Narodna Biblioteka 'Kiril i Metodiĭ', 1967-1971 (LCCN: 51-28342; OCLC: 2726881). Coverage since 1965.

Series 5. *Letopis na statiite ot bŭlgarskite spisaniiâ i sbornitŝi.* [Articles from Bulgarian Journals and Collections]. Sofiiâ : Narodna Biblioteka 'St. St. Kiril i Metodiĭ', 1991- . Fortnightly (LCCN: sn92-15206; OCLC: 25597005; ISSN 0324-0398). Continues *Letopis na statiite ot bŭlgarskite spisaniiâ i sbornitŝi.* Sofiiâ : Narodna Biblioteka 'Kiril i Metodiĭ', 1972-1990. Fortnightly (LCCN: 74-646953//r872; OCLC: 4695591; ISSN 0324-0398). Continues *Letopis na periodichnaiâ pechat.* Sofiiâ : Bŭlgarski bibliografski institut Elin Pelin, 1952-1971. (ISSN 0024-1180; OCLC: 1715164). Coverage since 1952.

Series 6. *Letopis na statiite ot bŭlgarskite vestnitŝi.* [Articles from Bulgarian Newspapers], 1991- . Sofiiâ : Narodna Biblioteka 'St. St. Kiril i Metodiĭ', 1991- . Monthly, with annual index (ISSN 0324-0347). Continues *Letopis na statiite ot bŭlgarskite vestnitŝi.* Sofiiâ : Narodna Biblioteka 'Kiril i Metodiĭ', 1972-1990. Monthly, with annual cumulation (LCCN: 74-

Sofi︠a︡ : Bŭlgarski bibliografski institut Elin Pelin, 1952-1971 (LCCN: 54-16150//r852; OCLC: 1715164; ISSN 0024-1180). Frequency varies. Coverage since 1952.

Series 7. *Bŭlgari︠a︡ v chuzhdata literatura–Bulgarika.* [Bulgaria in Foreign Literature], 1989- . Sofi︠a︡ : Narodna Biblioteka 'St. St. Kiril i Metodiĭ', 1991- . Annual (OCLC: 28613712; ISSN 0323-9969). Continues *Bŭlgari︠a︡ v chuzhdata literatura — Bulgarika.* Sofi︠a︡ : Narodna Biblioteka 'Kiril i Metodiĭ', 1978-1988. Sofi︠a︡ : Narodna Biblioteka 'Kiril i Metodiĭ', 1980-1990. Quarterly, with annual cumulation. [For the period 1982-1988 correction in ISSN 0204-9740.] Continues *Bulgari︠a︡ v chuzhdata literatura— Bŭlgarika, 1972-1977.* Sofi︠a︡ : Narodna Biblioteka 'Kiril i Metodiĭ', 1974-1978. Annual. Continues *Bŭlgarii︠a︡ v chuzhdata literatura. Bibliografski ukazater. 1964-1971.* Sofi︠a︡ : Narodna Biblioteka 'Kiril i Metodiĭ', 1966-1974. Annual (OCLC: 10703952). This title is not a series of the national bibliography for the period 1964-1971. Coverage since 1964.

Series 8. *Bibliografii︠a︡ na bŭlgarskata bibliografii︠a︡.* [Bibliography of Bulgarian Bibliographies]. Sofi︠a︡ : Narodna Biblioteka 'Kiril i Metodiĭ', 1989- . [Since 1990, Narodna Biblioteka 'St. St. Kiril i Metodiĭ'.] Annual (OCLC: 30128053; ISSN 0204-7373). Continues *Bibliografii︠a︡ na bŭlgarskata bibliografii︠a︡. Godishen ukazatel. 1967-1988.* Sofi︠a︡ : Narodna Biblioteka 'Kiril i Metodiĭ', 1973-1988. Annual (OCLC: 2418500; ISSN 0204-7373). Continues *Bibliografii︠a︡ na bulgarskata bibliografii︠a︡, knigoznanie i bibliotechno delo. 1963-1966.* Sofi︠a︡ : Narodna Biblioteka 'Kiril i Metodiĭ', 1964-1967 (LCCN: sn86-25766; OCLC: 13707958). Coverage since 1963.

Official publications were included in *Bŭlgarski Knigopis* until 1961, when coverage of official publications was then transferred to Series 2.

CIP is not practiced in Bulgaria.

LATEST ISSUE EXAMINED/CURRENCY: In a sampling of entries, imprint dates were from the latest two years. The latest issue examined was 8 February 1995.

AUTOMATION: *NBB* has been automated since 1992 (excluding series 3 and 8). *NBB* uses a local network IBM compatible and CDS/ISIS micro software

FORMAT AND SERVICES AVAILABLE: printed; disks (according to ISO 2709).

CURRENT LEGAL DEPOSIT LAWS: Decree No. 1367 on the Compulsory Deposit of Printed and Other Documents, published in *Durzhaven Vestnik* no. 78 of 1 October 1976; the Regulations to the Decree No. 1367 of 1976 on the Compulsory Deposit of Printed and Other Documents, published in *Durzhaven Vestnik* no. 42/29 of May 1979; Zapoved RD 09-562/22.12.1995 of the Ministry of Culture.[1]

AVAILABLE FROM: Narodna Biblioteka "St. St. Kiril i Metodiĭ", 1504 Sofi︠a︡, Boulevard "Vasil Levski" No. 88.

---

[1] *International Guide to Legal Deposit*, p. 70, and information in a letter dated 15 August 1996 to the author from Vera Gantcheva, Director, Narodna Biblioteka "St. St. Kiril i Metodiĭ."

VERIFIER: Vera Gantcheva, Director, Narodna Biblioteka "St. St. Kiril i Metodiĭ."

BURKINA FASO

No current national bibliography has been traced for Burkina Faso.

BURMA

No current national bibliography has been traced for Burma.[1]

Through 15 May 1971 a list entitled "Books Published in Burma between July 1 - September 30, 1969 and Registered under the Press Registration Law of 1962" appeared quarterly in *Pyihtaungsu Hsoshelit Thammata Myanma Naing Ngantaw ahtu amein pyan tan = The Socialist Republic of the Union of Burma Gazette Extraordinary.* (LC: 78-929005/SA/r82). This list included books and printed materials in Burmese.

Books published in Burma are listed in the accessions lists of Cornell University and Northern Iowa University.[2]

AL, SEA (ISSN 0096-2341) includes Burma within its scope.

BURUNDI

No current national bibliography has been traced for Burundi.

AL,ESA and *QIPL,ESA* (ISSN 1018-1555) include Burundi within their scope.

The Université du Burundi, Bibliothèque Centrale (recently renamed Bibliothèque Moammar Khadafi) has published its *Catalogue des publications sur le Burundi disponibles à la Bibliothèque de l'Université du Burundi: première partie: Les ouvrages.* - Bujumbara : Université du Burundi, 1984. This volume "lists many mémoires de fin des études, as well as publications." A second volume covering periodical literature is planned.[3]

---

[1] In the late 1980s the University Central Library and the Center for Research Library were beginning to coordinate responsibilities to compile a national bibliography; however, the project probably has not come to fruition according to May Kyi Win, Northern Illinois University, in a 14 July 1997 e-mail message to the author.

[2] Win e-mail message.

[3] Information was supplied to the author by James Armstrong, former Field Director, Library of Congress Office, Nairobi, Kenya in a letter dated 14 November 1985.

A compilation which may be of interest is F. Rodegem's *Documentation bibliographique sur le Burundi*. - Bologna : EMI, 1978.[1]

There are no legal deposit laws in Burundi.

CAMBODIA

No current national bibliography has been traced for Cambodia.[2]

AL,SEA (ISSN 0096-2341) includes Cambodia within its scope.

The Bibliothèque Nationale has published an inventory of its stock of almost 700 printed books in the Khmer language. This is largely from the collection of Prof. Cœdès, former director of the Ecole Française d'Extreme-Orient from 1929 to 1947. The bibliographic citation is Bibliothèque nationale (France). *Inventaire des libres imprimés khmers et thaï du Fonds George Cœdès* / par Manuel Mauriès, avec la collaboration d' Elisabeth Vernier. - Paris : Bibliothèque nationale, 1991 (LCCN: 92-177206//r932; OCLC: 26768270).[3] Citations are in Thai and Khmer with prefatory matter in French.

Helen Jarvis' "Restoring the bibliographic heritage of Vietnam and Cambodia, " *International Cataloguing and Bibliographic Control* 22 (no. 3 July/Sept. 1993): 42-45 gives an account of the international effort to restore the bibliographic infrastructure of the National Library of Cambodia after the Pol Pot years. This paper was also presented at IFLA General Conference (New Delhi, 1992; 032-BIBL-1-E+F).

CURRENT LEGAL DEPOSIT LAWS: Law (Kram) No. 106–NS of 14 June 1956 and 2 December 1958.[4]

CAMEROON

No current national bibliography has been traced for Cameroon.

---

[1] Armstrong letter.

[2] Dr. Helen Jarvis, School of Information Library and Archives Studies, University of New South Wales, Sydney, Australia stated in a 2 July 1997 e-mail note that there are some bibliographies listing legal deposit holdings for the French period which cover most of the publishing output from around 1920 to 1940. There is nothing which lists imprints for the current period, however. Helen Cordell, SOAS, London also states in a 23 June 1997 e-mail message that she knows of no national bibliography for the current period.

[3] Nicole Simon. "The Restoration of the Bibliographic Heritage of Vietnam and Cambodia: the Contribution of France." Paper given at the IFLA General Conference (New Delhi , 1992) for the Bibliographic Control Division. Unpublished.

[4] *International Guide to Legal Deposit*, p. 84. In this list Cambodia is listed as "Kampuchea."

Cameroon Imprints. Bulletin du Centre de Diffusion du Livre Camerounais. - no. 1- , Jan./Mar. 1978- . - Yaoundé : Centre de Diffusion du Livre Camerounais, 1978- . Quarterly. (LCCN: sn86-21925; OCLC: 62622059). It is stated in number 1, 1978 that this is a list of books, pamphlets and periodicals sent from Cameroon to the African Imprint Library Services. (Address given in January/March 1980 issue is 75 King Road, Falmouth, Massachusetts 02540 for orders sent from North America, Germany and Scandanavia.) From the first issue of 1979, *Cameroon Imprints* became the newsletter of the Centre de Diffusion du Livre Camerounais. The arrangement of the list, which includes both French and English titles, began as anlphabetical author listing and then changed to broad subject categories, with entries listed alphabetically by title within the subject categories. Entry information includes title, author, place of publication, publisher, date, pagination, illustrations, price (when known, indicated by a letter code), size, series. A note in the January/March 1980 issue stated that the compiler wanted to list entries by ISBD but found it too time-consuming to analyze. No. 6, 1979 is a checklist of periodicals received, with an asterisk (*) marking those titles received frequently. This list is alphabetically arranged; titles published more than once a year are capitalized; yearbooks, etc. are in lower case. It is stated that the list has no official status or backing. According to no. 4, 1978 this mimeographed newsletter is sent free to customers; others may subscribe by sending stamps, coupons, money orders or Unesco coupons. By no. 9, 1980 the need for financial support was mentioned. More current issues have not been located by the author in visits to Indiana University, University of Michigan, University of Minnesota, University of Wisconsin, Library of Congress, SOAS, and the British Library.

CANADA

TITLE: *Canadiana.* 1950- . - Ottawa : National Library of Canada / Bibliothèque Nationale du Canada, 1951- .
Eleven issues a year (July/Aug. combined) with multi-year cumulation replacing annual cumulation after December issue since 1982.
Issued in microfiche since 1978.
DDC: 015.'71; LC: microfiche, Z1365.C23; LCCN: 90-643621; OCLC: 3791032
ISSN 0225-3216

COMPILER: Acquisitions and Bibliographic Services Branch, National Library of Canada.

SCOPE AND COVERAGE: *Canadiana* lists publications of Canadian origin or interest published in Canada and materials published in other countries by Canadian citizens, a resident of Canada and/or material of Canadian subject content. Material which is subject to legal deposit regulations and has been published in Canada since 1950 is acquired and listed in the current *Canadiana.* Normally, only the first available printing is listed. The National Library has an agreement with the International Council of Canadian Studies to search for, acquire, and catalogue materials produced by major Canadian Studies programs and organizations outside Canada. ICCS notifies the National Library of materials that are within the scope of *Canadiana.*[1]

---

[1] Much of the information in this entry is included in the excellent "Introduction" of *Canadiana.*

Types of publications included in *Canadiana* are books (including selected mass market or trade paperbacks), pamphlets, serials (including newspapers), theses, atlases, microforms, kits, sheet music and scores, sound recordings, federal, provincial and municipal government publications, video recordings, CD-ROMs, and other electronic publications.

Excluded from *Canadiana* are publications with less than one-third Canadian content and foreign imprints which are not substantially Canadian in subject or content; travel books with only a small section on Canada; films, filmstrips and videotapes are not included after the December 1976 issue (when the National Library delegated responsibility for creating bibliographic records for these formats to the National Archives and later to the National Film Board); other visual non-book materials such as slide sets, transparencies and prints unless part of a kit; maps when they are separate publications; letters, unless in form of briefs; programmes or events of local or limited interest; most additional printings; sales catalogues, except those with information of subject and bibliographic interest; mass-market paperbacks if only printed in Canada and have no other Canadian connection; time-tables, course calendars; sound recordings subject to legal deposit in September 1969; kits subject to legal deposit in January 1978, video recordings and CD-ROMs subject to legal deposit in 1993.

CONTENTS: Table of contents, preface with information about scope, frequency, arrangement, cataloguing practices, and explanation of entry elements; Register 1: Canadian imprints; Register 2: Foreign imprints; Index A (authors, titles, series); Index B (English subject headings); Index C (French subject headings); Index D (International Standard Book Numbers); Index E (International Standard Serial Numbers), Index F (Dewey Decimal Classification numbers). The table of contents, introduction and DDC outline are presented in both English and French.

CATALOGUING RULES AND CLASSIFICATION SCHEMES USED: AACR2 (since 1980), the French version *Règles de Catalogage Anglo-américaines, deuxième edition* (RCAA2), *LCSH* and *Canadian Subject Headings* and in French from *Répertoire de Vedettes-matière*, and its *COM Supplément* are used in cataloguing *Canadiana*.

Canadiana uses DDC and the LC classification schemes, adapting for Canadian history, and Canadian literature.

ENTRY INFORMATION: COM register number in upper left corner, author, dates of author, title, place of publication, publisher, date, pagination, illustrations, size, series statement, notes including ISBN or ISSN, price if readily available, tracings. The Canadian control number appears at the lower right corner; below that is an indication if title is available as a machine-readable record; LC and DDC classification numbers are in lower left corner. An upper case "C" before a Dewey number represents Canadian literature, a lower case "j" preceding a Dewey number represents juvenile literature. An "o.o.p." appearing as the last note indicates that the title is out-of- print.

ARRANGEMENT: Both Register 1 (Canadian imprints) and Register 2 (Foreign imprints) of *Canadiana* are arranged by the COM register number. Within each class, main entries are arranged alphabetically.

The arrangement has varied over the years. Most recently, entries were arranged by DDC number. Prior to that, the bibliography was divided by format (monographs, serials, theses, etc.)

and included author/title/series index, English subject headings index, and French subject headings index.

INDEXES: Index A (author/title/series), Index B (English subject headings), Index C (French subject headings), Index D (ISBN), Index E (ISSN), and Index F (Dewey Decimal Classification numbers). Index entries provide basic bibliographical information. All indexes cover item listed in both registers. The indexes cumulate with each new issue. The user is referred to the complete register entry by noting the COM register number supplied in the index.

NOTES AND COMMENTS: The late 1960s and 1970s brought several changes to *Canadiana*. After a self-study, begun in 1975, new rules and format were adopted in the late 1970's, the biggest change being the five separate indexes. Automation also made available new dimensions and bibliographical services to users of *Canadiana*, including tape services and COM services (microfiche). International standards and recommendations were incorporated by Canadiana after the 1977 ICNB.

Canadiana succeeds *Canadian Catalogue of Books*, 1921-1949.

The 1950/51 volume (published in 1962) cumulates the "Canadian Catalogue, 1950" issued in the Canadian Library Association Bulletin, May 1950-March 1951 and Part 1, Trade, of *Canadiana* 1951.

The microfiche edition of *Canadiana* has been available since 1978. In 1980, changes instituted were more cross references, and arrangement of the information in one continuous column.[1] During the implementation of on-line bibliographic systems from DOBIS to AMICUS in 1995 no microfiche products were produced until the end of 1996. Missing issues of 1995 were issued as part of the 1991-1995 multi-year cumulation. The 1996 and 1997 issues were issued as an annual cumulation. Separate monthly issues will be issued beginning with the January 1998 issue.[2]

A printed guide to the history and use of *Canadiana* is available to subscribers.

Films were listed in *Canadiana* between 1964 and 1976 and are now collected and listed in *Film/ video Canadiana*. - 1985/1986. - Montreal : National Film Board of Canada for National Library of Canada, Moving Image and Sound Archives, la Cinémathèque québécoise, 1988- . Biennial (ISSN 0836-1002; OCLC: 18121299). This title continues *Film Canadiana*. - Vol. 1 (fall 1969)- 1983/84. - Montreal : National Film Board of Canada. Imprint varies. (ISSN 0015-1173; OCLC: 1983818). *Film/Video Canadiana* ceased as a paper product with the 1987/1988 issue. A CD-ROM version was produced annually from 1993 to 1995. Now that videotapes are subject to Canada's legal deposit regulations, entries are prepared from the actual

---

[1] For more information on changes introduced see "Canada: National Bibliography in Microfiche," *International Cataloguing* 10 (Jan./Mar. 1981):4.
[2] Information provided in a 22 August 1997 e-mail message to the author from David Balatti, Director, Bibliographic Services National Library of Canada.

item by the National Library's catalogues. At the present time, no one is compiling records for films.[1]

Canadiana includes publications in English and French.

Government publications are included in several sources, the first being in *Canadiana* in Part 1, since 1975. There is no identifying symbol, but by looking in the index under Canada and the issuing agency, one is able to identify many federal government publications. For an up-to-date listing of federal publications, see the Web site of Public Works and Government Services Canada Publishing at http://dsp-psd.pwgsc.gc.ca . *Canadian research index* / MICROLOG [computer file]. Toronto, Canada : Micromedia, 1995-   (ISSN 1206-1840; OCLC: 35045712) is an index and a documents delivery system which covers Canadian federal, provincial and local government publications. Also included are publications of non-government research institutions, professional associations and special interest groups. It is also available on the Internet at http://www.micromedia.on.ca .

CIP is used in *Canadiana* appearing in monthly issues in their preliminary and revised forms. Preliminary CIP records are not listed in the annual cumulations. Revision is done with book in hand and supersedes any previous record. "CIP" or "CIP rev." following the *Canadiana* control number identifies these entries.

ISSNs and key titles are assigned to Canadian serials by ISDS Canada, the Canadian Center for the International Serials Data System in the National Library.

A key to the level of treatment of material catalogued is given in the introduction, which determines the detail of descriptive cataloguing for types of material.

Beginning in 1982 multi-year cumulations began replacing the annual cumulations. The five-year cumulations now cover 1981-1985, 1986-1990, 1991-1995.

The *Canadiana* authorities (microfiche) product has been issued at the end of 1996. It will be regularly updated.

Quebec publishes its own national bibliography *Bibliographie du Québec* (ISSN 0006-1441; OCLC: 1532732) published by the Bibliothèque Nationale du Quebec. For Quebec titles not found in *Canadiana*, one may want to consult *Bibliographie du Québec*. Based on legal deposit this title includes books, pamphlets, microforms, printed music, maps, sound and electronic documents relating to Québec through the author or the subject. The bibliography is arranged by the LC classification, and then alphabetically within classes. Publications in series, atlases and electronic documents are arranged alphabetically. AACR2 are used in cataloguing. Subjects are according to Répertoire de vedettes-matière de la Bibliotheèque de l'Université Laval. Indexes are author/title/"vedettes secondaires" and subject.

LATEST ISSUE EXAMINED/CURRENCY: As stated in the introduction, *Canadiana* includes publications from 1950 to the present, with most imprints from the last two years.

---

[1] Information in a fax dated 25 August 1997 to the author from David Balatti, National Library of Canada,

The latest issue examined in July 1996 at the University of Wisconsin library was January/June 1995.

AUTOMATION: automated since 1973. Since 1995, AMICUS online bibliographic system is used.

FORMAT AND SERVICES AVAILABLE: microfiche, magnetic tape, Internet, online. The National Library plans to issue the national bibliography on CD-ROM by March 1998. Plans include both bibliographic and authority records, and records in the national bibliography not included before, e.g. maps from the National Archives Carto-Canadiana product, and records culled from the NUC. [1]

CURRENT LEGAL DEPOSIT LAWS: National Library Act, 1985, and National Library Book Deposit Regulations, 1995.[2]

AVAILABLE FROM: Canadiana Editorial Division, Acquisitions and Bibliographic Services Branch, National Library of Canada, 395 Wellington St., Ottawa, Ontario K1A ONA.

SELECTED ARTICLES: "Canada." *Commonwealth National Bibliographies. An Annotated Directory*. 2nd ed. London : Commonwealth Secretariat, Marlborough House, 1983:16-18.

"Canada: National Bibliography." *International Cataloguing* 11 (Apr./June 1982):15.

"Canada: National Bibliography in Microfiche." *International Cataloguing* 10 (Jan./Mar. 1981):4.

Wilson, Marion C. "Canadiana. Changes in the National Bibliography." *Canadian Library Journal* 34 (no. 6; Dec. 1977):417-419, 421.

VERIFIER: David Balatti, Director, Bibliographic Services, National Library of Canada.

CAPE VERDE

No current national bibliography has been traced for Cape Verde.

CENTRAL AFRICAN REPUBLIC

No current national bibliography has been traced for Central African Republic.

---

[1] Balatti e-mail
[2] Balatti fax.

CHAD

No current national bibliography has been traced for Chad.

The Bibliographie du Tchad was published by the Institut National Tchadien pour les Sciences Humaines in the series Études et documents tchadiens. Ser. A. Volume four was published in 1968 (OCLC: 1508666) and volume five (second edition, rev., corr.) by Jacqueline Moreau and Danielle Stordeur was published in 1970 (LCCN: 74-195032//r89; OCLC: 1207026).

The Educational Documentation Centre has published bibliographies of educational works and works on Africa and African culture.[1]

CURRENT LEGAL DEPOSIT LAWS: Presidental Decree of 1968 (governs freedom of press), article 7 (legal deposit for periodicals); Ordinance number 27/PR of 28 October 1968 (legal deposit for films and sound recordings.)[2]

CHILE

TITLE: *Bibliografía chilena.* - 1976/1979-   . - Santiago : Ministerio de Educación Pública, 1981-   .
Annual.
Continues: *Anuario de la prensa chilena.*
Publisher varies.
Microfiche since 1982/1984.[3]
Some years issued in combined form.
DDC: 015.83; LC: Z1701.S23; LCCN: sf93-92687; OCLC: 22497359
ISSN not found

COMPILER: Biblioteca Nacional.

SCOPE AND COVERAGE: Scope and coverage have varied throughout the years. At present, *Bibliografía Chilena (BC)* lists all titles published in Chile which are deposited within the period covered at the Biblioteca Nacional according to the legal deposit law, and works about Chile and by Chilean authors published elsewhere.

Types of publications listed in *BC* include books, pamphlets, official and government publications, periodicals and "diarios" (first issues and cessations), annual reports, statistics, and brochures.

CONTENTS: Preface, introduction, abbreviations, main bibliography, indexes. Some issues have an appendix.

---

[1] *Survey of Existing Legal Deposit Laws*, p. 24.
[2] Ibid.
[3] Ursula Schadlich. "The National Library of Chile." *Alexandria* 3 (3 1991):163.

CATALOGUING RULES AND CLASSIFICATION SCHEMES USED: In cataloguing, entries in *BC* follow AACR2 and its updates. Subject headings used are the authority data base of the Red Nacional de Información Bibliográfica (LEMB/RENIB).

DDC is the classification scheme used.

ENTRY INFORMATION: DDC number, author, title, place of publication, publisher, date, pagination, size, series statement, notes, including ISBN if known, tracings, internal numbers.

ARRANGEMENT: The main bibliography is arranged according to DDC numbers, within which entries are alphabetically arranged without regard to format.

The 1976-1979 volume was arranged chronologically, then by form of publication under each year covered. Subject indexes and appendices are placed at the end of each year.

INDEXES: Author index, title index, subject index are alphabetically arranged. The numbers refer the user to the right microfiche card and then an alfanumber which helps to locate the the the column where the entry appears, e.g., 001 J28, 004 M06.

1980 volume: general index, including authors, titles, and subjects, in a dictionary arrangement. Entries refer to the consecutive entry number. "Periódicos" and "revistas" are alphabetically arranged under the index entry "Publicaciones en Serie." The index does not include titles listed in the Appendix.

The 1976-1979 index treats subjects only using terms similar to the DDC headings.

NOTES AND COMMENTS: The national bibliography, *Anuario de la prensa chilena (AP)*, was published from 1952-1979 covering the years 1877/1885-1975. *AP* includes works by Chileans or about Chile printed abroad in volumes for 1891-1894 and 1896-1902, 1963 and 1964 (written by Chileans), and 1965-1975, in addition to the titles published and deposited at the Biblioteca Nacional. *AP* includes the same scope as *BC*, but from "1896-1900, enumerated 526 musical scores."[1] The first volume, 1877/1885, includes only books, pamphlets, and broadsides. Volumes for the years 1886-1890, 1903-1913, and 1915 included books, pamphlets, broadsides, newspapers and periodicals and other types of copyright registrations. Volumes for 1914, 1917-1921, 1922-1926, 1927-1931, 1932-1936, 1937-1941, 1942-1946, 1947-1951, 1952-1956, 1957-1961, 1962 list books and pamphlets. From 1963, the scope broadens to include periodicals once again, and since 1964, has included official publications.[2] (LCCN: sn85-23738; OCLC: 1644537).

The *AP* does not include university theses, dissertations, atlases, printed musical scores, films, tapes and recordings.[3]

---

[1] Juan R. Freudenthal, "Chilean National Bibliography: Origins and Progress," *Libri* 22 (1972, no. 4):276.

[2] Hensley C. Woodbridge, "Latin American National Bibliography," *Encyclopedia of Library and Information Science* 36, supp. 1 (1983):292.

[3] Ibid., p. 277.

AP ceased after 1916 and was not resumed until 1962. Volumes for those years not covered were done retrospectively from 1962-1964.

With the change of title to *BC*, there seems to be a concerted effort to conform to international bibliographic standards beginning with the 1980 volume. Many of the ICNB recommendations were adopted thus improving the quality and usefulness of this current national bibliography. The introduction explains the scope, arrangement and bibliographical standards of the *BC*. An analyzed entry would also be useful to the reader. One feature still missing that would be of benefit to bibliographers and librarians using this tool for acquisitions and collection development would be the addition of a list of publishers and their addresses. In the latest issue examined, the table of contents was not evident as in other volumes.

Until 1981 children's and juvenile books was a separate category in *BC* and entries were listed alphabetically by the main entry. From 1982, children's literature was incorporated into the main body, and the juvenile (young adult) literature appears as a subdivision of other subjects, e.g., Historia universal – literatura juvenil.

The appendix in some volumes lists works registered at the "Registro de Propriedad Intelectual" (copyright registration). Entries are in alphabetical order by main entry, and are assigned an entry number in a different sequence from that of the main bibliography. Information given includes author, title, inscription number and date. These entries are not included in the general index.

In the 1976-1979 volume there is a separate category for official publications. However, beginning with 1980, all titles are by DDC regardless of form. No symbol is used to designate government or official publications. One may identify many of them through the use of the index.

A title which may supplement *BC* is *Librao chilenos ISBN* - Santiago: Cámara Chilena de Libros, 1989-   (OCLC: 22340558). This title includes book in print including some government publications.

LATEST ISSUE EXAMINED/CURRENCY: The majority of the entries have imprints for the period covered. The shortcoming is in the time taken for publication and distribution of this title to libraries. This lag seems to have increased not decreased as one would wish with the microfiche format. There is a five year gap between coverage and publication for the 1985/1987 issue, whereas the 1976-1979 volume, published in 1981, was received by the British Library in December 1982. Generally, there has been a two year delay from the period covered until publication and then a further delay of up to a year until the title is received by the subscribing library. Since the imprint information is so current, it would be beneficial to speed up the production and distribution if this is at all possible. *BC* is following ICNB in every other way but the timeliness.

The latest volume examined at the University of Wisconsin in May 1995 covers 1985/1987, published in 1992.

AUTOMATION: Since 1984, the National Library uses the NOTIS system; translations into Spanish are done at RENIB.

FORMAT AND SERVICES AVAILABLE: Printed until 1981; from 1982, in microfiche. From 1997, the data bases of RENIB, and accordingly, the Biblioteca Nacional's database, is available on the Internet.[1]

CURRENT LEGAL DEPOSIT LAWS: The current legal deposit law is included in law number 16.643 of September 1967, Decreto Ley No. 100 modifies Articulo 4 of Ley No. 16.643, 1973; Ley no. 17.336, Art. 75, 1970.[2]

AVAILABLE FROM: Biblioteca National de Chile, Avenida Bernardo O'Higgins 651, Clasificador 1400, Santiago.

SELECTED ARTICLES: Freudenthal, Juan R. "Chilean National Bibliography: Origins and Progress." *Libri* 22 (no. 4 1972):273-280.

Villalobos R., Sergio. "La Bibliografia en Chile. Desarrolo de las Investigaciones Bibliograficas." *Cuadernos de Historia* 5 (July 1985): 69-70, 73.

Woodbridge, Hensley C. *Guide to Reference Works for the Study of the Spanish Language and Literature and Spanish American Literature.* 2d ed. NY: Modern Language Association of America, 1997. p. 193.

Woodbridge, Hensley C. "Latin American National Bibliography." *Encyclopedia of Library and Information Science* 36, suppl. 1 (1983):271-343.

VERIFIER: Justo Alarcon R., Sección Chilena, Biblioteca Nacional.

CHINA (PEOPLE'S REPUBLIC)

TITLE: *Chung-kuo kuo chia shu mu* [Chinese National Bibliography]. - 1985-   . - Pei-ching: Shu mu wen hsien ch'u pan she [Bibliography and Documentation Publishing House], [1986]- . Annual.
Publisher varies: 1992-   , Huayi Publishing House.
DDC: not found; LC: Z3101.C4918; LCCN: 95-646031/ACN/V; OCLC: 19051802
ISSN 0578-073X

COMPILER: Issues for 1985, 1987, 1987: Pei-ching t'u shu kuan "Chung-kuo kuo chia shu mu" pien wei hui chu pien; Pei-ching t'u shu kuan "Chung-kuo kuo chia shu mu" pien chi tsu pien chi. [The Chinese National Bibliography Editorial Committee of the National Library of China. The CNB Editorial Group of NLC]

---

[1] Information is included in a 13 August 1997 e-mail message to the author from Justo Alarcon R., Head of the Chilena Section, Biblioteca Nacional.
[2] *International Guide to Legal Deposit,* p. 72.

Issues for 1991- : Pei-ching t'u shu kuan "Chung-kuo kuo chia shu mu" pien wei hui chu pien; Pei-ching t'u shu kuan, t'u hsin shu mu shu ch'u chung hsin pien chi. [The Chinese National Bibliography Editorial Committee of the National Library of China; Bibliography Data Centre of New Technology Development Center of NLC]

SCOPE AND COVERAGE: *Chung-kuo kuo chia shu mu* [Chinese National Bibliography] (*CNB*) includes the publishing output which is deposited at the National Library of China according to legal deposit legislation, the collection of the National Library of China, and other bibliographic sources. Future issues plan to include publications written in other countries by Chinese citizens or publishing agencies, but to date only publications for mainland China are included.

Types of publications in the 1985 volume include only books; 1986 includes books serials, minority language books, doctoral dissertations, maps and atlases; 1987 includes books, minority languages books, maps and atlases; 1991 includes only books; 1992 includes books, minority language books, maps and atlases; 1993 includes only books. Later issues plan to expand coverage to include doctoral dissertations, selected scientific and technical papers, maps and atlases, photographs (of historical or reference value), materials in non-book form (microforms and audio-visual materials), materials in national minority languages and scripts (21 minority languages are issued annually totaling 1,200 titles), and braille books. Technical standards, patents and music books are planned to be within the scope.[1]

Excluded are reprints, ephemeral materials, and pamphlets under 49 pages. Important works, statutes or other works by Chinese leaders or foreign leaders will be included regardless of length. For historical reasons, publications from Taiwan, Hong Kong, and Macao are not yet obtainable through the depository system.[2]

CONTENTS: *CNB* (1985, 1986, 1987, 1991) is issued in two volumes. Vol. 1 includes members of the Chinese National Bibliography Editorial Committee, preface, explanations (which includes an explanation about information in a bibliographic entry), and the classified bibliography; vol. 2 includes the indexes. *CNB* (1992, 1993) has two main volumes and one index volume.

CATALOGUING RULES AND CLASSIFICATION SCHEMES USED: ISBD is used, and other national rules such as "General Bibliographical Description" (GB3792.1-1983), "Cataloguing Rules for Chinese General Books" (GB3792.2-1985), "Descriptive Cataloguing Rules for Serials" (GB3792.3-1985), "Cataloguing Rules for Non-book Materials"(GB3792.4-

---

[1] Huang Jungui. "Bibliographic Control in the People's Republic of China," trans. by Charles Aylmer. *BEASL Bulletin of the European Association of Sinological Librarians* 4 (1990):12. Information is also listed in National Bibliography Section, National Library of China, Beijing. "National Bibliography of China-Retrospect and Prospect." *International Cataloguing* 15 (no. 1 Jan./Mar. 1986):7.

[2] Huang Jungui, *International Cataloguing*, p. 7.

1985), and "Regulations for Atlases and Maps" (GB 3792.6-1986). The 1994 editions of these national rules, to be approved, are also used.[1]

Two classification numbers are given: the Chinese Library Classification number from the *Classification Rules for Books* and the Chinese Academy of Science Library Classification number from the Academy's *Library Classification Rules for Books.*

Descriptors are taken from the *Chinese Language Thesaurus and Classified Chinese Thesaurus.*

Since 1985, the National Library of China has adopted the national standard "Rules for Document Subject Indexing" for centralized cataloguing, compiling and printing of catalogue cards and the national bibliography.[2]

ENTRY INFORMATION: Chinese Library Classification number, author, title, publisher, date, pagination, size, notes including ISBN, price; tracings. In the 1985, 1986, and 1987 volumes each entry is assigned a serial number, comprising the NBC code, year and entry sequence number, e.g., CN85-00006. In the 1991,1992, 1993 volumes the serial number is a sequential number, e.g., 000014 which appears in the upper right corner. The Chinese Library Classification number and the Chinese Academy of Science Library Classification number are given at the end of each entry.

Each entry has access points by title, author, and classification number.

ARRANGEMENT: The bibliography is arranged according to 22 broad subject categories.

INDEXES: A separate volume includes title and author indexes arranged by Pin Yin sequence. When an entry has the same Pin Yin pronunciation but has different words, it will be arranged according to stroke order. When an author or title begins with an Arabic numeral, a year, Latin words, or Japanese kanji which has no Chinese equivalent, the entry will come at the end.

NOTES AND COMMENTS: The *CNB* is striving to follow international standards for national bibliographies. The scope of *CNB* has been defined to include the concept of "nation-language." Three factors for inclusion are all works 1) published on Chinese territory (including Taiwan and regions of Hong Kong and Macao) regardless of language, type of document and form of carrier, 2) co-produced by China and other countries, and 3) by Chinese citizens or Chinese publishers in foreign countries.[3]

The *CNB* for 1985 is described as a pilot national bibliography which was done manually. Volumes in print form were published annually. From 1988, the Library began the

---

[1] Information about the 1994 editions was included in Ms. Yuan Keli's notes to the author, received 31 January 1997.

[2] Huang Jungui, *BEASL*, p. 6.

[3] National Bibliography Section, National Library of China, Beijing. "National Bibliography of China-Retrospect and Prospect." *International Cataloguing* 15 (no. 1 Jan./Mar. 1986):7.

computerized cataloguing using CN-MARC. The volume published for 1992 was produced using the computer, and then information in volumes in between 1986 and 1992 were entered retrospectively using the computer. It is planned to also enter information for 1985 into the database and issue volumes for 1985-1995 as a special edition.

The *CNB* is available on two CD-ROM disks covering national bibliographic records from 1975-1987, and 1988 onwards.[1] It is updated twice a year. It uses ISO 10646 Character Set (including 20902 CJK characters) and UNIMARC/CNMARC format. Access points are by title, author, subject, keyword, classification numbers, classification scheme, ISBN/ISSN, Chinese Pin Yin of author and title, publisher, and the record number. Retrieval methods are by the following searches: general, truncated, Boolean, browsing, limited requirement search (by year of publication, or type of material), batch, or full text. The system arranges search results by stroke count and stroke order. Help is available in a printed handbook, and within a help module. To run the CD-ROM, the following is needed: IBM-compatible PC 386 or higher with at least 2 MB of RAM memory and a 40 MB hard disk; CD-ROM drive meeting ISO 9660 standards; PC-DOS or MS-DOS version 5.0 or higher; MS-DOS CD-ROM Extensions version 2.2 or higher, and Chinese system (e.g., ETen) version 3.0 or higher.

Before *CNB*, a bibliography which substituted as a national bibliography was *Ch'uan kuo hsin shu mu*. - 1950-   . - Beijing : China Publications Library, 1951-   . (OCLC: 3133964; ISSN 0578-073X). This is a monthly with an annual cumulation entitled *Ch'uan kuo Tsong shu mu*. The English title on the back cover is *New Books Catalogue of PRC*. The compiler is the Editorial Committee for New Books Catalogue of PRC, China Publications Library. Types of publications books, pamphlets, official and government publications, reports, maps and atlases, musical scores, children's books, foreign publications, translations, pictures and posters. Excluded are titles for internal circulation, reprints (included in earlier years), serials. A title and author index is arranged by stroke order.

China participates in the ISBN and ISSN programs.

LATEST ISSUE EXAMINED/CURRENCY: The latest issue examined is number 1992 at the University Library, Cambridge, England in November 1994. According to Mr. Aylmer, who had just returned from China, the years 1986-1991 were not yet published at that time. They since have been published. In December 1996, the volume for 1993 is the latest *CNB* published.

AUTOMATION: *CNB* has the Wenjin Integrated Library Management System using the Unix C/S. The server is a NEC UP4800/610 with UNIX SYSV R4.2 and Oracle 7.2, about forty clients are IBM-compatible PCs with Windows, protocol is TCP/IP. It now has about 470,000 titles (1975-1996). Another 400,000 titles (1949-1974) will be loaded in the system in 1998. Besides the cataloguing subsystem, the Wenjin Integrated Library Management System also has

---

[1] The CNB on CD-ROM disks covering records from 1949-1974 is planned to be completed in 1998, according to Ms. Yuan Keli.

acquisitions, circulation and retrieval subsystems. These subsystems are sharing the *CNB* and other data resources.[1]

FORMAT AND SERVICES AVAILABLE: printed, card form, CD-ROM, and machine-readable tape, disk.

CURRENT LEGAL DEPOSIT LAWS: In 1952 the State Council of the People's Republic of China promulgated "Provisional Regulations for Controlling the Publication of Books and Periodicals, Printing and Distribution Affairs." The Ministry of Culture required sample copies to be submitted to the National Library.

The regulations for collecting sample copies of books, periodicals and newspapers issued by the State Bureau for Publishing Administration on 18 April 1979 restate the rule that three copies of the first edition of all new publications must be sent to the National Library of China.[2]

AVAILABLE FROM: National Library of China, 39 Baishiqiao Road, 100081 Beijing.

SELECTED ARTICLES: Huang Jungui. "Bibliographic Control in the People's Republic of China." Trans. by Charles Aylmer. *BEASL Bulletin of the European Association of Sinological Librarians* 4 (1990):1-15.

National Bibliography Section, National Library of China, Beijing. "National Bibliography of China--Retrospect and Prospect." *International Cataloguing* 15 (no. 1 Jan./Mar. 1986):5-8.

VERIFIER: Ms. Yuan Keli, Cataloguing Dept., The National Library of China.

COLOMBIA

TITLE: *Anuario bibliográfico colombiano "Rubén Pérez Ortiz".* - 1963-   . - Bogota : Instituto Caro y Cuervo, Departamento de Bibliografía, 1966-   .
Annual.
Continues *Anuario bibliográfico colombiano.*
DDC: 015.9861; LC: Z1731.A58; LCCN: 94-655663; OCLC: 6419517
ISSN not found; ISBN 84-8271-208-X

COMPILER: Volumes for 1963-   are compiled by Francisco José Romero Rojas.

---

[1] Information is from a 6 February 1997 e-mail message from Mr. Zhen Xi Hui, Wenjin IT Research Center, National Library of China.
[2] Information from "National Bibliography of China-Retrospect and Prospect," p. 6, and from *BEASL*, p. 2.

SCOPE AND COVERAGE: *Anuario Bibliográfico Colombiano* (*ABC*) lists works published in Colombia in Spanish, and works of Colombian authors translated into other languages. It also includes books written by Colombian nationals or about Columbia printed abroad.

Types of publications included in *ABC* are books, pamphlets, official and government publications, theses, annual reports, new periodicals, maps, off-prints, non-book materials.

CONTENTS: "Presentación", bibliography, translations, new Colombian periodicals, "índice onomástico" [name index], title index.

CATALOGUING RULES AND CLASSIFICATION SCHEMES USED: The cataloguing follows the rules of ALA and Library of Congress with modifications. (1966 "Presentación"). Although ISBD is not used, the entry information given is complete.

No classification numbers are given in the entry information.

ENTRY INFORMATION: Main bibliography: author, joint author etc., title, place of publication, publisher, edition, date, pagination, illustrations, size, series, notes, including ISBN. Location of book in cooperating libraries is given in lower right corner: Biblioteca Nacional, Biblioteca Luis Angel Arango del Banco de la República, Biblioteca de la Academia Colombiana, Biblioteca del Departamento Nacional de Planeación, Biblioteca del Instituto Colombiano para el Desarrollo de la Ciencia y la Tecnología "Francisco José de Caldas", y la Librería Divulgación. No price, class number or entry number is given in the entries.

Complete bibliographical information is also given in the translation section and the new periodicals section.

ARRANGEMENT: The main bibliography is arranged alphabetically by main entry under the 100 classes of the DDC scheme.

The "Traducciones" section is arranged alphabetically by translator with full bibliographical information. The original title is given as a note.

The periodical list is alphabetically arranged by title.

The publishers' list (when one appears) is arranged alphabetically by city.

INDEXES: "Indice onomástico" includes personal and corporate authors, co-authors, translators and compilers and others if necessary; title index, anonymous works index. Indexes refer the user to the page number in the bibliography.

NOTES AND COMMENTS: The Colombian national bibliography began in 1951, issued by the Biblioteca "Jorge Garcés B." in Cali. (LCCN: 94-655686; OCLC: 30968289). From 1956-1962, *Anuario bibliográfico colombiano* is published in Bogotá by the Departamento de Bibliografía, Instituto Caro y Cuervo. (LCCN: 53-28591//r943; OCLC: 1481637; ISSN 0570-393X). The 1951 volume, edited by Pedro R. Carmona, was incorporated into a volume for 1951-56. The latter volume, plus volumes for 1957-58, 1959-60, 1961, 1962 were compiled by Rubén Pérez Ortiz. In 1963, the national bibliography is titled *Anuario bibliográfico colombiano "Rubén Pérez Ortiz."*

Government publications are not designated by any special symbols in the main bibliography. It is necessary to look under appropriate subjects and scan the entries. Many times notes in the entries will include the name of the minister of the government department, or other information that will help to identify entries as a government publication.

Basically, *ABC* has not altered its basic format throughout the years although there are a few changes worth mentioning. The translations of the 1951-56 volume are divided into Spanish, Latin and other languages, and there is no Instituto de Caro y Cuervo catalogue of publications included. With the 1961 volume, the "new periodicals" and the "addresses of bookstores and publishers" were added. The latest volume examined (1988-1989) does not include some features in these earlier volumes: abbreviations and symbols, publishers and book sellers list, anonymous index, publications of the Institute. Some of these features are suggested by the ICNB recommendations; it is anticipated that the abbreviations list will be included in later volumes.

The introduction of *ABC* would be more useful if it would explain in detail the scope of *ABC*, or would analyze an entry. Since this national bibliography is used by libraries in the country, it seems that it could serve as a classification guide better if it also included the classification number as part of the entry information.

In past years it was estimated that only about sixty percent of the national literature is received and registered in *ABC*. This is due to the lack of observation of the legal deposit law.[1] Listing the holdings of other cooperating libraries helps the *ABC* to have a more complete list of titles.

A publication that lists official publications of national, state, municipal, and autonomous agencies is *Bibliografía oficial colombiana. - no. 1- . - Medellín : Escuela interamericana de bibliotecología, 1964-* (ISSN 0067-6748).

Fichas para el Anuario Bibliográfico Colombiano for the years 1961-1964. Semiannual. (Biblioteca del bibliotecario) was compiled by Fermín Peraza Sarausa. Volume 1 was published in Medellín; volumes for 1962-1964 were published in Gainesville, Florida (LCCN: sf86-2016; OCLC: 6328191). The title was changed in July 1964 to *Bibliografía Colombiana, 1964-1972. - Gainesville, Fla., 1964-1980.* Annual, 1966-1972; semi-annual, 1964-1965. Compiler: Fermín Peraza Sarausa, 1964-1968 and Elna Vérez Peraza, 1969-1970 (LCCN: 64-4610//r862; OCLC: 7907665). The scopes of these two titles include "books and pamphlets published in Colombia or by Colombians living elsewhere and foreign materials dealing with Colombia. Official publications were included on a rather extensive basis. Arrangement is alphabetical by author with a detailed subject index."[2]

CIP does not exist in Colombia.

LATEST ISSUE EXAMINED/CURRENCY: There is a two to three year lag between the year covered and the publication date. The *ABC* could serve as an acquisitions and collection development tool better if this lag could be reduced.

---

[1] G. Pomassl, *Survey of Existing Legal Deposit Laws*, p. 26.
[2] I. Zimmerman, *Current National Bibliographies of Latin America*, p. 42. Also, *NST* 1986-88, v. 3, p. 3387.

The latest volume examined at Indiana University Library in March 1997 covers 1990/1991; it was published in 1995 and is the latest volume published to date.

AUTOMATION: Not automated at present, but the Instituto Caro y Cuervo plans to do so are in the near future.

FORMAT AND SERVICES AVAILABLE: printed; some years available on microfiche. The Instituto Caro y Cuervo has plans to put *ABC* on the Internet and on CD-ROM.

CURRENT LEGAL DEPOSIT LAWS: Legal deposit regulations have existed since 26 March 1834 which relate to deposition of national imprints in the National Library. The current laws mentioned in *ABC* are Ley 86 of 1946 concerning copyright and Decreto Numero 2840 of 14 November 1961 concerning the bibliographical functions of the Instituto Caro y Cuervo, and Ley 23 de 1982. The Decreto Numero 460 of 1995 (16 March) which regulates the registration of author rights and legal deposit excludes the Instituto Caro y Cuervo. This government decree forces the Institute to change the methodology for compiling the current national bibliography. [1]

AVAILABLE FROM: Departamento de Bibliografía, Instituto Caro y Cuervo, Carrera 11 no. 64-37, Bogotá 2.

VERIFIER: Francisco Jose Romero Rojas, Head of the Department of Bibliography, Instituto Caro y Cuervo.

COMOROS

No current national bibliography has been traced for Comoros.

AL,ESA (ISSN 1070-2717) and *QIPL,ESA* (ISSN 1018-1555) include Comoros within its scope.

Some current bibliographic works which list some publications from Comoros are as follows. *Annuaire des pays de l'océan indien* . -Aix-en-Provence : Presses universitaires d'Aix-Marseille, 1974-   . (ISSN 0247-400X). Some issues include bibliographies for Indian Ocean countries under "Bibliographie." For Comoros, see vol. 12 (1990-1991) for a listing of authors appearing in the bibliography, theses and dissertations, works and articles, collective works and anonymous works for the time period 1984-1991. *Ya Mkobe* (1984-   ), a semiannual published in Moroni by the Centre National de Documentation et de Récherche Scientifique, lists some current as well as retrospective publications. (LCCN: 85-981075; OCLC: 24396209). *Études océan indien: documents comoriens* published by Centre d'Etudes et de Recherches de l'Océan Indien Occidental, Institut National des Langues et Civilisations Orientales, Paris. (ISSN 0246-0092; OCLC: 13212190). *Asie du sud-est et monde insulindien* (LCCN: 73-642291//r82;

---

[1] "Presentación," *ABC* (1988-1989, published 1992), p. vii, and information from correspondence dated 12 March 1997 to the author from Francisco Jose Romero Rojas, Head of the Department of Bibliography, Instituto Caro y Cuervo.

OCLC: 5369835, #2257825) lists Comorian research and publications, e.g., volume 13, numbers 3-4 1981 (1983) are devoted to *Islam et littératures dans l'archipel des Comores.*[1]

CONGO

No current national bibliography was traced for the Congo.

LEGAL DEPOSIT LAWS: Décret D 66/249, 10 août 1966.[2]

CONGO (DEMOCRATIC REPUBLIC OF)

TITLE: *Bibliographie du Zaïre.* - 1987/1988-   . - Kinshasa-Gombe: La Bibliothèque nationale du Zaïre, 1990-   .
Annual.
"Collection Travaux"–t.p.
To be issued in 3 v.
DDC: 015.6751; LC: Z3631.B53; LCCN: 91-980342; OCLC: 31536236
ISSN not found

COMPILER: Bibliothèque Nationale du Zaïre.

SCOPE AND COVERAGE: *The Bibliographie du Zaïre (BZ)*[3] lists works published in Zaïre received through legal deposit.

Types of publications in volume 1 include books, pamphlets, and periodical articles. It is stated in preliminary pages that a projected volume 2 will include "mémoires et théses de doctorat" and volume 3 will cover audio-visual materials.

CONTENTS: Preface, classified bibliography, list of names and addresses of research institutions, publishers, and periodicals published in Zaïre, and the mission statement of the Bibliothèque Nationale du Zaïre.

CATALOGUING RULES AND CLASSIFICATION SCHEMES USED: International standards are followed.

---

[1] The author is grateful for the periodical titles which were included in an 11 September 1985 letter to the author from James Armstrong, former Field Director of the Library of Congress Office, Nairobi, Kenya.
[2] *International Guide to Legal Deposit*, p. 73.
[3] Since the writing of this entry the name of the country has changed to the Democratic Republic of Congo. A decision was made by the author to keep the title and country name in the entry as it was when examined.

The DDC system is used.

ENTRY INFORMATION: Author, title, place of publication, publisher, date, pagination, illustrations, size, series statement, DDC number in lower right corner. Periodical articles include the source, volume, number, date, and pagination.

ARRANGEMENT: Arranged by DDC number, and then alphabetically by the main entry.

INDEXES: There were no in the 1987/1988 issue.

NOTES AND COMMENTS: The *BZ* is to be issued in three volumes: 1, imprimés; 2, les mémoires et thèses de doctorat; and 3, les documents audio-visuels. To date, the first volume has been published. When the projected volumes are published, the scope will be widened to include memoirs, dissertations and audio-visual materials.

The *BZ* lacks several features that would make it easier to use. In the issue examined, there was no table of contents or preliminary material to help the user understand the scope and arrangement of the bibliography. An abbreviations list, and an explanation of the bibliographic entry, and an index would also be helpful to the user.

The *BZ* is a successor to the *Bibliographie nationale* (*BN*) which suspended publication since about 1979. *BN* was an annual which includes works published in Zaïre received through legal deposit, foreign publications about the country and works written by Zaïrian nationals published abroad. Types of publications included with the scope of *BN* are books, pamphlets, reports, periodical articles, new periodicals, official and government publications, school books, theses and dissertations, IGO publications (e.g. World Bank), local language publications. The bibliography is arranged in two lists: periodicals (arranged alphabetically), and classified. (LC: Z3635.B5; DT644; LCCN: 79-645478; OCLC: 5155750).

BN continues *Bibliographie nationale retrospective des publications zaïroises ou relatives à la République de Zaïre, acquises par la Bibliothèque Nationale.* Kinshasa-Gombe : Département de la culture et des arts, Direction des archives et bibliothèques, 1971-1973. (LC: Z3635.B5; DT644; LCCN: 79-645477//r91; OCLC: 5155709). This covers works published in Zaïre or works about Zaïre published between 1871-1960, and held by the *Bibliothèque Nationale. BN* began with no. 5, 1974, assuming the numbering of the retrospective bibliography.

LATEST ISSUE EXAMINED/CURRENCY: The Library of Congress received this first number in 1990; no others have been received since then. The volume covers 1987 and 1988 publications. *BZ* will be a contribution to bibliographic control for publications from Zaïre. As of now, it is an important historical record of publishing for the time period covered, but not a timely source for acquisitions purposes.

AUTOMATION: produced by computer.

FORMAT AND SERVICES AVAILABLE: printed.

CURRENT LEGAL DEPOSIT LAWS: Loi no. 74-003 du jan. 1974 relative au depot obligatoire des publications; loi no. 78-013 du juillet 1978.[1]

AVAILABLE FROM: Bibliothèque Nationale, Avenue Colonel Tshatshi, no. 10, B.P. 5432, Kinshasa-Gombe.

VERIFIER: No reply received.

COSTA RICA

TITLE: *Bibliografia Costarricense.* - 1994-   . - San José : Biblioteca Nacional, 1995-   .
Annual.
Continues *Annuario bibliográfico Costarricense.*
DDC: 015.7286; LC (090): F1453.A65; LCCN: not found; OCLC: 3679776
ISSN 1409-1097

COMPILER: Centro de Documentación y Bibliografia, Biblioteca Nacional Miguel Obregon Lizano.

SCOPE AND COVERAGE: *Bibliografia Costarricense (BC)* includes material deposited at the Biblioteca Nacional according to the legal deposit laws.

Types of publications included are monographs, pamphlets, periodicals, government publications, maps, theses and dissertations, audio-visual materials.

CONTENTS: Introduction, abbreviations, list of classification subjects, bibliography, indexes.

CATALOGUING RULES AND CLASSIFICATION SCHEMES USED: AACR2 to the second level has been used by the Department of Technical Processes in cataloguing entries. Subject headings are from the *Listas of Encabezamientos de Materias para Bibliotecas.*

The classification used is DDC.

ENTRY INFORMATION: DDC subject heading and number at the head of the entry, author, title, edition statement, place of publication, publisher, date, pagination, size, series statement, notes, subject headings, added entries, DDC number in lower left corner, and consecutive number of registration in the lower right corner.

ARRANGEMENT: The bibliography is arranged according to the subjects of DDC.

INDEXES: Author index, title index, subject index.

---

[1] The first law is cited in *International Guide to Legal Deposit*, p. 106. The second law is cited in *GIP-UNISIST Newsletter*, supplement on *BSTW* in 1978, p. 102.

NOTES AND COMMENTS: This title is a new one in the Latin America area; it is wonderful to have a current publication for Costa Rica. One hopes that solutions have been found to overcome difficulties with publishing, distribution and staffing, problems that continually plagued *Annuario bibliográfico costarricense*. The bibliographic entries are in two files on the disk named BIBLI95A and BIBLI95B. Other files include the introduction and a brief guide. *BC* is attractively presented in a double column lay-out with five to eight entries to a page when printed out.

As stated above, *BC* continues *Annuario bibliográfico costarricense*. - 1956-1972/74. - San José : Imprenta Nacional, 1958-1978. Annual (irregular); some issues combined. (LCCN: sn87-17231; OCLC: 1623802; ISSN 0066-5016). This title supersedes *Boletín Bibliográfico*, published by the Biblioteca Nacional in 1948-1956, covering titles appearing in the years 1946-1955. It provides an alphabetical list of publications which included books, pamphlets, periodicals, bulletins and a list of periodicals appearing in the year of publication.[1]

Annuario bibliográfico costarricense (ABC) was compiled by Comité Nacional de Bibliografía Adolfo Blen, Asociación Costarricense de Bibliotecarios.[2] *ABC* lists works published in Costa Rica during the year and deposited at the Biblioteca Nacional, the University of Costa Rica, and from the non-deposit collection of the library of the Central Bank. It also includes works written by nationals and works about Costa Rica published abroad, and publications that have not been included in *ABC* back to 1956. Types of publications included in *ABC* are books, pamphlets, official and government publications, IGO publications, maps, reports, conference papers, institutional and private publications, translations of works published in Costa Rica. Excluded are periodicals, ephemera, books under ten pages.

Contents of a typical volume of *ABC* would include a table of contents, "presentación," abbreviations, bibliography, author index. Although the introduction does not state the rules followed in cataloguing the bibliographical entries, entries are fully described with information conforming to ISBD, and they appear to follow rules similar to AACR. An alphabetical subject classification grouping is used. The arrangement of *ABC* by subject based on a lengthy alphabetical list of subject headings such as coffee, religion, yoga, etc. This arrangement commenced in 1959-1960; previously, the bibliography was organized by author and subject listings. Official publications are listed under the appropriate headings, such as "Administración", or "Administración publica." They may be located by looking in the author index under the issuing agency. No symbols are used to designate government publications. An author index completes the volume.

It would be useful to have a more expanded introduction to *ABC*. A discussion of scope and contents, rules followed, an analyzed entry, and any new changes in the current volumes would all be beneficial to the reader. In addition, a title index, and a publishers' list would aid in locating and purchasing books. It would help in the identification of foreign imprints included

---

[1] Information is taken from "Bibliografia Costarriense" which is a typed history of the bibliographic coverage of Costa Rica. This report has no author or date, but was sent to the author by Marco A. Chacón Monge, Biblioteca Nacional.

[2] According to a footnote in Zimmerman, *Current National Bibliographies of Latin America* (p. 75) most of the work of *ABC* has been carried on by Prof. Nelly Kopper. Her name is also mentioned in the introduction of the 1972/1974 volume.

in the bibliography if ICNB recommendation number 5 would be followed. This suggests marking foreign imprint titles with a symbol.

The *BC*, with the publication of retrospective titles, plans to cover periods where there is no bibliographic coverage. One recent title which aims to do this is Gioconda Garcia Bontempo, and Nydia Maria Jiménez Segura. *Bibliografia costarricense 1975-1983.* Práctica dirigida de Licenciatura en Bibliotecologia u Ciencias de la Información, Escuela de Administración Educativa, Facultad de Educación, Universidad de Costa Rica, 1989. 4 vols. The scope covers books, pamphlets, documents, maps, printed music, and periodical publications. The title has an author index, a title index, and uses DDC. Another title is *Bibliografia Costarricense 1937-1945,* compiled and published by the Centro de Documentación y Bibliografia in 1984 (LCCN: 84-196065; OCLC: 11785151). [1]

A current title which has been useful during the period between the inactivity of *ABC* and the birth of *BC* is *Catalogo nacional ISBN [   ] : Libros publicados en Costa Rica* / Agencia Nacional ISBN. - 1983/1984-   . - San José : La Agencia, 198? -   . Annual (DDC: 015.7286; LC: Z1451.C37; LCCN: 86-645008; OCLC: 14584172). This title includes all of the works that are sent to the Biblioteca Nacional by the closing of the issue of *Catalogo*. It is based on legal deposit. Types of publications included are monographs, pamphlets, official and government publications. The contents include a table of contents, introduction (includes scope, rules followed, and a list of abbreviations), alphabetical list of ISBN publishers in this edition, bibliography of books published in Costa Rica for the current year, author index, title index, subject index, and ISBN numerical index. The numbers used in the index refer the user to the consecutive entry numbers in the bibliography.

Cataloguing rules used in *Catalogo* are the *Boleta enviada por los Editores a la Agencia Nacional ISBN* and AACR2; classification follows *Clasificación Tabla de Materias ISBN,* selección y recap. Juan Carlos Merlo. Information given in the entries are consecutive entry number, author, title, edition statement, place of publication, publisher, date, pagination, size, series statement, notes, including DDC number and ISBN. The arrangement of the bibliography is in classification order. Although it has a more limited scope than *ABC*, it is helpful to have a list of current publications from Costa Rica in the void created when *ABC* was not published. The latest volume examined at the British Library in June 1997 is for 1990/91, published in 1991; the latest published volume available in September 1997 is for the year 1993, published in 1996.

LATEST ISSUE EXAMINED/CURRENCY: The latest volume examined is the *BC* 1995 disk, published 1997 which was sent to the author by the Biblioteca Nacional. Most entries are from 1994 and 1995, although earlier imprints are included. This new title is located in only one location on the OCLC database, University of New Mexico, at the time of writing this entry. As word of this title becomes known, libraries interested in Latin American studies should purchase this; this title will be useful to researchers and bibliographers, especially if it is a current publication. Publication on disk may help in its timeliness.

---

[1] Information is taken from "Bibliografia Costarriense" which is a history of the bibliographic coverage of Costa Rica. This typed report has no author or date, but was sent to the author by Marco A. Chacón Monge, Biblioteca Nacional.

AUTOMATION: *BC* is the product of the BICO database of Centro de Documentación y Bibliografia, and is processed by the Micro/ISIS version 3.04 of Unesco, using a Pentium 120, 8 MB of memory.

FORMAT AND SERVICES AVAILABLE: 1994, printed; 1995- , on disk (MS/Word v. 6).

CURRENT LEGAL DEPOSIT LAWS: The 1995 disk version of *BC*, published 1997, cites the legal deposit legislation Decreto No. 32, de 19-7-1902.

The legal deposit law is not effective due in part to the lack of a stated time period for deposition of materials.

AVAILABLE FROM: Biblioteca Nacional de Costa Rica, Apartado Postal 10,008-1000, Ave. 3 y 3B, Calle 15 y 17, San José.

SELECTED ARTICLES: Woodbridge, Hensley C. "Latin American National Bibliography: Costa Rica." *Encyclopedia of Library and Information Services*:36 (suppl. 1 1983):298-299.

VERIFIER: Marco A. Chacón Monge, Area de Formación Colecciones, Biblioteca National.

CÔTE D'IVOIRE

TITLE: *Bibliographie de la Côte d'Ivoire*. - 1969-   . - Abidjan : Bibliothèque Nationale, [1970]- .
Semiannual (1973-   ); annual (1969-1972).
First issue undated and unnumbered, but constitutes no. 1, 1969.
At head of title: Republique de Côte d'Ivoire. Ministère des affaires culturelles.
DDC: 015.666; LC: Z3689.B5; LCCN: 76-616932//r933; OCLC: 2495479
ISSN 0084-7860

COMPILER: Bibliothèque Nationale.

SCOPE AND COVERAGE: *Bibliographie de la Côte d'Ivoire (BCI)* lists publications produced in the Ivory Coast, publications about the Ivory Coast or written by Ivorians and published elsewhere, or emanating from IGOs of which the Ivory Coast is a member. It is based on legal deposit.

Types of publications included in *BCI* are books, pamphlets, periodical articles, official and government publications, periodicals and newspapers, theses and dissertations, posters, selected IGO publications as defined in the scope, maps and atlases, microforms, expositions catalogues, brochures, local language publications.

CONTENTS: 1975: table of contents, introduction, list of signs and abbreviations, list of periodicals indexed, classification scheme used in the bibliography, bibliography: books, periodical articles, official publications (part 1 and 2), index for [year], supplement(s) for [year], index(es) for supplement(s).

1972: table of contents, books, periodicals, periodical articles, official publications, other imprints, index 1972; supplement to number 3, 1971: books, periodical articles, official publications, other imprints, list of deposited periodicals, list of signs and abbreviations.

CATALOGUING RULES AND CLASSIFICATION SCHEMES USED: ISBD(M) has been used in cataloguing titles since 1972. AACR2 rules are followed.

For classification, broad subject groups, using 0, 1, 3, etc. numbers and headings resembling the order of DDC are used.

ENTRY INFORMATION: 1974: Section 1 (books): consecutive entry number, author, title, place of publication, publisher, pagination, illustrations, size, series statement, brief notes including ISBN if known, legal deposit number given in lower left corner (e.g., D.L. 74-9337). Price is usually not given. Section 2 (periodical articles): consecutive entry number, author, title, periodical title, volume and number, date and pagination. Section 3 (official publications), part 1 (government) and part 2 (organized state societies): consecutive entry number, issuing agency, title, place of publication, publisher, pagination, illustrations, size, series statement, brief notes.

No individual title classification numbers are given.

ARRANGEMENT: The entries are divided by types of publication: books, periodical articles, and official publications. All are arranged by the broad headings of DDC. Sections 1 and 2 are then arranged alphabetically by author; section 3 is arranged alphabetically by issuing agency.

INDEXES: One alphabetical index of authors (corporate and personal) and titles. Numbers in the index refer back to entry numbers in the bibliography.

NOTES AND COMMENTS: No *BCI* seems to have been published since the volume covering 1975. According to Mr. Gueye who presented a paper about *BCI* at the 1983 ASCOBIC conference the eight year delay in the appearance of the 1975 volume was due to problems with the low level of the operational budget, lack of technical personnel at a certain point and the legal deposit irregularity. Also, because of the high production costs of *BCI*, the whole process needed to be reviewed. In order to catch up with production of *BCI* it was decided to adopt the new format of 21 x 29.7 cm. and to make a less costly edition, to dispense with the periodical articles which will be included in a monthly or quarterly loose-leaf publication and to make a retrospective bibliography for the period 1977-1982. The *BCI* in this format should be published in January 1984.[1] The author was unable to locate *BCI* in this new format.

BCI is written in French, the language of the country.

As noted above, there is a separate section for official publications. Official publications are gathered from regular visits to various government departments.

---

[1] Mr. Gueye, "Côte d' Ivoire. Communication presentée par Monsieur Gueye. Bibliographie National de la Côte d'Ivoire," *Afribiblios* 7 (no. 1, June 1984):19-21. The author thanks David Wilkin, French Department, The College of Wooster, for translating this article.

It would be helpful to have a more complete introduction to *BCI* as in earlier years. Except for the "sommaire" there is very little to guide the reader in the use of *BCI* and to help them understand the purpose and scope of the bibliography. A publishers' list would also be useful.

There is no special symbol for foreign imprints. It is necessary to look for the imprint information, or for the legal deposit number for Ivory Coast imprints.

Users need to be aware of the supplements included in each volume. For title verification, it is necessary to check each volume after the title's date of publication.

The title *BCI* in the Ivory Coast may be a source for some confusion until it is realized that the Université d'Abidjan has also issued a publication by that same title. According to Joanne Zellers, Area Specialist, African Section, African and Middle East Division, Library of Congress, the university title is based on their accessions. Each volume is on a specific topic such as "Sciences de la terre" and "Sciences de l'homme." The volumes are published as they are completed. The university bibliography is not based on legal deposit.

LATEST ISSUE EXAMINED/CURRENCY: The 1974 volume was published in 1977 and received at the British Library, London, 15 October 1978; the volume for 1975 was published in 1983 and received in 1985 by SOAS.

Issues include imprint dates for the year covered. In earlier issues, titles were included in supplements for [year] at the end of the current bibliography. Supplements for several years may be included in one volume. The latest volume examined is the volume for 1975.

It is unfortunate that the lag before publication and receipt of the bibliography in a library relegates this timely current national bibliography to an historical record rather than an acquisitions tool and a record of publishing in the country.

AUTOMATION: not known.

FORMAT AND SERVICES AVAILABLE: printed.

CURRENT LEGAL DEPOSIT LAWS: Decree 62-68 of 2 February 1962; Decree 73 of 15 January 1969.[1] Enforcement of the legal deposit is Decree 69 of 15 January 1969.

Part of the delay of the national bibliography is due to the ineffectiveness of the legal deposit laws. There are efforts to modify the law and bring it under the National Library.[2]

AVAILABLE FROM: Information about *BCI* may be obtained from Bibliothèque Nationale, BPV 180, Abidjan. Subscription payments should be directed to: Société Générale de Banque en Côte d'Ivoire, B.P. 1355, Abidjan.

VERIFIER: No reply received.

---

[1] *International Guide to Legal Deposit*, p. 84.
[2] *International Cataloguing* 8 (Apr./June 1979):15.

CROATIA

TITLE: *Hrvatska bibliografija. Niz A, Knjige* [Croatian bibliography. Series A. Books]. - 1/3, 1991-   . - Zagreb: Nacionalna i sveučilišna biblioteka, 1991-   .
Hrvatska bibliografija is divided into three separate series: *Niz A, Knjige.* - 1/3- , 1991-   . - 1991-   ; *Niz B, Prilozi u časopisima i zbornicima.* - 1- , 1990-   . - 1991-   ; *Niz C, Serijske publikacije.* 1- , 1991-   . - 1992-   . [1]
Monthly.
Some nos. issued in combined form.
Continues in part *Bibliografija knjiga tiskanih u SR Hrvatsko.*
DDC: 015.4393; UDC: 015(497.13)(05)540.1; LC: Z2901.H78; LCCN: 93-645960; OCLC: 28305967
ISSN 1330-0423

COMPILER: Nacionalna i sveučilišna biblioteka u Zagrebu. The library changed its name to Nacionalna i sveučilišna knjiznica in November 1995.

SCOPE AND COVERAGE: *Hrvatska bibliografija. Niz A, Knjige* (HB.A) lists books of Croatia which are deposited at the Nacionalna i sveučilišna knjižnica according to legal deposit, as well as books published abroad which are written by Croatian authors and in the Croatian language.

Types of publications include books, catalogues of art exhibitions, graphical maps, printed music, maps and atlases, tourist guides, and selected pamphlets.

Information about additional coverage is included in Notes and Comments.

CONTENTS: Preface, abbreviations, table of contents, classified bibliography, indexes.

CATALOGUING RULES AND CLASSIFICATION SCHEMES USED: The bibliographic description is according to ISBD(M), ISBN(NBM), ISBD(CM), ISBD(PM). National cataloguing rules by Eva Verona are used (cited as PPIAK in *UNIMARC Manual*); entry information is in the UNIMARC format.

Classification scheme used is the UDC.

ENTRY INFORMATION: Author, title, edition statement, place of publication, publisher, date, pagination, illustrations, size, series statement, notes including number of copies printed, bibliographic references, ISBN, national bibliography number in lower right corner, and UDC number in lower left corner.

ARRANGEMENT: The classified bibliography is arranged alphabetically within the UDC numbers.

INDEXES: Author, title/series, subject, ISBN indexes.

---

[1] In this entry, *Niz A* will be analyzed; information will be given for *Niz B* and *Niz C* in Notes and Comments.

NOTES AND COMMENTS: *Hrvatska bibliografija* since its beginning has recorded Croatian national production regardless of the political situation within the country. The National and University Library was the national library within the state of former Yugoslavia, and had the obligation stated by Croatian law to publish the national bibliography. The *Bibliografija Jugoslavije* was a compilation of Yugoslav imprints over which the national libraries had no control or influence.[1]

As earlier stated, *HB.A* continues in part *Bibliografija knjiga tiskanih u SR Hrvatskoj /* Nacionalna i sveučilišna biblioteka u Zagrebu. - Zagreb : Biblioteka, 1978-1984. Monthly (LCCN: sn86-25217; OCLC: 10884562; ISSN: 0350-8722). This title continues *Bibliografija knjiga tiskanih u Narodnoj Republici Hrvatskoj za godinu....* 1(1945)-5(1950). - Zagreb : Jugoslavenska akademija znanosti i umjetnosti, 1948 [e.g. 1949]-1956. Annual (LCCN: 51-3165//r93; LC: Z2938.L5B5; OCLC: 5071886; ISSN 1330-2736). This title continues in part *Hrvstska bibliografija.* - God. 1 (1941)- god. 4 (1944). - Zagreb : Hrvatska državna tiskara : Hrvatsko bibliotekarsko društvo, 1941-1944 (LCCN: 64-39883; OCLC: 5163881).

Hrvatska Bibliografija has two additional series. Following is information about these.

Hrvatska bibliografija. Niz B. Prilozi u časopisima i zbornicima [Croatian bibliography. Series B. Articles in Journals and Proceedings] / Nacionalna i sveučilišna biblioteka u Zagrebu. 1- , 1990- . - Zagreb : Biblioteka, 1991- . Monthly (LCCN: 93-646025; DDC: 015.05783; ISSN 1330-0415). This title continues *Bibliografija rasprava, članaka i književnih radova u časopisima SR Hrvatske.* - 1978-1982. - Zagreb : Nacionalna i svenčilišna biblioteka, 1979-1985. - (Hrvatska bibliografija. Niz B). Monthly (ISSN 0351-0115) which continues *Bibliografija rasprava, članaka i književnih radova u časopisima Narodne Republike Hrvatske za godinu....* - Knj. 1 (1945/46)- knj. 7 (1952). - Zagreb : Jugoslavenska akademija znanosti i umjetnosti, 1948-1956. - (Hrvatska bibliografija. [Niz B ; Knj. 1-7]) Annual (ISSN 1330-2744). Series B lists articles in journals and proceedings which are deposited at the Nacionalna i svenčilišna knjiznica according to legal deposit law. Contents include preface, user guide, table of contents, list of journals and proceedings processed in a particular issue, classified bibliography, author and subject indexes. Guidelines followed include ISBD(CP) and ISBD(S). Information given is author, title, illustration statement, notes including whether there is a bibliography, and summaries if different from the language of the title. Also given is the title of the source, ISSN, volume, date, number, and pagination of the article, and national bibliography number in the lower right corner. Organized by UDC subjects, entries are alphabetically listed within the headings.

Hrvatska bibliografija. Niz C. Serijske publikacije [Croatian bibliography. Series C. Serial publications] / Nacionalna i sveučilišna biblioteka. 1- , 1991- . - Zagreb : Biblioteka, 1992- . Semiannual and annual. Godoišnje i polugodišnje. (LCCN: 93-646029; OCLC: 28474643; ISSN 1330-0431). Series C lists serial publications (except newspapers) published in Croatia which are deposited at the Nacionalna sveucilisna knjiznica according to legal depposit, and serial publications in the Croatian language or edited by a Croatian editor (individual or corporate) published abroad. Contents include preface, alphabetical bibliography of titles, indexes (publisher, UDC, ISSN). Entries are according to ISBD(S). Entry information given is title, statement of responsibility, numbering, place of publication, publisher, date, size, series statement, notes including frequency statement, bibliographic history of titles with ISSN and

---

[1] Information included in a 22 July 1997 fax to the author from Mirna Willer, National Library.

key titles, current ISSN and key title, and national bibliography number in lower right corner, UDC number in lower left corner.

Series D of the national bibliography, to include dissertations, is in the planning stage.

Official publications are bibliographically covered by the Government of Croatia. Croatian Information Documentation Federal Agency.

Another title which is useful to locate new Croatian titles is *CIP bilten* / Nacionalna i sveučilišna biblioteka u Zagrebu. - Zagreb : Biblioteka, 1992- . Monthly (LCCN: sn92-25992; OCLC: 26498905; ISSN 0205-0275). This title is not part of the national bibliography.

LATEST ISSUE EXAMINED/CURRENCY: The latest issue of *HB.A* examined at the University of Illinois, Urbana in June 1996 is no. 10, 1993, which was published in 1995. Most imprints were for the time period covered. Some monographic series had earlier imprints. The latest issue of *Niz C, Serijske publikacije* examined is no. 2, 1994 , published in 1996, which was sent to the author by Ms. Willer.[1]

AUTOMATION: The bibliography has been automated since 1981. In 1991 the library installed a new automated system CROLIST developed by the National and University Library and the software firm EA (now renamed UNIBIS). CROLIST uses ORACLE RDBMS and UNIX client/server system. The test CROLIST fourth generation WEB OPAC is available on the Internet. The current hardware in use is COMPAQ Proliant 4500J.[2]

FORMAT AND SERVICES AVAILABLE: printed, magnetic tape (ISO 2709 and UNIMARC formats), Internet (http://www.nsk.hr).

CURRENT LEGAL DEPOSIT LAWS: Obavezno dostavljane tiskanih stvari i druge bibliotečne grade ('Službeni list SR Hrvatska' 25/1973).[3]

AVAILABLE FROM: Nacionalna i sveučilišna knjižnica, Hrvatska, 10 000 Zagreb, Hrvatske bratske zajednice bb (P.O. Box 550).

SELECTED ARTILCES: *Savetovanje Tekuce Bibliografije u Jugoslaviji: Zbornik Saopstenja, Beograd, 18-19. Novembar 1986.* Beograd : Jugoslovenski Bibliografski Institut, 1987.

VERIFIER: Mirna Willer, Nacionalna i sveučilišna knjiznica.

---

[1] The National Library moved to new premises which is one of the reasons the bibliography is late. However, the database is up-to-date, and several issues are currently at the printer. This information was included in a fax to the author from Mirna Willer, National Library.

[2] Information in Ms. Willer's fax.

[3] *International Guide to Legal Deposit*, p. 106. In her fax, Ms. Willer states that a new law is in the parliament and is expected to be released by October 1997.

CUBA

TITLE: *Bibliografía cuba*. - 1937-   . - Habana : Consejo Nacional de Cultura, 1938-   .
Annual (1990-   ); irregular (1989); bimonthly (1982-1988) with annual cumulative index;
annual (1965-1981).
From 1937-1952, title was *Anuario bibliográfico cubano*.
Volumes for 1937-1963/1964 issued by the Departamento Colección Cubana for the Biblioteca
Nacional José Martí; 1965-   by Biblioteca Nacional.
DDC: not found; LC: Z1511.B5; LCCN: 71-378138//r862; OCLC:1519737
ISSN 0574-6086

COMPILER: Departamento de Bibliografía Cubana, Biblioteca Nacional José Martí.

SCOPE AND COVERAGE: *Bibliografía Cuba (BC)* includes titles written by Cubans and
foreign authors published in Cuba, and titles written by Cuban authors published abroad,
received on legal deposit by the Biblioteca Nacional.

Types of publications included in *BC* are books, pamphlets, periodicals (first issues), annual
reports, official and government publications, maps and atlases, IGO publications, printed music
scores, limited editions, films, sound recordings, posters, exhibition catalogues, programs of
activities, postage stamps issued within the country, disks, bibliographies of bibliographies
published in Cuba.

The posters, exhibition catalogues, postage stamps, disks, film were added to the scope in
beginning 1972, maps were added to the scope in 1977, and in 1980, printed music scores were
included in an alphabetical listing retrospective to 1972.[1]

Excluded are periodical articles which are indexed in *Indice General de Publicaciones
Periódicas Cubana*, compiled by the Departamento de Bibliografías de la Biblioteca Nacional
José Martí, currently Departamento de Bibliografía Cubana.

CONTENTS: From the 1989 volume: table of contents, [section one: bio-bibliographies,
omitted], section two: books and pamphlets of Cuban and foreign authors published in Cuba,
and serial monographs described as monographs, supplement listing books previous to 1989,
Cuban authors in other lands; section three: serial publications; section four: special materials;
indexes.

Volumes from year to year vary in contents. The 1982 volume, for instance, besides the above
contents, includes an introduction, abbreviations and signs; section one: books, pamphlets,
maps, drama, etc. about José Martí, all of which are not included in 1989. The organization of
the bibliographic contents of the 1979 volume is slightly different. Section one: books and
pamphlets; section two: serial publications; section three: indexes; section four: bio-
bibliographies; section five: special materials; section six: indexes. The supplements are in a
separate section at the end of the volume, chronologically arranged.

---

[1]   Araceli Garcia Carranza and Xonia Jimenez Lopez. "The Contribution of the National
Library of Cuba to Current and Retrospective Bibliography." Paper presented at the IFLA
General Conference, 1994. (096-BIBL-3-E), pp. 6-8.

CATALOGUING RULES AND CLASSIFICATION SCHEMES USED: Beginning with 1982, the classification scheme used for books and pamphlets is based on the *Clasificación Biblioteco-Bibliografía de la URSS (BBK)* which has very general classes. This classification was used until *BC* began using the DDC with the 1992/1993 issue.[1]

Prior to 1982, serials, annuals, and monographic series were catalogued following AACR, British text (1967). Entries are set out according to the rules of the *Bibliographical Handbook of the Dag Hammarskjöld Library*.[2]

Beginning with 1982, the maps, sound recordings, posters, musical works are described according to the rules set by the Sección de Materiales Especiales del Departamento de Procesamiento Técnico de la Biblioteca Nacional José Martí. Exposition catalogues, postage stamps, films, and programs of activities follow rules set by the Departamento de Investigaciones Bibliográficas de la Biblioteca Nacional.

ENTRY INFORMATION: For books and pamphlets: entry number, author, title, place of publication, publication, date, pagination, size, illustrations, notes including other authors and series note given. No price information.

ARRANGEMENT: Beginning with the 1982 issue: The bibliography is arranged in broad subject arrangement based on *Clasificación Biblioteco-Bibliográfica de la URSS (BBK)*, then alphabetically arranged.

Prior to 1982, the bibliography was arranged by broad DDC subject headings.

INDEXES: Analytic index (including author, title, subject in capital letters); index of collections; series; publishers. The number used refers the reader to the entry number.

NOTES AND COMMENTS: From 1937 until 1952, the Cuban national bibliography appeared under the title *Anuario Bibliográfico Cubano*. In 1953, the title was changed to *Bibliografía Cubana*. For political reasons, there were two current national bibliographies by the same title for the period 1959-1966. One was compiled by the Biblioteca Nacional José Martí in Habana. The other was published by Fermín Peraza y Sarausa, the former editor of *BC*, who left Cuba for Colombia and then Florida where he died in 1969. The last volume of *Bibliografía Cubana* edited by Dr. Peraza, published by him in Gainesville, Florida, covered 1965 and was published in 1966. Dr. Peraza was responsible for organizing *Revolutionary Cuba: A Bibliographical Guide*. The first volume covering 1966 was published in 1967; the volume for 1970 appeared in 1979, and was edited by his wife Elena V. Peraza.[3] This title includes books and pamphlets published in or about Cuba for the year covered.

The 1982 volume of *BC* has an introduction, signs and abbreviations, and "bio-bibliografías" of authors who died during the year. This is an excellent biographical source for contemporary

---

[1] Information is included in a 23 May 1997 letter to the author from Xonia Jiménez, Vice-Directora of Biblioteca Nacional Jose Marti.

[2] *BSTW, Supplement 1980*, p. 25.

[3] Information from I. Zimmerman, *Current National Bibliographies of Latin America*, pp. 105-106, and from A. Nilges, *Nationalbibliographien Lateinamerikas*, p. 94.

Cuban authors. The introduction and bio-bibliografías do not appear in the 1986 and 1989 volumes.

The introduction in *BC* for the 1979 volume explains the difference in scope and arrangement from other volumes. It also explains cataloguing principles followed for locations of bibliographic entries. For example, films are entered under the director. In addition, it would be helpful to include an explanation of an entry as part of the introduction.

From 1979-1981, *BC* is published in two volumes. Volume 1 includes books and pamphlets, serials and bio-bibliographies; volume 2 includes maps, postage stamps, exposition catalogues, sound recordings, films and cultural activity programs of note. Each volume is accompanied by analytic, title, collection, series and publisher indexes.

The 1982 volume brought about change for *BC*. The introduction in the first number of 1982 summarizes the following changes: rearranging works about José Martí into "national" and "international", rather than "activa" and "pasiva", a new norm for describing books and pamphlets, a different classification scheme, and an integrated titles and analytic index. Entries for maps are to be compiled bimonthly and treated in accordance to the work. According to the introduction, the "bio-bibliografías" will continue to be compiled annually.

Government publications have been included since 1967.

Maps are included in a cartobibliography appearing in the 1977 volume which covers maps from 1959-1976. This bibliography appears again in the 1990 volume of *BC* covering maps from 1977-1991.[1]

In 1989, any earlier titles which have not been listed in the national bibliography are now listed in the main bibliography and not in a supplement.

The National Library compiled a national bibliography for the period 1917-1936 as a retrospective bibliography. It was published in four periods of four years each: 1917-1920, 1921-1924, 1925-1932, and 1933-1936. These were arranged alphabetically, and each volume was indexed.[2] This continues Carlos M. Trelles y Govín. *Bibliografía Cubano del Siglo XX [1900-1916].* 2 v. (OCLC: 1410019).

CIP is not practiced.

LATEST ISSUE EXAMINED/CURRENCY: Generally, publication of *BC* was one to two years after the date of coverage. If *BC* could be more timely, it could serve an acquisitions and collection development function for libraries worldwide.

Imprints are from the year covered with newly acquired titles from earlier years also listed in the main bibliography rather than bibliographical supplements as in earlier years.

---

1 Nilges, ibid., p. 92, and Garcia Carranza and Jimenez Lopez, p. 7 and 9.
2 Araceli Garcia Carranza and Xonia Jimenez Lopez. "The Contribution of the National Library of Cuba to Current and Retrospective Bibliography." Paper presented at the IFLA General Conference, 1994. (096-BIBL-3-E), p. 6.

The latest issue examined in March 1995 at the University of Minnesota Library is no. 1, for 1989, published in 1990.

AUTOMATION: No information was supplied by the Biblioteca Nacional José Martí. No. 1, 1989 was not automated.

FORMAT AND SERVICES AVAILABLE: printed.

CURRENT LEGAL DEPOSIT LAWS: Decree 3387 of 17 March 1964.

AVAILABLE FROM: Biblioteca Nacional "José Martí", Apdo 6881, Avenida de Independencia entre 20 de Mayo y Aranguren, Plaza de la Revolución José Martí, Habana.

SELECTED ARTICLES: Garcia Carranza, Araceli and Jiménez Lopez, Xonia. "Contribucion de la Biblioteca Nacional de Cuba a la bibliografia corriente y retrospectiva," *ICBC* 23 (Apr./June 1994): 23-26. This article is based on a paper given at IFLA General Conference Havana 1994. The author has the English translation "The Contribution of the National Library of Cuba to Current and Retrospective Bibliography." (096-BIBL-3-E).

VERIFIER: Xonia Jiménez, Vice-Directora of Biblioteca Nacional Jose Marti.

CYPRUS

TITLE: *Kypriakē vivliographia* [Cyprus bibliography]. - 1983/1984-   . - Leukōsia : Vivliographikē Hetaireia Kyprou [Bibliographic Society of Cyprus], 1985-   .
Annual.
DDC: not found; LC: Z3496 K95 ; LCCN: 89-648626; OCLC: 19540262
ISSN not found

COMPILER: Nikos Panagiōtou.

SCOPE AND COVERAGE: *Kypriakē vivliographia* (*KV*) includes the publishing output of Cyprus described by the compiler. This title is viewed as the beginning of a current national bibliography.[1]

Types of publications include books, pamphlets, official and government publications, periodicals, and newspapers.

Turkish Cypriot publications are not included.

CONTENTS: Listing of series' titles, table of contents, introduction including abbreviations list, bibliography, index.

---

[1] Lillian Sciberras. "Efforts towards Bibliographic and Library Cooperation in the Mediterranean Region." *ICBC* 17 (no. 2 April/June 1988):24.

CATALOGUING RULES AND CLASSIFICATION SCHEMES USED: ISBD is followed without the punctuation of AACR2.

No classification number is assigned to entries.

ENTRY INFORMATION: Consecutive entry number, author, title, edition statement, place of publication, publisher, date, series statement, size, pagination, illustrations, notes, e.g., index.

ARRANGEMENT: Arrangement is by DDC broad subject headings. Within the subject, the entries are alphabetical arranged within languages with Greek language publications listed first.

INDEXES: Author index. Numbers used refer the user to the consecutive entry numbers in the main bibliography.

NOTES AND COMMENTS: *KV* is part of the Bibliographic Society of Cyprus' series. Following is a list of volume numbers with the bibliographic list included: 2, 1983/84; 3, 1985; 5, 1986; 6, 1987; 8, 1988; 9, 1989; 11, 1990; 12, 1991; 13, 1992; 14, 1993; 15, 1994; 16, 1995.

In 1987 first steps were taken to establish a national library for Cyprus called the Cyprus Library. It is to be a depository for newly published materials and eventually be responsible for publishing the national bibliography and running the ISBN and ISSN Centers.[1]

KV is a good source for many publications from Cyprus. Greek, English, and French titles were noted in issues examined. If Turkish Cypriot publications are not recorded in another bibliography, it should be a consideration for *KV* to include these. It also would be useful for *KV* to include a classification number. Possibly these points should be considered when the Cyprus Library assumes the responsibility for the national bibliography. The Bibliographic Society of Cyprus is to commended for the undertaking of this bibliography.

In *Bibliography '84: Papers and Proceedings of a COMLA [Commonwealth Library Association] Regional Workshop, Msida, Malta, 13-16 November 1984*, edited by Paul Xuereb. Valletta, Malta : Ghaqda Bibljotekarji, 1985, it was mentioned on page 6 that a 1983 Cypriot bibliography was in preparation by Kostas Stephanou and S. Petrides. Stephanou has compiled *Kypriakē Vivliographia* (OCLC: 6625854; ISSN 0454-8035) as part of the *Vivliographikon Deltion* beginning with 1960/61- published in 1962. This bulletin, based on library collections, includes books, pamphlets, government publications, and IGO publications.

LATEST ISSUE EXAMINED/CURRENCY: The latest issue examined at the University Library, Cambridge, England in June 1997 is for 1995, published in 1996.

Imprint dates cover 1995.

AUTOMATION: not known.

FORMAT AND SERVICES AVAILABLE: printed.

---

[1] John Harvey. "New Cyprus National Library Approved." *International Leads:* 2 (spring 1988):5.

CURRENT LEGAL DEPOSIT LAWS: Statute Laws of Cyprus, Cap. 79, III.[1]

AVAILABLE FROM: Bibliographic Society of Cyprus, % Ministry of Education and Culture, Pedagogical Institute, Gregoris Afxentiou Street, 1413 Nicosia.

VERIFIER: No reply received.

CZECH REPUBLIC

TITLE: *Česká národní bibliografie. Knihy* [Czech national bibliography. Books]. - 1994-   . - V Praze : Národní knihovna, 1994-   .
Monthly.
Some nos. combined.
Continues *Národní bibliografie České republiky. Knihy.*
Frequency and publisher varies.

DDC: not found; LC: Z2131.N37; LCCN: 96-646582; OCLC: 32398506
ISSN 1210-8898

COMPILER: Národní knihovna České republiky.

SCOPE AND COVERAGE: *Česká Narodní Bibliografie. Knihy* [*CNB.K*] lists the publishing output of Bohemia, Moravia, and part of Silesia, Czech Republic that is deposited at the Národní Knihovna according to legal deposit legislation.

Types of publications included in *CNB.K* are books, pamphlets, first issues of annual reports, limited editions, brochures, calendars, official and government publications, specialized periodical publications, handbooks, directories.

Omitted are IGO publications, internal documents.

CONTENTS: Table of contents (in Czech, German, Russian and English), preface (in Czech, English, German) classified bibliography, indexes.

CATALOGUING RULES AND CLASSIFICATION SCHEMES USED: Cataloguing rules follow AACR2R (since 1995); before then, national rules were followed.   Complete bibliographic information is given.

The classification scheme used is UDC (top level).

ENTRY INFORMATION: Consecutive entry number in upper left corner, classification number in upper right corner, author, title, place of publication, publisher, date, pagination, illustrations statement, series statement, notes including ISBN, price, binding, number of books

---

[1] *International Guide to Legal Deposit*, p. 74.

printed, subject headings. The number at the bottom left is the identification number of the record in the Aleph database. The number at the bottom right is the shelfmark.

ARRANGEMENT: Arrangement is by ten subject divisions (UDC- top level).

INDEXES: *Názvovy rejstřík* (title index), *jmenný rejstřík* (names index), *předmtový rejstřík* (subject index), *rejstřík korporací* (corporate body index) at end of each issue. Numbers refer to the entry numbers in the classified bibliographic section. Annual cumulation of author, illustrator, translator, title and subject indexes. The 1992 published in 1994, however, is the last one which will be published since a decision was made to cancel the annual cumulated index.[1]

NOTES AND COMMENTS: The Czech Republic became independent on 1 January 1993. Before then, the Czech Republic was part of Czechoslovakia which was made up of two national republics—Czech and Slovak. Each republic has its own national bibliography.

As stated above, *CNB.K* continues *Národní bibliografie České republiky. Knihy,* 1993 (LCCN: 94-646882//r996; OCLC: 30772054; ISSN 1210-8898). Continues *Bibliografický katalog ČSFR. České knihy,* 1990-1992 (OCLC: 29180336; ISSN: 0862-9218) which continues *Bibliografický katalog ČSSR. České knihy,* 1960-1989 (OCLC: 11465864; LCCN: sn84-46155). Continues *Bibliografický katalog ČSR. České knihy,* 1955-1959 (OCLC: 7940080; ISSN 0528-6247), which continues *Bibliografický katalog ČSR. Česká kniha,* 1952-1954 (OCLC: 11465939). Continues *Česká kniha,* 1951 (OCLC: 7939508) which continues *Bibliografický katalog ČR. Knihy české,* 1933-1950 (OCLC: 20843857). Continues *Bibliografický katalog,* 1922-1928 (OCLC: 6320192).

The current title *CNB* has been analyzed in this entry. With the continuation of titles, the national bibliography began coverage in 1922. Other parts of the national bibliography are identified as follows.

Česká národní bibliografie. Hudebniny. - Praha : Národní knihovna České republiky, 1994- . - Annual (OCLC: 34713447; ISSN: 1211-1236). Continues *Národní bibliografie České republiky. Hudebniny = National Bibliography of the Czech Republic. Printed Music,* 1993- . - Annual (OCLC: 33296210; ISSN 1210-8855). Continues *Bibliografický katalog ČSFR. České hudebniny, gramofonové desky a kompaktní disky* [Czech Music, Gramophone Records and Compact Disks], 1990-1992. - Praha : Národní knihovna v Praze. Quarterly (OCLC: 28642869; ISSN 0862-8580) is a continuation of *Bibliografický katalog ČSSR. České Hudebniny a Gramofonové Desky* [Czech Music and Gramophone Records], 1965-1989. Quarterly (OCLC: 5512377; ISSN 0323-1569). This title is a continuation in part of *Bibliografický Katalog ČSSR. České Hudebniny.* 1951-1954. - Státní knihovna České Socialistické Republiky, 1955-1959 which supersedes in part the earlier *Bibliografický Katalog ČSSR. České a Slovenské Hudebniny. Státní Knihovna České Socialistické Republiky,* 1946-1950 (about ten issues a year). Coverage was provided in *Bibliografický Katalog Československé Republiky* from 1937-1945. Weekly (irregular).

Česká národní bibliografie. Články v českých časopisech [Articles in Czech Periodicals]

---

[1] Information in an e-mail letter dated 1 November 1996 to the author from Dr. Bohdana Stoklasová, Head of Cataloguing and National Bibliography, Národní Knihovna České Republiky.

1994- . (ISSN 1210-8995). The publishing in printed form was stopped in 1990. Starting from 1992 this is accessible only in machine-readable form, on CD-ROM, floppy disk, and on the Internet. Continues *Národní bibliografie České republiky. Články v českých časopisech* [Articles in Czech Periodicals], 1991-1993 (ISSN 1210-8995). Only in machine-readable form, on CD-ROM and floppy disk. Continues *Bibliografický katalog ČSFR. Články v českých časopisech* [Articles in Czech Periodicals], 1990. Praha : Národní knihovna v Praze, 1990 (LCCN: sn94-33087; OCLC: 29817523). Continues *Bibliograficky katalog ČSSR. Články v českých časopisech*, 1961-1989. - Praha : Státni Knihovna ČSSR, 1960-1989 (LCCN: sn88-21474; OCLC: 17641846). Continues *Bibliografický katalog ČSR. Články v českých časopisech*, 1955-1960 (OCLC: 9224812; ISSN 0006-1115). Continues *Bibliografický katalog ČSR. České časopisy*, 1953-1954 (LCCN: sn88-21472; OCLC: 9225644).

Česká národní bibliografie. Grafika. 1994-   . Praha : Národní knihovna České republiky, 1996-   (ISSN 1211-1341). It is planned that the maps, which were a part of this series until 1994 will be a part of the *Česká národní bibliografie. Kartograficke dokumenty serie*, which will be created in 1997.[1] *Grafika* continues in part *Národní bibliografie České republiky. Grafika a mapy*, 1993 (OCLC: 35061874; ISSN 1210-8936) which continues *Česká Grafika a mapy* [Czech graphic art and maps], 1958-1992. Prague : Státní Knihovna České Socialistické Republiky and Národní Knihovna v Praze, 1958-1992. Annual (OCLC: 3006213; ISSN 0577-3504).

Česká národní bibliografie. Disertace a autoreferáty. 1994-   (ISSN 1210-8995), only in machine-readable form. Continues *Národní bibliografie České republiky. Disertace a autoreferáty*, 1990-1993 only in machine-readable form. Continues *Bibliografický katalog ČSFR. České disertace* 1989 (published 1993; OCLC: 28602419; ISSN 0862-8599). The publishing in printed form was stopped in 1989. Starting from 1990, information has been accessible only in machine-readable form, and on CD-ROM. Continues *Bibliograficky katalog ČSSR. České disertace*, 1979-1989. - Praha : Státní knihovna ČSR v Nakl. a vydavatelství Panorama, 1980-1990 (OCLC: 10987770; ISSN 0232-041X). This continues *Bibliografický katalog ČSR. Československé Disertace*. [Czechoslovak theses]. 1964-1978. [Praha] : Státní knihovna ČSR, [etc.], 1965-1979. Annual. Dissertations omitted from previous volumes and covering years 1974-1984 are issued in a separate volume of the later title *České disertace*, published in 1987. Annual (OCLC: 2469708; ISSN 0232-041X).

Bibliografický katalog ČSSR. Noviny a časopisy v českých krajích. - 1976-1984. - Praha : Státní knihovna ČSSR. Cumulated for five years. Continues *Bibliografický katalog ČSR. Noviny a časopisy v českých krajích.* [Newspapers and periodicals in Bohemia and Moravia]. - 1951-1976. - Praha : Státní knihovna ČSR, 1952-1981. Biennial. (LCCN: sn84-44291; OCLC: 4723369).[2]

Česká národní bibliografie. Soupis bibliografií. - 1994-   . - Praha : Národní knihovna, 1995-   . Annual (ISSN 1211-1325). Continues *Národní bibliografie České republiky. Soupis českých bibliografií.* 1993 (ISSN 1210-8944). Continues *Bibliografický katalog ČSRF. Soupis českých bibliografií*, 1990-1992. (OCLC: for 1991: 28614020; ISSN 0862-9234). Continues

---

[1] Stoklasová e-mail.
[2] Some dates given by Stoklasová correspondence from 1 November and 1 October 1996 differ from the OCLC record; dates used are supplied by Dr. Stoklasová.

Bibliografický katalog ČSSR. Soupis českých bibliografií. 1960-1989. (1983-1989, ISSN 0323-1860). Continues *Bibliografický katalog ČSR. Soupis českých bibliografií = Bibliography of the Czech Bibliography.* - 1951/55-1960. - Praha : Narodní knihovna v Praze, 1955-1961 (ISSN: 0323-1860; OCLC: 19760130).

Česká národní bibliografie. Zahraniční bohemika. - 1994-   . - Praha : Národní knihovna, 1996-   . Annual (ISSN 1211-4375). Continues *Národní bibliografie České republiky. Zahraniční bohemika,* 1993 published in 1995. (ISSN 1210-8987). Continues *Bibliografický katalog ČSFR. Zahraniční Bohemika.* - 1990-1992. - V Praze : Národní knihovna v Praze, 1993-1995 (LCCN: 94-646180//r95; OCLC: 28240693; ISSN 1210-4523). From 1973-1989 *Zahraniční bohemika* was not published.[1] Continues *Bibliografický katalog ČSSR. Zahraniční Bohemika a Slovacika v roce....* [Foreign publications about Bohemia and Slovakia]. - 1964-1972. - [Praha] : Státní knihovna ČSSR, 1965-1973. Annual (OCLC: 5376776). Continues *Zahraniční bohemika a slovenika.* - 1962-1963. - V Praze, Národní knihovna, 1963-1964 (OCLC number: 5376597). Continues *Zahraniční bohemika.* 1961. - V Praze L Národní knihovna, 1962 (LCCN: 60-21623; OCLC: 53790913). *Bibliografický katalog ČSR. Zahraniční bohemika v roce....* - 1956-1958. - Praha : Státní Knihovna Ceské Socialistické Republiky, 1957-1959. Annual. Cumulation was published in 1968 with the title *Bibliografický katalog ČSSR. Česká kniha v cizině* 1939-1965.

Česká narodní bibliografie. Zvukové dokumenty. 1994- . - Praha : Národní knihovna, 1996-   . Annual. (ISSN 1211-1333). Continues *Národní bibliografie České republiky. Zvukové dokumenty.* 1993. Annual (ISSN 1211-1384). This title is a continuation in part of *Bibliografický katalog ČSFR. České hudebniny, gramofonové desky a kompaktní disky* since 1993.

The national bibliography assumed a new look with the volume for 1983. Indexing was expanded, and the bibliographic descriptions followed ISBD. Since 1995 the national bibliography has been processed according to the international standards AACR2 and UNIMARC.

The National Library in Prague is the first East European national library to contribute records to OCLC. It will contribute the national bibliography to the OCLC Online Union catalog beginning with 1995 data. Loading backfiles are under consideration.[2]

LATEST ISSUE EXAMINED/CURRENCY: The latest *CNB.K* issue was examined at the Biblioteksjänst AB Library, Sweden in September 1997. It was number 4 for 1997.

AUTOMATION: *CNB* has been automated since 1982 using CDS/ISIS. Since 1995, *CNB* is using ALEPH. Entries are structured under the international exchange format UNIMARC.

FORMAT AND SERVICES AVAILABLE: printed, online, CD-ROM (since 1994), floppy disk (updates of the quarterly CD-ROM is produced monthly on floppy disk). Books and articles are available on the Internet: http://www.nkp.cz

---

[1] Stoklasová e-mail.

[2] "National Library in Prague to Contribute Czech National Bibliography to OLUC." *OCLC Newsletter* (March/April 1995):19-20.

In the future serials will be added.

CURRENT LEGAL DEPOSIT LAWS: Legal deposit law (Decree No. 140-64 SDG of 17 June 1964); Vsem nakladatelskym a vudavatelskym organizacím v ČR (Č.j. 3 654/90-III/I), 22 brezna 1990. Zákon České národní rady c. 106/1991 SB. o neperiodických publikacích; Zákon č. 37/1995 SB. o neperiodických publikacích.[1]

AVAILABLE FROM: Národní knihovna České Republiky, 110 01 Prague 1, Klementinum 190.

SELECTED ARTICLES: "Czech Bibliography: the 20th Century." In Ryznar, Eliska and Croucher, Murlin. *Books in Czechoslovakia: Past and Present.* Wiesbaden: Otto Harrassowitz, 1989. pp. 70-74.

VERIFIER: Dr. Bohdana Stoklasová, Head of Cataloguing and National Bibliography, National Library of the Czech Republic.

DENMARK

TITLE: *Dansk bogfortegnelse.* - 1841/58-   . - Ballerup : Dansk BiblioteksCenter, 1861-   .
Monthly, with quarterly, annual, multi-year cumulations.
Title varies.
Publisher varies.
DDC: 015.489; UDC: 015 (489); LC: Z2561.D191; LCCN: 03-9839//r613; OCLC: 1565885
ISSN 0106-2743

COMPILER: Dansk BiblioteksCenter [Danish Library Center] in collaboration with Det kongelige Bibliotek [The Royal Library].

SCOPE AND COVERAGE: *Dansk Bogfortegnelse (DB)*, the *Danish National Bibliography, Books*, lists the books and serials in book form, microform and from 1996 computer-readable publications which are published in Denmark and received directly from the publishers on a voluntary basis. The Royal Library supplements this material with publications received from printers deposited according to legal deposit legislation. Publications are listed whether they are sold by booksellers or not. Titles of original works by Danish authors published abroad or titles published abroad in Danish were included until 1990.

Types of publications include books (including reprints, revisions and new editions), official and government publications, periodicals and newspapers (new titles, title change, and cessations), annuals (each issue), printed music which emphasizes the text, text matter for AV material if

---

[1] Information is from the *Survey of Existing Legal Deposit Laws*, p.29, *International Guide to Legal Deposit*, p. 74, and updated in an 1 October 1996 letter to the author from Dr. Vojtech Balík, Director of Národní Knihovna České Republiky. Information in the letter is also supplied by Dr. Bohdana Stoklasová, Head of Cataloguing and National Bibliography, Národní Knihovna České Republiky.

distinguished as being primary material, IGO publications, song and hymn books if the notes are only intended for the melody line with or without text, latest reprint listed (first reprint is listed in weekly list), maps in book form, dissertations (if published), computer-readable publications on a physically fixed medium, e.g., CD-ROM, which contain text or where the text is considered predominant in the case of mulitmedia. Publications of this type published abroad are included if they are intended for the Danish market.

Excluded are books not sold by booksellers that have fewer than 17 pages, ephemera and short-term interest publications, e.g., election pamphlets, calendars, programmes, advertising publications, publications of a temporary or archival character, e.g, prepublications, administrative materials, publications appealing to a narrow circle or internal affairs (local directories, timetables, private or ordinary annual reports), publications from municipal and county authorities dealing with current administrative and physical matters, e.g., planning publications, statutes, and statistics, audio-visual materials, art files, art sheets, educational guides, and course materials.

Multi-year: coverage is the same as the annual list with the exception that newspapers, periodicals and foreign publications sold on a commission basis are omitted. These titles are transferred to the multi-year catalogue *Dansk Periodicafortegnelse*. Foreign books sold on a commission basis are omitted from the quinquennial list. Only the latest edition of non-fiction books are given, with notes to previous editions; all editions of fiction books within a five year period are listed. The last edition in book form is 1981/1985 (published 1987); subsequent issues are in microfiche.

CONTENTS: Monthly and quarterly: verso of cover: (in Danish and English) preface (including purpose, scope, and illustrated example of an entry), abbreviations and symbols, publishers' addresses, ISBN publisher identifiers, alphabetical section with complete bibliographical information, classified index section, list of misprinted ISBNs, back cover included Danish decimal classification schedules. No table of contents, or indexes.

Annual: (in Danish and in English) contents, abbreviations and symbols, preface, "how to use *DB*," outline of classification, book statistics, publishers' addresses, list of publishers' ISBN identifiers, alphabetical bibliographical section, classified index section, list of misprinted ISBNs, *The Greenlandic Book List*, *The Faroese Book List*, *The Danish National Bibliography*. *Cartographic materials*.

CATALOGUING RULES AND CLASSIFICATION SCHEMES USED: Since 1976, cataloguing rules used are "Katalogiseringsregler og bibliografisk standard for danske biblioteker" [Cataloguing rules and bibliographical standard for Danish libraries]. Part 1, headings, is based on AACR, British text, with substantial changes as agreed upon based on AACR2. Changes since 1991 have resulted in no personal authors in new serial records, and corporate bodies no longer appear as main entry headings. Part 2 "Beskrivelse" (Descriptions) is based on AACR2.

"Katalogiseringsregler og bibliografisk standard for dansk biblioteker: Periodica" [Cataloguing Rules and Bibliographical Standard for Danish Libraries: Serials] is based on AACR2.

Filing rules follow "Alfabetiseringsregler for danske biblioteker og bibliografier" [Filing Code for Danish Libraries and Bibliographies].

The classification scheme used is Decimalklassedeling [Danish Decimal Classification], 5th ed.

ENTRY INFORMATION: Main entry (if personal author, includes year of birth if known; corporate bodies may have explanatory addition in parentheses), title, edition, place of publication, publisher's address, publisher, date, pagination, illustrations, size, series statement, decimal class number, notes, ISBN or ISSN, type of binding, price including VAT (net after the price means no discount to booksellers), FAUST number, e.g., a computer-identification number. An asterisk (*) indicates that Dansk BiblioteksCenter supplies information and order form sets for the title. The main entry in the alphabetical section provides the most complete bibliographic information.

ARRANGEMENT: The bibliography section is arranged alphabetically by main entry.

INDEXES: Classified index.

NOTES AND COMMENTS: From 1851-1855, *DB* was also issued under the title *Maanedlig Dansk Bogfortegnelse*.

During the period of 1856-1975, the *DB* was published by G.E.C. Gads Forlag, which continues to sell these volumes.

DB is cumulated from alphabetical weekly listings in the periodical *Bogmarkedet*. Monthly lists are cumulated into the quarterly list as follows: No. 1, 2, 1/3, 4, 5, 4/6, 7, 8, 7/9, 10, 11, 10/12. Entries are arranged in an alphabetical main section, with a classified index section.

Faroese titles published in the Faroe Islands, publications in the Faroese language, literature dealing with Faroese matters together with original works by or translations of Faroese writers published abroad are listed in the annual list entitled *Færøsk Bogfortegnelse*. Only Faroese titles published in Denmark are listed in all parts of *DB*. The *Færøsk Bogfortegnelse* is prepared by the National Library, the Faroe Islands, and catalogued and classified according to the rules of their library. Information is organized in an alphabetical main section, and a classified index section.

Greenlandic titles are listed together with the Danish titles in the weekly and monthly/quarterly lists. The annual cumulation *Grønlandsk Bogfortegnelse* includes publications published in Greenland and publications in the Greenlandic language together with original works by Greenlandic writers published abroad. In the annual cumulation, these titles appear in a separate list; the Danish section only includes titles in Greenlandic published in Denmark. *Grønlandsk Bogfortegnelse* is arranged by an alphabetical section and a classified index.

Dansk Kortfortegnelse [Danish National Bibliography. Cartographic Materials] lists Danish, Faroese and Greenlandic maps in sheet and book forms. The list is arranged topographically and prepared by the curators of the map collection at the Royal Library. The list is also published separately by the Royal Library. Maps in book form are also listed in *DB* and in the Greenland and Faroe lists.

ICNB recommendations 5, 6, 8, 9, 10, 13 are followed. The preface, given both in Danish and English, includes an analyzed entry.

Volumes of *DB* for 1915/19-1930/34 include *Islandsk Bogfortegnelse* for the same dates.

"See" references are used abundantly throughout the alphabetical and systematic sections.

Government and official publications are not designated by any symbols.

Other sections of the Danish national bibliography supplement *DB*. Briefly these are as follows.

Anmeldelsesbasen [The Review Database] lists reviews from newspapers, periodicals and annuals. Compiled and published by Dansk BiblioteksCenter. Available online only. 1990- . Previously, this information was in paper as *Dansk Anmeldelsesindeks* (ISSN 0106-1488).

Artikler i Bøger [The Danish National Bibliography. Articles in Books]. 1981-1989. Published by Bibliotekscentralen, 1983-1990. Annual. (ISSN 0108-0261) Lists articles in books.

Artikelbasen [The Article Database]. 1981- . - Ballerup : Dansk BiblioteksCenter, 1981- . Lists articles from newspapers, periodicals and annuals available online and on CD-ROM. From 1979-1993 also published annually as *Dansk Artikelindeks* [The Danish National Bibliography. Articles]. Continues *Dansk Tidsskrift Index* 1975-1978, and *Avis Kronik Index* 1940-1978. (ISSN 0106-147x; OCLC: 8325590).

Bibliografi over Danmarks Offentlige Publikationer. 1948- . - Ballerup : Dansk BiblioteksCenter, 1949- lists publications issued by the Danish government and municipalities of Copenhagen and Århus, arranged by issuing ministry. Publisher varies. Indexed. Annual. (ISSN 0067-6543; OCLC: 1519726).

Dania Polyglotta 1945- lists foreign-language literature (books and periodicals) of Danish interest published abroad about Denmark as well as books and serials written by, illustrated by or edited by Danes or being in other ways connected with Danish literature published abroad. As of 1990/91 (new series 22/23), this list also includes Danish, Faroese or Greenlandic language books and periodicals published abroad. Compiled by the Danish Department, Royal Library. Annual. (ISSN 0070-2714) A separate file for *Dania Polyglotta* within the REX database is maintained by the Royal Library, and is accessible on line to users of the Royal Library and accessible nationally and internationally via the telecommunication network.[1]

Dansk Billedfortegnelse [The Danish National Bibliography. Visual recordings] includes slice series, overhead transparencies, motion pictures, video recordings and video discs which are for sale, loan or rent. Published by Dansk BiblioteksCenter.

Dansk Lydfortegnelse [The Danish National Bibliography. Sound Recordings] 1982/84- lists phonorecords, recorded tapes, and compact discs in which music does not have the primary function. Published by Dansk BiblioteksCenter. (OCLC: 13087727). Since 1989, this information is only available online and on CD-ROM.

Dansk Musikfortegnelse [The Danish National Bibliography. Music] 1931/33- includes sheet music. Compiled by the Music Department, Royal Library and published by Dansk

---

[1] [English introductory remarks], *Dania Polyglotta*, 1990/91, p. 4.

BiblioteksCenter, 1934-   . Annual. (DDC: 016.7817489; LC: ML120.D3D3; LCCN: 45-33260/MN/r83; ISSN 0105-8045; OCLC: 4428679).

Dansk Periodicafortegnelse [The Danish National Bibliography. Serials] lists newspapers, periodicals, and annuals together with certain monographic series. It is compiled by the Danish Department, Royal Library and published by Dansk BiblioteksCenter. 1972-   . There have been two. The latest covers 1976-1985, and is compiled by Det Kongelige Biblioteks Danske afdeling.[1] New and ceased serials first appear in a weekly list along with the weekly list of *DB* which serves to keep the *Dansk Periodicafortegnelse* up-to-date. Since the latest full edition, Bibliotekscentralen has issued supplements called *Dansk Periodicafortegnelse. Supplement*, the latest in 1990 covered 1970/71 to 1976/80. (ISSN 0084-9596; OCLC1028149).

Danske Musikoptagelser: Grammofonplader og lydbånd [Danish National Bibliography. Music Recordings: Gramophone Records and Sound Tapes]. 1975-   lists music recordings. Published by Dansk BiblioteksCenter, 1978-1983. Quarterly, with annual cumulations. Only available online and on CD-ROM, 1984-   . Continuation of *Danske Kassettebånd* (covering 1973-74, published 1974-76) and *Danske Grammmofoplader* (covering 1967-1974, published 1973-75; ISSN 0105-9688).

Grønlandsk Avis- og Tidsskrift-Index [Greenland's Newspaper and Periodical Index]. 1950/1954-   lists articles relating to Greenland and Greenlandic matters. Kobenhavn : Det kongelige Bibliotek, 1974-   . (ISSN 0105-9599).

LATEST ISSUE EXAMINED/CURRENCY: The latest monthly list of *DB* examined was no. 1, 1996 received from the Dansk BiblioteksCenter, April 1996. The annual cumulation for 1993, published 1994 was the latest examined in the University of Minnesota Library on 25 March 1995.

AUTOMATION: The *DB* is produced from information in *DANBIB*, the library's bibliographic database.[2]

FORMAT AND SERVICES AVAILABLE: All titles in the main lists of *DB* are accessible online, and on CD-ROM from the Danish Library Centre. Both formats cover publications from 1970 to the present.[3] REX, the Royal Library Information system, includes titles in the *DB*. All Danish and Greenlandic titles from *DB* are accessible online in DANBIB via connection to the library automation system for the Danish public libraries. The *DB* is available also on magnetic tape.

CURRENT LEGAL DEPOSIT LAWS: Act of Legal Deposit ("Preface," *DB*, 1983). *Survey of Existing Legal Deposit Laws* (p. 30) cites Lov (Nr. 160-1. Juli 1927).

AVAILABLE FROM: Dansk BiblioteksCenter , Tempovej 7-11, 2750 Ballerup.

---

[1] Information in a letter to the author dated 13 September 1990 from Ann Welling, research librarian, Det Kongelise Bibliotek.
[2] Information from Kirsten Waneck, Deputy Directory, Dansk BibliotekCenter.
[3] Ibid.

SELECTED ARTICLES: Madsen, Mona. *Nationalbibliografi, formål og funktion--med en oversigt over dansk national bibliografi.* Kongelige Danmarks Biblioteksskole, 1994.

Optagelseskriterier for Dansk Bogfortegnelse og Dansk Periodicafortegnelse. 4 udg. Ballerup : Dansk BiblioteksCenter, 1995.

Waneck, Kirsten. *The Danish National Bibliography* (28 May 1996). Translation of the Danish BiblioteksCenter's annual report to the Danish National Library Authority.

Waneck, Kirsten. "The Role of the National Bibliographic Agency." In *ISBN Review*: 15 (1994).

Waneck, Kirsten; Hansen, Randi Digest. "Bibliographic Control in Denmark." *ICBC* 26 (no. 2 April/June 1997):28-31.

VERIFIER: Kirsten Waneck, Deputy Director, BiblioteksCenter.

DJIBOUTI

No current national bibliography has been traced for Djibouti.

Djibouti is included within the scope of *AL,ESA* and the *QIPL,ESA*.

DOMINICA

No national bibliography has been traced for Dominica.

Dominica is within the scope of *CARICOM Bibliography*, vol. 1/2 (1977/1978)- vol. 10 (nos.1-2, 1986) (ISSN 0254-9646).

DOMINICAN REPUBLIC

TITLE: *Anuario bibliográfico dominicano.* - 1946-   . - Santo Domingo : Biblioteca Nacional, 1947-   .
Annual (interrupted 1948-1977).
Publisher varies: 1946, Oficina de Canje y Difusion Cultural; 1947, Seccion de Canje y Difusion Cultural de la Secretaria de Estado Educación y Bellas Artes.
Continues *Boletín Bibliográfico Dominicano*
DDC: not found; LC: Z1533.A58; LCCN: sn91-25351
ISSN not found

COMPILER: Departamento de Bibliografía Nacional, Biblioteca Nacional.

SCOPE AND COVERAGE: *Anuario Bibliográfico Dominicano* (*ABD*) lists works published in or about the country and deposited at the Biblioteca Nacional according to legal deposit legislation. Since the legal deposit law is not closely observed *ABD* also includes titles written by national authors that must be acquired by the Biblioteca Nacional. Titles about the country but published abroad are also included and some articles about Dominican Republic matters in foreign periodical titles which are subscribed to by the Biblioteca Nacional.

Types of publications included in *ABD* are books, pamphlets, official and government publications, theses and dissertations, selected periodical articles (as noted above), and university publications.

Excluded from coverage in *ABD* are serial publications, beginning with the 1978 volume. Some earlier volumes, e.g., 1946 and 1947, included periodicals and newspapers.

CONTENTS: 1980-1982: introduction, instructions for use including rules used and an analyzed entry, bibliography, author index, subject index.

1946 volume: Part l: bibliography arranged by subject; Part 2: theses presented at the University of Santo Domingo for 1945-1946; Part 3: periodicals and newspapers appearing in the Dominican Republic during 1946, index.

CATALOGUING RULES AND CLASSIFICATION SCHEMES USED: AACR2 rules are followed.

No classification scheme is used in the 1980-1982 volume. The bibliography is organized by subjects without any classification numbers. The 1946 volume used broad subjects.

ENTRY INFORMATION: 1946: Part 1: author, title, place of publication, publisher, date, pagination, series, illustrations, entry number in lower right corner. No price, size, notes.

1980-1982: Consecutive bibliographic entry number, author, title, place of publication, publisher, date, pagination, series.

ARRANGEMENT: *ABD* 1946, Part l is arranged alphabetically by broad subject classification, with entries alphabetically arranged by main entry within the subjects; Part 2, theses, is divided into University of Santo Domingo theses of 1945-1946, and theses of the exact sciences faculties; Part 3 is alphabetical by title.

ABD 1980-1982 is organized by alphabetical subjects.

INDEXES: 1946: author index; 1980-1982: author index, subject index. Numbers in the author index refer to the consecutive entry numbers; numbers in the subject index refer to the page number where the subject is located in the bibliography.

NOTES AND COMMENTS: *ABD* has appeared very sporadically over the years with the latest publication covering 1980-1982, retrospectively covering 1979 and earlier listing titles not included in a previous volume; the issue was published in 1984 by the Biblioteca Nacional. This was the first appearance of *ABD* since 1978. *ABD* continues *Boletín Bibliográfico*

Dominicano (no. 1, July/Aug. 1945; no. 2, Sept./Dec. 1945). Ciudad Trujillo : [s.n.], 1947 (OCLC: 7563260).

Bibliografía Actual del Caribe (ISSN 0070-1866) includes the Dominican Republic within its scope. Even though this title is not current, it helps to fill the void created by the interruption of *ABD* between 1948-1977.

Information on periodical publications is listed in "Bibliografía de Publicaciones Periódicas" by Pablo Lorenzo, published in no. 12-13, April-Sept. 1979 of *El Papiro: órgano de la Asociación Dominicana de Bibliotecarios, Inc.* - No. 1, June 1976-   . - Santo Domingo : La Asociación, 1976-   (LCCN: 84-646061; OCLC: 5279734).

It is good to see *ABD* has been updated along some of the ICNB guidelines. According to H. Woodbridge, the 1978 *ABD* was arranged by DDC;[1] one wonders why the 1980-1982 volume is now organized once again by an alphabetical subject sequence. Since this is a national bibliography, it would be helpful to include a classified bibliography for the benefit of other libraries within the country as well as abroad. This sharing of expertise particularly by librarians cataloguing from the work itself would aid the library community. If frequency can be improved especially through an improved and more effective legal deposit legislation, this title will be counted upon by librarians, bibliographers and research students to help identify publications from and about the Dominican Republic.

LATEST ISSUE EXAMINED/CURRENCY: In a sample of entries from the 1980-1982 volume, the "retrospective character" mentioned in the instructions for use was apparent. Sixty-four percent of the entries were from 1976 or earlier, with some imprints from the 1930's; the oldest entry noticed was 1899. Only twelve percent of the entries analyzed were from the period covered; twenty-four percent were from 1977-1979.

The latest issue examined was the 1980-1982 volume published in 1984 and received on 31 October 1984 by the Benson Latin American Collection, University of Texas, Austin.

AUTOMATION: not automated.

FORMAT AND SERVICES AVAILABLE: printed.

CURRENT LEGAL DEPOSIT LAWS: Law number 112 of 15 April 1971 (*Gaceta Oficial*, no. 9223, 23 April 1971).

AVAILABLE FROM: Biblioteca Nacional, César Nicolás Penson, Santo Domingo.

VERIFIER: no reply received.

---

[1] Information for the 1978 volume was taken from H. Woodbridge, "Latin American National Bibliographies" in *Encyclopedia of Library and Information Sciences*, vol. 36, suppl. 1 (1983):303.

ECUADOR

TITLE: *Anuario bibliográfico ecuatoriano.* - 1982-1987. - Cuenca : Banco Central del Ecuador, Centro de Investigación y Cultura, 1984-1991.
Continues: *Ecuador, bibliografía analítica.*
DDC: 016.9866; LC: Z1761.E57; LCCN: 86-640202, OCLC: 12729368
ISSN not found

COMPILER: Rodrigo Abad Gómez.

SCOPE AND COVERAGE: *Anuario bibliografico ecuatoriano* (*ABE*) includes titles published in or about Ecuador; it is based on legal deposit.

Types of publications within the coverage of *ABE* are books, pamphlets, official and government publications, periodicals (first issues), periodical articles, essays in collections.

CONTENTS: Table of contents, introduction, bibliography, index of journals included in *ABE*, name and corporate author index.

CATALOGUING RULES AND CLASSIFICATION SCHEMES USED: ISBD (M) and ISBD (S) are used in cataloguing entries.

No classification scheme is used.

ENTRY INFORMATION: For monographs: entry number in upper left corner, author, title, place of publication, publisher, pagination, illustration statement. No size or price information is given.

For periodical articles: entry number in upper left, author of article, title of article, title of periodical in which article appeared, place of publication, volume, pagination, date.

For periodical publications: entry number, e.g., 2383, title, place of publication, publisher, first issue, date, frequency, price.

ARRANGEMENT: Entries are arranged alphabetically under broad subject headings and their subdivisions of the DDC: general works, philosophy, religion, social sciences, languages, pure sciences, applied sciences and technology, "bella artes," literature, history and geography.

INDEXES: The table of contents is called the "general index." At the end are the index of journals included in *ABE*, and the name and corporate author index. The numbers refer back to the entry numbers.

NOTES AND COMMENTS: *ABE* continues *Ecuador, bibliografía analítica.* - Cuenca : Centro de Investigación y Cultura del Banco Central del Ecuador, 1979-198?. (LCCN: 80-647066//r862; OCLC: 6834871). This title lists national and foreign publications on Ecuador.

Books and periodical articles are listed separately and arranged by the DDC system. Name and subject indexes are given, with the last issue including a cumulative index. With the 1982 volume, the title has changed to *Anuario Bibliográfico Ecuatoriano*.

Bibliografía ecuatoriana. - No. 1 (Jan./Feb. 1975) - (1981?). - Quito: Biblioteca General de la Universidad Central del Ecuador, 1975-1981? Semiannual (irregular) (1976-1981?); bimonthly (1975). (LCCN: 77-649113//r83, OCLC: 4432658). The final issue is the annual cumulation *Anuario Bibliográfico Ecuatoriana*. *Bibliografía Ecuatoriana* (*BE*) includes titles published in or about Ecuador. Beginning with number 7, specialized bibliographies include titles about books or Ecuadorian authors which include works published in Ecuador and from other parts of the world on the subject covered. This title was an effort to update the *ABE*.

In the last few years, it appears that the majority of entries are analytical. This is useful as a periodical or collections index, but one wonders how many books are published in Ecuador and the effectiveness of the legal deposit law. Although *ABE* is attractively done, there are a few improvements that could be added to make this meet ICNB recommendations. A list of publishers and addresses would be a helpful addition, as would an analyzed entry in the introduction. It would also be helpful to add classification numbers to each entry as done in the *Bibliografia ecuatoriana*. Including a list of abbreviations would be beneficial to the user. Most important, however, would be the wish that this bibliography continue as a timely current national bibliography. At present it is ceased.

Diccionario bibliográfico ecuatoriano. - Vol. 1-   . - Quito : Biblioteca Ecuatoriana "Aurelio Espinosa Pólit," 1989-   is publishing a catalogue of "Ecuatoriana."[1] (LCCN: 90-174147//r97; OCLC: 22112339).

Prior to *ABE*, there were other attempts to begin a current national bibliography. One of the titles was *Boletín Bibliográfico Ecuatoriano*, designed to be a quarterly. It lasted only for two issues: Jan./March and April/June 1967.

LATEST ISSUE EXAMINED/CURRENCY: The last issue examined in May 1995 at the University of Wisconsin is the volume for 1986 published in 1989.[2]

CURRENT LEGAL DEPOSIT LAWS: Legislative decree of 21 March 1934; 1958 Copyright Statute, Art. 24-32. Few comply with these ineffective laws.

AVAILABLE FROM: no longer published.

VERIFIER: ceased publication.

---

1 "Ecuador," *Information Sources in Official Publications*, pp. 107-108.
2 Ibid. It states that Ecuador's national bibliography ceased with coverage of 1987.

EGYPT

TITLE: *Nashrat al-īdā'.* - 1974-   . - [al-Qāhirah]: Dār al-Kutub wa-al-Wathā'iq al-Qawmīyah [Egyptian National Library], 1974-   .
Frequency varies: monthly, with annual cumulative index (Jan. 1996-   ), semi-annual (1990-1995), quarterly (Jan. 1974- Dec. 1989).
Added title page: *Legal deposit bulletin.*
Continues: *Nashrat al-īda' al-shahrīyah* [Legal deposit monthly bulletin].
DDC: not found; LC: Z3651.N36; LCCN: 78-641280/NE/r90; OCLC: 3735020
ISSN 1012-5639

COMPILER: National Bibliography Section, Egyptian National Library.

SCOPE AND COVERAGE: The *Nashrat al-īdā'* or *Legal Deposit Bulletin* (*LDB*) is based on materials of national imprint received at the National Library according to legal deposit legislation.

Types of publications received are books, pamphlets, official and government publications, annual reports, school books, research reports, brochures, and maps.

Excluded are non-book materials, publications under 25 pages, serials, IGO publications, music and films.

CONTENTS: The *LDB* includes two parts: Africa (Arabic), and Foreign Languages. The Arabic part is from right to left, and the Foreign Languages part is from left to right. Through 1989, each of these parts may have the following sections: main, government, school, children. Beginning in 1990, the school books have been excluded from the main section. Beginning in 1995, the children's books have been excluded from the *LDB* and issued separately. A table of contents, list of abbreviations, and indexes are included in both parts. Additional information is included in the Arabic part.

CATALOGUING RULES AND CLASSIFICATION SCHEMES USED: ALA cataloguing rules with use of corporate headings are followed.

An adaptation of the DDC system is used by *LDB* to classify entries.

ENTRY INFORMATION: Author, title, edition statement, place of publication, publisher, date, pagination, illustrations, size, series, notes including bibliography, ISBN, accession or shelf-mark in lower left corner, e.g., H37868-37869, DDC number in lower right corner. The consecutive serial number is in the upper right corner of the main entry.

ARRANGEMENT: The main section is divided into the DDC broad subject areas, e.g., general works, social sciences, language, pure sciences, technical arts, literature, history. Entries are arranged alphabetically within each of these divisions.

INDEXES: Author index, title index, subject index, publishers index. The index number refers the user to the consecutive serial number in the main bibliography. Serial numbers used are preceded by a number and a letter which denote successively the issue number and section in which the bibliography entries occur, e.g., 1 S 43, 44, 51-53. Letters used are: G = government publications section; J = children and juvenile books section; M = main; S = school book section. Indexes cumulate in the final issue of the year. The "List of Publishers" also serves as an index since serial numbers for books produced by various publishers are listed under the publisher's name.

Beginning in 1996, an annual cumulative index will be published. This includes author, title, subject headings, and publishers.[1]

NOTES AND COMMENTS: The predecessor of *LDB* (analyzed in this entry) is *Nashrat al-īdāʿ al-shahrīyah* [Legal deposit monthly bulletin]. - Jan. 1969 - Jan./Dec. 1973. - [al-Qāhirah], Dar al-Kutub wa-al-Wathāʾiq al-Qawmīyah, 1969-1974. (LCCN: 78-641281/NE/r90; LC: Z3651.L496; OCLC: 3734999). Monthly (Jan. 1969 - Dec. 1973, with annual cumulations for 1969, 1970, 1971, and 1972 appearing under the title *Egyptian Publications Bulletin*). A cumulative index was published for 1973. The *Nashrat al-īdāʿ al-shahrīyah* was an attempt to update the *Egyptian Publications Bulletin* in a more timely fashion.

The *Egyptian Publications Bulletin* (LCCN: ne63-1777//r903; LC: Z3651XC3; OCLC: 3076060; ISSN: 0575-1306) started as a quarterly first appearing in 1956 covering 1955 imprints. This title continued with irregularity through cumulations from 1955 to 1960, 1961-1962, 1961-1965, 1966-1967, and 1968. In an effort to create a more timely publication, the National Library began the publication of the *Nashrat al-īdāʿ al-shahrīyah,* a monthly. The annual cumulations for 1969, 1970, 1971, and 1972 appear under the title *Egyptian Publications Bulletin.*

The *LDB* is published in English (left to right) and Arabic (right to left). About two-thirds of each issue is in Arabic.

The *LDB* issues that were examined had no introduction or explanation in English (or any other foreign language) of the scope and contents of the issue, although it appears that some explanation was given in the Arabic part. Since there are several different kinds of numbers used in an entry, it would be helpful to have an English explanation for users. Sections do have brief notes at the beginning, but a general introduction following ICNB recommendation numbers 9 and 10 would be useful. The latest issue examined did not include an English preface; however, earlier issues included a preface which gave an historical note regarding the relationship to *Egyptian Publications Bulletin* but does not include further descriptive information about the national bibliography.

---

1 Information received in a March 1997 letter to the author from Mrs. Laila Hemeida, Chief of Central Management, National Library.

In some (not all) issues, government publications have their own separate section and includes publications of government authorities, departments, and the public sector.

Children's are listed in a separate section until 1995. Not every issue has this section. From 1995, children's books are listed in an annual publication *Bulletin for children's books*.[1]

Another separate section is the school books section. Only those books issued by the Minister of Education are in this section, according to a note at the section's beginning. Other educational materials such as scientific research, university textbooks and reprints of university periodical articles are under the author in the main bibliography.

The *AL,ME.* - Vol. 1 (1963)-vol. 31 (1993) published by the Library of Congress Field Office in Cairo includes Egypt within its scope and, until its cessation, was a good supplement to the Egyptian national bibliography.

Another reliable title is *Dalil al-kitab al-Misri* [Egyptian Books in Print] (LCCN: 72-960043/NE/r842), which is an annual volume begun in 1972, listing books in print.

LATEST ISSUE EXAMINED/CURRENCY: At the SOAS Library, London, England, the latest issue examined in April 1995 was for October, November, December 1988. This was published in 1992. If the publication date could be closer to the date of coverage, it would enable the *LDB* to be used as an acquisitions tool.

An analysis of the English imprint dates included mostly 1988 dates with a few entries for the earlier 1980s.

AUTOMATION: From 1990 to 1995, information for the *LDB* was stored on disks. From July 1995 to June 1996 the National Library conducted a pilot project using CDS/ISIS to set up a common communication format prepared by Unesco Bibliographical Communications. Currently, the National Library is setting up an integrated information system to produce its printed form.

FORMAT AND SERVICES AVAILABLE: printed.

CURRENT LEGAL DEPOSIT LAWS: Law No. 354/1954, Law No. 14/1968 has been amended by Law No. 38/1992 putting into effect the Minister of Culture's Decree No. 453/1995.[2]

AVAILABLE FROM: Egyptian National Library, Sharia Corniche El-Nil Street, Boulac, Cairo.

---

[1] Hemeida letter.
[2] Hemeida letter.

SELECTED ARTICLES: Van de Vate, Katherine. "Bibliographic Control [Egypt]." In *Books from the Arab World: A Guide to Selection and Acquisition*, pp. 16-18. 1988.

Wein, Charlotte. "Det egyptiske nationalbibliotek– eller noget om arabisk informationsstruktur." *DF-Revy* 17 (no. 1 Feb. 1994):7-9.

VERIFIER: Mrs. Laila Ibrahim Hemeida, Chief of the National Library Central Management.

EL SALVADOR

No current national bibliography has been traced for El Salvador.

Several attempts to create an on-going current national bibliography have not met with success. Following are some titles with descriptive notes that may be useful.

The most recent on-going project is the *National Salvadorean Bibliography*, 1800-1990 (*NSB*). The Gallardo Library purchased the unfinished bibliographic project of 18,000 El Salvadorean records from the Latin American Bibliographic Foundation. The work was done by George Elmendorf and Bernardo Melero who were forced to halt their work because of insufficient funding. The scope of this project includes works published by Salvadoreans in El Salvador or about El Salvador between 1800-1983; the Gallardo Library plans to extend the time period to 1990 and add additional material within the scope. The Gallardo Library project, which officially began in 1991, is based on the model used for the *Nicaraguan National Bibliography / Bibliografía Nacional Nicaragüense, 1800-1978*. Standards and procedures are being worked through. At various stages, review of the work provides opportunity to correct procedures as necessary. The on-going problem has been the reduction of the number of trained staff who are able to continue working on the project. Therefore, the project is moving slowly towards completion. Because the collections of principal libraries in El Salvador are being consulted it will also serve as a collective catalogue. At completion, it is estimated that the *NSB* will include 30,000 entries, and will be available in print and on disk.[1]

Anuario bibliográfico salvadoreño. - 1950-   . - San Salvador : Biblioteca Nacional, 1952-   . (LCCN: sn87-17232; OCLC: 6275966) was conceived as an annual publication listing works published in El Salvador, works by Salvadorean authors published elsewhere, and works about El Salvador. Types of publications included in *Anuario bibliográfico salvadoreño* (*ABS*) are books, pamphlets, official and government publications. The volume covering 1952 includes a summary, catalogue of materials by alphabetical index of subjects, abbreviations, and a catalogue of authors. Entry information given is author, title, place of publication, publisher, pagination, and notes. No price information is given. Bibliographic information is available by author as well as by subject. On the verso of the title page are the words "Anexo de *Anaqueles*. Epoca V, no. 4, 1954." Bibliographies of works printed in El Salvador during the early 1950's appeared in *Anaqueles* in 5. época, no. 2, May 1951/April 1952 covering publications in 1950, 5. época, no. 3, May 1952/April 1953 covering publications in 1951 and 5. época, no. 4,

---

[1] Emmanuelle Bervas-Rodriguez. "The National Salvadorean Bibliography, 1800-1990." Paper given at IFLA 1994 General Conference, Cuba (156-BIBL-4-E).

covering publications in 1952.[1]   The volume of *ABS* covering 1952 was published in 1954, and received by the British Library in May 1956. This is the latest volume available at the British Library and the Library of Congress. Earlier publications of this list for the late 1940's appeared in the Biblioteca Nacional's publication *Revista* under the title "Bibliografía Salvadoreña" in 4. época, vol. 1 (Jan./April 1948), 4. época, vol. 2 (May/Aug. 1948), 4. época., vol. 5 (May/Aug. 1949) and in *Anaqueles* 5. época, no. 1 (Jan./April 1951).[2] According to *BSTW, 1975-1979* the Biblioteca Nacional has published *Bibliografía Salvadoreña* annually since 1956. This title lists books, maps and atlases. However, at the present time this appears to have been suspended.[3] The author was not able to verify this title.

Guión Literario. - año 1, no. 1- . - San Salvador : Departamento Editorial del Ministerio de Cultura, 1956- . (ISSN 0017-5447) includes a section listing the Ministerio's publications during the period covered.[4] This, however, is not a complete list of Salvadorean literature.

Beginning in 1968, the quarterly *Boletín Bibliografíco* was published by Biblioteca Nacional, listing titles published in El Salvador and about El Salvador which were received on legal deposit. Types of publications included within its scope were books, pamphlets, periodical articles, government publications, dissertations. It followed AACR for cataloguing entries and used DDC (18th ed.) for its classification scheme. *Boletín Bibliografíco* was arranged in two sections: publications from El Salvador and from Central America; and international publications. However, it was interrupted in Jan./June 1970.[5]

CURRENT LEGAL DEPOSIT LAWS: Ley de Imprenta of 16 September 1886, amended by Decree No. 12 of 6 October 1950, Art. 140.[6]

AVAILABLE FROM: Correspondence may be directed to: Departamento de Medios de Comunicación, Biblioteca Nacional, Calle Delgato y 8a Avenida Norte, San Salvador.

EQUATORIAL GUINEA

No current bibliography has been traced for Equatorial Guinea.

---

[1] H. Woodbridge, "Latin American National Bibliography," *Encyclopedia of Library and Information Science*, vol. 36, suppl. 1, p. 332, and Annemarie Nilges, "El Salvador." *Nationalbibiliographien Lateinamerikas*, p. 75.

[2] Nilges, p. 76.; *Union List of Serials*, volume 1, p. 358, states that *Anaqueles* was formerly titled *Revista* for series 4, 1948-1949.

[3] *BSTW, 1975-1979*, p. 174.

[4] I. Zimmerman, *Current National Bibliographies of Latin America*, p. 78.

[5] *BSTW, Supplement 1980*, p.34. Also, Annemarie Nilges, "El Salvador." *Nationalbibliographien Lateinamerikas*, pp. 73-76, especially p. 74.

[6] *International Guide to Legal Deposit*, p. 80; also in G. Pomassl, *Survey of Existing Legal Deposit Laws*, p. 32. In 1974, according to Pomassl, only twelve percent of the books published were deposited at the Biblioteca Nacional.

ERITREA

No current national bibliography has been found for Eritrea.

AL,ESA with its *Serial Supplement* (ISSN 1074-3820) and *QIPL,ESA* include Eritrea within their scopes.

ESTONIA

TITLE: *Eesti rahvusbibliograafia. Raamatud = The Estonian national bibliography. The books.* 1(1994)-   . - Tallinn, Estonia : Eesti Rahvusraamatukogu, 1994-   .
Quarterly.
Continues *Raamatukroonika* [The Chronicle of books].
DDC: 015.474 ; LC: Z2533.R36; LCCN: 95-651330; OCLC: 32619953
ISSN 1024-0160

COMPILER: Eesti Rahvusraamatukogu [National Library of Estonia].

SCOPE AND COVERAGE: *Eesti rahvusbibliograafia. Raamatud (ER.R)* includes the publishing output of Estonia which is deposited at the national library according to legal deposit laws.

Types of publications include books, pamphlets, and government publications. See the Notes and Comments section for how other formats are covered.

CONTENTS: *ER.R* includes the preface in Estonian and in English, table of contents, UDC tables, classified bibliography, ISBN corrections list, name index.

CATALOGUING RULES AND CLASSIFICATION SCHEMES USED:
International ISBD standards are followed.

The classification scheme used is the UDC.

ENTRY INFORMATION: UDC general heading number and heading, consecutive entry number, title, statement of responsibility, edition statement, place of publication, publisher, date, place of printing, printer, pagination, illustrations, size, series statement, notes including bibliography pagination, ISBN. Entries do not have individual class numbers assigned.

ARRANGEMENT: The classified bibliography is arranged alphabetically (first in the Latin alphabet, and then in Cyrillic) under the UDC headings.

INDEXES: Alphabetic name index in both the Latin and Cyrillic alphabet.

NOTES AND COMMENTS: Before the break-up of the USSR, Estonian imprints were included within the scope of the *Knizhnaîa letopis'*, and in the then regional bibliography of *Raamatukroonika = Knizhnaîa letopis'.* - 1946-1991, 4. - Tallinn : Eesti Riiklik Kirjastus, 1946-

1993. Entries are in Estonian and Russian. Frequency and publisher varies. (LCCN: 60-43080//r95; LC: z2533.R3; OCLC: 2827141; ISSN 0201-6877).

The following national bibliography series are presently available only on offline databases in the National Library of Estonia. International ISBD standards are followed.[1]

Estonian periodicals. The database is compiled since 1994, and comprises Estonian periodicals published in and outside Estonia.

Estonica. The database is compiled since 1990, and comprises monographs about Estonia or written by Estonian authors published outside Estonia as well as articles from foreign periodicals.

Estonian sheet music. The compiling of the database was started in 1995.

Estonian maps. The compilation of the database started from 1990. A bibliography of Estonian maps from 1990-1996 will be published in 1997.

Estonian posters. The compilation of this database started in 1995.

Estonian postcards. The compilation of this database started in 1995.

Articles and sound recordings are listed in separately printed parts of the national bibliography. Descriptions of these follow this entry for *ER.R.*

LATEST ISSUE EXAMINED/CURRENCY: The latest issue examined in November 1996 at Indiana University is for January - March, 1, 1996. Imprints are from the time period covered, and also include several 1995 dates in this first issue of 1996.

During this period of transition to automation, problems with hardware and software affected the currency of the national bibliography. Missing issues from these transition years will be issued at a later date.

AUTOMATION: From 1994, *ER.R* is compiled on the basis of the offline database "Kroonika" [The Chronicle]; the annual growth is about 2700 entries.

The implementation of the integrated library system in 1997 will enable the library to transfer the offline databases from PC to the new system and provide online access via Internet.

FORMAT AND SERVICES AVAILABLE: printed. In the future, the Estonian national bibliography will be available on CD-ROM.

More information about the databases can be found on the library's homepage: http://www.nlib.ee

---

[1] Information about the offline databases was received by the author in a letter dated 17 December 1996 from Dr. Ivi Eenmaa, General Director, National Library of Estonia.

CURRENT LEGAL DEPOSIT LAWS: Decree of the Government of the Republic of Estonia no. 142 of May 8, 1992 on Temporary Regulations of Legal Deposit will be replaced by the Legal Deposit Law in 1997.[1]

Law on the National Library of Estonia, 9 May 1994.[2]

AVAILABLE FROM: The *ER.R*, *ER.A*, and *ESR* (the latter two listed below) are available from the National Library of Estonia, EE0100 Tallinn, Tönsmägi 2.

§

TITLE: *Eesti rahvusbibliograafia. Artiklid* [The Estonian national bibliography. Articles from serials]. - 1993, 1- . - Tallinn : Eesti Rahvusraamatukogu, 1993- .
Monthly.
Continues *Artiklite ja retsensioonide kroonika* [Chronicle of articles and reviews].
DDC: not found; LC: AI19.E77T3; LCCN: sn94-31272; OCLC: 31204397 ISSN 1022-517X

COMPILER: Eesti Rahvusraamatukogu.

SCOPE AND COVERAGE: *Eesti rahvusbibliograafia. Artiklid* (*ER.A*) records reviews and articles from Estonian periodicals of the current month. Scientific and problem articles, and articles on cultural heritage are preferred. Each issue has a list of the periodicals indexed. An annual list is included in the last issue of the year.

CONTENTS: *ER.A* includes the preface in Estonian, Russian and English, UDC outline, articles listing, list of serials, name index, table of contents.

CATALOGUING RULES AND CLASSIFICATION SCHEMES USED: Bibliografitsheskoe opisanie dokumental GOST 7.1-84. This will be changed in 1997.

Since 1992, the classification scheme used is UDC.

ARRANGEMENT: The classified bibliography is arranged alphabetically (first in the Latin alphabet, and then in Cyrillic).

ENTRY INFORMATION: UDC general heading number and heading, consecutive entry number, author, title, annotation, statement of responsibility, host item, date and/or number of host item, pagination, series statement, notes including bibliography pagination.

INDEXES: Alphabetic name index, both in Latin and Cyrillic letters; annual name index.

The name index includes authors, compilers, interviewers, persons interviewed, translators, commentators, illustrators, etc.; the personalia entry numbers are in brackets.

---

[1] *Riigi Teataja* no. 22. 10 June 1992, pp. 609-613. Information in Dr. Eenmaa's letter.
[2] *Legal Acts of Estonia*. No. 1, 9 February 1995. pp. 7-11. Information in Dr. Eenmaa's letter.

NOTES AND COMMENTS: As stated above, *ER.R* continues *Artiklite ja retsensioonide kroonika*. - 1952-1991. - Tallinn : Eesti Riiklik Kirjastus, 1952-1996. Publisher varies. Monthly (LC: AI19.E77T3; LCCN: 92-649018; OCLC: 5141393; ISSN 0571-2068).

The number attached to each periodical title listed indicates how fully it has been cited: (1) fully cited, (2) partially cited, (3) selectively cited, with an emphasis on cultural history.

If an article has several subjects, it is located under the main subject with other subjects marked by an asterisk (*).

LATEST ISSUE EXAMINED/CURRENCY: The last issue examined from Indiana University in the autumn of 1996 is no. 1, 1996.

AUTOMATION: *ER.A* is compiled on the basis of the offline database "Artikkel," the annual growth is about 25,000 entries.

FORMAT AND SERVICES AVAILABLE: printed.

§

TITLE: *Eesti helisalvestised = Estonian sound recordings*. - 1993-   . - Tallinn : Eesti Rahvusraamatukogu, 1996-   .
Annual.
LC: not found; LCCN: not found; OCLC: not found
ISSN 1406-118X

COMPILER: Eesti Rahvusraamatukogu [National Library of Estonia].

SCOPE AND COVERAGE: *Estonian Sound Recordings* (*ESR*) registers cassettes and CDs of Estonian composers and performers, as well as cassettes with texts in Estonian produced in a certain year regardless of the place of publication.

CONTENTS: *ESR* includes the preface in Estonian and English, sound recordings listing, name index, publisher index.

CATALOGUING RULES AND CLASSIFICATION SCHEMES USED: ISBD(NBM) is followed.

ARRANGEMENT: *ESR* is arranged alphabetically.

ENTRY INFORMATION: Consecutive entry number, title, statement of responsibility, place of publication, publisher, date of publication, specific material designation and extent, other physical details, accompanying material statement, production number, notes.

INDEXES: Alphabetic name index, both in Latin and Cyrillic letters; publisher index.

LATEST ISSUE EXAMINED/CURRENCY: This issue was not examined by the author; information is from the Director General of The National Library. The latest issue in December 1996 is the annual bibliography for 1994.

AUTOMATION: *ESR* is compiled on the basis of an offline database.

FORMAT AND SERVICES AVAILABLE: printed.

SELECTED ARTICLES: Eenmaa, Ivi. "The National Library of Estonia," *Alexandria* 3 (3, 1991):169-177.

Riuitel, A. "Zakon Estonskoi Respublici o natsional noi biblioteke Estonii." [Law of the Estonia Republic Concerning the National Library of Estonia] *Bibliotekar* 1991 (no. 9):31-32.

VERIFIER: This entire entry has been verified by Dr. Ivi Eenmaa, General Director, National Library of Estonia.

ETHIOPIA

TITLE: *Ethiopian Publications = Ba'Ityopya yatatamu sehufoc.* - vol. 1-   . - Addis Ababa : Provisional Military Government of Socialist Ethiopia, Ministry of Culture and Sports, [1980-   ].
Annual (irregular)
Cover title.
DDC: 016.963; LC : Z3521.E83, DT373; LCCN: 83-980121//r90; OCLC: 10021858
ISSN not found

COMPILER: Legal Deposit and Bibliography Section, The Department of National Library and Archives, Addis Ababa.

SCOPE AND COVERAGE: *Ethiopian Publications* (*EP*) includes titles published in Ethiopia and deposited at the National Library according to the legal deposit law. Titles published in Amharic, English, Italian, French, German, Arabic, Geez, and Tigrinya are included in *EP*.[1]

Types of publications included in *EP* are books, pamphlets, official and government publications, periodicals, newspapers, maps, and IGO publications about Ethiopia. Periodicals and non-book publications are usually included in a separate part from the books.

CONTENTS: Volume 11, part 3: introduction (in Amharic), bibliography (in Amharic), bibliography (in English), index.

The language of the introduction varies from volume to volume. Some volumes have an introduction in Amharic, English, and/or French.

---

[1] The author is grateful for the help of Fentahun Tiruneh, Amharic Specialist, Hebraic Section, African and Middle East Division, Library of Congress for his help in translating the text.

CATALOGUING RULES AND CLASSIFICATION SCHEMES USED: Cataloguing rules followed are not stated in the foreword. National standards and AACR67 are used.[1] Subject headings used for the organization of the bibliography appear to follow DDC.

No classification scheme is evident.

ENTRY INFORMATION: Author, title, place of publication, publisher, date, pagination, illustrations, size, series. No classification number is given.

ARRANGEMENT: The bibliography is arranged by subject headings following DDC.

INDEXES: Author and title index in Amharic and in English. The numbers refer to the page number.

NOTES AND COMMENTS: Ethiopia has two titles published by separate institutions called *Ethiopian Publications*. The author has chosen to analyze in detail the title published by the Department of National Library and Archives since this is the body usually responsible for a national bibliography. The other *Ethiopian Publications* is published by the Institute of Ethiopian Studies; it is described in more detail later. The roles of the two publications are not always clearly defined.[2] Both are useful in identifying publications in Ethiopia.

The title by the National Library and Archives has varied. The first three volumes in four parts, all published in 1980, are called *Ethiopian Publications*; the fourth part published in June 1980 without a volume number is called *Ethiopian Publications by Legal Deposit*. Volume 4, published in 1982, only has the Amharic title which is not translated into English. Part 1 of volume 4 includes non-book publications, Ethiopian periodicals, and government publications. Part 4 of volume 4 includes the subjects of history, philosophy, and literature.[3] From volumes 5 to 9 the titles have distinct titles: volume 5 (1982), *Bibliography on Geography and History in English and Amharic*, volume 6 (1983), *Author Index in Amharic*, volume 7 (1983), *Title Index in Amharic*, volume 8 (1984), *English Language*, volume 9 (1985), *Foreign Language Publications received by the Legal Deposit Section in the years 1980-1984*. Volume 10 (1987) and 11 (1989) are titled *Ethiopian Publications in Amharic and English*. Part 2 of volume 11 covers periodicals and non-book publications.[4]

---

[1] *BSTW, Supplement 1981-1982*, p. 124.

[2] For a more detailed discussion of this point see the article by Sushma Gupta. "The National Bibliography of Ethiopia: Current Status." *International Information & Library Review* 24 (1992):45-56.

[3] Volume 4 is called *Ethiopian Publications*. The author is indebted to Fentahun Tiruneh, Amharic Specialist, Hebraic Section, The Library of Congress for his help in better understanding the contents of vol. 11 in particular and the series in general. The Library of Congress does not have a complete run of all parts.

[4] Information received in a letter dated 22 January 1986 from James Armstrong, former Library of Congress Field Director, Nairobi, Kenya to Elizabeth Widenmann, a copy of which was sent to the author. Titles for volumes 10 and 11 are taken from Sushma Gupta. "The National Bibliography of Ethiopia: Current Status." *International Information & Library Review* 24 (1992):55, Appendix III.

A retrospective bibliography published in 1977 by the National Library is called *Ethiopian Publications: Books and Journals Published in Ethiopia, 1943-1975*, vol. 2.[1] The National Library received an Unesco grant to compile a companion volume retrospective national bibliography covering the period 1975-1985; *Bibliography of Published Materials in Ethiopia* was published in 1986 (LCCN: 89-980000).

The Institute of Ethiopian Studies, Addis Ababa University has been compiling a bibliography by the same title *Ethiopia Publications* (ISSN 0071-1772; OCLC: 2349312) in the absence of a national bibliography. This title was first published in 1965 covering titles for 1963 and 1964. It includes books, pamphlets, annuals, official publications, conference papers, theses, and periodical articles published during the year of coverage. The first of two sections includes Ethiopian publications which are arranged by author; the second section lists foreign publications and is arranged by DDC. An author index is provided for both sections. Basic bibliographic information is provided for both monographs and periodical articles. AACR2 punctuation is followed. This series appears to be over ten years late in its publication schedule. Several libraries which have this title do not have a complete set, particularly of current volumes. This *Ethiopian Publications*, however, is located in more libraries than the National Library title.

Ethiopia is within the scope of *AL,ESA* and *QIPL,ESA*.

LATEST ISSUE EXAMINED/CURRENCY: The latest volume examined in April 1997 is vol. 11, part 3 for 1989 received by the Library of Congress. It includes publications for 1989.

A wide range of imprints is evident; books are listed when they are received.

The latest Institute of Ethiopian Studies' *Ethiopian Publications* examined at the University of Wisconsin in May 1995 was No. 12 published in 1984 covering 1975/1976.

AUTOMATION: not automated.

FORMAT AND SERVICES AVAILABLE: printed.

CURRENT LEGAL DEPOSIT LAWS: Deposit of Printed Materials Act of 1975.

AVAILABLE FROM: National Library and Archives, P.O. Box 717, Addis Ababa.

SELECTED ARTICLES: Sushma Gupta. "National Bibliography of Ethiopia: Current Status." *International Information & Library Review* 24 (1992):45-56 .

VERIFIER: Fentahun Tiruneh, Amharic Specialist, Hebraic Section, African and Middle East Division, The Library of Congress, and Solomon Mulugeta, Department Head, National Library.

---

[1] Gupta, Appendix III, p. 55.

FIJI

TITLE: *Fiji national bibliography*. - 1970/1978-1986. - Suva, Fiji : Library Service of Fiji, Ministry of Education, Dec. 1979-1986.
Annual.
DDC: 015.96/11; LC: Z4651.F54; LCCN: 80-649972//r83; OCLC: 6509604
ISSN not found

COMPILER: Library Service of Fiji.

SCOPE AND COVERAGE: *Fiji National Bibliography* (*FNB*) covers publications published in Fiji from 1970 to the current volume, and monographs published outside Fiji which are about Fiji or include at least a substantial section on Fiji, and monographs written by Fiji citizens wherever published.

Types of publications included in *FNB* are monographs, new serials, theses about Fiji and presented to Fiji institutions, government and official publications, and legal notices, statutes, etc.

Excluded are articles in serials which are covered by *South Pacific Periodicals Index*. - Suva, Fiji: Pacific Information Centre, University of the South Pacific, 1981-   (LCCN: 85-641342; OCLC: 11434038). This title continues *Bibliography of Periodical Articles Relating to the South Pacific*. - Suva, Fiji : University of the South Pacific Library, 1974-197?. (LCCN: 77-151147//r85; OCLC: 3725669).

CONTENTS: Table of contents, acknowledgment, introduction, abbreviations, bibliography; author, title and series index; subject index, periodicals, legal notices, directory of printers and publishers.

CATALOGUING RULES AND CLASSIFICATION SCHEMES USED: *FNB* uses the AACR2 (1980). Subject headings are from the *LCSH*. (9th ed.).

The classification system used is DDC (19th ed.).

ENTRY INFORMATION: DDC number in upper left corner, accession number in upper right corner, e.g., F106-86, author, title, place of publication, publisher, date, pagination, illustrations, size, tracings.

The periodicals list includes full cataloguing information for periodicals. The DDC number and accessions numbers are not given.

The "Legal notices, statutes, etc." list gives the title, place of publication and publisher, date, then lists the number of the legal notice, title, year and/or location within the title.

ISBN is given for foreign publications if it is known.

ARRANGEMENT: The monographs in the bibliography are arranged in DDC order. Periodicals are arranged alphabetically with complete bibliographic information. Legal notices, statutes, etc., are arranged numerically in the legal notice number order.

INDEXES: Author/ title/series index; subject index. The accessions number is used to refer readers to the main bibliography. Since the accession numbers are in numerical order this provides a simple way of locating the entry needed.

NOTES AND COMMENTS: Although the preface to the first edition (1979) states the chief librarian's intention to have the *FNB* become a semiannual publication from 1980, it remained an annual until it ceased. The latest issue located is for 1986.[1]

It seems that the compilers are striving to make Fiji's bibliographic record from 1970 to 1986 as complete as possible. The 1983 volume states in the introduction that the catalogues of the University of the South Pacific (USP) Library have been scanned to find titles not included in previous issues, and the current titles at USP Library have been catalogued to supply more information to *FNB*. The 1986 volume states that while most of the publications in that volume were published 1984-1986, there are entries dating back to 1950 because the title is still current and is important, and has not been previously recorded.

The statement that the *FNB* is based on legal deposit does not appear on any of its preliminary pages. Although the USP Library is a depository library, the library's legal deposit role for *FNB* is not clearly stated.

In looking at the *FNB*, it was not apparent that it includes material in the languages/scripts of its diverse cultures.

It would be helpful for *FNB* to include a summary of the DDC tables that are used in organizing and classifying the entries in the main bibliography.

If a user is looking for a title published in 1970, for example, it would be necessary to check all volumes published; each year covers 1970 to the present, and even earlier (1950s) if a previously unrecorded important title is current and important to users.

It would be helpful to include the titles from the periodicals list and the legal notices, statutes, etc., list in the index. If a reader is not aware of these lists of materials located at the end of the bibliography, they could easily overlook this valuable and otherwise hard-to-locate information. CIP is not used in *FNB*.

The *FNB* is an attractively presented national bibliography with the unique function of listing the publications of Fiji for a given year. It would seem important to continue the bibliographic control through this publication to the rest of the world. For the present, the *South Pacific Bibliography* (see separate entry) includes Fiji within its scope, and during the last decade it is the only title which records the current publishing of Fiji.

---

1   SOAS, University of London received a note from the publisher stating that the title is temporarily suspended. Although a 1995 issue of the Fiji Library Association Newsletter stated that it was to be published again in 1995, the author's latest correspondence by e-mail (25 February 1997) with Esther Williams, University of the South Pacific, states that no one is undertaking the production of this title now. In a 16 July 1997 e-mail message from Jayshree Mamtora, Pacific Information Centre, he states that the Library Service of Fiji is not planning to revive *FNB*. At present, *FNB* has ceased. Entries for *FNB* originate from the *South Pacific Bibliography*.

AL,ESA, its *Serial Supplement*, and *QIPL,ESA* include Fiji within their scopes.

LATEST ISSUE EXAMINED/CURRENCY: Approximately one to two year's lag from the time it is published to the time it is received by a library (overseas), combined with the span of years covered (1970-1983 for the 1983 volume) makes this an historical record rather than an acquisitions tool. The majority of entries from the 1983 volume were from earlier years. The 1986 volume included entries mostly from the 1984-1986 years.

The latest volume examined was for 1986, the latest received by SOAS in November 1994.

AUTOMATION: not known.

FORMAT AND SERVICES AVAILABLE: printed.

CURRENT LEGAL DEPOSIT LAWS: Libraries (Deposit of Books) Act, No. 48 of 1971. Deposit of Books (Exemption Order) Legal Notice No. 155 of 1971.

AVAILABLE FROM: Library Service of Fiji, 162 Ratu Sukuna Road, Suva.[1]

VERIFIER: Jayshree Mamtora, Librarian, Pacific Information Centre, Suva.

FINLAND

TITLE: *Suomen kirjallisuus = Finlands litteratur = The Finnish national bibliography.* - 1544/1877-   . - Helsinki : Helsingin Yliopiston Kirjasto [Helsinki University Library], 1878- . Frequency varies. Since 1972 issued monthly, three numbers of which are double numbers (1/2, 6/7, 8/9); annual cumulation (*Vuosiluettelo Årskatalog*); five year cumulation.
DDC: not found;   LC: Z2520.S955 (annual); Z2520.S95 (monthly);   LCCN: 74-645541 (annual);   OCLC: 1794592 (annual); 1606212 (monthly)
ISSN 0355-0001 (annual); ISSN 0355-001X (monthly)

COMPILER: Bibliographic Department, Helsinki University Library.

SCOPE AND COVERAGE: *Suomen kirjallisuus = Finlands Litteratur = The Finnish National Bibliography* (*SK*) lists the publishing output of Finland based on legal deposit copies delivered by the printers to the Deposit Copy Office of the Helsinki University Library. The *SK* also includes new books published abroad with a Finnish author, in Finnish or about Finland.[2]

Types of publications included since automation are books, atlases, printed music such as song-books with notes which are intended for schools, and guides for music teachers, new volumes of multi-volume works, material not available for sale in bookstores, IGO publications.

---

[1] Address was supplied to the author in a 19 July 1995 e-mail message from Esther Williams, USP. There are still copies of *FNB* available per information from Jayshree Mamtora's 16 July 1997 e-mail.
[2] "Preface," *SK*, no. 12, 1994.

Before automation, types of publications included were books, pamphlets and duplicated material (of sixteen pages or more), official and government publications, maps and atlases, printed music such as song-books with notes which are intended for schools, and guides for music teachers, annual reports, new volumes of multi-volume works, material not available for sale in bookstores, IGO publications, calendars, yearbooks, microforms.

Excluded are commercial and advertising publications such as lists of goods, price lists, shopping guides, internal publications of firms and societies, and occasional publications such as programmes and timetables.

Annual and five year cumulations include some materials not listed in the monthly issues. For instance, new impressions of titles are listed in the five year cumulation, duplicated materials which do not belong to any series, and pamphlets of less than sixteen pages. Newspapers, periodicals and foreign publications are included in the five year cumulation which is the most complete form of the Finnish national bibliography.[1]

According to the preface of the 1983 *Vuosiluettelo Årskatalog*, maps and musical scores, usually included in the annual volume, were to be filed and produced as a separate catalogue. However, as of 1997 no separate catalogues have been printed for musical scores and maps. The *Viola* database covers Finnish printed music from 1977 onwards. Serials, usually included in the multi-year catalogues were also to be listed separately, but no separate catalogue has been issued to date. At present, serials are within the scope of the *Fennica* database.

CONTENTS: Monthly: preface (Finnish, Swedish, English), contents (Finnish, Swedish, English), outline of classification, classified bibliography, list of publishers additions, list of ISBNs, publisher prefixes additions.

Alphabetical section (Annual 1993): contents (Finnish, Swedish, English), preface (Finnish, Swedish, English).

Systematic section (Annual 1993): contents (Finnish, Swedish, English), systematic groups, index, list of books, publishers' address list, publisher prefixes, list of invalid ISBNs.

CATALOGUING RULES AND CLASSIFICATION SCHEMES USED: The national cataloguing rules, *Suomalaiset luettelointisäännöt* for different materials (Helsinki 1989-1991), follow ISBD international standards and recommendations. Cataloguing format is FINMARC.

The classification scheme used is the abridged Finnish edition of UDC entitled *Yleinen Kymmenluokittelu.*

ENTRY INFORMATION: Author (including dates if known), title, place of publication, publisher, date, pagination, size, series, notes including ISBN, the year of an earlier edition; complete classification number given in lower left corner.

---

[1] The following updated information about these cumulations was received in a letter dated 4 April 1997 to the author from Pirkko Korttinen, Librarian, *Suomen kirjallisuus.* The publishing of the printed annual bibliography *Vuosiluettelo Årskatalog* has ceased with the 1994 issue. The only five year cumulation which has been published is the cumulation for 1967-1971; there are no plans to publish further cumulations.

The letter K (K) after an ISBN indicates that the number has been corrected.

ARRANGEMENT: Monthly: The bibliography is arranged by the UDC classification system. Before 1982, monthly issues were arranged in alphabetical order.

Annual (1993): entries are arranged alphabetically in the first volume, and then by UDC subject in the systematic volume.

INDEXES: Monthly: Current monthly issues do not include indexes. Before automation, SK included an author/title index, and a key to subjects index. The number given refers the reader to the UDC number in the bibliography.

Annual (l993): the first volume is an alphabetical section, and the second volume is a classified subject section.

Since 1986 *Vleinen suomalainen asiasanasto* [The Finnish General Thesaurus] is used for indexing 2/3 of the book material. The latest edition is 1994.

NOTES AND COMMENTS: *SK* has existed since 1878, covering from 1544/1877 onwards. The Bibliographic Department has published *SK* as described above since 1972. *SK* began automation in 1978. From the beginning of 1979 the preparation of bibliographic records for titles received on legal deposit has been decentralized to the university libraries of Helsinki, Turku and Jyväskylä, each responsible for a third of the material received on legal deposit. Later, Joensuu, the Parliament Library and the Finnish Library Service also participated. The records from these libraries, based on legal deposit copies delivered by the printers and publishers, are entered into the national bibliography database *Fennica*.

The reorganization due to automation has caused a few changes in the scope of *SK*. The *SK* now includes only books. The original plan was to list separately serials (usually included in the multi-year cumulations), maps and musical scores (usually included in the annual volume).[1] Literature on Finland published abroad, formerly included in the multi-year cumulations, will now appear in the monthly catalogues. This list will include new books published in Finnish as well as works written, illustrated or translated by Finns, or about Finland, which have been published abroad.[2]

Publications about Finland published abroad are extracted from the national bibliography database to produce *Fennica Extranea*.

---

[1] According to *SK*'s *Vuosiluettelo Årskatalo*1990 "Preface," serials, maps and musical scores were to be filed and produced in separate catalogs. However, no separate catalogues have been published, according to P. Korttinen's 4 April 1997 letter. Serials, maps, and musical scores are included within the scope of the *Fennica* database. Finnish printed music from 1977 onward is included also in the Viola database.

[2] "Preface," *SK*, no. 12, 1994. In the *SK Vuosiluettelo Årskatalo*1990 "Preface," it stated that literature on Finland published abroad, will be in a separate catalog. It appears as if this material may be covered in both the monthly catalogue as well as the separate catalogue *Fennica Extranea*.

Government publications are not distinguished by a symbol in *SK*. However, *Valtion Virallisjukaisut =Statens Oficiella Publikationer = Government Publications in Finland* is an annual bibliography published by the Library of Parliament, first published in 1962 covering the year 1961.[1] It lists all titles published by government offices and public institutions except maps and charts. (LCCN: 66-57016//r96; LC: Z2520.A3F25; OCLC : 1781524; ISSN 0430-5094).

The University of Jyväskylä prepares an annual *Suomalaisten äänitteiden luettelo = Catalogue of Finnish recordings*. This is a catalogue of recorded music which began in 1983.[2] (LCCN: 88-651522; LC: ML156.4N3F57; OCLC: 18764210; ISSN 0782-1875). This title continues *Suomalaisten äänilevyjen luettelo. Catalogue of Finnish records. - 1902/1945-1982. -* Helsinki : [Suomen Äänitearkisto], 1945-1982. (LCCN: 79-640954/MN/r904; LC.: ML156.4N3F57; OCLC: 4400367).

Because of the legal deposit method of acquisition, the annual volume may include titles published at the end of the preceding year. For instance, the 1993 annual may have some 1992 titles.

An auxiliary number (07) indicates a textbook and an auxiliary number (024.7) indicates literature for children or young people.

Finland has been assigning ISBNs to books since 1972. If a book does not have an ISBN, a national bibliographic number will be used, e.g., F790044.

ISSNs have been assigned to serials since 1974. *SK* has included them in the series statement since 1977.

SK follows most of the ICNB recommendations. One addition to consider is adding an analyzed entry to the preface.

The microfiche edition of *SK* has a slightly different scope than the printed *SK*. From 1985, it includes pamphlets "under 16 pages as well as duplicated material that is not included in any serials."[3] This publication has ceased.

An important development that has taken place in Finland is the cooperation among Helsinki University Library, University of Jyväskylä Library, and Turku University Library to participate in the joint cataloguing programme which contributes cataloguing of legal deposit material to the national bibliography database. In addition, a supply service company for public libraries, Kirjastopalvelu Oy, "contributes to the project by providing staff and in exchange receives the right to sell bibliographic records to public libraries."[4]

---

[1] Esko Häkli. "Helsinki University Library – The National Library of Finland." *Alexandria* 2 (1):34, and in and Henrik Schauman, and Kaarina Puttonen, "Finland," In *Official Publications of Western Europe*, p. 40.

[2] Häkli, p. 35.

[3] Maria Forsman. "The Finnish National Bibliography" In *Guide to Nordic Bibliography. Supplement 1*, p. 23.

[4] Häkli, p. 34.

The CD-ROM version of the national bibliography is called *Fennica : Suomen kansallisbibliografia = Finlands nationalbibliografi = The Finnish national bibliography* [computer file]. Helsinki : Helsingin yliopiston kirjasto; BTJ–Kirjastopalvelu Oy; Kirjavälitys Oy, 1990- . Quarterly. The scope includes books and serials. Searchable in Finnish, Swedish, and English. Includes Boolean operators, and appropriate search keys. The 1997/1 *Fennica* covers the period 1930 – 5 December 1996.

The retrospective conversion of the *Finnish National Bibliography* from 1828 will be completed by the end of 1998.[1]

LATEST ISSUE EXAMINED/CURRENCY: Out of a sample of twenty entries in the December 1994 issue, all were published in 1994. A sample of 38 entries from the May 1995 issue showed 23 titles from 1994, 14 from 1995, and one n.d. It appears that the decentralizing of the bibliographic records is efficient and timely. *SK* can be used effectively for current acquisitions and collection development.

The latest monthly issue examined was no. 5 for 1995 in Sept. 1997 at the Bibliotekstjänst AB Library. The latest annual examined at the University of Minnesota Library in 1995 is for 1993, published in 1994. A five year volume was not examined.

AUTOMATION: The Helsinki University Library installed an integrated online library system (VTLS) in late 1989. A Hewlett Packard 3000/950 computer makes it possible to use the new system to produce the national bibliography. All academic libraries in Finland as well as some other libraries have the same system and are linked as a unified network.[2]

FORMAT AND SERVICES AVAILABLE: printed, CD-ROM, magnetic tape, on-line as KOTI. The *Fennica* database is currently available on the Internet, but plans are to close it and keep this database as a working database. All of the national bibliography material is available in the union catalogue of Finnish university libraries (*LINDA*) and by the end of 1997, this information will also be available in the catalogue database *HELKA* of the libraries, University of Helsinki.

CURRENT LEGAL DEPOSIT LAWS: Deposit copy law of 12 June 1980 effective 1 January 1981 (Ask 420/80), and Statute on Free Copies of 5 December 1980 (Ask 774/80).[3] These include book and non-book materials such as audiovisual materials and sound recordings within its scope.

AVAILABLE FROM: monthly: Edita oy, PL 800, 00043 Edita, Finland; CD-ROM: BTJ-Kirjastopalvelu oy, PL 84 00211 Helsinki.

---

[1] Korttinen letter.

[2] Häkli, p. 35.

[3] *International Guide to Legal Deposit*, p. 76; according to P. Korttinen's letter of 4 April 1997, these continue to be the current laws.

SELECTED ARTICLES: "Finland: National Bibliographic Control." *International Cataloguing* 8 (Oct./Dec. 1979):40.

Forsman, Maria. "The Finnish National Bibliography" In *Guide to Nordic Bibliography. Supplement 1 (1983-1986)*, pp. 23-27.

Häkli, Esko. "A finn koenyvtari-informacios rendszer es informacios politika. Tervezes, iranyitas, finanszirozas." [The Finnish library and information system and information policy: planning, administration and financing] *Tuudomanyos es Mueszaki Tajekoztatas* 38 (7 July 1991):263-266.

Häkli, Esko. "Das finnische nationalbibliographische System." *Informationsmittel für Bibliotheken (IFB)* 1994: 492-500. (Besprechungsdienst und Berichte 2). This is an article in a festschrift for Professor Häkli.

Häkli, Esko. "Helsinki University Library- The National Library of Finland." *Alexandria* 2 (1 1990):29-39. See esp. "Bibliographic Activities" and "Automation."

Karstu, Eeva-Marjatta. "The National Bibliography of Finland" In *Guide to Nordic Bibliography*, pp. 43-45.

Selleck, Roberta. "The Scandinavian National Bibliographies as Tools for Research and Book Selection." *Collection Management* 6 (spring/summer 1984):125-134.

Suhonen, Irja-Leena. "Kansallisbibliografian kansalliset ja kansainvaliset tehtavat. National and international duties of a national bibliography." *Signum* 27(2 1994):36-39.

VERIFIER: Mrs. Irja–Leena Suhonen, Head of the Bibliographic Department, Finnish National Bibliography, Helsinki University Library.

FRANCE

TITLE: *Bibliographie nationale française. Livres. Notices établie par la Bibliothèque Nationale de France à partir des documents déposés au titre du dépôt légal.* - Paris : Méreau, 1990- .
Biweekly.
Subtitle varies: beginning with no. 1 Feb. 1, 1990 *la Bibliothèque Nationale de France à partir des documents déposés au titre du dépôt légal.*
Continues *Bibliographie de la France. Bibliographie officielle. Livres. Publications reçues par le service du dépôt légal de la Bibliothèque Nationale.*
DDC: 015.44; LC: Z2165.B5725; LCCN : 90-64900; OCLC: 21224800
ISSN 1142-3250

COMPILER: Bibliothèque Nationale de France.

SCOPE AND COVERAGE: *Bibliographie nationale française. Livres* (*BNF*) lists the publishing output of France which is received at the Bibliothèque Nationale according to legal deposit legislation. It also includes titles published in Monaco received on voluntary legal deposit.

Types of publications include books, pamphlets, official and government publications, translations, conference proceedings, exhibition catalogues.

Maps, periodicals and series, official and government publications, music are in the appropriate supplements of *BNF*.

CONTENTS: Classification schedule, brief explanation of symbols, classified bibliography, author index, title index, subject index.

CATALOGUING RULES AND CLASSIFICATION SCHEMES USED: The Association française de normalisation (AFNOR) and ISBD rules are followed.

The classification scheme used is UDC. In the near future, DDC will be used in the national bibliography.

ENTRY INFORMATION: Consecutive entry number, author, title, place of publication, publisher, date, pagination, illustrations, size, series, BN-OPALE numbers are at the end of the entry on the lower right, e.g., BN 1790721, and replaces the Bibliothèque Nationale number from *Bibliographie de la France. Bibliographie officielle. Livres* in the same position, e.g., 16 Lc1. 474 , notes including ISBN and ISSN, price, tracings.

An asterisk (*) at the beginning of an entry indicates an official publication. An "J" indicates a work for young people; an "S" within a box indicates a scholarly work.

ARRANGEMENT: The classified bibliography is alphabetically arranged within UDC subject groups.

INDEXES: Bi-weekly issues have author index, title index and subject index. Indexes cumulate quarterly on microforms, and into an annual printed index. Numbers refer to the entry numbers.

NOTES AND COMMENTS: The French current national bibliography has existed since 1811. Issues include the ongoing "année" number. Reorganizations have taken place, the latest major change occurring in 1990.

As stated earlier, *BNF* continues *Bibliographie de la France. Bibliographie officielle. Livres. Publications reçues par le service du dépôt légal de la Bibliothèque Nationale* (1977-1989; ISSN 0150-1402). *Bibliographie de la France (1975). 1ère partie, Bibliographie officielle. Livres* and in part *Bibliographie de la France. Biblio* and *Journal général de la librairie et de l'imprimerie*.

Following are supplements of the national bibliography. All follow the same entry format and symbols as *Livres*.

Bibliographie nationale française. Publications en série, 1992-   . Monthly. Arranged by large UDC divisions and subdivisions, title index, "collectivités"- author index, subject index. Annual index. The scope includes new titles of journals, reviews, annuals and monographic series. (LCCN: sn 93-33508; OCLC: 25727939; ISSN 1142-3269).   Recent preceding titles: *Bibliographie nationale française. Supplément I. Publications en série*, no. 1, 1990-no. 12, 1991 (LCCN 90-650213; OCLC: 21465148; ISSN 1142-3269); *Bibliographie de la France. Supplément I. Publications en séries. 1977-1989. Index annuel* (LCCN: 84-642630; OCLC: 5585081; ISSN 0150-1399).

Bibliographie nationale française. Publications officielles, 1992-   . Bimonthly. Arranged by nine divisions (budgets, lois et traités; assemblées constitutionnelles; cours et juridictions; administration centrale; administration locale; administration locale; établissements publics; et entreprises nationalisées; organisations intergouvernementales) and title index, "collectivités"- author index, subject index, personal names index. Annual index. The scope includes official publications of an administrative nature, and publications of the chief intergovernmental organizations--European and international-- which have their headquarters in France. (LCCN: sn 94-31504 ; OCLC: 25728501; ISSN 1142-3277). Recent preceding titles: *Bibliographie nationale française. Supplément II. Publications officielles*, no. 1,1990-no. 12, 1991. Bimonthly.   Annual index (LCCN: 90-649594; OCLC: 21881338; ISSN 1142-3277); *Bibliographie de la France. Bibliographie officielle. Supplément II. Publications officielles, 1977-1989*. Bimonthly (LCCN: 84-642628; OCLC: 5585688; ISSN 0150-5955).

Bibliographie nationale française. Musique, 1992-   . Three times a year. Arranged by the following divisions: A. Œuvres instrumentales, B. Œuvres vocales, C. Œuvres scéniques, D. Œuvres théoriques, E. Œuvres pédagogiques, F. Brouillons et esquisses, G. Collections, H. Divers. Parts A-C are subdivided. Author index, title index, uniform title index. Annual index. (LCCN: sn 94-31065; OCLC: 28083159; ISSN 1142-3285).   Recent preceding titles: *Bibliographie nationale française. Supplément III. Musique*, no.1, 1990-no. 3, 1991. Three times a year. Annual index (LCCN: sn 90-18239; OCLC: 22411739; ISSN 1142-3285); *Bibliographie de la France. Bibliographie officielle. Supplément III. Musique. 1977-1989.* Quarterly; three times a year <1987>-1989. (LCCN: 84-642638; OCLC: 5585108; ISSN 0150-5971).

Bibliographie nationale française. Atlas, cartes et plans. 1993-   . Annual. Arranged in three main divisions (ciel, mers, terre, with terre subdivided into Afrique, Amérique, Asie, Europe. Europe is subdivided into countries, France is further subdivided into regions.) Arranged alphabetically by regions and geographic names. Categories of maps are arranged as follows: topographical - by "échelles en order décroissant," general - in chronological order, and thematic - by themes. Author index, geographic index, thematic index (LCCN: sn 93-33515; OCLC: 28228110; ISSN: 1142-3293). Recent preceding titles: *Bibliographie nationale française. Supplément IV. Atlas, cartes et plans*, 1990-1992. Annual (LCCN: sn 92-19395 ; OCLC: 25732459; ISSN 1142-3293); *Bibliographie de la France. Bibliographie officielle. Supplément IV. Atlas, cartes et plans. 1977-1989.* Annual (LCCN: 84-642639; OCLC: 5585122; ISSN 0150-5998).

An introduction explaining the scope and coverage would be helpful for users. A publishers' list would also be convenient for those who use the bibliography as an ordering tool. Entry information is explained in a brief paragraph at the beginning of the bibliography.

PROMPTNESS RECEIVED/CURRENCY: Receipt of current issues and the coverage of imprints for the period covered have improved with the reorganization of the *BNF*. The latest issues examined in Sept. 1997 at the Bibliotekstjänst AB Library is: *BNF. Livres*, 18 juin 1997, *BNF. Atlas, cartes et plans*, 1996, *BNF. Musique*, 26 mars 1997, and *BNF. Publications officielles*, 18 juin 1997.

AUTOMATION: The *BNF* is automated by the GEAC system. The BN OPALE database was developed on GEAC from 1984-1987 following specifications of the Bibliothèque Nationale.

FORMAT AND SERVICES AVAILABLE: print, microfiche, magnetic tape or disk, CD-ROM (La Bibliographie nationale française depuis 1970). Since February 1992 BN-OPALE and BN-OPALINE have been available online through an external server: Serveur bibliographique national.[1] Since March 1995 BN-OPALE and BN-OPALINE are accessible on the RENATER / INTERNET network.[2]

The music, and maps and plans department provides access to references via BN-OPALINE. This has also been extended to the department of prints and photography; other specialized departments may use this in future.[3]

CURRENT LEGAL DEPOSIT LAWS: Loi du 20 Juin 1992, décret du 31 décembre 1993.[4]

AVAILABLE FROM: Méreau, 175 bd Anatole France, BP 189, 93208 Saint-Denis Cedex, Paris.
Magnetic tape service available: Bibliothèque Nationale de France, 58, rue de Richelieu, 75084 Paris, Cedex 02.

CD-ROM available through Chadwyck-Healey France.

VERIFIER: Isabelle Boudet, Bibliothèque Nationale de France.

FRENCH GUIANA

No current national bibliography was traced for French Guiana.

GABON

No current national bibliography has been traced for Gabon.

---

[1] "France," *International Guide to MARC databases and services*, national magnetic tape, online and CD-ROM services, 1993 (3d rev. and enl. ed.), p. 190.
[2] Information from the brochure *Bibliothèque nationale de France. Produits bibliographiques*.
[3] *Livres hebdo*. (no. 32-35, 25-8-89):27
[4] Information supplied by Isabelle Boudet, Bibliothèque Nationale de France.

THE GAMBIA

TITLE: *The Gambia national bibliography.* - Banjul : The National Library of the Gambia, 1988-   .
Annual.
Title from cover.
Continues with same ISSN : *National bibliography of the Gambia.*
DDC: not found; LC (090): Z3735.N37; LCCN: not found; OCLC: 6716143
ISSN 0796-014X

COMPILER: National Library of the Gambia.

SCOPE AND COVERAGE: According to the preface, *The Gambia National Bibliography* (*GNB*) lists every new work published and also materials by and about the Gambia and Gambians that are deposited at The National Library of The Gambia under the legal deposit law, describes each work in detail and gives the subject matter of each work as accurately as possible.

Types of publications include books, pamphlets, first issues and subsequent title changes of periodicals, newspapers, annual reports; government publications, theses and dissertations, maps and atlases, periodical articles (photocopies or reprints).

Excluded are gazettes, acts, bills and parliamentary debates published in the Gambia, audiovisual materials, and musical scores.

CONTENTS: Contents, preface, abbreviations and symbols, DDC scheme, classified subject section, index, list of Gambian publishers/printers.

The contents vary in some years.

CATALOGUING RULES AND CLASSIFICATION SCHEMES USED: The AACR2 and ISBD(M), ISBD(S) are followed in cataloguing the material.

The DDC (20th ed.) is used for classification.

"All articles have been indexed using terms from *OECD Macrothesaurus.*"[1]

ENTRY INFORMATION: DDC number in upper left, author, title, edition, place of publication, publisher, date, pagination, illustrations, size, series, ISSN or ISBN, number of copies held by the library, subject terms, legal deposit number, e.g., L.D., 92-37.

An asterisk (*) by the place of publication indicates the title was published outside the Gambia.

The preface states that prices are given but they are not part of the entry information given.

---

1 "Preface," *The Gambia National Bibliography*, p. iii. (1992)

ARRANGEMENT: The main bibliography is arranged by the major classes of the DDC system.

INDEXES: One alphabetical index includes authors (including joint authors, editors), titles (for main entries only) and series. References are to the classification number in the main bibliography.

Information given in the index entries includes author, title, DDC number and legal deposit number.

NOTES AND COMMENTS: The preface of the *GNB* is clearly written and includes the elements suggested by ICNB recommendation number 6, 9, and 10.

GNB continues *National bibliography of The Gambia: Current national bibliography.* - Vol. 1, no. 1 (Jan./Dec 1977)-1987. - Banjul : The National Library of The Gambia, 1978-1988. Annual (1982-1988), semi-annual, with second issue being the cumulation (1977-1981). (DDC: 015.6651034; LC: Z3735.N37; LCCN: 83-647808; ISSN 0796-014X). In examining issues of the *National bibliography of The Gambia* over a period of years, it is apparent that the number of publications has decreased in recent years. The last issue (1987) includes several features not found in the *GNB*:, e.g., publisher's address, cataloguing-in-publication data for the *GNB*, list of publishers and/or printers.

A publishers' list would be a helpful feature to include in the *GNB* since publishers' addresses may not be easily available outside the country.

No symbols mark government publications.

The National Library of the Gambia uses CIP for publications they produce, although there was no symbol in the abbreviations and symbols list to designate a CIP entry.

Local languages, e.g., Mandinka, are listed. There are eight known languages and dialects in The Gambia.[1]

LATEST ISSUE EXAMINED/CURRENCY: At the University Library, Cambridge, England annual volumes are received about nineteen months from the period covered. If this national bibliography is meant to be used as an acquisitions tool or for selection of titles in area studies and collection development, the timeliness of the bibliography needs to be improved. The time lapse in publication and distribution creates a large gap difficult to overcome.

The latest volume consulted is 1993.

AUTOMATION: not automated.

---

[1]   Sally N'je, "Publishing in The Gambia and Cataloguing-in-Publication," International Cataloguing-in-Publication Meeting, Ottawa, 16-19 August 1982. (IFLA/UBC/CIP/ID3):[1].

FORMAT AND SERVICES AVAILABLE: printed.[1]

CURRENT LEGAL DEPOSIT LAWS: The Gambia Library Board Act No. 31 of 1976.

The legal deposit law is not as effective as one would wish. Although publishers are becoming aware of it gradually, it is often necessary for librarians to go directly to the publishers to obtain copies of titles that have been published. Because The Gambia is a small country and because relations between The Gambia Library Board and the publishers are cordial, this method works well. This method, however, consumes the staff's time and causes delays in producing the national bibliography. In recent years, there has been a slight awareness that if publishers list their titles in the *GNB* they will sell more copies. Possibly this awareness will lead to greater voluntary cooperation in supplying a legal deposit copy.[2]

AVAILABLE FROM: National Library of the Gambia, Reg Pye Lane, Private Mail Bag 552, Banjul.

SELECTED ARTICLES: Bankole, Beatrice S. "Current National Bibliographies of the English Speaking Countries of Africa." *International Cataloguing* 14 (Jan./Mar. 1985):5-10.

VERIFIER: Chief Librarian, The National Library of The Gambia.

GEORGIA

TITLE: *Tsignis Matiane = Knizhanīā letopis'* [Book Chronicle] . - 1917/1925-   . - Tbilisi : Tsignis Palata [Book Chamber], 1925-   .
Monthly (1927-   ); 3 vols. a year (1926); annual (1925).
DDC: not found; LC: not found; OCLC: not found
ISSN 0136-0787

COMPILER: Tsignis Palata [Book Chamber].

SCOPE AND COVERAGE: *Tsignis Matiane* (*TM*) includes the publishing output of Georgia, which is deposited at the Tsignis Palata according to legal deposit laws.

Types of publications include books, pamphlets, and new serials.

---

[1] It is hoped that the 1995 edition of *The Gambia National Bibliography* will be produced on the computer according to a letter dated 17 July 1996 written to the author from the Chief Librarian.

[2] Information gathered from Sally N'je, Chief Librarian, The Gambia, in an interview with the author held during the IFLA General Conference, Chicago, IL, 20 August 1985. This method was also mentioned in "Gambia," *Afribiblios* 9 (no. 1 June 1986):3. Information in a letter dated 17 July 1996 to the author from the Chief Libarian indicates that a draft amendment to the legal deposit law has been forwarded to the necessary authorities by The Gambia Library Board.

CONTENTS: Table of contents (in Georgian for Georgian books and Russian for Russian books), abbreviations, classified bibliography, indexes.

CATALOGUING RULES AND CLASSIFICATION SCHEMES USED: Soviet bibliographic rules are followed.

The classification scheme used is Edinnaîa Klassifikatsîa Literaturi dlîa Knigopechatanîa v SSSR [Union Classification of Literature for Book-Publishing in the USSR].

ENTRY INFORMATION: Author, title, place of publication, publisher, date, pagination, illustrations, size, series statement, notes including number of copies printed, ISBN.

ARRANGEMENT: Arrangement is by Soviet subject headings.

INDEXES: In Georgian for books published in Georgian and in Russian for books published in Russian: author index, title index, subject index, geographical index.

NOTES AND COMMENTS: Since Independence, Georgia libraries have been going through financial hardships and are not able to afford the purchase of the national bibliography. The libraries were the main buyers of the bibliography; therefore, the bibliography has not been published since 1992, although the *TM* has been prepared on an annual basis and stored in the Book Chamber. The Georgian government is in negotiations with the Book Chamber to agree on a money allocation for the Georgian libraries to make it possible for them to afford the purchase of the national bibliography.

The Automation Department of the National Library of Georgia has maintained a database of books published from 1991 to the present. It follows the UNIMARC format.

Since Independence, many private publishers have come into existence and are not aware or do not heed the legal deposit laws. Therefore, it is necesary for the Collection Development Department of the National Library of Georgia to visit these new publishers and inform them of the legal deposit laws.

Books written in Georgian, Russian, Armenian, and other languages found in the country are included in *TM*; this follows ICNB Recommendation no. 6.

Before Independence, the USSR *Knizhnaîa letopis* listed selected titles which were published in Georgia.[1]

Of note for earlier books is *Kartuli Tsigni. Bibliograpia* [Georgian Book. Bibliography]. This title is published in three multi-part volumes and covers books published in Georgia from 1629 to 1950. Vol. 1 and 3 are published by Tsignis Palata, and vol. 2 is published by Tekninka da Shroma [Technique and work].

---

[1] In 1988 Teimuraz Chkhenkeli, Deputy Director of the National Library of Georgia, compared titles in *TM* and *KL*. Only about 30% of the titles listed in *TM* were found in *KL*.

LATEST ISSUE EXAMINED/CURRENCY: No issue was available for examination.[1]

AUTOMATION: not automated.

FORMAT AND SERVICES AVAILABLE: printed.

CURRENT LEGAL DEPOSIT LAWS: Decree no. 321 (26 April 1993) titled "On regulation of sending out of free control and paid mandatory copy of printed production."

AVAILABLE FROM: Tsignis Palata, Tbilisi, Georgia. The latest issue available is 1992. Negotiations are in progress to update the national bibliography.

VERIFIER: Nina Chkhenkeli, USIS librarian, American Center of Information Resources; Teimuraz Chkhenkeli, Deputy Director, National Library of Georgia.

GERMANY

TITLE: *Deutsche Nationalbibliographie und Bibliographie der im Ausland erschienenen deutschsprachigen Veröffentlichungen.* Hrsg: Die Deutsche Bibliothek, 1991 ff. [Auslieferung über die] Buchhändler-Vereinigung GmBH, Frankfurt am Main.
Weekly.
Title from cover.
Reihe A: Monographien und Periodika des Verlagsbuchhandels. Wöchentliches Verzeichnis. (DNB. Reihe A) (DDC: not found; LC: Z2221.D4752; LCCN: sn91-22768; OCLC: 23132339; ISSN 0939-0421).
Reihe B. Monographien und Periodika außerhalb des Verlagbuchhandels. Wöchentliches Verzeichnis. (DNB. Reihe B) (DDC: not found; LC: Z2221.D4753; LCCN: sn91-22769; OCLC: 23132331; ISSN 0939-043X).

COMPILER: Die Deutsche Bibliothek (Deutsche Bücherei Leipzig, Deutsche Bibliothek Frankfurt am Main, Deutsches Musikarchiv Berlin)

SCOPE AND COVERAGE: *Deutsche Nationalbibliographie und Bibliographie der im Ausland erschienenen deutschsprachigen Veröffentlichungen* (DNB) includes the publishing output of Germany since 1913 which is deposited at the Deutsche Bibliothek according to legal deposit legislation at Leipzig and Frankfurt am Main. In the future this will include video tapes and electronic publications. *DNB* also includes all titles in the German language produced or published in Austria, Switzerland, and elsewhere since 1913; all translations of German language publications published or otherwise produced in other languages since 1913; all foreign language titles about Germany published or produced abroad since 1913; printed works published or written by German-speaking emigrants from 1933 to 1945.

---

[1] The author is indebted to Nina Chkhenkeli, USIS Librarian, Tbilisi, Georgia, and Tjeimwaz Chkhenkeli, Deputy Director of the National Library of Georgia for the national bibliography information from Georgia, and to Mr. Lee Avdoyan, Library of Congress, who put me in contact with Ms. Chkhenkeli.

DNB. Reihe A: includes the titles available within the publishers' trade. *DNB. Reihe B*: includes the titles from outside the publishers' trade.

Types of publications included in *DNB. Reihe A* and *Reihe B* are books, pamphlets (over six pages), periodicals (new and ceased), official and government publications, annual reports, atlases, standards, literary recordings, audio-visual materials, microforms and electronic publications.

Not included are films (except video), patents, publications with ten or less in a print run (except publications on demand), publications with less than four pages (except maps), musical scores; original art maps with no text or title, travel brochures, posters, "Akzidenzschriften," daily newspapers which are not filmed. Some of these categories are included in another series of *DNB*. See the Notes and Comments section.

CONTENTS: *DNB. Reihe A* and *DNB. Reihe B*: outline of subject classification scheme, introduction, classified bibliography. Indexes are published separately.

CATALOGUING RULES AND CLASSIFICATION SCHEMES USED: For descriptive cataloguing *DNB* uses *Regeln für die alphabetische Katalogisierung in wissenschaftlichen Bibliotheken*. 2., überarb. Ausg. (*RAK-WB*) (ISBN 3-87068-436-4), and *RAK-NBM*. ISBD is followed. Subject cataloguing uses *Regeln für den Schlagwortkatalog*. 2., erw. Aufl. (*RSWK*) ISBN 3-87068-397-X.

DNB uses the classification scheme according to the ten main classes of UDC, 2 ed.

ENTRY INFORMATION: *Reihe A* and *Reihe B*: title number in upper left, CIP number (if applicable) follows consecutive title number, author, title, edition statement, place of publication, publisher, date, pagination, illustration statement, size, series statement, ISBN or ISSN, binding, price, *DBN* identification number. Other information is given in smaller type below the entry, e.g., NE introduces additional information about the entry, keywords are introduced with SW, GT indicates a decision for a complete title tracing. Cross-references of authors whose pseudonyms are known are introduced with VW. Symbols are explained, e.g., § indicates official publications, and ∞ indicates the paper follows ISO 9706.

ARRANGEMENT: *Reihe A* and *Reihe B*: arranged alphabetically within 65 subject groups.

INDEXES: *Reihe A* and *Reihe B* combine to form one index which is published separately titled *DNB. Monographien und Periodika des Verlagbuchhandels und außerhalb des Verlagbuchhandels. Wöchentliches Verzeichnis. Wochenregister zu Reihe A und Reihe B.* Weekly, including monthly cumulation. The last issue of each month is the monthly cumulation called *Monographien und Periodika des Verlagbuchhandels und außerhalb des Verlagbuchhandels. Monatregister zu Reihe A und Reihe B.* (DDC: 015.43/034; LC: Z2221.D477; LCCN: 91-640137; OCLC: 23284960; ISSN 0939-0480). The weekly and monthly indexes list corporate and personal authors, titles, subject headings, and keywords in one alphabetical sequence. They include a list of ISSN/ISBN in ascending order and an alphabetical list of publishers (for *Reihe A*). Instructions for using the index are given at the beginning of the index section.

Indexes to other series are mentioned with the bibliographic information under the Notes and Comments section.

NOTES AND COMMENTS: The unification of the Deutsche Bücherei Leipzig and the Deutsche Bibliothek Frankfurt am Main has produced, since 1991, a unified German national bibliography composed of general and special bibliographies which are arranged in series with specific scopes and coverages, and varying frequencies. Currency, quality and completeness in a single, well-ordered system guarantees significantly more efficient access to the published material which is available through legal deposit. Costly and time-consuming duplication is avoided.

The Deutsche Bibliographie. Wöchentliches Verzeichnis was published as *Bibliographie der Deutschen Bibliothek*, 1947-1952. The *Deutsche Nationalbibliographie und Bibliographie des im Ausland erschienenen deutschsprachigen Schrifttums* continues, with change in title and scope, the *Wöchentliches Verzeichnis*, 1842-1930.

DNB. Reihe A is formed by the merger of *Deutsche Bibliographie. Wöchentliches Verzeichnis. Reihe A, Erscheinungen des Verlagsbuchhandels.* Frankfurt am Main : Buchhändler-Vereinigung, 1947-1990 (DDC: 015.43; LC: Z2221.D475; LCCN: 82-645154; OCLC: 8734867; ISSN 0170-1037) and *Deutsche Nationalbibliographie und Bibliographie des im Ausland erschienenen deutschsprachigen Schrifttums. Reihe A, Neuerscheinungen des Buchhandels.* Leipzig : Deutsche Bücherei, 1931-1990 (DDC: 015.43; LC: Z2221.H67; LCCN: 86-644852; OCLC: 1585746; ISSN 0323-3596).

DNB. Reihe B is formed by the merger of : Deutsche Bibliographie. Wöchentliches Verzeichnis. Reihe B, Beilage, Erscheinungen außerhalb des Verlagsbuchhandels. Frankfurt am Main: Buchhändler-Vereinigung, 1947-1990 (DDC: 015.43; LC: Z2221.F752; LCCN: 82-645155//r872; OCLC: 8735154; ISSN 0170-1053), and *Deutsche Nationalbibliographie und Bibliographie des im Ausland erschienenen deutschsprachigen Schrifttums. Reihe B, Neuerscheinungen außerhalb des Buchhandels.* Leipzig : Deutsche Bücherei, 1931-1990 (DDC: 015.486; LC: Z2221.D495; LCCN: 86-644852; OCLC: 11066953; ISSN 0323-3642).

Information for other *DNB* series follows.

Reihe C. Karten —Vierteljährliches Verzeichnis. Hrsg: Die Deutsche Bibliothek, 1991 ff. [Auslieferung über die] Buchhändler-Vereinigung GmBH, Frankfurt am Main. Quarterly. Cumulated semiannually in Reihe D. (DDC: not found; LC: Z2221.F7522; LCCN: 91-640147//r93; OCLC: 23853403; ISSN 0939-0553). Maps are arranged alphabetically by title. Includes author, title, keyword index, and an ISSN/ISBN index. Entries are catalogued according to *RAK-WB* and *RAK-Karten. Reihe C* appears together with Series A and B but can be purchased separately. Atlases are listed in group 62 of *Reihe A* and *Reihe B*.[1]

Reihe D. Monographien und Periodika — Halbjahresverzeichnis. Hrsg: Die Deutsche Bibliothek, 1991 ff. [Auslieferung über die] Buchhändler-Vereinigung GmBH, Frankfurt am Main. Semiannual. This index is issued in two parts: 1. Teil. *Alphabetisches Titelverzeichnis* (title index alphabetically arranged); 2. Teil. *Schlagwort- und Stichwortregister* (subject

---

[1] *Deutsche Nationalbibliographie = German National Bibliography* / Die Deutsche Bibliothek. - Frankfurt-a.-M. : Buchhändler-Vereinigung GmbH, [1997]. p. 7.

heading and keyword index). Cumulates: *Reihe A, Reihe B, Reihe C* (DDC: not found; LC: Z2221.F73; LCCN: 92-640100; OCLC: 25469604; ISSN 0940-2721).

Reihe E. Monographien und Periodika — Fünfjahresverzeichnis. 1986-1990. Hrsg: Die Deutsche Bibliothek, 1991 ff. [Auslieferung über die] Buchhändler-Vereinigung GmBH, Frankfurt am Main. Every five years. This index is issued in two parts as is Reihe D: alphabetical title index, and subject heading and keyword index with a systematic overview of the subject headings used. (DDC: 015.43075; LC: Z2221.D49; LCCN: 93-640033; OCLC: 27307480; ISSN 0942-4318).

Reihe F, Periodika — Fünfjahresverzeichnis. "Indexes all new periodical publications and periodicals issued in modified form in German and German-speaking countries during the reporting period. Ordered by subject groups. Last issue: 1981-1985, Part I (ISSN 0170-1002). Future frequency for issue now under discussion."[1] Author, title, subject heading, keyword index.

Reihe G, Fremdsprachige Germanica und Übersetzungen deutschsprachiger Werke —— Vierteljährliches Verzeichnis. Hrsg: Die Deutsche Bibliothek, 1991 ff. [Auslieferung über die] Buchhändler-Vereinigung GmBH, Frankfurt am Main. Quarterly (DDC: 016.943/005; LC: Z2221.D498, DD17; LCCN: 92-640293; OCLC: 26899384; ISSN 0939-057X). Part 1 includes foreign language publications published abroad about Germany and people in the German-speaking countries. Part 2 includes translations published abroad of works originally written in German. Organized by 65 subject groups, and then alphabetical within the groups. Author, title, subject heading, and keyword index, language index, and publisher index in each issue which are cumulated separately in an annual index. This series includes titles published after 1989; plans are to include important earlier publications in the 1991-1995 index on a one-time basis.[2]

Reihe H. Hochschulschriften — Monatliches Verzeichnis. 1991 ff. Monthly (DDC: 011/.75; LC: Z5055.G29, D478; LCCN: 91-640151//r93; OCLC: 23459934; ISSN 0939-0588). Reihe H lists dissertations and habilitation papers from German institutions of higher learning and German language dissertations and habilitation papers published abroad regardless of the form in which they have appeared. As of 1993, German-language university publications from Austria and Switzerland are included. Arranged alphabetically within 65 subject groups. Author, title, subject headings, keyword index is cumulated separately in an annual index.

Reihe M. Musikalien und Musikschriften — Monatliches Verzeichnis. 1991 ff. Monthly. (DDC: not found; LC: (090) ML5.D43; LCCN: not found; OCLC: 23665749; ISSN: 0939-0596). Part 1 of *Reihe M* includes printed music deposited at the Deutsches Musikarchiv Berlin and the Deutsche Bücherei Leipzig, including items not available for sale. Part II includes written works about music. Part I is arranged by 11 subject groups; Part II includes publications about music arranged alphabetically. The index for Part I includes index of publishers, index of names and titles of musicalia; the index for Part II includes an author, title, subject heading, and keyword index for publications about music. Cumulated separately in a two-part annual index.

---

[1] The author is grateful for information and clarification for this and other series supplied in a letter dated 16 May 1995 from Michaela Michel, Die Deutsche Bibliothek.
[2] *Deutsche Nationalbibliographie = German National Bibliography.* p. 10.

Reihe N. Vorankündigungen Monographien und Periodika (CIP) — Wöchentliches Verzeichnis. Hrsg: Die Deutsche Bibliothek, 1991 ff. [Auslieferung über die] Buchhändler-Vereinigung GmBH, Frankfurt am Main. Weekly. (DDC: not found; LC: Z2221.D4763; LCCN: sn91-26465; OCLC: 23361432; ISSN 0939-0634). Pre-publication notifications for selected monographs and periodicals (CIP) organized by subject groups. Not included are music, "Musiktonträger", maps, school books, religious pamphlets, offprints from journals, daily newspapers, light fiction in partial form such as a title without ISBN, and unchanged new editions. Author, title, and keyword index, ISSN/ISBN index, index of publishers. Cumulated in a monthly index (except the publisher index).

Reihe T. Musiktonträger — Monatliches Verzeichnis. Monthly (DDC: not found; LC: (090) ML156.2, D47; LCCN: sn91-17108; OCLC: 23575867; ISSN 0939-0642). Reiht T lists music recordings, including those not for sale, which are deposited at the Deutsches Musikarchiv Berlin and the Deutsche Bücherei Leipzig. Arranged alphabetically within 11 subject groups. Compact disks, compact cassettes, music videos, and records. Index of companies, names and titles index. Cumulates separately in an annual index.

Reihe BB. Bibliographie der Bibliographien [Bibliography of bibliographies] Annual. (DDC: not found; LC: not found; LCCN: not found; ISSN 0301-4614). Index of bibliographies and literature lists (whether issued independently or not). Arranged by subject groups. Each issue contains a subject heading index.

LATEST ISSUE EXAMINED/CURRENCY: The latest issues examined at Bibliotekstjänst AB Library in September 1997 are *A*, 14 August 1997; *B*, 14 August 1997; *C*, Juni 1997; *N*, 14 August 1997. Entries include titles received during the period covered. Most are published during the current year, but there also are numerous titles from earlier years.

AUTOMATION: The *Deutsche Bibliographie.Wöchentliches Verzeichnis*, one of the predecessors of the *DNB*, was automated since 1966, thus claiming to be the first national bibliography to be automated. The *DNB* is produced by the same *EDV* data base.

FORMAT AND SERVICES AVAILABLE: printed, title cards, floppy disk and magnetic tape; online service: through the database BIBLIODATA using MESSENGER retrieval system; compact disk: *Deutsche Nationalbibliographie CD-ROM aktuell (DNB-CD)*, 1986ff; *Deutsche Nationalbibliographie CD-ROM Musik (DNB-Musik);* CD-ROM of university publications catalogued by Die Deutsche Bibliothek 1945-1992 (Diss-CD); cataloguing files from Der Deutschen Bibliothek available in USMARC through cooperative effort between Der Deutschen Bibliothek and Library of Congress Cataloging Distribution Service.

CURRENT LEGAL DEPOSIT LAWS: "The Gesetz über die Deutsche Bibliothek Bibliothek (Law regarding the Deutsche Bibliothek) of 31 March 1969 described the functions and duties of the Deutsche Bibliothek, establishing it as the central archival library with headquarters in Frankfurt am Main. The Gesetz über die Deutsche Bibliothek was precised by the Veordnung über die Pflichtablieferung von Druckwerken an die Deutsche Bibliothek (Pflichtstückverordnung - PflStV=Legal Deposit Directive) of 14 December 1982 and expanded to include the provisions of the law of the Treaty of Unification of 23 September 1990.

AVAILABLE FROM: Printed and CD-ROM editions from Buchhändler-Vereinigung GMBH, Grosser Hirschgraben 17-21, 60311 Frankfurt am Main.

Other services and information from Die Deutsche Bibliothek, Zentrale bibliographische Dienstleistungen, Zeppelinallee 4-8, D-60325, Frankfurt.

SELECTED ARTICLES: *Deutsche Nationalbibliographie = Germany National Bibliography* / Die Deutsche Bibliotek. Frankfurt-a.-M. : Buchhändler-Vereinigung, [1997].

Lehmann, K-D. "Die Deutsche Bibliothek: Germany's National Library and National Bibliographic Agency." *Alexandria* 5 (3 1993), pp. 161-174.

VERIFIER: Michaela Michel, Die Deutsche Bibliothek.

GHANA

TITLE: *Ghana national bibliography bi monthly.* - vol. 20, no.1 (Jan./Feb. 1987)- . - Accra : Ghana Library Board, 1987- .
Bi-monthly, with annual cumulation titled *Ghana national bibliography.*
Title from cover.
Continues: *Ghana: A current bibliography*, v. 1-19 (Sept./Oct. 1967-Nov./Dec. 1986) and assumes its numbering.
Duplicated.
DDC: not found; LC: Z3785.G445; LCCN: sn88-17215; OCLC: 17743634
ISSN 0855-0093[1]

COMPILER: George Padmore Research Library on African Affairs, Ghana Library Board, Accra.

SCOPE AND COVERAGE: The *Ghana National Bibliography Bi monthly* (*GNBB*) lists books and pamphlets deposited according to the legal deposit law at the George Padmore Research Library on African Affairs, and acquisitions, in whatever form or language, originating from Ghana by Ghanaians or non-Ghanaians, and publications by Ghanaians or non-Ghanaians published abroad about Ghana.[2]

Types of publications included are books, pamphlets, new periodical titles, articles with Ghana subject content from books, pamphlets, periodicals and newspapers.

CONTENTS: Preface, abbreviations; Section One, classified subject section; Section Two, author, title and series index; Section Three, subject index; Section Four, appendix 1 — list of publishers and their addresses.

Cataloguing of material follows AACR2, ISBD(M) and ISBD(S). For subject headings the *LCSH* is used. DDC20 is followed.

---

[1] In a letter dated 1 November 1996 to the author Mrs. Sarah Kanda, Acting Director of Library Services stated that there has been typing errors on a number of issues regarding the ISSN; 0855-0225 is an erroneous ISSN.
[2] "Preface," *GNBB* Nov./Dec. 1993 (vol. 26, no.6), p. ii

ENTRY INFORMATION: DDC number, author, title, place of publication, publisher, year, pagination, size, series, ISBN, tracings, *GNB* number.

For periodical articles, complete bibliographic information necessary for location of the articles is given.

ARRANGEMENT: Section One includes full bibliographic information and is arranged by the DDC system. Section Two is arranged alphabetically; Section Three is arranged alphabetically by subject.

INDEXES: Author, title, and series index; subject index.

NOTES AND COMMENTS: With the beginning of *GNBB* the national bibliography has become more timely but it still has problems to overcome before it will have a current national bibliography which can serve as a selection and acquisitions tool for other libraries. To date, Ghana has no national library. The George Padmore Research Library on African Affairs, a wing of the Ghana Library Board, has been performing the functions of a national bibliographic center. An ineffective legal deposit law which is not enforced affects the lateness of the current bibliography. Precious staff time must be spent in locating elusive publications that should be deposited automatically. The legal deposit law doesn't extend to unclassified government publications, so government departments are not under obligation to deposit documents. Since it is estimated government publications constitute sixty percent of the national imprint, this is a sizable group of titles to track down by already overworked staff members.[1] There is no centralized government agency in charge of publications. Another contributing factor to the delay of annual cumulations is the shortage of printing materials, e.g., plates and paper.[2]

Ghana: A Current Bibliography. -v. 1-v. (Sept./Oct. 1967) - 19, no. 6 (1986) - Accra : Research Library on African Affairs, 1967-1986. (DDC: 016.9166703; LC: Z3785.G445; LCCN: 73-643917; OCLC: 1786969), a bi-monthly issued as a supplement to *Ghana National Bibliography* (ISSN 0072-4378), first appeared in November 1967. The scope as stated in the introduction of the November/December 1977 issue is based on the acquisitions of the Research Library within the specified period, on material deposited with the Library under the Book and Newspaper Registration Act, 1961, and on the accessions lists of libraries both in and outside Ghana. According to A.N. Deheer, this duplicated list was the only means of updating the *Ghana National Bibliography* which has been delayed by several years because of production problems mentioned above.[3] It is now continued by *GNNB*.

Ghana national bibliography. - 1965-19 . - Accra : Ghana Library Board, 1968-19 . Annual. (ISSN 0072-4378; LC: Z3785.G4; OCLC: 1751202) is the annual issue of the national bibliography which is supplemented to keep it current by *Ghana: A Current Bibliography*, and now by *GNNB*. Its scope and coverage include legal deposit material deposited at the Research

---

[1] Gerhard Pomassl, *Survey of Existing Legal Deposit Laws* (Paris: Unesco, 1977), p. 35.

[2] Beatrice S. Bankole, "Current National Bibliography of the English Speaking Countries of Africa," *International Cataloguing* 14 (Jan./Mar. 1985):6. Mrs. Kanda stated in her letter that the lack of timeliness is due currently to lack of professional staff, and finances. These are also the stated reasons in Christiana Kwei, "Ghana," *Afribiblios* 8 (no. 2 Dec. 1985):51-52.

[3] A.N. Deheer, "Ghana," *Afribiblios* 7 (no. 7 June 1984):15

Library on African Affairs, material traced in other libraries, e.g., "extracts from the catalogues of the University of Ghana, Legon and certain special libraries in Accra."[1] It includes all material, in whatever form or language, originating from Ghanaians and about Ghana, published in Ghana and abroad. Types of publications covered are books, pamphlets, new periodicals and periodical and newspaper articles, theses, Ghanaian language publications, official and government publications, IGO publications, unpublished materials, maps and atlases. Since 1977, an asterisk (*) is used for materials published abroad.[2] The section on Ghanaian languages includes Ewe, Fante, Ga-Adangme, Kasem, Nzema and Twi. Changes occurred in the *Ghana National Bibliography* with the 1974 volume. The introduction states that the use of ISBD was begun, a new group of subjects was introduced, monographs were separated from serials, periodical articles were assigned a separate section, a local publishers' list with addresses was added, and changes were made to conform with initial standards and promote bibliographical control. Most of the government publications are listed in one section and therefore do not have a specialized symbol. One may also check the index under Ghana to identify publications and their issuing agencies.

The Ghanaian National ISDS Centre, begun in 1981 is actively assigning ISSNs to newspapers and periodicals that have survived the slump in the printing industry.

In analyzing the type of material listed in the *GNBB*, there is a high percent of periodical and newspaper articles as compared to books.

A ten year gap exists in the coverage of annual issues, e.g. 1979-1988. This gap will be bridged by two five year cumulations; currently 1979-1983 is in progress.[3]

Plans are developing for a Ghanaian CIP program.[4]

LATEST ISSUE EXAMINED/CURRENCY: The latest volume examined is vol. 29, no. 4 (July/Aug. 1996) published in 1996 and received by the Indiana University Library, in Dec. 1996. This is much more timely than the former *Ghana National Bibliography* which was received an average of thirteen months after publication.

AUTOMATION: not automated.

FORMAT AND SERVICES AVAILABLE: printed.

CURRENT LEGAL DEPOSIT LAWS: Book and Newspaper Registration Act of 1961 (Act 73) as amended in 1963 (Act 193).[5]

---

[1] "Introduction," *Ghana National Bibliography*, from the volume covering 1973, published 1975.
[2] Bankole, p. 6.
[3] Kanda letter.
[4] Bankole, p. 6. However, in Mrs. Kanda's letter, she stated that the CIP program has not been established yet.
[5] "Preface," *GNBB* Nov./Dec 1993, p. ii.

AVAILABLE FROM: George Padmore Research Library on African Affairs, P.O. Box 2970, Accra.

SELECTED ARTICLES: Bankole, Beatrice S. "Current National Bibliographies of the English Speaking Countries of Africa." *International Cataloguing* 14 (Jan./Mar. 1985):5-10.

Kisiedu, Christine O. "Ghana and the Knowledge Explosion — The Problem of Bibliography." *African Research Documentation*, no. 8/9 (1975), pp. 34-41.

Kwei, Christina. "Ghana," *Afribiblios* 8 (no. 2 Dec. 1985):51-52.

VERIFIER: Sarah D. Kanda, Acting Director of Library Services, Ghana Library Board.

GREECE

TITLE: *Hellenike ethnike vivliographia.* - Athenai : To Grapheio , 1989-   .
Annual; (semiannual, the last issue being the annual cumulation, 1989-1990?).
Added title page: *Greek national bibliography / National Library of Greece, Cataloguing Department, National Bibliographic Office.*
DDC: not found; LC: Z2285.H45; LCCN: 92-649773; OCLC: 26498788
ISSN 1105-3046

COMPILER: Ethnike Vivliotheke tes Hellados. Tmema Katalogon, Grapheio Ethnikes Vivliographias. [National Library of Greece. Cataloguing Department. National Bibliographic Office].

SCOPE AND COVERAGE: *Hellenike ethnike vivliographia (HEV)* lists the printed library material published in Greece within the current and preceding two years which is received under legal deposit at the National Library of Greece.

Types of publications included in *HEV* are books, pamphlets over 16 pages, official and government publications. Excluded are first issues and changes of title of serials and newspapers, pamphlets of under 16 pages unless they form a series, reports of research and other similar projects.

CONTENTS: Contents (in Greek and English), introduction (although in Greek and English, the Greek is more detailed and includes an analyzed entry with both Greek and English notations), classification scheme, bibliography, indexes.

CATALOGUING RULES AND CLASSIFICATION SCHEMES USED: Descriptive cataloguing is based on AACR2. The subject headings "come from the list of Greek subject headings, developed by the Cataloguing Department of the National Library of Greece and modelled on the *LCSH*."[1]

---

[1] "Introduction," *Hellenike ethnike vivliographia* (Jan./June 1990), p. 10

Records in the UNIMARC format were begun with the 1991 *HEV*.[1]

The classification scheme used is DDC.

ENTRY INFORMATION: Serial number in left margin, DDC number in upper left corner, author, title, responsibility statement, place, publisher and/or printer, date, pagination, size in standard book format, e.g., 8 ov. and in centimeters, notes, subject headings, call number in lower left corner, national bibliography number in lower right corner.

ARRANGEMENT: Alphabetically arranged within the subject groups.

INDEXES: Author, title and series index; subject index; publishers index; ISBN index; year of publication index. Indexes refer the user to entry information by giving the serial number.

NOTES AND COMMENTS: Before *HEV*, several attempts to establish bibliographic control were established.

Hellenike Vivliographia. - Athens : Vivliographike Hetaireia tes Hellados, 1972- 198?. was an attempt by the Bibliographical Society of Greece to fill the need of a national bibliography until *HEV* was established in 1989. (LC: Z2281.H44; LCCN: 79-641804//r89; OCLC: 4919459).

During the 1960's the *Greek Bibliography.* - Athens : National Printing Office, 1960-1968. (ISSN 0017-3851) was an English-language edition of *Deltion Hellenikes Vivliographias,* a classified bibliography which included books, pamphlets, official and government publications, maps and atlases. Indexed.

Some specific bibliographical problems with the Greek language are determining the proper declination of names (not easy without good biographical sources), proper spelling and accents for names (names given all in capital letters do not use accent marks), and establishing the proper order of names when both names given could be the surname.

A bibliography worth mentioning is l'Institut Français d'Athènes. *Bulletin Signalétique de Bibliographie Helleníque* (LCCN: sc83-6403). This continues the Institute's *Bulletin Analytique de Bibliographie Helleníque* (1945-1973). The 1973 volume was published in 1980. The *Bulletin Signalétique* provides a selected list of Greek works and translations. The volume for 1973 was published in 1980.

LATEST ISSUE EXAMINED/CURRENCY: Entries include the period covered as well as the two preceding years. If *HEV* could be received in a more timely manner in libraries around the world it could be used as an acquisitions tool and collection development aid. The latest issue examined was January/June 1990.

---

[1] Bokos, George. " National Library of Greece: Automation and Choice of Format," *ICBC* 21 (no. 2):25

AUTOMATION: " ...a new automated system is expected to be installed in the Library during the first part of 1992."[1]

FORMAT AND SERVICES AVAILABLE: printed

CURRENT LEGAL DEPOSIT LAWS: Legal deposit 880/1943.[2] Non-book materials are not included.[3]

AVAILABLE FROM: The National Library of Greece, 32 Panepistimiou Av., 106 79 Athens.

SELECTED ARTICLES: Bokos, George. "National Library of Greece: Automation and Choice of Format," *ICBC* 21:2 (April/June 1992): 24-28.

VERIFIER: Associate Professor Panayotis G. Nicolopoulos, Director, National Library of Greece.

GUATEMALA

No current national bibliography has been traced for Guatemala.

Attempts to sustain a current national bibliography have not been successful. *Índice bibliográfico guatemalteco.* - Guatemala : Biblioteca Nacional, 1952-61 (ISSN 0445-9059; OCLC: 4078926) was an irregular publication which included books, pamphlets, and periodical articles issued in Guatemala, and material about Guatemala from elsewhere. Publication was suspended 1953-1957. *Anuario bibliográfico guatemalteco.* - Guatemala (City) : Biblioteca Nacional, 1961 (ISSN 0518-0775; OCLC: 4652308) resulted in only one volume covering 1960 as far as the author can determine. Included in the scope are books, pamphlets, official and government publications, theses, and periodicals. The periodicals are listed in a separate section. Arrangement of both the book and the periodical sections is alphabetical by the main entry. At the end of the volume is an historical list of printers and publishers important in Guatamala's history. Addresses for current publishers and printers are given. *Revista Biblioteca Nacional*, 4th ser., vol. 1, no. 1, 1962, pp. 137-167 may be the last attempt to compile a current national bibliography.[4]

"Collección bibliográfica del tercer centenario de la fundación de la primera imprenta en Centro América" is a series which combines older works with new compilations to cover publishing in

---

[1] Ibid, p. 26. A letter dated 23 July 1996 to the author from the Director of the National Library of Greece states that the automation system, made for the needs of the National Library of Greece, is used in the production of *HEV*.

[2] "Introduction," *HEV* (Jan./June 1990):10

[3] Cabral, Maria Luisa. "Les Bibliothèques nationales du sud de l'Europe: situation présente et évolution probable," *ICBC* 17 (no.1, Jan./Mar. 1988):10

[4] H. Woodbridge, "Latin America National Bibliography," *Encyclopedia of Library and Information Science*, vol. 36, suppl. 1, pp. 307-308.

Guatemala from 1660 to 1960.[1] The series title *Bibliografía Guatemalteca, y catálogo general de libros, folletos, periódicos, revistas publicados en Guatemala*. - Guatemala : [Tip. Nacional], 1960-1964 (OCLC: 12441041) is a ten volume work giving "detailed bibliographical information with annotations about books, pamphlets, etc. and in many cases the texts of decrees, official notices, etc."[2] Much of this work is based on work done by Gilberto Valenzuela Reyna. Title varies in earlier volumes. Horacio Figueroa Marroquín. *Appéndice a la Bibliografía guatemalteca*. - Guatemala : Tip. Nacional, 1988 includes works which are not in *Bibliografía guatemalteca*.

CURRENT LEGAL DEPOSIT LAWS: Ley de Emisión del Pensamiento of 2 May 1966, Decree no. 9, Artículo 60 (*El Gualtemateco*, vol. 176 of 2 May 1966, No. 53, p. 497).[3]

GUINEA

No current national bibliography has been traced for Guinea. Mention of two volumes of the national bibliography published in 1975 and 1976 is made in the "Guinea Republic" country report which appeared in *Afribiblios* 8 (no. 2, Dec. 1985):58.

CURRENT LEGAL DEPOSIT LAWS: Decree no. 290/PRG, dated 9 November 1973.[4]

GUINEA-BISSAU

No current national bibliography has been traced for Guinea-Bissau.

GUYANA

TITLE: *Guyanese national bibliography*. - Jan.-Mar. 1973-   . - Georgetown : National Library, 1973-   .
Quarterly, the fourth issue being an annual cumulation.
DDC: 015.88/1; LC: Z1761.G88; LCCN: 74-646314; OCLC: 1462419
ISSN 0376-5202

COMPILER: National Library, Georgetown.

---

[1] I. Zimmerman, *Current National Bibliographies of Latin America*, p. 80.
[2] R. Balay, *Guide to Reference Books*, 11th, entry AA481 describes the volume contents.
[3] G. Pomassl, *Survey of Existing Legal Deposit Laws*, p. 36, and *International Guide to Legal Deposit*, p. 80.
[4] "Guinea Republic," *Afribiblios* 8 (no. 2, Dec. 1985):58.

SCOPE AND COVERAGE: The *Guyanese National Bibliography* (*GNB*) lists all works printed in the Republic of Guyana based on materials received at the National Library under legal deposit legislation.

Types of publications included in *GNB* are books, pamphlets, first issue and title changes of periodicals, annual reports, official and government publications, printed theses, maps and atlases, musical scores, motion pictures, filmstrips, phonorecords.

Omitted from the scope of *GNB* are periodicals and annual reports (except as mentioned above), certain government publications, e.g., gazettes and restricted publications.

CONTENTS: Preface; list of terms, definitions and abbreviations; outline of the DDC; classified subject section; alphabetical section; list of publishers; appendix: list of single bills, acts, subsidiary legislation and parliamentary debates.

CATALOGUING RULES AND CLASSIFICATION SCHEMES USED: Cataloguing rules followed in *GNB* are AACR2 and ISBD (M). ISBD was first used in 1975.

The classification scheme used is the DDC (19th ed.).

ENTRY INFORMATION: Fullest information is given in the classified subject section and includes the following: analyzed classification number with appropriate headings, author, title, edition, place of publication, publisher, date, pagination, illustrations, size, series, notes including bibliography, binding, price information, pseudonyms, "literary text in Akawaio and English", etc. The serial number in the legal deposit collection is given in parentheses in the lower right corner.

"See" notes are used throughout the alphabetical section.

Information given in the appendix section for bills, parliamentary debates, acts, orders, regulations, resolutions, proclamations includes number and short title, pagination, and the date, and page number where it is found in the *Official Gazette*.

ARRANGEMENT: The classified subject section is arranged by the DDC scheme.

The appendix is arranged by type of government publication, arranged chronologically.

INDEXES: The alphabetical section is an index which includes authors, joint authors, editors, translators, illustrators, titles, and series arranged in one alphabetical sequence. The author entries provide title, publisher, date and price. Classification numbers at the extreme left refer to the classification number in the subject section. The number in parentheses at the extreme bottom right corner is the serial number in the legal deposit collection.

The large number of cross references in the index aid the user in finding the information needed. For title and entries other than the main entry, the user is referred to the main entry where the classification number in the classified subject section is given.

Subject entries are not included in the index.

"The List of Publishers" includes addresses and telephone numbers of Guyana publishers.

NOTES AND COMMENTS: Non-book materials were added to the scope of *GNB* in 1975. The 1981 annual cumulation included a non-book material section preceded by list of abbreviations for non-book materials, following the List of Publishers. The non-book material is divided into: motion pictures and filmstrips; phonorecords. Most entries were for motion pictures, with a summary statement added to other details given: title, producer/director, distributor, reels, length, sound, color, millimeter, narrator, sound track, sponsor, date. The serial number for the legal deposit collection is not given. For phonorecords, the serial number for legal deposit collection is given. Detailed information also includes: name, title, speed, contents, size, playing time, producer, title on container, engineer, etc.

GNB is duplicated.

Publications written in languages and dialects of the country, such as the Carib-speaking group Akawaio, are included; *GNB* is in the English language, which is the official language of Guyana.

No symbol designates government publications in the subject section. However, one may look in the index under Guyana and the issuing agency for identification of most government publications listed in any issue.

Due to "severe staff constraints at both the professional and technical levels" the National Library has not been able to keep current. The latest issue available in June 1995 is for the quarter January - March 1991. The National Library intends to publish the outstanding issues of the *GNB* at a later date.[1]

LATEST ISSUE EXAMINED/CURRENCY: Annual cumulations arrived at the University Library, Cambridge, eleven to twelve months after the year covered, with the January-December 1990 arriving in 1992. This was the latest issue available at the University Library in November 1994. Entries in the issues examined were mostly for the year covered, with only a few for the previous year.

AUTOMATION: There are plans for automation of the *GNB*.

FORMAT AND SERVICES AVAILABLE: printed.

CURRENT LEGAL DEPOSIT LAWS: The Law Revision Act, 1972 (Act No. 4 of 1972) designated the National Library as a legal depository. Publications and Newspapers Act (Chap. 21:01 of the Laws of Guyana, rev. ed. 1973) and of non-book material is the legal deposit law. ("Preface", iii)

AVAILABLE FROM: Chief Librarian, National Library, P.O. Box 10240, Georgetown.

VERIFIER: Gwyneth Browman, Chief Librarian

---

[1] Information is taken from an undated letter to subscribers of the *Guyanese National Bibliography* sent to the author by the Chief Librarian in May 1995.

HAITI

No current national bibliography has been traced for Haiti.

"Bibliographie Haitienne [   ]" appears in *Conjonction*. - Port-au-Prince, Haiti : L'Institut Francais d' Haiti periodically since 1961 covering the years 1950 to the present. The lists are compiled by individuals in the best manner possible, which may mean going to bookstores, etc. to see what books are available. Legal deposit law is not effective; Haiti has been waiting for a revision for many years. Problems in production and distribution of publications cause bibliographic control to be almost non-existent.[1]

Lists examined in *Conjonction* (ISSN 0304-5757) are: number 160 (Jan. 1984) "Bibliographie Haitienne 1981-1982," by Patrick Tardieu, pp. 53-76; number 154 (June 1982) "Bibliographie Haitienne en 1981," by Jean Wilfrid Bertrand and Patrick Tardieu, pp. 91-94; number 147 (Dec. 1979) "Les Livres de l'année 1979," by Wilfrid Bertrand, pp. 85-91; number 152 (Jan. 1982) "Pour une Bibliographie des Études Littéraires Haitiennes," by François Hoffman, pp. 45-57; numbers 141/142 (Feb. 1979) "Publications Haitiennes 1978," by Wilfrid Bertrand, pp. 102-107; number 134 (June/July 1977) "Pour une Bibliographie des Études Littéraires Haitiennes," by François Hoffman, pp. 5-54; number 132 (Dec. 1976/Jan. 1977) "Bibliographie 1976: Publications Haitiennes ou concernant Haiti," pp. 81-83. Earlier numbers included bibliographies that were compiled by Max Bissainthe.[2]

Changes in organization of the *Conjonction* list have occurred. In 1981-1982, there are 160 titles (180 entries) listed by subject. It was decided to change from UDC used in previous lists to the DDC scheme beginning with the 1981/1982 list (number 160, January 1984). The compiler has also tried to separate titles written by the Haitian authors and Haitian imprints from the titles published abroad or written by foreign authors. Previously, there was no attempt to make any distinction. A decision was also made to include works with Haitian themes from the U.S. and Canada since 1980.

Patrick Tardieu mentions in the introduction to the 1981-1982 compilation that it was thought this list might be included in the catalogue of the "Sociedad Dominicana de Bibliofilos" until it was realized that in that title no distinction is made regarding the date of publication. Instead, an appendix will be added to this title.

Entry information given for the titles listed is author, title, place of publication, publisher, date, pagination, occasional note. Classification number is given at the beginning of each class.

---

[1] Jean Wilfrid Bertrand and P. Tardieu, "Bibliographie Haitienne en 1981," *Conjonction* (no. 154 1982):91.

[2] For citations in earlier numbers see the section on Haiti in H. C. Woodbridge, "Latin American National Bibliography," *Encyclopedia of Library and Information Science* 36 (Suppl. 1 1983):271-343, especially 309. In his article, Woodbridge also states that with the loss of the compiler M. Bissainthe from Haiti to New York, there was no complete list published from the early 1960's until 1972 was covered in number 119.

The list for 1981 by Jean Wilfrid Bertrand and Patrick Tardieu also appeared in number 4/5 (July/December 1981) of the *Bulletin d'information de l'Association des archivistes, bibliothécaires et documentalistes francophones de la Caraïbe* (Section Haiti) Quarterly (ISSN 0254-1078). This is another source of bibliographic information for Haiti. It is a duplicated periodical. Number 1 covers 20 October 1979 - 20 October 1980. In number 6/7 (January/June 1982) a list appears entitled "Publications reçues," pp. 25-26 which lists eight titles.

Lygia M. Ballantyne authored *Haitian Publications: An Acquisitions guide and bibliography*. - Washington, DC : Library of Congress, 1979. (OCLC: 6225641). This publication also appears in the SALALM bibliography and reference series, no. 6 in 1980. (OCLC: 7252216). A particularly helpful feature in this bibliography is an annotated list of periodicals; a checklist of Haitian monographs 1970-1979 extends the time coverage of the retrospective bibliographies by Max Bissainthe. *Dictionnaire de bibliographie haitienne*. - Washington, DC: Scarecrow Press, 1951. (OCLC: 1416029) and the supplement *Dictionnaire de bibliographie haitienne premier supplement*. - Metuchen, NJ : Scarecrow, 1973. (OCLC: 1028483) which cover the time period 1764-1949, and 1950-1970 with updates for pre-1950, respectively.

Notes Bibliographiques Caraibes (ISSN 0180-4103) includes Haiti within its scope.

CURRENT LEGAL DEPOSIT LAWS: "A law makes it compulsory for printers to deposit with the Department of Interior books and brochures published in Haiti. There are also laws covering the deposit of official documents."[1] This law is not effective.

HONDURAS

TITLE: *Anuario bibliográfico hondureño*. - 1961-   . - Tegucigalpa : Ministerio de Cultura y Turismo, Dirección General de Cultura, Biblioteca Nacional, 1963-   .
Annual, some issues combined; interrupted 1972-1979.
Publisher varies.
1961 issued originally under title *Anuario bibliográfico*; later reissued in 1961-1971 cumulated volume as *Anuario bibliográfico hondureño*.
DDC: 015.7283/034; LC: Z1471.H6; LCCN: 86-640122//r912
ISSN 0570-3948

COMPILER: 1981/1983, Luis Roberto Castellanos, Director, Biblioteca Nacional; earlier volumes compiled by Miguel Angel García.

SCOPE AND COVERAGE: *Anuario Bibliográfico Hondureño* (*ABH*) lists works published in Honduras during the period covered. Although it is not specifically stated in the introduction, the bibliography is compiled from titles deposited at the Biblioteca Nacional according to the legal deposit law.

---

[1] Pomassl, *Survey of Existing Legal Deposit Laws*, p. 38. There is no citation of a current law in *International Guide to Legal Deposit*.

Types of publications included in *ABH* are books, pamphlets, official and government publications, university publications, dissertations, textbooks. Mimeographed titles are also listed.

Not included within the scope of *ABH* are audio-visual materials, microforms, maps, and periodicals.

CONTENTS: For 1981/1983: "presentación," bibliography.

CATALOGUING RULES AND CLASSIFICATION SCHEMES USED: The cataloguing rules are not stated. Basic bibliographic information is given, although this information is not presented in AACR2 format.

No classification scheme is used in the volume for 1981-1983.

ENTRY INFORMATION: Author, title, place of publication, publisher, date, pagination. If the title is not published, the term "mimeografiado" is used in place of the publisher. A thesis is usually identified by the word "tesis" before the date.

ARRANGEMENT: For 1981/1983: the arrangement is chronological, and then is arranged alphabetical by author.

INDEXES: No index in the 1981/1983 volume.

NOTES AND COMMENTS: Miguel Angel García, former Director of the Biblioteca Nacional, was responsible for editing *Anuario Bibliográfico Hondureño* 1961-1971. - Tegucigalpa : Banco Central de Honduras, 1971. Originally issued annually, these volumes were superseded by the 1961-1971 cumulation issued to commemorate the 152nd anniversary of the independence of Honduras. This title includes entries arranged chronologically, then arranged by DDC, and finally arranged alphabetically under the subject. Books, pamphlets, periodicals, bulletins, government publications (from 1963), mimeographed reports, and newspapers are included within the scope. Information about ceased periodicals is listed separately. Information given for entries is author, title, place of publication, publisher, date, pagination, size, and illustrations. Occasional notes are given, but no price, or subject information is mentioned. In 1965, government publications were separately listed after the classification scheme. The 1961 issue was originally titled *Anuario Bibliográfico*.

ABH was in hiatus from 1972-1979. During these years Honduras was not covered by an official current national bibliography. There have been several attempts by bibliographers to fill this void and also to complement *ABH*. Although some of these should be considered retrospective national bibliographies, an attempt to fit these bibliographic tools into a chronological pattern which covers from the present time back to 1620 is as follows.[1]

---

[1] Information received by the author in a telephone conversation 22 August 1986 from Rachel Miller, Latin American Specialist, Watson Library, University of Kansas indicated that during her trip to Honduras in the summer of 1984 she had a conversation with Luis Roberto Castellanos, Director of the Biblioteca Nacional, who indicated that he was planning to compile a bibliography for the years 1972-1979.

Since the early 1980's there have been two bibliographies published in Honduras with the exact same title. One is compiled by the Biblioteca Nacional as described above; the second is compiled by Mario Argueta. *Anuario bibliográfico hondureño.* - 1980-   . - Tegucigalpa : Universidad Nacional Autónoma de Honduras, Sistema Bibliotecario, 1982-   . This work lists titles acquired by the Universidad Nacional Autónoma de Honduras. It is supplemented with bibliographical information from authors, publishers, libraries, etc. ("Presentación"). Types of publications include books, pamphlets, official and government publications, periodicals, and university publications. Contents for the 1981/1982 volume include the "presentación," books listed by author and by subject, government publications listed by author and by subject, periodical publications listed by issuing agency. These bibliographic sections are repeated for each of the two years included. At the end is an addendum for books printed in 1980 that were not listed in the *ABH* for 1980. The cataloguing rules are not stated; information is not presented in AACR2 format, but the basic bibliographic information of author, title, place of publication, publisher, date, series is given. No classification scheme is used; however, in the subject bibliography, broad subjects are alphabetically arranged. Arrangement is chronological by type of publication and by author and subject. Authors and broad subjects are alphabetically arranged in the books and in the government publications sections. Periodical publications are arranged alphabetically by the issuing agency. The 1980 volume is arranged by author and by subject. Although there is no index, the bibliographic entries are listed in an author and a subject approach. The latest volume examined is for 1981/1982, published in 1985, and received as a personal copy by John Hébert, Assistant Chief, Hispanic Division, Library of Congress.[1] Two advantages of Argueta's publication over the one compiled by the Biblioteca Nacional are the inclusion of periodicals and the subject approach of the bibliographic listings. Neither of these is apparent in the 1981/1983 volume compiled by the Biblioteca Nacional.

Before the 1980 volume of *ABH*, Jorge Fidel Durón published "Las Publicaciones Hondureñas de [   ]" in the *Boletín de la Academia Hondureña de la Lengua* (ISSN 0065-0471; OCLC: 3248828) for a number of years.[2] This bibliography includes works published in Honduras during the time period covered. It also includes bibliographic sources published abroad which list Honduran works.

An earlier title done by Jorge Fidel Durón which helps assimilate the Honduran imprints is *Indice de la Bibliografía Hondureña.* - Tegucigalpa : Imprenta Calderón, 1946 which largely supersedes, but not completely, the *Repertorio Bibliográfico Hondureño.* - Tegucigalpa: Imprenta Calderón, 1943 done by the same author (OCLC: 1416298). He also wrote bibliographic essays from time to time which appeared in *Honduras Rotaria* (LCCN: 54-31305;

---

[1] According to information received in a letter dated 21 June 1986 from Mario Argueta to the author he is compiling information for a 1983-1984 volume.

[2] The earliest citation found for this list is in *HLAS* (no. 38), entry 78. This compilation is for the year 1971, published in 1972. Continuing citations are given in the national bibliography list issued by SALALM. The latest citations seen are in Lionel V. Loroña. *Bibliography of Latin American and Caribbean Bibliographies 1987-1988*, entry no. 103 and 104 for the years 1984 and 1985.

OCLC: 3734409) and included books, government publications and periodicals for the year covered.[1]

A retrospective bibliography done by Miguel Angel García is *Bibliografía Hondureña.* - Tegucigalpa : Banco Central de Honduras, 1971-1972 (2 vols.). Volume 1 covers 1620-1930, volume 2 covers 1931-1960 (OCLC: 33175416). The *ABH* 1961-1971 continues this work.

Official publications are listed in *La Gaceta.*[2]

LATEST ISSUE EXAMINED/CURRENCY: The 1981/1983 copy examined was collected personally in the summer of 1984 from the Biblioteca Nacional by Rachel Miller, Latin American Specialist, Watson Library, University of Kansas. This is the latest volume examined and, as far as the author can determine, the latest volume issued.

Entries are from the years covered.

AUTOMATION: not automated.

FORMAT AND SERVICES AVAILABLE: *ABH*, compiled by Biblioteca Nacional, is a duplicated list.

CURRENT LEGAL DEPOSIT LAWS: Law of 20 July 1958.[3] This law is not effective.

AVAILABLE FROM: Biblioteca Nacional de Honduras, Ave. Cristobal Colón, Calle "Salvador Mendieta," POB 1117, Tegucigalpa.

VERIFIER: no reply received.

HONG KONG

TITLE: *A Catalogue of books printed in Hong Kong. Special supplement number 4 to the Hong Kong Government Gazette.* - Oct./ Dec. 1964-   . - Hong Kong : H. Meyers, Government Printer, 1965-   .
Quarterly.
DDC: not found; LC (090): J8.B55a suppl. 4; LCCN: not found; OCLC: 2434873
ISSN not found

COMPILER: New Territories Public Libraries, Cultural Services Department.

---

[1] "Los Libros y Publicaciones de 1960" appeared in *Honduras Rotaria* for May/June 1961; "Los Libros y Publicaciones de 1967" appeared in *Honduras Rotaria* in Feb./April 1968. These were cited in Zimmerman. *Current National Bibliographies of Latin America*, p. 83.
[2] *BSTW, 1975-1979*, p. 227.
[3] Ibid., p. 226.

SCOPE AND COVERAGE: *A Catalogue of Books Printed in Hong Kong. Special Supplement Number 4 to the Hong Kong Government Gazette* (*CBPHK*) includes the publishing output of Hong Kong which is deposited according to legal deposit legislation. Titles printed in Hong Kong for foreign publishers are also included.

Types of publications include books, pamphlets, periodicals (first issues and title changes or a first issue of a periodical originally printed outside Hong Kong), official and government publications, musical scores, and reprints.

Excluded are separate bills, ordinances, regulations, leaflets, loose-sheets, posters, periodicals (except first issue and title change or first issue of periodicals originally printed outside Hong Kong).

CONTENTS: [Brief introduction], abbreviations list, bibliography.

The fourth quarter includes an annual index and a periodicals supplement.

CATALOGUING RULES AND CLASSIFICATION SCHEMES USED: Cataloguing rules followed are AACR2 and ISBD(M). An exception to AACR2 is made for publications issued by the Hong Kong Government Departments which are entered under the name of the departments. The Liu cataloguing scheme (modified) is used for Chinese books.

A classification scheme is not used.

ENTRY INFORMATION: Consecutive serial number, author, title, edition, place of publication, pagination, size, series, statement, notes including ISBN, price, binding information; legal deposit number in lower right corner, e.g., HK83-1611.

The Periodicals list includes English title, Chinese title, frequency, language, price, publisher, the numbers deposited and the dates of the issues. At the end of this list is a list of Chinese titles.

ARRANGEMENT: The bibliography is arranged in two sections: English and Chinese. The English section is arranged alphabetically by the main entry; the Chinese section is arranged by stroke sequence.

The annual list of periodicals deposited in the period covered includes English titles alphabetically arranged and Chinese titles arranged by stroke. Supplement to *Gazette* no. 6, vol. CXXXV (12 February 1993) is a bibliographic compilation of Chinese and English periodicals deposited in 1991. The publishers' names and addresses, and printers' names and addresses are given in separate listings. Separate English and Chinese indexes follow.

INDEXES: Quarterly issues do not include an index. Annual cumulated indexes are given in the fourth quarter issue. In the 1982 issue English author index, Chinese author index (arranged by strokes), printers' name and address (English first, then Chinese), publishers' name and address (English first, then Chinese), periodicals deposited in 1982 under terms of Ordinance. Numbers refer to the serial number in the upper left corner of the entry information.

NOTES AND COMMENTS: Government publications are not designated by a symbol. Only by looking at the imprint is one able to determine whether it is a government publication, since not all titles are listed under Hong Kong and the issuing agency.

The Chinese titles of periodicals deposited includes the English translation of Chinese periodical titles. This is a helpful source of information for librarians, researchers and other people who could benefit from a translation of the Chinese title, or who need to see a visual image of the Chinese title and its English equivalent.

In looking through several years of the *Hong Kong Government Gazette*, no particular pattern for the appearance of the "Catalogue of Books" was apparent.

The user of the "Catalogue of Books" would benefit from a more detailed introduction. An expanded explanation of the scope and contents, and an analyzed entry would be helpful.

Besides the listing of the *CBPHK*, the *Hong Kong Government Gazette* includes other recurring lists such as lists of dental practioners.

LATEST ISSUE EXAMINED/CURRENCY: Entries are for the period covered in the *CBPHK*.

The latest number examined was 11 June 1993 received by the University Library, Cambridge, England, on 19 July 1993. An average of one to two months elapses between the date of publication of *Hong Kong Government Gazette* and the date of receipt. However, the time lag between the imprints in the *CBHK* and the date of appearance in the *Special Supplement No. 4* is substantial, although variable. The supplement to *Gazette* no. 6/1993 (vol. CXXXV) lists imprints for 1991.

AUTOMATION: not known

FORMAT AND SERVICES AVAILABLE: printed

CURRENT LEGAL DEPOSIT LAWS: Books Registration Ordinance (Chap. 142) of the Laws of Hong Kong.

AVAILABLE FROM: *Ulriches International Periodicals Directory* for 1994/95 gives the following subscription address: Director of Information Services, Information Services Dept., 1 Battery Path, G-F, Central, Hong Kong.

VERIFIER: no verification requested.

HUNGARY

TITLE: *Magyar nemzeti bibliográfia. Könyvek bibliográfiája. - 32.évf. 16.füz. (31 Aug. 1977)* - . - Budapest : Országos Széchényi Könyvtár, 1977- .
Fortnightly (twenty-four issues per year), with annual cumulative index until 1991.

Continues *Magyar nemzeti bibliográfia = Bibliographia Hungarica* (Jan./March 1946-15 Aug. 1977) monthly (1947-1960), quarterly (1946), ISSN 0373-1766.
DDC: 015.439; LC: Z2141.M258; LCCN: 78-644066//r912; OCLC: 4710012
ISSN 0133-6843

COMPILER: Országos Széchényi Könyvtár.

SCOPE AND COVERAGE: *Magyar Nemzeti Bibliográfia. Könyvek Bibliográfiája (MNB.K)* [Hungarian National Bibliography. Bibliography of Books] includes titles published in Hungary deposited at the National Széchényi Library through legal deposit.

Types of publications listed in *MNB.K* are books, brochures (of at least A5 size), official publications, and printed theses. First issues and title changes of serials and annuals are published in *Magyar Nemzeti Bibliográfia. Új Periodikumok* [Hungarian National Bibliography. Bibliography of New Periodicals] in the monthly supplement to the Bibliography of Books (ISSN 1219-6835). Maps and atlases are published in the *MNB.K* as a quarterly appendix under the title *Térképek bibliográfiája.*

Omitted from *MNB.K* are school books, textbooks and materials of primary adult education, offprints (except those published in series), trade literature, standards (except collected editions), patents, propaganda publications and ephemera, exhibition catalogues (except permanent collections), research reports, fold-out booklets, and dimension picture books.

CONTENTS: Until 1992, the first issue of the year included: contents, guide to the bibliography, list of subject groups, alphabetical index of subject groups, list of abbreviations, list of abbreviations of publishers' names in the publication area, list of Hungarian publishers, index of ISBN prefixes of Hungarian publishers, classified bibliography; alphabetical index, index of standard numbers, subject contents. All issues included explanatory prefaces in Hungarian, English, German, and Russian, classified bibliography, alphabetical index of authors and titles, and an ISBN, ISSN index. Serials appear in a monthly appendix, and descriptions of maps and atlases appear four times a year.

With the change from an external computer center to the online integrated library system, which does not have an output program for producing the national bibliography, temporary changes to the national bibliography are necessary. Since 1992, contents include "For our users' attention," and an alphabetical list of newly published books deposited at the national library.

CATALOGUING RULES AND CLASSIFICATION SCHEMES USED: For decisions on headings for bibliographic entries the national standard family MSZ 3423 Leíró katalógusok bibliográfiai tételeinek szerkesztése [Choice of headings for descriptive catalogues], for the form of heading, prescriptions of the national standard family MSZ 3440 A bibliográfiai leírás besorolási adatai [Heading elements of the bibliographic description] are followed; entries are arranged by national standard MSZ 3401 A bibliográfiai tételek betürendbe sorolásának szabályai [Bibliographic filing rules]; the data elements and punctuation of the bibliographic description are defined by national standards MSZ 3424/1 Bibliográfiai leirás. Könyvek [Bibliographic description. Monographic publications] and MSZ 3424/2 Bibliográfiai leírás. Időszaki kiadványok [Bibliographic description. Serials]. All national bibliographic standards are based on ISO standards, ISBD and IFLA guidelines.

Data elements for an entry written in a non-Latin alphabet are transliterated according to ISO standards and standard drafts. Abbreviations follow MSZ 3432 Szavak és szókapcsolatok røoviditése a bibliográfiai leírásban [Abbreviation of words and compound terms used in bibliographic description]. Subject content information is based on the Hungarian adaptation of the Universal Decimal Classification, and on the series of "Extensions and Corrections to the Universal Decimal Classification."

The classification scheme used is UDC.

ENTRY INFORMATION: Entry number, author/contributor, title, place of publication, publisher, date, pagination, illustrations, size, series statement, brief notes including language, ISBN and/or ISSN, UDC number. Since April 1992, an identification number has been added at the end of the items, e.g., [*MNB KB* 94768]. This number is given automatically by the software DOBIS/LIBIS. Also additional filing information is given at the end of the bibliographic descriptions with abbreviations, e.g., Tft. [other main entries], Mt. [added entries].

An incorrect ISBN is printed ISBN [! ISBN.....(corrected ISBN)]. When there is no standard number printed on the publication, the Hungarian ISBN agency assigns it and it is shown as ISBN (ISBN.....*).

ARRANGEMENT: Entries of the bibliography are alphabetically arranged within subject groups according to UDC. Since April 1992, when use of DOBIS/LIBIS began, it has been necessary to tailor the acquisition list program to publish up-to-date lists of newly published books while work is done on a compatible output program. These lists are arranged alphabetically.

INDEXES: An alphabetical index of authors, contributors, titles, series and subjects is in each issue, cumulating in an annual index. Numbers refer the user to the entry numbers which are consecutive throughout the year. Data elements of secondary entries appear in the index. During the temporary phase beginning in 1992, no indexes are provided.

NOTES AND COMMENTS: From 1992 there has been a modification in the structure and publishing of the national bibliography while the National Széchényi Library develops an output program compatible with the integrated system. In order to continue providing current service for newly published material, it has been necessary to arrange the entries alphabetically, provide no indexing, attach identification numbers at the end of the entries, include no separate entries about series, put additional filing information at the end of the bibliographic descriptions (Tft: other main entries, Mt.: added entries), and the list does not include analyzed entries for collections. "Bibliography of new periodicals" and "Bibliography of maps" are regularly published appendixes.

Prior to this, the first issue of the year includes a detailed guide to use of the bibliography, a list of abbreviations, a list of publishers in Hungary in addition to the classified bibliography.

Each bibliography has a brief explanation of standards used in cataloguing entries, and other helpful notes. Since 1992, these explanations appear in Hungarian and English. Previously, the explanations appear in Hungarian, English, German and Russian.

The Acquisitions & Cataloguing Division, in addition to producing the national bibliography, also maintains the Hungarian ISBN agency (since 1974) and Hungarian ISSN Agency (since 1976) which allocate international standard numbers. The first ISBN appeared in the volume for 1975.

There is no separate listing of government publications. The best approach in identifying publications is through the index. By looking under issuing agencies, a user is able to pinpoint entries included in that issue of the national bibliography, and then use the entry number to gain complete bibliographical information.

The printed annual cumulation is entitled *Magyar Könyvészet: A Magyarországon megjelent könyvek bibliográfiája.* [Hungarian bibliography: Bibliography of books published in Hungary]. 1961/1962-1991. Budapest : Országos Széchényi Könyvtár, 1963-1992. Annual. (ISSN 0133-3496). This will no longer be published in printed form. The first cumulated CD-ROM version was published in 1994, and its regular publishing update began in 1996.

Since 1996 a floppy version of the national bibliography appears which includes the same bibliographic entries as that of the printed issues. The records are in HUNMARC data exchange format and in ISO 2709 record format on the disks. The floppy version can be subscribed with four types of character sets: extended IBM 852, extended ASCII (OCLC), ISO 8859/1, ISO 8859/2.[1]

Bibliographic information on the floppy version is as follows: *Könyvek nemzeti bibliográfiája floppyn* [computer file] [Hungarian national bibliography of books on floppies]. -1.évf. 1.sz. = 51.évf. 1.sz. (1996-   ). - Budapest : Országos Széchényi Könyvtár, 1996-   . Fortnightly (24 floppies a year). (ISSN 1219-6444).

Bibliographic information on the CD-ROM version is as follows: *Magyar nemzeti bibliográfia. Könyvek* [computer file] = *Hungarian national bibliography. Books.* - CD-ROM. - 1976/1991- . Budapest : Országos Széchényi Könyvtár, 1994-   . Frequency varies (ISSN 1218-2192). It is planned that next year's edition [1995] will include bibliographic records covering the years 1992-1995. Beginning in 1996, the CD-ROM added database information for *MNB. Időszaki kiadványok bibliográfiája.*[2]

The national bibliography for Hungary is divided into several parts. For this guide, only the main series has been annotated. Other parts of the current national bibliography of Hungary are listed below.

Hungarika irodalmi szemle. [Selected bibliography of articles related to Hungary published abroad]. - 6.évf, 1.füz. (Jan./March 1977)-19évf. 4.füz. (Oct./Dec. 1989). -.Budapest : Országos Széchényi Könyvtár, 1977-1989. Quarterly (LCCN: 77-644966//r85; LC: Z2143.H84; DB906; OCLC: 3719474; ISSN 0133-7505). Preceding title: *Hungarica külföldi folyóiratszemle*

---

[1] Information from a letter dated 26 August 1996 to the author from Susanne Berke, Head of Acquisitions and Cataloguing Division, National Szévhényl Library.

[2] "Preface," HNB/CD Hungarian National Bibliography. Books on CD-ROM = Magyar Nemzeti Bibliográfia Könyvek CD-ROM Adatbázisa. User Manual. 1994, and from Susanne Berke's letter of 1 October 1996 to the author.

[Repertory of serials published abroad in Hungarian language]. - Budapest : Országos Széchényi Könyvtár, 1971-1976. From 1990, title changed to *Magyar nemzeti bibliográfia. Külföldön megjelenö hungarikumok. Cikkek*, with the first volumes appearing at the end of 1996.[1]

Külföldi magyar nyelvü kiadványok. [Hungarian publications published abroad in Hungarian language]. - 6.évf. 1.füz. (Jan./March 1977)- 9.évf. 4.füz. (Oct./Dec. 1989). - Budapest : Országos Széchényi Könyvtár, 1977-1989. Quarterly (ISSN 0133-333X). Preceding title: *Külföldi magyar nyelvü folyóiratok repertóriuma* [Repertory of serials published abroad in Hungarian language]. 1976. Preceding supplement to the *Külföldi folyóiratok repertóriuma*, 1972-1975. From 1990, title changes to *Magyar nemzeti bibliográfia. Külföldön megjelenö hungarikumok. Könyvek*, with the first volumes appearing at the end of 1996.[2]

Magyar nemzeti bibliográfia. Idöszaki kiadványok bibliográfiája [Hungarian national bibliography. Bibliography of serials]. - 1981-1990. - Budapest : Országos Széchényi Könyvtár, 1983-1994. Annual (LCCN: sc85-008204; OCLC: 10418181; ISSN 0231-4592). Beginning in 1996 this title is continued on the *MNB* CD-ROM which then includes information about both books and serials. Preceding title: *Kurrens idöszaki kiadványok* [Current serials in Hungary]. Budapest : Országos Széchényi Könyvtár, 1976-1980. Annual. (LCCN: 78-649891//r85; LC: Z6956.H8K87; PN5355.H8; OCLC: 4562169; ISSN 0134-0247).

Magyar nemzeti bibliográfia. Idöszaki kiadványok repertóriuma. [Hungarian national bibliography. Repertory of serials]. - 32.évf. 15.füz. (15 Aug. 1977)- . - Budapest : Országos Széchényi Könyvtár, 1977- . Monthly (ISSN 0133-6894). Preceding title: *Magyar folyóiratok repertóriuma. Repertorium bibliographicum periodicorum Hungaricum.* [Repertory of Hungarian Serials]. - Budapest : Országos Széchényi Könyvtár, 1945-1977. Fortnightly. (LCCN: sn84-46274; OCLC: 1590112; ISSN 0025-0112).

Magyar nemzeti bibliográfia. Zenemüvek bibliográfiáya [Hungarian national bibliography. Bibliography of music scores and records]. - 8.évf. 3.füz. (30 Sept. 1977)- . - Budapest : Országos Széchényi Könyvtár, 1977- . Quarterly (ISSN 0133-5782). Supplement to the *Magyar nemzeti bibliográfia. Kónyvek bibliográfiája* until 1994. Preceding title: *Magyar zenemüvek bibliográfiája.* [Hungarian bibliography of music]. - Budapest: Országos Széchényi Könyvtár, 1970-1977.

Two parts of the national bibliography which have ceased are listed below.

A Magyar bibliográfiák bibliográfiája. [Bibliography of Hungarian bibliographies]. 1956/1957-1974/1976. - Budapest : Országos Széchényi Könyvtár, 1960-1979. Frequency varies. Ceased (ISSN 0541-9093).

Magyar könyvészet. Tankönyvek. [Hungarian bibliography. Textbooks]. 1965/1966-1971/1972. - Budapest : Országos Széchényi Könyvtár,1968-1976. Frequency varies. Ceased (ISSN 0133-4611).

---

[1] Berke letter.
[2] Ibid.

A cumulation of books from years preceding 1961 and the addition of the year 1945 was published as *Magyar könyvészet: A Magyarországon nyomtatott könyvek szakosított jegyzékee* [Hungarian bibliography: Classified list of books printed in Hungary]. 1945-1960. vol. 1-5. Budapest : Országos Széchényi Könyvtár, 1964-1968.

LATEST ISSUE EXAMINED/CURRENCY: The latest issue examined was for 1 March 1996 at the University of Illinois, Urbana-Champaign in June 1996. The Országos Széchényi Könyvtár should be commended on efforts to keep the bibliographic information current even though it is not in the format they would prefer. It is anticipated that the 1997 *MNB* will be prepared using the new program.

AUTOMATION: The acquisitions list program is produced using the computer centre of the national library. The national library has the NEKTAR system (Integrated Information System) from 1990. The library installed an IBM 9221/150 mainframe computer and the DOBIS/LIBIS integrated library system. From the database of books, which serves as the OPAC, the data file of new records can be downloaded regularly. The format of printed issues are produced from this file by using a PC program developed by the library's programmers.[1]

FORMAT AND SERVICES AVAILABLE: printed; CD-ROM; floppy. Database of books published from 1992 online (OPAC for library users); Internet access via http://www.oszk.hu/mnbkb/

CURRENT LEGAL DEPOSIT LAWS: Legal deposit was first established on 28 December 1802. The most recent legal deposit legislation is A müvelödési miniszter 17/1986. (VIII.20.) MM számú rendelete 700/1986. (Müv. K. 18.) MM számú irányelv. A new legal deposit law is under preparation.[2]

AVAILABLE FROM: Országos Széchényi Könyvtár [National Széchényi Library], H-1827 Budapest, Budávri Palota F-épület.

SELECTED ARTICLES: Benyei, M. "A kurrens magyar nemzeti bibliografia otven eve" [Fifty years of the Hungarian current national bibliography]. *Könyvtari figyelö* 42 (3 1996):391-402.

Berke, Barnabásné. *A kurrens Magyars Nemzeti Bibliográfiai rendszer mai problémái* [Current issues of the Hungarian National Bibliography system]. In *Könyvtári figyelö* 41 (5 1995):585-590.

Berke, Susanne. "Hungarian National Bibliography." Paper delivered at the International Conference on Library Automation in Central & Eastern Europe, April 11-13, 1996, Budapest, Hungary. (publication forthcoming)

---

[1] Ibid, and from S. Berke. "Hungarian National Bibliography," unpublished talk given at the International Conference on Library Automation in Central & Eastern Europe, April 11-13, 1996. p. 6.
[2] *International Guide to Legal Deposit*, p. 82. Ms. Berke mentioned in her August 1996 letter that a new legal deposit law is under preparation; it is hoped that it will be accepted by the Hungarian Parliament by the end of 1996.

VERIFIER: Susanne Berke, Head of Acquisitions and Cataloguing Division, Országos Széchényi Könyvtár.

ICELAND

TITLE: *Íslensk bókaskrá = The Icelandic national bibliography*. - 1974-   . - Reykjavík : Landsbókasafn Íslands, 1975-   .
Annual, with five year cumulations.
Supplement issued separately: Íslensk Hljóðritaskrá = *Bibliography of Icelandic sound recordings*.
DDC: 015.491/2 19; LC: Z2590.A3I84; LCCN: 83-645423; 83-645424; OCLC: 2134340; 8839969
ISSN 0254-1378

COMPILER: Útgáfu annast Landsbókasafn Íslands, Háskólabókasafu Skráningardeild [The National and University Library of Iceland. Cataloguing Department]. The change in the compiler's name from The National Library of Iceland to the above became effective 1 December 1994.

SCOPE AND COVERAGE: *Íslensk Bókaskrá = The Icelandic National Bibliography* (*INB*) lists titles published in Iceland and deposited at the National and University Library according to the legal deposit legislation, and titles printed abroad for Icelandic publishers.

Works about Iceland published elsewhere and foreign translations of Icelandic works are not included.[1]

Types of publications included in *INB* are books, pamphlets (of more than five pages), official and government publications, theses and dissertations, research reports, new serials and serials with title changes, handbooks, maps and charts, offprints, annual publications that are regarded as handbooks, musical scores, standards, sound recordings. (Since 1979 sound recordings are listed in the supplement.)

From 1974-1978 periodicals and newspapers were not included in the annual volumes; however, they were included in the first five year cumulation for the years 1974-1978.

Excluded are ephemeral materials (unless of unusual importance), IGO publications, and items less than five pages (unless they belong to a catalogued series).

CONTENTS: Contents (in Icelandic and in English), preface (in Icelandic and in English), abbreviations and unabbreviated terms, list of publishers, books: statistical summaries, alphabetical section, classified section; serials: new titles; maps and charts.

CATALOGUING RULES AND CLASSIFICATION SCHEMES USED: The book description follows ISBD(M). Serial entries follows ISBD(S). Maps and charts follow

---

[1] *Guide to Nordic Bibliography*, Supplement 1, #18.

ISBD(CM). Recordings are according to ISBD(NBM). The main entries are chosen according to AACR2.

The classification scheme used is DDC (20th ed.); only a few variations which are common practice in Icelandic libraries are used. ("Preface," 1992, p. 6)

ENTRY INFORMATION: Author, title, edition statement, place of publication, publisher, date, pagination, illustrations, size, notes, price in lower left corner, six digit computer identification number (in italics) and the classification number, preceded by a square bracket, e.g., [808.81, in lower right corner; ISBN.

A plus sign (+) indicates that the title may have more than one classification number assigned to it. An asterisk (*) indicates that the classification number has been revised since the preliminary edition. The juvenile books are marked with a "B" before the classification number.

ARRANGEMENT: Books are arranged in an alphabetical list and in a classified list. Serials are arranged alphabetically by main entry; maps and charts are alphabetical by title.

Juvenile books are placed at the end of the classified section.

INDEXES: No separate index for *INB*. However, there is access to the entries through alphabetical and classified arrangement. The Supplement has an index.

NOTES AND COMMENTS: According to the preface, the *INB* is published in three stages: a preliminary edition appears in a monthly order list from "Thjónustumiðstöð bokasafna," published as a photocopy after a list from the National and University Library of Iceland; an annual volume subsequently published by the National and University Library of Iceland, and a five year cumulation.

Selected information from the annual bibliography appeared 10 December 1983 as a supplement to *Morgunblaðið* under the title "Bækur 1983" sponsored by the Icelandic Publishers' Association, but it ceased in 1987.[1]

The volume for 1979 introduces computerization of the *INB*, the new serials section and the supplement which lists recordings.

The supplement information is as follows: *Íslensk Hljóðritaskrá = Bibliography of Icelandic sound recordings* / Útgáfu annast Landsbókasafn Íslands. Skráningardeild. Fylgir Íslenskri bókaskrá. Reykjavík : Landsbókasafn Íslands Háskólabókasafu, 1980- . (DDC: 016.7899/12/094912; LC: ML156.2.I84; LCCN: 83-64-5422/MN; OCLC: 7634062; ISSN 0254-4067). The scope includes disks, cassettes, and compact disks. New serial titles and titles not received in time for an earlier volume are included. Contents: Preface, abbreviations and unabbreviated terms, record publishers, recordings, index. The numbers in the index refer to the entry number. The recordings section is alphabetical by main entry.

---

[1] "Preface," *INB* 1983, p. 5. Cessation information was in a 6 March 1995 note from H. G. Eythórsdottir, the editor of *Íslensk Bókaskrá.*

The statistical summaries are based on the items published in Iceland and received at the National and University Library according to the legal deposit legislation. Offprints and works printed in Iceland for foreign publishers are not included in the statistical summaries. Revisions of statistical summaries for previous years are included if necessary. The numbers in each column indicate volumes, not titles. Books are defined as having forty-nine pages or more, pamphlets, five to forty-eight pages.

The most complete information is found in the alphabetical section.

Entries for Icelandic names are under their given names, not under surnames or patronymics. In filing, a second forename and/or a patronymic given before a family name is ignored unless two or more authors have the same first forename and patronymic or family name.

Entries are entered under the main classification number as well as other numbers assigned to the volume.

The national bibliography of Iceland for the period 1887-1943 was listed in *Ritaukaskrá Landsbókasafnsins* [the *Accessions Catalogue of the National Library*]. *INB* is a continuation of "Íslenzk rit" which was included in the *Arbok Landsbókasfn Íslands* for the years 1945-1975 and the Booksellers' Association *Bókaskrá Bókaslafélags Íslands*, 1937-1973.[1]

Official publications are not designated by any special symbol.

Five year cumulations are available for 1974-1978, 1979-1983 (published 1992), and 1984-1988 (published 1994).

LATEST ISSUE EXAMINED/CURRENCY: The latest volume of *INB* examined in September 1997 at the Bibliotekstjänst AB Library is for 1995 published in 1996. Entries are for the year covered, as well as earlier publications which were not received in time for inclusion in previous issues.

Volumes were scheduled for publication as follows: 1992 volume in March 1995, 1993 volume in May 1995, 1994 volume in August 1995, 1995 volume in 1996.[2]

AUTOMATION: Introduced with the 1979 volume. From the volume for 1992, the library is using a new computer system called Libertas (Bristol, England). The Icelandic name for the computer system is "Gegnir".

FORMAT AND SERVICES AVAILABLE: Printed. The database, which includes entries from 1880 to the present, is searchable online using Libertas through a modem connection, and is also available at the following Internet address: saga@bok.hi.is Soon it is anticipated that *INB* may be available on CD-ROM disks.

---

1 *Guide to Reference Books* (11th), AA720, p. 80.
2 Contract agreements between the National and University Library of Iceland and the printing company Steinholt Ltd.

CURRENT LEGAL DEPOSIT LAWS: Law No. 43/1977, the Legal Deposit Act. (Preface, 1991, p. 5)

AVAILABLE FROM: The National Library and University of Iceland, Arngrímsgata 3, 107 Reykjavík.

SELECTED ARTICLES: Hannesdóttir, Sigrún Klara. "The National Bibliography of Iceland," *Guide to Nordic Bibliography*, pp. 34-36.

VERIFIER: Hildur G. Eythorsdóttir (editor).

INDIA

TITLE: *Indian national bibliography*. - Oct./Dec. 1957-   . - Calcutta : Central Reference Library, 1958-   .
Frequency varies: monthly, with annual cumulation (1984-1987, 1989-   ); biannual (1980-1981, 1982-1983); annual (1978, 1979); monthly, with annual cumulation (1964-1977 except 1968-1970); quarterly, with annual cumulation (1958-1963).
DDC: 015.54; LC: Z3201.A2I5; LCCN: sa68-6846//r892; OCLC: 1645018
ISSN 0019-6002

COMPILER: Central Reference Library, Ministry of Human Resource Development. Department of Culture.

SCOPE AND COVERAGE: The *Indian National Bibliography* (*INB*) lists India's current publishing output in fourteen major Indian languages including English which are received by the National Library, Calcutta according to the legal deposit legislation.

Types of publications included are books, pamphlets, annual reports, periodicals and newspapers (first issue or title changes), official and government publications, theses and dissertations (if printed).

Excluded from *INB* are maps, musical scores, periodicals and newspapers (except first issues or title changes), keys and guides to textbooks, telephone directories, trade catalogues, company reports, brochures, IGO publications, etc. The monthly issues do not specify these exclusions in the preface.

CONTENTS: Monthly: preface, abbreviations and language symbols, classified bibliography, author and title index, subject index.

Annual: table of contents, preface, outline of DDC, transliteration tables, bibliography, Colon classification scheme, list of publishers, text of the legal deposit law, language fascicles, subscription rates.

CATALOGUING RULES AND CLASSIFICATION SCHEMES USED: AACR2 is followed since January 1988 with little modification.

DDC (19th ed.) is used since January 1988 with little modification. The Colon Classification number (6th ed.) is also assigned to each entry.

ENTRY INFORMATION: DDC number with DDC headings given at the beginning of each different number, author (dates of birth and death if known), title, statement of responsibility, place of publication, publisher, date, pagination, illustrations, size, series statement, notes, ISBN/ISSN when it appears in the document, the nature of binding, and price. The Colon number is located at lower right corner. The language of the book is indicated by a symbol enclosed in parentheses in the lower left corner of the entry information, e.g. (H) for Hindi, (T) for Tamil, (E) for English.

ARRANGEMENT: The bibliography is arranged by the DDC classification system.

INDEXES: Author and title index; subject index. Numbers refer to the DDC number in the classified bibliography. Prior to 1974, the index was combined into one.[1]

NOTES AND COMMENTS: "The *INB* is not only a bibliographical tool, but also a potential source and instrument of national integration. It cuts across state boundaries, languages, sex, religion and political beliefs and economic conditions of the Indian population and contributes to national solidarity. The outside world depends to a large extent on this vital tool for information or on the intellectual activity and output, and recorded and codified information."[2]

Multiple scripts representing Indian languages and how to present them in the national bibliography was a problem studied by the creators of *INB*. Eventually it was decided to Romanize the scripts so that authors and titles of books in all Indian languages could be presented in one sequence. Entries are transliterated into Roman script with diacritical marks and then arranged in one alphabetical order under each class. Although this makes the information more accessible to users not familiar with the many scripts, this does not follow ICNB recommendation 6. For *INB*, however, this seems to be a wise decision although additional diacritical marks not easily found in Roman typesetting fonts were needed to distinguish between words spelled alike but with different meanings in the various languages. The use of the symbol in the lower left corner helps to identify the original language of the title which is in the spirit of the ICNB recommendation.

The *INB* is now published by a photo-offset process.

There is no plan at present to publish the *INB* for the years 1968-1970, "though the material for these years is still available in the *INB* offices."[3] Issues for 1988 have not been published with the exception of January 1988.

An analysis of the *INB* shows there are a few features that would be helpful to add. The preface does not indicate the type of publications that are included within its scope. This information

---

[1] The *Indian National Bibliography* 1958-1992, p. 6.

[2] C.G. Viswanathan, "What Ails the Indian National Bibliography?" *Library Association Record* 81 (July 1979):333.

[3] Downing, "The Indian National Bibliography—its Present State and Future Prospects," *Library Resources & Technical Services* 28 (Jan./March 1984):20

may seem to be stating the obvious, but is important information to users of the bibliography. Only by analyzing the titles listed is one able to deduce what may be within the scope. Exclusions are listed in the 1977 annual cumulation, but this information should be repeated in the preface of each issue. A table of contents would be useful to include. A publishers' list would be a helpful addition; if this seems impractical to include in the monthly issues, certainly in the annual cumulations. It was included in the 1977 annual. Other items to consider adding to the monthly issues are the outline of the DDC scheme and the Colon classification explanation. Both would be used by people consulting *INB* issues.

Since 1973 the classified section fo the bibliography appears in one sequence. Previously, the bibliography was in two parts: non-official and official publications.

Government publications are not designated by any symbol. Since 1973 they have been integrated with other publications. The imprints help to identify titles as government publications.

Languages included in the language symbol list are Assamese, Bengali, English, Gujarati, Hindi, Kannada, Malayalam, Marathi, Oriya, Punjabi, Sanskrit, Tamil, Telugu and Urdu.

A quinquennial edition of *INB* entitled *Cumulated Index, 1958-1962* was published in 1970.[1]

AL,SA included India within its scope.

LATEST ISSUE EXAMINED/CURRENCY: Entries analyzed indicated that most were for the year covered or for the previous two years.

The latest monthly issue examined was January 1991 published January 1993 and received January 1994 by the University Library, Cambridge, England. It would be more timely if issues were mailed to libraries as they were published and not mailing two or three issues at once which seems to be the way the University Library, Cambridge receives them. It is important to speed up the availability of *INB* to users. This is especially important for acquisitions and collection purposes; many titles included in *INB* are not printed in large quantities and therefore not available for very long.

AUTOMATION: not automated.

FORMAT AND SERVICES AVAILABLE: printed.

CURRENT LEGAL DEPOSIT LAWS: Delivery of Books (Public Libraries) Act of 1954 and its amendment, Act No. 99 of 1956.

AVAILABLE FROM: Central Reference Library, Ministry of Human Resource Department, Department of Culture, Belvedere, Calcutta-700027.

---

[1] Information included in a letter dated 24 April 1995 to the author from the Librarian, Central Reference Library.

SELECTED ARTICLES: Downing, Joel C. "The Indian National Bibliography—its Present State and Future Prospects." *Library Resources & Technical Services* 28 (Jan./March 1984):20-24.

Downing, Joel C. "Reorganization of the Indian National Bibliography." *SALG Newsletter* (June 1983):1-4.

The Indian National Bibliography, 1958-1992. Calcutta: Granthalaya Pvt. Ltd. for Govt. of India, 1992. [pamphlet]

VERIFIER: Y. Acharya, Librarian, Central Reference Library.

INDONESIA

TITLE: *Bibliografi nasional Indonesia = Indonesian national bibliography.* - 1953-   . - Jakarta : Proyek Pengembangan Perpustakaan, Departemen Pendidikan den Kebudayaan, 1953-   .
Quarterly, with annual cumulations (1978-   ); before 1978, multi-year cumulations: 1973-1977, 1964-1972, 1964-1965, 1945-1963 compiled from several sources.
Publisher varies.
Continues *Catalogus dari buku-buku jang diterbitkan di Indonesia*, 1945/9-1954, published 1950-1955.
Former title: *Berita Bulanan dari Kantor Bibliografi Nasional*;1953-1962 (monthly).
DDC: not found; LC: Z3273.B52; LCCN: not found; OCLC: 3487263
ISSN 0523-1639

COMPILER: Perpustakaan Nasional R.I.

SCOPE AND COVERAGE: *Bibliografi Nasional Indonesia = Indonesian National Bibliography* (*BNI*) lists the publishing output of Indonesia that is acquired by the National Library through gifts, purchases, and exchanges. *BNI* is based on legal deposit legislation since 1990.

Types of publications included in *BNI* are books, pamphlets, official and government publications, periodicals (first issues) and other serials, theses and dissertations (printed only), research reports, conference proceedings, maps and atlases (first issues), music (printed), standards, patent specifications, reviews, reports.

Excluded from *BNI* are theses and dissertations (unless printed), phonorecords, audiovisual materials, artistic prints, articles in periodicals, comics, posters, popular magazines, and other ephemeral which have little informational and historical value.

CONTENTS: Preface (in Indonesian and English), table of contents, abbreviations, Secondary summary of DDC, classified bibliography, author and title index, subject index.

CATALOGUING RULES AND CLASSIFICATION SCHEMES USED: AACR2 format is followed with some local modification for Indonesian names, geographic names and corporate bodies. Here the *Authority File of Indonesian Names* (Jakarta: Perpustakaan Nasional, 1985), and *List of Uniform Headings for Geographic Names and Indonesian Corporate Bodies* (Jakarta: Pusat Pembinaan Perpustakaan, 1981) are followed. Beginning in 1977, ISBD(M) was introduced in *BNI*. The National Library uses the *List of Subject Headings for Public and School Libraries*, and adaptation of the *Sears Subject Headings* to establish subject headings.[1]

The classification scheme used is DDC (20th ed.), with modifications for Islam, geography and history of Indonesia, and the Indonesian language and literature. *The Expansion and Adaptation of the Notations of Some Sections of the DDC related to Indonesia* (Jakarta: Pusat Pembinaan Perpustakaan, 1982) is used.

ENTRY INFORMATION: DDC number (upper left); author, title, edition statement, place of publication, publisher, pagination, illustrations, size, brief notes including original title for translated titles, index, and ISBN or ISSN; accession number, e.g., 91-736/173/92, in lower right position.

ARRANGEMENT: The classified bibliography is arranged by DDC.

Adult fiction and children's fiction sections are listed after the 900's in the classified bibliography.

Prior to 1978, *BNI* was divided in two sections: monographs arranged alphabetically by the main entry within DDC headings, and serials arranged alphabetically according to title.

INDEXES: Author and title index; subject index. Numbers used refer to the classification numbers in the bibliography.

A publishers' list is in the annual cumulation.

NOTES AND COMMENTS: *Catalogus dari buku-buku jang diterbitkan di Indonesia*, compiled by G. Ockeloen, covered Indonesian publications from 1870-1954. This work became the foundation from which the current bibliography was able to continue the listing of Indonesian publications.

From 1963, *Berita Bulanan* (as the national bibliography was then titled) was very irregular in publication and was not published at all during the last quarter of 1964 and suspended publication from April 1965 until it resumed publication in 1970 under the present title. Cumulated editions for 1964-1965 and later 1964-1972 were published to cover this period.

Indonesia is plagued by problems common to many developing countries trying to produce a current national bibliography—shortage of qualified staff, high costs of printing and other production expenses, lack of national funds available for bibliographic activities, and an inadequate communication network for dissemination of information within the country. The

---

[1] Information is taken from the Preface of *BNI* (vol. 41, no. 3 (Sept. 1993) and from Dady P. Rachmananta, "Bibliographical Standards of Indonesia: Implementations and Progress," In *The Library in the Information Revolution*, pp. 174-175.

national bibliography does not have a high priority, sometimes even within the library profession.[1] In the late 1970s it was estimated that only about twenty percent of the national imprint was covered by *BNI*.[2] One of the main reasons, which remains valid today, for this low rate of coverage was the lack of a legal deposit law until 1990.

The bilingual preface is thorough in its coverage of scope, contents, entry information and arrangement.

CIP is given.

Each quarterly issue includes 500-800 entries, about 75 percent of which are commercial publications.[3]

Government publications are not designated by any symbol. Many of these titles can be located by looking in the index under Indonesia and the issuing department.

Publications in English and Indonesian are included in *BNI*. There are "over 400 local languages and dialects, some of them with their own scripts but without transliteration schemes. Books in non-Roman scripts are for the time being not listed in the national bibliography."[4] Arabic scripts are Romanized.

"The Indonesian National Centre for the International Serials Data System" (ISDS) is administered by the National Scientific Documentation Centre (Pusat Dokumentasi Ilmiah Nasional- PDIN) and is responsible for promoting the use of the International Standard Serial Number (ISSN) and achieving total coverage in the registration of Indonesian serials."[5]

It is worth noting *Indeks berita dan artikel surat kabar bidang ilmu-ilmu sosial dan kemanusiaan = Press Index in Social Sciences and Humanities*, 1970- . (ISSN 0216-7573), and *Indeks Majalah Ilmiah Indonesia = Index of Indonesian Learned Periodicals* (current) 1980- . (ISSN 0216-6216; OCLC: 10355089). *The Press Index* is a quarterly which indexes eight newspapers published in the capital city.

The Katalog Induk Nasional = National Union Catalog (LCCN: 81-942098/SA/r85) is an on-going cooperative project, with 1993 being a continuation of the *National Union Catalog* 1988-1991. This project was initiated from about 1980 to 1987.

AL,SEA (0096-2341) included Indonesia within its scope.

---

[1] Mastini Hardjo Prakoso, "The Development of National Bibliographies in Indonesia," *International Cataloguing* 10 (July/Sept. 1981):36.

[2] J.N.B. Tairas and Soekarman Kertosedono, "National Bibliographic Control in Indonesia," *International Cataloguing* 6 (Oct./Dec. 1977):47.

[3] Information supplied in a letter dated 4 July 1996 to the author from Ms. Mastini Hardjo Prakoso, Director.

[4] Tairas, p. 47.

[5] Rachmananta, p. 175.

LATEST ISSUE EXAMINED/CURRENCY: Entries in the September 1993 issue generally have imprints from 1992 and earlier. December 1993 was the latest issue received by the Department of Information and Library Studies, Aberyswyth, Wales in November 1994, and is the latest issue examined.

AUTOMATION: not known.

FORMAT AND SERVICES AVAILABLE: printed.

CURRENT LEGAL DEPOSIT LAWS: Act No. 4/1990 declares that each publisher in the country, government and commercial, should submit at least two of their latest publications to the National Library, or to the Regional Library located in every province (26 regional libraries).[1]

AVAILABLE FROM: Perpustakaan Nasional R.I. = National Library of Indonesia, Jl. Salemba Raya 28A, POB 3624, Jakarta Pusat 10002.

SELECTED ARTICLES: Hardjo-Prakoso, Mastini. "The Development of National Bibliographies in Indonesia." *International Cataloguing* 10 (July/Sept. 1981):35-36.

Rachmananta, Dady P. "Bibliographic Standards of Indonesia: Implementation and Progress," pp. 170-178. In *The Library in the Information Revolution*. Singapore, Maruzen Asia, 1983.

Tairas, J.N.B. and Kertosedono, Soekarman. "National Bibliographic Control in Indonesia." *International Cataloguing* 6 (Oct./Dec. 1977):47-48.

VERIFIER: Mastini Hardjo Prakoso, Director.

IRAN

TITLE: *Kitābshināsī-'i millī-'i Īrān.* - 1970-   . - Teheran : National Library of Iran, 197?-   . Biannual (irregular, 1983-   ); annual (1981- 1982); irregular (1963-1980). Continues *Kitābshināsī-i millī* [National bibliography, Iranian publications]. Absorbed *Sūrat-i kitābhā-yi fihrist shudah dar sāl-i....* DDC: 015.55; LC: Z3366.K4; LCCN: 93-650376/NE; OCLC: 28732718 ISSN 0075-0522

COMPILER: Kitābkhānah-i Millī-i Jumhuri-i Islami-i Īrān [National Library of the Islamic Republic of Iran].[2]

---

[1] Prakoso letter.

[2] Information in a 30 July 1997 letter to the author from Poori Soltani. The latest national bibliography the author examined was before the November 1990 name change; it was called *Kitābkhānah-i Millī-i-i Īrān.* [National Library of Iran].

SCOPE AND COVERAGE: The *Kitābshināsī-'i millī-'i Īrān.* or *Iranian National Bibliography* (*INB*) includes titles published in Iran and deposited at the National Library under legal deposit legislation, and purchased books in Persian bought from abroad.

Types of publications in *INB* are books, pamphlets, new serials and title changes, selected official and government publications, talking books, braille books.

Omissions are non-book materials.

CONTENTS: Introduction, list of contents, classified bibliography, children's books section, section for pamphlets, indexes. Additional sections have been added for talking books (since 1994) and braille books (from 1997).

CATALOGUING RULES AND CLASSIFICATION SCHEMES USED: Cataloguing rules followed are AACR2 with Iranian amendments.

Each entry includes a DDC number and an LC number. Classifications sections relating to Iran have been expanded as needed, or newly compiled.

ENTRY INFORMATION: Entry number, author, title, place of publication, publisher, date, pagination, size, series statement, notes including price and ISBN, subject and added entries, DDC number is in lower right corner, LC classification number in lower left corner. For those entries written in Persian, the information in right and left corners are reversed, e.g., LC classification is in the lower right corner.

ARRANGEMENT: The classified bibliography is arranged by detailed subject headings of the DDC scheme, e.g., chain indexing.

INDEXES: The subject index, title index, personal names and corporate body index, and publisher index (with addresses) are alphabetically arranged. Since 1994 the publishers' index has been dropped.

NOTES AND COMMENTS: In 1983 the National Library of Iran and the Tehran Book Processing Centre (TEBROC) amalgamated. With this joining of resources, there have been some decisions and plans to implement change in the *INB* to bring it into line with the Unesco's *Guidelines for the National Bibliographic Agency and the National Bibliography.* As reported in a June 1985 letter from Mrs. Poori Soltani to the author, and in *International Cataloguing* 14 (Apr./June 1985):18, the following decisions for number 51 (1983) and subsequent issues are listed below.[1]

1. The *National Bibliography of Iran* will be published biannually from 1983 onwards until conditions are right to bring it out quarterly. It is not thought that the frequency will change for several years.

2. The scope of the *National Bibliography* will be to cover all Iranian imprints regardless of the language.

---

[1] These have been updated according to Mrs. Soltani's letter of 30 July 1997.

3. ISBDs, and AACR2 will be fully used, taking into consideration the Persian adaptation made by Ex-TEBROC, and new additions and changes made by the National Library of Iran.

4. Publications of more than five pages will be counted as books and included in the *Bibliography*.

5. In order to cooperate with the related International Agencies, Unesco, IFLA, etc. different statistics will be taken in the process of time.

6. Books will be arranged in classified sequence.

7. The full edition of the most recent Dewey Decimal Classification edition will be used in the classified system.

8. Each entry will have the following item (sic): a) main entry according to our authority file; b) full descriptive cataloguing (ISBD); c) all necessary notes; d) Persian subject headings; e) all necessary added entries; f) DDC classification number; g) Library of Congress classification number plus work mark; h) the National Library of Iran card number.

9. The Roman alphabet equivalent of all foreign names whose works have been translated will appear in main and added entries in front of the Persian form.

10. Subject, title and author index will be included to increase the accessibility.

11. List of publishers plus their addresses will be included at the end.[1]

12. Periodicals will not be included in the *National Bibliography*. The *Directory of Iranian Periodicals and Newspapers* will be published separately as usual.

13. The *Bibliography* will only contain books, since no other materials are deposited to the Library. Since 1994 talking books are also included even though the depository law does not cover them.

14. The size of the printed *Bibliography* will be twenty-one by thirty centimetres and each page will contain two columns.

15. Children's books and school text-books will be included in the *Bibliography*, though children's books are classified in a separate section under the title "Children's Books."

16. Subject authority file and name authority file are kept and published annually as the by-products of the *Iranian National Bibliography*.

---

[1] As mentioned earlier, this list has been eliminated since 1994, when the National Library became computerized.

Number 4 of these provisions has not been realized. The *INB* has treated pamphlets in a separate section.[1]   It is encouraging to see the positive changes in *INB* since no. 51 when international guidelines were adopted.

Kitābshināsī-'i millī-'i [National bibliography, Iranian publications]. - v. 1-5 (1963-1970). - Teheran, National Library, 1964-1970 (OCLC: 2086909; ISSN 0075-0522) is continued by *Kitābshināsī-'i millī-'i Īrān*. in 1970. This was published at irregular intervals through 1977, with 1968 and 1969 not published. The Revolution of 1978 delayed the volume for 1978. The spring issue of 1978, no. 45, was published in 1993, the summer issue, no. 46 in 1980, the autumn and winter issue, no. 47 as a six month issue in 1983. 1979 and 1980, no. 48, was published in one cumulation in 1983-1984; volumes for 1981, no. 49, and 1982, no. 50, were published in 1984; 1983 was published in two numbers (nos. 51 and 52) in 1986 and 1987; 1984 (nos. 53 and 54) were published in 1987 and 1990 respectively, 1985 (nos. 55 and 56) were published in 1992 and 1995 respectively, 1986 (nos. 57 and 58) were published in 1988 and 1989; 1987 (nos. 59 and 60) were published in 1988 and 1991; 1988 (nos. 61 and 62) were published in 1991 and 1990; 1989 (no. 63) was published in 1992; 1990 (no. 65) was published in 1993; 1991 and 1993 (nos. 67 and 68) were published in 1993 respectively, and 1992 (nos. 71 and 72) were published in 1993 and 1995. No. 83, part one, 1995 was published in 1996. Some numbers are still to be published: 69, 70, 73, 74, 84, 85, and 86 are finished and waiting to be published.   A special project in the Cataloguing Department is working on processing the retrospective uncatalogued books for nos. 76, 77, and 78 which are still in process. Because the National Library is computerized, the bibliographic information of all materials catalogued including the unpublished ones exist in the Library's database, 16 disks, and a CD-ROM updated to March 1997.[2]

The introduction of *INB*, written in Persian, explains the aims and objectives, and how to use the national bibliography.

The first non-official annual national bibliography of Iran was founded and edited by Iraj Afshar and collaborators in 1954.   The first volume of *Bibliographie de l'Iran* was published by the Anjaman-i Kitāb (Book Society of Iran). With volume 3 the name changed to *The Bibliography of Persia*. With volume 6 the format was changed, e.g., entries were given serial numbers, and printing in two columns was abandoned. The efforts of Afshar produced twelve volumes of the *The Bibliography of Persia*, with volume 12 produced in 1966. In 1967 the ten-year cumulation was published.

In the late 1970's, the *INB* was in hiatus.   Librarians, bibliographers, and researchers who depended on it for current publishing in Iran, had to find appropriate substitutes. One new and timely publication which appeared during this time seems to reflect an accurate, but limited view on Iranian publications. *Nashr-i-dānish*. - Tehran, Iran : Markaz-i Nashr-i Dānishgāhī, 1980-1995.   (LCCN: 83-930690/NE; OCLC: 10153141; ISSN 0259-9090)   was a bimonthly journal published in Persian by Iran University Press, sponsored by the Cultural Revolution Council.   Its scope includes articles and reports on new policies for books and university

---

[1] Poori Soltani, "Iranian national bibliography: an approach to new standards." *ICBC* 18 (no. 2 April/June 1989):30.
[2]   Information was provided by P. Soltani, *op. cit.*, and in her 30 July 1997 letter, and Jill Butterworth, Middle East Bibliographer, University Library, Cambridge in November 1994.

publications since the Islamic Revolution, plus reviews on recently published books, a classified bibliography of latest publications in Iran and news on cultural activities. Other information given is the level at which the book is aimed, pagination, publisher, analyses and description. It is arranged by an Iranian modification of DDC. *Nashr-i-dānish* covered publications in Iran approved by the Revolution. With its cessation and with the resurgence of the *INB*, it is hoped that librarians will be able to once again rely on the national bibliography.

The national library publishes the *Directory of Iranian Periodicals* which is a record of periodical publications in Iran, and the *Directory of Iranian Newspapers*, a listing of the newspapers published in Iran. Since 1994 these two titles have now been amalgamated into one title under the title *The Directory of Iranian Periodicals and Newspapers.*[1]

AL,ME (vol. 1, 1963- vol. 31, 1993; ISSN 0041-7769) included Iran within its scope.

LATEST ISSUE EXAMINED/CURRENCY: The latest copy examined at the University Library, Cambridge in 1995 is number 62, part two (1988) published 1990. Entries were not analyzed for currency.

AUTOMATION: The National Library was computerized in 1994. The hardware is a P.C., and Persian software is Pars-Azarakhsh which is based on CDS/ISIS.

FORMAT AND SERVICES AVAILABLE: printed. The National Library has its database available on 16 disks, and CD-ROM.

CURRENT LEGAL DEPOSIT LAWS: The 1907 legal deposit legislation was revised in 1965 and in 1970, according to Bibliography, Documentation Terminology (no. 1, 1970). Law of month of Muharram 1326/1908. Amended. In Qanun al-Matbuʻat (Law of Publications) Article 14 ratified in fifth month of 1358/1979, provides for legal deposit material to go to the National Library, not to the Ministry of Islamic Guidance.[2] Currently, ten legal deposit copies are given to the Ministry of Culture and Islamic Guidance, two copies of which are given to the National Library.[3]

AVAILABLE FROM: National Library of Iran, 30 Tir Street, P. Code 11364, Tehran.

SELECTED ARTICLES: "National Bibliographies, Iran." *Current Research in Library and Information Science* (formerly *RADIALS Bulletin*), no. 3 (1984):54, entry 533D55; 84/3/103.

Soltani, Poori . "Iranian national bibliography: an approach to new standards," *ICBC* 18 (April/June 1989):30-32.

VERIFIER: Poori Soltani, National Library of Iran.

---

[1] Soltani letter.
[2] Information provided by Katherine Van de Vate, Department of Oriental Manuscripts and Printed Books, The British Library, during a conference with the author in June 1985.
[3] Soltani letter.

IRAQ

TITLE: *al-Bibliyūghrāfīiah al-waṭanīyah al-'Irāqīyah.* - no. 1-   . - Baghdad : National Library, 1971-   .
Three times a year (1982-), quarterly, with annual cumulation (1977-1981?), annual (1971-1976).
At head of title, no. 26/27- : Ministry of Culture and Information, National Library, Baghdad.
Added title page: *Iraqi national bibliography.*
Title varies.
DDC: not found; LC: (090) Z3036.N3; LCCN: not found; OCLC: 8580560
ISSN not found

COMPILER: Bibliography and Statistic Section, National Library.

SCOPE AND COVERAGE: The *Iraqi National Bibliography* (*INB*) is based on legal deposit and includes titles published in and/or about the country or written by Iraqi authors published elsewhere.

Types of publications listed in *INB* are books, pamphlets, serial publications, selected official publications and government publications, selected theses, maps and atlases, school publications, general publications in Arabic, Turkoman and Kurdish languages, and other foreign languages.

Omitted from *INB* are musical scores, films, recordings, microforms, standards and patents, extracts and articles copied by a duplicating machine.[1]

CONTENTS: European languages section: table of contents, introduction (not included in 1981 or 1982). The parts vary. For 1982: Part I. Books and pamphlets in English, Part II. Theses in European languages issued in Iraq, Part III. Theses in European languages issued outside Iraq. Author index, title index. Arabic section: table of contents, introduction; Part I. Publications in Arabic issued in Iraq: general publications, government publications, school publications, children's publications. Part II. Theses issued in Iraq. Part III. Publications printed outside Iraq by Iraqi authors. Part IV. Theses done outside Iraq. Part V. Kurdu and Turkoman publications. Part VI. Current serials, or recent serial cessations. Part VII. Foreign publications. Author index, title index.

CATALOGUING RULES AND CLASSIFICATION SCHEMES USED: The cataloguing rules used are not stated. It appears that AACR rules may be followed, although AACR2 punctuation is not used. The cataloguing form is not consistent.

Classification numbers are according to the DDC scheme. The broad subject field divisions are also DDC. It is not stated which edition of DDC is used.

ENTRY INFORMATION: Dewey number in upper left corner, entry number (in parentheses) in upper right corner, author, title, place of publication, publisher, date, pagination, illustrations, series statement, notes, tracings. No price is given.

---

[1] "Introduction," *Iraqi National Bibliography* no. 23 (1979):4.

ARRANGEMENT: European languages section: Part I is arranged by types of publications and then by subjects. Parts II and III are arranged by broad general subjects according to the DDC scheme. The Arabic section is also arranged by the DDC scheme.

INDEXES: An author index and a title index are used in both the European languages section and in the Arabic section. The numbers used in the indexes refer to entry numbers of the titles listed in *INB*.

NOTES AND COMMENTS: The European languages section, the first section in *INB* running from left to right, is predominantly written in English with titles from other Western languages present on occasion. In number 26/27 this section accounted for about 100 pages, one-sixth of the volume. The rest of the volume, right to left, includes publications written in Arabic, Kurdish, Turkoman and other indigenous languages. This section, the largest, accounts for five-sixths of number 26/27.

The title of this publication has had several changes in its brief life: *Nashrat al-īdā 'lil-matbū'āt al-Irāqīyah* (1-13, 1971-1976), *al-Bibliyūghrāfīyah al-Waṭanīyah al-'Irāqīyah* (14-16, 1976-1977), *al-Fihris al-waṭanī lil-matbū'āt al-Irāqīyah* (17-25, 1977-1980), and the current title is adopted with number 26/27, 1981.

English added titles have also varied: *The Bulletin of Iraqi Publications Depository* (1-4, 1971-1973), *Depository Bulletin of Iraqi Publications* (7-13, 1974-1976), *The National Bibliography of Iraq* (14-18, 1976-1977), *Iraqi National Bibliography* (19, 1977), *Index of Iraqi Publications* (20-23, 1978-1980), *National Iraqi Bibliography* (26/27, 1981), and *Iraqi National Bibliography* (29, 1982).

Prior to *Nashrat al-īdā 'lil-matbū'āt al-Irāqīyah* an Iraqi national bibliography was produced by the Central Library of the University of Baghdad under the title *al-Nashrah al-Irāqīyah lil-Matbū'āt* [Iraqi Publications Bulletin], 1963-   ; this is still being published.

Two types of publications that may not be listed as completely as they should be in the national bibliography are government publications and university publications. In her unpublished paper, Katherine Van der Vate quotes the Library of Congress's *Annual Report*, Cairo Office, fiscal year 1983, p. 11: "Several universities are worth a visit for their faculty publications" after it was implied in the report that these are difficult to obtain.

Kurdish languages are included in *INB* as they pertain to Iraq's legal deposit laws. Another location for Kurdish literature can be found at the Kurdish Library's home page http://www.marebalticum.se/Kurd/index.htm

AL,ME (Vol. 1, 1963- vol. 31, 1993; ISSN 0041-7769) included Iraq within its scope.

LAST ISSUE EXAMINED/CURRENCY: Statistics given in number 23 (covering July-September 1978, published 1979) indicate about half of the entries listed are before the 1970 legal deposit law; of the current titles listed less than fifty percent of those are from 1978. The rest is from 1971-1977. In total, about twenty five percent are from the current year.

The latest issue examined was number 29, 1982. This is the latest issue found in the U.S. and in England. It is from the University of Chicago.

AUTOMATION: not known.

FORMAT AND SERVICES AVAILABLE: printed.

CURRENT LEGAL DEPOSIT LAWS: Legal deposit law number 37 of 1970 (promulgated 4 March 1970), Law no. 3 on Copyright, 1971, art. 8.[1]

AVAILABLE FROM: National Library, Bab-el-Muaddum, Baghdad.

VERIFIER: no reply received.

IRELAND

TITLE: *Irish publishing record.* - 1967-1988. - Dublin : University College, 1968-1989; 1989-
. - Dublin : National Library of Ireland, 1990-   .
Annual.
Publisher varies: vols. for 1967-1975 issued by School of Librarianship, University College, Dublin; vols. for 1976-1988 issued by: Library, University College, Dublin; vols. for 1989 - issued by the National Library of Ireland.
DDC: 015/.415; LC: Z2034.I87; LCCN: sn91-14415; OCLC: 2157914
ISSN 0579-4056

COMPILER: National Library of Ireland.

SCOPE AND COVERAGE: *Irish Publishing Record* (*IPR*) lists the publishing output of both the Republic of Ireland and Northern Ireland within the preceding year. Reprints of books published prior to 1967, the first issue of the *IPR*, are also included. Works deposited according to legal deposit legislation under the copyright law and works acquired or brought to the attention of the compilers by publishers, booksellers and individuals are listed.

Types of publications included in *IPR* are books, pamphlets, new periodical titles (including changes of title), official and government publications of general interest, annuals, yearbooks, maps, and musical scores, school textbooks, juvenile literature.

Maps published by the Ordnance Survey of Ireland and the Ordnance Survey of Northern Ireland are not included.

CONTENTS: Contents, introduction, classified list, name index, title index, list of publishers and addresses. Separate listings for new serials titles, juvenile books, and school textbooks are given following the classified list.

In earlier volumes, the scope and coverage was stated in the introduction (not currently the case), a statistical summary by subject of items recorded during the period covered was included.

---

[1] *International Guide to Legal Deposit*, p. 83.

CATALOGUING RULES AND CLASSIFICATION SCHEMES USED: Cataloguing rules used are not stated in the introduction. The records are in UKMARC format.

The classification scheme used is the DDC.

ENTRY INFORMATION: The DDC number is listed at the beginning of sections, followed by the consecutive entry number in the left margin, author, title, place of publication, publisher, date, pagination, illustrations, size, series, notes including bibliography and indexes, ISBN. In parentheses at the lower left is the National Library of Ireland record number.

In earlier volumes the DDC number is given with the subject heading at the beginning of the subject category.

ARRANGEMENT: Bibliographic entries are alphabetically arranged within the DDC sections.

For earlier volumes, separate sections at the end of the classification are used for new serials titles, juvenile books and school textbooks.

INDEXES: Name (including personal and corporate) index, title index. Numbers refer to the entry numbers.

A list of publishers and addresses is also supplied.

NOTES AND COMMENTS: The 1990 issue "marks a new phase in the title's history."[1] It was a cooperative project in conjunction with Trinity College, using relevant records from its online Dynix database, and University College, Dublin; Linen Hall Library, Belfast; Queen's University, Belfast; and North-eastern Education and Library Board.[2] using records from its BLCMP database, under a preparatory project called the Action Plan for Libraries (APL) of the Commission of the European Communities. The project is looking for other ways to cooperate and to provide timely bibliographical tools.

IPR includes publications in Irish and English, both official languages of the country. This follows ICNB recommendation 6.

Government publications are not designated by a special symbol. It is possible to locate a few by looking under corporate headings in the index. Only those government publications "of general interest" are included. A more complete listing is found in the annual *Catalogue of Government Publications* published by the Stationery Office.

LATEST ISSUE EXAMINED/CURRENCY: Entries include imprints for the time period covered. The latest issue examined is 1992, published 1994. Each issue includes titles published during the period covered.

---

[1] "Introduction," *Irish Publishing Record* 1990, p. 1.

[2] Information of other BLCMP sites in addition to University College, Dublin was given to the author in a 21 July 1995 letter from Brian McKenna, Keeper-Systems, National Library of Ireland.

AUTOMATION: Funding sources for the Commission for the European Communities APL project enabled both hardware and software to be installed at the National Library of Ireland to facilitate the exchange of information from various databases and for record conversion software.

FORMAT AND SERVICES AVAILABLE: printed. There are no immediate plans for output in other formats.[1]

CURRENT LEGAL DEPOSIT LAWS: Copyright Act of 1963.

AVAILABLE FROM: The Editor, *Irish Publishing Record*, National Library of Ireland, Kildare Street, Dublin 2.

SELECTED ARTICLES: Peare, J.D. Trevor; McKenna, Brian; Cullen, Clara, "Producing the Irish Publishing Record at the National Library of Ireland," *Program* 26 (no. 3 July 1992): 271-278.

VERIFIER: Brian McKenna, Keeper-Systems, National Library of Ireland.

ISRAEL

TITLE: *Ḳiryat Sefer: riv'on bibliyografi shel Bet ha-sefarim ha-le'umi yeha-universiṭa'i bi-Yerushalayim*. - 1924- . - Yerushalayim : Bet ha-sefarim, 1924- .
Quarterly, with separate annual index cumulation.
Publisher varies.
Text in Hebrew and English.
DDC: 016.8924; LC: Z6367 .K57; DS102.5; LCCN: 54-51497//r832; OCLC: 1755169
ISSN 0023-1851

COMPILER: Jewish National and University Library.

SCOPE AND COVERAGE: *Ḳiryat Sefer* (*KS*) lists all Israeli printed works as received on legal deposit at the Jewish National and University Library, and foreign publications that relate to areas of Judaism.

Types of publications included in *KS* are books, new serials, theses and dissertations, atlases, official publications and government publications.

Omitted are musical scores, films, filmstrips, slides.

CONTENTS: On both of the versos of the front cover in English and the front cover in Hebrew are abbreviations lists. Next, in both sequences is the Contents. The Bibliography is listed in one sequence, from back to front, followed by sections entitled Book Notes, Book Reviews; Studies; Notes; From the Library's Collection. Each issue does not include every

---

[1] Ibid.

section, and section names vary slightly. Beginning with volume 65, the following sections have been eliminated: Book Notes, Book Reviews, Studies, Notes, From the Library's Collection.

CATALOGUING RULES AND CLASSIFICATION SCHEMES USED: Since volume 61, the format of the entries conform in principle to ISBD.

Classification is arranged according to twenty-three broad subject divisions such as Bible; Midrashic and Halakhic literature; Jewish philosophy and religion; prayers and liturgy; ethics and sermons; juvenile literature; science and technology; publications in Arabic. Beginning with volume 65, publications in Arabic are no longer listed. Entries are not given any classification numbers. The classification headings are written in both Hebrew and in English.

ENTRY INFORMATION: Consecutive entry number, author, title, place of publication, publisher, date, pagination, illustrations, size, series statement, notes including ISBN.

An entry may be listed more than once. Full information is given under the principle heading assigned. Other listings of the same entry will refer user to the principle heading for complete bibliographic information.

The asterisk (*) used in front of some entry numbers is not explained in the abbreviations list. An assumption by this user is that it indicates that the title has been printed abroad and is not part of the Israeli imprint.

Books written in Hebrew and in languages other than Hebrew are supplied with a brief note about the book; this note is written in Hebrew.

ARRANGEMENT: The bibliography is arranged in broad subject headings, with subdivisions as needed, e.g., literature: Hebrew literature from the Middle Ages to the Enlightenment; modern Hebrew literature. Entries are consecutively numbered and alphabetically arranged under the various headings and subheadings.

INDEXES: The index is an annual volume published separately after the end of the year covered. In the index volume, there is a contents page listing the headings covered in the quarterly issues with the page numbers given where these headings appear in each issue. The index volume includes an index of Hebrew and Yiddish authors; index of Hebrew titles; index of Arabic authors; index of non-Hebrew authors, index of non-Hebrew titles, index of Russian authors and Anonymous works, and index of Greek authors (as needed). The numbers in the indexes refer the user to the consecutive entry numbers. Beginning with the index for volume 65, the index of Arabic authors has been discontinued.

In addition to indexing the divisions by the index volume, contents page and the various indexes mentioned above, through volume 64 the *KS* index volume also indexes the following divisions which appear in the quarterly issues: reviews; studies; from the Library collections; notes. However, beginning with volume 65, the index volume no longer indexes the divisions that have been eliminated.

Indexes have been periodically cumulated: vols. 1-15, studies and reviews; vols. 16-25, studies and reviews; vols. 26-35, studies and reviews; vols. 1-40, studies, notes and reviews. Supplement to vol. 41 (published 1967).

NOTES AND COMMENTS: Although official and government publications may be listed in *KS*, the major source for these publications is Israel Government Publications. - No. 1- . Jerusalem : State Archives, 1956- . (OCLC: 1753995). This began as a monthly, changed to a quarterly and is now an annual. It is not an exhaustive publication but is the most complete listing of official and government publications available. IGO publications are not listed.

In looking at the recommendations of the ICNB, it would be helpful to have an introduction which includes the scope and coverage, and to have indexes included in the quarterly issues of the journals in addition to the existing annual index. It also would be beneficial to bibliographers and librarians to have the library's classification numbers and subject headings included in this bibliography as part of the general information given. Many of these titles are unique to Israel, and guidance on classification and subject headings from librarians in the country where the book originated and is "in hand" would be extremely helpful.

The Hebrew and Western languages bibliography is given in the Hebrew sequence.

On the English title page of *KS*, vol. 66, no. 1: Bibliography of all the Publications in Israel and of Judaica from Abroad.

On occasion, some books written in Hebrew have translations of the author's name and titles. This information is included in the notes.

ISSN has been used since 1977.

From 1924-1975, a variation on the spelling of this title was *Kirjath Sepher*.

Periodical articles are indexed in *Index of Articles on Jewish Studies*. - Vol. 1- . Jerusalem : Editorial Board, *Kiryat Sefer*, Jewish National and University Library, 1966- (LCCN: sn88-14278; OCLC: 10166775; ISSN 0073-5817) and in *Index of Hebrew Periodicals*. - Vol. 1. (1977)- . - Jerusalem : Centre for Public Libraries, 1978- . Annual.

LATEST ISSUE EXAMINED/CURRENCY: The latest examined was volume 66, no. 1, 1996. It was published in 1996 and received by the author from The Jewish National and University Library.

In the two libraries that were checked (University of Wisconsin Madison, and the University Library, Cambridge, England) issues arrived ten to nineteen months after the period covered. The index volume has more of a delay; the index for 1988-1989 was published in 1994.

The currency of *KS* declined during the period of its computerization. This process has been completed, and the delay in the listing of new entries has largely been eliminated. New entries are now catalogued directly into the *KS* computerized database. The index is now published approximately one month after the final volume of each year, and should arrive in libraries in a more timely fashion.[1]

It was not possible for the author to check dates for the books in Hebrew which one would assume would be more current than foreign imprints listed. The verso of the title page states that vol. 66, no. 1 includes books published since 1988.

AUTOMATION: The hardware is the mainframe computer of the Hebrew University of Jerusalem, and the software is a bibliography program called ALEPH (Automated Library Expandable Program), produced by Ex Libris, a Jerusalem-based company.[2]

FORMAT AND SERVICES AVAILABLE: printed, Internet (telnet to 128.139.31.5; user name is "aleph"; no password required. Personal computer or mainframe needs software for reading Hebrew text).

CURRENT LEGAL DEPOSIT LAWS: Press Ordinance, 1934; Press Ordinance (amendment) Law, 5713-1953.[3]

AVAILABLE FROM: Jewish National and University Library, P.O.B. 34165, Jerusalem 91341.

VERIFIER: Raya Gutfreund, Director, The Jewish National & University Library

ITALY

TITLE: *Bibliografia nazionale italiana. Monografie.* - 1994, fasc. 1 (genn. 1994)-   . - Roma : Istituto centrale per il catalogo unico delle biblioteche italiane i per le informazioni bibliografiche. - 1994-   .
Monthly, with annual cumulation under title *BNI. Catalogo Alfabetico Annuale.*
Issues for 1994- called: *Nuova serie del Bolletino delle pubblicazioni italiane ricevute per diritto di stampa; Anno* [ ], *fasc.* [ ] which continues the numbering of *Bibliografia nazionale italiana.* [*Pubblicazione mensile*].
Continues in part: *Bibliografia nazionale italiana.* [*Pubblicazione mensile*].
Issued with a computer disk.
DDC: 0155.45/005; LC: Z2341.B583; LCCN: 96-650444; OCLC: 31912783
ISSN 1125-0879

COMPILER: Biblioteca Nazionale Centrale di Firenze.

---

[1] Information received in a 6 March 1997 letter to the author from Raya Gutfreund, Director of The Jewish National & University Library, Hebrew University of Jerusalem.
[2] Gutfreund letter.
[3] *International Guide to Legal Deposit*, p. 83. There has been no change in the legal deposit law according to Director Gutfreund's letter.

SCOPE AND COVERAGE: *Bibliografia nazionale italiana. Monografie. (BNI.M)* lists the publishing output of Italy that is deposited at the Biblioteca Nazionale Centrale di Firenze according to the legal deposit legislation. It lists the current year's publications and titles from the preceding year.

Types of publications in *BNI.M* include books, pamphets, selected official and government publications, selected maps and atlases, selected IGO publications, translations, phonorecords and audio-visual material if submitted.

Publications in series (first issues), and theses (if printed), children's books, and musical scores (from 1997) are included in other series of the national bibliography. See Notes and Comments section.

Excluded from *BNI.M* are titles of internal interest for specific groups, of special interest to certain groups of people only, titles of ephemeral interest, and non-book materials, official, administrative, and IGO publications of an internal nature, non-official editions of laws, decrees, and regulations (exempted are certain collections from specialized editors), publications of political parties, chambers of commerce, and cultural and religious groups which are of internal interest, pastoral letters and other official documents of religious authority, minor religious publications, consumer literature and "rosa" literature, publications not for sale but distributed outside of the normal channels of sale (such as subscription), reprints, preprints, etc. unless they have not been described previously, books to honor a person when works are republished in a special edition and previous works have been described, test materials of schools, biographical writings of limited destination of occasional or devout character, calendars of limited interest, patents, extracts (even in a series), exhibition catalogues, tourist information, educational catalogues or antique catalogues of historical or scientific interest, publications of commercial nature unless they are the only sources of information in certain fields (e.g., coin collecting, art), musical arrangements, speeches tied to a specific occasion, stenciled documents or communications printed on poor quality material mainly of a propagandistic nature, maps.

CONTENTS: Monthly: introduction, corrections, floppy disk guide, classified bibliography, separate indexes (not tipped in).

CATALOGUING RULES AND CLASSIFICATION SCHEMES USED: The *Regole Italiane di Catalogazione per autori*, and *Soggettario per i cataloghi delle biblioteche italiane* are used in cataloguing. ISBD is followed.

The classification scheme used is the DDC.

ENTRY INFORMATION: Author, title, place of publication, publisher, date, pagination, illustrations, size, series statement, notes including ISBN and price when known, tracings, DDC number in lower left corner, consecutive *BNI* number in lower right corner (e.g., BNI 96-7111).

From 1960 to 1984 an asterisk (*) in front of an entry identifies volumes successive to the first volume of a continuation.

ARRANGEMENT: The classified bibliography is arranged according to the DDC. Entries are alphabetically arranged within the subject categories.

INDEXES: Author and title index, subject index, publishers' index. The number refers to the *BNI* number in the classified bibliography.

NOTES AND COMMENTS: National bibliographic coverage for Italy has been in existence since the late 19th century. The scope has been fairly stable. Changes of title for the national bibliography are as follows. *BNI.M* continues in part *Bibliografia nazionale italiana.* [*Pubblicazione mensile*]. - Anno. 1, fasc. 1 (genn. 1958)- anno 36, fasc. 12 (dic. 1993). - Roma : Istituto centrale per il catalogo unico delle biblioteche italiane i per le informazioni bibliografiche [e] a cura della Biblioteca nazionale centrale di Firenze. - 1958-1993 (OCLC: 1519749; ISSN 1125-0879). From 1958-1975, the publisher's name was Centro nazionale per il catalogo unico delle bibioteche italiane e per le informazioni bibliografiche. This title absorbed *Bibliografia nazionale italiana. Pubblicazioni non descritte nella bibliografia nazionale italiana. 2., Testi musicali* and continued *Bollettino delle pubblicazioni italiane ricevute per diritto di stampa.* - [Firenze, Italy : Presso la Biblioteca nazionale centrale di Firenze, 1886-1957]. (LCCN: 05-29458//r; OCLC: 1347265).

BNI is now covered by the following parts. *BNI.M* is described in detail in this entry. The other titles are as follows. All are published in Rome by the Istituto centrale per il catalogo unico delle biblioteche italiane e per le informazioni bibliografiche, and issued by the Biblioteca Nazionale Centrale di Firenze. Beginning in 1998 publication of the *BNI* will be by the Biblioteca Nazionale Centrale di Firenze. In 1996, the ISSN changed from ISSN 006-1077 for all series to separate ISSNs for each series.

Bibliografia nazionale italiana. Libri per ragazzi. - 1995- . Monthly (10 nos. a year) (LCCN: 96-650683; OCLC: 35869005; ISSN 1125-2480). This title includes children's books, game books, and first books. Author/title index, subject index, general index (emphasizes general themes different from actual subjects), publishers' index. Issued with floppy disk.

Bibliografia nazionale italiana. Periodici e seriali. - 1995- . Semiannual (DDC: 015.45/034; LC: Z6956.I8B495; LCCN: 96-650445//r97; OCLC 33859300; ISSN: 1125-0887). Includes first issues of periodicals and publications in series. Author/title index, subject index. Issued with floppy disk. This title continues in part *Bibliografia nazionale italiana* (OCLC: 1519749) when periodicals were included with the monographs from 1958-1993.

Bibliografia nazionale italiana. Tesi di dottorato. - 1995- . Semiannual (LC: Z2341.B53; LCCN: 96-650657; OCLC: 34459549; ISSN: 1125-0895). Includes published theses and dissertations. Author/title index, subject index following the codified list in *Gazzetta ufficiale.* Following this is a table listing the subjects by the alphanumberic codes, e.g., L22B stands for Tibetologia, P01E, is Econometria. These codes and subjects are intended to facilitate use of well-known terms in the university setting. No coverage for dissertations exists prior to this title since the legal deposit law affecting dissertations was not in existence until recently. Issued with floppy disk.

Bibliografia nazionale italiana. Annunci di pubblicazioni di prosssima edizione [Announcement of forthcoming books]. - 1995- . - Monthly (OCLC: 34796405; ISSN 1125-2499). This title is distributed as an insert to *BNI.M*. It includes an author and title index, and publishers' index, but no subject index. Arrangement is by DDC system.

Bibliografia nazionale italiana. Supplemento. - 1995- . Annual (ISSN 1123-6175). This lists legal deposit materials published two years and earlier than the coverage of the current year. For instance, *BNI..M* 1997 lists books for 1996 and 1997. The *Supplemento* lists books for 1995 and earlier. Author/title index, subject index, publishers' index. Issued with a disk. Continues *BNI. Supplementi* - Firenze : Biblioteca Nazionale Centrale, 1971-199?. Eight numbers in separate issues. Includes additional entries for the period 1958-1971. (ISSN 1123-6175). This was suspended from 1974-1982; volume 9 (1986) includes the years 1958-1982, and volume 10 (1988) includes 1983, prevalently, and 1958-1982, subordinately.

Available for use with the issues is a floppy disk; instructions for installation and use are included in the national bibliography. The disk includes bibliographic information of publications listed in the issue. The data can be accessed by author, title, subject, classification number, parallel title, parallel subject, collections, ISBN, and publisher.

From 1958-1962 published music was compiled into pamphlets from *BNI*. From 1963-1986, no pamphlets were separate from *BNI* (one series until 1993, and from 1994-1996, in *BNI.M*). A new publication *Bibliografia nazionale italiana. Musica a stampa* is planned for autumn 1997; this will separate music from *BNI.M*. Its coverage will begin from 1995, and DDC will be used.[1]

The *Bibliografia Nazionale Italiana su CD-ROM* (ISSN 1125-2561) is available in both DOS and Windows environments. Users can search by more than 20 different access points including personal author, corporate author, title, place of publication, date of publication, series, publisher, country of publication, language, DDC number, DDC description, DDC edition, subjects, type of publication, and ISBN/ISSN. Boolean operators, operators for adjacency and proximity, truncation and wildcards can be used in searches.[2]

Annual cumulations are issued under title *BNI. Catalogo Alfabetico Annuale.* - Vol. 1 (1958)- . - Roma : Istituto Centrale per il Catalogo Unico delle Biblioteche Italiane e per le Informazioni Bibliografiche, 1961-   (OCLC: 1519750; ISSN 1123-6205).

BNI. Soggetti: liste di aggiornamento, 1956-1985 [Subjects: list of updates]. - Firenze : Biblioteca nazionale centrale, 1988 includes subject headings used in the *BNI*. (OCLC: 23006610).

Beginning in 1998 publication of the *BNI* will be by the Biblioteca Nazionale Centrale de Firenze.

Improvements since the 1980s have included an introduction and a publishers' list in the monthly issues.

Government publications are not designated by any symbols.

In 1996, ISSN changed from ISSN 006-1077 for all series to separate ISSNs for each series.

---

[1] Information in a 23 August 1997 letter from Dr. Gloria Cerbai Ammannati.
[2] Taken from an announcement in *ICBC* 24 (no. 3 July/Sept. 1995):52. The ISSN is supplied by Biblioeca Nazionale Centrale di Firenze.

BNI is photo-composed by ILTE–Moncalieri. It is arranged in an attractive double column lay-out with main entries in bold face, and adequate spacing between entries.

BNI does not participate in CIP.

LATEST ISSUE EXAMINED/CURRENCY: The latest issues printed in August were sent to the author by the Biblioteca Nazionale Centrale i Firenze: *BNI.M* April 1997; *Supplemento* 1996; *Tesi di dottorato* 1996/2; *Libri per ragazzi*, April 1997; and *Periodici* 1997/1. All were accompanied by the disk versions. The imprint dates listed in *Monografia* were for 1996 and 1997.

The latest issue examined in March 1997 at the University of Michigan Library is for September 1996. Most of the entries had imprints for 1995 and 1996 which is within the stated scope. Monthly issues are received by University of Michigan Library four to six months after publication which is an improvement of several months earlier than in the 1980s. Now this publication can be used as a collection development and acquisitions tool, and for research.

AUTOMATION: automated. The Servizio Bibliotecario Nazionale (SBN) archives is derived from the BNI records deposited at the Biblioeca Nazionale Centrale.

FORMAT AND SERVICES AVAILABLE: printed, floppy disk, magnetic tape (UNIMARC format), CD-ROM. BNI can not be reached by Internet because it is a subproduct of SBN; however, the database of Biblioteca Nazionale Centrale is available at http://www.bncf.firenze.sbn.it

CURRENT LEGAL DEPOSIT LAWS: N. 374: Legge 2 febbraio 1939 (*Gazzetta Ufficiale della Repubblica Italiana* del 6 marzo 1930, n. 54), amended by N. 660: Decreto Legislativo Luogotenenziale 31 agosto 1945 (*Gazzetta Ufficiale della Repubblica Italiana* del 27 ottobre 1945, n.129); N. 2052 Regio Decreto 12 dicembre 1940; N. 82: Decreto Legislativo Luogotennenziale 1 marzo 1945; Legge 29 dic. 1949, n. 958 covers cinematography, which was modified with Legge 31 luglio 1956, n. 897 and 4 nov. 196, no. 1213, :egge 10 maggop 1983. m/ 182, legge 14 gennario 1994, n. 26, and legge 1 marzo 1994, n. 153; Legge 21 feb. 1980, no. 28 (*Gazzetta Ufficiale della Repubblica Italiana* , 25 feb. 1980, n. 54) covers doctoral theses.[1]

AVAILABLE FROM: Biblioteca Nazionale Centrale, Piazza Cavalleggeri 1, 50121 Firenze.

The CD-ROM is also available from Chadwyck-Healey outside of Italy.

SELECTED ARTICLES: Martinucci, Andrea. "La nuova BNI." *Bollettino AIB* 34 (no. 4 Dic. 1994):449-452.

Peruginelli, Susanna. "Role and Function of the National Bibliography in the Italian System (SNB: Servizio Bibliiotecario Nazionale)." *Bibliographic Access in Europe: first International*

---

[1] *Survey of Existing Legal Deposit Laws*, p.45, *International Guide to Legal Deposit*, p. 83, and information in a 23 August 1997 letter addressed to the author from Dr. Gloria Cerbai Ammannati.

Conference: The Proceedings of a Conference Organised by the Centre for Bibliographic Management and held at the University of Bath 14-17 September 1989. Lorcan Dempsey, ed. Aldershot, England, Gower, 1990. pp. 125-127.

VERIFIER: Dr. Gloria Cerbai Ammannati, direttore responsabile della BNI, Biblioteca Nazionale Centrale di Firenze.

JAMAICA

TITLE: *Jamaican national bibliography*, Vol. 1 (Jan./Mar. 1975)-   . - Kingston : National Library of Jamaica, 1975-   .
Quarterly, the fourth issue being an annual cumulation.
Supersedes Institute of Jamaica, Kingston, West India Reference Library. *Jamaica national bibliography.*
DDC: 015.7292; LC: Z1541.J35; LCCN: sf87-92095; OCLC: 4760593
ISSN 0075-2991

COMPILER: National Library of Jamaica.

SCOPE AND COVERAGE: *Jamaican National Bibliography* (*JNB*) lists materials published in Jamaica, works about Jamaica, or by Jamaicans published outside the country received in the National Library of Jamaica. In the absence of a legal deposit law, the Library has undertaken to collect all material pertinent to Jamaica, whether by purchasing items or by soliciting donations. It is the library's policy to include material published since 1979 whenever it is received by the National Library.[1]

Types of publications included are books, pamphlets, first issues and title changes of periodicals, annual reports, official and government publications, maps and atlases, audio-visual materials, ephemera.

Omitted from the scope of *JNB* are periodicals (except as noted above), annual reports, certain government publications, e.g., bills, acts, subsidiary legislation, gazettes and parliamentary debates.

CONTENTS: Preface, outline of DDC, classified subject section, author and title index.

CATALOGUING RULES AND CLASSIFICATION SCHEMES USED: AACR2, ISBD(M) and ISBD(S) are used in cataloguing *JNB* entries.

Classification follows DDC (19th ed.). Prime marks are used to allow libraries to abridge the numbers if needed.

Filing is according to the ALA Filing Rules, 1980.

---

[1] The library policy information was given in a 24 November 1995 letter to the author from Director John A. Aarons.

ENTRY INFORMATION: Dewey Decimal Classification number and headings in upper left corner, author, title, editor, place of publication, publisher, date, pagination, illustrations, series statement, size, notes including ISBN or ISSN, price, and binding. In the lower left corner is the *JNB* serial number, e.g., JM87-31.

An asterisk (*) in the left hand margin indicates those works with a foreign imprint.

ARRANGEMENT: The classified subject bibliography is arranged according to the DDC scheme using the 100 subject categories.

INDEXES: Author/title index, alphabetically arranged. Entry information given in a shortened form includes author, translator, illustrator, title, and/or series statement as well as edition of work, publisher, price, classification number and the *JNB* serial number. The numbers used refer the reader to the *JNB* serial number in the classified bibliography.

NOTES AND COMMENTS: *JNB* is similar in style and format to the former CARICOM Bibliography and to the other Caribbean national bibliographies. ICNB recommendations are followed. The introduction includes the scope, arrangement and sample bibliographic and index entries. It would be helpful to the user to have the bibliographic entry analyzed.

Prior to the January - December 1986 issue, the annual cumulation of *JNB* included a list of articles from selected Jamaican periodicals and a list of Ministry Papers tabled in the House of Representatives. Information given in the selected periodicals list, arranged alphabetically by author's name, includes author, title, pagination, size, periodical title, number and year.

Information given in the Ministry paper section includes the definition of a Ministry or White Paper and, arranged chronologically, the Government's decision on a measure prepared for final action by Parliament, the title and the order in which it was laid on the table in the House of Representatives and the name of the Minister of Government who laid it on the table. With the 1986 cumulation, these items were discontinued.

National bibliographic control for Jamaica is aided by the following additional sources. *The Jamaican national bibliography*, 1964-1974 / The Institute of Jamaica. - Millwood, N.Y.: Kraus International Publications, c1981 (ISBN 0-527-45166-5) is a compilation of titles from *JNB*, 1964-1970, published by the West India Reference Library, the Institute of Jamaica, and titles from three Jamaican libraries (Institute of Jamaica, the Jamaica Library Service and the University of the West Indies at Mona) during the 1970-1974 period. Prior to this, the West India Reference Library, Institute of Jamaica was responsible for the publication of *Jamaica Accessions*. 1964-1967. - Kingston : Institute of Jamaica, 1965-1967.

CIP entries are indicated by the words "CIP entry" before the *JNB* serial number. When the book is acquired by the National Library and subsequently edited, the entry is marked "CIP rev.". (Preface, *JNB* 1987, no. 1; p. ii).

LATEST ISSUE EXAMINED/CURRENCY: There seems to be an increased delay in publishing the quarterly issues from the 1980s when quarterly issues were published ten to fourteen months after the date of coverage. The January/March 1987 was published in 1991.[1]

In the issues examined, entries included are from the last three years, with approximately 60% of the entries at least a year old; over the years there has been a slight increase in the number of titles published during the period covered.

The latest issue examined in May 1995 was January/March 1987, published in 1991, and received by University of Wisconsin, 5 June 1991.

AUTOMATION: *JNB* is automated for internal use only.[2]

FORMATS AND SERVICES AVAILABLE: printed.

CURRENT LEGAL DEPOSIT LAWS: There is no legal deposit law. Legal deposit is based on British Act, 1915. Pomassl mentions the Books (Preservation and Registration of Copies) Law (*Survey of Existing Legal Deposit Laws*, p. 46) which dates back to 1887. However, legal deposit is not in existence according to the "Preface" (i; 1991). This may be one of the contributing factors for the delay in publication of issues of the *JNB*.

AVAILABLE FROM: National Library of Jamaica, P.O. Box 823, Kingston.

SELECTED ARTICLES: Bandara, S.B. "Jamaican National Bibliography." *International Library Review* 13 (1981):311-321.

VERIFIER: John A. Aarons, Director, National Library of Jamaica.

JAPAN

TITLE: *Nihon zenkoku shoshi.* - 1988-1 = no. 1622- . - Tokyo : Kokuritsu Kokkai Toshokan, [1988]- .
Weekly.
Added title: *Japanese national bibliography weekly list*
Continues *Nihon zenkoku shashi shukanban.*
DDC: not found; LC: Z3301.N77; LCCN: sn88-35883; OCLC: 17723816
ISSN 0389-4002

COMPILER: Kokuritsu Kokkai Toshokan [National Diet Library].

SCOPE AND COVERAGE: *Nihon Zenkoku Shoshi* (*NZS*) lists the publishing output of Japan which is deposited at the National Diet Library (NDL) according to the National Diet Library

---

1 In his letter to the author, Director Aarons stated that the delay has been due to personnel problems.
2 Ibid.

Law Article 24, number 2, and Article 25, recording the publishing output of Japan which is supplied, donated, purchased, or given to the NDL.

Types of publications include books, selected pamphlets, official and government publications, periodicals, theses and dissertations, braille books, non-book materials, and musical scores in book form.

Excluded from the *NZS* are maps, musical scores in sheet form, and musical recordings (such as CDs).

CONTENTS: *NZS* includes introduction, bibliography, analyzed entry.

CATALOGUING RULES AND CLASSIFICATION SCHEMES USED: In the late 1980s the National Diet Library adopted ISBD. Previous to that, entries were described by the National Diet Library Classification Rules with modifications, National Diet Library Cataloguing Rules for Serials, Nippon Indexing Rules (new ed.), National Diet Library List of Subject Headings, and ISBD standards.

The classification scheme used is the Nippon Decimal Classification system. For official and government publications *Shokuinroku* (Directory of Government Officials) is used.

ENTRY INFORMATION: Ordinary entries include order number in upper right corner, title, author, place of publication, publisher, date, pagination, size, series, price, pronunciation of Chinese characters by Japanese syllabary, subjects, National Diet Library Classification number (marked with a circled 1), Nippon Decimal Classification number (marked with a circled N), Japanese National Bibliography number in parentheses (JP95-20935). An asterisk (*) indicates ordinary arrangement; entries not marked with an asterisk (*) use the simplified arrangement.

Simplified entries include title, author, place of publication, publisher, date, pagination, size, series, price, pronunciation of Chinese characters by Japanese syllabary, and the Japanese National Bibliography number.

ARRANGEMENT: The bibliography is arranged by the subjects according to the Nippon Decimal Classification system. Foreign works are at the end of the Japanese syllabary and are arranged alphabetically according to the Roman alphabet.

INDEXES: From 4 April 1997, no. 1997-13 each weekly issue includes a title index and an author index. Books in languages other than Japanese are listed at the end of each index. *NZS* had quarterly indexes up to the first quarter of 1997. *Nihon Zenkoku Shoshi Shukanban. Sakuin = Japanese National Bibliography Weekly List. Quarterly Indexes* includes a title index and an author index. Both indexes are divided into books, and children's literature. The title and author indexes exclude examination materials and books described with the simplified arrangement. (LC: Z3301.N771; LCCN: sn89-11651; OCLC: 8335142; ISSN 0389-4002). This title continues *Nohon shuho: sakuin. Japanese national bibliography: quarterly indexes*, 19??-1980. (LCCN: 78-647964/J/r862; OCLC: 8335142; ISSN 0385-3292).

Arrangement is by the Japanese syllabary. Foreign works are at the end of the Japanese syllabary and are arranged according to the Roman alphabet. The Japanese National Bibliography number refers the user to the classified bibliography.

Nihon Zenkoku Shoshi-choshamei sakuin is a title and author index of NZS. It is based on the JAPAN/MARC tapes that NDL produces, and issued by the Japan Library Association under the supervision of the National Diet Library.[1]

Publishers' list is also included.

NOTES AND COMMENTS: The *NZS* continues *Nihon zenkoku shoshi shukanban = Japanese national bibliography weekly list.* -1981-1-1987-50 = no. 1273-no. 1621. - Tokyo : Kokuritsu Kokkai Toshokan, [1981-1987]. (LCCN: sc83-4284; OCLC: 7654154; ISSN 0389-4002). This title continues *Nohon shuho* [Weekly deposit report]. - no. 1-1272 (June 18, 1955-1980). - Tokyo, Kokuritsu Kokkai Toshokan, 1955-1980 (LCCN: sn85-11730; OCLC: 2265153; ISSN 0385-3292). This title supersedes *Kokunai shuppanbutsu mokuroku.* - [Tokyo] : Kokuritsu Kokkai Toshokan Ukeire Seiribu, 1951-1955 (LCCN: 74-817985/J/r86; LC: Z3303.K7; OCLC: 1797026). The first Japanese national bibliography was published in September 1948 under the title *Nohon Gepppo* [Monthly deposit report].

It would be helpful to have a bilingual presentation of the preliminary information, especially the introduction which explains the scope, coverage and arrangement. An analyzed entry, clearly labeled is given as part of the preliminary information in the government section, and most recently, in the weekly lists. It is also helpful to have indexes in each weekly list; this began in the second quarter of 1997. ICNB recommendations 5, 6, 8, 9, 10, 11, 13 are followed.

Earlier volumes of the annual volume included audio-visual materials. In 1975, a supplement (1948-1969) was published to list those publications dropped out of the regular editions of the annual bibliography during that time period. Currently Appendix C, published once a year, includes non-book materials.

The verso of the cover of the annual volume has an analyzed entry which is helpful to the user.

In collaboration with the Japan Library Association the NDL developed JAPAN/MARC in the 1980s. On a commercial basis beginning in April 1988, the NDL began distribution of J-BISC, a quarterly CD-ROM product using JAPAN/MARC. Information retrieval, production of printed catalogue cards, editing of bibliographic records, and downloading to floppy or hard disk are functions that can be performed by using J-BISC. The scope covers Japanese monographs published and acquired by the NDL from 1948 to the present; these are divided into retrospective and current disks. Boolean operators permit refined searches from 12 index/search options: title, author, NDL Subject Headings, NDL Classification, Nippon Decimal Classification, publisher, ISBN, Government Code, call number, printed catalog card number and JP-record number on JAPAN/MARC. Instructions are displayed only in Japanese. A user manual is available. (LCCN: 87-647454/AJ; OCLC: 12395043).[2]

---

[1] Information was received in a 28 May 1997 and a 19 September 1997 letter from Fumio Ishikawa, Director, Processing Coordinating Office, Acquisitions Department, NDL.
[2] Information received in a 18 December 1990 letter to the author by Hiroshi Imon, Director, Library Cooperation Department, NDL, and also by using J-BISC.

PROMPTNESS RECEIVED/CURRENCY: In looking at the annual volume entries, about eighty-eight percent were from the period covered, ten percent were from the previous year, and the remainder were for earlier years.

The latest *NZS* examined in June 1997 was 1997, no. 17, sent to the author by the NDL.

AUTOMATION: The Weekly List has been automated since January 1977. The 1977 annual volume is the first automated annual.

Hardware products are the products of Hitachi Co., Ltd. Software programs used for automation are developed by the NDL.[1]

The NDL began to distribute Japanese MARC tapes in April 1981.[2]

FORMAT AND SERVICES AVAILABLE: print, magnetic tape (since 1988), and CD-ROM (J-BISC). The past one year data of the National Diet Library holdings of Japanese books is available from the Library home page on the Internet. It is updated every month.[3]

CURRENT LEGAL DEPOSIT LAWS: National Diet Library Law (Law No. 5, 9 February 1948) with amendments, the latest being Law No. 3, 28 January 1955).[4]

AVAILABLE FROM: MARC tape: Japan Library Association, 1-1-10 Taishido, Setagaya-ku, Tokyo 154.

Distributor: Kinokuniya Co., Ltd. International Business Division, 38-1 Sakuragaoka 5-chome, Setagaya-ku, Tokyo 156.

Also available through: Kinokuniya Publications Services of New York Co., Ltd., 10 West 49th Street, New York, New York 10020, USA, and Maruzen Co., Ltd. International Division Export Division, 3-10 Nihombashi 2-Chome, Chuo-ku, Tokyo 103.

CD-ROM: Kinokuniya and Maruzen (see above).

SELECTED ARTICLES: Koo, Ja Young. "The Problems and Solutions of National Bibliographies in the East Asian Countries: Current Bibliographic Controls in China, Japan, Korea." In *Proceedings of IFLA Worldwide Seminar May 31-June 5, 1976*. Seoul: Korean Library Association, 1976. pp. 210-227.

Maruyama, Shojiro. "National Bibliographic Control in Japan. Past and Present, an Approaching Effort to UBC." In *Proceedings of IFLA Worldwide Seminar May 31-June 5, 1976*. Seoul: Korean Library Association, 1976. pp. 427-433.

---

[1] Information about automation was received in Ishikawa letter.

[2] "The Present State of JAPAN/MARC on CD-ROM (*J-BISC*)."National Diet Library, August 1990. This is a one page flyer that the author received in 1990 from the NDL in reply to queries on J-BISC.

[3] Information about the Internet was received in Ishikawa letter.

[4] *International Guide to Legal Deposit*, p. 84.

Niki, K. "National Bibliographic Control of Current Publications in Japan." *Bulletin – Association for Asian Studies.* Committee on East Asian Libraries, no. 90 (June 1990):9-18.

VERIFIER: Fumio Ishikawa, Director, Processing Coordinating Office, Acquisitions Department, National Diet Library.

JORDAN

TITLE: *al-Bibliyūghrāfiyā al-waṭanīyah al-Urdunīyah* -1979-   . - 'Amman : The Jordan Library Association, 1980-   .
Annual.
Added title page: *The Jordanian national bibliography: the annual register of book production in Jordan.*
From 1994, issued by the Department of the National Library.
DDC: 015.5695; LC: Z3471.B524; LCCN: 83-643650/NE/r89; OCLC: 9560109
ISSN not found

COMPILER: Department of the National Library (1994-   ), National Bibliography Committee, Jordan Library Association (1979-1993).

SCOPE AND COVERAGE: *al-Bibliyūghrāfiyā al-waṭanīyah al-Urdunīyah* or *The Jordanian National Bibliography* (*JNB*) lists titles published in Jordan by individuals, private and official organizations for the benefit of librarians, publishers and others. It is not based on legal deposit.

Types of publications included are books, pamphlets, theses, official and government publications, and serials.

Omissions include school textbooks and audio-visual aids.

CONTENTS: *JNB* includes a Western (all in English) and an Arabic section which is bound tête-bêche. For the 1991 volume the Western contents are: contents, classified bibliography, indexes. The Arabic section is similarly organized.

CATALOGUING RULES AND CLASSIFICATION SCHEMES USED: The *JNB* is catalogued according to AACR2 and ISBD.

The classification scheme used is DDC with Arabic amendments.

ENTRY INFORMATION: For theses: serial number, author, title, place of publication and publisher if known, date, pagination, note indicating the degree and where thesis is submitted, class number, subjects.

For books: serial number, author, title, place of publication, publisher, date, pagination, illustration statement, class number, subjects. Prices are not included.

ARRANGEMENT: The arrangement is by DDC 100 broad headings, then alphabetically by author.

INDEXES: Western section: author index; title index, subject index. The number refers the reader to the serial number in the bibliography. Arabic section: author and title index; subject index.

NOTES AND COMMENTS: Beginning in 1994, the Department of the National Library is issuing the *JNB*. From 1979-1993 the Jordan Library Association is to be commended for its efforts in producing a national bibliography which aids in universal bibliographic control. The volumes of the *JNB* vary somewhat with each issue. The 1991 volume has been prepared and compiled by the National Bibliography Committee of the Jordan Library Association. It includes a subject index in the Western section; this is a addition not seen since 1982. *JNB*, however, does not include an introduction which should explain the scope and coverage of the bibliography; this feature is very helpful to users of the *JNB*. From 1983, the *JNB* has been done by a voluntary committee earlier called Special Committee for Bibliographic Control. Beginning with the 1983 volume, there are differences from earlier issues. Some of the enhancements suggested by international standards are not included. It does not include an abbreviations list for the Western section as found in 1981, it does not include a subject index for the Western section as in the 1982 volume, it does not include a list of bookshops, publishers and presses in Jordan as found in the 1982 volume. The scope and arrangement statements are clearly spelled out, though briefly, in the 1982 volume. The 1983 introduction stresses the voluntary compilation by JLA members but does little else to explain the scope of *JNB*. However, recently the voluntary committee has reinstated some of the helpful features; an explanatory introduction, including scope, coverage, standards, abbreviations used, etc. in each issue would also be a valuable contribution.

The *JNB* is divided into Western and Arabic sections. The Western section ranges from about one-tenth to one-half of the book; the rest of the book comprises the Arabic section.

An earlier volume has a special supplement on Jordanian publications published abroad.

The only literary form in the Western section for 1983 is the theses done for degrees at Jordanian universities. The 1984 volume has both theses written at Jordanian universities, as well as other dissertations relevant to Jordan awarded from Arab and foreign universities. The 1982 volume has more of a variety of literary forms in its Western section.

Government publications are not specifically designated by a symbol or a section. However, by checking in the index under Jordan and the department needed, it is possible to find many of the government publications listed.

Mahmud al-Akhras has written *al-Bibliyūghrāfiyā al-Filastīnīyah al-Urdunīyah, 1900-1970*, published in 1972 (JLA publication no. 3), and *al-Bibliyūghrāfiyā al-Filastīnīyah al-Urdunīyah, 1971-1975*, published in 1976 (JLA publication no. 4). These were a compilation of annual lists which appeared in the JLA *Risālat al-Maktabah* from 1970 to 1978. The translated English titles are *Palestine-Jordan Bibliography, 1900-1970*, and *Palestine-Jordan Bibliography, 1971-1975*. These volumes include works written by Palestinian and Jordanian authors regardless of the place of publication or domicile. ISBD information is given for each entry. Arrangement is first by DDC (18th ed.) with modifications, then alphabetically arranged by main entry. Access to the entries is by author, title, and subject indexes.[1] Most titles are in Arabic. Annual updates of this work appeared until 1978 in *Risālat al-Maktabah*.[2]

Bibliyūghrāfiyā al-waṭanīyah al-Urdunīyah ('Amman, Jordan: 1980). - 1980. 'Amman : Department of Libraries, Documentation and National Archives, 1981. (LC: 83-643650/NE/r89) with the added title *National Bibliography of Jordan* (*NBJ*) is the first attempt by the Department of Libraries, Documentation and National Archives (DLDNA) to produce an official national bibliography. According to the introduction, compilation of the bibliography was hindered by the ineffectiveness of the by-law legal deposit clause which states that one copy of every item published in Jordan should be deposited at the DLDNA free of charge. To date, this is the only volume published, and according to George Atiyeh, former Head, African and Middle East Division, Library of Congress, this title is no longer being published. It has appeared only once. It is based on legal deposit and includes titles published in Jordan and selected titles published outside Jordan. Types of publications included are books and pamphlets, school books, theses and graduation projects, official and government publications, current periodicals.

NBJ is divided into Western language and Arabic sections. Both sections are similarly arranged and include table of contents, introduction, list of abbreviations, classified bibliography (general works published in Jordan, Jordanian school books, university theses and graduation projects, government reports, guides, pamphlets, and statistics, current national periodicals, sample of national works published outside of Jordan). The DDC tables are given in the Arabic section but not in the Western languages section. The Western language section is about twenty percent of the volume. English is the only Western language observed in this edition of *NBJ* .

Information in the entries of *NBJ* includes entry number, author, title, place of publication, publisher, date, pagination, illustration statement, occasional notes, e.g., In Arabic and English. The bibliography is arranged by subject headings. Indexes include author and title index, subject index for both the Western languages and the Arabic sections. The number in the author and title index refers to the DDC number; the number in the subject index refers to the entry number.

Jordan is included within the scope of *AL,ME* (ISSN 0041-7769, 1963-1993), and the *Arab Bulletin of Publications* (OCLC: 2239670).

LATEST ISSUE EXAMINED/CURRENCY: The latest volume of the *JNB* examined at Princeton University Library in April 1995 is for 1991, published in 1992.[3]

In the issues examined, the majority of entries were within a two year period from the time period covered.

---

[1] "Review," *Risālat al-Maktabah* 10 (No. 1, March 1975):23-24.

[2] Katherine Van de Vate, "Jordan." In *Books from the Arab World. A Guide to Selection and Acquisition.*, p. 32.

[3] In a 1 June 1997 letter to the author, Moha'd Khair I. Rajab, Assistant Director General for Library Affairs, Department of the National Library, states that, since assuming responsibility for the *JNB*, the Department has published issues for 1994 and 1995.

AUTOMATION: not automated.

FORMAT AND SERVICES AVAILABLE: printed.

CURRENT LEGAL DEPOSIT LAWS: Legal deposit law 27 effective 1 January 1983.[1]

AVAILABLE FROM: Department of the National Library, P.O. Box 6070, 'Amman.

SELECTED ARTICLES: Van de Vate, Katherine. "Jordan." In *Books from the Arab World. A Guide to Selection and Acquisition.* Durham: Middle East Libraries Committee, 1988, pp. 31-32.

VERIFIER: Moha'd Khair I. Rajab, Assistant Director General for Library Affairs, Department of the National Library.

KAZAKHSTAN

TITLE: *Baspasóz shezhīresī = Letopis' pechati.* - 1938-   . - Alma-Ata : Gos. Knizh. palata Kazakhsko i SSR, 1938-   .
DDC: 015.5845; LC: not found; LCCN: not found; OCLC: not found
ISSN 0136-0825

COMPILER: Gosudarstvenny i Komite Kazakhsko i SSR po delam izdatel stv, poligrafii i knizhno i torgovl i, Gosudarstvennaia knizhnaĭa palata Kazakhskoi SSR.

SCOPE AND COVERAGE: *Baspasóz shezhīresī* (*BS*) includes the publishing output of Kazakhstan which is deposited at the national library. Concentration is on the social sciences. Publications in Kazakh and Russian are included.

Types of publications include books, pamphlets, serials (first issues) and dissertations.

Omitted from BS are journals and newspapers which are covered in *Letopis' zhurnalnykh statei* and *Letopis' gazetnykh statei.*

CONTENTS: Classified bibliography of books, periodicals, indexes, table of contents in Kazakh and Russian. Information for combined issues are presented issue by issue. The contents of issues vary.

CATALOGUING RULES AND CLASSIFICATION SCHEMES USED: Cataloguing rules follow the national cataloguing standard laws of Russia.

Classification scheme used is DDC.

---

[1] Van de Vate, p. 31.

ENTRY INFORMATION: Consecutive entry number, author, title, place of publication, publisher, date, pagination, size, ISBN number, number of copies published, price, internal number [92-806], and symbols, e.g., ba indicates cards are to be printed. An internal number is listed in lower right corner.

ARRANGEMENT: Arranged alphabetically within the subject scheme.

INDEXES: Author index, subject index.

NOTES AND COMMENTS: Before the breakup of the USSR, publications of Kazakistan were recorded in *Knizhnaĭa letopis'* and *Baspasôz shezhīresī = Letopis' pechati.* Since Kazakistan established its independence, the primary record of Kazakistan's publishing output is recorded in *BS.*

Since 1993 journal articles are listed in *Zhurnal Maqalalarii shezhīresī = Letopis' zhurnal'ih stateĭ* (ISSN 0136-0833). Periodical articles were covered in *BS* before then.

Since 1993 newspaper articles are listed in *Gazet Maqalalarii shezhīresī = Letopis' gazetnykh stateĭ* (ISSN 0136-0833). Newspaper articles were covered in the *BS* before then.

Since 19?? reviews are listed in *Maqalalar men retŝenziĭalar shezhīresī = Letopis' stateĭ i retŝenziĭ* (LCCN: 88-644403//r972; OCLC: 18830355; ISSN 0136-0833). Before then, reviews were covered in *BS.*

PROMPTNESS RECEIVED/CURRENCY: The latest copy of *BS* examined at the University of Illinois in June 1996 is for 9-10/1992, published in 1992. The majority of imprints were from the period covered; a few were from 1991. The latest copy of the review articles seen is no. 12, 1991; the latest copy of the journal articles seen is nos. 7/8, 1994, and the latest copy of the newspaper articles seen is no. 1, 1994.

AUTOMATION: not known.

FORMAT AND SERVICES AVAILABLE: printed.

CURRENT LEGAL DEPOSIT LAWS: not known.

AVAILABLE FROM: Gos. Knizh. palata, 480100, g. Alma-Ata, ul. Tole Be, 40.

VERIFIER: no reply received. The author is grateful for the help of Helen Sullivan and Patricia Thurston, Slavic Reference Service, Univerity of Illinois Library, Urbana-Champaign.

KENYA

TITLE: *Kenya national bibliography.* - 1980-   . - Nairobi : Kenya National Library Service, National Reference & Bibliographic Department, 1983-   .
Annual.

Subtitle: *A classified subject bibliography of current publications produced in Kenya & foreign materials of interest to Kenya and/or written by Kenyans, arranged according to the Dewey Decimal Classification and catalogued according to the Anglo-American Cataloguing Rules, with a full author & title index.*
DDC: 015.676/2034, in *Kenya National Bibliography*: 015.676205; LC: Z3587.K47a; LCCN: 83-980780; OCLC: 9997044
ISSN not found

COMPILER: National Reference & Bibliographic Department, Kenya National Library Service.

SCOPE AND COVERAGE: The scope of the *Kenya National Bibliography* (*KNB*) covers current publications produced in Kenya and foreign materials of interest to Kenya and/or written by Kenyans. Legal deposit publications as well as materials acquired through purchase, gift, exchange or donation for the Kenya Collection (Kenyana) are included.

Types of publications included in *KNB* are books, research reports, theses, dissertations, conference proceedings, pamphlets, government publications, maps, first issues of new serials and subsequent title changes (including annual reports, yearbooks, biennials), and selected exhibition catalogues.

All publications with a Kenyan imprint emanating from regional organizations (African Development Bank, East African Wild Life Society, African Medical Research Foundation, etc.) based in Kenya are included.

Omissions include brochures, routine government publications (parliamentary bills, amendments of bills, parliamentary debates, individual acts, etc.), calendars, programmes, advertising matter/trade literature with product information only, and other ephemeral publications. Publications produced locally by international inter-government and private organizations (United Nations Environment Programme, International Laboratory for Research on Animal Disease, United Nations Centre for Human Settlements, etc.) based in Kenya are not included in the *KNB* except for materials by these agencies with significant Kenyan subject content (approximately one-third content). Articles from periodicals, reissue of an edition if text is unchanged, sales catalogues (except those with information on subject or bibliographic interest), diaries, books without text, time-tables, coloring books, stamps, bank notes are also not included.

CONTENTS: Preface (which includes scope and coverage, an analyzed entry, and a list of indigenous languages), list of abbreviations, outline of the Dewey Decimal Classification, classified subject sequence, author and title index, list of publishers.

CATALOGUING RULES AND CLASSIFICATION SCHEMES USED: *KNB* is catalogued according to AACR2 (1978). ISSNs are included as they apply to relevant foreign imprints and local subsidiaries of multi-national publishers; an ISSN agency has not been set up in Kenya. Descriptive format follows ISBD.

The classification scheme used is the DDC (19th ed.). Slight modification of the 800 class number (literature) accommodates fiction in indigenous languages, e.g., 896.3923K shows fiction in kiswahili. A list of the abbreviations used for indigenous languages is given in the Preface.

ENTRY INFORMATION: DDC number in upper left corner, author, title, place of publication, publisher, date, pagination, illustrations, size, series statement, notes including legal deposit registration number of the entry, ISBN, price, tracings, *Kenya National Bibliography* serial number in brackets in the lower left corner, e.g., [KE90-098].

Foreign publications of interest to Kenya and work by Kenyans published abroad are marked with an asterisk (*) in the main classified subject sequence.

The letter "F" is added to the classification numbers for all fiction in foreign languages.[1]

ARRANGEMENT: Arrangement is by classified subject sequence of main entries according to the DDC (19th ed.).

INDEXES: Author (including personal, corporate, joint authors, translators, editors, compilers, illustrators) and title index are arranged in one sequence. Series are also listed in the index. Cross references are used. The numbers used in the index refer the user to both the DDC number and the *KNB* serial number in the subject sequence of entries, e.g., 620.80951/KE90-229. There is no alphabetical subject index. The author and title index is filed according to *ALA Rules for Filing Catalog Cards*, 2d ed., 1968.

NOTES AND COMMENTS: The 1980 *KNB* is the first issue of a current national bibliography for Kenya. Publications in and before 1979 will constitute materials for the retrospective *KNB* "planned to appear in ten year cumulations, starting with 1979 running backwards".[2] F. W. Ochola has expressed the hope that the *KNB* will be current by 1985, and then the National Reference & Bibliographic Department could begin the retrospective editions covering the decennial periods.[3] Publications missed in either current or retrospective *KNB* will be recorded in subsequent editions/cumulations.

When the *KNB* is on schedule, it is hoped that its frequency will become quarterly.[4]

Current serial titles published in Kenya are listed in the first issue (1980). In subsequent *KNB* editions, only new serial titles and name/title changes of current periodicals will be included.

KNB follows ICNB recommendations 5 and 6 (with the exception of the less used Hindi and Arabic scripts Romanization), 9, 10, and has set as a goal meeting recommendation number 8.

---

1 "Preface," *Kenya National Bibliography* 1990, p. viii.
2 F. W. Ochola, "The Kenya National Bibliography," *International Cataloguing* 13 (July/Sept. 1984):29. It was confirmed that this project is in progress in a letter to the author dated 24 March 1995 from Mrs. Larissa Odoyo, Head, Reference and Bibliographic Department.
3 Julian Witherell, "Report of a Trip to Africa, March-June 1984, part 3," *Africana Libraries Newsletter* no. 42a (July 1985):2.
4 F. W. Ochola, "The Kenya National Bibliography and Universal Bibliographic Control," *Maktaba* 7 (no. 2 Dec. 1980 (Feb. 1983):15.

Kenyan Periodicals Directory. - Nairobi : Kenya National Library Service, National Reference & Bibliographic Dept., 1984-   , a biennial sister publication of *KNB*, lists titles of current serials and periodical cessations in two separate classified subject sequences. Although this is the only volume published to date, a retrospective *Periodicals Directory* was due for publication in 1995.[1]

Although the legal deposit law is now adequate enough to be effective in gathering the government publications which are available, it lacks the effective enforcement machinery.[2] An attempt to rectify this is being made with a further amendment to the law which would penalize non-compliant publishers.[3]

Government publications listed in the *KNB* can be located by looking in the index under corporate author, or by scanning the subject sequence. No special mark is given to government publications.

At present, there is no CIP program in Kenya.

AL,ESA and *QIPL,ESA* include Kenya within their scopes.

In March 1995, the volume for 1991 was at the printers, and the volume for 1992 will go to the printers in May 1995.[4]

LATEST ISSUE EXAMINED/CURRENCY: Entries are from the period covered. The latest volume examined covers 1990, published 1993 and received at the University Library, Cambridge 1 February 1994.

AUTOMATION: *KNB* is not automated although it is compiled by using a computer.[5]

FORMAT AND SERVICES AVAILABLE: printed.

CURRENT LEGAL DEPOSIT LAWS: The Books and Newspapers Act (Legal Deposit Law, Cap. 111), revised edition, 1980. Amended in 1987.[6]

AVAILABLE FROM: Kenya National Library Service, National Reference & Bibliographic Department, P.O. Box 30573, Nairobi.

---

[1] Odoyo letter, op.cit.

[2] Ochola, "The Kenya National Bibliography," *International Cataloguing* 13 (July/Sept. 1984):30. In a letter to the author dated 24 March 1995, op. cit., Mrs. Larissa Odoyo stated that the 1987 amendment to the legal deposit law still in inadequate since it does not cover the legal deposit of government publications, works in braille, audio-visual materials, and other non-print media.

[3] Witherell, p.2.

[4] Odoyo letter, op. cit.

[5] Ochola, "Kenya," *Afribiblos* 8 (no. 2 Dec. 1986):61, and Odoyo letter, op. cit.

[6] "Preface," *Kenya National Bibliography* 1990, p. vii. Amendment information was in a letter dated 5 April 1995 to the author by Mrs. Odoyo.

SELECTED ARTICLES: Ochola, Francis W. "The Kenya National Bibliography." *International Cataloguing* 13 (July/Sept. 1984):29-31.

VERIFIER: Mrs. Larissa Odoyo, Head, National Reference and Bibliographic Department, Kenya National Library Services.

KOREA (DEMOCRATIC PEOPLE'S REPUBLIC)

No current national bibliography has been traced for the Democratic People's Republic of Korea.

Ms. Inkyong Ahn, Senior Reference Librarian, Korean section, Asian Division, Library of Congress, verifies that no title exists.

KOREA (REPUBLIC)

TITLE: *Taehan Min`guk ch'ulp'anmul ch'ongmongnok.* - 1945/1962- . - Seoul : Kungnip Chungang Tosŏgwan, 1965- .
Annual.
Added title page: *Korean national bibliography.*
DDC: 015.519; LC (090): Z3316.T3; LCCN: sn85-21317; OCLC: 12139381
ISSN 0496-6945

COMPILER: Kungnip Chungang Tosŏgwan [National Library of Korea].

SCOPE AND COVERAGE: *Taehan Min`guk ch'ulp'anmul ch'ongmongnok* or the *Korean National Bibliography* (*KNB*) lists the publishing output of the Republic of Korea which has been deposited at the National Library of Korea according to legal deposit legislation.

Types of publications included in *KNB* are books, pamphlets, official and government publications, periodicals (first issues), musical scores, finding aids (guides, inventories, indexes, checklists), manuals, handbooks, children's books, limited editions, non-book materials, IGO publications, limited editions, newspapers.

Excluded are theses and dissertations, foreign publications, maps, periodical articles and titles published outside of Korea.

CONTENTS: Cataloguing information about *KNB*, introductory remarks, table of contents (and outline of classification scheme), main bibliography (divided by form of publication: official publications, general publications, books for children, textbooks, special publications (including non-book materials and serials publications) and title index.

CATALOGUING RULES AND CLASSIFICATION SCHEMES USED: *Korean Machine Readable Cataloguing Rules for Descriptive Cataloguing.*

The classification scheme used is the Korean Decimal Classification (KDC) edited by the Korean Library Association.

ENTRY INFORMATION: Author, title, place of publication, publisher, date, pagination, size, series. Price is given when known, as is the ISBN. The number in triangle brackets in the lower left corner is an index number which links to government publications, general publications, and children's books, e.g., <H00010>.

ARRANGEMENT: The official publications are arranged by issuing agency; the other sections (general publications, books for children, textbooks, non-book materials and serial publications) are arranged by headings from the Korean Decimal Classification; within each section they are arranged alphabetically. Serials are entered by title. Western language publications are at the front of each section.

INDEXES: An index is supplied for each of the separate sequences, including the titles and authors. Numbers are the index numbers which link to titles and authors in the text.

NOTES AND COMMENTS: Current acquisitions is aided by the publication of monthly issues of *Nappon wŏlbo*. - Vol. 23-No. 1 (1994, 1)-   . - Seoul : Kungnip Chungang Tosŏgwan, 1994-   . Monthly (LCCN: 94-657663/AK/V; LC: Z3316.M86; OCLC: 30879295; ISSN 1227-5247). *Nappon wŏlbo*, which cumulates into the annual current national bibliography, continues *Munhŏn Chŏngbo = Literary Information*. - 1972-yŏn 1-wol [Jan. 1972]- 1993 yŏn 12 wol [Dec. 1993]. - Seoul : Kungnip Chungang Tosŏgwan, 1972-1993. Monthly (LCCN: 79-646902/K/V/r943; LC: Z3316.M86; OCLC: 471040; ISSN 1225-0090). This title includes both domestic and translated works. One section under the division "New Information" is entitled "National Information." Published by the Central National Library as its accessions list, Munhŏn Chŏngbo is based on legal deposit. This title was established in 1972 and was formed by the union of *Chongch'aek charyo sokpo* and *Ch'ulp 'anmul nappon wŏlbo*. (LCCN: sn85-20704; OCLC: 11828658).

In the introduction of the *KNB*, it states that all Korean words are arranged alphabetically, all Chinese words are translated into Korean, and Japanese and European words are pronounced in Korean and arranged by alphabetical order.

Periodicals articles are listed in *Chŏnggi kanhaengmul kisa saegin = Korean periodicals index*. - 1969, 1/3-   . - Seoul : Taehan Min guk Kukhoe Tosŏgwan   [National Assembly Library], 1969-   (OCLC: 4561753). From 1963-1968 the title was *Kungnae kanhaengmul kisa saegin* (OCLC 4561676); this title continues *Haksul chapchi saegin* published since 1963 covering 1960-1968 (OCLC: 9411789). In 1982, a volume of *Chŏnggi kanhaengmul kisa saegin* covering 1910-1945 was published (OCLC: 22816790). The current *Korean periodicals index* is now automated quarterly. Earlier frequencies varied. Its scope includes government publications, and university, college and social organization journals. Arrangement is by subjects and authors.

Chŏngbu kanhaengmul mongnok or the *Government Publications in Korea*, issued by the National Assembly Library, 1948/79 (vol. 13) is an annual list based on legal deposits made at the library. (LCCN: 70-825140/K/V/r94; LC: Z3317.C44; OCLC: 3902090). From 1980-1989 it was also published by the Ministry of Culture and Information under the same title on an annual basis. At present *Chŏngbu kanhaengmul mongnok* is published by the Ministry of Information annually.[1]

LATEST ISSUE EXAMINED/CURRENCY: Volumes include imprints from the period of time covered. The latest volume examined at the National Library of Wales in November 1994 is 1992, published 1993. In June 1997, the latest volume to be published is 1995, published in 1996.

AUTOMATION: During 1982, the automation of *KNB* was established. The hardware used to produce the *KNB* is "Tandem NonStop Cyclone/R." The software used to produce the *KNB* is CENTLAS (CENtral Library Automation System) which was developed by the National Library of Korea.

FORMAT AND SERVICES AVAILABLE: printed, magnetic tape, CD-ROM in Korean characters, and Internet (which will retrieve general publications, theses, and dissertations).

CURRENT LEGAL DEPOSIT LAWS: Article 17 of The Library and Reading Promotion Act (Legislation No. 4746, 24 March 1994) outlines the submission of materials for legal deposit to the National Library of Korea.[2]

AVAILABLE FROM: The National Library of Korea, 60-1, Panpo-Dong, Seocho-Gu, Seoul, 137-702.

SELECTED ARTICLES: Choo, Yong Kyu. "National bibliographic control of current publications in South Korea." *Bulletin, Association for Asian Studies*. Committee on East Asian Libraries. No. 90 (June 1990):19-23.

Kim, Young Kuy. "A Study on the script and pronunciation of Japanese person's name in library cataloguing: about index of "Korean National Bibliography." *Do-seo-gwan-hak Non-jip* [Journal of the Korean Library and Information Science Society] 20 (1993):285-315.

Koo, Ja Young. "The Problems and Solutions of National Bibliographies in the East Asian Countries: Current Bibliographic Controls in China, Japan and Korea." pp. 210-227. In *Proceedings of IFLA Worldwide Seminar May 31 - June 5, 1976*. Seoul : Korea Library Association, 1976.

Lee, Pongsoon and Young Ai Um. "The State of Bibliographic Control and Services." pp. 105-115. In *Libraries and Librarianship in Korea*. Westport, CT: Greenwood Press, 1994.

Lee, Seong Duk. "A Study on Korean National Bibliography." Seoul : Sook Myung University, 1993. (Master of Library and Information Science)

VERIFIER: Director Gi-young Jeong, National Library of Korea.

---

[1] Current information about *Chongbu kanhaengmul mongnok* was received in a 22 May 1997 letter to the author by Choon-seop Kim, Chief, Planning & Cooperation Division, National Library of Korea.
[2] *The Library and Reading Promotion Act* was received with Choon-seop Kim's letter.

KUWAIT

TITLE: *al-Bibliyūjrāfiyā al-waṭanīyah al-Kuwaytīyah : sijill al-intāj al-fikrī fī al-Kuwayt khilāla'ām* [   ] [*Kuwaiti national bibliography: record of intellectual production in Kuwait during the year* [   ]]. - 1983-   . [Kuwayt] : Dawlat al-Kuwayt, al-Majlis al-Waṭanī lil-Thaqāfah wa-al-Funūn wa-al-Ādab, Idārat al-Maktabāt al-'Āmmah, 1985-   .
Annual, with cumulation every five years.
DDC: not found; LC: Z3028/K87B53 1985; LCCN: 87-964695/NE; OCLC: 20260206
ISSN not found

COMPILER: [i'dād al-Maktabah al-Markazīyah lil-Dawlah] [State Central Library].

SCOPE AND COVERAGE: *al-Bibliyūjrāfiyā al-waṭanīyah al-Kuwaytīyah* (*BWK*) includes the publishing output of Kuwait which is deposited at the national library according to legal deposit laws.

Types of publications include books and pamphlets.

Omitted from *BWK* are serials.

CONTENTS: Preface, introduction, classified bibliography, indexes, DDC subject headings.

CATALOGUING RULES AND CLASSIFICATION SCHEMES USED: International standards are followed. The Arabic subject heading list / Indexing Dept., King Saud University, Riyadh , a subject list compiled by Ibrahim Al-Khazindar, and the subject headings from Yafet Memorial Library, American University, Beirut are used.

The classification scheme used is DDC.

ENTRY INFORMATION: Serial number, author, title, place of publication, publisher, date, pagination, illustrations, size, series statement, notes.

ARRANGEMENT: Arrangement of the classified bibliography is by DDC, with modifications for Islamic religion, Arabic literature, history, and geography.

INDEXES: Author index, title index, subject index. The serial number is used to refer the user to the entries in the classified bibliography.

NOTES AND COMMENTS: For many years the author has heard there may be a national bibliography for Kuwait but subject specialists consulted have not been able to verify the title. This appears to be a national bibliography for Kuwait. This 1983 list includes 360 books by Kuwaiti and Arab authors. If distribution of this national bibliography could be improved, it would be helpful to scholars and bibliographers interested in publications from Kuwait.[1]

---

[1] The author is indebted to George Selim, Near East Section, Library of Congress African and Middle East Division for sending me a copy of pages from this title, and to Abdullah Bushnaq, student at The College of Wooster for assistance in translating pages from this work.

A monograph which covers six years is *Qā'imah bibliyūjrāfīyah bi-al-kutub al-'Arabīyah al-manshūrah fī al-Kuwayt khilāla al-'awam* (1977/1978/1979/1980/1981/1982) [Bibliographic list of Arabic books published in Kuwait through years 1977-1982] / idad wa-tajmī' Murāqabat al-Shu'ūn al-Thaqāfīyah [Collected and prepared by Cultural Affairs Supervision. National Council for Culture, Arts, Literature]. - [Kuwait] : Dawlat al-Kuwayt, al-Majlis al-Waṭanī lil-Thaqāfah wa-al-Funūn wa-al-Ādāb, [198-]. (LCCN: 86-107770/NE; OCLC: 13580786). This title lists 1418 books all published in Kuwait during the years 1977-1982. They are divided by subject headings from the Arabic subject heading list / Indexing Dept., King Saud University, Riyadh, and a subject list compiled by Ibrahim Al-Khazindar. Subject headings are listed alphabetical in this list except under divisions which have historical divisions in chronological order. Entries include author, title, place of publication, publisher, date, pagination, illustration statement, edition number, and series statement. The list has three indexes: subject headings, author, and title. The number in front of the titles or author's name is the serial number for the book.

The *Copyright Bulletin*'s "List of National or Regional Bibliographies" includes *Selected Bibliography on Kuwait and Arabian Gulf*, 1969, and *Source Book on Arabian Gulf States: Arabian Gulf in General, Kuwait, Bahrain, Qatar, and Oman*, 1975, both published by the Libraries Department, Kuwait University. According to the *Copyright Bulletin* "List," the contents of both bibliographies include books and pamphlets, maps and atlases. According to *BSTW, 1975-1979* (p.270) the *Source Book* also includes official and government publications, periodicals, theses and dissertations. The above years are the only issues of these titles that the author is able to verify.

According to Mr. George Atiyeh, former Head, Near East Section, African and Middle Eastern Division, Library of Congress, there is an annual book fair catalogue which lists Kuwait imprints and books about Kuwait. The title, translated from the Arabic, is *The Catalog of the [ ] Arabic Book Fair in Kuwait... on the ground of International Fairs*. The Mashrif District Sixth Circle, under the auspices of the National Council for Culture, Arts and Literature. The 7th book fair issue, 4-13 November 1981 is the latest copy examined.

The Ministry of Information compiles a list of publications that is received on legal deposit, which, according to Muḥammed al-Shattī, includes about 60-70 percent of titles published in Kuwait during the period 1972-1982.[1]

AL,ME (1963-1993, ISSN 0041-7769) and *The Arab Bulletin of Publications* (OCLC: 2239670) include Kuwait within their scopes.

LATEST ISSUE EXAMINED/CURRENCY: The latest issue examined from The Library of Congress in August 1997 covers the year 1983; it was published in 1985.

Imprint dates cover from the period covered.

AUTOMATION: automated.

---

[1] Katherine Van de Vate. *Books from the Arab World: a Guide to Selection and Acquisition.* Durham : Middle East Libraries Committee, 1988. On page 35, she makes reference to Muḥammed al-Shattī, "Taṭawwur ḥarakat al-nashr fi al-Kuwayt," [The Development of Publishing in Kuwait] in *'Ālam al-Kutub* 3 (no. 4 Jan./Feb. 1983):607.

FORMAT AND SERVICES AVAILABLE: printed.

CURRENT LEGAL DEPOSIT LAWS: [Legal deposit law of March 1972].[1]

AVAILABLE FROM: Kuwait Central Library, POB 26182, 13122 Safat.

VERIFIER: Mr. George Selim, Near East Section, African and Middle Eastern Division, The Library of Congress.

KYRGYZSTAN

TITLE: *Kyrgyz Respublikasynyn basma sòz zhylnaamasy = Letopis' pechati Kyrgyzskoĭ Respubliki* [The Republic of Kyrgyzstan's Chronicle of the Printed Word]. - 19??- . - Bishkek: Kyrgystan Book Chamber, 19?? - .
Monthly.
DDC: not found; LC: not found; LCCN: not found; OCLC: not found
ISSN 0136-085X

COMPILER: State Book Chamber, Kyrgyz Republic.

SCOPE AND COVERAGE: *Kyrgyz Respublikasynyn basma sòz zhylnaamasy* (*KRBSZ*) includes the publishing output of Kyrgyzstan deposited at the national library according to legal deposit laws.

Types of publications include books, pamphlets, periodicals, and newspapers.

CONTENTS: Preface, classified bibliography, periodical titles list, indexes, table of contents by type and subject.

CATALOGUING RULES AND CLASSIFICATION SCHEMES USED: ISBD is followed.

The classification scheme used is UDC.

ENTRY INFORMATION: Consecutive entry number, author, title, edition statement, place of publication, publisher, date, pagination, size, series statement, notes, including ISBN, language of publication if other than Kyrgyz or Russian, or if translated for *KRBSZ*, number of copies printed, Kyrgyz Republic Book Chamber registration number, indication of origin of publication and method of printing, classification number in lower right corner. Some entries have analytic table of contents.

ARRANGEMENT: Arrangement is by 50 subject headings.

INDEXES: Name index, subject index, geographic index.

---

[1] Van de Vate, p. 35.

NOTES AND COMMENTS: Before the breakup of the former USSR, *Knizhnaîa letopis'* included selected publications from Krygyzstan. The regional bibliography for Kyrgyzstan was *Kyrgyz Respublikasynyn basma sôz zhylnaamasy = Letopis' pechati Kyrgyzshoĭ Respubliki* (ISSN 0136-085X). When Kyrgyzstan became independent, *KRBSZ* became their national bibliography. This was a difficult title to locate.[1]

PROMPTNESS RECEIVED/CURRENCY: The latest issue examined in August 1997 is nos. 3/4, 1994 from Harvard College Library. Imprint dates are from 1994.

AUTOMATION: not automated.

FORMAT AND SERVICES AVAILABLE: printed.

CURRENT LEGAL DEPOSIT LAWS: No information available.

AVAILABLE FROM: Kyrgyzstan Book Chamber, 720000, G. Bishkek, ul. Sovetskaîa 170, a/ia 806.

SELECTED ARTICLES: Beynen, G. Koolemans. "The National Bibliographies of the Turkic Republics of the Soviet Union." *Government Information Quarterly* 3 (No. 2 1986):141-152. See especially pp. 147-148.

VERIFIER: David Zmijewski, Middle Eastern Division, Harvard College Library.

LAOS

TITLE: *Bannánukrom háéng Sát = National bibliography of Laos.* - 1968-1974 - Vientiane : Ho Samut Háéng Sát, 1969?-1974.
Biennial, with some issues combined.[2]
Ceased publication.[3]
DDC: not found; LC: (090) Z3226.L3B21; LCCN: not found; OCLC: 11478132

---

1 In a 28 July 1997 e-mail message, Irina Egorova, head of the Moscow office on CIS publications for East-View Publications, informed Kirill Fessenko, periodicals, East View Publications, that the national bibliography or any substitute title is not available and is not published currently because of financial difficulties. The author is grateful to David Zmijewski, Middle Eastern Division, Harvard College Library, who had a 1994 issue of the title, Carl Horne, Indiana University Library, and Mary Stevens, University of Toronto Library for their help. Valentina Antonova, a student at The College of Wooster, translated parts of the bibliography for the author. The author received no reply to two letters written to libraries in Bishkek.
2 The introduction for the 1968 volume stated that the bibliography was planned to be published yearly. However, in reality, volumes exist for 1968, 1970/71, 1972, and 1974.
3 When asked the status of the national bibliography in 1985, the National Library stated that this title is in a period of hiatus with plans to continue at a future date. However, OCLC record 11478132 now states that this publication has ceased. See Notes and Comments.

ISSN not found

COMPILER: Ho Samut Háéng Sát [Bibliothèque Nationale].

SCOPE AND COVERAGE: *Bannánukrom háéng Sát = National Bibliography of Laos* (*BHS*) includes the publishing output of Laos which is deposited at the Bibliothèque Nationale according to the legal deposit legislation. Laotian, English and French language publications are listed.

Types of publications include books, pamphlets, official and government publications, periodicals (from 1972), annuals, theses and dissertations by Lao students submitted to universities of the world, conference papers, and reports.

Excluded from *BHS* are broadsheets, microfilms, audio-visual materials, maps and plans, music, artistic prints and posters, IGO publications, internal documents.

CONTENTS: 1972: Classified monographs, classified serials, official publications, conference reports and research reports, alphabetical index of authors and titles. 1974: Classified monographs, classified serials, index of authors and titles.

CATALOGUING RULES AND CLASSIFICATION SCHEMES USED: No explanation is given. The descriptions appear to be pre-ISBD, with headings. AACR is used for Western materials. National cataloguing rules are used for Lao names only.

The classification scheme used is DDC.

ENTRY INFORMATION: DDC number in left margin, author, title, place of publication, publisher, date, pagination, illustrations, size. Complete information is not always supplied.

ARRANGEMENT: Arrangements differ in the various volumes. 1974 is arranged in two parts—classified monographs, and classified serials. 1972 volume is arranged in the two parts with a third part including official publications, conference reports and research reports. 1970-1971 is arranged in one classified sequence. 1968 is arranged in three parts—classified, alphabetical listing of authors, editors and issuing bodies, and an alphabetical order of titles.

INDEXES: Alphabetical index of authors and titles (all volumes except 1968).

NOTES AND COMMENTS: Although *BHS* is currently ceased, there are plans to resume its publication in the future. Because information on *BHS* was hard to locate, it was felt that it may be useful to include it, especially in light of plans for a future publication from Laos. It is through correspondence with Judith Szilvássy, Head, Department of Interlibrary Services, Union Catalogue of Periodicals, Hungarian National Library, Budapest, Hungary, that the most information was received. On a consultatory trip to Laos, she was able to confer with colleagues at the National Documentation Centre, Laos. Subsequent letters dated 22 October 1985 and 29 December 1985 included much of the information in this description. The author is grateful for her generous help. It is through a 1997 letter from Ms. Szilvássy (now Director, Information and Documentation Centre, Council of Europe) that the author was encouraged to contact the IFLA/ALP which is supporting a Laotian national bibliography project.

Under funding by IFLA/ALP, the National Library of Laos, under supervision of the Ministry of Information and Culture and the Department of State Printing and Distribution House, is collecting printed materials from 1975-1990 to produce a national bibliography for that period. Unlike the existing *BHS* which is based on the National Library's collection, this project is designed to collect material from all parts of Laos and from private printing houses and government publishers. The national bibliography will include bibliographic records for printed materials organized in volume I, 1975-1980; volume II, 1981-1985; volume III, 1986-1990, and a supplementary volume for the National Liberation period.[1]

The author also met with Helen Cordell, Principal Assistant Librarian, Southeast Asia and Pacific specialist at the University of London, School of Oriental and African Studies Library, London. Since the bibliography is written in Laotian script, the author is grateful to her for her interpretation of some of the material included in *BHS*.

Problems with the ineffectiveness of the legal deposit law have plagued the efforts to have a complete listing of Laotian imprints. Many publishers, private institutions and ministries ignore the legal deposit legislation. It is pointed out by Ms. Szilvássy that the old law has been abolished and the 1969 law has not been approved.

In many entries, the bibliographic information given is incomplete. It takes valuable staff time to try to trace missing information such as a year or place of publication, or to establish the correct form of the Laotian author's name.

In future issues, it would be beneficial to include preliminary information and to have it presented bilingually. This prefatory material should include some of the ICNB recommendations such as a table of contents, an introduction with explanations of the scope and coverage, rules followed, an analyzed entry, and abbreviations.

In addition to the official bibliography described, the following bibliographies with the same title have been published: *Bibliographie du Laos* / par Thao Kéne. - s.l. : Comité Littéraire, 1958 and *Bibliographie du Laos* / Pierre Bernard Lafont. - Paris : École Française de l'Extrême-Orient, 1964.[2]

A bibliography which updates the *BHS* slightly is *Bibliographie du Laos.* / Pierre-Bernard Lafonte. - Paris : Ecole Française d'Extreme-Orient, 1964-1978. (Publications–'Ecole Française d'Extreme-Orient, v. 50). 2 v. (OCLC: 851431). This comprehensive work includes books and and periodical articles by subject heading arrangement in all fields of knowledge. Volume 1 includes material to 1961, volume 2 covers works from 1962 to 1975. Author index.

AL,SEA included Laos within its scope.

PROMPTNESS RECEIVED/CURRENCY: The 1970/1971 issue examined by the author included imprints from the 1960's as well as from the time period covered. Most imprints were for earlier years.

---

[1] Bounleuth Thammachak. "Reports on Implementing the National Bibliography Project 1975-1990." *IFLA/ RSAO Newsletter* 8 (no. 2 Dec. 1996):11-13.
[2] Information in Ms. Szilvássy's 29 December 1985 letter from Vientiane.

The latest volume examined by the author was 1973 published in 1974, received by the University of London SOAS Library 31 January 1979. No later copies were located at the Library of Congress, British Library, SOAS, University of Michigan, University of Minnesota, Cornell University, or University of Wisconsin.

AUTOMATION: not automated.

FORMAT AND SERVICES AVAILABLE: printed.

CURRENT LEGAL DEPOSIT LAWS: Loi sur le dépot légal culturel. Decret 271 du 17 Janvier, No. 5029 du 4 Octobre 1927 et No. 5 du 3 Janvier 1928, later supplemented or replaced (?) by Loi du dépot légal [as part of] Arrété ministériel sur l'education nationale au Laos, No. 160/ED du 26 Février 1969, concernant la création de la Bibliothèque nationale. The old law has been abolished and this new law has not been approved.

AVAILABLE FROM: Not currently being published. Information may be received from Bibliothèque Nationale, BP 704, Vientiane.

SELECTED ARTICLES: Phonthipasa, B. ["Prerequisites of creation, contemporary state and perspectives of development of the National Bibliography of Laos People's Democratic Republic"]. In [National Bibliography, publishing activity and librarianship in the countries of Asia and Africa.] St. Petersburg: Library of Russia Academy of Sciences, 1992. pp. 89-103. In Russian.

Thammachak, Bounleuth. "Reports on Implementing the National Bibliography Project 1975-1990." *IFLA RSAO Newsletter* 8 (no. 2 December 1996): 11-13.

VERIFIER: no reply received.

LATVIA

TITLE: *Latvijas preses hronika = Letopis' pechati Latvii.* - 1-   . - Rīga : Institūts, 1990-   .
Monthly.
Issues for 1994 also have English title: *Latvian press chronicle.*
Continues *Latvijas PSR Preses chronika.*
DDC: 015.474; LC: Z2535.L365; LCCN: 91-649614; OCLC: 24169088
ISSN 0130-9226

COMPILER: Latvijas Nacionālā Biblioteka. Latvijas Bibliogrāfijas Institūts. [The Bibliographic Institute was incorporated into the National Library of Latvia in December 1993, and is reflected in *Latvijas preses hronika* from no. 2, 1994.]

SCOPE AND COVERAGE: Types of publications included in *Latvijas preses hronika Grāmatu hronika (LPH.GH)* are books, pamphlets and brochures, catalogues, anniversary programmmes, prospectuses, etc. of significant cultural or historical events published in Latvia. Volumes of art reproductions and photographs are entered in both the *LPH.GH* and the

Chronicle of Pictorial Works. Anthologies are analyzed with entries for all authors and translators. Entries for collections of abstracts have only Latvian authors or those living in Latvia.

Omitted from *LPH.GH* are some kinds of ephemera.

CONTENTS: Preface (in Latvian, English, Russian), table of contents, classified bibliography, indexes.

CATALOGUING RULES AND CLASSIFICATION SCHEMES USED: International standards ISBD(G), ISBD(M), ISBD(S), ISBD(CM), ISBD(CP), and UK MARC are used.

The classification scheme used is from *Universal Decimal Classification: International Medium Edition: English text: Part 1-2.* 2nd ed., 1993.

ENTRY INFORMATION: Consecutive entry number, author, title, place of publication, publisher, date, pagination, illustrations, size, series statement, number of copies printed, price, internal number, (e.g., 94-56), UDC number in lower right corner.

Entries are numbered separately according to an annual scheme. Book numbers start with 1, periodicals and series start with 3001, printed music start with 3501; pictorial works start with 4001, journal and newspaper articles start with 5001, reviews start with 40001, Latvia and Latvians in the world press start with 40501.

An asterisk (*) indicates that the materials are described by other bibliographic sources or received at the Institute in a exchange arrangement from other republics and states.

ARRANGEMENT: Arrangement is by type of material presented in separate sections. Entries are arranged by UDC.

INDEXES: Each volume includes a personal index, title index of books, printed music, albums and series; ISBN index, language index of publications in the section "Latvia and Latvians in world press", and the index of periodicals and series appearing in the issue. Once a year a separate edition *The Latvian Press Chronicle. Auxiliary indexes* is issued.

NOTES AND COMMENTS: *LPH* continues *Latvijas PSR prese chronika = Pechat' Latviisko i SSR / Latvijas PSR Kulturas ministrija [un] Latvijs PSR Grāmatu palāta pie LPSR Valsts bibliotēka.* Rīga : Latvijas Valsts izdevniecība, 1958-1989 (LC: Z2535.L365; LCCN: 57-47180//r91; OCLC: 24168353; ISSN: 0130-9226).

LPH includes the following sections which are issued in a common issue; not all sections are in every issue. Descriptive information is taken from the *LPH* English preface.

Grāmatu hronika [Book chronicle] is analyzed above.

Periodisko un turpinājumu izdevumu hronika [Chronicle of periodicals and series] appears annually in issue no. 12 of *LPH*. Entries give summary information about the whole item.

Nošu hronika [Chronicle of printed music] includes entries for separate editions of musical scores, publications of printed music for use in educational institutions, and includes information about printed music published in books, periodicals, newspapers, etc. published in Latvia. It appears quarterly in issues 3, 6, 9, and 12.

Attēlizdevumu hronika [Chronicle of pictorial works] includes information about artist produced posters, audio-visual materials, portraits, reproductions of paintings (separate and collective) and postcards.

Žurnālu un avīžu rakstu hronika [Chronicle of articles in journals and newspapers] gives a selective overview about articles in periodical issues. All fiction is recorded. Information about articles appearing in parallel editions in several languages is given only in Latvian.

Recenziju hronika [Chronicle of reviews] includes information about a selection of literary reviews published in periodicals and newspapers. Entries include a description of the work under review, followed by information about the review itself.

"Latvija un latvieži pasaules presē" ['Latvia and Latvians in the world press'] reflect information about the political, economic and cultural life of Latvia published outside Latvia during the previous two years. This includes entries not only for Latvian authors living in Latvia, but also those living abroad. Entries for materials not published within the two year period defined are arranged in a supplement at the end of each classified subsection.

Each entry is given in the language of origin with brief annotations in Latvian if necessary. Entries in other character systems are transliterated in the Roman or Cyrillic alphabet.

Authors' summaries of dissertations, are included in the *Gramata hronkia*.

It would be of help to the user to have a summary of UDC headings listed in the prefatory material.

A publication which gives annual statistics about publishing in Latvia is *Latvijas prese / Latvijas Nacionālā Bibliotēka, Latvijas Bibliogrāfijas Institūts*. - Rīga : Latvijas bibliogrāfijas institūts, 1990-   . (LC: Z375.L3L316; LCCN: 94-651266; OCLC: 25401380; ISSN not found). This title continues *Latvijas PSR prese = Pechat' Latviisko i SSR / Latvijas PSR Kūltūras ministrija [un] Latvijas PSR Grāmatu palāta pie LPSR Valsts bibliotēkas*. Rīga : Latvijas Valsts izdevniecība, 1958-1989. This title covers 1940/1956-1988 (LC: Z375.L3L316; LCCN: 88-641097//r942; OCLC: 15028776; ISSN: not found).

LATEST ISSUE EXAMINED/CURRENCY: The latest issue been is for June 1994 at Columbia University in August 1995. The entries are from the period covered.

AUTOMATION: Integrated library system ALISE [Advanced Library Information System] is implemented in the Bibliographic Institute.

FORMAT AND SERVICES AVAILABLE: printed.

CURRENT LEGAL DEPOSIT LAWS: The Law of the Republic of Latvia "About the National Library" stipulates: "all the printing houses must send 5 copies of all printed works to the National Library free of charge."[1]

AVAILABLE FROM: Bibliographic Institute of Latvia, Anglikanu Street, 5, LV-1816 Rīga.

VERIFIER: Dzintra Mukane, Director of the Bibliographic Institute, Deputy Director of the National Libary of Latvia.

LEBANON

No current national bibliography has been traced for Lebanon.

Lebanon is within the scope of *AL,ME* published from vol. 1 (1963)-31 (1993), and *The Arab Bulletin of Publications.*

Throughout the literature, references are made to a national bibliography active in the 1960s and early 1970s for Lebanon. David H. Partington in "National Bibliographies from the Middle East" mentions a national bibliography published by the National Library (Dar al-Kutub al-Waṭanīyah) which is part of the Ministry of National Education (Wizārat al-Tarbiyah al-Waṭanīyah). *Al-Nashrah al-Bibliyūghrafīyah al-Lubnānīyah lil-Intāj al-Fikrī wa-al-Tibā'ī fī Lubnān* [The Lebanese Bibliographic Publication for the Intellectual and Printing Production in Lebanon] begins coverage with part 1 for 1964, published in 1965. Part 3, issued 1971, and part 4, issued 1972, are in mimeographed form. The bibliography is in Arabic. According to Mr. Partington, the presentation of the material for the 1964 volume is in two parts. Part I lists books by Lebanese nationals, regardless of place of publication; part II lists books printed in Lebanon by non-Lebanese nationals. Appendixes include an index to Lebanese authors, and an index of Lebanese translators and editors. The volume for 1965 is in one alphabetical listing, arranged by Dewey, with an author index.[2]

Speaking of the same publication, Mohammed M. Aman states that the Lebanese National Bibliography "first appeared in 1965 covering the year 1964. The bibliography includes books written or translated by Lebanese and books published in Lebanon regardless of language or nationality of the author. The Lebanese National Bibliography is arranged in approximate Dewey Decimal Classification but without decimal numbers."[3]

---

1 Information in a letter dated 10 October 1996 to the author from Dzintra Mukane, Director of the Bibliographic Institute.

2 David H. Partington, "National Bibliographies from the Middle East, part 1," *Foreign Acquisitions Newsletter* 46 (no. 45):5. Information also taken from a letter to the author from Mr. Partington, dated 4 February 1986.

3 Mohammed M. Aman, "Bibliographical Services in the Arab World," *College & Research Libraries* 31 (July 1970):251.

Another listing of the same title but cited differently is seen in Pomassl's *Synoptic Tables* (Table 11). Bibliothèque Nationale. *Al-Nasra al-bibliogrāfīja al-Lubnānija. Bulletin bibliographique libanais des œuvres intellectuelles et des imprimés au Liban.* (1964-   ) 1965-   . According to Pomassl, this title includes books, non-book trade material, official publications, and publishing relating to Lebanon.

The "List of National or Regional Bibliographies" listed in the *Copyright Bulletin* 18 (no. 4 1984) includes a listing for Lebanon entitled National Bibliography. According to information supplied to the compilers as late as 31 March 1984, this title is an annual, published by the National Library, Place de l'Etoile, Beirut, and includes books and pamphlets.

In spite of the above *Copyright Bulletin* claim, the Middle East specialists at the University Library, Cambridge, the Library of Congress, Washington, DC., UCLA, the British Library Social Sciences Division, London, and SOAS, London have verified that there is no known current national bibliography at the present time. According to George Selim, Near East Section, African and Middle East Division, Library of Congress, the closest title to a national bibliography which lists current imprints is *al-Kitāb al-'Arabī fī Lubnān. Manshūrāt Jadīdah* (The Arabic Book in Lebanon. New Publications). The first volume of this catalogue appeared in 1980, and includes current imprints displayed at an annual book publishers' exhibition sponsored by the al-Nādi al-Thaqāfī al-'Arabī [Arab Cultural Club]. It is arranged by DDC, each entry is annotated, and has an author index and a list of publishers with addresses and telephone numbers. The latest held by the Library of Congress is for 1982. According to David Partington, the scope of this catalogue does not include government, corporate entries, or periodical titles.[1] (LC: Z3466.K57; LCCN: 81-642663; OCLC: 7621650).

CURRENT LEGAL DEPOSIT LAW: 1953 (Pomassl. *Synoptic Tables*, Table 11); 1952 (Aman, "Bibliographical Services...", p. 251). The *International Guide to Legal Deposit*, p. 86) cites [1924 Decree 2385 (amended 1946), art. 158-162]. Abdullatif Abdulhakeem Samarkandi's thesis cites a legislative decree number 134 of 6 December 1959, clause 41 as the depository law.[2]

LESOTHO

TITLE: *Lesotho index.* - No. 10, 1989-   . - Roma, Lesotho: Documentation and Publications Division, Institute of Southern African Studies, National University of Lesotho, 1989-   .
Quarterly (irregular).
Continues: *Lesothana.*
Cover title: *Lesotho index. An annotated bibliography of new and newly located Lesotho materials.*

---

[1] Information on *al-Kitāb al-'Arabī fī Lubnān. Manshūrāt Jadīdah* is taken from letters to the author from George Atiyeh, dated 2 December 1985 and David Partington, dated 4 February 1986.

[2] Abdullatif Abdulhakeem Samarkandi. "National Bibliography in Saudi Arabia, Egypt and Tunisia: Analytical and Comparative Study with a View to Planning a Saudi Arabian National Bibliography." Dissertation. Loughborough University of Technology, 1990. p. 45.

DDC: not found; LC: not found; LCCN: 90-80819; OCLC: 20456410
ISSN not found

COMPILER: Documentation and Publications Division, Institute of Southern African Studies, National University of Lesotho.

SCOPE AND COVERAGE: The scope of *Lesotho Index* (*LI*) includes those titles published in Lesotho, and those about Lesotho published elsewhere.

Types of publications included in *LI* are monographs, annual reports, pamphlets, workshop publications, government publications.

CONTENTS: Foreword, bibliography, indexes.

CATALOGUING RULES AND CLASSIFICATION SCHEMES USED: Cataloguing rules are not stated, although most information included in an AACR2 record is found in these entries.

No international classification scheme is used.

ENTRY INFORMATION: Entry number, e.g., 002, accession number, shelf location or classification number?, e.g., 11/1, 8/4, author, title, publisher, date, pagination, keywords, brief annotation.

ARRANGEMENT: The arrangement of the bibliography appears to be by accession number, e.g., 89/001, 89/002.

INDEXES: Author index, corporate author index, subject index. Numbers in the indexes refer back to the entry numbers.

NOTES AND COMMENTS: Although no current national bibliography has been traced for Lesotho, *LI* is a subject bibliography which includes all publications that have come to the attention of the Documentation and Publications Division, Institute of Southern African Studies, National University of Lesotho since the last issue regardless of the imprint date. Some issues are devoted to special topics. *LI* includes some analyzed entries, i.e., specific contributions within a workshop publication. *LI* is not based on legal deposit law since there is no legal deposit law in Lesotho.

LI continues the subject bibliography *Lesothana. An Annotated Bibliography of New and Newly Located Lesotho Materials*. No. 1 (Aug. 1982) -9 (May 1987). - Roma : National Library of Lesotho, Institute of Southern African Studies, 1982-1987. Quarterly. As stated in the first issue of *Lesothana*, this is intended to update the bibliography by Shelagh M. Willet and DavidP. Ambrose entitled *Lesotho: A Comprehensive Bibliography*. - Oxford : Clio Press, 1980. The scope of the quarterly will include titles published in Lesotho, and publications about Lesotho from the Institute and from information gathered from collections such as the National University of Lesotho Library, the Jacot Guillarmod Collection in Grahamstown, the LASA Library in Fort Collins, Colorado,[1] Yale University Libraries, Melville J. Herskovits Library of African Studies, Northwestern University, and SOAS Library, University of London. At the beginning, the priority of the compilers is to list the substantial backlog of material. Each of the first issues concentrates on specific subjects (e.g., history: general; history: early history). As the backlog is absorbed into the bibliography, then timeliness of entries and the coverage of the complete classification scheme will be a bigger consideration. In addition to bibliographic information (entry number and subject heading, author, title, location symbol, place of publication and publisher, date, pagination, Dewey number for those holdings of the Documentation Centre) each entry includes a brief annotation and tracings.

The *AL,ESA* and *QIPL,ESA* include Lesotho within their scopes.

LATEST ISSUE EXAMINED/CURRENCY: The latest issue examined in 1995 was *LI* no. 14 (July 1990) received 18 December 1990 at the University of Wisconsin, Madison library.

The shortage of staff is the main problem for delays.[2]

AUTOMATION: The software used in compiling the bibliography is "not at all user-friendly."[3]

FORMAT AND SERVICES AVAILABLE: printed.

CURRENT LEGAL DEPOSIT LAWS: none.

AVAILABLE FROM: Documentation and Publications Division, Institute of Southern African Studies, National University of Lesotho, P.O. Roma 180.

VERIFIER: no reply received.

LIBERIA

No current national bibliography has been traced for Liberia.

CURRENT LEGAL DEPOSIT LAWS: The *International Guide to Legal Deposit* cites the Legal Deposit Law in 1963, and the Presidential Message of 1965 (p. 86).

---

[1] LASA refers to the now-defunct Lesotho Agricultural Sector Analysis program of the Agricultural and Natural Resources section, Department of Economics, Colorado State University. Some LASA materials are in the University library, and a complete set is in the library of the Office of International Programs, Department of Economics, Colorado State University. This information was gathered in a series of telephone conversations with various departments at Colorado State University 4 June 1986.

[2] "Foreword," *Lesotho Index*, no. 10.

[3] Ibid.

LIBYA

TITLE: *Bibliyūghrāfīyah al-waṭanīyah al-ʿArabīyah al-Lībīyah lī-ʿām....* [The Libyan Arab national bibliography]. - 1982- . - Benghāzī : Dār al-Kutub al-Waṭanīyah, 1983- .
Triennial (1984/1985/1986-); annual (1982-1983).
Continues *Bibliyūghrāfīyah al-ʿArabīyah al-Lībīyah* [The Libyan Arab bibliography].
DDC: not found; LC: (090) Z3971.B53; LCCN: sn90-14238; OCLC: 21284491
ISSN not found

COMPILER: Dār al-Kutub al-Waṭanīyah [National Library of Libya – Benghāzī].

SCOPE AND COVERAGE: *Bibliyūghrāfīyah al-waṭanīyah al-ʿArabīyah al-Lībīyah lī-ʿām....* or the *Libyan Arab National Bibliography* (*LANB*) includes the publishing output of Libya, which is deposited at the national library according to legal deposit laws.

Types of publications include books, pamphlets, current periodicals, official and government publications, theses and dissertations, annual reports, children's books, foreign publications, reports, maps and atlases, standards, all types of material which include bibliographies or indexes, research.

Omitted are non-book materials and IGO publications.

CONTENTS: The Arabic section includes a table of contents, preface, introduction, terms and abbreviations used, summary of Dewey classification, bibliographic statistics, classified bibliography, indexes. The section written in English includes table of contents, terms and abbreviations used, summary of Dewey classification, bibliographic statistics; it does not include the introduction.

In a multi-year volume, such as 1990/1991/1992 bound in one volume, each year has a title page and the following sub-sections: trade (commercial, university, etc.) publications, official publications, periodicals, curriculum and school books (manuals and children's books), theses and dissertations, foreign language publications. Indexes are included in each section.

CATALOGUING RULES AND CLASSIFICATION SCHEMES USED: ISBD was adopted in 1978. The second level of bibliographic description is according to the first Arabic edition of the AACR, done by the Jordan Library Association in 1983.

Arabic subject headings are taken from lists prepared by Ibrahim Ahmed El-Kazindar, Kuwait, and Nassir Mohammed Eswaydan, Saudi Arabia. Other lists include *The Greatest Arabic Subject Headings List*, and the *LCSH* for foreign publications.

Also used is *Symbols of Authors and Books : Rules prepared by the Technical Department. Cataloguing, General Index and Technical Print*. National Library of Libya–Benghazi.
The classification scheme used is DDC, with amendments from the DDC in religion, history, language and literature for Arabic subjects.

ENTRY INFORMATION: Entry number, DDC number, author, title, translation note, place of publication, publisher, date, pagination, size, illustrations, series statement, tracings.

ARRANGEMENT: Arrangement is by DDC within the sections of trade books, official publications, periodicals, curriculum, theses and dissertations, and foreign language publications.

INDEXES: Separate author and title indexes are given for trade books and periodicals, scholastic and college books, and foreign language books. The numbers used in the index refer back to the entry numbers in the bibliography.

NOTES AND COMMENTS: *LANB* continues *Bibliyūghrāfīyah al-'Arabīyah al-Lībīyah* (*BAL*) [Libyan Arab Bibliography]. - 1971- 1981. - Tripoli : National Library, 1972- 1984. Annual. (LCCN: 78-643868 NE). In some volumes there is an added title page: *The Arab bibliography of Libya for 19[ ]*, and in other volumes, the added title page reads *The Libyan Arab Bibliography for 19[ ]*. The 1981 volume was prepared by the National Library in Benghazi. The compiler for 1976-1980, with a slight variation for 1976, is the Documentation and Technical Processing Section, Administrative Committee for Revolutionary Information Cultural Affairs, Tripoli. From 1973-1975, the compiler is the National Library and National Documents, Tripoli. The 1972 volume was compiled by The Section of Jamahiri Culture, Tripoli, and the 1971 volume was prepared by National Cultural Centers Department, Ministry of Information and Culture, Tripoli. The *Libyan Arab Bibliography* from 1971 included books, reports, and research taken from the *Libyan National Bibliography* 1951-1971, and volumes for 1972-1981 included books, reports, research, and periodicals.

English titles for the current national bibliography as listed by the National Library of Libya, and the date of publication are as follows: *Libyan Arab Bibliography for 1971*. 1972. *Libyan Arab Bibliography. The Official Directory of Libyan Intellectual Production*. 1973. *Libyan Arab Bibliography. The Official Directory of Libyan Intellectual Production*. 1975. *Libyan Arab Bibliography. The Official Directory of Libyan Intellectual Production*. 1974. *Libyan Arab Bibliography. The Official Directory of Libyan Intellectual Production*. 1976. *Libyan Arab Bibliography for 1976. The Official Directory of Libyan Intellectual Production*. 1977. *Libyan Arab Bibliography for 1977. The Official Directory of Libyan Intellectual Production*. 1978. *Libyan Arab Bibliography for 1978*. 1980. *Libyan Arab Bibliography for 1979. The Official Directory of Libyan Intellectual Production*. 1983. *Libyan Arab Bibliography for 1980. The Official Directory of Libyan Intellectual Production*. 1984. *Libyan Arab Bibliography for 1981. The Official Directory of Libyan Intellectual Production*. 1982. *Libyan National Bibliography for 1982*. 1983. *Libyan Arab National Bibliography for 1983*. 1985. *Libyan Arab National Bibliography for 1984/1985/1986*. 1987. *Libyan Arab National Bibliography for 1987/1988/1989*. 1996. *Libyan Arab National Bibliography for 1990/1991/1992*. 1996. *Libyan Arab National Bibliography for 1993/1994/1995*. 1996.

The scope and coverage of the *BAL* includes publications printed in Libya that are gathered by staff members as a result of a letter by the compilers to publishers requesting a copy of their publications. Types of publications covered are the same as *LANB*. As with *LANB*, the *BAL* is divided into an English and an Arabic section. The classified bibliography is arranged by DDC within the various sub-sections. An author index, title index, subject index for monographs, title and subject indexes for periodicals are provided.[1]

---

[1] The author appreciates the help of Abdullah Bushnaq, student at The College of Wooster, for his help in the translation of this text.

al-Bibliyūghrāfīyah al-waṭanīyah al-Lībīyah or the *National bibliography of the Libyan Arab Republic: Current and Retrospective* was published in two parts in 1972. Part one includes periodicals through 1972, Arabic and English coverage from 1827-1971. Part two covers 1951-1971, and includes books, reports and research. (LCCN: 78-643867/NE; LC: Z3971.B53; OCLC: 4204399).

The Annotated Bibliography for the Current Works of the Libyan Arab Authors, prepared by the Technical Processing Section, General Administration of Culture, was issued in two editions: 1976 and 1980 (revised and enlarged).

Libya is included within the scope of *The Arab Bulletin of Publications* and *AL,ME*, vol. 1 (1963)-vol. 31 (1993). Also some Libyan publications are included in the *Annuaire de l'Afrique du nord* . - 1 (1962)- . Paris, Centre national de la recherché scientifique, 19 - . (LCCN: 65-36969//r66; LC: DT181.A74; OCLC: 1481450; ISSN 0066-2607). An extract of this publication appears under the title *Chroniques et documents libyens* : 1969-1980 / par Hervé Bleuchot ; préface de M. Flory. - Paris : Editions du Centre national de la recherché scientifique, 1983. (LCCN: 88-109673; LC: DT236.B58 1983; OCLC: 11718705).

CIP is not practiced.

According to Director Saleh M. Najim, future plans for the National Library of Libya include establishing an ISBN program, and having ISSNs for the periodicals.

Titles in English, French, Italian and Arabic languages are included in *LANB*.

LATEST ISSUE EXAMINED/CURRENCY: The latest issue examined at the Princeton University Library in December 1996 is for 1987/1988/1989 published in 1996.

In looking at the English section for 1987/1988/1989 issue, most of the English entries were from the year covered. If the frequency of publication could be increased and distribution of *LANB* could be improved, *LANB* would be a useful current awareness source.

AUTOMATION: Not automated, although it is hoped to be automated in the near future.

FORMAT AND SERVICES AVAILABLE: printed.

CURRENT LEGAL DEPOSIT LAWS: Law No. 11 (Publications Act) of 14 June 1959. Amended by Royal Decree of 22 November 1962.[1]

---

[1] Confirmation that this is the current law was received in a letter dated 27 March 1997 to the author by Director Saleh M. Najim, National Library of Libya– Benghazi. *International Guide to Legal Deposit*, p. 86.

A legal deposit decree is not effective; there is no effective legal deposit law. The lack of an effective legal deposit law is the cause of delays in production of the national bibliography. A lot of time is spent gathering the publications that should automatically be deposited at the national library.

AVAILABLE FROM: Gift and Exchange Section, Acquisition Department, National Library of Libya– Benghazi, P.O. Box 9127, Great Socialist People's Libyan Arab Jamahiriya.

SELECTED ARTICLES: Attia, Ridha. "National Bibliographies in the Maghreb: A Survey of their Contents and Perspectives." Paper presented at the 50th IFLA General Conference, Nairobi, Kenya, 19-24 August 1984.

Schlüter, Hans. "Nationale bibliographie Libyens." *ZIBB* 22 (no. 1 1975):47-49.

Van de Vate, Katherine. *Books from the Arab World: a Guide to Selection and Acquisition.* Durham: Middle East Libraries Committee, 1988. See pp. 28-29.

VERIFIER: Mr. Saleh Mohammed Najim, Director, National Library of Libya

LIECHTENSTEIN

TITLE: *Liechtensteinische Bibliographie.* - Vaduz : Liechtensteinische Landesbibliothek, 1974- .
Annual.
DDC: 016.9436/48/005; LC: Z2124.L53L53; DB540.5; LCCN: 77-642540; OCLC: 3237500
ISSN (No ISSN assigned)

COMPILER: Liechtensteinische Landesbibliothek.

SCOPE AND COVERAGE: *Liechtensteinische Bibliographie* (*LB*) includes the publishing, printing and duplication output of Liechtenstein, works written by citizens of Liechtenstein or about Liechtenstein that are held by the Liechtensteinische Landesbibliothek.

Types of publications include new appearances of books, pamphlets, periodicals (new and changes of title, place of publication, frequency, publisher, etc.), periodical and newspaper articles about the history, people or of general cultural interest about Liechtenstein, official and government publications, maps and plans, scores, audiovisual media, typed theses and dissertations sent to the Landesbibliothek, translations.

Excluded are postcards, posters, brochures, reviews, encyclopedia articles, reviews, typed "Diplomarbeiten" and dissertations which were not sent to the Landesbibliothek, publications which are outdated quickly such as telephone directories, travel schedules, price lists; programs of festivities without special contributions or articles, publications without documentational value.

CONTENTS: Table of contents, foreword, user's guide, subject groups, bibliography: part 1, about Liechtenstein; part 2, works published in Liechtenstein, index, price and source of supply for *LB*.

CATALOGUING RULES AND CLASSIFICATION SCHEMES USED: The cataloguing rules used are not stated; ISBD rules adapted by the Vereinigung Schweizerisher Bibliothekare (VSB) are used. [1]

The classification scheme used is as follows: Part 1 uses a special version of the decimal classification used by the *Bodensee-Bibliographie*; Part 2 uses a simplified version of the International Decimal Classification, e. g., 1.1, 2.0.

ENTRY INFORMATION: Teil 1 and 2: consecutive entry number in upper left corner, author, title, year, place of publication, publisher, date, pagination, illustrations, size, notes including series, internal location number (e.g., FL H 897, A, B; FL X 1450/6, A) in lower left corner.

Translated titles include information about the original work.

ARRANGEMENT: Bibliographic entries are divided in two parts. Part 1 includes titles relating directly to Liechtenstein. The arrangement follows the *Bodensee-Bibliographie* published since 1977. Entries are divided into ten broad subject groups such as general, history, literature and art, population, religion and church. These subjects are subdivided. Groups 11 and 12 arrange entries by personal and family name, and place name. All are alphabetically arranged within the subjects. Part 2 includes titles that do not relate directly to Liechtenstein but were published in Liechtenstein. This part is categorized in ten subject groups and their subdivisions.

The titles are arranged alphabetically within both subject groups.

INDEXES: The index is an alphabetical listing of authors, editors, collaborators, publishers, series titles, anonymous titles, keyword index. Numbers refer to the consecutive entry number.

NOTES AND COMMENTS: *LB* is printed, and is presented in an attractive format. The preliminary remarks explain the scope and contents of the bibliography. An analyzed entry would be a helpful addition. For instance, it would be useful to know the proper name of the number in the lower left corner of each entry.

Official and government publications are not marked with any symbols.

Retrospective cumulations of Liechtenstein imprints which cover the years preceding *LB* are as follows. The years not yet covered bibliographically are from 1910-1959.

Heidi Roeckle. *Liechtensteinische Bibliographie, 1960-1973.* - Vaduz : Liechtensteinische Landesbibliothek, 1979. (LCCN: 81-154558; OCLC: 6856320).

---

[1] Information is given in a 1 August 1997 fax to the author by Marc Ospelt, Liechtensteinische Landesbibliotek.

Katalog der in den Bibliotheken der regierenden Linie des fürstlichen Hauses von und zu Liechtenstein befindlichen Bücher aus dem XVI.-XX. Jahrhundert. Im Auftrage seiner Durchlaucht des regierenden Fürsten Franz von und zu Liechtenstein. Bearb. von Hanns Bohatta [*Catalogue of Books from the XVI to the XX Century Contained in the Libraries of the Ruling Line of the Princely House von and zu Liechtenstein*]. Wien : Fürstlich Liechtensteinische Gemälde-Galerie [Princely Liechtenstein Picture Gallery], 1931. 3 v. (OCLC: 14700046).

LATEST ISSUE EXAMINED/CURRENCY: Bibliographic entries are for the period covered with few exceptions. The latest issue examined at the University of Minnesota in 1995 was for 1990.

AUTOMATION: Since 1981 the *LB* has been produced by SIBIL (Système informatisé pour Libraries).

FORMAT AND SERVICES AVAILABLE: printed.

CURRENT LEGAL DEPOSIT LAWS: "LGBl. 1961 Nr. 25."[1]

AVAILABLE FROM: Liechtensteinische Landesbibliothek, FL-9490 Vaduz, Liechtenstein.

A list of the available volumes, prices, and where to order them is given at the end of *LB*.

VERIFIER: Marc Ospelt, *Liechtensteinische Bibliographie,* Liechtensteinische Landesbibliothek.

LITHUANIA

TITLE: *Bibliografijos žinios. Knygos : Lietuvos valstybinės bibliografijos rodyklė = Bibliographical news. Books : Lithuanian national bibliographical index.* - Vilnius : Centras, 1996- .
Monthly.
Continues in part *Bibliografijos žinios = Bibliographical news = Bibliograficheskii vestnik.*
DDC: not found; LC: Z2537.B584; LCCN: 96-651340; OCLC: 35325070
ISSN 1392-1738

COMPILER: Lietuvos Respublikos Kultūros ministerija, Lietuvos nacionalinė Martyno Mažvydo biblioteka. Bibliografijos ir knygotyros centras [Ministry of Culture of the Republic of Lithuania, Martynas Mazvydo National Library. Centre of Bibliography and Book Science].

SCOPE AND COVERAGE: The *Bibliografijos žinios. Knygos (BZ.K)* includes books published in Lithuania which are deposited at the Lietuvos nacionalinė Martyno Mažvydo biblioteka. Bibliografijos ir knygotyros centras according to legal deposit laws.

---

1 The legal deposit law citation was included in a 5 August 1997 fax to the author by Marc Ospelt, Liechtensteinische Landesbibliotek.

Types of publications include books and pamphlets.

Excluded from *BZ.K* are departmental literature of limited usage, instructions, informative advertising publications, poster-like exhibition prospectuses, some publications of special technical character, such as standards, technical publications on separate technological processes, typical construction projects, posters of limited departmental application, posters of different events.

Serials, articles, and information about Lithania published in Lithuania and elsewhere are listed in other parts of the national bibliography which are analyzed after this title.

CONTENTS: Table of contents (also listing the UDC classes used in this issue), classified bibliography, index.

CATALOGUING RULES AND CLASSIFICATION SCHEMES USED: Cataloguing rules follow ISBD(M) for monographs, ISBD(CM) for maps, and ISBD(PM) for sheet music.

The classification scheme used is UDC.

ENTRY INFORMATION: Consecutive entry number, author, title, place of publication, publisher, date, place of printing and printer, pagination, illustrations, size, series statement, notes including number of copies printed, and ISBN, UDC number in lower right corner.

ARRANGEMENT: Arrangement is by UDC. The UDC table is published in the first issue.

INDEXES: Each issue has a name index. Annual indexes: name, title, collective author and geographic indexes. Annual cumulative indexes of the names of persons, titles, series, etc. are published in a separate publication.

NOTES AND COMMENTS: Prior to 1996, all Lithuanian imprints were included within the scope of *Bibliografijos žinos = Bibliographical news = Bibliograficheskii vestnik*. - Vilnius : Biblioteka, 1992-1995 (LC: Z2537.S62; OCLC: 28502763; ISSN 1308-0308). Before the break-up of the USSR, entries were listed in *Knizhnaîa letopis*, and in the then regional bibliography of *Spaudos metraštis = Letopis' pechati*. - 1957-1992, no. 12. - Vilnius : Valstybinė politinės ir mokslinės literatūros leidykla, 1957-1992 Entries are in Lithuanian and Russian. Monthly (LCCN: 91-649474//r93; LC: Z2537.S62; OCLC: 3723474; ISSN 0135-1354). The first issue of each year includes information about the title. Each issue includes sections (arranged by subject): Knygų metraštis [Books], Žurnalų ir laikraščių straipsnių metraštis, Recenzijų metraštis, Tarybinės lituanikos metraštis, with some issues including Periodinių leidinių metraštis, Gaidų metraštis, Vaizduojamojo meno spaudinių metraštis. This title was formed by a merger of *Knygų metraštis* (LCCN: 61-43669//r91; OCLC: 23026309), and *Žurnalų ir laikraščių straipsnių metraštis*. 1949-1956. - Vilnius : Lietuvos TSR Knygų Rūmai, 1949-1957 (LCCN: 58-53510//r91; LC: AI19.L5Z8; OCLC: 23026581; ISSN: not located).

Three other parts of the *Bibliografijos žinios* are analyzed after this entry. They are *Lituanika, Serialniai leidiniai* and *Straipsniai*.

Before Lithuania's independence, The Centre of Bibliography and Book Science was known as the Lithuanian Book Chamber.

LATEST ISSUE EXAMINED/CURRENCY: The latest issue examined is no. 7, 1996 received at the Library of Congress in January 1997.

Publishing and printing delays prevent *BZ* from being as timely as the Centre would desire.[1]

AUTOMATION: *BZ* is automated using a PC and Procite (LC). In 1997, plans are to change the national bibliography according to the Lithuanian Integrated Library Information System (LIBIS) which was installed in 1996. For the creation of the national bibliographic data bank, Lithuania will be using the ALEPH software, and the UNIMARC format.[2]

Records of the national bibliography will be sent to the Union Catalogue of Lithuania for rendering information services to all libraries and national bibliographic agencies of foreign countries, following agreements between countries regarding the exchange of bibliographic and authority records.

FORMAT AND SERVICES AVAILABLE: printed, CD-ROM, machine-readable form.

CURRENT LEGAL DEPOSIT LAWS: 1993 is the latest regulation.[3]

AVAILABLE FROM: Lietuvos nacionalinė Martyno Mažvydo biblioteka, Bibliografijos ir knygotyros centras, K. Sirvydo g. 4, 2600 Vilnius.

SELECTED ARTICLES: Bourne, Ross. "National Bibliographies and the Technological Gap," *ICBC* 24 (no. 2 April/June 1995):26-29.

Bulavas, V. and Varniene, R. *Lithuanian Integrated Library Information System*. Vilnius : 1995. p. 35.

Bulavas, V. and Varniene, R. "The Lithuanian Integral Library System (LIBIS)." *Bulletin of the American Society for Information Science* 21 (1 1994):25-26.

Varniene, R. "UBC and UNIMARC activities in Lithuania." *ICBC* 24 (no. 1 Jan./March 1995):8-9.

Varniene, R. "International UBC. UNIMARC Seminar in Vilnius. New Ways for implementation of modern techniques in bibliography." Paper presented at 61st IFLA General Conference, 20-26 August 1995, Istanbul. (Booklet 4, pp. 9-15).

§

---

[1] Bourne, Ross. "National Bibliographies and the Technological Gap," *ICBC* 24 (no. 2 April/June 1995):27.

[2] Information was received in a letter dated 14 February 1997 to the author from Dr. Regina Varniene, Centre of Bibliography and Book Science, National Library of Lithuania.

[3] Bourne, p. 26.

TITLE: *Bibliografijos žinios. Lituanika : Lietuva pasaulio spaudoje = Bibliographical news. Lituanica : Lithuania in the world press.* - 1996, nr. 1-   . - Vilnius : Centras, 1996-   .
Monthly.
Continues in part *Bibliografijos žinios = Bibliographical news.*
DDC: not found; LC: Z2537.B585; LCCN: 96-651342; OCLC: 35394022
ISSN 1392-1762

COMPILER: Lietuvos Respublikos Kultūros ministerija, Lietuvos nacionalinė Martyno Mažvydo biblioteka. Lituanistikos skyrius [Ministry of Culture of the Republic of Lituania, Martynas Mažvydo National Library. Department of Lithuanian Publications].

SCOPE AND COVERAGE: The *Bibliografijos žinios. Lituanica (BZ.L)* includes books about Lithuania published elsewhere and received at the Lietuvos nacionaline Martyno Mažvydo biblioteka. Bibliografijos ir knygotyros centras. It also includes articles from foreign periodicals and journals about Lithuania or written by Lithuanians abroad.

Types of publications include books, pamphlets, and articles.

CONTENTS: Table of contents (also listing the UDC classes used in this issue), periodicals and journals from which information is taken, classified bibliography, index.

CATALOGUING RULES AND CLASSIFICATION SCHEMES USED: Cataloguing rules follow ISBD.

The classification scheme used is UDC.

ENTRY INFORMATION: Consecutive entry number, author, title, place of publication, publisher, date, place of printing and printer, pagination, illustrations, size, series statement, notes including number of copies printed, and ISBN, UDC number in lower right corner.

ARRANGEMENT: Arrangement is by UDC.

INDEXES: Each issue has an name index. Annual indexes: name, title, collective author and geographic indexes.

NOTES AND COMMENTS: Prior to 1996, all Lithuanian imprints were included within the scope of *Bibliografijos žinios = Bibliographical news.* - Vilnius : Biblioteka, 1992-1995. (LC: Z2537.S62; OCLC: 28502763; ISSN 1308-0308).

LATEST ISSUE EXAMINED/CURRENCY: The latest issue examined is no. 6, 1996 received at the Library of Congress in January 1997.

AUTOMATION: Not automated, but a decision has been made to use Unesco's CDS/ISIS in order to apply UNIMARC.[1]

FORMAT AND SERVICES AVAILABLE: printed; CD-ROM.

---

[1] Bourne, p. 27.

§

TITLE: *Bibliografijos žinios. Serialiniai leidiniai. Lietuvos valstybinės bibliografijos rodyklė = Bibliographical news. Serials : Lithuanian national bibliographical index.* - 1995-   . - Vilnius : Centras, 1996-   .
Annual.
Continues in part *Bibliografijos žinios = Bibliographical news.*
DDC: not found; LC: Z6956.L5B53; LCCN: 96-651341; OCLC: 35325239
ISSN 1392-1754

COMPILER: Lietuvos Respublikos Kultūros ministerija, Lietuvos nacionalinė Martyno Mažvydo biblioteka. Bibliografijos ir knygotyros centras [Ministry of Culture of the Republic of Lituania, Martynas Mažvydo National Library. Centre of Bibliography and Book Science].

SCOPE AND COVERAGE: The *Bibliografijos žinios. Serialiniai leidiniai. Lietuvos valstybinės bibliografijos rodyklė = Bibliographical news. Serials : Lithuanian national bibliographical index (BZ.SL)* includes serial publications issued in Lithuania which are deposited at the Lietuvos nacionaline Martyno Mažvydo biblioteka. Bibliografijos ir knygotyros centras according to legal deposit laws.

Types of publications include newspapers, magazines, research works, collections, and bulletins.

Excluded are wall-newspapers, meteorological, agrometeorological, hydrometeorological bulletins, information leaflets and technical information leaflets of different organizations.

Books, articles, and information about Lithania published in Lithuania and elsewhere are listed in other parts of the national bibliography which are analyzed separately.

CONTENTS: Preface, table of contents, newspapers, magazines, periodical and continued collections, periodical and continued bulletins and other reference books, serials in braille, indexes.

CATALOGUING RULES AND CLASSIFICATION SCHEMES USED: Cataloguing rules follow ISBD(S).

No classification scheme is used.

ENTRY INFORMATION: Consecutive entry number, title, responsibility statement, editor, beginning issue, place of publication, publisher, date, notes including ISSN for magazines..

ARRANGEMENT: Arrangement is by types of publications: newspapers, magazines, periodical and continued collections, periodical and continued bulletins and other reference books, serials in braille. Entries are then arranged alphabetically under each category.

INDEXES: Editors, title index, ISSN, joint authors, and places of publication.

NOTES AND COMMENTS: Prior to 1996, all Lithuanian imprints were included within the scope of *Bibliografijos žinios = Bibliographical news.* - Vilnius : Biblioteka, 1992-1995 (LC: Z2537.S62; OCLC: 28502763; ISSN 1308-0308). This is in accordance with the National

Library of Lithuania Scientific Council's resolution of 29 November 1995 which reorganized the national bibliography.

Until 1996, the Serials section was called Periodicals.

Text in Lithuanian, Russian, with some English entries.

LATEST ISSUE EXAMINED/CURRENCY: The latest issue examined is 1995, published in 1996 and received at the Library of Congress in January 1997.

Most imprints have the previous year's imprint since the publications of the previous year are the titles registered. Some serials which are registered late are included in the year following their publication.

AUTOMATION: Automated. Currently using Procite, with plans to use ALEPH (UNIMARC format).[1]

FORMAT AND SERVICES AVAILABLE: printed.

§

TITLE: *Bibliografijos žinios. Straipsniai : Lietuvos valstybinės bibliografijos rodyklė = Bibliographical news. Articles : Lithuanian national bibliographical index.* - 1(1996)-   . - Vilnius : Centras, 1996-   .
Monthly.
Continues in part *Bibliografijos žinios = Bibliographical news.*
DDC: not found; LC: Z2537.B5857; LCCN: 96-651368; OCLC: 35547803
ISSN 1392-1746

COMPILER: Lietuvos Respublikos Kultūros ministerija, Lietuvos nacionalinė Martyno Mažvydo biblioteka. Bibliografijos ir knygotyros centras [Ministry of Culture of the Republic of Lithuania, Martynas Mažvydo National Library. Centre of Bibliography and Book Science].

SCOPE AND COVERAGE: The *Bibliografijos žinios. Straipsniai : Lietuvos valstybinės bibliografijos rodyklė = Bibliographical news. Articles : Lithuanian national bibliographical index* (*BZ.S*) includes articles published in selected serials of Lithuania which are deposited at the Lietuvos nacionaline Martyno Mažvydo biblioteka. Bibliografijos ir knygotyros centras according to legal deposit laws.

Types of publications cover articles from newspapers, magazines, periodical and continued collections which include documentary material, fiction, reviews, sheet music published in serial publications. A few publications use the Cyrillic alphabet.

Serials, books, and information about Lithania published in Lithuania and elsewhere are listed in other parts of the national bibliography which are analyzed separately in the Lithuania entry.

CONTENTS: Table of contents, classified bibliography, indexes, title abbreviations list.

---

[1] Varniene letter.

CATALOGUING RULES AND CLASSIFICATION SCHEMES USED: Cataloguing rules follow ISBD. Articles are described according to *Guidelines for the Application of the ISBDs to the Description of Component Parts*.

No classification scheme is given for individual articles.

ENTRY INFORMATION: Consecutive entry number, author of the article, title, serial title, illlustrator's name given if applicable, ISSN if known, date, number, pagination. An asterisk (*) identifies newspapers and periodicals which are issued in different languages.

ARRANGEMENT: Articles are arranged by the ten basic UDC classes, with some categories broken down to the second summary as needed. The UDC table is published in the first issue of the Articles.

INDEXES: Serial titles (separate newspapers and journals sections arranged alphabetically) and specific issues indexed in this issue, name index. Annual cumulative indexes of names of persons, joint authors, etc. appears in a separate publication.

NOTES AND COMMENTS: Prior to 1996, all Lithuanian imprints were included within the scope of *Bibliografijos žinios= Bibliographical news*. - Vilnius : Biblioteka, 1992-1995. (LC: Z2537.S62; OCLC: 28502763; ISSN 1308-0308). *BZ.S* continues in part *Bibliografijos žinios*.

Including a preface in each issue would helpful to the user.

LATEST ISSUE EXAMINED/CURRENCY: The latest issue examined is no. 6, 1996 received at the Library of Congress in January 1997.

AUTOMATION: Not automated, but a decision has been made to use Unesco's CDS/ISIS in order to apply UNIMARC.[1]

FORMAT AND SERVICES AVAILABLE: printed, CD-ROM.

VERIFIER: Dr. Regina Varniene, The Centre of Bibliography and Book Science, National Library of Lithuania.

LUXEMBOURG

TITLE: *Bibliographie luxembourgeoise*. - 1944/45-   . - Luxembourg : Bibliothèque nationale, 1945-   .
Annual.
DDC: not found; LC: Z2461.B5; LCCN: 51-39615; OCLC: 2066422
ISSN not found

COMPILER: Luxemburgensia Department, Bibliothèque Nationale.

---

[1] Bourne, p. 27.

SCOPE AND COVERAGE: *Bibliographie luxembourgeoise* (*BL*) lists titles that are published, edited, printed or mimeographed in Luxembourg, written by Luxembourgers or concerning Luxembourg, that are received by the Bibliothèque Nationale either through legal deposit or by acquisition.

Types of publications included in *BL* are books, pamphlets, periodicals (new titles or titles not previously listed and changes in title, publisher or frequency), official and government publications (since 1963 covering 1962), maps and atlases, musical scores, audio-visual material such as disks, video cassettes, and music cassettes; periodical articles and other materials of scientific worth or concerning local history and folklore, IGO publications if they relate to Luxembourg, published theses and dissertations by citizens of Luxembourg abroad or by foreigners whose subject concerns Luxembourg provided that the National Library possesses a copy.

Excluded from *BL* are ephemeral materials such as telephone directories, timetables, price lists; postcards, publications published for European Community organizations established in Luxembourg but which do not relate to Luxembourg, festivities programs without articles of content, unpublished theses and scientific memoirs (unless a copy has been deposited at the National Library), publicity materials which have no documentary interest.

CONTENTS: Table of contents, avertissement [introductory information], abbreviations list, bibliography by subjects, periodical section, audiovisual section, author, collections, and anonymous index, subject indexes, publishers' and printers' list, and list of Luxembourg ISBN numbers.

CATALOGUING RULES AND CLASSIFICATION SCHEMES USED: Cataloguing rules followed are not stated in the introduction. AACR2 format is used, and basic bibliographic information is given.

The classification scheme used is broad general subjects.

ENTRY INFORMATION: Consecutive entry number, author, title, place of publication, publisher, date, series, pagination, illustrations, size, notes. Price is not given.

For articles in collections: author and title of article, title of the collection, place of publication, year and page numbers for the article.

For periodical articles: author and title of article, periodical title, volume, year, number, pagination.

If periodicals are published in "Luxembourg-Ville," the place of publication is not given.

ARRANGEMENT: *BL* is arranged by eighteen broad subject categories, and additional categories which list the new or changed periodical titles, audio-visual materials, and indexes. Most of the broad subjects are subdivided. Entries are alphabetically arranged within the categories.

INDEXES: Author, contributors, anonymous works and collections; subject index. Recent subject indexes are alphabetical; in earlier years the subject index was divided into part A:

subjects of general interest and part B: subjects concerning Luxembourg. Numbers refer to the consecutive entry number in the bibliography.

NOTES AND COMMENTS: The *BL* includes titles from preceding years that have entered the Bibliothèque Nationale's collection during the year of publication.

Official and government publications are not designated by any symbol.

BL is in a pleasing format, and meets ICNB recommendations 5, 6, 9-11. A future consideration might be to include an analyzed entry in the introductory remarks.

CIP does not exist in *BL.*

LATEST ISSUE EXAMINED/CURRENCY: Entries are for the period covered with some titles listed that have not been included previously. On four sample pages, all of the titles except two were for the period covered. The latest issue examined from Miami University, Oxford, OH is for 1994, published 1995.

AUTOMATION: not automated.

FORMAT AND SERVICES AVAILABLE: printed. Internet accessibility is available from the end of September 1997.

CURRENT LEGAL DEPOSIT LAWS: Règlement grand-ducal du 10 août 1992 réglementant le dépôt en faveur de la Bibliothèque Nationale en tant qu'agence bibliographique.[1]

AVAILABLE FROM: Bibliothèque Nationale, 37 Boulevard F.D. Roosevelt, 2450 Luxembourg. Fax: (+352) 475672

VERIFIER: Jean-Claude Muller, Director, Bibliothèque nationale.

MACEDONIA (FORMER YUGOSLAV REPUBLIC OF)

TITLE: *Makedonska bibliografija. 1. Serija monografski publikacii.* - 1980, Sv. 1-   . - Skopje : NUB "St. Kliment Ohridski," 1981-   .
Frequency varies: currently semiannual; biennial, 1950-1971.
Makedonska bibliografija published in 3 series. See Notes and Comments.
Continues *Makedonska bibliografija. 1 del, Monografski publikacii.*
DDC: not located; UDC: 015 (497.17); LC: Z2911.M35; LCCN: 95-646633; OCLC: 9097949
ISSN 0351-417X

COMPILER: Narodna i univerzitetska biblioteka "Kliment Ohridski" Skopje.

---

[1] Information about the new legal deposit law was sent in a 9 September 1997 letter to the author by Director Muller.

SCOPE AND COVERAGE: *Makedonska bibliografija. 1. Serija monografskii publikacii* (*MB.1*) includes the publications of Macedonia, irrespective of language or script, which is deposited at the national library according to legal deposit laws.

Types of publications include books, pamphlets, maps, published and manuscript dissertations, and note materials.[1]

Omitted from *MB.1* are periodicals and periodical articles, which are included in other national bibliography series which are described in the Notes and Comments section. Titles published outside Macedonia written by Macedonian authors are included in *Bibliography Makedonika*, also described in the Notes and Comments section.

CONTENTS: Foreword, abbreviations, classified bibliography, indexes, UDC subject heading index.

CATALOGUING RULES AND CLASSIFICATION SCHEMES USED: ISBD(M), and Macedonia guidelines consistent with International Federation of Documents rules are followed, as are the descriptive cataloguing guidelines by Eve Verona,

The classification scheme used is UDC.

ENTRY INFORMATION: Title, responsibility statement, place of publication, publisher, date, pagination, illustrations, size, series statement, notes including original heading of translated publication, number of copies printed, number of bibliographic references, summary, ISBN, UDC number in lower left corner, etc.

ARRANGEMENT: Arrangement is by UDC categories; multiple entries under a UDC number are arranged alphabetically.

INDEXES: Author, title (1980-   ), UDC subject heading index (1993-   ), ISBN, UDC subject heading index (1993-   ), publisher and printer (1994-   ).

NOTES AND COMMENTS: Before the break-up of Yugoslavia, the National and University Library has been recording Macedonian production in *Makedonska bibliografija* as prescribed under legal deposit law. Since 1991, prepared and issued under the independent Macedonia Republic. The *Bibliografija Jugoslavije. Knjige, brosure i muzikalije* is a compilation of Yugoslav imprints on which national libraries had no control or influence.

MB.1 has been described above. This title continues *Makedonska bibliografija. 1 del, Monografski publikacii.* 1975-197? Skopje : NUB "St. Kliment Ohridski," 1979-   . (LCCN: sc84-01623; OCLC: 9097911) which continues *Makedonska bibliografija za ...godina. 1 del, Knigi, brosuri, separati, muzikalii i albumi.* - 1962 i 1963-1974. - Skopje : Biblioteka, 1967-1977. Frequency varies (LCCN: sc84-1593; OCLC: 9097849). This title continues in part *Makedonska bibliografija za ... god.* - 1950-1951-1960 i 1961. - Skopje : Biblioteka, 1962-1966. Biennial (LCCN: 52-43456//r842; OCLC: 9097789). This title continues *Makedonska*

---

[1] The author appreciates the help of Stefan Tzanev, a student at The College of Wooster, in translating information for this entry.

bibliografija od osloboduvanjeto do krajot na ... godina. - Skopje : Drzavno knigoizdatelstvo na NR Makedonija, 1951 (LCCN: sf84-26; LC: Z2854.M3S6; OCLC: 1216057; ISSN 0580-499X).

Since 1980 there have been three series in the Macedonia bibliography. Bibliographic information on the other two follows.

Makedonska bibliografija. 2. Serija Statii i prilozi [Articles and appendixes]. - 1980 - , Sv. 1- . - Skopje : NUB "St. Kliment Ohridski," 1981- . Quarterly (DDC number: not located; UDC: 015 (497.17); LC: Z2957.M3M34; LCCN: 90-646183; OCLC: 117335674; ISSN 0351-4196). This continues in part *Makedonska bibliografija za ... god.* - 1950-1951-1960 i 1961. - Skopje : Biblioteka, 1962-1966. Biennial. (LCCN: 52-43456; OCLC: 9097789). This is a selected bibliography based on particular scientific periodicals (70-80 titles). The selection of articles is by previously determined criteria. Periodical articles and periodicals from proceedings of scientific meetings are included. Before the break-up of Yugoslavia, Macedonian articles and appendixes were included within the scope of *Bibliografija Jugoslavie : clanci i prilozi u seriskim publikacijama, serija A,B,C.* - Beograd : Jugoslovenski bibliografski institut, 1950- .

Makedonska bibliografija. 3. serija. Seriski publikacii [Serial publications]. 1944/1984 - , Sv. 1- . - Skopje : NUB "St. Kliment Ohridski," 1993- . Every one or two years (DDC: not located; UDC: 015 (497.17); LC: Z2913.M33; LCCN: sn94-31119; OCLC: 31065968; ISSN 0351-4188). This title includes serials published and printed in Macedonia. It does not include monographic serials.

In addition to the current national bibliography, the national library has published since 1985 the *Bibliography Makedonika*, covering titles from 1975. *Bibliografija Makedonika 1 serija Jugoslovenski publikacii za Makedonija* (UDC: 015(497.17):497.1; ISSN 0352-4124), and *Bibliografija Makedonika 2 serija Stranski publikacii za Makedonija* (UDC: 015(497.17):100; ISSN 0352-4132) includes titles that fulfill one of the following criteria: works written in the Macedonian language published in the former Yugoslav Republics, works published by Macedonian authors outside Macedonia, and works on Macedonia or Macedonians.[1] Types of publications include books, pamphlets, published and manuscript dissertations (series 1) note material, maps and articles. From 1991, two serials will be included in one serial *Stranski publikacii za Makedonija.*[2]

The retrospective bibliography of Macedonia is an on-going project which is planned to cover from the beginning of publishing in Macedonia up to 1944. The first volume covered books and was published in 1970: *Retrospektivna bibliografija na Makedonija. Knigi* (LCCN: 74-970092; LC: Z2957.M3R48; OCLC: 4064306). This covers book production of the geographic territory and ethnic Macedonia from the first published book up to 1913, and the book production from the Republic of Macedonia up to 1944 which are in libraries in Macedonia and abroad. Types of publications include books, pamphlets, note material, almanacs, calendars, etc. Contents include foreword, entries, appendix on the Jewish contribution, indexes, contents. A second volume which covered serials was published in 1993: *Retrospektivna bibliografija na Makedonija. Seriski publikacii* [v.2, pt. 1]. (LCCN: 96-165385; LC: Z2911.P67 1993;

---

[1] Stana Jankoska and Viktorija Kostovska. "The St. Clement of Ohrid National University Library: Macedonia's National Library." *Alexandria* 8 (2 1996): 124-125.
[2] Kalajlievska letter.

OCLC:35673815; ISSN 0351-4188). This covers book production of the geographic territory and ethnic Macedonia up to 1944 in Serbian and Bulgarian languages.

LATEST ISSUE EXAMINED/CURRENCY: The latest issue of *MB.1* examined is 1993, no. 2, at the University of Michigan Library in March 1997; the latest issue of *MB.2* examined is 1991, no. 2. Imprint dates cover from 1989 to 1991.

AUTOMATION: Since 1990 *MB* has been produced by a word processor and is part of the Yugoslav bibliographic database *YUBIB*.

FORMAT AND SERVICES AVAILABLE: printed.

CURRENT LEGAL DEPOSIT LAWS: Zakon za zadolzitelen primerok vo Sluzben vesnik na Republika Macedonija. - Skopje. - br. 11 (8 mart 1994); str. 291-293.

AVAILABLE FROM: Narodna i univerzitetska biblioteka "St. Kliment Ohridski" Skopje.

VERIFIER: Vera Kalajlievska, Director, National and University Library.

MADAGASCAR

TITLE: *Bibliographie nationale de Madagascar.* - 1970/71-   . - Antananarivo : Bibliothèque universitaire et Bibliothèque nationale, 1979-   .
Frequency varies: quarterly (1983-), biennial (1970/71-).
From 1983-   issued by Bibliothèque nationale.
Parallel title: *Rakitahirinkevi-pirenen' i Madagasikara* (1983-   )
Continues *Bibliographie annuelle de Madagascar.*
DDC: 015.69/1; LC: Z3701 .B5, DT469.M26; LCCN: 79-649190; OCLC : 5881201
ISSN 0067-6926.

COMPILER: Bibliothèque Nationale.

SCOPE AND COVERAGE: The *Rakitahirinkevi-pirenen' i Madagasikara = Bibliographie Nationale de Madagascar* (*BNM*) strives to include all publications printed in Madagascar and deposited at the Bibliothèque Nationale according to legal deposit legislation. Materials printed abroad about Madagascar are also within the scope regardless of subject, level or scholarly interest.

Types of publications within the scope of *BNM* are books, pamphlets, official and government publications, reports, first issues of periodicals, mimeographed and typed materials of permanent value such as lectures.

Omitted from *BNM* are IGO publications, maps, plans, phonograph recordings, theses and internal documents, and from 1983, periodical articles and newspaper articles.

CONTENTS: Introduction (in Malagasy and in French), UDC tables, indicator numbers for Madagascar by region and city, bibliography: monograph section, publications in series, author indexes, abbreviations.

CATALOGUING RULES AND CLASSIFICATION SCHEMES USED: ISBD has been used in the national bibliography since 1979.[1] The National Library adopted ISBD(M) in 1976 and ISBD(S) in 1977.[2]

The classification system used is the UDC.

ENTRY INFORMATION: For monographs: consecutive entry number, author, title, place of publication, publisher, date, size, pagination. If not printed, method of production noted (e.g., ronéot). Price is not given.

Publications in series (new titles): consecutive entry number, title, author, frequency, number, issue date, edition, pagination, format, notes.

Serial publications (new titles): title, frequency, numbers and dates of publication.

For periodical articles: consecutive entry number, author (if known), title, periodical title, place of publication, number, date, pagination of article.

Although not currently used, earlier issues included some entries are marked with an asterisk (*) or with two asterisks (**). There is no abbreviations list to indicate the significance of these symbols. In the particular issue that these symbols were first noted, there was no introduction which might have explained the symbols. One ascertains by looking at the marked entries that these symbols are identifying foreign imprints.[3]

ARRANGEMENT: "Monographs" and "Publications in series" are in separate parts. The monographs are arranged by UDC number, then arranged alphabetically by main entry. The publications in series is divided into "new publications" and "publications in progress." The new publications are arranged by UDC number, then arranged alphabetically by main entry; the publications in progress are alphabetical by main entry.

INDEXES: "Monographs" and "Publications in series" have separate sections within the first two indexes: index of authors and other responsible persons, index of subjects, and table of systematic classes of publications in series. The number used refers back to the entry number in the classified bibliography.

NOTES AND COMMENTS: *BNM* continues *Bibliographie Annuelle de Madagascar* (*BAM*) (ISSN 0067-6926; OCLC: 2497124) from the first volume covering 1964, published in 1966, to

---

[1] *International Cataloguing* 11 (Jan./Mar. 1982):2.

[2] *IFLA Journal* 5 (no. 3 1979):255.

[3] In a 14 July 1997 letter written to the author by Jeannette Ramananiary, Head of the Department of Bibliographies and Catalogues, Documentary Research and Information Operations, Bibliothèque Nationale, one asterisk indicates works or articles published in Madagascar, and two asterisks mark works published outside of Madagascar.

another volume covering 1969, published in 1973. It was renamed *BNM* with the 1970/71 volume published in 1979.

Because of the long delay in publication of *BNM*, the Bibliothèque Nationale began publishing *Rakitahirinkevi-Pirenen' i Madagasikara*, the first issue being for the first "trimestre" 1983. Other issues to date are the second "trimestre" 1983, and the second "semestre" 1983, which appeared in 1984/1985. This title is mimeographed and has been published in a very small edition. This title does not attempt the broad coverage of *BNM*, e.g., periodical articles. Although foreign titles are within its scope, there are few to be found. Since 1983 *Rakitahirinkevi-Pirenen' i Madagasikara* has been the first listed title of parallel titles, the second being *Bibliographie national de Madagascar*.

The 1972-1982 gap in *BNM* has been partially covered by the following two titles: *Rakitahirinkevi-pirenen' i Madagasikara = Bibliographie nationale de Madagascar* 1972-1975, and *Vao niseho = Vient de paraitre* 1977-1980. The years 1976, 1981, and 1982 have not been included although bibliographic records exist for this period.[1]

Although the *BAM* only began in 1966 (covering 1964) there is bibliographical coverage from 1500-1955 in *Guillaume Grandidier's Bibliographie de Madagascar* (3 v. reprint, OCLC: 26696921), and from 1956-1963 with Jean Fontvieille's continuation of this title up to the commencement of the current bibliography coverage (OCLC: 13391716).

Government publications have been included since the first issue of *BNM*. These are not marked by a symbol, but can be identified by the corporate headings used in the index and the classified bibliography.

Languages used in *BNM* are French, German, English and Malagasy.

AL,ESA and *QIPL,ESA* include Madagascar within their scopes.

LATEST ISSUE EXAMINED/ CURRENCY: Promptness is a problem with this national bibliography. The gap is shorter with the narrower scope of *BNM*. The latest issue examined is for the second quarter of 1989, published in 1990, and received 30 April 1991 at Indiana University. This is the latest published.[2]

Most volumes include titles for the year covered, with an addendum for titles from earlier years.

AUTOMATION: not automated.

FORMAT AND SERVICES AVAILABLE: printed.

---

[1] Information about coverage of the existing records is taken from a letter to the author by James C. Armstrong, Field Director, Library of Congress Office, Nairobi, Kenya, dated 11 September 1985.

[2] Information received in the 14 July letter written to the author by Jeannette Ramananiary. The *BNM* is now printed by computer which should help with the regularity of the bibliography's publication schedule.

CURRENT LEGAL DEPOSIT LAWS: Loi no. 90-031 du 21 décembre 1990 sur la Communication (Chapitre II : Du Dépôt Légal).[1]

AVAILABLE FROM: Bibliothèque Nationale, Anosy, P.O. Box 257, Antanararivo.

SELECTED ARTICLES: Lyutova, K.V. "Stanovlenie Natsional'noi Bibliografii v Demokraticheskoi Respublike Madagaskar." ("The Establishment of a National Bibliography in the Democratic Republic of Madagascar.") *Sovetskaya Bibliografiya* no. 2 (1976):109-114.

Nucé, M. S. de. " La Bibliographie Nationale à Madagascar." In *The Bibliography of Africa. Proceedings and Papers of the International Conference on African Bibliography, Nairobi, 4-8 December 1967*, edited by J. D. Pearson and Ruth Jones, pp. 120-125. London: Frank Cass & Co., 1970.

Rahary, Espree. "Madagascar. " *Afribiblios* 9 (no. 1 June 1986):7.

Rakoto Rzafindrakotohasina Rabakonirina. "Rapport présenté a Dar-es-Salaam par le représentant de Madagascar." *Afribiblios* 7 (no. 1 1984):22-24.

VERIFIER: Jeannette Ramananiary, Head of the Department of Bibliographies and Catalogues, Documentary Research and Information Operations, Bibliothèque Nationale.

MALAWI

TITLE: *Malawi national bibliography.* 1967-   . - Zomba : National Archives of Malawi, 1968-   .
Subtitle: *List of publications deposited in the Library of the National Archives.*
Continues: *List of publications deposited in the Library of the National Archives.*
Annual, with cumulations; biennial (1977-1980).
DDC: O15.689/7; LC: Z3577.N37a; DT857; LCCN: 77-642555; OCLC: 2588837
ISSN 0542-3058

COMPILER: Staff members of the National Archives of Malawi, e.g., 1986: Dick D. Najira.

SCOPE AND COVERAGE: The *Malawi National Bibliography* (*MaNB*) lists all titles published in Malawi and received by the National Archives during the calendar year. Every effort is made to make this bibliography as complete as possible.

Types of publications included are books, pamphlets, new serials, official and government publications, annual reports and other publications of statutory bodies, clubs and societies, churches, etc.

Excluded are school magazines which appear sporadically and under varying titles, advertising brochures, maps and non-print materials, IGO publications.

---

[1]   14 July 1997 letter.

CONTENTS: 1984-1990: introduction, table of contents, bibliography, first issues of periodicals, periodical cessations and changes, author index, subject index, directory of publishers in Malawi, appendix: the *Printed Publications Act*. Earlier issues included statistics on book production.

CATALOGUING RULES AND CLASSIFICATION SCHEMES USED: Since 1982, AACR2 has been adopted for cataloguing entries.

The *MaNB* uses the 100 main subject divisions of the DDC scheme.

The *LCSH* (12th ed.) has been used for subject headings, with local adaptions as appropriate.

ENTRY INFORMATION: Entry number, author, title, place of publication, publisher, date, pagination, illustrations, size, series statement, For 1986, entry number is listed at lower right corner, e.g., MNB-056. The 1983 and earlier issues only list a number, e.g., 56. Prices have not been given in issues after the 1982 issue.

Occasional notes such as a title translation or contents notes are given.

In some issues, addresses of smaller publishers are given in entry information rather than in the major publishers' list.

Entries do not include a classification number but entries are grouped under one of the 100 classification headings in the main section of new publications.

ARRANGEMENT: In the main section, entries are arranged alphabetically within a classified order following the 100 divisions of the DDC scheme.

In the Periodical Cessations and Changes Section, entries are alphabetically arranged.

INDEXES: 1984-1990 includes an author index and a subject index. For 1986 issued separately: The author/editor/title/series index is in one alphabetical arrangement. An exception was 1979/80 which had a separate author and a title index. From 1979, index numbers refer to entry numbers, a precise way of pinpointing the entry needed. Earlier volumes referred to page numbers. The classification number was not given and it was necessary for a reader to scan an entire page which might include several classification numbers.

Before the mid-1970's, there was no index.

NOTES AND COMMENTS: *List of Publications Deposited in the Library of the National Archives* began in 1961 covering the Federation of Rhodesia and Nyasaland and was published in 1963 by the National Archives of Rhodesia and Nyasaland. Malawi imprints for 1965 onwards have been listed in *MaNB*. Issues for 1965 and 1966 appeared in mimeographed form under the title *List of Publications Deposited in the Library of the National Archives*.[1]

---

[1] K.M. Mtapiko, "Introduction," *Malawi National Bibliography*. 1986. Zomba: National Archives, 1988. p. [i].

Since 1991 the National Archives has been the ISBN Agency for Malawi. The *MaNB* plans to include the ISBN in future issues.

The publishers' list was first included in the 1975 volume.

Malawi. Printing and Stationery Department. *Catalogue of Publications* (1976?-   ). (LCCN: 80-642746) lists most of the government publications published by the government printer.

There is no identification of official or government publications in the Main Section. However, many are traced by checking the index under Malawi and then the issuing government departments.

QIPL,ESA, AL,ESA, and its predecessor *AL,EA* include Malawi within their scopes.

The *MaNB* 1984-1990 (which incorporates the separately published 1984 and 1986 issues) is printed as are some previous issues; however, the 1984 and 1986 issues first appeared separately in duplicated format.

The *MaNB* includes publications in other languages and dialects, particularly Chichewa.

Statistics on book production began appearing in the 1983 *MaNB*. Figures on book statistics included in the statistical table are based on publications received during the period covered, regardless of publication date. Figures for periodicals include annual reports. For 1986, 156 books and pamphlets and 42 periodicals were recorded. These statistics are not included in the *MaNB* 1984-1990 cumulation.

LATEST ISSUE EXAMINED/CURRENCY: In the mid-1980s, the annual volumes were available for use in libraries consulted fifteen to eighteen months following the period of time covered. However, this gap appears to be widening. The latest volume examined at SOAS, University of London in April 1994 is for the period 1984-1990, published in 1994. This includes the 1984 and the 1986 issues which were issued earlier in duplicated form.

A sample of entries from the *MaNB* for 1986 listed titles published primarily from 1985 and 1986 which is for the period covered.

AUTOMATION: not automated.

FORMATS AND SERVICES AVAILABLE: printed.

CURRENT LEGAL DEPOSIT LAWS: Printed Publications Act 1947 (Cap. 19:01 of the consolidated Laws of Malawi) . A new proposal has been submitted for consideration which seeks to include new forms and media not covered by the existing legislation.[1]

AVAILABLE FROM: The Government Archivist, National Archives of Malawi, P.O. Box 62, Zomba.

---

[1] Dick D. Najira, "Malawi," *Afribiblios* 7 (no. 1 June 1984):25. This is mentioned in the 1986 "Introduction". In a letter to the author dated 27 April 1995, D.D. Najira states that the legal deposit law has not yet been revised or replaced.

SELECTED ARTICLES: Bankole, Beatrice S. "Current National Bibliographies of the English Speaking Countries of Africa." *International Cataloguing* 14 (Jan./Mar. 1985):5-10.

Najira, Dick D. "Malawi." *Afribiblios* 7 (no. 1 June 1984):25-26.

VERIFIER: D.D. Najira, Librarian, National Archives of Malawi.

MALAYSIA

TITLE: *Bibliografi negara Malaysia = Malaysian national bibliography.* - 1967-   . - Kuala Lumpur : Perpustakaan Negara Malaysia, 1969-   .
Quarterly (1985-   ); quarterly, with fourth issue being the annual cumulation (1975-1984); annual (1967-1974).
Publisher varies.
Cumulative publication on CD-ROM (1966-1988).
DDC: 015.595; LC: Z3261.B5; LCCN: sn91-27118; OCLC: 3323781
ISSN 0126-5210

COMPILER: Perpustakaan Negara Malaysia [National Library of Malaysia].

SCOPE AND COVERAGE: *Bibliografi Negara Malaysia = Malaysian National Bibliography* (*MNB*) lists the publishing output of Peninsular Malaysia, Sabah and Sarawak which is deposited at the National Library of Malaysia in accordance with the provisions stipulated under the *Deposit of Library Material Act, 1986* (Act 331). It includes materials published in Malay, English, Chinese, Tamil and East Malaysian languages.

Types of publications included in *MNB* are books, research reports, textbooks, children's books, official and government publications, first issues of serials, conference proceedings, standards, charts, and maps. Starting with the first quarter for 1989, audio-visual materials, e.g., cassettes, video, gramophone records and films are listed. Popular magazines, comics with educational contents, pamphlets, souvenir programmes, commemorative and travel brochures are selectively included.

Excluded are publications without a Malaysian imprint, trade catalogues, posters, as well as other ephemera which have little historical or informational value, periodical and newspaper articles, theses and dissertations, artistic prints, internal documents, IGO publications.

CONTENTS: Contents, preface (in Malay and in English), DDC outline (in Malay, English, Chinese, Tamil), DDC Malaysian expansion schedules for languages and literature, geographic area codes, abbreviations (in Malay and English), format designations (in Tamil, Malay, English), bibliography (Roman script section, and non-Roman script section), list of publishers with addresses (fourth quarter).

CATALOGUING RULES AND CLASSIFICATION SCHEMES USED: AACR2 rev. ed. is followed. Malay names are catalogued in accordance with AACR2 using the modification of rule 22.27D, while Iban names are cataloged in accordance with the *Rules for Iban Names* prepared by the Cataloguing and Classification Committee of the National Library of Malaysia. The body of the entry follows ISBD(M) for books, ISBD(S) for serials, ISBD(CM) for maps, and ISBD(NBM) for non-book materials.

LCSH and *Tajuk Perkara Tempatan* are followed for subject headings.

Malay, Chinese, Tamil, Jawi or other vernacular language publications are catalogued in the language and script of the publication. Transliteration of author/title are provided for Jawi, Chinese and Tamil entries to facilitate filing. The *ALA Rules for Filing Catalog Cards* is used for all alphabetical arrangements of earlier publications until 1982 and for the non-Roman section. With the computerization of *MNB*, the arrangement of entries is based on "ASCII" filing (American Standard Code for Information Interchange).

The classification scheme used is DDC (20th ed.), in addition to the historical, geographical, language and literature expansions for Malaysia drawn up by the Cataloguing and Classification Committee of the National Library of Malaysia.

ENTRY INFORMATION: Author, title, place of publication, publisher, date, pagination, illustrations, size, series statement, notes, binding, price, subject headings, added entries, DDC number in lower left corner, internal number in lower right corner, e.g., M90-1370.

ARRANGEMENT: The 1990 volume is arranged in two sections. The first section consists of Roman script entries alphabetically arranged under author, title, series, and subject heading. The second section consists of non-Roman script entries arranged alphabetically under author, title, series, and subject headings.

Earlier years vary in the arrangement. For example, the bibliographies in the volumes for 1979 and 1980 are in sections. The first is the classified section arranged alphabetically within the DDC scheme. The second section is the author, title, and series index arranged in alphabetical order, and the third section is the subject index. A list of publishers' addresses of those whose works are recorded within the bibliography is also included as a final section.

INDEXES: In 1990, the two sections serve as indexes; there are no separate indexes. Earlier volumes include an author/title/series index, and a subject index; the number used refers to the DDC number in the classified section.

NOTES AND COMMENTS: From 1967-1969 *MNB* was arranged in 2 parts: classified section and an alphabetical section, with a publishers' list appended. The 1967 and 1969 volumes state that they include all books received regardless of the publication date. Since 1970, the *MNB* has been arranged in three sections until the volume for 1982 which is in two sections. With the automation in 1983, its annual cumulation is divided into two volumes.

The bilingual preface discusses the important points of scope and coverage, arrangement, and cataloguing rules followed. It is helpful to have this detailed information, including an analyzed entry.

MNB includes materials published in Bahasa Melayu, English, Chinese, Tamil, and East Malaysian languages, thus meeting ICNB recommendation 6. The old Bahasa Melayu spelling is retained. The word "[sic]" is added to indicated that the old spelling is used.

According to Donald Wijasuriya, *MNB* is selective and on the average, only about sixty-three percent of the material deposited at the National Library is recorded in *MNB*.[1]

For 1982, only one quarterly issue and the annual cumulation were produced.

Government publications until 1978 can be identified by the letter "G" on the registration number (G70-37). From 1979 onwards all government publications are identified with '1', e.g., (M901-280).[2]

In many respects, *MNB* is to be commended in meeting most of the ICNB recommendations. The *MNB* has been one of the most successful national bibliographies that presents publications in the language in which they were written. The one drawback of the bibliography is its timeliness; this may be addressed with the migration to CD-ROM format. The 1990 volume, published in 1994, is the last printed issue. The National Library of Malaysia (NLM) is testing the feasibility of publishing all issues only on CD-ROM. [3]

From 1996, the NLM has issued *MNB* on CD-ROM. *Bibliografi negra Malaysia* [computer disk]. - 1968/1988-   . - Kuala Lumpur : Perpustakaan Negara Malaysia, 1996-   includes 35,000 cumulative records of books, government publications, new serial titles, standards, maps, conference papers, and proceedings from 1966-1988 in Bahasa Melayu, English, Chinese, Tamil and East Malaysian languages. A selection of popular magazines, souvenir programmes, pamphlets, commemorative and travel brochures are also listed. There are three ways to search for bibliographic records: field search (about 20 qualifiers), Boolean search, and browse. Results may be displayed in three formats: card, tagged (MARC) and labeled. The user has a choice of viewing the search results by brief citations or full contents of the records. If the new format aids the timely appearance of *MNB*, it makes *MNB* a valuable resource for acquisitions, for collection development, and as a historical record.

Indexes on CD-ROM. - Kuala Lumpur : Perpustakaan Negara Malaysia, 1996-   . Irregular (ISSN 1394-5599) is a title that has combined the resources of several titles based on legal deposit: *Indeks majalah Malaysia = Malaysian periodicals index* (1984 to June 1991), *Indeks suratkhabar Malaysia = Malaysian newspaper index* (1988-June 1991), and *Indeks persidangan Malaysia = Index to Malaysian conferences* (1988-1994). The indexing database for the inclusive titles will be maintained and updated.

A brief description and history of four tools that are based on legal deposit are as follows: *Indeks majalah Malaysia = Malaysian periodicals index*. - 1973-1991. - Kuala Lumpur : Perpestakaan Negra Malaysia, 1974-1996. Semiannual (DDC: 059.4992/8, 015.595; LC: AI3.I26; LCCN: 76-643146/SA; OCLC: 3347214; ISSN 0126-5040). This indexes articles in periodicals deposited at the National Library under the legal deposit legislation. This title, which is no longer

---

[1] D.E.K. Wijashriya, "National Bibliographic Systems: A Review of Arrangements in Relation to Malaysia," In *Conference on Universal Bibliographical Control in Southeast Asia*, p. 49.

[2] Information received in a letter dated 26 February 1997 to the author from Dahlia Zainal, Technical Services Division, National Library of Malaysia.

[3] In a 30 July 1997 letter from Carole Ann Goon, Director, Serials Division, mentions that both the *Indexes on CD-ROM* and the *Bibliografi Negara Malaysia on CD-ROM* are intended to test the feasibility of publishing these titles in this format.

published in paper form and is available on *Indexes on CD-ROM,* continues in part *Indeks majallah kini Malaysia Singapura dan Brunei = Index to current Malaysian, Singapore, and Brunei periodicals.* - 1967-1968. - Kuala Lumpur : Persatuan Perpustakaan Malaysia/Persatuan Perpustakaan Singapura, 1969-1971 (LCCN: sn85-20034; LC: Z6958.M3I38; OCLC: 3346454; ISSN 0019-3984).

Indeks persidangan Malaysia = Index to Malaysian Conferences. - 1976-   . - Kuala Lumpur : Perpustakaan Negara, 1976-   . Annual (DDC: 015.595; ISSN 0127-4880). The *Index to Malaysian Conferences* is an index of working papers of conferences, seminars, symposiums and workshops which are deposited at the National Library of Malaysia under the provisions of the *Deposit of Library Material Act, 1986.* Working papers presented in Malaysia, as well as those outside the country but deposited at the National Library are indexed. It consists of two sections: subject, and author/title. Both are arranged alphabetically. The 1995 issue is the latest printed. It is available on CD-ROM with a cumulative contents from 1988-June 1994. Only entries in romanized script are included.[1]

Terbitan bersiri kini Malaysia (bukan kerajaan) = Malaysian current serials (non-government). - 1981-   . - Kuala Lumpur : Perpustakaan Negara Malaysia, 1981-   . Irregular (LCCN: 88-650343; OCLC: 9126525; ISSN 0127-1555). Lists Malaysian serials received at the National Library according to legal deposit legislation. Entries are alphabetically arranged by main entry and follow AACR2 format. Includes entries in Chinese, English, and Malay. This title continues *Majalah kini Malaysia: bukan kerajaan = Current Malaysian serials : non-government.* - 1976. - Kuala Lumpur : Perpustakaan Negara Malaysia, 1976 (OCLC: 5700655).

Terbitan bersiri kini Malaysia (kerajaan) = Malaysian current serials (government). - 1982-   . - Kuala Lumpur : Perpustakaan Negara Malaysia, 1983-   . Irregular (LCCN: 83-942024/SA/r88; OCLC: 10510944; ISSN 0127-2691). Includes journals, annual reports, statistics, government gazettes, etc. deposited at the National Library according to legal deposit legislation. This title continues *Majalah kini Malaysia: kerajaan = Current Malaysian serials: government.* - 1973. - Kuala Lumpur : Perpustakaan Negara Malaysia, 1974. Irregular (LCCN: 75-940667/SA/r84; OCLC: 2401123).

AL,SEA included Malaysia within its scope.

LATEST ISSUE EXAMINED/CURRENCY: Although most entries are for the period covered, there are several entries for earlier years.

The latest issue examined in April 1995 is the October - December issue for 1990, published in 1994 and received by Princeton University Library.

AUTOMATION: *MNB* became automated in 1983, with an exchange format (MALMARC) based on the international standard ISO 2709. In 1993 the library system was changed to VTLS (Virginia Technology Library System) which runs on a Hewlett Packard 900.[2]

---

[1] Zainal letter.

[2] Zainal letter.

FORMAT AND SERVICES AVAILABLE: printed through 1990. In 1996, the *MNB* is available on a cumulative CD-ROM which covers the period 1966-1988.

The *Index to Malaysian Conferences* is available on CD-ROM covering 1988-1994.

CURRENT LEGAL DEPOSIT LAWS: Deposit of Library Material Act, 1986 (*MNB* "Preface," iii, 1990).

AVAILABLE FROM: University of Malaya Cooperative Bookshop Ltd., Library Building, University of Malaya, P.O. Box 1127, Jalan Pantai Baru, 59700 Kuala Lumpur.

SELECTED ARTICLES: Kadir, Mariam Abdul. "National Bibliography of Malaysia: Problems and Prospects." In *Conference on National and Academic Libraries in Malaysia and Singapore: Proceedings of a PPM and LAS Conference held at Sains Malaysia, Penang, 1-3 March 1974.* Edited by Lim Huck Tee and Rashidad Begum. Penang: Persatuan Perpustakaan Malaysia, 1975, pp. 69-76.

VERIFIER: Carole Ann Goon, Director, Serials Division, National Library of Malaysia; Dahlia Zainal, Librarian, National Library of Malaysia.

MALDIVES

No current national bibliography has been traced for Maldives.

AL,SA included Maldives within its scope.

MALI

No current national bibliography has been traced for Mali.

CURRENT LEGAL DEPOSIT LAWS: Law No. 85-04/AN-RM of February 11, 1985.[1]

MALTA

TITLE: *Bibljografija nazzjonali ta' Malta = Malta national bibliography.* - 1983-   . - Valletta: National Library of Malta, 1984-   .
Annual.
Text in English and Maltese.

---

[1] Diallo, Abdoul Aziz. "Mali, National Library of." Translated by Mildred S. Myers. *Encyclopedia of Library and Information Science* 45 (Suppl. 10 1990):253.

DDC: 015.4585; LC: not found; LCCN: not found; OCLC: 29949418
ISSN not found

COMPILER: John B. Sultana...[et al.]

SCOPE AND COVERAGE: *Bibljografija nazzjonali ta' Malta = Malta national bibliography* (*MNB*) includes publications produced in Malta during the current year, works about the Maltese Islands and those written by Maltese nationals published abroad and received by legal deposit.

Types of publications included in *MNB* are monographs and pamphlets of eight pages or more of text, government publications, and periodicals (first issues). Each edition of a serial, e.g. *Annual abstract of statistics*, a yearbook, a directory or an annual report, is catalogued as a separate work. Works and parts of works about the Maltese Islands or written by Maltese nationals but published abroad are within *MNB*'s scope and are marked by an asterisk (*).

CONTENTS: Preface; abbreviations; classified bibliography; index of authors, titles, series; subject index; "Select List of Periodical Articles."

The preface includes an explanation of the scope of *MNB*, and an analyzed entry.

CATALOGUING RULES AND CLASSIFICATION SCHEMES USED: AACR2 is used in cataloguing titles; the *Sears List of Subject Headings* is used for subject headings.

For classification purposes, *MNB* uses DDC (20th ed.).

ENTRY INFORMATION: In the classified bibliography: DDC number, author (sometimes including dates of birth and/or death), title, place of publication, publisher, date, pagination, illustrations, size, series statement, notes which may include contents, bibliography information, ISBN, price information; tracings, and a consecutive entry code number in lower right corner, e.g., 91-122.

Information about new periodicals in the classified bibliography includes DDC number, title, publisher, volume number, beginning date, illustrations, size, frequency, notes, tracings and entry code number.

In the "Select List of Periodical Articles": author, title of article, title of periodical, volume, number, date, pagination. There is no classification or code number in these entries. The titles of Maltese periodicals indexed in this issue are given at the beginning of the section. Articles under two printed pages in length are excluded; local newspapers have not been indexed.

ARRANGEMENT: The entries in the classified bibliography are arranged by DDC headings and numbers, then alphabetically arranged. The "Select List of Periodical Articles" is arranged by the DDC ten broad subject headings, e.g., 1 Philosophy and related disciplines; 2 Religion, etc.

INDEXES: The author/title/series index includes personal and corporate authors, editors, compilers, translators, illustrators and contributors as well as titles and series, in an alphabetical sequence. The subject index, also alphabetically arranged, includes general subjects, e.g., Maltese essays; Painting, Maltese, under which books on a particular subject can be found in the classified bibliography. In both indexes, the numbers given refer the reader to the code number assigned to the entries by the compilers. These code numbers are in consecutive order in the classified bibliography.

Information in the "Select List of Periodical Articles" is not included in the indexes.

NOTES AND COMMENTS: The *MNB*, from its 1983 pilot edition to present day, is a well-planned and carefully executed document intended from the beginning to be based upon the ICNB recommendations. Pages are attractively arranged in double column lay-out, with main entries printed in boldface type for easy reference.

A valuable by-product in the production of the national bibliography is the *Authority List of Maltese Names for Libraries Using AACR2*, compiled by Lillian Sciberras and Victor Magri. Msida: University of Malta Library, 1984.

Publications in Maltese and English (the official languages of Malta), Italian, Arabic and French have appeared in *MNB*.

There is no symbol for government publications, but checking in the author index under Malta and then the issuing agency will help to locate many government titles. The *Gazzetta tal-Gvern ta' Malta = The Malta Government Gazette* also publishes a list of all official publications.

It would be helpful to include a list of publishers and their addresses in the *MNB*. Since this is also a ICNB recommendation, it may be forthcoming in future issues. It would also be useful to have the current legal deposit law cited in the "Preface."

The pilot edition of 1983 indexed seventeen periodicals; the 1991 MNB indexes over 55 periodicals for the compilation of the "Select List of Periodical Articles." A selection of titles indexed are: *The Architect; Central Bank of Malta Quarterly Review; Commercial Courier; Design and Decor; Education; Forum, Heritage; Il-hsieb; Hyphen; L-Imnara; Industry Today; Journal of Mediterranean Studies; Pastor; Problemi ta' llum; The Teacher; Tomorrow; The Year Book.*

LATEST ISSUE EXAMINED/CURRENCY: The latest issue examined in April 1995 at the SOAS library is for 1991, published in 1993.

Publications received by legal deposit during the period covered are included in *MNB*. Over 90% of the entries in the issue examined were for the year covered.

AUTOMATION: not automated. *MNB* is produced using Microsoft Word on a 486 PC.

FORMAT AND SERVICES AVAILABLE: printed.

CURRENT LEGAL DEPOSIT LAWS: Public Libraries' Ordinance (first promulgated in 1925, Chapter 92 of the Laws of Malta).[1]

AVAILABLE FROM: National Library of Malta, 36 Old Treasury Street, Valletta.

SELECTED ARTICLES: Sciberras, Lillian. "The Malta National Bibliography: Headings and Descriptive Cataloguing, Problems and Solutions." *International Cataloguing* 14 (Jan./Mar. 1985):11-12.

Sciberras, Lillian. "The Malta National Bibliography" In *A Marketing Tool for the Information Industry* ... London : University of London, 1986.

VERIFIER: John B. Sultana, Director, Biblijoteka Nazzjonali.

MAURITANIA

No current national bibliography has been traced for Mauritania.

Liste mensuelle des nouvelles acquisitons (LMNA). Juil. 1973-   . - Nouakchott: Bibliothèque nationale, 1973-   includes titles published in Mauritania, and titles published abroad about Mauritania. It is based on legal deposit and acquisitions of the Bibliothèque Nationale. Types of publications included in *LMNA* are books, official and government publications, and periodicals. Ruth Freitag states that this publication is suspended, but efforts are being made to resume issuance or to begin a new periodical.[2]   Efforts by the author to locate this title have not been successful.

Official publications are listed in *Journal Officiel de la République Islamique de Mauritanie.*

CURRENT LEGAL DEPOSIT LAWS: Law No. 63-109 of June 1963, and Loi 65-047, 1965.[3]

AVAILABLE FROM: Bibliothèque Nationale, B.P. 20, Nouakchott.

---

[1] *BSTW, 1975-1979.* pp. 285-286. The *International Guide to Legal Deposit* cites a 1983 amendment, p. 87.
[2] Ruth Freitag. "National Bibliographies" in *A.L.A. World Encyclopedia of Library and Information Sciences*, p. 389.
[3] *International Guide to Legal Deposit*, p. 88.

MAURITIUS

TITLE: "Bibliography of Mauritius, supplement no. [ ]." In *Annual Report of the Archives Department for the year 19*[ ], 1955- . - Port Louis : Archives Department of Mauritius, 1950- . Annual.
DDC: not found; LC: CD2355.M3A33; LCCN: 55-17744; OCLC: 2414801
ISSN 0076-5481

COMPILER: Archives Department of Mauritius.

SCOPE AND COVERAGE: The scope of the "Bibliography of Mauritius" ("BOM") includes all publications registered in the Archives Department under legal deposit legislation produced in Mauritius and publications of interest to Mauritius published elsewhere.

Types of publications included in "BOM" are books, pamphlets, articles in periodicals and newspapers, periodicals, IGO publications, official and government publications, theses and dissertations, atlases, administrative documents, conference papers, newsletters.

Omitted in recent issues are plans, maps and charts.

CONTENTS: In "BOM" supplement no. 40 of 1995 the scope note and contents page are followed by these sections: A. Private publications, B. Periodicals, newspapers and serials, C. Government and semi-official publications, D. Publications issued abroad.

Earlier supplements include two other sections: Manuscripts and archivalia; Plans, maps and charts. Also, in earlier supplements "Publications issued abroad" was included with section A, "Private publications."

Most theses and dissertations, periodical and newspaper articles, conference papers, and newsletters appear in section D, Publications issued abroad.

CATALOGUING RULES AND CLASSIFICATION SCHEMES USED: "BOM" includes no statement about cataloguing rules. Information given in the supplement for 1995 appears to be compatible with ISBD.

Entries are not classified or organized in any classified arrangement.

ENTRY INFORMATION: Section A. Private publications: author, title, edition statement, place of publication, publisher, date, pagination, size, illustration statement. Section B. Periodicals, newspapers and serials: title, frequency, first issue date, holdings, publisher, brief notes. Section C. Government and semi-official publications: monographs information: issuing agency is at the beginning, then title, place of publication, publisher, date, pagination, size, illustration statement. Serials information: issuing agency is at the beginning, title, frequency, issue number and year. Section D. Publications issued abroad: same as for A or B.

New entries in B and new headings in C are marked with an asterisk (*).

Prices are not given. In earlier issues prices were included.

ARRANGEMENT: The sections are arranged alphabetically as follows. Private publications: by author; periodicals, newspapers and serials: by title; government and semi-official publications: by issuing agency, and publications issued abroad: by author. For earlier years, manuscripts and archivalia were listed alphabetically by corporate body and then arranged chronologically. Plans, maps and charts were arranged by region.

INDEXES: No index.

NOTES AND COMMENTS: The "BOM" has been a supplement to the *Annual Report of the Archives Department* of Mauritius since 1955. However, under a different title there has been a legal deposit publications list in the *Annual Report* since 1950. "The List of Publications Printed in Mauritius and Deposited in the Archives Office" for 1949 was organized into sections for government publications, semi-official publications, private organizations, and periodicals.

The "BOM" continues to update A. Toussaint and H. Adolphe's *Bibliography of Mauritius, 1502-1954* published in 1956.

The "BOM" since 1985 appears in the *Annual Report of the Archives Department* (*AR*) as follows: "BOM" suppl. no. 31 (1985) is in *AR* for 1985, no. 12 of 1986; "BOM" suppl. no. 32 (1986) is in *AR* for 1986, no. 13 of 1987; "BOM" suppl. no.33 (1987) is in *AR* for 1987, no. 12 of 1988; "BOM" suppl. no.34 (1988) is in *AR* for 1988, no. 10 of 1989; "BOM" suppl. no. 35 (1989) is in *AR* for 1989, no. 3 of 1991; "BOM" suppl. no. 36 (1990) is in *AR* for 1990, no. 1 of 1991; "BOM" suppl. 37 (1991) is in *AR* for 1991, no. 7 of 1993; "BOM" suppl. no. 38 (1992) is in *AR* for 1992, no. 22 of 1994; "BOM" suppl. no. 39 (1993) is in *AR* for 1993, no. 2 of 1996; and "BOM" suppl. no. 40 (1995) is in *AR* for 1995, no. 8 of 1996.

Titles published abroad and thus not under the legal deposit law are listed separately in section D. This follows the ICNB recommendation number 5.

The "BOM" includes publications in English, French, Creole and other local languages, thus adhering to ICNB recommendation 6.

It would be of help to users if the "BOM" would follow ICNB recommendation 10 which includes guidelines for an introduction. The "BOM" does not state the type of publications included or omitted, the frequency of the publication, or bibliographic and cataloguing tools used.

The addition of an index, a list of publishers including addresses, and an analyzed entry in the introduction would greatly enhance the use of this otherwise excellent bibliography. The list of publishers would aid librarians in using the "BOM" as an acquisitions tool.

"Memorandum of Books Printed in Mauritius and Registered in the Archives Office" (ISSN 0465-398X, OCLC no. 4262711) is published quarterly by the Archives Department and included in the *Government Gazette of Mauritius*. This title does not include serials. The bibliography is divided into publications issued by government and public institutions, and publications issued by private individuals and organizations. This list is cumulated by the "BOM" in the *Annual Report of the Archives Department*.

Mauritius is included within the scopes of *AL,ESA* and *QIPL,ESA* .

LATEST ISSUE EXAMINED/CURRENCY: The latest issue examined at Rhodes House Library, Oxford University is the *Annual Report of the Archives Department for 1995* published in 1996; this "BOM" was supplement no. 40 of 1995.

Coverage is designed to include current legal deposit titles, as well as to supplement Toussaint and Adolphe's earlier work. Current titles and earlier titles are in the same alphabetical arrangement and are not in any chronological order. In spite of the broad date range, the majority of the titles listed are from the current year covered or from the previous year.

AUTOMATION: not automated.

FORMAT AND SERVICES AVAILABLE: printed.

CURRENT LEGAL DEPOSIT LAWS: As stated in the scope note of supplement number 40 (1990): Ordinance 71 of 1952.

AVAILABLE FROM: Government Printer, La Tour Koenig, Pointe-aux-Sables.

VERIFIER: Dr. P. H. Sooprayen, Chief Archivist, Archives Department, Development Bank of Mauritius Complex, Petite Rivière, Mauritius.

MEXICO

TITLE: *Bibliografía mexicana* [computer file]. - 1992-   . - México : Universidad Nacional Autónoma de México, Biblioteca Nacional, 1992-   .
Annual.
Continuation of the printed *Bibliografía mexicana.*
DDC number: 015.7205; L.C. classification number: Z1411.B53; LCCN: sn95-30988; OCLC number: 33316664
ISSN not found

COMPILER: Universidad Nacional Autónoma de México, Biblioteca Nacional.

SCOPE AND COVERAGE: *Bibliografía Mexicana* (*BM*) lists all titles published in México received on legal deposit at the National Library. [1]

Types of publications included in *BM* are books, pamphlets, official and government publications, IGO publications issued in México, maps and atlases, serial publications (new

---

[1] The author is grateful to Miguel A. Lopez S., Departamento de Informatica, Biblioteca Nacional de Mexico for sending the author the latest *BM* bibliography via ftp file and for helping to access the information on the disk. For the latter, the author also appreciates the help of Mustafa Hasham and Robert Maclean, two College of Wooster students.

titles, title changes, cessations), theses and dissertations, microforms, musical scores, sound recordings, postage stamps.

Omitted from the scope of *BM* are filmstrips, video tapes, etc.

CONTENTS: Bibliographic entries.

CATALOGUING RULES AND CLASSIFICATION SCHEMES USED: *BM* uses AACR2 and ISBD for cataloguing entries.

The classification scheme used is DDC.

ENTRY INFORMATION: DDC number, author, title, place of publication, publisher, date, pagination, illustrations, size, series, notes including ISBN, subject and added entries, legal deposit number in lower right (e.g., 95-0646-00).

ARRANGEMENT: The bibliographic entries are arranged by date of entry into the data base.

INDEXES: No index.

NOTES AND COMMENTS: *BM* continues the printed edition *Bibliografía mexicana.* - ene./feb. 1967- jun., 1989. - México : Universidad Nacional Autónoma de México, Instituto de Investigaciones Bibliográficas, Biblioteca Nacional e Hemeroteca Nacional, 1967-1991. Publisher and frequency varies. Some years include supplements (DDC number: 015.7205; LC classification number: Z1411.B53; LCCN: 92-655528; OCLC number: 1519748; ISSN 0006-1069). From 1967-1978, *BM* only listed monographs. Types of publications after that are the same as the computer file version described above. The contents are arranged by the broad DDC headings—general works, philosophy, religion, social sciences, languages, pure sciences, technology (applied science), arts and recreation, literature, geography and history, analytical index, "sumario" (table of contents). The main bibliography is arranged by DDC, and then alphabetical within the class. An analytical index, arranged as a dictionary, includes author, title, subject. The number used in the index refers to the entry number in the main bibliography. Subject entries are in all capital letters.

Publishers for the *BM* 1967-1991 vary. 1967 was published by Universidad Nacional Autónoma de México (UNAM), Biblioteca Nacional e Instituto Bibliográfico Mexicano; 1968-1978 by UNAM, Biblioteca Nacionale e Instituto de Investigaciones Bibliográficas; 1979-1991 by UNAM, Instituto de Investigaciones Bibliográficas, Biblioteca Nacional e Hemeroteca National.

It would be useful, especially for those unfamiliar with *BM*, to add a separate file which would include an introduction or a preface explaining the scope, types of publications included, frequency, an analyzed entry, changes which occur in the volume, abbreviations and symbols used, and a table of contents. The disk version follows the printed version in not including these. These additions would be in line with the ICNB recommendations.

No symbols mark government publications in the bibliography. However, by searching for "México" and the issuing agency, one is able to locate many of the government publications included in that particular issue. México does not have a centralized government publisher, and combined with problems of legal deposit non-compliance, it is difficult to compare the percentage of government publications available with those publications actually listed in *BM*.

Supplements for the printed edition are published much later than the period covered. Supplement 1 for 1968 (published in 1974), Supplement 2 for 1968 (published in 1979) listed titles that have been received by the compiler since *BM* was issued for the year 1968.

Anuario Bibliográfico is an annual (irregular) publication published by Biblioteca Nacional (covering 1958-1960) and the Instituto de Investigaciones Bibliográficas (covering 1961-1969). According to information given in OCLC record 1033476 *Anuario Bibliográfico* has been absorbed by *BM*. One assumes that *Anuario Bibliográfico*, once it could become a timely publication, was intended to be an annual cumulation of publications received on legal deposit by the Biblioteca Nacional, thus complementing *BM*, which does not have annual cumulations. However, because of the large lag between the date of coverage and the publication date, it never was able to fulfill its goal of complementing *BM*. *Anuario Bibliográfico* acts as more of a retrospective national bibliography than as an annual cumulation for a current national bibliography. Because of its perspective, the coverage is quite complete, having the advantage of being able to gather and add titles to the appropriate volume as they are identified.

LATEST ISSUE EXAMINED/CURRENCY: Most of the entries in *BM* were for the period covered.

The latest issue examined during September 1997 was for 1995 when the author was sent files to examine.

AUTOMATED: automated. Details not known. Entries are in MARC format.

FORMAT AND SERVICES AVAILABLE: As of 1992, disks in three formats: ASCII, ISO 2709 suitable for CDS/ISIS and MiniIsis, and a disk suitable for ALEPH, DYNIX, TINLIB, etc.

CURRENT LEGAL DEPOSIT LAWS: The legal deposit law of 1957 was supplemented by Decree of 11 January 1965; the 1956 Copyright Law, amended 1963, art. 122, 130, 134.[1]

AVAILABLE FROM: Correspondence to: Instituto de Investigaciones Bibliográficas, Biblioteca Nacional, Seccion de Ventas y Distribución Insurgentes Sur s/n, Centro Cultural, Ciudad Universitaria, México 20, D.F.

VERIFIER: no reply received.

MICRONESIA (FEDERATED STATES OF)

No current national bibliography has been traced for Micronesia.

---

[1] *International Guide to Legal Deposit*, p. 88.

The Federated States of Micronesia (Kosrae, Pohnpei, Truk, Yap) are included in the scope of the regional *South Pacific Bibliography* (ISSN 0257-9149).

MOLDOVA

TITLE: *Bibliografia Moldovei: cărţi, albume, hărţi, note muzicale, discuri, seriale. etc.* - Ian./Feb. 1992- . - Chişinău : Biblioteca Naţională a Republicii Moldova, 1992- .
Bimonthly.
In Romanian (Moldovian), Russian, and other languages.
DDC: not found; LC: Z2514.M6.B48; LCCN: 94-656029; OCLC: 29557719
ISSN not found

COMPILER: Biblioteca Naţională a Republicii Moldova [National Library of the Republic of Moldova].

SCOPE AND COVERAGE: *Bibliografia Moldovei: cărţi, albume, hărţi, note muzicale, discuri, seriale. etc.* (BM) includes the publishing output of Moldova, which is deposited at the National Library of the Republic of Moldova according to legal deposit laws.

Types of publications include books, pamphlets, new serials, musical scores, recordings, maps, art publications, catalogues, calendars, placards, diplomas, labels, postcards, etc. Analytical materials concerning Moldova from the foreign press are included in the "Exteriorica" division. Materials from South Bessarabia and North Bucovina (Ukraine) are also included.

CONTENTS: Argument, bibliography, index, abridged table of UDC.

CATALOGUING RULES AND CLASSIFICATION SCHEMES USED: International cataloguing standards are followed. Text in scripts other than Latin are transliterated according to international standards.

The classification scheme used is UDC.

ENTRY INFORMATION: Consecutive registration number, author, title, publisher, place of edition, editor, date, place of publication, place of printing, pagination, illustrations, size, series statement, notes including price, edition, ISBN, inventory number, and UDC number.

ARRANGEMENT: Arrangement is by the UDC system within types of documents.

INDEXES: Name index, book title index, serials title index (biannually). The "exteriorica" division includes names index, and toponymical index of publications.

NOTES AND COMMENTS: Since 1992 the Biblioteca Naţională a Republicii Moldova has published *BM*. From 1964 to 1990 the National Library collaborated with the National Book Chamber of the Republic of Moldova to compile *Moldavia Sovietica in presa Uniunii RSS = Sovetskaia Moldavia v pecati SSSR* [Soviet Moldova in Soviet Union Press], a division which was included in *Cronica Presei RSSM = Letopis' pecati MSSR* (OCLC: 4839404).

In 1991, the National Library published *Moldova in publicatiile straine* [Moldova in foreign publications].[1]

LATEST ISSUE EXAMINED/CURRENCY: The author has communicated with the National Library for information on this title. No copy has been examined.

AUTOMATION: BM is partly automated; total automation is expected by the end of 1997 with format in an international format (MARC or otherwise) and the use of Windows. Books, albums, and musical scores are currently in MARC format from the database of the Catalogue Department. Recordings, serials, and group materials are done by hand and then typed out.

FORMAT AND SERVICES AVAILABLE: printed.

CURRENT LEGAL DEPOSIT LAWS: "Legea depozitului legal" [Legal deposit law] is up for approbation by the Republic of Moldova government.[2]

AVAILABLE FROM: National Library of the Republic of Moldova, Str. 31 August 78A, 2012 Chişinău.

SELECTED ARTICLES: Leich, Harold M. "Bibliographic systems of the Soviet Republics: Moldavia and Tajikistan." *Government Information Quarterly* 2 (no. 3 1985): 291-298.

VERIFIER: Tatyana Iskymjy, Deputy Director, National Library of the Republic of Moldova.

§

TITLE: *Cronica presei.* - 1991-   . - Chişinău : Camera de Stat a Cărţii din Republica Moldova, 1991-   .
Monthly.
Added title page: *Letopis' pechati*
No. 3, 1993-   issued by Camera Naţională a Cărţii din Republica Moldova.
Continues *Letapis' pechati Moldavskoĭ SSR.*
In Moldavian, Romanian, and Russian; summaries in Russian.
DDC: 015.4985; LC: Z2514/M6:47; LCCN: 94-656025; OCLC: 28613819
ISSN 0261-6761

COMPILER: Camera Naţională a Cărţii din Republica Moldova [National Book Chamber of the Republic of Moldova].

SCOPE AND COVERAGE: *Cronica presei (CP)* includes the publishing output of Moldova, which is deposited at the Archives of the National Book Chamber of the Republic of Moldova according to legal deposit laws.

---

[1] Information in 14 August 1997 letter to the author from Tatyana Iskymjy, Deputy Director, National Library of the Republic of Moldova.
[2] Information included in Iskymjy letter.

Types of publications include books, pamphlets, new serials, musical scores, fine arts, journal articles, and newspaper articles.

CONTENTS: Introduction (in Russian and Moldovian), classified bibliography, index.

CATALOGUING RULES AND CLASSIFICATION SCHEMES USED: ISBD is followed; the descriptions conform to Russian standards.

The classification scheme used is UDC.

ENTRY INFORMATION: Consecutive entry number, author, title, place of publication, publisher, date, pagination, illustrations, size, series statement, notes including price, number of copies printed, ISBN, and legal deposit number, e.g., [94-4]. In the lower right corner is the complete classification number.

ARRANGEMENT: Arrangement is by the UDC subject headings and classification system.

INDEXES: Name index, title index, subject index, alphabetical index of book dealers and publishers.

NOTES AND COMMENTS: Before the breakup of the USSR, publications of Moldova were recorded in the following nine sections: *Knizhnaĭa letopis' = Kronika kertsii* [Bibliography of books], *Letopis' periodicheskikh izdaniĭ Moldavskoĭ SSR = Kronika editsiilor periodiche al RSSM* [Bibliography of Moldavian SSR serial publications], *Letopis' not = Kronika publikatsiilor de note* [Bibliography of musicalia], *Letopis' izoizdaniĭ = Kronika editsiilor de arta plastike* [Bibliography of graphic materials], *Letopis' zhurnal'nykh stateĭ = Kronika artikolelor de reviste* [Bibliography of journal articles], *Letopis' gazetnykh stateĭ = Kronika artikolelor de gazete* [Bibliography of newspaper articles], *Letopis' retsenziĭ = Kronika rechenziilor* [Bibliography of reviews], *Bibliograficheskie posobiĭa MSSR = Materiale bibliografiche din RSSM* [Bibliography of bibliographies], *Sovetskaĭa Moldaviĭa v pechati SSSR = Moldova sovetike in presa Uniunii RSS* [Soviet Moldavia in the press of the USSR]. - 1958-1991. - Kishinev : Kartĭa moldoveniăske, 1958-1991 (LCCN: 76-220501//r942; LC: Z2514.M6L47; OCLC: 4839404; ISSN 0201-6761).[1] Since Moldova established its independence, Moldova's publishing output is recorded in *Cronica presei* and in the National Library of the Republic of Moldova's *Bibliografia Moldovei: Carti. Albume. Harti. Note muzicale. Discuri. Seriale.*, etc. (See entry above.)

CP continues Letopis' pechati Moldavskoĭ SSR, which had its added title page of *Kronika preseĭ RSSM* until 1989, and from 1990, *Cronica presei R.S.S. Moldoveneşti.*

The introduction includes the scope and coverage, and explains some of the abbreviations used in the bibliography, e.g., p = first edition, d = second edition, of = offset printing, lt = lithography, ft = photocopy, tn = first printing, ta = last printing.

---

1 Harold M. Leich. "Bibliographic systems of the Soviet Republics: Moldavia and Tajikistan." *Government Information Quarterly* 2 (no. 3 1985): 297.

LATEST ISSUE EXAMINED/CURRENCY: The latest issue examined on 11 November 1996 is no. 1, 1994 from the University of Illinois.

AUTOMATION: not known.

FORMAT AND SERVICES AVAILABLE: printed.

CURRENT LEGAL DEPOSIT LAWS: "Legea depozitului legal" [Legal deposit law] is up for approbation by the Republic of Moldova government.

AVAILABLE FROM: Camera Naţională a Cărţii din Republica Moldova, prospekt Stefan Chenmari, 180, g. Chişnău.

SELECTED ARTICLES: Leich, Harold M. "Bibliographic systems of the Soviet Republics: Moldavia and Tajikistan." *Government Information Quarterly* 2 (no. 3 1985): 291-298.

VERIFIER: no reply received from the National Book Chamber of the Republic of Moldova. Verified in part by Tatyana Iskymjy, Deputy Librarian, National Library of the Republic of Moldova.

MONACO

No current national bibliography was traced for Monaco.

Monaco publications are listed in the *Bibliographie nationale française*.

Paul Lavagna is the author of *Bibliographie nationale de la principauté de Monaco, 1761-1986*. - Monaco : Impr. Testa, 1988. (LC: Z2191.L38 1989; LCCN: 89-200757; OCLC: 21556570). This title is a one-time compilation of the publishing output in Monaco, particularly high quality editions, from 1761 to 1986. Through the cooperation of publishers, printers, booksellers, and libraries the compiler was able to describe titles in the Bibliothèque Louis Notari and in the library and archives of the Palace of the Prince. Gaps in coverage occur despite the best efforts of everyone.[1] The contents include an essay on the history of printing in Monaco since its origins, history of publishing houses in Monaco, alphabetical bibliography (over 300 pages), works coming from the library and archives of the Palace of the Prince, list of printers, list of publisher, list of newspapers, journals, and periodicals. The foreword by the mayor of Monaco lauds the patience and persistence of Paul Lavagna and his work in helping the world to learn about the social, economic, and cultural development and history of Monaco through its publications.

From 1930-1980, Monaco publications are listed in the national bibliography of France.

---

[1] Information in a 23 September 1997 letter to the author from Hervé Barral, Conservateur, Bibliothèque Louis Notari.

CURRENT LEGAL DEPOSIT LAWS: Legal deposit law no. 87 of January 1925. This is not effective and the nation's collections depend on the good will of the publishers. [1]

VERIFIER: Hervé Barral, Conservateur, Bibliothèque Louis Notari.

MONGOLIA

TITLE: *BNMAU-d khélégdsén Mongol nomyn burtgel [   ]* . - 1913/1944-   . - Ulaanbaator : Shinzhlekh Ukhaany Akademiin Khevleli Gazar [Academy of Sciences Publishing House], 1945?-   .
Compiler varies.
Title varies.
Publisher varies.
Frequency varies.
DDC: not found; LC: Z3121.B585; LCCN: 91-645076 (1976/1979-); OCLC: 23455473 (1976/1979-)
ISSN or ISBN not found

COMPILER: 1980/1984, M. Baianzul, D. Enkhtor; editor: Sh. Bazar.

SCOPE AND COVERAGE: *BNMAU-d khélégdsén Mongol nomyn burtgel [   ]* (*BNM*) includes the publishing output of Mongolia which is deposited at the State Public Library presumably according to legal deposit laws.

Types of publications include books and pamphlets.

Earlier volumes may also have included periodicals within the title's scope.[2]

CONTENTS: Bibliography according to general subject groups such as Marxist-Leninist thought, communist party of the Soviet Union, Mongolian Communist Party, other Communist Parties and movements, Mongolian Communist Youth League, philosophy, religion, social sciences, statistics, political science, international relations, economics, military science, education, linguistics, mathematics, physics, chemistry, biology, technology and engineering, agriculture, arts, sports, history, geography, library science, Mongolian belle-lettres, Soviet belles-lettres, other foreign belles-lettres; contents page.

CATALOGUING RULES AND CLASSIFICATION SCHEMES USED: Basic information is given.

No classification scheme appears with the entries or subject headings used. The subject groups are very general categories, e.g., Marxist-Leninist thought, philosophy, religion, social sciences, and history.

---

[1] Ibid.
[2] The author is grateful to Robert Dunn, Area Specialist, Asian Division, Library of Congress for the scope information.

ENTRY INFORMATION: Author, title, place of publication, publisher, date, pagination, number of copies printed, an internal number, e.g., Y-3, Y-1, cost.

ARRANGEMENT: Arrangement is alphabetical by main entry within the subject groups.

INDEXES: No indexes appear in the issues examined.

NOTES AND COMMENTS: *BNM* has covered the years 1913/1944, 1945/1958 (in two parts), 1959/1960, 1961/1962, 1963/1964, 1965/1967, 1968/1970, 1971/1972, 1973/1975, 1976/1979, and 1980/1984. No later volumes have been verified, but it is anticipated that others will be published.[1]

The 1976/1979 volume is catalogued as a serial. Earlier volumes were treated as monographs under the following identity numbers. LCCN: 85-927567 (1973/1975), 85-92787 (1971/1972), 85-927589 (1968/1970); OCLC: 17879366 (1973/1975), 17133422 (1971/1972); 17133455 (1968/1970).

In earlier volumes, the title in Russian appears on the verso of the title page as follows: *Bibliografiiâ mongol'skikh knig izdannykh v MNR.*

To more closely follow the recommendations of the ICNB, it would be helpful to the user if this bibliography included an abbreviations list, and an introduction which explains the scope and coverage, legal deposit law citation, and an analyzed entry. The use of an international classification scheme in conjunction with the subject groups would be an enhancement to the bibliography. An index would also be useful to the researcher or bibliographer. However, it is good to see this listing of titles published in Mongolia even if these suggestions cannot be accomplished.

LATEST ISSUE EXAMINED/CURRENCY: The latest issue examined is 1980/1984, published in 1987, held by Indiana University.

AUTOMATION: not automated.

FORMAT AND SERVICES AVAILABLE: printed.

CURRENT LEGAL DEPOSIT LAWS: No information available.

AVAILABLE FROM: State Public Library, Ulaanbaatar.

VERIFIER: Carl Horn, Central Eurasian Areas Studies Specialist, Indiana University Libraries.

---

[1] The author is grateful to Carl Horn, Central Eurasian Areas Studies Specialist, Indiana University Libraries, Indiana University for his help in writing this entry. In the near future, Indiana University will have access to most of the volumes of this series through an arrangement with a private collection.

MOROCCO

TITLE: *Bibliographie nationale marocaine. -* 1961- . - Rabat : Bibliothèque Générale et Archives du Maroc, 1962- .
Monthly (irregular?), with annual cumulated index.
DDC: 015.964 B47; LC: Z3836.B53; LCCN: 73-297810; OCLC: 2487226
ISSN 0483-7991

COMPILER: Bibliothèque Générale et Archives du Maroc.

SCOPE AND COVERAGE: The scope of the *Bibliographie Nationale Marocaine (BNM)* includes publications produced in Morocco, or publications about the country, deposited at the Bibliothèque Générale et Archives du Maroc.

Types of publications covered in *BNM* since 1984 are books, pamphlets, official and government publications, periodicals, periodical articles, theses and dissertations, maps and atlases, musical scores, guides, inventories, textbooks, microforms.

There have been changes in the scope over the years. In the 1960s the bibliography included mainly periodical and newspaper articles.

Omitted from the *BNM* scope are IGO publications.

CONTENTS: *BNM* is in two parts: French and Arabic. Both parts include an explanation of the entry, classified bibliography, and subject index.

CATALOGUING RULES AND CLASSIFICATION SCHEMES USED: Since 1976, ISBD has been used.

The classsification system is UDC.

ENTRY INFORMATION: Bibliothèque Générale number in upper right corner, author, title, place of publication, publisher, pagination, size, illustrations, series statement, UDC number in lower left corner, legal deposit number and the "inventaire" number in lower right corner.

ARRANGEMENT: The bibliography is arranged according to the UDC system in both the Arabic and French sections.

INDEXES: Subject; no author or title indexes until 1984. Number used refers to UDC number.

NOTES AND COMMENTS: During the years under French rule, 1912-1956, the national bibliography of France included most of the French publications produced in Morocco.

The *BNM* has undergone several changes of scope and contents in its recent history. At one time in the 1960's, it concentrated on periodical articles and analytical entries from monographs, thus functioning more as an index. Then in the 1970's the emphasis was shifted to monograph entries. In 1984, another format was effected when, according to Attia, *BMN* changed to an alphabetical listing of author and titles, with author and subject indexes. All types of documents are included in this alphabetical sequence.[1]

A title which may be more accessible and helpful than *BNM* is *al-Kitāb al-Maghribī* [*Le livre Marocain*]. - no. 1- . - Morocco : l'Association des Auteurs Marocains pour la Publication [AAMP], 1983- (LC: 84-642097). This annual journal includes "Isharat bibliyughrafiyah" [Bibliographical notices], a substantial section on recent Moroccan publications. Articles and reviews of publications are also included. Introductory pages are in both French and Arabic. The advantages of this title is its timeliness. Number 11/12 (1995), the latest seen by the author, includes mostly 1995 publications. It is readily apparent that *al-Kitāb al-Maghribī* is filling a need in identifying current Moroccan publications in a timely fashion. In the introductory pages, the staff asks for donations of books to this publication as well as to the national library. This publication is available from *Le Livre Marocain*, 53, Avenue Allah Ben Abdellah-Rabat, BMCE No 61002/23 Rabat, Morocco.[2]

The years 1934-1953 were covered by a list entitled "Bibliographie Marocaine" published in volumes 26, 30, 34, 38, 42 of the periodical *Hesperius* and volume 3 of *Hesperius-Tamuda*. After a gap in coverage from 1954-1961, the list for 1962 was compiled and eventually produced by off-set in 1966.[3]

A list of legal deposit works has been published annually in two different titles and in three different formats: 1. Ouvrages édités au Maroc de 1939 à 1947 (duplicated; alphabetically by author). 2. Liste des publications déposées à la Bibliothèque générale et archives au titre du depôt légal au cours de l'année...Rabat, 1948-1959 (annual; duplicated). Published in two parts: official publications and other publications. 3. Liste des publications déposées a la Bibliothèque générale et Archives au titre du dépôt légal au cours de l'année... 1960- 1966. Published in two parts: works in Arabic; works in French and foreign languages. Dewey decimal classification.[4] A new series began in 1968.[5] In addition to the above list, from 1931 to 1962, the Bibliothèque Générale has issued *Informations Bibliographiques Marocaines*. Fortnightly. Prior to 1959, this was only in French; since this time, it is in French and other languages and in Arabic. Broad subject headings are used.

Morocco is included within the scope of *AL,ME* (Vol. 1, 1963-vol. 31, 1993; ISSN 0041-7769), and the *Arab Bulletin of Publications* (LCCN: 73-960585/NE).

---

[1] Ridha Attia, "National Bibliographies in the Maghreb: A Survey of their Contents and Perspectives." Paper presented at IFLA General Conference. Nairobi, Kenya, 19-24 August 1984. (55-Bib-1-E):10-11.

[2] This publication was first pointed out to me by Katherine Van der Vate in her monograph *"Books from the Arab World. A Guide to Selection and Acquisition*, and later emphasized by George Atiyeh, former Head, Near East Section, African and Middle Eastern Division, Library of Congress as an important title for Moroccan bibliographic control.

[3] Wanda Auerbach, "The National Bibliography of Morocco," *African Library Journal* 3 (pt. 1 spring 1972):11.

[4] Auerbach, p. 11.

[5] David H. Partington, "National Bibliographies from the Middle East," *Foreign Acquisitions Newsletter* no. 45 (spring 1977):6.

LATEST ISSUE EXAMINED/CURRENCY: The latest issue of *BNM* examined is April 1984, received by Columbia University. Date of receipt is not available, but this is the latest that they have received as of August 1995. This may be caused by inadequate distribution; all libraries that were checked did not have anything later. The gap in time between the time covered and the time that the title is delivered to subscribing libraries is not acceptable as an acquisitions tool. One must rely on other sources for current bibliographic coverage.

The latest issue of *Le Livre Marocain* examined at Princeton University in June 1997 is for nos. 11/12, 1995.

AUTOMATION: *BNM* has no plans to automate.

FORMAT AND SERVICES AVAILABLE: printed.

CURRENT LEGAL DEPOSIT LAWS: For official publications: Decree 2.72.640 of 11 Kaada 1392 (18 December 1972); other publications: the Decree of 7 October 1932, amended in 1944 and augmented by Decree of 10 April 1951.[1] Attia cited a 1956 French legal deposit law as the current law.[2]

AVAILABLE FROM: Bibliothèque Générale et Archives du Maroc, BP 1003, Avenue Ibn Battouta, Rabat.

SELECTED ARTICLES: Aman, Mohammed M. "Bibliographical Services in the Arab Countries." *College & Research Libraries* (July 1970):249-259.

Auerbach, Wanda. "The National Bibliography of Morocco." *African Library Journal* 3 (pt. 1 spring 1972):7-13.

Van de Vate, Katherine. "Acquisition from individual countries: Morocco," In *Books from the Arab World. A Guide to Selection and Acquisition.* Durham: Middle East Libraries Committee, 1988, pp. 26-28.

VERIFIER: no reply received.

MOZAMBIQUE

No current national bibliography has been traced for Mozambique.

---

[1] *BSTW, 1975-1979*, p. 294, and *International Guide to Legal Deposit*, 89.
[2] Attia, p. 10.

Some titles which include Mozambique within their scopes are *AL,ESA*, its *Serial Supplement,* and *QIPL,ESA*. *Boletim Bibliográfico* was being planned by the Biblioteca Nacional de Moçambique, C.P. 141, Maputo in 1982.[1]

The Arquivo Historico de Moçambique has recently created a database of Mozambican monograph holdings from their collection. The Arquivo has cited and abstracted all chapters, pages, books, etc. pertaining to Mozambique, excluding journal articles which be their next project.[2]

This title may be useful to verify serials. Ilídio Rocha. *Catálogo dos periódicos e principais seriados de Moçambique da introdução da tipografia á independência, 1854-1975*. - Lisboa : Edições 70, 1985. (LCCN: 86-114926; OCLC: 13279429) which is an enlarged edition of *Catálogo dos periódicos e principais seriados editados em Moçambique da introdução da tipografia á independência, 1854-1975*. Maputo : Centro Nacional de Documentação e Informação de Moçambique, 1980 (LCCN: 81-115060; OCLC: 8242932).

NAMIBIA

TITLE: *Namibia national bibliography*. - 1990/1992-   . - Windhoek: National Library of Namibia, 1996-   .
DDC: 015.6881; LC: not found; LCCN: not found; OCLC: not found
ISSN 1026-0773

COMPILER: National Library of Namibia.

SCOPE AND COVERAGE: The *Namibia National Bibliography* (*NNB*) lists publications received by legal deposit at the National Library of Namibia during the period covered. It also includes titles received at selected other libraries which were not deposited at the National Library. The first issue includes all of the serials currently received by the National Library. Subsequent issues will include only new serial titles, changes in titles, and cessations. Titles about Namibia published elsewhere which include significant Namibian content (approximately one-third content) of material about Namibia, and titles written by Namibians but published elsewhere are included. These titles are set apart from the national imprint by an asterisk (*).

Types of publications included in *NNB* are books, pamphlets over five pages, periodicals, newspapers, published dissertations and theses, official and government publications, conference proceedings, IGO and NGO publications produced in Namibia if they have significant Namibian content (approximately one-third content), maps, audio visual materials, exhibition catalogues, and translations.

---

[1] Information supplied to the author in an 11 September 1985 letter from James Armstrong, former Field Director, Library of Congress Office, Nairobi, Kenya. The author can not verify that this title currently exists.
[2] Information included in a 26 October 1994 letter to the author from Ruth Thomas, Field Director, Library of Congress Office, Nairobi, Kenya.

Omitted are periodical articles, acts, bills, pamphlets of less than five pages, local church and school newsletters duplicated and intended for a limited audience, duplicated materials with a limited distribution, single sheet newsletters, reprints, calendars, programs, advertising/trade literature with product information only, coloring books, stamps, sales catalogues (except those with information on subject or bibliographic interest), preliminary survey reports, and drafts of titles subsequently published, reports intended for internal use, and other ephemeral publications.

CONTENTS: Contents, introduction including scope, coverage, and an analyzed entry, legal deposit ordinance, list of abbreviations and acronyms, language and library codes; DDC (second summary headings), classified bibliography, indexes, list of local publishers.

CATALOGUING RULES AND CLASSIFICATION SCHEMES USED: Cataloguing is based on AACR2. Classification scheme used is the DDC. *LCSH* is used for subject headings.

ENTRY INFORMATION: Master File Number, DDC number, author, title, place of publication, publisher, date, pagination, size, ISBN or ISSN, *LCSH*, added entries, National Library shelf list number. If the title is held by another library, not the National Library, that library's symbol and shelf number are given. An asterisk (*) by the Master File Number indicates it is not a Namibian imprint.

ARRANGEMENT: The bibliography is arranged according to the DDC system, and then alphabetically arranged.

INDEXES: The author/title index includes authors, editors, compilers, joint authors, contributors, and titles arranged in alphabetical order. Subject and series indexes, and an index of languages (other than English) are also included. Reference numbers are to the consecutive entry numbers in the classified bibliography. Cross references are used when needed.

NOTES AND COMMENTS: After Namibia gained its independence in 1990, it was decided that they should have a national bibliography to record its national imprint. The first issue is designed to cover the period of time 1990-1992, the second issue will cover 1993-1995, and the third issue will begin annual coverage with 1996.

The *NNB* includes a variety of languages in its national bibliography. There is the possibility of over 20 languages and dialects in which books could be written.

Before the present title, Namibia did not have an official current national bibliography. Namibia has been fortunate in having two comprehensive sources that have helped identify both the nation's imprint and titles about Namibia. The first is a computer database begun by Werner Hildebrecht. NAMLIT includes titles published in Namibia or about Namibia published elsewhere which have come to the attention of the compiler regardless of date or format. Articles, dissertations, books, pamphlets, official and government publications, serials (sometimes single issues which are analyzed) are included. Responsibility for this database now resides with the National Library. Some special collections are analyzed and included. The scope of this database is wider than a national bibliography. *NAMLIT* has developed its own thesaurus. The scope has changed over the years--e.g., from recording the serials holdings of the National Archives when Mr. Hildebrecht worked there, to now currently including the current holdings of the National Library where Mr. Hildebrecht currently works.

The second source is *NNB: Namibische national-bibliographie = Namibian national bibliography* / Erkhard Strohmeyer. 1971/1975-1978/1979. Basel : Basler Afrika Bibliographien, 1978-1981, which has appeared in 1978, 1979, and 1981. (DDC: 016.91688; LC: Z3771.S77; ISSN 0170-5091). The *Namibische National-bibliographie* attempts to list all titles published in Namibia and those publications of Namibian interest published elsewhere that the author has seen and catalogued himself. All entries have the location where he first saw the volume. Any publication at any bibliographic level is considered. This bibliography is not based on legal deposit and has a wider scope than many national bibliographies.

Types of publications included in *Namibische National-bibliographie* are books, pamphlets, periodicals, scientific research presented as journal articles, reports, papers, journal articles, government publications. Omitted are those titles that Strohmeyer has not seen. Contents of *Namibische National-bibliographie* include a foreword (in German and English), symbols for the location of title entries, abbreviations, German table of contents including a classified list of DDC headings, English table of contents including a classified list of DDC headings, bibliography, author and title index. Entry information includes: consecutive entry number, author, title, place of publication, publisher, date, pagination, size, library location symbol, notes including ISSN when known. For journal articles, appropriate and complete bibliographic information is given. Entries do not include a classification number. The entry numbers are continuous from volume to volume. The bibliography is arranged by DDC headings and then alphabetically arranged. Both the English and German languages are used throughout the bibliography. An attempt has been made to include indigenous languages. According to Strohmeyer, publishing in local languages has been increasing. New aspects of these languages need to be dealt with further in future volumes.

In the 1976/77 volume, there is a supplement for books published during 1971/75.

These titles are part of the publisher's series *Mitteilungen der Basel Afrika Bibliographien* series: 1971/75 is volume 20, 1976/77 is volume 21, 1978/79 is volume 24.

The *AL,ESA*, its *Serial Supplement*, and *QIPL,ESA* include Namibia within their scopes.

LATEST ISSUE EXAMINED/CURRENCY: The first issue was published in 1997; it is anticipated that subsequent issues will be published in a more timely manner so that the source can be used as an acquisitions tool.

AUTOMATION: The database in mounted on a DOS based system. Unesco's CDS/ISIS is used to build the database.

FORMAT AND SERVICES AVAILABLE: printed; other formats are being considered.

CURRENT LEGAL DEPOSIT LAWS: South West Africa Ordinance No. 10 of 1951. Concerning deposit of printed material. The legal deposit law is from the South African administration, and is not effective. It is being rewritten, and will be submitted to Parliament in the near future.

AVAILABLE FROM: National Library of Namibia, Private Bag 13349, Windhoek.

SELECTED ARTICLES: Bell, Barbara L. "The Making of the Namibia National Bibliography." *ICBC* 25 (no. 2 April/June 1996):31-33.

VERIFIER: Louise Hansmann, Editor, *Namibia National Bibliography*.

NEPAL

TITLE: *Nepalese national bibliography for... . -* 1981-   . Kathmandu : The Library and The Centre, c1983-   .
Annual (irregular).
Some issues have title: *Nepalese national bibliography*.
Also included in *JNRC*: *Journal of the Nepal Research Centre*, beginning with vol. V/VI, 1981/82.
DDC: 016.954./6/005; LC: Z3210.44; DS493.4; LCCN: 87-658419//r92; OCLC: 17211315
ISSN not found

COMPILER: Compilation done by the staff of Tribhuvan University Central Library and Nepal Research Centre.

SCOPE AND COVERAGE: The *Nepalese National Bibliography* (*NNB*) includes the publishing output of Nepal that is acquired by or has been brought to the attention of Tribhuvan University Central Library and the library of the Nepal Research Centre. It is not based on legal deposit legislation.

Types of publications in *NNB* are books, official and government publications, IGO titles published by IGO headquarters based in Nepal, volunteer service publications in Nepal.

Excluded from *NNB* are periodicals, periodical articles, newspapers, maps, musical scores, textbooks and guides to textbooks, school books, ephemeral material such as trade catalogues, telephone directories, public relations pamphlets, etc.

CONTENTS: Preface, introduction which includes the coverage, transliteration policy, arrangement, and an analyzed entry; abbreviations used, addenda for earlier year, bibliography, author index, subject index, title index.

CATALOGUING RULES AND CLASSIFICATION SCHEMES USED: Cataloguing rules used are not mentioned in the introduction, but full bibliographical description is given in AACR1 format.

The classification scheme used is DDC (16th ed.).

ENTRY INFORMATION: DDC number, verbal extension of class number, author, title, place of publication, publisher, date, pagination, price, language symbol.

ARRANGEMENT: The bibliography is classified according to the DDC subject headings. Entries are alphabetically arranged by the main entry within the class.

Books in all languages are listed in one sequence under subject headings.

INDEXES: Author index; subject index; title index. The numbers refer the user to the DDC number in the classified bibliography.

NOTES AND COMMENTS: 1981 is the first year of an annual bibliography cooperatively sponsored by Tribhuvan University Central Library and the library of the Nepal Research Centre. Until now, occasional bibliographies listed publications of Nepal. The compilers feel that scholars worldwide need to have a reliable and regular source to consult which lists titles published in Nepal. Without a legal deposit law, it is hard to know that all publications have been included, but a concerted effort has been made to locate elusive titles. It is thought that any title missed could be listed in an addendum in subsequent issues. In the future, a periodicals list, also including periodical articles, will be issued. These are not included within the *NNB* scope at present. This list is a noble effort to create a current national bibliography.

Publications in English, Devanagari, Nepali, Sanskrit, Newari and Maithili languages are included in *NNB*. All languages are transliterated if necessary and are listed in one sequence under subject headings. Davanagari script is transliterated into Roman script with diacritical marks; Nepali titles are transliterated according to the Turner system; Newari titles are transliterated according to a "slightly modified system of the usual transliteration of Sanskrit." [1]

The introduction follows ICNB recommendation 10. Clear statements of coverage and exclusions, treatment of transliteration, arrangement of the *NNB*, entry information given, an analyzed entry and a list of abbreviations used are all included.

In the absence of any legislation requiring a deposit copy, it is difficult for the compilers to know what publications are available especially if the titles are not available commercially. Many international and national agencies often do not sell their publications commercially so it is difficult to locate these titles. Limited editions are quickly out of stock and therefore may never be brought to the attention of the compilers. Titles listed in the *NNB* were acquired by or called to the attention of the Tribhuvan University Central Library, and the library of the Nepal Research Centre.

The *NNB* appears in separately bound offprint copies as it appeared in the *Journal of the Nepal Research Centre* (*JNRC*), and also as a separately numbered part of the *JNRC*. To date, the national bibliography for 1981 is included in vol. V/VI (1981/82); 1982 is included in vol. VII (1985); 1983 is in VIII (1988), and 1984-1986 are included in vol. IX (1993). The irregularity of the journal in recent years has been a problem. In 1993 Trivhuvan University Central Library has acquired a laser printer and updated software which may make it possible to produce a print quality draft of the national bibliography at the library, thus not relying on the *JNRC*. [2]

AL,SA included Nepal within its scope.

---

1 "Introduction" for 1984-1986, p. 3.
2 "Preface", p. 2 of the 1984-1986 *NNB*. In a letter to the author dated 1 July 1996, Ms. Bhandary stated that *NNB* is now available separately.

LATEST ISSUE EXAMINED/CURRENCY: Entry imprint dates are from the period covered, with late entries belonging in the previous bibliography listed in an addenda.

The latest copy examined in May 1995 at the University of Wisconsin Madison was in *JNRC* vol. IX (1993) which included the *NNB* for 1984-1986.

AUTOMATION: Data is in machine readable format.

FORMATS AND SERVICES AVAILABLE: printed.

CURRENT LEGAL DEPOSIT LAWS: No legal deposit law or copyright law.

AVAILABLE FROM: Tribhuvan University Central Library, Kirtipur, Kathmandu. FAX: +977-1-226964; email: k_mani@npl.helthnet.org.

SELECTED ARTICLES: Jacob, Louis A. "Nepalese Bibliography Now Available." *Library of Congress Information Bulletin* 42 (3 Oct. 1983):340.

VERIFIER: Krishna Mani Bhandary, Chief Librarian, Tribhuvan University Central Library.

NETHERLANDS

TITLE: *Brinkman's cumulatieve catalogus van boeken. Nederlandse bibliografie bevattende de in Nederland en Vlaanderen uitgegeven of herdrukte boeken, die werden ontvangen door het Depot van Nederlandse Publikaties van de Koninklijke Bibliotheek te 's-Gravenhage.* - Alphen aan den Ryns : Samsom, 1930- .
Monthly (eleven numbers a year) with quarterly, half-yearly, annual, and five year cumulations. Publisher varies; current place of publication & publisher: Houten : Bohn Stafleu Van Loghum.
Annual cumulation continues consecutive numbering: *Brinkman's alphabetische lijst van boeken.*
DDC: 015.492; LC: Z2431.B8; LCCN: 81-640034//r84; OCLC: 7081010
ISSN 0007-0165

COMPILER: "Redactie Brinkman [Brinkman Editorial Board]," of the division "Depot van Nederlandse Publikaties & Nederlandse Bibliografie [Depository of Dutch Publications and Dutch Bibliography]," Koninklijke Bibliotheek [Royal Library].

SCOPE AND COVERAGE: *Brinkman's Cumulatieve Catalogus van Boeken* (*BCCB*) is the current Dutch national bibliography. This title, appearing weekly and monthly, respectively, as List A and List B and cumulated yearly, is based on publications published in the Netherlands and received by the Koninklijke Bibliotheek (Royal Library) Depot van Nederlandse Publikaties (Deposit of the Dutch Publications) in the Hague. *BCCB* also lists books published in Flanders, and Dutch-language books published abroad or translated from the Dutch.

Types of publications included in *BCCB* are books from the Netherlands and Flanders, periodicals (first issues, title changes, and theme numbers), pamphlets, official and government publications (local and national), published dissertations, other university papers, published reports, reprints, translations, and electronic publications. A bibliography of musical scores appears in nos. 3, 6, 9 and in the annual cumulation.

Excluded from *BCCB* are postcards, audio-visual material, microforms, and IGO publications.

CONTENTS: Introduction which includes scope, rules and contents of *BCCB*, bibliography, bodies and unions index, subject index.

CATALOGUING RULES AND CLASSIFICATION SCHEMES USED: Rules for the title description follow ISBD and are according to the Federation of Organizations of the Library, Information and Documentation (FOBID), The Hague, NBLC (Dutch Centre of Public Libraries), 1978-1982. 1) Description rules for non-serial publications. 2) Description rules for serial publications. 3) Rules for catalogue construction.

The 32 categories used in the *A-lijst* and *B-lijst* have been recommended by UNESCO, to which "educational appliances" has been added as category 33; further additions to the *A-lijst* categories are musical scores, Dutch books in translation, and electronic publications.

ENTRY INFORMATION: Author, title, place of publication, publisher, date, pagination, illustrations, size, series statement, brief notes including ISBN and ISSN, price if known, CIP. Internal number code, e.g., B8467867, in lower right corner.

ARRANGEMENT: Arrangement in *BCCB* is alphabetical by entries. Arrangement in *A-Lijst* and *B-Lijst* is by the 37 groups, e.g. trade, ethnology and folklore, pure science and history of science, poetry, biology. Entries are alphabetical within the categories.

INDEXES: The bodies and union index ("Instanties en verenigingen") in *BCCB* (corporate register in *B-Lijst*) includes two kinds of entries: an enumeration of publications for which the body or union is responsible, and cross-references to different names of the same body or union, or to different bodies and unions with which a body or union is connected through the organization.

The topic index ("Onderwerpenregister") is an alphabetical list of subjects, personal names and geographic terms, all found in the main bibliography. Cross-references for synonyms of topic terms used in the topic index are used.

A-lijst and *B-lijst* include an author/title index.

NOTES AND COMMENTS: The annual cumulation of *BCCB* continues the consecutive numbering of *Brinkman's alphabetische lijst van boeken* (1881-1929). This title continues *Alphabetische naamlijst van boeken, plaat-en kaartwerken* , and *Alphabetische naamlijst van boeken* (1790-1832; OCLC: 9120379).

The five-year cumulation *Brinkman's catalogus van boeken en tijdschriften* (OCLC: 1537095) supersedes *Alphabetische naamlijst van boeken, plaat-en kaartwerken* and the annual *Brinkman's cumulatieve catalogus van boeken*.

The Dutch national bibliography is named after the first compiler and publisher of the catalogue, C.L. Brinkman (10 September 1820 - 29 September 1881).

Publishers cooperate with the Depository of Dutch Publications, Royal Library and *BCCB*. Books that publishers send to *BCCB* are placed in the Royal Library Depository. Therefore, *BCCB* is a complete list of books received on this voluntary deposit program.

In the introduction, the editors give helpful hints for easier use of the bibliography. Some specific points explained are the filing of diacritical marks and that if the first word of a title is a number, it will be filed before the alphabetical entries. It would be helpful if an analyzed entry and an abbreviations list could be included in the introduction. In looking at the entry information, it was unclear what some of the abbreviations in an entry meant, e.g., Met lit. opg., (W), NUGI 694, and why a proper name should appear in the internal numbering code. From other information read by the author, it seems that the understanding of this number might be useful for readers. It was suggested that since 1974 one is able to identify official publications by the third and fourth numerals.[1]

Information for some of the abbreviations are: (A)=Algemeen=General, (S)=Schoolbook, (W)=Wetenschappclijk=Scientific book, and NUGI =Nederlandse Uniforme Genre Indeling (Netherlands Uniform Genre-Classification). For example, NUGI 694 means criminal law. The letters and NUGI code are determined by the publishers and are of use to the bookseller.[2]

A-lijst (A-list) is a weekly classified list included within *Boekblad. Nieuwblad voor het boekenvak* (ISSN 0167-4765). The purpose of *A-lijst* is to include books, and first numbers and theme numbers of the Dutch and Flemish periodicals published in the Netherlands and Flanders which are distributed and available commercially. After a month, these titles are included in *BCCB*.

Nederlands bibliografie B-lijst (The Dutch Bibliography B-list) begun in 1983 is a monthly list compiled by the editors of *BCCB* and of the division "Depot van Nederlandse Publikaties & Nederlandse Bibliografie" of the Royal Library; it is published by the Nederlands Bibliografisch Centrum" (Dutch Bibliographic Center). The *B-lijst* includes publications of the Netherlands issued by governmental authorities (national and local), scientific institutes and similar organizations, privately published dissertations and other university papers. Materials in List B are generally not distributed through the conventional commercial channels. The bibliography is divided into 33 categories; entries are alphabetically arranged within these categories. Entries in the title/author and corporate indexes give reference to the category in "Bibliografie" and to the main entry. Titles marked with CIP have already been listed in *Uitgaven in voorbereiding/CIP* (which was ceased in April 1996). Cumulations of *B-lijst* will be included in number 6 and the cumulated edition of *BCCB*.

A portion of the preliminary pages is given in English as well as in Dutch.

---

[1] *Survey on the Present State of Bibliographic Recording*, p. 73.
[2] Information is given in a 29 July 1997 letter to the author from Kees van der Berg, Head, Acquisitions and Processing, Koninklijke Bibliotheek.

The contents of each number is as follows: 1– Jan., 2– Jan./Feb., 3–Jan./Feb./Mar., 4–Apr., 5–Apr./May, 6–Jan./Feb./Mar./Apr./May/June, 7–July, 8–July/Aug., 9–July/Aug./Sept., 10–Oct., 11–Oct./Nov.

Brinkman's Cumulatieve Catalogus op CD-ROM [Brinkman's Cumulative Catalogue on CD-ROM] is available on two disks, a back file (from 1981/1989) and a current file (1990-). These disks include the full A and B lists, as well as titles not published in the A and B lists. Complete bibliographic information is given. The searching access points are title and sub-title, ISBN, ISSN, author, corporate authors, publisher, year and place of publication, NUGI reference, key word, national bibliography numbers, etc. Boolean operators AND, OR, and NOT can be part of the search which can be done in Dutch or English language. Features such as "Save search" and "New records search" are available. A browsing feature is available. OPTI-WARE'S retrieval and interface software developed by Online Computer Systems, Inc. is used. Minimum hardware requirements are an IBM-compatible PC with a 286 processor or above, 430 KB of free memory, and a hard disk with 1 MB of free space, CD-ROM player with Microsoft extensions, PC capability of DOS version 3.10 or higher.

Maps separately published in the Netherlands can be found in *Bibliografie van in Nederland verschenen kaarten* [Bibliography of Dutch Maps] published from 1975-1982 by the Royal Library, The Hague (ISSN 0377-8975) and from 1991 published as an inlay in *BCCB*.

Official publications are listed in *Bibliografie van in Nederland verschenen officiële uitgaven bij Rijksoverheid en provinciale besturen* [Bibliography of Dutch Governmental Publications] by the Royal Library, The Hague (ISSN 0165-2958). This title ceased publication after 1987.

Titles in the CIP program were listed in *Uitgaven in voorbereiding/CIP* [Cataloguing in Publication] by the Royal Library, The Hague until April 1996 when the CIP program ceased.

For a complete listing of titles published in Flanders, one should consult the national bibliography for Belgium.

LATEST ISSUE EXAMINED/CURRENCY: The majority of the entries are for the period covered. A statement on the title page indicates that additions for earlier years are also included.

The 1993 cumulation was the latest examined in June 1997 at the University Library, Cambridge. The latest five year cumulation examined in June 1997 was 1986-1990. *B-lijst* for Jan./Feb. 1997 was the latest monthly examined; it was received at the University Library on 22 April 1997.[1]

 AUTOMATION: The production of the *BCCB* takes place in the framework of the Shared Cataloguing System in the Netherlands. Automation is by the Pica-bureau, Leiden. Alfa Base Publikatie Processors, Alphen aan den Rijn is responsible for the photographic set-up of *BCCB*.

FORMAT AND SERVICES AVAILABLE: printed; CD-ROM. The bibliography as such is not available on the Internet. However, the catalogue of the Koninklijke Bibliotheek, which

---

[1] The 1996 cumulation was published in June 1997, and the latest five year cumulation (1991-1995) was published in 1996.

includes the catalogue of the *Deposit of Dutch Publications*, is available on the Internet. Catalogue entries from the *Deposit* are the basis for the bibliography.

CURRENT LEGAL DEPOSIT LAWS: No legal deposit law.[1] Publications are deposited on a voluntary basis through an agreement with publishers.

AVAILABLE FROM: Intermedia bv, P.O. Box 4, 2400 MA Alphen aan den Rijn.

SELECTED ARTICLES: Heijligers, A. and Owen, J. Mackenzie. "Bibliographic Control in the Netherlands," pp. 41-43. Based on a paper by A. L. van Wesemael. In *The Interchange of Bibliographic Information in Machine Readable Form.* London, The Library Association, 1975.

Maanen, A. Van and Willemsen, A.W. "Cataloguing-in-Publication in the Netherlands." Background Paper number 8 presented at the International Cataloguing-in-Publication Meeting, Ottawa, 16-19 August 1982. Organized by IFLA in association with Unesco (IFLA/UBC/CIP/BP8). Mimeographed.

VERIFIER: Kees van den Berg, Head, Acquisitions and Processing, Koninklijke Bibliotheek.

NEW ZEALAND

TITLE: *New Zealand national bibliography.* - 1966- . - Wellington, N.Z. : National Library of New Zealand, 1967- .
Monthly (eleven numbers a year 1981- , Feb.-Dec.); from 1983- cumulates monthly, and annually in December.
Supersedes in part: Current national bibliography section of *Index to New Zealand periodicals and current national bibliography of New Zealand books and pamphlets*, and *New Zealand General Assembly Library. Copyright publications.*
Available only in microfiche from June 1983- .
DDC: 015.931; LC: Z4101.N57; LCCN: 90-657630//r91; OCLC: 10756728
ISSN 0028-8497

COMPILER: New Zealand National Bibliography Section, National Library of New Zealand.

SCOPE AND COVERAGE: The *New Zealand National Bibliography* (*NZNB*) is a selected list of New Zealand and Tokelau works which are deposited at the Legal Deposit Office. Works published overseas about New Zealand (if one fifth of its subject content relates to New Zealand), and by authors normally resident in New Zealand or who have been recognized as New Zealander authors are also listed. Most of those not published in New Zealand have been purchased by the National Library and the Alexander Turnbull Library. Only current publications are included, e.g., items published from the current and preceding five years. Books and serials need to be four pages or more in length and to be "published."

---

[1] *International Guide to Legal Deposit*, p. 90.

Types of publications included in *NZNB* are books, pamphlets, official and government publications, serials (first issue and subsequent name changes), newspapers, maps and charts, atlases, videos, sound recordings, musical scores, art prints, CD-ROMs, kits and pictures.

Excluded are publications under four pages and folded sheets, unless forming part of a series, newsletters of local societies unless the title includes research, publications meant for internal circulation within an organization, and IGO publications.

CONTENTS: Microfiche: The microfiche edition is divided into five sections: Introduction/how to use the microfiche; Register; Subject index; Author/title index; Publishers address list. This arrangement has evolved since the 1983 edition which had separate sections for author and title, and the 1984 edition which was divided into: Register, Subjects, Author/title and Non-book. Addresses. The non-book materials for the years 1986 and 1987 are included in *NZNB* for 1988; the delay was due to software limitations on *New Zealand Bibliographic Network* (*NZBN*) database. Later, this non-book material section has been integrated into the register, subject index, and author/title index.[1]

Printed (produced until 1982): introduction, abbreviations and symbols, bibliography: section I: books, art prints, music scores, sound recordings, corrections to earlier volumes of *NZNB*, section II: atlases, maps and charts, section III: serials, authority file for new serial and corporate body headings (beginning in 1981), publishers' addresses, index of titles, series and selected added author entries for section I and section III.

CATALOGUING RULES AND CLASSIFICATION SCHEMES USED: Microfiche: AACR2 and *LCSH* are followed, with some specific New Zealand subject headings used.

The classification scheme followed is DDC (20th ed.).

Printed: *NZNB* used AACR2 in cataloguing, and *LCSH* are followed with some New Zealand specific headings. If a subject is used and not included in this list, it is identified with an asterisk (*). ISBD(M) has been followed since 1974, ISBD(S) and ISBD(NBM) since 1978, ISBD(CM) since 1979.

The classification scheme followed is DDC, and 301-307 Sociology Expanded Version based on Edition 19 with extensions for place from the New Zealand Library Association expansion for New Zealand. Where desirable, a secondary classification is added in parentheses. The McColvin classification number is given for music, and the letter "J" is used to indicate works intended for users up to the fourth form.

When transliteration schemes are used, they are noted.

ENTRY INFORMATION: Microfiche (Register entry): register number, author, title, place of publication, publisher, date, pagination, illustrations, size, series statement, notes, ISBN/ISSN, subject entries, added entries, DDC number and edition of Dewey used, e.g., the last two numbers of 657.436 20 indicates DDC (20th ed.) is used. The *NZNB* number is given in square

---

1 Alison Fields, "The National Bibliography in New Zealand. Part I: Development and Description," *New Zealand Libraries* 48 (no. 3, Sept. 1995):50.

brackets at the end of the entry, e.g., [zbn9282224]. The register entry is the most complete entry information and is the only entry to include the classification number.

Early microfiche editions have had slight variations. For example, the DDC number is in lower left corner. Also, in addition to the DDC number, the LC number and another number, usually the LCCN, are listed if they are included in an overseas agency record.

Entry information for the subjects and the author/title sections only includes bibliographic description through the pagination or illustration statement.

Microfiche: (Subjects): The subjects are given in capital letters, then the author, title, place of publication, publisher, pagination and illustrations. The monthly issues have "1995 NZNB" in lower left; lower right are the *NZNB* number, e.g., zbn85-001876, and the register number, e.g., 00000540.

Microfiche: (Author/Title): author, title, edition, place of publication, publisher, date, pagination, illustrations, size, *NZNB* number (beginning in 1985) and the register number. This list includes all added title entries.

Microfiche: (Publishers Addresses) This is an alphabetical list of publishers who are represented by several titles. Each microfiche has its own alphabetical index in the lower right hand corner. Through most of the 1980s this section appeared to an adjacent section of non-book items: Section a: author, artist or musician, title, description, price, tracings; Section b: atlases, maps and charts; Section c: publishers' names and addresses.

Printed: Bibliography, section I: author, title, edition statement, place of publication, publisher, date, pagination, illustrations, series statement, notes including price, binding, DDC number, ISSN and ISBN, tracings. Section II: geographical entry heading, name, edition, scale, place of publication, publisher, description, series, notes, price, tracings. No classification number is given. Section III: title, number and volume, beginning date, place of publication, publisher, year, volume, illustrations, size, description, ISSN, tracings, price, frequency. No classification number is given.

Prior to 1983, the printed *NZNB* used an "o" in the margin for works of non-New Zealand origin. This practice is not continued with the microfiche edition.

Items known to be out-of-print, privately circulated, limited or restricted circulation, or gratis are identified with appropriate notes.

Entries preceded by "CIP" are prepared from cataloguing-in-publication data; on publication of the title, a full entry is supplied. *NZNB* ceased doing CIPs since 1993.[1]

Entries in section III preceded by "d" are discontinued.

A dash (—) preceding an entry indicates incomplete bibliographic information.

---

[1] Information from e-mail correspondence dated 5 January 1996 to the author from Karen Rollitt, Editor-in-Chief, New Zealand National Bibliography Collection Services, National Library of New Zealand.

ARRANGEMENT: Microfiche: Register: arranged in register number (accession) order. Subject: arranged alphabetically by subject headings. Author/Title: alphabetical order. Publishers Addresses: alphabetical order.

Printed: all sections of the bibliography are alphabetically arranged: section I by author, section II by geographical area, section III by title.

INDEXES: Microfiche: The subject, author/title sections serve to index the entries, giving access to the full bibliographic descriptions in the register section. These indexes are alphabetically arranged. Each monthly issue cumulates for the year. Cross references are used. The register number refers the user to the register section where these numbers are numerically arranged.

Printed: index of titles, series and selected added author entries.

NOTES AND COMMENTS: "New Zealand is one of the few countries in the world which can claim to have national bibliographic coverage for the entire span of its written history. Together the range of national bibliographies covers the entire period from the first known publication about New Zealand in 1668 through to the present day."[1] The *NZNB* (1966-) was preceded by the *Current National Bibliography* (1950-1965), *Copyright Publications* (1933-1965), and the *New Zealand National Bibliography to the year 1960*.

From 1966 until the first half of 1983 the *NZNB* was published and available in printed format. From June 1983 the *NZNB* is available only on microfiche.[2] Information for the *NZNB* is entered directly into the *NZBN* database which had the facility to create computer output microforms."[3]

A microfiche edition was produced retrospectively for the years 1961 to 1982; this was made by photographing pages from the printed pages. A cumulated copy of the microfiche, for the years 1983-1993, was produced in 1994.[4]

Microfiche: The *NZNB*, June 1983- has improved its presentation and arrangements from the first microfiche editions which had no introduction or explanation about the scope, coverage, exclusions, arrangement, table of contents and entry analysis.

The first two issues of the microfiche edition in June and July 1983 were entitled *NZBU Catalogue*. August 1983 to November 1983 were entitled *NZ Bibliography*. Only with the cumulation for all of the 1983 issues was the national bibliography entitled *New Zealand National Bibliography*.

---

[1] Fields, p. 46.

[2] It should be noted that in a letter dated 13 February 1996 to the author from Karen Rollitt, *NZNB*, she mentions that since 1983 *NZNB* has produced a paper printout--a list of the bibliographic items catalogued in the last month arranged in the order that catalogue records have been added to the database. It is produced mainly for Acquisitions Librarians for selection purposes.

[3] Fields, p. 50.

[4] Rollitt letter.

The fiche headers are color-coded for easy identification.

Numbers carry the prefix for the originating agency, e.g., anb = *Australian National Bibliography*, bnb = *British National Bibliography*, zbn = *New Zealand Bibliographic Network*.[1]

Each monthly set of microfiche cumulates with the previous month, which makes this easier to consult. The last set cumulates the year. This monthly cumulation is a difference from the earlier printed copies. If one is using this as an acquisitions guide, it would be helpful to mark current monthly entries with a symbol to help the user locate quickly the new entries for each month. The paper printout was created to aid the selection process.

Printed: The authority file for new serial and corporate body headings is a guide for names whose form has changed with AACR2 and helps to identify newly established headings. Personal names and unaltered serials are not included.

The annual cumulation includes statistics on book production in New Zealand.

NZNB has ceased providing the LC number on overseas records.[2]

South Pacific Bibliography includes materials on the indigenous people of New Zealand.

LATEST ISSUE EXAMINED/CURRENCY: Microfiche: The latest microfiche examined was for May 1995 at the University of Wisconsin, Madison library.

The *NZNB* on microfiche is accomplishing the timeliness needed to become an acquisitions and selection tool as well as an historical record of the nation's publishing output.

Printed: The printed annual was usually received ten to twelve months from the period covered. The monthly issues were received three months after the period covered.

AUTOMATION: *NZNB* is generated directly from the *NZBN* database using WLN (Western Library Network) software; it is produced on an Amdahl mainframe.

FORMAT AND SERVICES AVAILABLE: microfiche; magnetic tape service; online through the *New Zealand Bibliographic Network* (*NZBN*), paper printout (since 1983). *NZNB* database can be accessed via telnet.

In the future it is planned to offer *NZNB* on CD-ROM, and via the Internet.

CURRENT LEGAL DEPOSIT LAWS: Legal Deposit is compulsory, under the National Library Act 1965, Section 30A, amended 1994.[3]

---

[1] Information received in a letter to the author from K.S. Williams, Librarian-in-charge, *NZNB*, dated 23 December 1985.

[2] Rollitt letter.

[3] As cited on the verso of the cover in *Information for publishers and writers*, published by the National Library of New Zealand. n.d.

AVAILABLE FROM: Publications, Public Affairs Group, National Library of New Zealand, PO Box 1467, Wellington 6000.

SELECTED ARTICLES: Fields, Alison. "The National Bibliography in New Zealand. Part I: Development and Description." *New Zealand Libraries* 48 (no. 3 Sept. 1995):46-51.

"The National Bibliography in New Zealand. Part II." *New Zealand Libraries* 48 (no. 6, June 1996) pp. 107-110.

VERIFIER: Karen Rollitt, Editor-in-Chief, *New Zealand National Bibliography*

NICARAGUA

TITLE: *Bibliografía nacional de Nicaragua.* - 1979/1989-   . - Managua : Instituto Nicaragüense de Cultura, 1991-   .
Irregular.
DDC: 016.97285; LC: Z1481.B53; LCCN: sn94-35678; OCLC: 31007889
ISSN not found

COMPILER: Biblioteca Nacional Ruben Dario.

SCOPE AND COVERAGE: *Bibliografía nacional de Nicaragua* (*BNN*) includes the publishing output of Nicaragua which is deposited at the national library, and over 20 other sources. The title includes books by Nicaraguan authors regardless of where they live, and books about Nicaragua by foreign authors.

Types of publications include books, pamphlets, theses and dissertations.

Omitted from *BNN* are periodicals.

CONTENTS: Introduction, location codes where the books can be found, bibliography, indexes.

CATALOGUING RULES AND CLASSIFICATION SCHEMES USED: AACR2 is followed for cataloguing. For subject headings, "Listas de encabezamiento de materia para bibliotecas" compiled by Carmen Rovira and Jorge Aguayo, and the *Index Medical Latinoamericano*, edited by the Centro Latinoamericano de Información en la Ciencia de la Salud de Sao Pablo, Brasil.

No classification scheme is used.

ENTRY INFORMATION: Consecutive entry number, author, title, place of publication, publisher, date, pagination, series statement, notes including where subject and where theses are written, tracings, location code.

ARRANGEMENT: The bibliography is divided into two sections: bibliography, and theses from the different universities in the country. Both are alphabetically arranged by the main entry.

INDEXES: Author index, title index.

NOTES AND COMMENTS: It appears that the *BNN* 1979/1989 is the beginning of a current national bibliography which will continue to appear on a regular basis. The information in this issue has been added to the database of the retrospective national bibliography *Nicaraguan National Bibliography / Bibliografia Nacional Nicaragüense, 1800-1978* . Books and pamphlets printed in Nicaragua, written by Nicaraguans and written about Nicaragua, laws, decrees, agreements, treaties, Presidential publications, serials, budgets, census material is included within its scope. It was published in three volumes by the Latin American Bibliographic Foundation and Biblioteca Nacional Ruben Dario, 1986-1987.

It is delightful to see the coverage of Nicaraguan bibliography in the above titles in the last decade. One suggestion would improve the current national bibliography's usefulness. So that specific subjects could be located quickly it would be helpful to have the bibliography include classification numbers from an universal system (such as DDC or UDC, for example), or include a subject index with references to the tracings in the entries. The former would be preferable and would adhere to the ICNB recommendation no. 11.

Boletín Nicaragüense de Bibliografía y Documentación. - no. 1- July/Sept. 1974-   . - Managua: Biblioteca, Banco Central de Nicaragua [etc.], 1974-   is intended to establish the basis for a national bibliography to continue to work begun by Biblioteca Americana de Nicaragua's *Bibliografía de libros y folletos publicados en Nicaragua (en 1942, o antes según fecha de publicación), que se encuentran en algunas bibliotecas particulares de Nicaragua. A bibliography of books and pamphlets published in Nicaragua (with 1942 or earlier as date of publication) to be found in certain private libraries of Nicaragua.* Managua: Ed. Nuevos Horizontes, 1945, and *Bibliografía de trabajos publicados en Nicaragua... A bibliography of works published in Nicaragua. 1943-45/47.* Managua: Ed. Nuevos Horizontes, 1944-1948, "and to begin a methodical inventory of Nicaraguan culture."[1] Numbers also include an informative essay on areas such as painting and sculpture, drama, and archeology. This title is an "organo oficial" of the Biblioteca del Banco Central de Nicaragua.

LATEST ISSUE EXAMINED/CURRENCY: The latest issue examined at Indiana University Libraries in March 1997 is for 1990/1992, published in 1993.[2]

Imprint dates are from the period covered.

AUTOMATION: For automation, the format IBERMARC is used in the MicroIsis program.

---

[1] *HLAS: 50*, entry number 82.
[2] The author talked to a reference librarian at the Nettie Lee Benson Latin American Collection, University of Texas, Austin in July 1997. The Collection has received the 1993-1995 issue, published in 1996.

FORMAT AND SERVICES AVAILABLE: printed.

CURRENT LEGAL DEPOSIT LAWS: No legal deposit was traced.

AVAILABLE FROM: Biblioteca Nacional Ruben Dario, Apdo. Postal 101, Managua.

VERIFIER: no reply received.

NIGER

No current national bibliography has been traced for Niger.

NIGERIA

TITLE: *The National bibliography of Nigeria.* 1973-   . - Lagos : National Library of Nigeria, 1973-   .
Monthly, with quarterly, semiannual and annual cumulations.
Continues: *Nigerian publications: current bibliography* (0078-0812).
Subtitle: *Current national bibliography*
DDC: 015.669; LC: Z3553.N5N37, DT515.A2, Z3597.N277; LCCN: 76-643253
ISSN 0331-0019

COMPILER: National Library of Nigeria.

SCOPE AND COVERAGE: *The National Bibliography of Nigeria (NBN)* includes publications published in Nigeria and received under legal deposit legislation, books written by Nigerians in any part of the world and items on Nigeria published abroad.

Types of publications covered are books, pamphlets, government publications, new serials, local language publications, conference papers, maps and plans, tape recordings, newspapers. With the 1988 volume, phonorecords are added.

Omitted from the *NBN* are some non-print materials such as films.

CONTENTS: Table of contents, preface, abbreviations and symbols, outline of LC classification scheme, outline of DDC scheme, extract from the National Library of Nigeria Classification Scheme, classified sequence, author, title and series index, subject index, new serials titles, list of publishers and printers, National Library Decree, and statistical tables.

CATALOGUING RULES AND CLASSIFICATION SCHEMES USED: The cataloguing of materials in the bibliography follows the AACR2 (since 1982), ISBD(M) and ISBD(S), ISBD(CM), and ISBD(NBM).

The latest edition of the DDC system is used, and arrangement of entries is by DDC. Each entry also has been assigned LC classification numbers. For government publications, the National Library of Nigeria classification scheme is used in addition to the DDC and LC classifications. This number is preceded by OD DT515.

NBN first began using ISBD(M) and ISBD(S) in 1974. ISBNs were first shown in the national bibliography covering the year 1976 (published 1977) although the National Library had been issuing ISBNs to publishers since 1974 when the ISBN Centre was established.

The *LCSH* is followed for the subject headings that appear in each entry.

ENTRY INFORMATION: DDC number in upper left corner, author, title, edition, statement of responsibility, place of publication, publisher, date, pagination, illustration statement, size, series statement, paperback notation, notes including ISBN and ISSN if known, price if known, subject and added entry tracings, LC classification numbers in lower left corner within brackets, legal deposit number in lower right corner.

Material published abroad is marked by an asterisk(*).

ARRANGEMENT: Since 1976, the classified sequence of the *NBN* is arranged by the DDC scheme. Arrangement for earlier volumes followed a pattern originating from the University of Ibadan and maintained by the National Library until 1976. Information was alphabetically arranged within categories of: works in English language; government publications; works in vernacular; Nigeriana published outside the country and acquired by the Library; Nigerian periodicals and newspapers. Some of the categories were further subdivided.

From the 1994 annual cumulation, materials in the *NBN* are to be arranged by format, e.g., monographs, serials, sound recordings.[1]

INDEXES: Author/title/series index; subject index. Both indexes are arranged alphabetically.

NOTES AND COMMENTS: *Nigerian Publications: Current National Bibliography.* - 1950/52-1972 was published by Ibadan University from 1953-1970, and by the National Library of Nigeria from 28 June 1970-1972. Frequency was weekly, with quarterly and annual cumulations (1953-1972). The first volume was a cumulation of the years 1950-1952. From 1950-1954 the scope listed only books deposited at the National Library; periodicals, maps and newspapers were excluded. This title did not have subject headings or subject classifications from 1950/52-1970, and was alphabetically arranged by author.

Nigerian Periodicals and Newspapers 1950-1970 lists periodicals and newspapers deposited at the Ibadan University Library.

Nigeria has been a member of the ISDS since December 1977. The Nigerian National Serials Data Centre, established in the National Library since 1976, is responsible for assigning ISSNs to serials published in Nigeria.

---

[1] Information included in a letter to the author dated 28 June 1996 from M.Wali, National Librarian.

The statistical information at the back of the volume gives an account of publishing in Nigeria during the past ten years. Information is given for official publications, non-official publications in English, Nigerian language publications, serial publications and titles published outside Nigeria.

Through 1973, the current national bibliography issued a narrative summary of publishing in Nigeria. A statistical section in tabular form still gives numerical output, but is not as detailed as the previous summaries for 1973 and earlier.

NBN no longer includes a separate section for government publications. A separate section for government publications since 1962 (when the national bibliography was called *Nigerian Publications*) made it an easy task to determine the output of various government agencies. Before 1962, government publications were arranged in the English language section under "N" for Nigeria.

In Nigeria, although English is the official language, and the Hausa language is spoken by over forty percent of northern Nigeria, there are over 250 languages and dialects; some estimates have indicated the figure to be closer to 400.[1] The enormity of locating, identifying, and cataloguing so many languages is staggering. It is not known how many of these languages are in print, but a count of language headings used in *NBN* from 1950/52 to 1972 accounts for fifty-two.[2] That figure is updated by Shoyinka (p.85) to sixty-one in her 1979 article. The problem of not having staff members who are familiar with the lesser known dialects is a real one.

Nigeria has been a leader in Black Africa where it was the first country to have a current national bibliography.[3] *NBN* has strived to conform to international standards and has continued to produce a current national bibliography which reflects the publishing output of the country. Even with the tremendous effort of staff members, it is still estimated that only fifty percent of the publishing output is recorded in the *NBN*.[4]

Periodicals which ceased or changed titles were noted in *Nigerian Publications* in volumes before 1970. After that this information was to be included in *Serials in Print in Nigeria*, which has now ceased publication. Currently, the National Serials Data Centre records title changes and cessations of serials, and new titles are listed in *NBN*.

From January 1987, monthly issues are produced from a camera-ready computer printed list.[5]

Nigeria has participated in CIP since May 1983.

[1] Patricia H. Shoyinka, "Bibliographic Control in Nigeria," *International Library Review* 11 (1979):85.

[2] Sam O. Oderinde, "Cataloguing of National Materials: Problems of Compiling Nigeria's National Bibliography," *International Cataloguing* 5 (July/Sept. 1976):8.

[3] C. C. Aguolu, "National Bibliography in Nigeria: its Growth, Development and International Dimensions," *African Research and Documentation* no. 28 (1982):2.

[4] Beatrice S. Bankole, "Bibliographic Control and Documentation." A paper presented at the Nigerian Library Association Seminar on Collection Development at Enugu, 2-6 November 1981. p. 15.

[5] Beatrice S. Bankole, "Nigeria," *Afribiblios* 9 (no. 1 June 1986):12

A total of 5,012 publishers have been assigned ISBN from inception in 1974 through June 1996.[1]

The University of Lagos systematically acquires non-book materials in Nigeria as much as is possible.

Theses and dissertations are included in the National Library's *Theses and Dissertations Accepted for Higher Degrees in Nigerian Universities* 1966/67- . 1969- .

LATEST ISSUE EXAMINED/CURRENCY: Annual volumes are received in the University Library, Cambridge, England, on an average of three years after the year covered. Monthly issues are equally delayed. In April 1995, the latest copy received by the University Library, Cambridge was the 1988 annual cumulation published in 1991 and received 22 April 1992. One of the major reasons for the delay in receiving *NBN* is because of incomplete bibliographical data.[2]

This same reason, plus a lag between publication date and deposition of materials at the National Library may be why the *NBN* has included entries which are several years behind the year covered. This has improved from 1973 when a sample page included a title from 1973, 1972, 1971, 1970, 1969, 1968, and 1966. A sample page from the September 1980 issue showed four entries from 1979 and two from 1980; in the 1988 volume, a sample page included one entry from 1983, five entries from 1987, one from 1988. This means that a user needs to check several volumes to locate materials for a given year. It also makes it hard to use the *NBN* as a selection tool for collection development purposes.

In a tabular appendix to her article, Shoyinka states that breakdowns of titles listed in the national bibliography from 1950-1976 were thirty-four point five percent official publications, fifty percent non-official publications and fifteen point four percent Nigerian language publications. Eighty-four point six percent of the titles were English language, fifteen point four percent were Nigerian language.

AUTOMATION: Beginning with the 1995 *NBN*, the data input is entered on CDS/ISIS application software using the Techmedia system.[3]

FORMATS AND SERVICES AVAILABLE: printed.

CURRENT LEGAL DEPOSIT LAWS: National Library Decree, (No.29) as cited in *Federal Republic of Nigeria Official Gazette* 57 (no. 27; 14 May 1970): A134.

AVAILABLE FROM: The Director, National Library of Nigeria; P.M.B. 12626, Lagos.

---

[1] Wali letter.
[2] Shoyinka, op. cit., p. 82.
[3] Wali letter.

SELECTED ARTICLES: Abimbola, S. O. "National Bibliography of Nigeria, Past, Present and Future." *Nigerbiblios* 1 (Oct. 1976):10-12, 16, 18-19, 22.

Aguolu, C.C. "National Bibliography in Nigeria: its Growth, Development and International Dimensions." *African Research and Documentation* no. 28 (1982):2-9.

Anyanwu, Virginia. "The Bibliographic Control of Nigerian Government Publications." *Government Publications Review* 19 (no. 5 Sept./Oct. 1992):505-512.

Bankole, Beatrice S. "Current National Bibliographies of the English Speaking Countries of Africa." *International Cataloguing* 14 (Jan./Mar. 1985):5-10.

Bankole, Beatrice S. "Nigeria." *Afribiblios* 9 (no. 1 June 1986):11-17.

Nweke, Ken M.C. "Legal Deposit Laws in Nigeria and Bibliographic Control of Nigeriana since 1950." *Government Publications Review* 18 (no. 4 July/Aug. 1991):339-345.

Shoyinka, Patricia H. "Bibliographic Control in Nigeria." *International Library Review* 11 (1979):77-91.

VERIFIER: Mu'azu H. Wali, National Librarian, National Library of Nigeria.

NORWAY

TITLE: *Norsk bokfortegnelse. Årskatalog. = The Norwegian national bibliography. [Yearbook].* - 1814/47-   . - Oslo : Den norske bokhandlerforening, 1848-1994; Oslo : Universitetsbiblioteket i Oslo, 1995-   .
Annual; monthly (1973-1993), with quinquennial cumulation (1921/25-1971/75).
Continues *Aarskatalog over norsk litteratur.*
DDC: 015.481; UDC: 015 (481); LC: Z2591.N86; LCCN: not found; OCLC: 16582364
ISSN 0029-1870

COMPILER: Universitetsbiblioteket i Oslo, Bibliografisk avdeling [University of Oslo Library, Bibliographic Services Department, Oslo].

SCOPE AND COVERAGE: *Norsk bokfortegnelse. Årskatalog = The Norwegian National Bibliography. [Yearbook]* (NB.A) lists the publishing output of Norway (in Norwegian and in other languages) which is deposited at the University Library according to legal deposit legislation. Titles printed abroad for Norwegian publishers, original works by Norwegian authors published abroad, and reports published in other countries from congresses which were held in Norway are also included. From the volume covering 1995 works published abroad are published in a separate volume called *Norsk bokfortegnelse. Årskatalog. Norvegica extranea.* This volume also includes translations of Norwegian authors which are published abroad, and works by foreigners which are published abroad and are about Norway or Norwegian topics.

Types of publications included in *NB.A* are books, pamphlets, monographic series, some official and government publications, theses and dissertations, research reports, sound recordings of books, calendars, microforms which replace books, and machine-readable files.

Maps are included in the *Årskatalog* in a separate section entitled "Kart."

Musical scores (until 1970's) were included in the quinquennial cumulations. Musical scores are now included in *Norsk musikkfortegnelse. Notetrykk = The Norwegian national bibliography of printed music*.

Excluded are newspapers, films and sound recordings, school books for elementary and secondary school, correspondence courses, off prints, account books, rules and membership lists of local associations, tourist brochures, time tables, concert, movie and theater programs, forms, price lists, films and videos. New legal deposit legislation may change the status of non-book materials. Even though internal documents for various institutions, advertisement folders, brochures, exhibition catalogues, and programmes are not listed in the *NB.A*, they are under bibliographic control in the University of Oslo Library and are accessible to users.[1]

New and changed periodical titles and ceased periodicals were listed in a periodicals section in *NB.A* through 1992. They are now omitted and are published in their own publication *Norsk periodikafortegnelse* [Norwegian list of serials].

CONTENTS: Annual: table of contents, foreword, part 1- Books, etc.: alphabetical listing, classified index, place index; part 2: maps, subject index with reference to the DDC number; statistics on books and pamphlets registered for the year covered.

The ISBN list and publisher addresses can be found through 1991 in *NB.A*. Currently, these are now published in a separate volume.

CATALOGUING RULES AND CLASSIFICATION SCHEMES USED: Since 1 January 1977, ISBD(M) has been followed. Since January 1984 AACR2, translated and edited for Norwegian use (1983 with 1987 and 1990 revisions), has been followed.

Since 1 January 1984, the classification scheme used is DDC, fourth Norwegian abridged edition, revised edition (Oslo, 1986). Corrections and additions which are gradually adopted and published by the Norwegian Committee for Classification and Indexing (earlier the Norwegian Dewey Committee) is used in the classification as well as a revised table for electronic data handling (004-006 Data handling, 621.39 Computers and Computer (data) technique (Oslo, 1988)) and a revised table for 780 Music (Oslo, 1994). In certain areas where subjects are divided geographically, there have been divisions added which follow the *Geographical Divisions of Norway after Melville Dewey's System: Auxiliary Tables*, prepared by the Norwegian Dewey Committee (Oslo, 1983).

ENTRY INFORMATION: Books: author (dates given if known), title, place of publication, publisher, date, pagination, illustrations, size, series statement, DDC number, notes including

---

[1] Erling Grønland, "Norway: National Bibliographic Control in a Small Country," *International Cataloguing* 6 (July/Sept. 1975):7-8.

ISBN, price when known. From 1977, *NB.A* no longer includes the nationality identification for foreigners as part of the information given.

Maps: title, responsibility statement, scale, place of publication, publisher, date, collation, illustration statement, size, series statement, DDC number, notes.

ARRANGEMENT: Books, alphabetical list: The main bibliography is arranged alphabetically by main entry. In addition, book titles, joint authors, editors, and other collaborators, series titles, persons and corporations, and alternative personal and corporate names are listed in the alphabetical list with references to the main entries.

The classified list is based on DDC. Complete bibliographical information is given in the alphabetical section, with shortened entries given in the systematic list.

Maps, alphabetical list: The main entry and references (from title and publisher) are arranged in one alphabetical list. Atlases are listed first, followed by individual maps under place name; Norwegian and foreign names are in the same alphabetical listing.

INDEXES: Part 1: The classified index is divided into two lists: literature for adults arranged by Dewey numbers 001-999, and literature for children and young people. A 'U' is added after the number in the latter section. In the 800 Literature (both in the "adult" and the children /youth parts) the entries are divided into two lists: first, literary history and criticism, and then by works of literature. The works of literature have an "S" added after the number.

The Place index is divided into two alphabetical lists: Norway, and Foreign Countries. Complete bibliographic information is listed in the alphabetical list. Titles may be found under the name of the place and the municipality in the Norway section, and under the name of the place and the country name in the Foreign Countries section.

Part 2: The subject index is according to the DDC system. Reference is to the DDC number listed in the classified index.

NOTES AND COMMENTS: The former title of the *NB Årskatalog* is *Årskatalog over norsk litteratur*, 1903-1951 (OCLC: 1460517; ISSN 0805-7001). This title continued *Kvartalskatalog over norsk literatur*, 1-10 Aarg., 1893-1902 (OCLC: 16582417).

NB was cumulated from weekly entries in *Norsk bokhandlertidende*. - Oslo : Norske Bokhandlerforening from 1880 until 1976 (ISSN 0029-1889; OCLC: 1604090). The weekly lists were cumulated to monthly lists, and appeared from 1977 to April 1994 as a supplement to *Bok og Samfunn* [Book and Society] (LCCN: 77-640831//r80; OCLC: 2833027). From April 1994 the monthly lists are superseded by the fortnightly *Norsk bokfortegnelse. Nyhetsliste. List of new books* (LCCN: sn96-31219; OCLC: 34175966; ISSN 0805-6978), published by Universitetsbiblioteket i Oslo. This lists books catalogued by the Bibliographic Services Department during the last 14 days.

In addition to the paper edition, *NB* is published in microform edition under the title *Norske trykk*. This edition, available every two months, is slightly different from the paper form which lists the new titles. The microform edition is cumulative; because of this feature, it is difficult to distinguish the new titles listed for the month from titles previously listed. If one uses the *NB* to locate new titles for acquisition purposes, the paper copy may be more useful. Two editions covering several years are available on microfiche: 1971/75 and 1984/93 (LCCN: sn87-19219; OCLC: 11141707; ISSN 0332-5385).

A CD-ROM edition comprising all parts of the national bibliography from the time the University of Oslo was computerized is published quarterly by the University of Oslo Library from 1990. Its name is *Nasjonalbibliografiske data = Norwegian national bibliographic file* (ISSN 0803-2637).[1]

The database *Norbok* containing *NB.A* can be searched online in the service UBO:BOK and is included in the CD-ROM *Nasjonalbibliografiske data.*

From March 1994 the electronic BIBSYS catalogue is used as the registration tool and entries are transferred to the national bibliographic database every night. As BIBSYS is a system shared by about 70 Norwegian university, college and research libraries (among them the University of Oslo Library and the National Library, Rana Branch), all using the Norwegian translation of AACR2 and several using the Dewey Decimal classification, this has increased the production of the national bibliography by more than 50%. Thus substantial backlogs of unprocessed titles from the 1980s and 1990s are slowly diminishing.[2]

From 1 January 1978, foreign Norwegian material has been entered into the data base. This information, previously accessible only in card catalog form, is now available in a volume similar to Denmark's *Dania Polyglotta* or Sweden's *Suecana Extranea.* In 1995, the second of three volumes of *NB* is titled *Norvegica extranea–verker utgitt i utlandet = Works published abroad.* It includes books published by Norwegians – original works and translations– published outside the country and/or about the country written by foreigners.

Information about other parts of the *NB* follows. *Norsk musikkfortegnelse. Notetrykk.* - 1993-   . - Oslo : Universitetsbiblioteket i Oslo, 1994-   . Annual (LCCN: 94-658125; DDC: 016.7817481; LC: ML120.N6N67; OCLC: 30824835; ISSN 0804-6328). This title continues *NB Musikktrykk.* - 1981/1983-1992. - Oslo : Universitetsbibliotek, 1985-1993. Annual (LCCN: 86-650542/MN/r94; LC: ML120.N6.N67; DDC: 016.7817481; OCLC: 19860317; ISSN 0800-9805). Includes musical scores, which were included in the *NB* quinquennial volumes until 1970.

Notetrykk is available online as the database *Nornoter* in the service UBO:BOK and is included in the CD-ROM *Nasjonalbibliografiske data.*

Norsk musikkfortegnelse. Lydfestinger = The Norwegian national discography. - 1990/91-   . - Oslo : Universitetsbiblioteket i Oslo, 1993-   . Annual. (ISSN 0804-5631). Includes sound recordings of music. Also available online as the database *Lydopptak* in the University of Oslo's service TRIP and included in the CD-ROM *Nasjonalbibliografiske data.*

---

[1] Information about the CD-ROM *Nasjonalbibliografiske data* was received in 14 March 1997 letter to the author from Anne M.H. Langballe, Bibliographic Services Department, University of Oslo Library.

[2] Langballe letter.

Norsk periodikafortegnelse = Norwegian list of serials. - 1993-   . - Oslo, Universitetsbiblioteket i Oslo, 1995-   . Annual (ISSN 0805-3340). Includes new, ceased and changed serial titles. Serials were included in *NB.A* until 1993.

Norske tidsskriftartikler = The Norwegian index to periodical articles (*NOTA*) Jan./Mar. 1980 - . Oslo : Universitetsbiblioteket, 1980-   . Quarterly (1980-1993); annual (1994-   ). (LCCN: 88-647102; ISSN 0332-978X; OCLC: 9677346). Continues *Norsk tidsskriftindex.* - Oslo : Steenske Forlag, 1918-1965. Articles in periodicals. Arranged by DDC. Subject index. Cumulative author index. Irregular (LCCN: 21-13026//r522; LC: AI13.N6; OCLC: 9694555). *HelseNOTA : bibliografi over artikler i norske helse-og sosialtidsskrifter* [Health NOTA ; bibliography of articles from social services and health journals]. - 1992-   . - Oslo : Universitetsbiblioteket i Oslo, 1992-   . (ISSN 0803-6568). Together, these two indexes list articles from 440 journals in most subject fields. They are available together online as the database *Norart* in the service UBO:BOK, via Internet, and are included in the CD-ROM *Nasjonalbibliografiske data.*[1]

Government publications are not designated by any symbols in *NB*.

Bibliografi over Norges offentlige publikasjoner. - [1 årg.] (1956)-32 (1987) for part 1, 35 (1990) for part 2. - Oslo : Universitetsbiblioteket, 1956-1991. Annual. (LCCN: sn86-26351; LC: Z2599.O8; OCLC: 1761555; ISSN 0474-8050) is a listing of all official publications. Based on legal deposit, it includes internal publications, limited editions, pamphlets and brochures, monographs and serials, each issue of annual reports, maps, and IGO publications published in Norway. Since 1975, it is arranged in two parts: part 1: institutions (main entries) in alphabetical order according to books, series, annual reports, and part 2: circulars, and memos between departments and directorates, etc. Annual.

The bibliographic database *ESOP* (password needed, not on the Internet) of Statens forvaltningstjeneste [Government Administration Service, Documentation Service] registers the official publications.[2]

The new publications of the government and the departments are found in full text via the Web server *ODIN : offentlig informasjon og dokumentasjon i Norge* [Official documentation and information from Norway]. Internet address : http://odin.dep.no/

The ISBN was added to information given in *NB* by 1971. *NB. Årskatalog. ISBN–liste* includes all the ISBNs assigned to publishers since then. The list is in two parts: alphabetical by name and numerical by publisher number. Information given includes ISBN–publisher's name, address, telephone, and publishing house number. In 1992-1993, and 1995- this list was issued as a separate volume. ISBNs are also available online as the database ISBNforlag in the service TRIP, via Internet and are included in the CD-ROM Nasjonalbibliografiske data.

Many cross references are used in the bibliographic sections.

---

[1] Information about *HelseNOTA* was included in Langballe's letter.
[2] This information and the information about ODIN was received in a 14 March 1997 letter to the author from Øivind Berg, Head, Bibliographic Services Department, University of Oslo Library.

The introductions at the beginning of the annual volumes include a lot of information that is beneficial to the user. One wishes that the *NB* might follow the Danish example of presenting the preliminary material bilingually. As it is, all of the information in *NB* is only in the Norwegian language, a handicap for users who do not know Norwegian. This is not meant to be a criticism, but a suggestion which might reflect the importance of *NB* and the use made of it internationally.

Statistics on books and pamphlets indexed in *NB.A* include three tables: indexed books and pamphlets by subject, indexed books by original language and subject, and indexed literary books and pamphlets by type (genre).

In 1995 a project was launched by the National Librarian to convert the printed quinquennial volumes of *NB* back to 1920 by scanning OCR-program and conversion to NORMARC records by an in-house developed program. By spring 1997, the years 1941/45 and 1966/70 A-M have been added to *Norbok* and the CD-ROM.[1]

LATEST ISSUE EXAMINED/CURRENCY: The *Årskatalog* for 1993 published 1994 was the latest examined at the University of Minnesota Library in March 1995. Imprint dates included from 1991-1993. Imprint dates included in an annual volume may go five years back in time. The CD-ROM *Nasjonalbibliografiske data* is published in February and then quarterly, *Norsk bokfortegnelse. Årskatalog* in April; the other parts of the *NB* are published also during the spring.

AUTOMATION: All parts of *NB* are automated in two online services: UBO:BOK (an in-house developed system) and TRIP (originally a Swedish system). The automation started with *NB.A* (the database Norbok in UBO:BOK) in 1971. The format used is NORMARC, based on USMARC. The systems for the national bibliography are run on a Digital Alpha computer under the operation system Open VMS.[2]

FORMAT AND SERVICES AVAILABLE: print, microfiche (under the title *Norske trykk*), CD-ROM (under the title *Nasjonalbibliografiske data = Norwegian national bibliographic file*), online searching through UBO:BOK, and available on the Internet: http://www.nbo.uio.no/baser/

CURRENT LEGAL DEPOSIT LAWS: The Act on Legal Deposit of Public Accessible Documents of 9 June 1989 (in force from 1 July 1990) replaces the Norwegian provisions on legal deposit and the earlier law of 1939. It covers videos, films, records, cassettes, EDP-documents, combined documents, photographs and broadcasts in addition to printed materials. **AVAILABLE FROM:** Universitetsbiblioteket i Oslo, Bibliografisk avdeling, N-0242 Oslo.

SELECTED ARTICLES: Grønland, Erling. "Norway: National Bibliographic Control in a Small Country." *International Cataloguing* 6 (July/Sept. 1975):7-8.

Langballe, Anne M.H. "Nytt om de nasjonalbibliografiske produktene." *Bok og bibliotek* 1994, no. 2:23.

---

[1] Langballe letter.
[2] Berg and Langballe letters.

MARCposten : informasjon fra Bibliografisk avdeling, Universitetsbiblioteket i Oslo (1984, no. 1- , ISSN 0800-9767, usually two numbers a year) regularly gives information on the national bibliography.

Rugaas, Bendik. "Developing a New National Library in Norway." *Alexandria* 2 (1 1990):41-49.

Strøm, Ola. "Store huller i vår nasjonalbibliografi." *Bok og bibliotek* 47 (no. 3 1980):185-187.

VERIFIER: Anne M.H. Langeballe, Bibliographic Services Department, University of Oslo Library.

OMAN

No current national bibliography has been traced for Oman. George Selim, Near East Section, African and Middle East Division, Library of Congress has assisted me in searching the Library of Congress holdings; no national bibliography was located.

Oman is included within the scope of *AL,ME*. - Vol. 1 (1963)—vol. 31 (1993). - Cairo : Library of Congress Office, Cairo, 1963-1993. (ISSN 0041-7769). There is also an unnumbered volume for 1962.

al-Nashrat al-'Arabiyah lil-matbu'at [The Arab Bulletin of Publications] (LCCN: 73-960585/NE; LC: Z3013.N3) includes Oman within its scope. Studies about Oman are available in the literature. One serial publication is *Oman studies bibliographic info* / Oman Studies Centre for Documentation and Research on Oman and the Arabian Gulf. – Tübingten, [Germany], 1982- . Annual (LCCN: 88-646131; LC: Z3028.05O54; OCLC: 9708443).

PAKISTAN

TITLE: *Pakistan national bibliography*. - 1962-   . - Karachi : Government of Pakistan, Department of Libraries, National Bibliographical Unit, 1962-   .
Annual (irregular).
DDC: 015.549; LC: Z3191.P33; LCCN: sn92-10092; OCLC: 2190777
ISSN 1019-0678 (1989-   )

COMPILER: National Bibliographical Unit, Department of Libraries.

SCOPE AND COVERAGE: The *Pakistan National Bibliography* (*PNB*) lists new titles published in Pakistan which are received in the Delivery of Books and Newspapers Branches of the National Library of Pakistan at Islamabad under Copyright Ordinance during the year covered. Earlier issues state that new titles from Liaquat Memorial Library, Karachi were listed. Pakistani publications acquired through other sources by the National Library of Pakistan but not received according to the Copyright Ordinance are also listed. Pakistani publications in

English, Urdu, Bengali, Sindhi, Pushtu, Punjabi, Baluchi, Persian, Arabic and other languages are included.

Types of publications included are books, pamphlets, periodicals (first issue and title change), official and government publications, reports, press conferences.

Excluded from *PNB* are keys and guides to textbooks and ephemeral materials such as publicity pamphlets, periodicals and newspapers (except first issue of new periodicals and title change), maps, musical scores, theses, audio-visual material, and foreign publications written by Pakistanis or about Pakistan.

CONTENTS: Preface, list of abbreviations and language symbols, DDC outline (second summary), classified section, index, list of prominent booksellers and publishers. With the 1989 volume, the English language publications section and the publications written in Urdu, and other Pakistani and Oriental languages appear en tête bêche; the contents are supplied for each section.

CATALOGUING RULES AND CLASSIFICATION SCHEMES USED: AACR2 and ISBD are used in cataloguing entries.

Transliteration of entries other than English into Roman script is based on *Cataloguing of Pakistani Names* by Dr. Anis Khurshid.

Author headings follow recommendations of IFLA's *Names of Persons: National Usages for Entry in Catalogues.*
The classification scheme used is DDC (20th ed.).

ENTRY INFORMATION: DDC number and heading, author or corporate author, title, place of publication, publisher, date, pagination, illustrations, price, series statement, symbol of the language of the book (other than English) given in lower left corner, accessions number is shown in parentheses in lower right corner. The number is preceded by a D (depository) or N (acquired by the National Library of Pakistan). Earlier volumes included the accessions number of each book received and the responsible library's symbol is shown in parentheses, e.g., (L-2178 [from the Liaquat Memorial Library, Karachi]) in lower right corner.

The entry appearing in the classified section under the main entry includes the most complete information.

ARRANGEMENT: The classified bibliography is arranged by the DDC system. From 1989, the issue is divided into two sections: those titles written in the English language, and publications written in Urdu, and other Pakistani and Oriental languages. These two sections appear téte bêche.

The 1962 volume is arranged in two sections: non-government publications, and government and quasi-government publications.

INDEXES: An alphabetical index including authors, editors, translators, compilers, titles, subjects and series entries is given for each section. In some cases an entry is also made under the name of the institution responsible for the publication. Abbreviated entry information for most of the information in the classified section is given for the author index entries. Numbers refer to the classification number of the entries in the bibliography. Cross references are used throughout the index.

NOTES AND COMMENTS: *PNB* lags behind in its publication by several years. For a time the delay was due to the move from Karachi to Islamabad. Because of this lag, a monthly issue of the national bibliography, *Accessions List Pakistan,* (LC: Z3199.A65, DS376.9, LCCN: 87-657534, OCLC: 15995083) began to appear in 1985.[1] Previously, the six monthly accessions lists of the National Library in Islamabad and the Liaquat Memorial Library in Karachi have been relied upon to help fill this gap. Because one function of a current national bibliography is to identify new titles for bibliographers and researchers, it is important for the timeliness of *PNB* to continue to improve; it has improved from ten years ago.

PNB is a printed bibliography, presented in an attractive format. An explanation of entry information, rules followed, scope and contents is provided in the preface.

Government publications are not designated by any symbol. One is able to locate many titles by looking under the corporate name in the classified section and in the index under Pakistan and the name of the department.The 1962 volume was compiled on the basis of bibliographic particulars collected from prominent publishers, and the *Provincial Catalogues of Books and Periodicals* (registered under the *Press and Publication Ordinance 1960, xv of 1960*). This year is considered the first issue of *PNB*.

The second volume of *PNB* was 1968, published in 1970. To help fill the gap between these two volumes, a combined volume covering 1963/1964 was published in 1972. According to information on the verso of the title page of the 1978 volume, the volumes for 1965-1967 and 1970-1971 are not issued yet.

Entries for native scripts are Romanized.

A list of prominent booksellers and publishers giving their addresses is included at the end of the volume.

CIP is not practiced.

AL,SA included Pakistan within its scope.

The Pakistan Bibliographical Working Group has published the *Retrospective Pakistan National Bibliography* for 1947-1961. (LCCN: 73-166386; OCLC number: 701188) It was issued in fascicules covering DDC 000 to 399. Remaining fascicules containing the subjects from 400 to 999 are being published by the National Library of Pakistan and the Pakistan Bibliographical Working Group and are expected to come out within one year's time; these are a retrospective supplement to the *PNB*.

---

[1] Information included in a letter to the author from Ilse Sternberg, Assistant Keeper, Overseas English Section, English Language Branch, Department of Printed Books, The British Library, dated 29 April 1985.

LATEST ISSUE EXAMINED/CURRENCY: The latest volume examined in June 1997 was the 1989 volume published in 1992, and received by the University Library, Cambridge, England 14 October 1993.

AUTOMATION: not automated.

FORMATS AND SERVICES AVAILABLE: printed.

CURRENT LEGAL DEPOSIT LAWS: Copyright Ordinance, 1962. The preface of the 1969 volume indicated that this was the first *PNB* to be published after the Ordinance. The compilers felt that this ordinance was not effective and this volume did not reflect the publishing of Pakistan.

AVAILABLE FROM: National Library of Pakistan, Constitution Avenue, Islamabad-44000.

VERIFIER: M. Irshad Sherwani, Editor, Pakistan National Bibliography.

PALESTINE

TITLE: *al-Bibliyūghrāfiyā al-Filasṭīnīyah fī al-Waṭan.* - 1967/1980-   . - al-Quds [Jerusalem] : Jam'īyat al-Dirāsāt al-'Arabīyah [Arab Studies Society], 1981-   .
Annual (1983-   ).
Cover title: *Palestine—local bibliography.*
DDC: not found; LC: Z3476.B5, DS113.7; LCCN: 88-648429/NE; OCLC: 18397742
ISSN not found

COMPILER: Ḥusayn Ghayth.

SCOPE AND COVERAGE: *al-Bibliyūghrāfiyā al-Filasṭīnīyah fī al-Waṭan* or *Palestine— local bibliography* (*P-LB*) lists titles written by Palestinians from the West Bank, Gaza Strip, and Israel, written in Arabic and other languages.

CONTENTS: From 1984 volume (translated from the Arabic): foreword by the Arab Studies Association, introduction, abbreviations of terms, subjects by DDC: general knowledge, philosophy, religion, social science, language, theory sciences, practical sciences, art, literature, geography and history, indexes, appendices for previous years.

CATALOGUING RULES AND CLASSIFICATION SCHEMES USED: ISBD information is supplied. Exact size is not specified.

The DDC classification scheme is used in all of the volumes except vol. 1 (1967-1980).

ENTRY INFORMATION: Consecutive entry number, author, title, place of publication, publisher, date, pagination, size (small or big), illustrations.

ARRANGEMENT: Entries are arranged alphabetically within broad subjects following DDC. Within each appendix the entries are alphabetical. The DDC number is given.

INDEXES: Author and translator index, title index, subject index. Number refers to the consecutive entry number in the bibliography.

NOTES AND COMMENTS: Although this bibliography transcends geographical and political boundaries of the countries involved, and is not strictly a "national bibliography" issued by a national library based on legal deposit, it seems appropriate to include this bibliography in the country section.

To date, the following volumes have been published: 1967/1980 (pub. 1981), 1981/1982 (pub. 1983), 1983 (pub. 1984), 1984 (pub. 1985), 1985 (pub. 1986), 1986 (pub. 1987), 1987/1988 (pub. 1990), 1989/1992 (pub. 1993), and 1993/1996 (pub. 1997).

In the 1984 volume, a statistical table in the introduction shows that 1802 titles have been listed from the volumes covering 1967 through 1984. The 1984 subject breakdown shows the social sciences and literature categories to have the most titles, with the year's total standing at 175.

Also important to mention is *Mahmūd al-Akhras. al-Bibliyūghrāfiyā al-Filasṭīnīyah al-Urdunīyah, 1900-1970.* Added title page: *Palestine-Jordan Bibliography, 1900-1970* (Jordan Library Association publication 3), 1972, and his *al-Bibliyūghrāfiyā al-Filasṭīnīyah al-Urdunīyah,, 1971-1975.* Added title page: *Palestine-Jordan Bibliography, 1971-1975* (Jordan Library Association 4), 1976 (OCLC: 4725379). These titles include local and foreign imprints and are written mostly in Arabic.

The scope of *Yusrá Abū 'Ajamīyah's Bibliyūghrāfiyā al-Filasṭīnīyah.* Amman : Jordan Library Association, 1982 lists publications by Arabs in Palestine, 1948-1980 (LCCN: 84-143030/NE; OCLC: 11212186). It includes original works, translations, edited works, compilations, indexes of libraries inside and out of the occupied country, including Syria, Lebanon and Israel. It is arranged by a modified DDC scheme (e.g., entries can be found entered under the translator) and follows AACR2.

The *Arab Bulletin of Publications* (OCLC: 2239670) and *AL,ME* (1963-1993, ISSN 0041-7769) include PLO publications within their scope.

LATEST ISSUE EXAMINED/CURRENCY: The latest issue examined of *P-LB* at Princeton University in June 1997 is for the year 1984, published 1985. Later copies were sought in several other libraries without success.

AUTOMATION: not automated.

FORMAT AND SERVICES AVAILABLE: printed. The volumes will be available on internet in the near future.

CURRENT LEGAL DEPOSIT LAWS: Not applicable.

AVAILABLE FROM: Arab Studies Society, P.O. Box 20479, Jerusalem.

VERIFIER: Ishaq Budeiri, General Director, Arab Studies Society.

PANAMA

No current national bibliography has been traced for Panama.[1]

Although there is no official current national bibliography, the mid-1950's through the early 1960's yielded some compilations that are useful to mention. *Bibliografía Panameña existente en la Biblioteca de la Universidad* was compiled by Biblioteca Nacional de Panamá. Ministerio de Educación, Comité Nacional por Bibliotecas, 1954? (LCCN: 58-45300; OCLC: 4018337). *Bibliografía Panameña de Libros y folletos, 1955.* - Panamá : Oficina de Información y Publicaciones, 1958. Carmen D. Herrera compiled *Bibliografía Retrospectiva de libros y folletos 1957-1955.* Panama : Imprento Nacional, 1958 (LCCN: 63-35900/L; OCLC: 24994301). Carolina M. Rodríguez authored *Bibliografía retrospectiva de publicaciones periódicas aparecidas en la República de Panamá, 1960-1958.* - Panama : 1960 (OCLC: 15087879). Attempts have been made to list Panamanian titles in "Bibliografía Panameña [ ]" appearing in *Lotería.* - Panama: Lotéria Nacional de Beneficencia (ISSN 0456-5827; OCLC: 1756179). The list for 1961 appeared in *Lotería*, 2, época 7 (1962) and was compiled by Juan Antonio Susto; the list for 1960-1963 appeared in *Lotería*, 2, época 10 (1965), compiled by Francisco A. Herrera.[2] *Revista Lotería* continues *Lotería* and in checking issues for the first part of 1985, the author found no bibliography of Panamanian publications (ISSN 0024-662X). This title is continued by *Revista cultural lotería* (LCCN: 92-65553; OCLC: 23025839). A retrospective coverage was done by Juan Antonio Susto Lara, who compiled *Panorama de la Bibliografía en Panamá: 1619-1967.* Panama: Editorial Universitaria, 1971 (LCCN: 72-221657//r89; OCLC: 1079116). This title includes both Panamanian and foreign titles.[3]

CURRENT LEGAL DEPOSIT LAWS: Law No. 47 of 1946, Article 92; Law No. 11 of 10 February 1978, Article 80.[4]

---

[1] *BSTW, Supplement 1981-1982* states that the Biblioteca Nacional is planning to produce a national bibliography in 1985 (p. 221). No title or publication could be traced by the author through searches in databases, bibliographies, and in a conversation with Latin American specialist John Hebert, Library of Congress, in April 1997.

[2] Information included in a 25 April 1985 letter to the author from Margaret Johnson, Head, Hispanic Section, British Library.

[3] *HLAS*, no. 36, entry 53. For additional bibliographic titles about Panama before 1983 see the section on Panama in "Latin American National Bibliography," *Encyclopedia of Library and Information Services*, vol. 36, suppl. 1, p. 323-324.

[4] *BSTW, 1975-1979*, p. 316.

PAPUA NEW GUINEA

TITLE: *Papua New Guinea national bibliography.* - Mar. 1981-   . Waigani, [Port Moresby]: National Library Service of Papua New Guinea, 1981-   .
Semi-annual (with annual cumulation) 1990-   ; annual 1989; semi-annual 1988; quarterly (with annual cumulation) 1981-1987.
Continues in part: *New Guinea bibliography* / University of Papua New Guinea.
DDC: 015.953 (in vol.); 016.9953 (OCLC record); LC: Z4811.N48; LCCN: 81-649257; OCLC: 7626120
ISSN 0252-8347

COMPILER: National Library Service of Papua New Guinea.

SCOPE AND COVERAGE: The *Papua New Guinea National Bibliography* (*PNGNB*) includes all materials recently published in the country. Overseas publications by Papua New Guineans or with Papua New Guinea subject content are also included from 1981-1989. From 1990 onwards, only materials published in Papua New Guinea are included. Materials acquired for the Papua New Guinea Collection of the National Library Service form the basis of the bibliography, but items from the libraries of the University of Papua New Guinea, the Institute of Applied Social and Economic Research and the Department of Justice are also submitted for inclusion in *PNGNB*.

Types of publications included are monographs, serials (first issues and subsequent name changes), maps, audio-visual materials, theses, official and government publications, and pamphlets.

Omitted are sound recordings which are listed in *Commercial Recordings of Papua New Guinea Music*, and periodical articles which are included in *New Guinea Periodical Index*. - University of Papua New Guinea Library, 1968-   .

CONTENTS: Introduction, organization of the national bibliography including an explanation of entries, DDC explanation of historical and geographical expansions, DDC outline, classified sequence by DDC, author/title/series/added entry index, subject index, publishers list.

CATALOGUING RULES AND CLASSIFICATION SCHEMES USED: Augmented level of description following AACR2, 1988 (third level of description) and *LCSH* are used in cataloguing entries for *PNGNB*.

The DDC (20th ed.) is used for classifying material.

Filing rules used are *ALA Filing Rules*, 1980.

ENTRY INFORMATION: DDC number in uper left corner, main entry, title, place of publication, publisher, year, pagination, illustrations, size, series, notes, including the ISBN if known, tracings.

Subject headings marked with an asterisk (*) indicates that the subject headings are indigenous to Papua New Guinea and have yet to be established as valid by the Library of Congress.

The uniform title, usually enclosed in square brackets, is given at the beginning of entries where it is needed.

In the 1980s, titles not held by the National Library have the holding library's abbreviations in the upper right-hand corner of the entry, e.g., ED for Department of Education Research Library. However, this practice of listing items from other libraries has been discontinued in recent years.

ARRANGEMENT: The classified sequence is arranged by DDC number and then alphabetically arranged by main entry.

INDEXES: Author/title/series/added entry index, and a subject index. Numbers refer to the classification number in the classified sequence where the complete record for an index entry is located.

NOTES AND COMMENTS: This title continues in part the *New Guinea bibliography*, published by the University of Papua New Guinea from 1967-1980. The scope included publications from Irian Jaya and the Solomon Islands as well as New Guinea. The *PNGNB* no longer includes the two earlier locations within its scope.

It would be useful to have a table of contents to *PNGNB*.

Government publications are not designated by a symbol. It is necessary to look under Papua New Guinea and then the issuing agency in the index. One may also find a high proportion of these titles by checking the classified sequence under the 300's.

Entries in Melanesian and in English are included in *PNGNB* which follows ICNB recommendation number 6. ICNB recommendations 5, 8, 9, 10 and 11 are also fulfilled.

South Pacific Bibliography (see separate entry) includes Papua New Guinea within its scope.

LATEST ISSUE EXAMINED/CURRENCY: The latest issue examined was for 1993, received by University of London SOAS in November 1994.

In looking at a sample of three pages which included 26 entries from the 1991 volume, 14 had 1991 imprints, seven had 1990 imprints, and one had a 1989 imprint. This currency is much improved from an analysis of the 1983 volume which had most of the imprints spanning from 1976-1982 with very few published in 1983. The introduction of the legal deposit law should help with both the currency and the comprehensiveness of the *PNGNB*.

AUTOMATION: not automated.

FORMAT AND SERVICES AVAILABLE: printed.

CURRENT LEGAL DEPOSIT LAWS: Legal deposit was introduced with the National Library and Archives Act 1993. It was gazetted on 24 May 1994.

AVAILABLE FROM: Editor, *Papua New Guinea National Bibliography*, National Library Service of Papua New Guinea, P.O. Box 5770, Boroko. Available on subscription or exchange.

SELECTED ARTICLES: "Papua New Guinea: National Bibliographic Services." *International Cataloguing* 11 (Apr./June 1982):15.

VERIFIER: Karen Sereva, Bibliographical Services Librarian, National Library Service of Papua New Guinea.

PARAGUAY

No current national bibliography has been traced for Paraguay.

Although Paraguay has no current national bibliography, the Universidad Nacional de Ascunción, Escuela de Bibliotecología has compiled a retrospective national bibliography which may be useful. One hopes that this title eventually will be on-going and become the springboard for a current national bibliography in future years. This bibliography is not based on legal deposit.

Bibliografía Nacional Paraguaya: Obras Publicadas entre los años 1971-1977 (BNP) / Compilada por alumnos y profesores de la Escuela de Bibliotecología. - Ed. preliminar. - Asunción: Universidad Nacional de Asunción, Escuela de Bibliotecología, 1978 (DDC: 015.892; LC: Z1821.B5 1978; LCCN: 83-160959; OCLC: 10505106). *BNP* includes titles published in and about Paraguay listed in an alphabetical subject arrangement.

In the 1980s and early 1990s Margarita Kallsen has been compiling bibliographies which may be of assistance to researchers and bibliographers. Each volume typically covers a two-year period, although that varies. The titles are part of the Serie bibliografía paraguaya, 0257-7070. *Paraguay, dos años de bibliografia, 1990-1991.* - Asunción, Paraguay : [s.n.], 1993 (OCLC: 30833137); *Paraguay, dos años de bibliografías, 1988-1989.* - Asunción, Paraguay : [s.n.] 1990 (OCLC: 23015163); *Paraguay, un año de bibliografía*, 1987. - Asunción, Paraguay : Kallsen, 1988 (OCLC: 18905579); *Paraguay, dos años de bibliografía, 1985-1986.* - Asunción, Paraguay : Kallsen, 1987 (OCLC: 17700018); *Paraguay, cinco años de bibliografía, 1980-1984.* - Asunción : Paraguay : [s.n.], 1986 (OCLC: 14200597).

Carlos F. S. Fernández-Caballero has compiled a three volume retrospective bibliography which covers from 1724 to 1974 with the title *The Paraguayan Bibliography; a Retrospective and Enumerative Bibliography of Printed Works of Paraguayan Authors.* - Washington, Paraguay Arandú Books, 1970-1983 (OCLC: 186752). At the head of title for: v. 1, Aranduká ha kuatiañeé paraguái rembiapocué. The Paraguayan bibliography, v. 2, Paraguái tai hume, tove paraguái arandu taisarambi ko yvy apére. The Paraguayan bibliography, v. 3, Paraguái rembiapokúe ha paraguái rehegúa tembiapo oñembokuatiavaekúe. La Bibliografia paraguaya / Carlos F. S. Fernández-Caballero and Mariana Fernández-Caballero. Imprint for v. 2 is Amherst, Massachusetts : Seminar of the Acquisition of Latin American Library Materials, 1975, and this title is part of its series, Bibliography, 3. Imprint for v. 3 is Asunción, Paraguái.

Arandu Aranduka, 1983. Both foreign and Paraguayan authors who wrote about Paraguay and by Paraguayan authors writing on any subject are included. It includes books and articles.[1]

CURRENT LEGAL DEPOSIT LAWS: Ley No. 94: Derechos Intelectuales, 1951, Art. 50; Decreto No. 6.609, 1951; Código Civil, 1988, Art. 2184.[2]

PERU

TITLE: *Bibliografía peruana.* - 1984/1986-   . Lima : Biblioteca Nacional del Peru, Dirección General de Bibliografía Nacional y Ediciones, 1992- .
Irregular.
Continues *Anuario bibliográfico peruano.*
DDC: 015.85; LC: Z1851.A5; LCCN: 93-655669; OCLC: 28642487
ISSN not found

COMPILER: Biblioteca Nacional del Peru.

SCOPE AND COVERAGE: *Bibliografía Peruana* (*BP*) includes titles published in or about Peru, written by Peruvians and deposited at the Biblioteca Nacional according to the legal deposit laws. It also includes some materials acquired through purchase or gifts.

Types of publications included in *BP* are books, pamphlets, official and government publications, theses and dissertations, reports, maps and atlases, musical scores.

Excluded in *BP* are periodical publications and bio-bibliographies which will be published in separate publications.

CONTENTS: Introduction, abbreviations, table of contents, books and pamphlets, theses, indexes.

CATALOGUING RULES AND CLASSIFICATION SCHEMES USED: International bibliographic standards are followed. AACR2 to the second and third levels are used.

The classification scheme used is DDC.

ENTRY INFORMATION: For entries in the books and pamphlets classified bibliography: author, title, place of publication, publisher, date, pagination, illustrations, size, series statement, brief notes, consecutive entry number in lower right corner.

For entries in the theses classified bibliography: author, title, place, date, pagination, size, notes including the university and degree for which it was written, pagination of the bibliography; consecutive entry number in lower right corner.

---

[1] *HLAS*, no. 32, entry 57, and *HLAS*, no. 38, entry 79.
[2] *International Guide to Legal Deposit*, p. 92.

ARRANGEMENT: The classified bibliography for books and pamphlets is arranged by the DDC subject headings and then alphabetically by author. The theses section includes many of the same categories but also includes more specific categories, e.g., parques nacionales.

INDEXES: Name index, corporate author index, and publishers and printers index. Numbers used in the indexes refer the reader to the entry numbers in the classified bibliography.

NOTES AND COMMENTS: For a short period of time the monthly title *Bibliografía Nacional.* - 1978-1982. Lima : Biblioteca Nacional, Instituto Nacional de Cultura, 1978-1982 was established in an attempt to make the national bibliography more current than *Anuario Bibliográfico Peruano* was able to do. It is not as complete as *Anuario Bibliográfico Peruano*, and it is not *Anuario Bibliográfico Peruano's* continuation. *Bibliografía Nacional (BN)* was not automated. This bibliography was mimeographed, stapled and produced on newsprint quality paper. There was no introduction which would explain the purpose of *BN*, coverage and scope and any changes that may be relevant for the proper use of this bibliography. Only a limited number of copies were produced and available for distribution.

BN lists titles and articles published in or about Peru, written by Peruvians and deposited at the Biblioteca Nacional according to the legal deposit laws. It also includes some materials acquired through purchase or gifts. Types of publications included in *BN* books, pamphlets, periodicals (first issues), periodical articles, official and government publications, theses and dissertations, reports, maps and atlases, musical scores. The classification scheme used is the DDC. Both sections of the classified bibliography are arranged by the DDC subject headings and then alphabetically by author. Each issue has an author and a subject index; there is an annual cumulative index. (DDC: 015.85; LC: Z1851.P47a; LCCN: 80-647038; OCLC: 6022488).

As stated earlier, *BP* is a continuation of *Anuario bibliográfico peruano.* - 1943-1976. - Lima : Biblioteca National, Instituto National de Cultura, 1945-1986.[1] *Anuario Bibliográfico Peruano (ABP)* includes titles written by Peruvian authors, published within the years covered, and deposited at the Biblioteca Nacional according to the legal deposit laws. Books about Peru written by Peruvian authors, published abroad are also included. Types of publications included in *ABP* are books, pamphlets, periodicals, official and government publications, theses, music scores, newspapers, IGO publications when deposited, regional publications, maps and atlases, annual reports, limited editions. Frequency and publisher varies.

From 1970/1972 volume, contents for *ABP* are: [Preface]; table of contents; statistical table of Peruvian book production; classified bibliography: 1) Peruvian books and pamphlets, including official publications; 2) books and pamphlets about Peru; 3) periodical publications; 4) regional publications; 5) official periodical publications; bio-bibliography of Peruvian writers; indexes.

In *ABP*, ISBD is used to catalogue titles. Broad subject groups similar to DDC are used in the classified bibliography. Entry information supplied is author, title, place of publication, publisher, date, pagination, size, series, notes, entry number in lower right hand corner. Price is

---

[1] In a 30 September 1996 letter to the author from Ruth Ivazeta de Barnett, she states that *Anuario Bibliográfico Peruano* ceased with the 1986 issue which included imprints for the years 1973-1976.

given in earlier volumes, but not the later volumes. Full bibliographical information is given for periodical publications and for official publications.

ABP is arranged as follows: Peruvian books and pamphlets, books and pamphlets about Peru published abroad, and periodicals are arranged in a manner similar to DDC, including about 20 broad headings such as "obras generales," "filosofía," "religión," "historia," "geografía y viajes," "etnología y folklore," "legislation y estudios juridicos." Those of the periodical publications are classified under slightly different subject headings. Under the subject breakdown, the entries are listed alphabetically by the main entry. Regional publications are organized by regions, then by title. Official and government publications are arranged by issuing agency, and then alphabetically.

Indexes of *ABP* are title index covering periodicals; corporate author index; "onomástico" (name) index, "onomástico" index of the "bio-bibliografías," index of publishers and printers with works appearing in the current volume, organized by geographical locations, but complete addresses are not given. The number used refers the reader to the consecutive entry number in the classified bibliography, with the exception of the "bio-bibliografía" section, where the number refers to page numbers. Cumulative indexes are located at the back of the volumes (e.g., 1943-1972 is in the 1970-1972 volume). These are valuable for consulting bio-bibliographical information about deceased Peruvian writers covered in previous years, and for locating sections in previous volumes.

ABP is one of the most complete and useful national bibliographies in Latin America. Reference librarians and other people who need to know where hard-to-find information may be located should be aware of the "bio-bibliografías" section, a valuable section for both biographical and bibliographical information on Peruvian authors who have died during the period covered by *ABP*. Information includes a chronology of the author's life, a list of the author's works regardless of form, and a list of materials which discuss the author's work. This section forms a substantial portion of the *ABP*.

It is estimated that for the period covered seventy percent of publishing in Peru is represented in *ABP* ("Preface", v). According to information given in *Survey on the Present State of Bibliographical Recording in Freely Available Printed Form of Government Publications and Those of Intergovernmental Organizations*, about eighty percent of official publications are included (p. 80).

"Official publications previously included with other items were allocated a separate section 'Publicaciones oficiales' from the 1955-1957 volume."[1] More recently in *ABP*, official periodical publications are listed in a separate section; monographs are arranged by agency and included in the Peruvian books and pamphlets section.

On an average, the lag between the date of coverage and publication date for *ABP* was between three to six years; the lag from date of coverage to date of receipt at the libraries consulted is six to ten years. Because of the lag, *ABP* should be regarded as a retrospective bibliography.

LATEST ISSUE EXAMINED/CURRENCY: The imprints in *BP* are from the year covered.

---

[1] *Survey on the Present State of Bibliographical Recording in Freely Available Printed Form of Government Publications and Those of Intergovernmental Organizations*, p. 79.

The 1984/1986 volume was published in 1992, and was the most current available. In order for this title to be helpful as a selection source, it needs to become more current.

The latest issue examined in May 1995 is the 1984/1986 volume at the University of Wisconsin Madison Library.[1]

AUTOMATION: The *BP* is a product of *Base de Datos BIBNA*, produced with the Micro Isis program, and with the Ventura Professional Publisher program.

FORMAT AND SERVICES AVAILABLE: printed. It is a future goal to have it available on the Internet.

CURRENT LEGAL DEPOSIT LAWS: Ley 25326 Depósito Legal.[2]

One problem mentioned concerning legal deposit is the lack of clarity concerning whose responsibility it is to deposit material: the author's, editor's or publisher's.

AVAILABLE FROM: Suscripción y canje, Biblioteca Nacional del Peru, Avenida Abancay s/n, Apartado 2335, Lima.

VERIFIER: Ruth Ivazeta de Barnett, Sub-Jafa Instituccional, Biblioteca Nacional de Peru.

PHILIPPINES

TITLE: *Philippine national bibliography.* - Jan./Feb. 1974-   . - Manila : National Library of the Philippines, 1974-   .
Quarterly, with annual cumulations (1977-   ); bimonthly, with annual cumulations (1974 -1976).
DDC: 016.9599, in *Philippine National Bibliography*: 015.599; LC: Z3296.P53; LCCN: 77-648583//r892; OCLC: 2952148
ISSN 0303-190X

COMPILER: Bibliography Division, The National Library of the Philippines.

SCOPE AND COVERAGE: *The Philippine National Bibliography* (*PNB*) lists the publishing and printing output of the Philippines by Filipino authors or about the Philippines that is deposited at the National Library according to the legal deposit legislation. Unpublished material is also listed. Works in both English and Filipino and other Philippine languages, e.g., Tagalog, Ilocano, Cebuano, etc., are included.

Types of publications included in *PNB* are books, pamphlets, first issues of periodicals, newspapers, annuals, yearbooks, directories, etc.; official and government publications

---

[1] In her letter, Ms. Ivazeta de Barnett stated that the 1987-1990 volume was to be published "this month."
[2] "Introduccion," *BP* 1984/1986:iii.

including Presidential decrees, maps, plans and atlases, conference proceedings, seminar, and workshop papers, speeches, addresses, lectures, catalogues, musical scores, photographs, reprinted titles under Presidential Decree No. 285 as amended by Presidential Decree No. 1203, non-book materials copyrighted under Presidential Degree No. 49, the Decree on the Protection of Intellectual Property, and other material that reflects the intellectual and cultural growth of the Filipino nation.

In 1985, *PNB* began publishing *Part 2* which includes dissertations and theses deposited at the National Library as required by MECS Order No. 7 s. 1982.

Excluded are periodicals (except for first issues), certain government publications such as department, bureau, company and office orders, memoranda, and circulars; trade lists, catalogs, time tables and similar commercial documents, legal documents and judicial decisions, phonorecords.

CONTENTS: Table of contents, preface, list of abbreviations, DDC outline (2nd summary), classified bibliography sequence, author/title/series index, subject index, directory of printers and publishers' listed in the national bibliography.

Part 2 also has a list of degree abbreviations.

CATALOGUING RULES AND CLASSIFICATION SCHEMES USED: AACR2 has been used since 1980. Since the mid-1970's, ISBD(M) and ISBD(S) have been followed; ISBD(CM), ISBD(NBM), ISBD(G), ISBD(PM) have been adopted as they were published. *LCSH* is used. An authority file for Filipino subject headings has been established at the National Library.

The classification scheme used is DDC with expansions for the Philippine languages, literature, and history, and the LC classification schedules.[1]

ENTRY INFORMATION: DDC number in upper left corner, author, title, place of publication, publisher, date, pagination, illustrations, size, series statement, notes including ISBNs, price when known, subject headings and added entries. The entry number is in the lower right corner, e.g., 00427.

ARRANGEMENT: The main bibliography is classified according to the DDC subject headings. Entries are alphabetically arranged within the subject headings.

In issues for 1974 and 1975, the main bibliography is arranged alphabetically within the type of publication. Part I: Books, pamphlets, etc. Part II: Government publications. A. Books, pamphlets, etc. B. Periodicals, newspapers, annuals, etc. Part III: Theses and dissertations. Part IV: Musical scores. Part V: Titles reprinted in Philippines. Alphabetical arrangement within each section.

INDEXES: Author/title/series index; subject index. The numbers refer to the entry number in the classified bibliography. Prior to 1983, the *PNB* had an author/title/subject index.

---

[1] In a letter to the author dated 24 August 1995, Leonila Tominez, Chief, Bibliographic Services Division, National Library states that from the 1993 issue onwards, the *PNB* uses DDC (20th ed.) and the LC classification scheme.

NOTES AND COMMENTS: *The Philippine Bibliography, 1963-1972*, was "an effort toward establishing a national bibliography" (*Guide*, AA930). This title was superseded by the *Filipiniana Union Catalog, 1968-1973*, and the *Philippine Union Catalog, 1974-1975*, which is "an author list of Filipiniana materials currently acquired by the University of the Philippines Library and other libraries" (*Guide*, AA931). This later title is once again entitled *Filipiniana Union Catalog*. (1976-   ; OCLC: 3854902).

PNB, Part 2 is an annual listing of Philippine graduate theses and dissertations deposited by graduate schools to the National Library as required by MECS Order no. 7 s. 1982. The latest issue of *Part 2* published as of October 1995 is 1990. *Part 2* uses AACR2, DDC with expansions for Philippine languages, literature and history, LC classification scheme, and *LCSH*. It is arranged in a classified sequence with author/ title/ series, and a subject index.

The current *PNB* follows the ICNB recommendations 5, 6, 8, 9, 10, 11 and 13 established for a national bibliography. The preface includes an analyzed entry, scope and coverage and catalogue rules followed. One drawback is the lack of currency both in the entries and in the time lapse between the period of time covered and the receipt of the volume. Because of this gap, as illustrated below, the *PNB* can not be relied upon to be an acquisitions tool and an aid in building current collections.

The 1977 *PNB*, published in 1978, is the first volume to be produced by photo off-set from the National Library's computerized system.

Since the *PNB* does not include periodical articles within its scope, a title which complements the *PNB* is the *Index to Philippine periodicals*. - Vol. 1-   . - Manila : University of the Philippines Library, 1956-   . Semiannual (ISSN 0073-599X).

LATEST ISSUE EXAMINED/CURRENCY: The latest volume examined at the British Library was for 1995, published in 1995. In a sampling of 26 imprints, eight were 1995, six were 1994, 11 were 1993, and one was 1991.

AUTOMATION: The *PNB* is produced by photo off-set from camera ready press copy, using a DELL PC (486DX).

FORMAT AND SERVICES AVAILABLE: Available in print , and on disks (ISO 2709 format) upon request only.

CURRENT LEGAL DEPOSIT LAWS: Presidential Decree No. 812 (18 October 1975), effective 18 January 1976. Dissertations and theses are deposited as required by MECS Order No. 7 s. 1982.

AVAILABLE FROM: Acquisitions Division, National Library of the Philippines, P.O. Box 4118, Teodoro M. Kalaw Street, Ermita, Manila.

VERIFIER: Leonila Tominez, Chief, Bibliographic Services Division, The National Library.

POLAND

TITLE: *Przewodnik bibliograficzny.* - R.2 (14), no. 1/3- . - Warszawa : Biblioteka Narodowa, Instytut Bibliograficzny, 1946- .
Frequency varies. Currently weekly.
Supersedes *Urzędowy wykaz druków*, 1928-1939, and continues its numbering.
DDC: 015.438; LC: Z2523.P93; LCCN: 51-21471//r56; OCLC: 1605421
ISSN 0033-2518

COMPILER: Biblioteka Narodowa, Instytut Bibliograficzny.

SCOPE AND COVERAGE: *Przewodnik Bibliograficzny* (*PB*) lists the publishing output of Poland which is deposited at Bibliotek Narodowa according to legal deposit legislation. It also includes foreign publications about Poland which are received by Biblioteka Narodowa.

Types of publications include books, pamphlets, new periodicals, periodical articles, official and government publications, maps and plans, sheet music, illustrated works.

Omitted from coverage are single illustrations (drawings), monographs with fewer than 50 copies published, pamphlets of less than five pages, offprints, school and works' periodicals, local bulletins of political parties, local reports of no-research institutions, publishers' catalogues, library accessions lists, exhibition catalogues, theatre and other programmes if they are of local or ephemeral value.[1]

CONTENTS: Table of contents (in an entry paragraph before bibliographic entries), classified bibliography. At the end of number 1 is an explanation of scope, arrangement, classification scheme, indexes, etc.

CATALOGUING RULES AND CLASSIFICATION SCHEMES USED: The international bibliographic rules of ISBD(M), ISBD(PM) and ISBD(CM) as well as Polish national standards written by the Polish Committee for Standardization are used to give complete information.

The classification scheme used is UDC.

ENTRY INFORMATION: Author, title, place of publication, publisher, date, pagination, size, notes including ISBN and ISSN and price, subject headings, classification number in lower left corner, number of copies published, sequential number in lower right corner.

The symbol of a triangle Δ means that the bibliographic descriptions are late (opisy spóznione).

ARRANGEMENT: Since 1986, *PB* is arranged by UDC divisions, including some second and third level divisions.

For years prior to 1986 the bibliographic entries are arranged in twenty-six subject headings, including Marxism-Leninism, philosophy and psychology, history and ethnography, maps and plans.

---

[1] Barbara Karamac. "Bibliographic Control in Poland." *ICBC* 20 (no. 1 Jan./March 1991):3

INDEXES: *PB* has two annual indexes: an author/title alphabetical index, and a subject index. Each weekly issue has an alphabetical author/title index which cumulates into the annual alphabetical author/title index.

NOTES AND COMMENTS: Volume 1 for 1944-1945 of *PB* was published in 1955; it includes entries not previously listed in volumes for 1946-1947. Volume 2 was published in 1946.

It would be useful to have an introduction which would include the scope, contents, arrangement and rules followed in issues other than just number 1 of each year.

"The Polish national bibliography consists of five parts representing separate publications, each of which bears its own distinctive title; there is, however, no common title which would identify these serials as actual sections of the printed national bibliography."[1] The *PB* has been analyzed above. Other parts are as follows.

Bibliografia Wydawnictw Ciągłych Nowych, Zawieszonych i Zmieniajacych Tytuł [Bibliography of Serials: New, Ceased and Changed Titles]. Quarterly. Published as a loose inset in *PB* since 1977.

Bibliografia Wydawnictw Ciągłych [Bibliography of Polish Serials]. Annual. From 1958-1980 under its former title *Bibliografia Czasopism i Wydawnictw Zbiorowych*. Includes all currently published Polish serials.

Bibliografia Zawartości Czasopism [Index to Periodicals]. Monthly. 1951- .

Polonica Zagraniczne [Foreign Polonica]. Annual. 1956- . Includes printed items published outside Poland written in Polish or which have contents relating to Poland.

Since December 1994 *PB* exists on CD-ROM. The second CD-ROM published in 1996 covers the years 1985-1995.[2]

A special project was undertaken by the National Library in 1990 to list samizdats [underground publications during the mid-1970s through 1980s] in the national bibliography.[3]

CIP is practiced in Poland since 1988.

LATEST ISSUE EXAMINED/CURRENCY: The latest issue examined in June 1966 is 24-30 Marca 1996 received at the University of Illinois Library, Urbana-Champaign; the latest annual index seen is for 1992, published in 1993.

AUTOMATION: Data is in machine readable format since 1986. The records are accessed by Novell Netware in the National Library.[4]

---

[1] Karamac, p. 4.
[2] Information from a letter dated 5 August 1996 to the author from Dr. Sadowska.
[3] Karamac, p. 3-4.
[4] Sadowska letter.

FORMAT AND SERVICES AVAILABLE: printed, floppy disks, CD-ROM, Internet.

CURRENT LEGAL DEPOSIT LAWS: Article 32 and 33 of the Library Act of 9 April 1968; Order No. 234 of the Ministry of Culture and Arts of 2 August 1968. (*Monitor Polski*, no. 34, 1968, pp. 471-472). Zarzadzenie Ministra Obrony Narodowej Nr. 5/MON z dnia 16 stycznia 1971; Decyzja Nr. 22 Przesa Głównego Urzedu Geodezji i Kartografii z dnia 12 listopada 1981; Pismo Okólne Ministerstwa Lesnictwa i Przemysła Drzewnego z dnia 30 wrzesnia 1957 r. Nr. TE-2-086/2.[1]

AVAILABLE FROM: Biblioteka Narodowa, Instytut Bibliograficzny, Zaklad Przewodnika Bibliograficznego, 02-973 Warszawa, al. Niepodległości.

SELECTED ARTICLES: Karamac, Barbara. "Bibliographic Control in Poland," *ICBC* 20 (no. 1, Jan./March 1991):3-7.

VERIFIER: Dr. Jadwiga Sadowska, Head of the Polish National Bibliographic Agency.

PORTUGAL

TITLE: *Bibliografia nacional portuguesa* [computer disk]. - Agosto 1995-   . - Lisboa : IBL; Madrid : Chadwyck-Healey España [Distrib.], 1995-   .
Cumulating disk updated twice a year.
Supersedes *Boletim de bibliografia portuguesa. Monografias*, and *Boletim de bibliografia portuguesa. Publicações em série.*
Accompanied by *Bibliografia nacional portuguesa. Manual do utilizador* (1995: ISBN 972-565-204-5).
DDC: not found ; LC: not found; LCCN: not found; OCLC: not found.
ISSN 0873-3171

COMPILER: Instituto da Biblioteca Nacional e do Livro — Base Nacional de Dados Bibliográficos - PORBASE.

SCOPE AND COVERAGE: *Bibliografia Nacional Portuguesa* (*BNP*) covers the publishing output of Portugal which is deposited at the Biblioteca Nacional.

Types of publications included in *BNP* are books—including official and government publications, children's and juvenile materials, translations, theses and other academic works produced within Portuguese universities since 1987—and new periodical titles.

Excluded from *BNP* are reprints or printings from the same edition, commercial literature, printed music, periodical articles and non-book material.

CONTENTS: Written in Portuguese and in English, the user's manual accompanying *BNP* includes: contents, introduction, hardware and software requirements, general information about

---

[1] *Survey of Existing Legal Deposit Laws*, p. 62, and *International Guide to Legal Deposit*, p. 93.

operation, search instructions, how to print records, and export records. The Portuguese section includes more illustrated details, and examples. The English user is referred to appropriate illustrations in the Portuguese section.

The main menu includes options for oriented search, advanced search, print records, export records, general information, exit. For each of these, there is a help screen available.

CATALOGUING RULES AND CLASSIFICATION SCHEMES USED: Bibliographic description is according to *Regras Portuguesas de Catalogação* (1984) which implement ISBD, and adheres to AACR2.

The classification scheme used for subject retrieval is UDC. Alphabetical subject headings are assigned by *SIPORbase* (*Sistema de Indexção em Português* (2nd ed., Biblioteca Nacional, 1992).

ENTRY INFORMATION: Record number, author, title, numeration, place of publication, publisher, date, pagination, size, series, notes, ISSN/ISBN, subjects, UDC number.

ARRANGEMENT: Records are by register number with record information retrievable by various search options under the Oriented search and the Advanced search.

INDEXES: Under the Oriented search option, the user is able to search by title, author, series title, subject, UDC, publisher, place of publication, keyword, search terms dictionary, and free text.

NOTES AND COMMENTS: *BNP* supersedes *Boletim de bibliografia portuguesa. Monografias* / Biblioteca Nacional, 1981-1989. The last volume covers publications for 1987. (ISSN 0253-3413; OCLC: 9928760). The scope included books, pamphlets, official and government publications, dissertations (if printed), periodical articles, printed music, and translations.

Also superseded by *BNP* is *Boletim de bibliografia portuguesa. Publicações em série* / Biblioteca Nacional. (ISSN 0253-3421) which included new titles, cessations, and changes of serials within its scope.

The *Boletim de bibliografia portuguesa. Documentos não textuais* / Biblioteca Nacional. (ISSN 0253-343X) has ceased but at present the CD-ROM does not supersede this printed title. Cartography, iconography, foreign works written by Portuguese authors or about Portugal were within its scope.

It is obvious that a lot of thought went into the preparation of *BNP*. It is user-friendly, and the information is helpful and well organized. Help screens are available to the user at every stage. In choosing the General Information option one finds information about the database, contents of *BNP*, standards, and software requirements. It would be helpful to have a more complete statement under Contents of scope and coverage for publications included and those excluded. For example, are only new periodicals included, are periodicals included the year they cease, or have title changes? Are periodical articles, printed music, and maps included? Through correspondence it was determined that only new periodicals are included; if periodicals cease or have title changes, the existing record is updated. Periodical articles are not included, except as offprints; printed music is not included; maps are included only if they are atlases.[1]

A printed user manual is published in English and Portuguese. Instructions on use are also displayed on the screen, and a help function in the two languages is available. A ribbon at the bottom of the screen gives command options available.

The first CD-ROM disk includes over 40,000 records spanning 1989-1994. Each disk will cumulate. The second issue of the CD-ROM, published February 1996, includes more than 70,000 records, covering the years 1985-1995 (Sept.).[2]

Under the Advanced search option, searches can be refined by using Boolean operators, truncation, and by combining previous searches.

The user can display and print the brief citation format or a full record format (public format with labels), a single record or sequential records. It is possible to download records in the UNIMARC format.

BNP conforms to ISO 9660. Minimum hardware requirements to run *BNP* are IBM PC 286, 386, or 100% compatible, with at least 640 Kb RAM (with 512 Kb free), EGA or VGA card and monitor, preferably color, MS-DOS version 3.2 or higher, CD-ROM drive and controller card, printer recommended.[3]

BNP is extracted from Base Nacional de Dados Bibliograficos — PORBASE, a database which is both the online catalogue of the National Library (where the Portuguese bibliography is recorded) and the online union catalogue of the Portuguese libraries. PORBASE is currently the largest bibliographic database (over 800,000 records, March 1996) in Portugal, with 108 contributing libraries of all types and sizes, and includes information related to a wide range of different kinds of bibliographic materials, Portuguese and foreign, with no subject or chronological restriction. The database includes all works received by Legal Deposit since 1935 since this coverage is being permanently enlarged by means of a retrospective conversion programme being carried out. Old Portuguese materials are also being included through a special programme of retrospective cataloguing: the incunabula and the 16th century books are already available, while the 17th and 18th century collections are being recatalogued.[4]

Following are a few enhancement suggestions which would make this product even more helpful for users. One is to display a one-line prompt on the screen to indicate the current search in progress. Only when the author exited the search did it highlight the kind of search selected. For example, "You are searching by keyword using the terms bibliografia and national." This would be helpful when one is searching several different options, involved in a long search, or

---

[1] Information taken from a letter dated 12 May 1996 to the author from Fernanda Campos, Vice President, Instituto da Biblioteca National e do Livro.

[2] Figures for the second issue were supplied by Fernanda Campos in her letter.

[3] Information from publisher's flyer "Bibliografia Nacional Portuguesa em CD-ROM", and from page 38 of *BNP*'s *Manual do utilizador*.

[4] Information from Campos letter, and attachments "Base Nacional de dados bibliográficos - PORBASE" (December 1995).

when the user is interrupted in the search process. This could also be printed out when records are selected for printing. It would also be useful to have the number of the record in the search that is currently displayed appear with the total number of records found for that search. For example, #15 of 41 (fifteenth record of the 41 records found in the search).

LATEST ISSUE EXAMINED/CURRENCY: Entries in *BNP* are updated twice a year on a cumulating disk.

AUTOMATION: Information for *BNP* is generated for Chadwyck-Healey by the IBL using GLIS (GEAC Library Information System, in a GEAC-9000 machine) and software applications for UNIMARC records developed by IBL on CDS/ISIS 3.07 (Unesco).

FORMAT AND SERVICES AVAILABLE: CD-ROM; PORBASE is online on the Internet (free access by telnet: PORBASE.ibl.pt ; access times: 8.30 to 19.30, local time).

CURRENT LEGAL DEPOSIT LAWS: Decreto-Lei no. 74/82 de 3 Março, Decreto-Lei no. 75/82 de 3 de Março, Despacho no. 54/82, and Decreto-Lei no. 362/86 de 28 de Outubro. [1]

AVAILABLE FROM: Instituto da Biblioteca Nacional e do Livro, Campo Grande, 83, 1751 Lisboa CODEX, Portugal (for Portugal and Portuguese speaking African countries);

Chadwyck-Healey España, Juan Bravo, 18-2° C, 28006 Madrid, España (for Spain and Latin American countries);

Chadwyck-Healey France, 50 rue de Paradis, 75010 Paris, France (for France);

Chadwyck-Healey Inc., 1101 King Street, Alexandria, VA 22314, USA (for North America);

Chadwyck-Healey Ltd., The Quorum, Barnwell Road, Cambridge CB5 8SW, UK (for other countries).

SELECTED ARTICLES: Cabral, Maria Luísa. "The modernization of Portuguese libraries: five decisive years." *Program* (Belfast, Northern Ireland) 26 (no. 3 1992):249-258.

Campos, Fernanda Maria Guedes de ; Lopes, Maria Inês. "Biblioteca National: automation activities: progress report 1992." In Library Systems Seminar (17, 1993, Graz, Austria). *Library Systems Seminar: the virtual library..* Graz: Universitatsbibliothek der Karl-Franzens Universita, 1993, pp. 98-101.

Campos, Fernanda Maria Guedes de ; Lopes, Maria Inês. "Biblioteca Nacional: automation activities: progress report 1993. In Library Systems Seminar (18, 1993, Budapest). *Library Systems Seminar: library services in an electronic environment.* Budapest: National Széchényi Library, 1994, pp. 105-107.

---

[1] Information taken from *International Guide to Legal Deposit* (1991), p. 93, and confirmed as the current law by Fernanda Campos in her letter. Maria Luísa Cabral stated that the 1982 law of legal deposit also covers non-book materials. (53rd IFLA General Conference paper no. 94-Nat-3-E, pp. 10-11, subsequently published in *ICBC* 17 (no.1, Jan./Mar. 1988):10, "Les Bibliothèques nationales du sud de l'Europe: situation présente et évolution probable.")

Lopes, Maria Inês. "Base Nacional de Dados Bibliográficos — PORBASE." *Revista da Biblioteca Nacional* (S. 2) 9 (no. 2, Jul.-Dez. 1994):165-184.

Lopes, Maria Inês. "Base Nacional de Dados Bibliográficos — PORBASE." *Revista da Biblioteca Nacional* (S. 2) 10 (no. 1/2, Jan.-Dez. 1995):266-271.

VERIFIER: Fernanda Campos, Vice President, IBL.

PUERTO RICO

TITLE: *Anuario bibliográfico puertorriqueño.* - 1948-1974. - Rio Piedras : Biblioteca General, Universidad de Puerto Rico, 1950-1982.
Irregular.
Publisher varies.
DDC: 015.7295; LC: Z1551.A6; LCCN: sn87-29352; OCLC: 1481640
ISSN not found

COMPILER: Gonzalo Velázquez, Consultor en bibliografía, Biblioteca General, Universidad de Puerto Rico.

SCOPE AND COVERAGE: *Anuario Bibliográfico Puertorriqueño (ABP)* lists all titles published in Puerto Rico and foreign imprints about Puerto Rico.

Types of publications included in *ABP* are books, pamphlets, periodicals, government publications and newspapers.

CONTENTS: Table of contents, bibliography, publishers and printers of Puerto Rico, bookstores of Puerto Rico, abbreviations used.

CATALOGUING RULES AND CLASSIFICATION SCHEMES USED: There is no prefatory material to indicate the rules followed. It appears that standard bibliographic information is included, but not in the AACR2 format.

No classification scheme is apparent.

ENTRY INFORMATION: Author, title, edition, place of publication, publisher, date, pagination, illustrations, series, occasional brief notes. For periodicals, frequency may be given. Price and size are not given.

The most complete information is given under the main entry.

ARRANGEMENT: The main bibliography is arranged alphabetically by author, subject and title entries.

INDEXES: No separate index from the bibliography. The subtitle of the bibliography "Indice alfabético de libros, folletos, revistas y periódicos publicados en Puerto Rico..." indicates that the whole bibliography could be conceived of as an index.

NOTES AND COMMENTS: There are several features mentioned as recommendations by ICNB that do not appear in this bibliography. *ABP* does not include any introduction or prefatory material to help the user understand the scope, intent, and contents of the bibliography. It would be helpful to know if it includes foreign material about Puerto Rico without having to go through the bibliography checking the imprints, or if it is based on legal deposit legislation. The main bibliography is arranged alphabetically, and includes author, subject and title access thus functioning much as an index. It would be helpful to have the bibliography arranged in a classified scheme rather than in the present alphabetical arrangement. A bibliographer would be helped by looking under a specific classification arrangement, rather than having to scan the entire bibliography for appropriate headings or main entries. Indications of subject heading followed in the present bibliography are not given in any notes and would be useful information to include in an introduction.

All of the bibliographies thus far have been compiled by Gonzalo Velázquez.[1] It is realized that the compiling of this bibliography is a tremendous undertaking and the fine job that has been done is appreciated. Adding a few features mentioned in the ICNB recommendations, especially an introduction, and trying to overcome the gap of time between period covered and publication time, would add to the usefulness and value of this bibliography.

Foreign imprints are not designated with a symbol.

Bibliografía Actual del Caribe / Current Caribbean Bibliography / Bibliographie courante de la Caraïbe (ISSN 0070-1866), *Boletín Bibliográfico* (ISSN 0120-1204; OCLC: 2176868), *Fichero, Bibliografico hispanoamericano* (ISSN 0015-1592; OCLC: 1569143), includes Puerto Rico within their scopes. However, *Bibliografía Actual del Caribe / Current Caribbean Bibliography / Bibliographie courante de la Caraïbe* has experienced the same time-lag problem as *ABP*; the latest issue in several libraries consulted is for 1973.

LATEST ISSUE EXAMINED/CURRENCY: Entries included in *ABP* are from the period covered.

ABP is very late in appearing. In fact, because of this, it could be considered more of a retrospective bibliography. The 1965-1966 volume was published in late 1976, over ten years from the period that part of the volume covered. This is the norm, with the volume for 1967-1968 published in 1979, and the volume for 1973-1974 published in 1982. The volume for 1971-1972 was completed in 1979, but not printed until 1981. This has happened in at least one other instance. After it is published, it is received fairly promptly, even by overseas libraries. The University Library, Cambridge receives their copy on an average of five months after publication.

The latest volume available for examination in June 1997 was 1973-1974, published in June 1982, and received at the University Library, Cambridge, England in November 1982.

Bibliography of Latin American Bibliographies, 1983-1984, compiled by Lionel Loroña lists the volume *ABP* for 1973-1974, published in 1982. Although SALALM's "Annual Report on Latin

---

[1] According to Peter de la Garza, formerly of the Hispanic Acquisitions Program, Library of Congress, Mr. Velázquez, the compiler of *ABP*, has retired and, thus far, there have not been any further volumes compiled or published.

American and Caribbean Bibliographic Activities" for 1981, and again for 1982, lists an entry for the year 1978, the author believes this to be a publication date, and not a date of coverage.

AUTOMATION: not automated.

FORMAT AND SERVICES AVAILABLE: printed.

CURRENT LEGAL DEPOSIT LAWS: There is no legal deposit legislation, but Ley no. 5 of 8 December 1955 includes regulations for the National Archives. Copyright law dates from 1879 and amended in 1979 by [The laws of Puerto Rico. Title 3, chap. 41, set. 1013].[1]

AVAILABLE FROM: Departamento de Selección y Canje, Biblioteca General, Universidad de Puerto Rico, Rio Piedras, 00931.

VERIFIER: no verification requested.

QATAR

TITLE: *Qā'imat al-intāj al-fikrī al-Qaṭarī li-'ām* [List of intellectual production of Qatar]. - 1970-   . - Doha : Dār al-Kutub al-Qaṭarīyah [National Library of Qatar], 1971-   .
Annual.
DDC number: not found; LC: Z3038.Q2Q24; LCCN: 83-644575/NE; OCLC: 9710810
ISSN not found

COMPILER: Wizārat al-I'lām wa a-Thaqāfah, Dār al-Kutub al-Qaṭarīyah [Ministry of Media and Culture, National Library of Qatar].

SCOPE AND COVERAGE: The *Qā'imat al-intāj al-fikrī al-Qaṭarī li-'ām* [List of intellectual production of Qatar] (*LIPQ*) includes national imprints based on legal deposit as of 1982. Legal deposit also requires foreign imprints written by residents of Qatar to be deposited.

Types of publications included in *LIPQ* are books, pamphlets, dissertations, scientific research, serials, maps, music, official and government publications, audio-visual materials.

CONTENTS: The contents are divided into two sections: Arabic, and foreign languages (mainly English). Both sections have the same divisions beginning with general publications. Introduction, abbreviations, general publications (publications covering all subjects), government publications (all publications issued by the ministries), school publications (all school books issued by the Ministry of Education), periodicals, university theses, and children's books, indexes. In the years between 1981 and now, periodicals and university theses were added as new sections. Prior to number 12, 1981, the contents were general publications, school

---

[1] *Survey of Existing Legal Deposit Laws*, p. 64, and *International Guide to Legal Deposit*, p. 93.

publications, author, joint author, translator, editor index, title index, subject index, publishers' index.[1]

CATALOGUING RULES AND CLASSIFICATION SCHEMES USED: *LIPQ* uses *ALA Cataloguing Rules of Author and Title, L.C. Rules for Descriptive Cataloguing* and follows AACR2.

The DDC scheme, with modifications as needed, is used for classification purposes

ENTRY INFORMATION: DDC number, author, title, edition, place of publication, publisher, date, pagination, size, series statement, and legal deposit number. The price is not given.

ARRANGEMENT: The general section is arranged by the DDC scheme.

INDEXES: Author, joint author, translator, editor index (arranged by first name?), title index, subject index, publishers' index, index by university, index of theses (doctoral and masters). Prior to number 12, 1981, there were two indexes: author, and title.

NOTES AND COMMENTS: Qatar is included within the scopes of the *Arab Bulletin of Publications* and *AL,ME,* 1963-1993.

LATEST ISSUE EXAMINED/CURRENCY: The 1990 volume was published in 1991.

Entries were not analyzed for currency within the volume. The introduction stated that some publications are late in arriving and will be included in the next list. From that statement it seems that imprints are mostly from the period covered with a few imprints from earlier years.

AUTOMATION: not known.

FORMAT AND SERVICES AVAILABLE: printed.

CURRENT LEGAL DEPOSIT LAWS: Legal deposit law number 14, 1982 requires that three issues of books and periodicals published in the country be deposited at the National Library.

AVAILABLE FROM: Director, Qatar National Library, Box 205, Doha.

SELECTED ARTICLES: Aman, Mohammed M. and Sha'ban A. Khalifa. "Libraries and librarianship in Qatar." *International Library Review* 15 (1983):263-272.

VERIFIER: no reply received.

---

[1] Information was translated for me by Mr. Fawzi Tadros of the African and Middle East Division, Library of Congress, and Abdullah Bushnaq, student at The College of Wooster.

RÉUNION

No current national bibliography has been traced for Réunion.

The *AL,ESA* and *QIPL,ESA*, and *Annuarie des pay de l'océan indien* include Réunion within their scopes.

The Université de la Réunion. Service Commun de la Documentation publishes an exhaustive acquisitions list called *Iles du sud-ouest de l'océan Indien* (OCLC number: 31475747).[1]

Considerable bibliographic coverage of Réunion's publications is offered in *Fiches Bibliographiques* (ISSN 0750-0742) issued six times a year by the Institut National de la Statistique et des Etudes Economiques (INSEE), Service Départemental de la Réunion, and by Les Dossiers de l'Outre-mer, which continues *Bulletin d' Information du CENADDOM*. These publications emphasize the technical and social science areas and omit the literary areas of Réunion's publishing.[2]

ROMANIA

TITLE: *Bibliografia națională română. Cărți, albume, hărți.* Anul 42, nr. 1-   . - Bucareșt : Biblioteca Națională a României, 1993- .
Semimonthly.
Continues the numbering of *Bibliografia României. Cărți, albume, hărți.*.
Title and publisher varies since the national bibliography began in 1951; see Notes and Comments section.
DDC: 016.059591; LC: Z2923.B5; LCCN: 95-656039; OCLC: 30746478
ISSN 1221-9126

COMPILER: Biblioteca Națională a României.

SCOPE AND COVERAGE: *Bibliografia națională română. Cărți, albume, hărți.* (BNR.C) lists the publishing output of Romania that is deposited at the Biblioteca Națională a României according to the legal deposit legislation.

Types of publications in *BNR.C* include books, pamphlets, theses and dissertations, maps and atlases, and artistic prints.

Official publications, periodicals, periodical articles, music scores, cassettes, and "publicații apărute in Străinătate" are included in the other series of *BNR.C*.

---

[1] Information is from a letter dated 26 October 1994 to the author by Ruth Thomas, Field Director, Library of Congress Office, Nairobi, Kenya.
[2] Information is from a 11 September 1985 letter written to the author by the former Field Director James Armstrong, Library of Congress Office, Nairobi Kenya.

CONTENTS: Classified bibliography, personal names index, title index. At the end is a table of UDC numbers with subject headings.

CATALOGUING RULES AND CLASSIFICATION SCHEMES USED: There is no explanation of cataloguing rules used, but bibliographic entries follow international cataloguing rules. The ISBD order of elements is followed.

The classification scheme used is UDC.

ENTRY INFORMATION: Consecutive entry number, author, title, place of publication, publisher, date, pagination, illustrations, size, series, notes including ISBN, price; classification number(s) in lower left corner, legal deposit number (DL 936/94) and national bibliography number (BN 94-2876) in lower right corner.
ARRANGEMENT: Arranged by UDC subject headings.

INDEXES: An alphabetical index of names and a title index is included in each issue, and recently, an annual cumulated index is published; however, its continuing publication is uncertain.[1]

NOTES AND COMMENTS: The last few years have seen change in Romania. This is reflected in name changes for the country, national library, and a title change for the national bibliography. Following is the history of the *BNR.C* which has been continuous since 1952.

The current title, analyzed above, continues *Bibliografia României. Cărţi, albume, hărţi.* - Anul 40, 21 (1-15 Noem, 1991)-anul 41, 24 (16-31 Dec. 1992). - Bucureşti : Biblioteca, 1991-1992. Semimonthly (LC: Z2923.B5; LCCN: sn94-33068; OCLC: 29812733). This title continues *Bibliografia naţională a României. Cărţi, albume, hărţi.* - Anul 40, 1 (1-15 Ian. 1991) -anul 40, 20 (16-31 Oct. 1991). - Bucureşti : Biblioteca, [1991]. Semimonthly (LCCN: 93-656022//r95; OCLC: 25972375; ISSN 1220-5842). This title continues *Bibliografia României. Cărţi, albume, hărţi.* - Anul 39, 1 (1-15 Ian. 1990)-anul 39, 24 (15-24 Dec. 1990). Semimonthly (LCCN: 93-656023; OCLC: 25404542). This title continues *Bibliografia Republicii Socialiste România. Cărţi, albume, hărţi.* - Anul 17, 1 (1-15 Ian. 1968)-anul 38, 24 (16-31 Dec. 1989). - [Bucureşti] : Biblioteca Centrală de Stat a Republicii Socialiste România. Semimonthly (LC: Z2923.B5; LCCN: 75-647760//r882; OCLC: 2139516; ISSN 0524-8094). This title continues in part *Bibliografia Republicii Socialiste România. Cărţi, albume, hărţi, note muzicale.* - Anul 14, 16 (16-31 Aug. 1965)-anul 16, 24 (16-31 Dec. 1967). - [Bucureşti] : Biblioteca, [1965-1968]. Semimonthly (LC: Z2923.B82; LCCN: 88-656083; OCLC: 9246805; ISSN 0254-6035). This title continues *Bibliografia Republicii Populare Române. Cărţi, albume, hărţi, note muzicale.* - Anul 6, 1 (1/15 Ian. 1957)-anul 14, 15 (1/15 Aug. 1965). - Bucureşti : Biblioteca, [1957-1965] (LCCN: 57-22962//r882; OCLC: 9243061; ISSN 0254-6027). Continues *Buletinul bibliografic. Seria A, cărţi, broşuri, albume, hărţi, note muzicale.* - Bucureşti : Ministerul Culturii, Camera Cuărţii din R.P. R., 1954-1957. (OCLC: 26562495). Continues *Buletinul bibliografic al cărţii.* - Anul 3, 1 (15/31 Dec. 1953)-anul 3, 12 (1-15 Iunie 1954). - Bucureşti : Ministerul Culturii, 1953-1954 (OCLC: 26556497). Continues *Buletinul bibliografic al Camerei Cărţii din R.P.R. Cărţi, albume, plicure, pliante.* - Anul 1 [1951] -anul 2, 24 (31 Dec. 1953). - Bucureşti :

---

[1] In his 14 October 1996 letter to the author, Director Gheorghe-Iosif Bercan comments that the publication of the annual cumulated index is uncertain at the moment.

Comitetuo pentru Aşezămintele Culturale din R.P.R. de pe Lângă Consiliul de Miniştri, 1952-1953. Semimonthly (OCLC: 26556378).

The early 1970's saw a reorganization of the national bibliography. The previous six series were expanded or divided into several series. Each series is responsible for listing a specific type of publication. Recently, some of these series have merged. The initial project included ten series. However, several of the series were never published. The series that have been identified by the author are listed below although not all series have been examined and not all information is complete. These are published by the Biblioteca Naţională Românei and have the uniform name of the national bibliography in front of the title as shown in *BNR.C.*

Publicaţii seriale. - Anul 1, nr. 1 (1992) - . Annual. Includes all serials and is arranged according to UDC. (LCCN: sn93-30990; LC: AI19.R8; OCLC: 28446821; ISSN 1221-180X). *Note muzicale, discuri, casete.* 1968-   . Trimesterial. Includes sheet music, records and cassettes with subdivisions within each of these divisions. Arrangement is by UDC, with author and title index. (DDC: 016.059591; LCCN: sc82-3450; ISSN 1220-5877). Because the name of the national bibliography at the beginning of the title changes, there are several other OCLC records. The title *Note muzicale. Discuri. Casete* remains the same from 1978-   . Continues *Note muzicale, discuri.* - 1968-1978. Quarterly (LCCN: sn93-18033; LC: ML120.R64; OCLC: 6267197) Continues *Cărţi, albume, hărţi. note muzicale* which continues *Cărţi, albume, plicuri, pliante, note muzicale.* - Anul 3, 13 (16/30 Iunie 1954)-anul 5, 24 (5 Ian. 1957). 1954-1967. Semimonthly (OCLC: 26562495).

Teze de doctorat [Doctoral theses]. 1948/1970-   . - 1973-   . Annual. (LCCN: sn95-33116; sn96-17178; LC: Z2923; OCLC: 7369273; 34437607; ISSN 1223-7485). Since 1995, *Bibliografia Naţională Română* appears in front of *Teze de doctorat.*

Publicaţii oficiale. [Official Publications]. 1992-   . Biannual (LCCN: sn95-42684, sn95-42802; LC: Z2925.B52; OCLC: 32827035, 33261581; ISSN 1221-5309). Because the name of the national bibliography at the beginning of the title changes, there is more than one OCLC record. The title *Publicaţii Officiale* remains the same. Previously covered in *Cărţi, Albume, Hărţi,* and in *Articole din Publicaţii Periodice şi Seriale* as laws, decrees were published in newspaper articles.

The following title may be useful if one is looking for books by Romanians or about Romania. *Dacoromania.* 1973-   . - Freiburg : K. Alber. Publisher varies. Biennial. Includes publications relating to the country and written by Romanians published abroad (LCCN: 75-647726; OCLC: 2243880).

The following titles were intended as parts of the national bibliography, but never appeared as such.[1]

Atlase. Hărţi. [Atlases. Maps.] This title was prepared to be issued separately but was never published. Atlases and maps are convered in *Cărţi, Albume, Hărţi.*

Bibliografia bibliografiilor. To be published separately in several volumes as an independent work.

---

[1] Information verified in Bercan letter.

Foi volante. [Leaflets]. Annual. Not published.

Lucrări apărute in străinătate. Anul 1- . (1990)- . Bucuresti: Biblioteca Naţională a României, 1993- . Annual. (LCCN: sn95-32841; OCLC: 31636695; ISSN 1221-4515). This title began as *Lucrări apărute in străinătate*, became *Dacoromânia* in the 1970s, before continuing its former title. It is arranged according to UDC, and has author and subject indexes. Anul II, scheduled to appear in 1997, will cover 1991 to date and bear the title *Românica*.[1]

Publicaţii în serie. [Serials]. Annual. Previously covered in *Publicaţii Periodice si Seriale* since 1964. Replaced by *Publicaţii seriale*.
Stampe. Gravuri. [Prints. Engravings]. Annual. Not published.

The following series was discontinued. *Bibliografia Republicii Socialiste Româna. Articole din publicaţii periodice si seriale*. 1953-1988. Semimonthly. Includes articles in periodicals, serial publications and newspapers. Arrangement is by UDC, with an author index. Table of subjects (classified arrangement) follows the index. (LCCN: 79-646005//r83; LC: AI19.R8; OCLC: 2747358). Because there is a name change of the national bibliography at the beginning of the title there are several other OCLC records. The title *Articole din publicatii periodice si seriale* remains the same from 1959-1988). Continues *Bibliografia periodicelor din Republica Populara Romîna*. Anul 5, 1 (1/15 Ian. 1957) -anul 10, 24 (16/31 Dec. 1962). Continues *Buletinul bibliografic. Seria B. Articole si recenzii din presa*. 1953-1956. Bimonthly (OCLC: 10413140).

No preface or introduction is given in *BNR.C*. It would be helpful to the user if a short explanation of the scope and arrangement, analyzed entry, abbreviations list, and publishers' list were included.

LATEST ISSUE EXAMINED/CURRENCY: The latest issue examined was no. 8, 1997 at the Bibliotekstjänst AB Library, Lund, Sweden in September 1997. Bibliographic entries in this issue was mostly for 1996 and 1997.

AUTOMATION: Since 1979, the national library began automating its work. Between 1979 and 1982 the subsystems were established for the bibliographic control of the national bibliography, union catalogues of foreign imprints, collections of cultural material and historical material of books, and the library catalogues. The national bibliography was the first component to be implemented, beginning in 1982. Computer programs were written to run on Romanian minicomputers. The national library has been able to supplement these minicomputers with a few IBM-compatible PCs and a CORAL minicomputer. Presently, the software used for *BNR.C* and *Publicaţii seriale* series is TINLIB version for DOS, and CDS/ISIS for *Publicaţii oficiale. Note muzicale, discuri, casete* is published electronically.[2]

FORMAT AND SERVICES AVAILABLE: printed; magnetic tape.

---

[1] Information in a letter dated 21 October 1996 to the author written by Director Gheorghe-Iosif Bercan.
[2] The automation information is provided in Doina Banciu. "Automation of the Romanian National Library," *General Information Programme Unisist Newsletter*. Special edition: Romania [1990], p. 13-14, and in Director Bercan's 14 October 1996 letter.

CURRENT LEGAL DEPOSIT LAWS: Law No. 111/1995 published in *Monitorul Oficial– Partea I*, no. 280, 1995.[1]

AVAILABLE FROM: Outside Romania: RODIPET, S.A., P.O. Box 33-57, Piata Presei Libere nr. 1, Bucureşti. In Romania: Biblioteca Centrala de Stat, Str. Ion Ghica 4, Bucureşti. These titles are also available from East View Publications, 3020 Harbor Lane North, Minneapolis, MN 55447, USA.

SELECTED ARTICLES: Banciu, Doina. "Automation of the Romanian National Library." *General Information Programme. Unisist Newsletter.* Special edition: Romania [n.d.]: p. 13-14.

Ciorcan, Marcela. "National Bibliographies: Automation of the Bibliographical Work." *Probleme de Informare si Documentare* 28 (nos. 3/4 Jul./Dec. 1994): 114-116. Article also in Romanian, pp. 111-113.

"Romania: National Bibliography." *International Cataloguing* 10 (Jan./Mar. 1981):4.

Stefancu, Mircea. "Bibliografia naţională curenta." *Revista Bibliotecii Nationale* I (no. 1, 1995):23-24.

VERIFIER: Gheorghe-Iosif Bercan, Director, National Library of Romania.

RUSSIAN FEDERATION

TITLE: *Knizhnaĭa letopis'.* - 1- . - Moskva: Izd-vo "Kniznaĭa palata", 1907- .
Weekly.
Title varies.
Publisher varies.
Merger of: *Knizhnaĭa letopis'. Osnovnoĭ vypusk*, and *Knizhnaĭa letopis'. Dopolnitel'nyĭ vypusk. Knigi i broshiũry.*
DDC: not found; LC: Z2491.K55; OCLC: 27764339
ISSN 0869-5962

COMPILER: Rossiĭskaĭa knizhnaĭa palata [Russian Book Chamber]

SCOPE AND COVERAGE: *Knizhnaĭa letopis'* (*KL*) includes the publishing output of the Russian Federation and abroad when documents are published or imported for distribution within the Russian Federation and sent to the Russian Book Chamber according to the latest legal deposit legislation. Publications in all languages of the Russian Federation and foreign languages printed in Russia are included. Print runs must be 100 or more copies with the exception of scientific, fiction, children's and young people's books which are included without regard to the print run.

---

[1] Information provided in Bercan letter dated 14 October 1996 .

Types of publications included are books and pamphlets over five pages, official and government publications, technical conferences and seminars, reference and information literature, fiction, children's literature, standards, cultural, sporting and educational material published by the All-Union; IGO publications are included if written in Russian.

Theses and dissertations, periodicals, musical scores, maps and atlases, periodical articles, newspaper articles, bibliographies, art, reviews, translations are included in parts of the Russian national bibliography listed in the Notes and Comments section.

CONTENTS: Foreword (in first issue for the year), table of contents, classified subject bibliography, index for publications in non-Russian languages, enumeration index of bibliographic record of books and brochures for which no cards have been issued, ISBN corrections.

CATALOGUING RULES AND CLASSIFICATION SCHEMES USED: Russian State Committee on Standardization (Gosstandart) national standard *GOST 7.1-84* "Bibliographic Description of Publications."[1] This is in accordance with ISBD(M).

The classification scheme used is UDC.

ENTRY INFORMATION: Consecutive entry number, author, title, place of publication, publisher, pagination, size, series statement, notes, including ISBN, language of publication if other than Russian, or if translated for *KL*, number of copies printed, inventory number or Russian Book Chamber registration number, indication of origin of publication and method of printing, UDC number in lower right corner.

ARRANGEMENT: Arrangement is by UDC.

INDEXES: Weekly: name index; language index (for publications in non-Russian languages), enumeration index of bibliographic records for books and pamphlets for which no cards have been issued, incorrect ISBN index, and enumeration index of bibliographic records for foreign editions printed and distributed in Russian Federation. Numbers refer to the entry number.

Quarterly index: *Knizhnaĭa letopis'. Vspomogatel'nye ukazateli.* (LC: Z2491.K537; LCCN: 94-646864; OCLC: 30434892; ISSN 0869-5970). Formed by the merger of *Knizhnaĭa letopis'. Osnovnoĭ vypusk. Vspomgatel'nye ukazateli* (LCCN: 88647158; OCLC: 11957274; ISSN 0201-6153), and *Knizhnaĭa letopis'. Dopolnitel'nyĭ vypusk. Knigi i broshĭury* (LCCN: 88647159; OCLC: 7850611; ISSN O130-2329). Includes name, subject, geographical, incorrect ISBN indexes.

Annual index. *Knizhnaĭa Letopis'. Ukazatel' serii.* Foreword, alphabetical index of serial titles and bibliographic records of all editions within series (ISSN 0869-5989).

NOTES AND COMMENTS: As the former USSR national bibliography was divided into several parts, so also is the Russian Federation national bibliography. Each part has a specific purpose. A list of the major parts, in addition to the *KL* analyzed above, follows.

---

[1] Information received in a letter dated 1 March 1996 to the author by Mr. Alexander Dzigo, head of the Department of National Bibliography, Russian Book Chamber.

Letopis' avtoreferatov dissertatsiĭ. [Annals of Authors' Abstracts of Dissertations] / Rossiiskaia knizhnaĭa palata. Moskva: Izd-vo "Kniznaĭa palata", 1993-   . Monthly (LC: Z2495.K68; LCCN: 93-646164; OCLC: 27992823; ISSN 0869-5954).   Gives authors' abstracts of dissertations published in Russia.   Also includes dissertations sent to Russia but written elsewhere about Russia and on various topics.   Arrangement is according to the 20 subjects of the Russian dissertation classification.   Under each subject, the abstracts are divided into two groups: "Doktor nauk" and "Kandedat nauk" reflecting the doctoral dissertation and the masters thesis.   Indexes include name, and geographical (reflecting geographical names in the abstracts). Continues *Knizhnaĭa letopis'. Dopolnitel'nyĭ vypusk. Avtoreferaty dissertatsiĭ /* Gosudarstvennyĭ Komitet SSR po Delam Izdatel'stv, poligrafii, i knizhnoĭ torgovli [i] Vsesoiuznaĭa ordena "Znak Pocheta" knizhnaĭa palata. - Moscow : "Kniga", 1981-1992. (LCCN: 87656068; OCLC: 8030936; ISSN 0207-1126), which continues in part *Knizhnaĭa letopis'. Dopolnitel'nyĭ vypusk,* 1962-1980.

Ezhegodnik Knigi Rossiĭskoĭ Federatsii. [Bibliographic Annual of the Russian Federation Books]. - 1992-   . - Moskva: Izd-vo "Kniznaĭa palata", 1995-   . Annual (LC: Z2491.E9; LCCN: 96-646609; OCLC: 33982016; ISSN 0201-6354).   Publisher varies.   This cumulates *Knizhnaĭa letopis. Vspomogatel'nye ukazateli,* and *Knigi letopis',* and includes selected commercially available books published in the Russian Federation.   There are two volumes in three parts each for the 1992 edition.   Vol. 1 includes social sciences and humanities; vol. 2 includes technical sciences, and natural sciences.   Arrangement is alphabetical within subject groups.   Name, title, other than Russian materials, and subject indexes are in each volume.   1993 has three volumes.   The 1994 edition title will be changed to *Knigi Rossiĭskoĭ Federatsii. Ezhegodnik za...god."[1] Ezhegodnik* is a cumulation of 52 numbers of *KL* but does not include preprints, reissues of school textbooks, bibliographic indexes, book toys, coloring books within its scope.   From 1996, *Ezhegodnik* will be automated.   Then it will be a full cumulation of all *KL* records without any exclusions.   Former title was *Ezhegodnik knigi SSSR.* [Bibliographic Annual of the Soviet Book]. - 1925-1991. - Moscow : All-Union Book Chamber, 1927-1994. Annual.   Publication was suspended 1930-1934, 1936-1940.

Specific bibliographic serials and analytical indexes complementing *KL* are as follows.

Bibliografiĭa rossiĭskoĭ Bibliografii. [Bibliography of Russian Bibliographies]. - 1992-   . - Moskva, Izd-vo Kniznaĭa palata, 1994-   . Annual (LC: Z2491.A1B43; LCCN: sn 95-35274; OCLC: 31900745; ISSN 0204-3386).   Includes bibliographies published separately or including more than fifty entries as part of books or Russian periodical articles.   The first part is about bibliography written by scholars; the second part is a bibliography arranged by subject. Guidelines for selection are independently published bibliographies, current bibliographic publications; bibliographies found in journals, bibliographic lists attached to articles, and historic bibliographic reviews.   Classified by UDC; GOST 7.1-84 which prescribes bibliographic descriptions of documents is followed.   Former title: *Bibliografiĭa sovetskoĭ bibliografii.* [Bibliography of Soviet Bibliographies]. - 1939- 1991. - Moscow,1941-1991. Annual (LC: Z2491.A1V75; LCCN: 43-19002//r92; OCLC: 1519760; ISSN 0201-6346).

Kartograficheskaĭa letopis'. [Cartographical Annals]. - Moskva : Izd-vo Kniznaĭa palata, 1990-   . Semiannual (irregular).   Includes biographic, historic, and astronomy maps and atlases arranged by GOST 7.I 8-79 covering bibliographical description of map publications.   Includes

---

[1] Ibid.

territorial coverage (USSR) until 1992, from no. 1, 1992, includes RF. Arrangement is by continents, and then by countries. Indexes include names, geography, subject, and title. Volume two compiles indexes for both volumes as well as including bibliographic entries. Former title: *Kartograficheskaiā letopis'*. - Moscow : Vsesoiūznaiā Knizhnaiā Palata [All-Union Book Chamber], 1931-1989. Annual; 1931-1954. Irregular. (LCCN: sn91-37025; OCLC: 4177348; ISSN 0130-2086).

Letopis' gazetnykh stateǐ. [Annals of Newspaper Articles]. - Moskva, Izd-vo Kniznaiā palata, 1936-   . Weekly (LC: AI15.L35; LCCN: 54-41140; OCLC: 1714341; ISSN 0024–1172). Publisher and frequency vary. Classified index to newspaper articles from selected newspapers in the Russian language. Contents includes foreword (in first issue of each year), classified bibliography, and indexes (name, geographical, card index). The last issue (#52) of each year has an index of "temporary" subject headings which are for the anniversary of a special event for that year. Includes USSR territory coverage through no. 52, 1992; from 1993, this title is the state bibliographic index of RF. Arrangement is by UDC.

Letopis' izoizdaniǐ. [Annals of Reproduced Art]. - Moskva : Izd-vo Kniznaiā palata, 1934-   . Monthly (LC: Z5961.R9; LCCN: 76-649673//r872; OCLC: 2731061; ISSN 0134-8388). Title, publisher, and frequency varies. Arranged according to UDC, this title lists posters, printed reproductions of paintings, drawings, art postcards, portraits, art books with pictures, sculpture, comics, books for children, wall calendars with pictures, etc. published in the Russian Federation separately or in albums which are received on legal deposit. Contents include table of contents, foreword, classified bibliography, and indexes (name of artists or authors or persons depicted in a picture; title; index of museums where art is exhibited; index of journals and publications where pictures appear in this index. There is a separate annual compilation of indexes. Biographical sketches of artists and indexes to illustrators and authors whose works are listed are included.

Letopis' retsenziǐ. [Annals of Reviews]. - Moskva : Izd-vo Kniznaiā palata, 1934-   . Monthly (ISSN 0130-9242). A listing of book reviews and critical essays printed in major Russian journals, newspapers, and books. Contents include a foreword (in the first issue of each year), the UDC classified bibliography, and indexes (authors, editors, and titles of books published in Russia; authors, editors, and titles of books published abroad; names of reviewers). Publisher varies; previous ISSN 0507-4509.

Letopis' zhurnal'nykh stateǐ. [Annals of Periodical Articles]. - Moskva : Izd-vo Kniznaiā palata, 1926-   . Weekly (frequency varies) (ISSN 0024-1202). Publisher varies. Classified by UDC, this bibliography lists articles in periodicals, journals, non-periodical and continuing anthologies. Contents include a foreword, classified bibliography, and indexes (name, geographical, list of journals from which articles are taken). Quarterly indexes issued separately. Annual list of journals and collections indexed is published separately.

Notnaiā letopis'. [Annals of Music]. - Moskva : Izd-vo Kniznaiā palata, 1931-   . Bi-monthly (frequency varies) (LC: ML120.R9N92; LCCN:sn84-46056; OCLC: 7818864; ISSN 0130-7746). Includes published musical scores, musical textbooks, and books which have in its text the musical scores in a classified arrangement. Description is according to "Bibliographic description of musical publications" (GOST 7.16-79). Indexes within each issue include title, author, index of publications with scores. Included together in a separate publication is *Notnaiā letopis'.* "Supplementary Index", and *Notnaiā letopis'.* "List of titles and the first word of text of song." Previously called *Letopis' muzykal'noĭ literatury Velikoĭ Otechestvennoĭ Sovetskogo naroda* (LC: ML120.R8N6; LCCN:58-28032; OCLC: 2127764; ISSN 0029-4462).

Letopis' periodicheskikh i prodolzhaiushchikhsia izdaniĭ (LPPI) [The Chronicle of Periodical and Serial Publications]. - Moskva : Izd-vo Kniznaia palata, 1933-   . Quinquennial. Published in four parts:

1. *Zhurnaly* [Journals] (ISSN 0201-6257). Includes journals published during the five year period covered, e.g., 1986-1990. Titles are arranged in almost 50 subject categories, with complete bibliographic information supplied. Indexes include title, language, publishing organizations, titles by place of publication, and ISSN.

2. *Gazety* [Newspapers] (ISSN 0201-6389). Includes newspapers, local papers published in the republics, krais, oblasts and raions, city papers, military newspapers, some railroad and airline papers. Not included are newspapers from collective farms, and newsletters. Organized by administrative region. Complete bibliographic information supplied. Indexes include Russian title, non-Russian title, place of publication, subject, and administrative units.

3. *Sborniki* [Collections] (ISSN 0201-6389; same as *Gazety*). Includes collections, yearbooks, and other serial publications. Arranged in subject categories. Complete bibliographic information supplied. Indexes include title, language, publishing organization, place of publication.

4. *Biulleteni* [Bulletins] (ISSN 0201-6837). Includes bulletins, brochures and other information materials which have a press run of more than 200 copies. Indexes include title, language, publishing organization, and republic.[1]

Although the following title is not a numbered part of the *LPPI* series, it could be considered "number 5." *Letopis' periodicheskikh i prodolzhaiushchikhsia izdaniĭ. Novye, pereimenovannye i prekrashchennye izdaniem zhurnaly i gazety.* [Annals of Serial Publications and Continuing Publications]. - Moskva : Izd-vo Kniznaia palata, 1933-   . Annual, with various cumulations (LC: Z6956; ISSN 0201-6265). Beginning with 1955/1960, issued in two volumes: volume 1: *Zhurnaly, trudy, biulleteni* (journals); volume 2: *Gazety* (newspapers). Lists new periodicals and newspapers, title changes and title cessations in the Russian Federation for the year. Monographic series are included. Indexes include administrative divisions (geographical); place of publication; title; index of titles other than the Russian language; publishers; sponsors; interest groups, e.g., young people.

The following title is not part of the national bibliography, but may be useful. *Novye knigi* [New Books]. - Moskva : Mezhdunarodnaia Kniga, 1992-   . Semimonthly. (LCCN: sn93-42186; OCLC: 25958358; ISSN 0134-8396). Lists new titles published during the week. Also mentions titles soon to be published. Former title: *Novye knigi SSSR*. [New Books of the Soviet Union]. - Moscow : Gosudarstvennyi Komitet Soveta Ministrov SSSR po Pechati, 1956-1991. Weekly (ISSN 0134-8396).

No symbols are used to distinguish official and government publications.

LATEST ISSUE EXAMINED/CURRENCY: The latest issue of *KL* examined is no. 4, 1995 at the University of Minnesota in March 1995. All parts described above were examined and discussed with V. Frangulov, East View Publications.

---

[1] The following article explains this series and its availability: [Vladimir Frangulov], "Have you heard of *LPPI*s?," *Eurasian Press Monitor*, vol. 2, no. 3 (May 1995); p. 5.

AUTOMATION: The Russian Book Chamber forms databases on books, brochures, articles and all other types of publications from 1980 on the IBM PC 486. All national bibliographic and authority records distributed are in the UNIMARC and USMARC communication formats.

FORMATS AND SERVICES AVAILABLE: printed, magnetic tape, CD-Rom. During 1997-1998, it is planned for online availability via the Internet.

CURRENT LEGAL DEPOSIT LAWS: Federal Law of 1994 N77-F3 of 29 December 1994.

AVAILABLE FROM: Izd-vo Knizhnaĭa Palata, Kremlevskaĭa Nab. 1/9, Moskva.

Distributors for U.S.A. and the world except East Europe: East View Publications, 3020 Harbor Lane North, Minneapolis, MN 55447, USA.

SELECTED ARTICLES, BOOKS: Dzhigo, A. "Gosudarstvennaĭa bibliografiĭa strany - kul'turnoe bogatstvo obshchestva." *Kniga: Issledovaniĭa i Materialy* no. 65 (1993)22-26.

Dzhigo, A., Lenskii, B. "Novye tekhnologii v natsional'noĭ bibligrafii." *Kniga: Issledovaniĭa i materialy* no. 69 (1994):58-72.

Dzhigo, A. "Osnovnye funktsii natsional'nykh bibliograficheskikh tsentrov." *Kniga: Issledovaniĭa i materialy* no. 62 (1991):47-59.

Dzhigo, A. "Primenenie UDK v natsional'noĭ bibliografii Rossii." *Nauchnye i tekhnicheskie biblioteki* no. 4 (1994):32-37.

Dzhigo, A. "Sistema obĭazatel'nogo ekzemplĭara i sozdanie edinogo informatsionnogo prostranstva." *Informatsionnyĭ Bĭulleten' Bibliotechnoĭ Assotsiatsii Evrazii* no. 1 (1993):54-56.

Dzhigo, A. "Zakon "Ob obzĭatel'nom ekzemplĭare dokumentov." *Bibliografiia* no. 5 (1995):3-10.

Dzhigo, A. "Zakon "Ob obĭazatel'nom ekzemplĭare dokumentov - v deĭstvii." *Bibliotekovedenie* no. 2 (1995):3-10.

Dzhigo, A., Sukhorukov, K. "Obĭazatel'nyĭ ekzemplĭar i natsional'naĭa bibliografiĭa." *Bibliografiiano* 6 (1993):126-133.

Gruzinskaĭa, N., Dzhigo, A. "Kniga slov." *Sovetskaĭa Bibliografiĭa* no. 2 (1991):37-42.

Voprosy National'noŭbibliografii. Sost. A. Dzhigo, N. Gruzinskaĭa. Moskva: Knizhnaĭa Palata, 1991.

VERIFIER: A. A. Dzhigo, head of the department of national bibliography, Russian Book Chamber; K.M. Sukhorukov, senior bibliographer, Russian Book Chamber.

RWANDA

No current national bibliography has been traced for Rwanda. Although *BSTW 1975-1979* (pp. 354-357) indicates that the Centre de Bibliographie Rwandaise, a department of Library Services of the Université Nationale du Rwanda, plans to publish a current national bibliography incollaboration with the Minister of National Education, there are no plans to do so at the present time.[1]

Albert Lévesque has written *Contribution to the National Bibliography of Rwanda, 1965-1970.* London : G.K.Hall, 1979 which lists over 4500 items published in Rwanda or about Rwanda published abroad during the period covered. In the prefatory material it is stated that this work is intended to be a contribution to the future *Bibliographie Nationale Rwandaise.*

There is no national library nor any legal deposit law in Rwanda.

AL,ESA and QIPL,ESA include Rwanda within its scope.

SAUDI ARABIA

No current national bibliography has been traced for Saudi Arabia.[2] Selected current Saudi Arabian publications are included within the scope of *AL,ME,* vol. 1, (1963)-vol. 31, (1993) (ISSN 0041-7769). Yahya M. Sa'ati's *Publishing Trends in Saudi Arabia: a Subject Bibliography and an Analytical Study, 1970-1979.* - Riyadh : Riyadh Literary Club, 1979 is an analytical study on writing and publishing of all the Saudi as well as non-Saudi publications within the country during the period from 1970 to mid 1979.

"Excluding textbooks published by the Ministry of Education and the informative books by the different Ministries, this work can be termed as a national bibliography with its necessary indexes. The main object is a survey of all the publications of the said period, a study of all subjects, breaking down statistically by subjects, the role of publishing and printing houses and as well as the scientific society publications, the series that appeared during that period, and difficulies (sic) in acquiring these local publications."[3]

---

1 In a letter to the author dated 11 September 1985, James Armstrong, then the Field Director of the Library of Congress Office, Nairobi, Kenya verified that no current national bibliography exists, and in a second letter dated 14 November 1985 he further stated that there were no plans to produce a national bibliography. The author did not locate any existing national bibliography.

2 "National Bibliographies in Arab Countries." *International Cataloguing* 3 (Jan./Mar. 1974):3-4 states that the National Library published one issue of the national bibliography. Middle East specialists at the Library of Congress, the British Library and the University Library, Cambridge, England, were not aware of any current national bibliography today.

3 Yahya M. Sa'ati, "Summary." *Publishing Trends in Saudi Arabia: A Subject Bibliography and an Analytical Study, 1970-1979.* Riyadh : Riyadh Literary Club, 1979. p. 3.

Two other bibliographies which may prove useful are *Mu'jam al-matbū'at al-Sa'udiyah 1390-1399 A.H.* [Bibliography of Saudi Publications 1970-1979] by Shukri al-Anani, and *Fihris al-matbu'at al-hukumiyah: muqtanayat al-Maktabah al-Markaziyah* [Catalogue of Government Publications: Purchases of the Central Library], prepared by the Centre of Government Publications and Documentation, University of Riyadh (Riyadh, 1980), and reviewed in *'Alam al-Kutub* 1(1):92.[1]

In his doctoral thesis, Abdullatif Abdulhakeem Samarkandi identifies individuals and their attempts to compile lists of Saudi Arabian publications. These efforts are written by scholars for a specific purpose, such as to contribute to a book fair, or to fill a gap, and do not cover the entire national intellectual output for a particular time period based on legal deposit as a national bibliography would.[2]

The quarterly journal *'Ālam al-Kutub* [World of Books] (ISSN 0258-1159) is devoted to all aspects of the book concern of the Arab world including publishing, reviews, bibliographies, and related matters. Of special interest is the new books section. In volume 6, no. 1 (April 1985):68-85, Muhammad Fathi has compiled "al-Intaj al-fikri al-'arabi fi majal al-maktabat wa-al-ma 'lumat" (1983) [Arab intellectual production in the sphere of libraries and information. Part 1]. He is hoping to continue this bibliography which includes specialists' bibliographies, technical information and theses within its scope. This periodical is available from *'Ālam al-Kutub*, P.O. Box 1590, Riyadh.[3]

The *Accessions List of the Central Library of the King Saud University, Riyadh* is also cited by Van de Vate as an additional source of information. It may not be as available as *'Ālam al-Kutub*.[4]

CURRENT LEGAL DEPOSIT LAWS: Section No. 12 of Regulation M-17 on Publishing and Printing, issued on 13.04.1402 (19 February 1981) and approved by King Khalid is the legal deposit law. This law is not effective and is largely disregarded.

SENEGAL

TITLE: *Bibliographie du Sénégal.* - no. 40- . - Dakar : Archives du Sénégal, 1972- .
Frequency varies: annual (1972, 1976, 1978-); semi-annual (1973-1975, 1977).
Continues *Bulletin bibliographique des Archives du Sénégal* (Oct. 1964-Dec. 1971).

---

[1] Katherine Van de Vate, "Saudi Arabia," *Books from the Arab World. A Guide to Selection and Acquisition.* Durham : Middle East Libraries Committee, 1988. p. 34.
[2] Abdullatif Abdulhakeem Samarkandi, "National Bibliography in Saudi Arabia, Egypt and Tunisia: Analytical and Comparative Study with a View to Planning a Saudi Arabian National Bibliography." Dissertation, Loughborough University of Technology, November 1990. See especially chapter 7 "National Bibliography in the KSA", pp. 190-222.
[3] Information received in a conversation with Jill Butterworth, Middle East specialist, University Library, Cambridge, England, in November 1994.
[4] Van de Vate, *op. cit.*

Previous titles: *Liste des ouvrages et des revues dépouillées au cours du mois de* [ ] (Dec. 1962-Jan. 1963); *Liste des ouvrages reçus et des revues dépouillées au cours du mois de* [ ] (Feb. 1963-Feb. 1964).
DDC: O16.966'3; LC: Z3711.A73a; DT549; LCCN: 76-644514; OCLC: 2488705
ISSN 0378-9942
COMPILER: Archives du Sénégal.

SCOPE AND COVERAGE: *Bibliographie du Sénégal* (*BDS*) includes all Sénégal publications received by legal deposit plus other Senegalese works acquired by the Archives du Sénégal. Titles about Sénégal or written by Senegalese living abroad and published elsewhere are included. Translations of Senegalese works are also within the scope.

Types of publications listed are books, official and government publications, selected periodical articles, pamphlets, brochures, local language publications, theses and dissertations (since number 50), microforms, limited editions, new periodicals (since number 51), IGO publications.

CONTENTS: Table of contents, introduction, class schedule, abbreviations, bibliography, index of authors, index of corporate authors, index of titles, new periodicals supplement (since no. 52).

The combined numbers 59/60/61, and 62/63/64/65 covering 1987-1988-1989 and 1990/1991/1992/1993 respectively do not have a table of conents or introduction.

CATALOGUING RULES AND CLASSIFICATION SCHEMES USED: In cataloguing ISBD(M) and ISBD(S) is used beginning with number 52 (1980).

The Classification Universelle Décimale (UDC) is used beginning with number 52 (1980).

ENTRY INFORMATION: Consecutive entry number, author, title, edition, place of publication, publisher, year, pagination, illustrations, size, series, notes including ISBN, bibliographies, and indexes. Another number at the lower right is a local marking (e.g., bi I 8° 5306; bi I 4° 862) which was not identified in the introduction.

Full bibliographic information is given for the periodicals in the supplement.

ARRANGEMENT: Since number 52 the main bibliography is organized by UDC subject headings, then alphabetically arranged.

Number 48: The main bibliography is divided into retrospective official publications (arranged by corporate or subject headings within the year of publication); official publications of l'Afrique Occidentale Française, (l'A.O.F) (arranged chronologically); retrospective non-official publications (arranged by author); current official publications (arranged by corporate or subject heading within the year of publication), current non-official publications (arranged by author). The periodicals are placed at the head of each division.

Publications before 1977 are organized by year, and then alphabetized by broad subject.

INDEXES: Author; title. The numbers refer the user to the consecutive entry number in the main bibliography. Current periodicals are not included in the index.

NOTES AND COMMENTS: With number 52 (1980) *BDS* has established new guidelines, following recommendations of ICNB and meetings of ASCOBIC in 1978 and 1979. The title is now following a classified arrangement of UDC, and using ISBD(M) and ISBD(S).

A chart "Tableau Résumant l'Evolution du Bulletin Bibliographique des Archives du Sénégal" (n.p.) included in *BDS* number 48 summarizes very clearly the changes in title, frequency and new characteristics included in various issues. The chart covers from number 1-48.

It would be helpful to have the introduction include information suggested in ICNB recommendation number 10, especially the basis for the records, coverage, frequency, arrangement, outline of classified arrangement. Further help would be given if an analyzed entry was included in the prefatory material. This would identify various numbers used in the entries. A list of publishers would also be beneficial for persons needing names and addresses when ordering books.

There is no header identification on the pages. To make use a little easier, it would be helpful to have page headings which would help the reader know which section was being consulted without having to search for the section's beginning.

Several numbers include supplements. Examples of supplement titles are: 46, "Bibliographie. Planification du Sénégal. Ve plan de developpement"; 48, "Liste des periodiques Sénégalais reçus aux Archives"; 52, "Thèses et memories reçus aux Archives en 1980".

LATEST ISSUE EXAMINED/CURRENCY: The latest volume checked in April 1995 at the SOAS Library was combined numbers 62/63/64/65 (1990/1991/1992/1993), published 1995.

In examining a sample of entries in the latest volume, most imprint dates are within the date of coverage. This is an improvement over earlier years when a wide range of dates was included. If publication and distribution could be more timely, this title could be an effective acquisitions source for Sénégal publications.

AUTOMATION: not automated.

FORMAT AND SERVICES AVAILABLE: printed.

CURRENT LEGAL DEPOSIT LAWS: Law number 76.30 of 9 May 1976.[1] (published in *Journal Officiel de la République du Sénégal* 15 May 1976, 759-761).

AVAILABLE FROM: Exchange: Centre de Documentation, Archives du Sénégal, Immeuble Administratif, Avenue Roume, Dakar.

VERIFIER: M. Saliou Mbaye, Director, Archives du Sénégal.

---

[1] *BSTW, Supplement 1980*, p. 87. In his 8 August 1996 letter to the author Director M. Saliou Mbaye, Archives du Sénégal, stated that this continues to be the current legal deposit legislation.

SEYCHELLES

No current national bibliography has been traced for the Seychelles. *AL,ESA*, *QIPL,ESA* and *Annuaire de pays de l'océan indien* include the Seychelles within their scopes.

"Bibliographical notes" compiled by J.F.G. Lionnet appear periodically in the *Journal of the Seychelles Society* (ISSN 0582-9100). This lists books, pamphlets, periodicals, reports on the "natural history and related subjects of the Seychelles and neighbouring archipelagoes."[1] Some issues of this bibliography and the dates of its appearance are: no. 2 (Oct. 1962), no. 3 (Dec. 1963), no. 4 (Aug. 1965), no. 6 (Nov. 1968), no. 7 (Nov. 1971). According to Ms. Flavie Jackson, Librarian, Victoria, Seychelles, the *Journal of the Seychelles Society* is now "deeply dormant,"[2] and now has officially ceased publication in December 1984.[3]

The National Bookshop, P.O. Box 48, Victoria, Mahe, has a list of publications about the Seychelles in English, French and Creole languages. Information on Seychelles publications is also available from the Chief Librarian, P.O. Box 45, Victoria.[4]

SIERRA LEONE

TITLE: *Sierra Leone publications.* -1962/63-   . - Freetown : Sierra Leone Library Board, 1964-   .
Annual.
DDC: not found; LC: Z3553.S5S5; LCCN: 66-37297; OCLC: 5895485
ISSN 0583-2276

COMPILER: Sierra Leone Library Board.

SCOPE AND COVERAGE: *Sierra Leone Publications* (*SLP*) strives to include the national imprint published in English for the current year, January to December, received by the Sierra Leone Library Board under the legal deposit law. It also includes documents by Sierra Leoneans or about Sierra Leone published abroad. The 1987 issue has included some books in Kiro.

Types of publications included in *SLP* are books, pamphlets, first issues of periodicals, government publications, IGO publications, "Acts" and "Public Notices", annual reports, internal documents, maps and atlases.

---

[1] Ruth Freitag, "National Bibliographies," in *A.L.A. World Encyclopedia of Library and Information Services* (1980):390.
[2] Julian W. Witherell, "Report of a Trip to Africa, March-June 1984: part 3," *Africana Libraries Newsletter* no. 42a (July 1985):13.
[3] Judith Farley, "National Bibliographies," *A.L.A. World Encyclopedia of Library and Information Services* (2d ed. 1986):579.
[4] "Bibliographies," *Africana Library Newsletter* no. 42 (June 1985):4.

CONTENTS: Introduction (which includes an abbreviations list, the main classes of the DDC scheme, and an analyzed main entry), classified bibliography section, index, list of publishers.

CATALOGUING RULES AND CLASSIFICATION SCHEMES USED: Entries are catalogued according to AACR 1978 (British text), ISBD(M) since 1978, ISBD(S), ISBD(CM). The ISBN has been recorded when known. Subject tracings follow the *British National Bibliography* subject indexing system with some modifications.

Classification of entries is by DDC (19th ed.) since the 1990 volume.

ENTRY INFORMATION: DDC number, author, title, place of publication, publisher, date, pagination, illustrations, size, series statement, binding, price, ISBN if known, tracings.

Over the years, the use of the asterisk has had different meanings. The lack of explanation as to the meaning of the asterisks when used in some years (e.g., 1967 and 1968, 1969/71) is frustrating. In 1974/75, items received in 1972 are marked with one asterisk (*), and items received in 1973 are marked with two asterisks (**). Since the 1977/78 volume, an asterisk (*) is used only for works by Sierra Leoneans published abroad and works about Sierra Leone written by a foreigner which are acquired by the Library.

ARRANGEMENT: Since 1977/78 the classified subject section entries are arranged alphabetically by main entry within the classification numbers. In 1976/77, the main bibliography was alphabetically arranged by the main entry. In the 1960s up to the 1968 and 1969 volume the bibliography was arranged in two parts: official publications, alphabetically arranged by issuing agency, and semi-official and other publications, alphabetically arranged by main entry. The 1969/71 volume also had a section for the Commonwealth Parliamentary Association.

The 1975/76 volume has periodicals alphabetically arranged by title or issuing body.

INDEXES: Author/title/subject index. The numbers refer to the DDC number. Indexing is according to the *British National Bibliography* Precis indexing system with some modifications. The index appeared for the first time in the 1977/78 volume.

NOTES AND COMMENTS: The 1977/78 volume saw changes in its physical size and in its organization. In arrangement, it changed from the alphabetical listing to the ICNB recommendation of a classified arrangement.

Method of reproduction has varied over the past few years. The 1979/80 *SLP* was printed by the Government Printing Department, but volumes since have been typed and reproduced by the Sierra Leone Library Board.

Dates for including titles in *SLP* based on legal deposit receipt have changed. Earlier volumes state that *SLP* listed titles received from September to August of the current year for its current volume. Since 1981 the introduction states that it includes titles received on legal deposit from January to December of the current year; this has continued through the current volume.

The subtitle *A list of books and pamphlets in English received by the Sierra Leone Library Board under the Publication Amendment Act, 1962* was used until the 1977/78 volume.

Government publications, although not designated by a symbol, can be identified by looking in the index under Sierra Leone and then the issuing agency.

Government publications are also listed in the *Sierra Leone Government Official Diary*, and a selection is included at the back of the *Sierra Leone Gazette*.[1]

An additional source of bibliographical information is "List of New Accessions" found in the *Africana Research Bulletin*. This list first appears in volume 4, number 2, 1974 and covers material received from January 1971-January 1974. The scope of this occasional list includes material published in Sierra Leone and on Sierra Leone published elsewhere.[2]

No introduction appeared in the 1974/75 volume. The 1977/78 volume included an introduction which incorporates ICNB recommendation 10. This improvement, along with other modifications, shows the interest and desire of the Sierra Leone Library Board to meet international standards and to play an active part in contributing to the international bibliographical network.

Either by legal deposit or through personal contacts and visits to printers, the Sierra Leone Library Board is able to track down a high percentage of titles published each year.[3]

LATEST ISSUE EXAMINED/CURRENCY: The latest volume consulted in November 1994 was 1987, published in 1988 and received by the University Library, Cambridge, England, in October 1989. Taking a sample of 15 imprint dates from the 1987 volume, 10 of the 15 were from 1986 or 1987. Currency of entries has improved from earlier issues when it was necessary to have the asterisk symbol system. It is hoped that the recent lag in time from publication date to the subscribing library's receipt can be overcome so that *SLP* can be used by librarians for current acquisitions purposes.

Because of the low rate of publishing in the country, it has become difficult to publish *SLP* annually. "List of New Acquisitions" is displayed in the Library from time to time so that librarians can use it for acquisitions purposes.[4]

AUTOMATION: not automated.

FORMAT AND SERVICES AVAILABLE: printed.

CURRENT LEGAL DEPOSIT LAWS: Publications (Amendment) Act, 1962.

---

[1] "Sierra Leone," *Survey on the Present State of Bibliographic Recording in Freely Available Printed Form of Government Publications and Those of Intergovernmental Organizations*, 1977. p.87.

[2] According to information supplied in a 13 August 1996 letter written to the author by Marian Lisk, Deputy Chief Librarian, this list no longer appears in *Africana Research Bulletin*.

[3] Beatrice S. Bankole, "Current National Bibliographies of the English Speaking Countries of Africa," *International Cataloguing* 14 (Jan./Mar. 1985):7. Bankole cited information taken from Marian Lisk, *Sierra Leone: A Country Report* (ASCOBIC, 1983).

[4] Information supplied in a 13 August 1996 letter from Marian Lisk.

AVAILABLE FROM: Sierra Leone Library Board, P.O. Box 326, Freetown. Exchange inquiries welcomed.

SELECTED ARTICLES: "Sierra Leone Publications," *International Cataloguing* 13 (no. 3 July/Sept. 1984):27.

VERIFIER: Marian Lisk, Deputy Chief Librarian.

SINGAPORE

TITLE: *Singapore national bibliography.* -1967- . - Singapore : National Library, 1969- .
Print version: 1967- Jan./Mar. 1993.
CD-ROM version: 1967/1991- (cumulative).
Twice a year; CD-ROM cumulative (July 1993-). Print: quarterly, with annual cumulation (1977- Jan./Mar. 1993); annual (1967-1976).
DDC: 015.5957; LC: Z3285.S564; LCCN: sn94-18242; OCLC: 31629664; 29629614; 1643623 (print); OCLC: 29629614, 31629664 (CD-ROM)
ISSN 0128-6454; (print: 0129-315X)

COMPILER: National Library of Singapore.

SCOPE AND COVERAGE: The *Singapore National Bibliography* (*SNB*) lists all works published in the Republic of Singapore which have been deposited at the National Library under the legal deposit act. Publications in Malay, Chinese, Tamil and English are all included within the scope.

Types of publications included are books and pamphlets for sale (regardless of number of pages); books and pamphlets not for sale, including privately printed titles; society and church newsletters; publications of political parties, etc., government publications which include those for sale, for free distribution, and for limited distribution; first issues of current serials which include popular magazines, bye-laws and reports of associations, company accounts and reports, school magazines and house journals; maps, music, and any other material that may reflect the social, cultural or other aspects of the country. Some categories, such as programmes, art and trade catalogues are selectively included. IGO publications are listed if they are published in Singapore.[1]

Excluded are government publications of a routine nature: acts, bills, subsidiary legislations, parliamentary debates, gazettes and restricted publications; theses, microforms, audio-visual materials, periodical and newspaper articles.[2]

---

[1] Y. Wicks, "Official Publications of Singapore," *Singapore Libraries* 10 (1980):26.

[2] Chang Soh Choo, "The Retrospective Singapore National Bibliography, the Task Ahead," *International Cataloguing* 10 (Apr./June 1981):19, 22. See also J. Lee, "The Singapore National Bibliography: Problems and Prospects," 84. In *National and Academic Libraries in Malaysia and Singapore: Proceedings of a PPM and LAS Conference Held at Universiti Sains Malaysia,*

CONTENTS: CD-ROM User's Guide: System requirements, introduction, explanation on Windows and menu, Microsoft Window's glossary, getting started, exit windows or continue searching, best match search, field search, Boolean search, browse command; view, format and Window menu command, image.

Print: contents, preface (which includes scope, frequency, coverage, an explanation of the subject sequence, cataloguing, indexes), list of abbreviations, summary of classification schedule given in four languages, summary of classification expansions for languages and literatures of the Malay Archipelago and Oceania, and DDC historical expansion for Malaysia and for history, area notations for Malaysia, classified subject sequence, alphabetical author and title index, Chinese author and title index, Tamil author and title index, alphabetical subject index, list of publishers, list of Chinese publishers.

1993 was simplified: coverage, arrangement, main classified sequence, author, title and series index, subject index, list of publishers, ISBN/ISSN.

The 26th annual has two parts bound together: Part I is a computerized listing of entries in English, Malay and other Roman script languages while Part II lists the manually compiled Chinese and Tamil script entries. Each is divided into classified sequences; an author/title/series index; subject index; list of publishers.

CATALOGUING RULES AND CLASSIFICATION SCHEMES USED: *SNB* is catalogued according to AACR2r (1988 ed.). *LCSH* is used. Malay and Chinese names are entered in direct order according to AACR2R. On occasion the Chinese titles are given in a simplified script. No transliteration or translation is provided for non-Roman scripts. "Malay language and literature is classified by the expansion devised for the Joint Standing Committee on Library Cooperation and Bibliographical Services of the Library Associations of Singapore and Malaysia. The historical and geographical expansions for Malaysia follow that prepared by the National Library of Malaysia while the history expansion for Singapore is that used in the National Library of Singapore."[1]

ISBD(M) was used first in the 1974 issue of *SNB*.

The classification scheme used is DDC (20th ed.). Malay language, literature, history, geographical expansions are used.

ENTRY INFORMATION: CD-ROM: bibliographic information according to AACR2 is provided.

Print: DDC number in upper left corner, author, title, place of publication, publisher, date, pagination, illustrations, size, series statement, notes, ISSN (since 1976) or ISBN (beginning in 1980), price (Singapore dollars), notes, tracings. The registration number, e.g., S92-R2010, appears in the lower right corner.

Penang, 1-3 March, 1974, edited by Lim Huck Tee and Rashidah Begum. Penang: Persatuan Perpustakaan Malaysia, 1975. Lee also includes comics and posters in the scope of *SNB*.

[1] Preface iv-v, *SNB* 1992.

ARRANGEMENT: CD-ROM: Record information is retrievable by various search options which include best match search, field search, browse command, and image (viewing of Chinese and Tamil records).

Print: The classified subject section which is the main part of the bibliography is arranged by the second summary of DDC (20th ed.). Entries in the four languages are included in one sequence in the language of publication. Entries with the same classification number are filed in the following order: Roman, Jawi/Arabic, Chinese, and Tamil script.

INDEXES: CD-ROM: The Search by Field option displays 18 fields from which the user can choose: personal name, corporate name, meeting name, title, series title, subject heading, keyword, publisher, LC classification number, Dewey class number, record number, book number, serial number, publisher number for music, language, country of publication, year of publication, and format. Boolean operators can be used. Under the Browse command, 17 of the same fields are searchable; keyword is not included.

Print: Following the classified subject section are four indexes: alphabetical author and title index for English and Malay (Roman script), alphabetical author and title index for Chinese script arranged by the number of strokes of the character, and an alphabetical author and title index for Tamil script filed according to the order of the Tamil script. An alphabetical list of subjects in given in English. In all indexes, the DDC number is used to refer the user to the complete information in the classified subject section. Entry information in the indexes includes author, title and classification number.

From 1987 to the last printed issue: entries in Roman script are arranged alphabetically while those in the Chinese Index are arranged according to the number of strokes per character. Arrangement of the Tamil Index is according to the order of the Tamil script.

Earlier years of the *SNB,* e.g., 1970, had one alphabetical author, title, subject index in English and Malay and author and title indexes in Chinese and Tamil scripts.

NOTES AND COMMENTS: Singapore is a multilingual country and its national bibliography must reflect this. The printed *SNB* successfully integrated the published output of the four main languages (English, Malay, Tamil, Chinese) by using the classified subject arrangement. The CD-ROM edition includes images of Chinese and Tamil scripts titles catalogued from July 1993 onwards. The National Library hopes to list all Chinese and Tamil script records from 1967 onwards in the *SNB* CD-ROM soon.[1]

Since July 1993, the CD-ROM format has replaced the print version. Technical support requirements an IBM PC/AT/PS2 or compatible, DOS version 3.1 and Windows 3.1 or higher, five megabytes of free hard disk space, two megabytes of RAM, a CD-ROM drive which is compatible with MICROSOFT (DOS) extensions.

The *SNB CD-ROM: User's Guide* provides clear, helpful instructions in how to access the system and retrieve information. It is necessary to read and follow the *User's Guide* until familiar with the various searching techniques. A menu bar, tool bar, and title bar are part of the

---

[1] Information from Mrs. Chang Soh Choo, editor of the *Singapore National Bibliography*, in a letter to the author dated 19 April 1995.

main menu display screen. The latter gives the kind of search in progress. Help screens are available to the user at every stage.

Theses are recorded by the University of Singapore in bibliographies such as *Publications and Theses,* or *Dissertations, Theses and Academic Exercises Submitted to the University of Singapore and Deposited in the University of Singapore Library, 1947-1976.* The National University of Singapore, now has available in CD-ROM format *NUS Theses Collection 1947 -* which is produced as one of the three databases in a recent production entitled *SMC Ondisc: NUS Library Databases on CD-ROM.*[1]

Government publications are not marked with any designation. To discover titles of government publications one must consult the index under Singapore and then the corporate heading or the subject needed, scanning the information for government imprints and/or government corporate headings.

Official publications and government documents are listed in *Publications of Government Departments and Statutory Boards.* Singapore : Publicity Division, Ministry of Culture, 1978- .

Periodical articles are indexed in *Indeks Majalah Singapura = Singapore Periodicals Index* Singapore : National Library, 1973-1993. Annual (ISSN 0377-7928) which covers periodicals from Singapore and Brunei. Contents include introduction, abbreviations, list of periodicals indexed, subject list of articles (in English and in Malay), author section (in English and in Malay), subject list of articles (Chinese), author section (Chinese). This title is now available on CD-ROM, published in June 1996, and convering 1981-1994. It contains indexes to some 55,200 articles in English, Malay and Chinese.[2]

Before the existence of *SNB*, the Singapore *Government Gazette* published a quarterly list of books deposited under the Printers and Publishers Act. Although it is complete bibliographically, it is organized by the legal deposit registration number and makes access to a particular title difficult unless one knows the legal deposit number. The first list appeared in the *Straits Settlements Government Gazette*, 20 May 1887.[3]

From 1974-1979, the entry in the classified subject section of *SNB* has two numbers: the lower left number is the legal deposit registration number; the number on the lower right (e.g., S79-103) is the *SNB* serial number.

LATEST ISSUE EXAMINED/CURRENCY: CD-ROM: Entries in *SNB* are updated twice a year on a cumulating disk. The latest cumulation was examined at the University of Michigan in April 1997.

---

[1] Chang Soh Choo, "The Retrospective Singapore National Bibliography, the Task Ahead," p. 22.

[2] Information about the CD-ROM from a letter dated 30 July 1996 to the author from Mrs. Chang Soh Choo.

[3] Lee, *National and Academic Libraries in Malaysia and Singapore*, 83. Mrs. Chang Soh Choo's letter of 30 July states that this list is no longer published with the enactment of the *National Libray Act 1995.*

Print: The introduction of Part I and Part II seems to have helped a more timely production and distribution. The 1992 cumulated issue was published in 1993, and received by University Library, Cambridge 27 May 1993.

AUTOMATION: "Floppy disks from SILAS are sent to the vendor to be run on a software called Compound Document Processing System (CDPS) developed by the vendor. The data is sent in turn to another vendor to master the disk and duplicate the *SNB* CD-ROM copies."[1]

FORMATS AND SERVICES AVAILABLE: Magnetic tape service (SILAS), cartridge tape or floppy disk. This service is presently available on exchange basis to the Australian and New Zealand bibliographic networks for their national bibliographic records; CD-ROM format.

CURRENT LEGAL DEPOSIT LAWS: National Library Board Act 1995 (No.5 of 1995), Section 10 Deposit of Library Materials. This includes non-print and audio-visual materials.[2]

AVAILABLE FROM: National Library Board, 91 Stamford Road, Singapore 0617.

SELECTED ARTICLES: Khoo, George. "The Singapore National Bibliography." *Singapore Libraries* 1 (1971):55-57.

Lee, Judy. "The Singapore National Bibliography: Problems and Prospects." In *National and Academic Libraries in Malaysia and Singapore: Proceedings of a PPM and LAS Conference Held at Universiti Sains Malaysia, Penang, 1-3 March, 1974*, edited by Lim Huck Tee and Rashidah Begum. Penang: Persatuan Perpustakaan Malaysia, 1975, p. 83-93.

VERIFIER: Mrs. Chang Soh Choo, Assistant Head, Technical Services Division, National Library Board.

SLOVAKIA

TITLE: *Slovenská národná bibliografia. Séria A: Knihy.* - roc. 21- . - Martin : Matica Slovenská, 1970- .
Monthly, with separately issued annual cumulated index as no. 13.
Continues *Bibliograficky katalog ČSSR. Slovenské knihy.*
Frequency and publisher varies.
DDC: not found; LC: Z2124.S56S53; LCCN: 73-646907//r913; OCLC: 1789152
ISSN 0231-9780

COMPILER: Slovenská národná knižnica v Matici slovenske. Národný bibliografický ústav [Slovak National Library at Matica Slovenská. National Bibliographic Institute].

---

[1] Information from Mrs. Chang Soh Choo's 19 April letter.
[2] Mrs. Chang Soh Choo sent the author a copy of the new legislation which appeared in the Republic of Singapore *Government Gazette Acts Supplement* no. 9, Friday, 24 March 1995.

SCOPE AND COVERAGE: *Slovenská Národná Bibliografia. Séria A: Knihy* (*SNB.K*) lists the publishing output of Slovakia deposited at the Slovak National Library at Matica Slovenská according to legal deposit legislation.

Types of publications in *SNB.K* include books and pamphlets.
Maps, periodicals, periodical articles, dissertations, phonorecords, librettos, films and graphics are all included in other series cited in Notes and.Comments

CONTENTS: Classification scheme explanation (only in the first issue of each year), bibliography, name index, title index, subject index, table of contents.

CATALOGUING RULES AND CLASSIFICATION SCHEMES USED: National standards are followed. New national standards are being prepared following AACR2 rules.[1]

The classification scheme used is UDC.

ENTRY INFORMATION: Upper left corner lists the consecutive entry number, upper right corner gives the classification number, author, title, edition, place of publication, publisher, date, pagination, size, notes including ISBN, and number of copies printed if available; subject entries in small print, internal number, e.g., SB 52649/1 D1.

ARRANGEMENT: Arrangement of the bibliography follows UDC, alphabetically arranged by main entry within the subject groups.

INDEXES: Monthly issues include name, subject and title indexes. An annual cumulated index is issued as "čislo" 13 which includes the following: author index, compiler index, register of authors of introductions and forewords, illustrator index, title index, translations index (from Slovak into other languages, and from other languages into Slovak), publishers' list (no addresses are given but this lists the entry numbers in the bibliography for which the publisher is responsible), series and editions index, subject index. Number refers to the consecutive entry number.

NOTES AND COMMENTS: Slovakia became independent on 1 January 1993. Before then, Slovakia was part of Czechoslovakia which was made up of two national republics—Czech and Slovak. Each republic has its own national bibliography. The Slovakia national bibliography did not change its title since becoming a nation. It has continued to upgrade its bibliographic description, e.g, adding ISBNs.

SNB continues *Bibliografický katalog ČSSR. Slovenské knihy.* 1960-1969 (LCCN: sn80-1254; OCLC: 5766938) which continues *Bibliografický katalog ČSR. Slovenské knihy.* 1955-1960 (LCCN: sf94-91382; OCLC: 10903839). This continues *Bibliografický katalog ČSR. Slovenské kniha.* 1952-1954. (LCCN: sn80-2822; OCLC 5538889) which continues *Bibliografický katalog. Slovenská kniha.* 1946-1951.

---

[1] Information supplied in a letter of 22 August 1996 to the author from Ing. Daniela Slizová, Director of the Slovak National Library.

Slovakia is the home of over 500,000 Hungarians and 40,000 Ukrainians. Their literary output is included in *SNB*. Selected periodicals are also included in the journal articles index.[1]

The Slovak exile literature as well as literature referring to Slovak issues published abroad is reflected in the work of the National Bibliographic Institute of the Slovak National Library and in the Slovak National Bibliography System. This database has become a component of the *SNB*. Since 1990 an additional row of the *SNB.K* has been published under the subtitle *Zahranicné slovaciká* which appears annually.[2]

Statistics of the annual Slovak book production appear in no. 13 of *SNB.K*.

Since the early 1980s, the current computerized *SNB* has been restructured from earlier years and is divided into series A-J (K) as follows. Series B-J (K) are united quarterly in a common issue since 1984. All are published by the Slovak National Library at Matica Slovenská. (LC: Z2137.S6S548; LCCN:87-640682//r91l; OCLC: 12406079).

Séria A. Knihy. [Books] This series is analyzed in the above text.

Séria B. Periodiká. [Periodicals] Quinquennial, cumulation, 1981- . (LC: Z6956.S63S5; LCCN: 59-27220; OCLC: 5460209).

Séria C. Mapy. [Maps] Quinquennial, 1976- . (LC: Z2137.S6S546; LCCN: 90-646177; OCLC: 22234391).

Séria D. Dizertačné práce. [Theses and dissertations] Annual, 1978- . (LC: Z2137.S6S575; OCLC: 28606339).

Séria E. Špeciálne tlače. [Special publications, e.g., theatre programmes, exhibition catalogues, and publications for the blind] Annual since 1986; before 1986, one number as quadrennial, one number as biennial (1984). 1982?- . (LC: Z1029.5.S58; LCCN: sn92-38012; OCLC: 25111478).

Séria F. Firemná literatúra. [Trade catalogues and technical newsletters] Annual, 1980- . (LC: Z7164.B93S58; LCCN: sn92-38014; OCLC: 25178755).

Séria G. Grafika. [Graphic and fine arts] Annual since 1986- . (Before 1986, one number as quadrennial 1980, and one number as biennial 1984.) (LC: Z5956.G73S58; LCCN: sn92-38013; OCLC: 25111424).

---

[1] Mária Okálová. "Literárna Produkcia Národnostnych Mensín na Slovensku a jej Odraz v Automatizovanom Systéme Slovenskej Národnej Bibliografie." *Knižnice a Informácie* 25 (c. 5 1993):218-221.

[2] Milos Kovacka. "Zahranicní Slováci (Zahranicné Slovaciká) v Programe Národného Bibliografického Ústavu SNK MS a v Národnom Bibliografickom Systéme Slovenska a Slovákov ." *Knižnice a Informácie* 26 (c. 2 1994), pp. 60-63. Information about *Zahranicné slovaciká* is from Ing. Daniela Slizová's 22 August 1996 letter.

Séria H. Hudobniny. [Sheet music, books on music] Annual, 1981- . (LC: ML120.C9S59; LCCN: 87-640684/MN; OCLC: 15218110)

Séria I. Oficiálne dokumenty. [Official documents] Biennial, 1981- . (LC: J338.A12.S56; LCCN: sn94-30490; OCLC: 28606337) Since 1994, *Oficiálne dokumenty a normy* [Official documents and standards].[1]

Séria J. Audiovizuálne dokumenty. [Audio-visual materials] Annual, 1983- ; biennial, 1981-82. 1981- . (LC: ML156.2.S575; LCCN: 87-640683/MN/r91; OCLC: 15217993)

Séria K. Slepecké tlače [Braille script prints]. Triennial, 1993- .[2]

Another title also includes helpful information. *Slovenská národná bibliografia. Rozpisový rad Články.* - Martin : Matica Slovenská . Monthly (14 issues; 13 and 14 are name and subject indexes.). 1986- . Includes periodical and newspaper articles and reviews. Superseded *Slovenská národná bibliografia. Články,* 1978-1986. From 1955-1969, constituted part of *Bibliografický Katalog ČSSR.* Supersedes *Slovenské Časopisy.*

Before the restructuring in the early 1980s, *Slovenská národná bibliografia* was divided into the following series. *Séria A* has already been analyzed in the above entry.

Séria A. Knihy. - 1946- . Corresponds to new *Séria A.*

Séria B. Periodiká. - Martin : Matica Slovenská, 1958- . Quinquennial. Lists periodical titles. (LC: Z6956.S63S5; LCCN: 59-27220; OCLC: 5460209) Corresponds to new *Séria B.*

Séria C. Články. - Martin : Matica Slovenská, 1954-1977. Monthly. Includes periodical and newspaper articles and reviews. From 1955-1969, constituted part of *Bibliografický Katalog ČSSR.* Supersedes *Slovenské Časopisy.* This old series C corresponds to *Rozpisovy rad Články.*

Séria D. Speciálne tlače. - Martin : Matica Slovenská, 1970- . Annual. Includes dissertations, "firemná literatúra", patents, phonorecords, librettos, films, maps and atlases, graphics and "drobné tlače". This series was never realized.[3]

Séria E. Veda a kultúra na Slovensku. - 1971 / Dusan Katuscák, comp. - (LCCN: 79-646079//r912; LC: Z2137.S6V42; OCLC: 5292006). Only volume published.

Slovenské Hudobniny. [Slovak Music]. Martin : Matica Slovenská, 1960-1970. Annual. Continues *Bibliografický Katalog CSSR. Slovenské Hudobniny.* [Bibliography Catalogue. Slovak Music]. 1955-1959. This superseded in part *Bibliografický Katalog CSSR. Ceska a Slovenské Hudobniny.* Státni Knihovna Ceské Socialistické Republiky, 1933-1954. About ten issues a year. Dates from 1971-1980 are processed now as a retrospective bibliography.[4] This series is continued by the new *Séria H. Hudobniny.*

---

[1] Information in Ing. Daniela Slizová's 22 August 1996 letter.

[2] Slizová's 22 August 1996 letter.

[3] Slizová's 22 August 1996 letter.

[4] Slizová's 16 September 1996 letter.

LATEST ISSUE EXAMINED/CURRENCY: In a sample of entries from number 7/8, 1995 of *SNB.K* all imprint dates were from the period covered.

The latest issue examined was number 8 for 1995 at the University of Illinois Library, Urbana-Champaign.

AUTOMATION: *SNB* has been automated since 1976, currently using ALEPH system since 1995. Earlier records from CDS/ISIS are being transferred to ALEPH.

FORMAT AND SERVICES AVAILABLE: printed; online. After the transfer of records is completed from CDS/ISIS to ALEPH, the *SNB* will be available on CD-ROM. *Slovenská národná bibliografia* is available by Internet: http://www.matica.sk:4000/ALEPH

CURRENT LEGAL DEPOSIT LAWS: Edict of the Ministry of Education and Culture of 17 June 1964 is the latest legal deposit legislation.[1]

AVAILABLE FROM: Národny bibliografický ústav, Slovenská národná kniznica v MS, 03652 Martin, Novomeského 32.

SELECTED ARTICLES: Celkova, Lúdmila. "Zakladne Slovenské Narodne Bibliografie." *Citadel'* 30 (nos. 77-8 1981):suppl. I-VIII.

Durovcik, Stefan. "Projekt Automatizovaneho Systemu Slovenskej Narodnej Bibliografie." *Citadel'* 27 (no. 9 1978):318-320.

Katuščák, Dušan. "New Developments in Librarianship and Bibliographic Control in Slovakia." *ICBC* 25:1 (Jan./Mar. 1996):16-19.

"Slovak Bibliography from 1918 to the Present." In Ryznar, Eliska and Croucher, Murlin. *Books in Czechoslovakia: Past and Present.* Wiesbaden: Otto Harrassowitz, 1989. pp. 94-97.

VERIFIER: Ing. Daniela Slizová, Director of Slovak National Library, 03652 Martin.

SLOVENIA

TITLE: *Slovenska bibliografija. Knjige.* [Slovenia Bibliography. Books]. - št. 1/3 (1985)- . - Ljubljana : Narodna in univerzitetna knjižnica, 1985- .
Quarterly (1986-); monthly (1985).
Separate index published each year.
Continues *Slovenska bibliografija. B, Knjige.*
DDC: 015.4973; LC: in process; LCCN: 90-646277; OCLC: 13766759
ISSN 0353-1716

---

[1] *BSTW, Supplement 1981-1982*, p. 112. *International Guide to Legal Deposit* states that a new law is in the process of being approved, p. 74.

COMPILER: Narodna in univerzitetna knjižnica Ljubljana [National and University Library Ljubljana]

SCOPE AND COVERAGE: *Slovenska bibliografija. Knjige* (*SB.K*) lists the publishing output of Slovenia which is deposited at the Narodna in univerzitetna knjižnica.

Types of publications include books, pamphlets (more than eight pages), and government publications.

Omitted from *SB.K* are pamphlets (under eight pages) and periodicals. Periodicals are covered in *Slovenska bibliografija. A, Serijske publikacije.*

CONTENTS: Preface, table of UDC classification scheme, classified bibliography, indexes.

CATALOGUING RULES AND CLASSIFICATION SCHEMES USED: ISBD are followed.

UDC is used.

ENTRY INFORMATION: Author, title, place of publication, publisher, date, place of printing, printer, pagination, illustrations, size, series statement, notes including bibliographies, ISBN; UDC number in lower left corner followed by an internal number, national bibliography consecutive number in lower right corner.

ARRANGEMENT: Arranged by UDC general numbers and headings.

INDEXES: A name index and a subject index is published quarterly. A separate annual index includes an author index, title index, and subject index.

NOTES AND COMMENTS: The CD-ROM version of *SB.K* first appeared in 1995 and covered imprints from 1989-1994. CD-ROM 2 appeared in 1996 and covers imprints from 1989-1995; CD-ROM 3 was issued in September 1997 and covers imprints from 1989-1996.[1]

The national bibliography of Slovenia is divided into parts; *SB.K* has been analyzed above. Following is bibliographic information about other parts, and earlier parts of *SB.K*. Before 1985, the *Slovenska Bibligrafija* included books, articles (to 1980), serials, maps, music, audio cassettes, and records. From 1985, the national bibliography divided its scope into the parts listed below.

SB.A, Serijske publikacije [Serials]. - 32-33 (1978-1979)-   . Ljubljana : Narodna in univerzitetna knjižnica, 1985-   . (LCCN: 90-646281; LC: Z2957.S6S56; OCLC: 13766325; ISSN 0353-1724). This title continues in part *Slovenska bibliografija : casopisje in knjige, članki in leposlovni prispevki v casopisju in zbornikih.* - [1] (1945/1947)-31, 2. del (1977). - Ljubljana : Državna založba Slovenije, 1948-1985. Annual. (LCCN: 52-19448//r90; LC: Z2957.S6S55; OCLC: 1765635; ISSN 0350-3585).

---

[1] Information in a 24 September 1997 e-mail to the author from Matjaz Hocevar, Slovenia Bibliography Department, Narodna in Univerzitetna Knjižnica.

SB.K continues *SB.B, Knjige* [Books]. - 32-33 (1978-1979)- 39 (1984). - Ljubljana : Narodna univerzitetna knjižnica, 1986-1995. (LCCN: sn87-21892; LC: Z2957.S6S624; OCLC: 16350149; ISSN 1318-0479) Biennial. *SB.B, Knjige* continues in part *Slovenska bibliografija : casopisje in knjige, članki in leposlovni prispevki v casopisju in zbornikih.* - [1] (1945/1947)-31, 2. del (1977). - Ljubljana : Državna založba Slovenije, 1948-1985. Annual. (LCCN: 52-19448//r90; LC: Z2957.S6S55; OCLC: 1765635; ISSN 0350-3585).

SB. Članki in leposlovni prispevki v serijskih publikacijah in zbornikih [Articles and literature contribution in serial publications and composite books]. 32-33 (1978-1979). - Ljubljana : Narodna in univerzitetna knjižnica, 1989. (LCCN: sn90 25383; LC: Z2957.S6S625; OCLC: 22425045; ISSN 0353-4340). This title continued in part *Slovenska bibliografija : casopisje in knjige, članki in leposlovni prispevki v casopisju in zbornikih.* - [1] (1945/1947)-31, 2. del (1977). - Ljubljana : Državna založba Slovenije, 1948-1985. Annual. (LCCN: 52-19448//r90; LC: Z2957.S6S55; OCLC: 1765635; ISSN 0350-3585).

SB.D, Ostalo in neknjižno gradivo. [Varied and non-book materials] This title continued in part *Slovenska bibliografija.* - [1] (1945/1947)-31, 2. del (1977). - Ljubljana : Državna založba Slovenije, 1948-1985. Annual. (LCCN: 52-19448//r90; LC: Z2957.S6S55; OCLC: 1765635; ISSN 0350-3585). This part, which was to include maps, music, audio cassettes, records, etc., has never been issued.[1]

The articles in newspapers were within the scope of *Slovenska Bibligrafija* until 1980, and are still analyzed but exist only in a catalogue drawer in the library. From 1991, articles are listed in COBISS.

Beginning in 1997 the Narodna in Univerzitetna Knjižnica began contributing national bibliographic records to OCLC. Monographs from 1989 onward will be sent on a quarterly basis.[2]

LATEST ISSUE EXAMINED/CURRENCY: The latest issue of *SB.K* examined is no. 1, 1995, at the University of Illinois, Urbana-Champaign in June 1996.

AUTOMATION: The national bibliography has been automated since 1988 and is produced by the COBISS system through the host IZUM (Institut informacijskih znanosti Maribor).

FORMAT AND SERVICES AVAILABLE: printed; CD-ROM. The union catalogue, from which the *SB.K* records are produced, is accessible through telnet: //nuk.uni-lj.si and through the Internet: http://www.izum.si/cobiss [3]

CURRENT LEGAL DEPOSIT LAWS: Zakon o obveznem pošiljanju tiskov ('Uredni list SRS' št. 55/72, 42/86)[4]

---

[1] Information received in a letter dated 20 March 1997 to the author from Lidija Wagner, Chief, Slovenia Bibliography Department, Narodna in Univerzitetna Knjižnica.

[2] Wagner letter and Hocevar e-mail.

[3] Hocevar e-mail.

[4] *International Guide to Legal Deposit*, p. 106. At 1996 IFLA meetings in Beijing, the author was told by Matjaz Hocevarjua, a Slovenian delegate from the national library, that an effort to upgrade the legal deposit law is currently in debate.

AVAILABLE FROM: Narodna in Univerzitetna Knjižnica, 61000 Ljubljana, Turjaska 1.

VERIFIER: Lidija Wagner, Chief, Slovenia Bibliography Department, Narodna in Univerzitetna Knjižnica.

SOMALIA

No current national bibliography has been traced for Somalia.

AL,ESA and *QIPL,ESA* include Somalia within their scopes.

Somalia reports, post-Barre period. Part 1- . - [microform]. New Delhi : Library of Congress Office ; Washington, D.C. Available from the Library of Congress. Photoduplication Service. 1994. (LCCN: 94-982404; LC: DT407.S6488 1994; OCLC: 35450243) is a collection of reports issued largely by non-governmental organizations documenting conditions in Somalia in the post-Barre period from 1991 onwards. The "Guide to Contents" appears on the first microfiche. These reports have been collected and assembled by the Library of Congress' Nairobi Office. Additional materials issued by organizations included in Part 1 may be found, along with reports by new organizations, in Part 2- of this collection. The plan for this microfiche collection is to film the publications in groups of 500; each group will be assigned consecutive part numbers. The table of contents of the "Guide to the contents" lists: project background, register of publications and explanatory notes, geographical index, issuing body directory, subject index, and map of Somalia. Types of documents include project proposals, evaluations and reports, results of assessments and surveys, situation reports, internal agency memos, trip reports, newsletters and press releases. There is wide-ranging subject matter. Statistical charts are included. The "Register of Publications – Explanatory Notes" analyzes a descriptive entry; information given is the document number, source, organization, title, date, notes, regions, index terms.[1]

The following may be of help for government publications: *Bibliography on Somali documents based on documents available in the Documentation Centre.* 1984. (LCCN: 90-981526; LC: Z33526.B53 1984; OCLC: 26396248).

The current legal deposit legislation was established in 1977.[2]

---

[1] The author is indebted to Nancy Jean Schmidt, African subject and area librarian, Indiana University for calling this collection to my attention.

[2] *BSTW, 1975-1979*, pp.373-374. No information was available in *International Guide to Legal Deposit*.

SOUTH AFRICA

TITLE: *SANB. South African national bibliography = SANB. Suid-Afrikaanse nasionale bibliografie.* 1959-   . Pretoria : State Library, 1960-   .
Quarterly, with final issue being an annual cumulation.
At head of title: *SANB.*
Continues *Publications received in terms of Copyright Act No. 9 of 1916* (1933-1958).
DDC: 015.68; LC: Z3603.P7; LCCN: sn90-12617; OCLC: 1715459, 29801457
ISSN 0036-0864

COMPILER: State Library.

SCOPE AND COVERAGE: The scope of the *South African National Bibliography* (*SANB*) includes all material published in South Africa and received within the current and preceding two years under the legal deposit legislation.[1]

Types of materials covered in *SANB* are books, pamphlets, periodicals, government publications, microforms, maps, technical reports, South African Bureau of Standards specifications, theses, audio-visual materials, as well as some publications of limited circulation. Unpublished conference proceedings were included through 1984.

Excluded are parliamentary bills and papers; amendments to bills, individual entries to annual reports which are treated as serials, unpublished conference proceedings, picture strips, trade catalogues, sheet music, ephemera, pamphlets of less than five pages, house journals and school magazines. Theses which are not legal deposit material and which are listed in the *Union Catalogue of Theses and Dissertations of South African Universities,* are also not included. Since 1992, reprints are no longer included, unless the book was published before 1959.[2] Unpublished conference proceedings from 1985 are not included.

CONTENTS: Table of contents, introduction, abbreviations, guide to the main classes of the DDC, key to the Unesco subject divisions, statistics, text in classification order, index, subject index, list of publishers. All of the above except the subject index are given in English and Afrikaans. The subject index is in English only.

CATALOGUING RULES AND CLASSIFICATION SCHEMES USED: AACR2 is used in cataloguing since 1980. Afrikaans and multilingual works are catalogued in the official language of the title proper, as suggested by ICNB recommendation number 6. ISBD(M) was implemented in 1972.

From 1990, *SANB* uses DDC 20th ed. for its classification of titles, with the exception of 496 (African languages) and 896 (African literatures). A special schedule used in conjunction with the DDC has been compiled by D. Fivaz and P.E. Scott. These schedules are applied to the DDC number where there are instructions to add from Tables 5 or 6.

---

[1] The following is no longer valid and has been deleted from the introduction beginning with 1994: Also included are publications from Bophuthatswana, Ciskei, Transkei, Venda.
[2] "Introduction," *SANB* 1992, p. v.

LCSH is used in compiling the subject index.

ENTRY INFORMATION: Consecutive entry number, DDC number in upper left corner, author, title, place of publication, publisher, pagination, illustrations, size, series statement, notes, ISBN or ISSN, price, subject headings, accession number in lower right corner.

Symbols used: J = books for children and young people; schoolbooks; G = ceased or superseded publication; S = class number for series.

ARRANGEMENT: The main bibliography is arranged in a classified sequence according to the DDC system.

INDEXES: An alphabetical index includes author, editors, illustrators, compilers, joint authors, title (if significant) and series (if significant). Entries with an insignificant title are listed under the corporate body. From 1992, there is a subject index which uses *LCSH*, with "see" and "see also" references. Before 1992 there was no alphabetical subject index; subject access was gained by using the DDC schedules. Entries in the index were followed by the Dewey number and the main entry term, e.g., a work by George Randell was indexed under Randell, George: Gentlemen of the law - 340.0922 Randell.

The alphabetical index is as multilingual as possible. The subject index is in English only.

NOTES AND COMMENTS: The introduction to *SANB* is helpful in understanding the aims and contents of this national bibliography. With the first quarterly issue of 1994, the *SANB* has included a clear entry analysis which will help users to understand the bibliographic information presented.

Although government publications are not marked with a symbol, it is possible to look in the index under South Africa and then the issuing agency to locate many titles. It is also possible to identify many government publications by the accession number, e.g., OP/7583.

Subject headings are not assigned to the following: maps, periodicals, newspapers, school textbooks, and adult and children's literature, including fiction, short stories, school readers, drama, poetry, and collections. However, literary criticism, history, study guides, and similar publications do receive subject headings.[1]

The 1962 volume was the first volume to include book production statistics in South Africa. This is based on books received by the State Library as legal deposit.

The *SANB* has a weekly card service which consists of full entries for publications currently received, provided in standard catalogue format, together with additional information such as periodicals which have ceased publication. The card service has not included foreign publications about South Africa since 1983.

From September 1958-1969, the South African Public Library, Cape Town issued a quarterly publication called *Africana Nova*. This was based on the accessions of this library as well as legal deposit material. Previous to this, the library issued their *Quarterly Bulletin*, September

---

[1] "Introduction," *SANB* 1993, p. vi.

1946-June 1958. During the years 1959-1969, the *Africana Nova* and *SANB* duplicated each other to a great extent. There is one distinct difference, however, which may be helpful to remember. *Africana Nova* included titles about South Africa that were printed abroad. *SANB* includes titles published only in South Africa.[1]

Since the *SANB* does not include periodical articles and foreign publications within its scope, two titles which complement the *SANB* are as follows. *The Index to South African Periodicals = Repertorium van Suid-Afrikaanse Tydskrifartikeis* (Johannesburg : State Library, 1940-   ) is done in collaboration with Johannesburg Public Library, CSIR, Human Sciences Research Council, Medical Research Council and University of South Africa. *Bibliografie van Buitelandse Publikasies oor Suid-Afrika, Insluitende Publikasies van Suid-Afrikaners en Vertalings van Suid-Afrikaanse Werke in die Buiteland Uitgegee = Bibliography of Overseas Publications about South Africa, including Publications by South Africans and Translations of South African Works Published Abroad. - 1972-1978/80.* Pretoria: State Library, 1974-1981. This lists titles about South Africa "acquired by the State Library, including *inter alia* foreign publications about South Africa or with content relating to South Africa."[2]

LATEST ISSUE EXAMINED/CURRENCY: The 1993 annual cumulation, the latest volume consulted, was published in 1994 and received at the University Library, Cambridge, England, on 28 April 1994. The latest quarterly issue consulted is Jan./Mar. 1994. Quarterly issues that were checked all arrived four to five months from the period of time covered in the *SANB* issue. With this timeliness, the *SANB* could be used as an acquisitions tool as well as an historical record.

About fifty percent of the entries were for the year covered, with most of the remainder of the entries from the previous year. As mentioned above, the scope includes the current year plus the previous two years.

AUTOMATION: In 1968, *SANB* was one of the first national bibliographies to become computerized. With the 1983 volume, the State Library took over all aspects of production of the national bibliography. From 1988 the *SANB* is compiled on the DOBIS/LIBIS (Dortmunder Bibliothekssystem/Leuvens Integraal Bibliotheek Systeem) computer system.

FORMATS AND SERVICES AVAILABLE: printed; *SANB* is available online on SABINET as a separate *SANB* database since May 1991 (records from 1989 onwards); magnetic tape.

CURRENT LEGAL DEPOSIT LAWS: Legal Deposit of Publications Act, no. 17 of 1982, promulgated in 1984.[3]

AVAILABLE FROM: State Library, P.O. Box 397, Pretoria 0001.

---

[1] R. Musiker, "South African Bibliography: A Review," *College & Research Libraries* 24 (Nov. 1963):497-498 .

[2] Shirley Behrens, "National Bibliographic Control in South Africa," *Mousaion* 9:1 (1991):50.

[3] "Introduction," *SANB* 1992, p. v, and from a 12 April 1994 letter to the author by Barbara Kellerman, Programme Manager, Bibliographic Control, The State Library, Pretoria.

SELECTED ARTICLES: Behrens, Shirley, "National Bibliographic Control in South Africa," *Mousaion* 9:1 (1991):42-54.

Westra, P.E., Zaaiman, R.B. "The Two National Libraries of South Africa." *Alexandria* 3: (2 Aug. 1991), pp. 101-119.

VERIFIER: Barbara Kellerman, Programme Manager, Bibliographic Control, The State Library, Pretoria.

SPAIN

TITLE: *Bibliografía española. Monografías.* - Enero 1993-   . - Madrid : Biblioteca Nacional, 1993-   .
Monthly, with annual cumulative indexes.
Continues: *Bibliografía española.* - 1958-1992.
DDC: 015.46 B583;   UDC: 015(460);   LC: Z2685.B583;   LCCN: 96-655589;   OCLC: 32873083
ISSN 1133-858X

COMPILER: Biblioteca Nacional.

SCOPE AND COVERAGE: *Bibliografía Española. Monografías (BE.M)* lists the materials produced in Spain and deposited at the National Library according to legal deposit legislation.

Types of publications included in *BE.M* are books, pamphlets, brochures, official and government publications, limited editions, annual reports, atlases, theses and dissertations (when printed), conference proceedings, exposition catalogues, other works of a selective character.

Maps and plans, periodicals, printed music and voice recordings are included in supplements to *BE.M*, described under the Notes and Comments section.

Currently "grabados, dibujos, fotografías, y videograbacione" are included only in the *ARIADNA* database.[1]

Excluded are IGO publications, "las publicaciones menores" (such as festival programs, popular consumer literature known as "literatura de quiosco"), and items that require special treatment such as stamps, standards and patents, opera scores [partituras], periodical and newspaper articles.

CONTENTS: Introduction, abbreviations used in the text, index of subject headings as they appear in the text, classified bibliography, with juvenile literature at the end of the bibliography, indexes for author, subject, title, and series.

---

[1] Information from a letter dated 10 April 1995 to the author by Pilar Dominguez, Biblioteca Nacional.

CATALOGUING RULES AND CLASSIFICATION SCHEMES USED: Bibliographic description is according to ISBD(M). From 1985, *Reglas de Catalogación*. - Madrid : Ministerio de Cultura, Dirección General del Libro y Bibliotecas has been used. It apppeared in two volumes: volume 1 covered monographs and serial publications, volume 2 covered bibliographic descriptions of non-book materials. The revised edition of *Reglas de Catalogación* (ISSN 84-8181-065-7) was published in 1995 and includes rules for monographs, periodicals and special materials in one volume.

The classification scheme used is UDC. Subject headings used are from *Lista de encabezamientos de materia para Bibliotecas Públicas*.

ENTRY INFORMATION: Consecutive entry number in upper left corner, ARIADNA database number, e.g., BNE19921877845, in upper right corner, author, title, place of publication, publisher, date, pagination, size, series statement, notes including index, bibliography notes, legal deposit number, and ISBN, subject headings, added entries, UDC number at lower left corner.

Before the use of ARIADNA numbers, the legal deposit number, e.g., B. 4560-1978; M. 2272-1978, appeared in the upper right corner.

ARRANGEMENT: Arranged alphabetically by main entry within UDC subject groups. Children's literature appears at the end of the bibliography under UDC 087.5.

INDEXES: Since 1987, the *BE* (1958-1992) monthly issues have author, subject and title indexes. In 1992 a series index was added. The number refers to the bibliographic entry number in the main section. The cumulative annual indexes cover author, subject, title and series. The numbers used in the index refer to the bibliographic entry number. Before the mid-1980s, the annual index of *BE* (1958-1992) was arranged alphabetically; authors and translators names were entered in upper and lower case, titles were in italics, and subject entries were all in upper case.

NOTES AND COMMENTS: *BE.M* continues *Bibliografía española* (Madrid, Spain 1958). - 1958-dic. 1992. - Madrid : Ministerio de Educación Nacional, Dirección General de Archivos y Bibliotecas, Servicio Nacional de Información Bibliográfica, 1959-1992. Frequency varies (LCCN: 60-44645//r963; OCLC: 1519739). This title absorbed *Boletín del Depósito Legal de Obras Impresas* (ISSN 0006-6362; OCLC: 5580333).

The *BE* from 1958-1968 was compiled by Servicio Nacional de Información Bibliográfica, Biblioteca Nacional directed by Justo García Morales; the *BE* from 1969-1985 was compiled by Instituto Bibliográfico Hispánico directed by Vicente Sánchez. During this time it became the Nacional Bibliographic Agency. The *BE* (from1986) is compiled by Bibliographic Control Department, Biblioteca Nacional. Both publisher and frequency vary.

There were no volumes of *BE* published for 1964, 1965 and 1966, 1991 and only annual volumes were published for 1977, 1978, and 1987.[1] (OCLC: 1519739); Annual (ISSN 0523-

---

[1] This was verified in a 8 March 1995 letter to the author from Pilar Domínguez, Biblioteca Nacional.

1760); monthly (ISSN 0525-3675). The scope of *BE* (1958-1992) is continued by the new *BE.M.*

Since 1991 the *BE.M* is a subproduct of the ARIADNA database, the *BE. Publicaciones Periódicas* is a subproduct since 1994. Issues of *BE. Musica* and *BE. Cartografía* have been subproducts since December 1995. Information for subproduct titles are as follows.

BE. Monografías. Indices acumulativos. - 1993-   . - Madrid : Biblioteca Nacional, 1994-   . Annual. (UDC: 015(460); ISSN 1133-8563).

BE. Publicaciones periódicas. - 1993-   . - Madrid : Biblioteca Nacional, 1994-   continues *BE. Suplemento de publicaciones periódicas* / Instituto Bibliográfico Hispánico. – 1979-1992. – Madrid : Ministerio de Cultura, Dirección General del Libro y Bibliotecas, Subdirección General de Bibliotecas, Biblioteca Nacional. - 1979-1994 (ISSN 0210-8372). The new title is an annual publication which includes new periodical titles and periodical title changes published in Spain. Contents include general index (table of contents), introduction, index of subject headings which appear in the text, index of corporate and personal authors, index of titles. Bibliographic descriptions follow ISBD(S) and are arranged by UDC, then alphabetically by titles. (UDC: 016:(05)(460), 015(460); ISSN 1134-6620).

BE. Cartografía. - 1989/1991-   . - Madrid : Ministerio de Cultura, Biblioteca Nacional, 1994- (ISSN 1133-9519; OCLC: 32298886) continues *BE. Suplemento de cartografía.* – 1980/1987- . – Madrid : Ministerio de Cultura, Dirección General del Libro y Bibliotecas, Subdirección General de Bibliotecas, Biblioteca Nacional, 1989-   (ISSN 0214-4441). This earlier title's first issue covers 1980 to 1987 but is not retrospective before 1980.

The new title is an annual publication which includes maps and plans published in Spain. Not included in this supplement are atlases which are listed with books in *BE*, and minor publications within the scope. Contents include introduction, abbreviations used, index of subject headings that appear in the text, text, index of authors (includes both personal and corporate), subjects and places. Arranged by geographical area, then by type or kind of map, and date.

BE. Música impresa. - Madrid : Ministerio de Cultura, Biblioteca Nacional, 1995-   (ISSN 1135-7223; OCLC: 35297825) continues *BE. Suplemento de música impresa.* - 1985/1986 -   . - Madrid : Biblioteca Nacional, 1990-   continues *BE. Suplemento de música impresa.* -1985/1986-   . - Madrid : Ministerio de Cultura, Dirección General del Libro y Bibliotecas, Subdirección General de Bibliotecas, Biblioteca Nacional, 1990-   (LCCN: 91-655665/MN/r96; OCLC: 23134037; ISSN 1130-1392). This annual title includes printed music published in Spain. It does not include voice recordings which will be covered in another supplement.[1]

An excellent bibliography which lists publications from Catalonia is *Bibliografia national de Catalunya.* - No. 1/2 (1982)-   . - Barcelona, Departament de Cultura de la Generalitat de Catalunya, 1983-   . Quarterly (OCLC: 11587892; ISSN 0212-307X) This title lists monographs, sound recordings, and audio-visual materials published or produced during the period covered which arrive at the Institut Català de Bibliografia according to legal deposit regulations. Not included are periodicals, maps, theses, commercial exhibition catalogs,

---

[1] Dominguez letter.

ephemeral material, and since the end of 1988, most pamphlets, textbooks, reimpressions when the original is already listed, and newsstand literature. Entries are alphabetically listed with UDC arrangement, as adapted for use for Catalonia. Author/title index, and subject index are included. Bibliographic format is in CATMARC and bibliographic description follows ISBD(M). *Bibliografia nacional de Catalunya. Publicacions en sèries.* - Barcelona, Departament de Cultura de la Generalitat de Catalunya, 1983- is an annual supplement (OCLC: 11669157; ISSN 0212-5846).

LATEST ISSUE EXAMINED/CURRENCY: The majority of imprints are for the period covered, with some entries for one year earlier.

The latest monthly issue examined is for December 1994 sent to the author from the Biblioteca Nacional. The latest monthly issue examined at the University Library, Cambridge in November
1994 was the issue for January/June 1992. The latest annual issue examined at the University Library, Cambridge is for 1990. Monthly issues at the University Library were received an average of over two years from date of coverage.

AUTOMATION: In 1971 the Biblioteca Nacional initiated automation.[1] The name of the current database is ARIADNA; since 1991 the library management system software used by the Biblioteca Nacional is SIRTEX.[2]

FORMAT AND SERVICES AVAILABLE: paper, CD-ROM (*Bibliografía Nacional Española desde 1976 en CD-ROM,* OCLC: 31625809), magnetic tape, diskette, streamer, online using *Bibliografiá Española* database displayed in the IBERMARC format. The Biblioteca Nacional has a "Records Distribution Service" which offers bibliographic records in IBERMARC, UNIMARC, ISBD, and in paper, magnetic tape, streamer, and disk. It will also produce products for specific customer needs.

The OPAC is available via Internet at the following IP address: 193.144.3.10

By late 1995 *ARIADNA* also can be accessed by using x.25 or x.28 protocols.

Internet users can telnet: Aridana.bne.es

CURRENT LEGAL DEPOSIT LAWS: Decreto 642/1970 (*Boletín Oficial del Estado. Gazeta del Madrid* (BOE) de 16 marzo); Decreto 2984/1972 de 2 noviembre (BOE de 4 de noviembre); Ordenes Ministerial de 30 de octobre de 1971 (BOE de 18 de noviembre) y 20 de febrero de 1973 (BOE de 3 de marzo).[3] In the introduction of the 1989 BE Depósito legal V2.602-1968 is also mentioned.

AVAILABLE FROM: printed: BiblioLibrería (Biblioteca Nacional) Paseo de Recoletos, 20, 28001 Madrid.

---

[1] "Introducción," *Bibliografía Española.* Monografías. Indices acumulativos, p. III (1994).
[2] Information received in a letter dated 6 March 1995 from Pilar Domínguez, Biblioteca Nacional.
[3] *Survey of Existing Legal Deposit Laws,* p. 69

CD-ROM: distributed from Chadwyck-Healey España SL, Juan Bravo, 18, 28006 Madrid.

More information on other products mentioned under Formats and Services Available: Biblioteca Nacional. Unidad de Coordinación Informática, Paseo de Reoletos, 20-22, 28071 Madrid, España. Tel.: 34-1-580 78 86; fax: + 34-1-580 78 73; e-mail address: uci.correo@bne.es

VERIFIER: Pilar Domínguez, Biblioteca Nacional.

SRI LANKA

TITLE: *Śrī Laṅkā jātia grvntha nāmavaliya = Ilaṅkait tēcīya nūṟpattiyal = Sri Lanka national bibliography*. - No. 5/12, 1972-   . - [Kolamba, Śrī Lanka Jatikā Pustakāla Sēvā Maṇḍalaya, etc.], 1972-   .
Frequency varies: monthly (1994-   ), quarterly (1972-1993) with annual index cumulation.
Continues *Ceylon national bibliography*, and assumes its numbering.
Publisher varies; under former title: National Bibliography Division of the National Archives.
Text in English, Sinhala or Tamil.
DDC: 015.5493; UDC: 015 (548.7); LC: Z3211.A3; DS489; LCCN: 77-912495/SA; OCLC: 3582032
ISSN 0253-8229

COMPILER: National Library of Sri Lanka.

SCOPE AND COVERAGE: The *Śrī Laṅkā jātia grvntha nāmavaliya = Ilaṅkait tēcīya nūṟpattiyal = Sri Lanka national bibliography.= Sri Lanka National Bibliography* (SLNB) is an authoritative bibliographical record of current Sri Lanka publishing in Sinhala, Tamil and English. It is based upon the material deposited at the National Library of Sri Lanka according to the legal deposit legislation, voluntary deposit copies received by the National Library under the ISBN project, and information on new publications received from the publications division of the National Library and Sri Lankan publishers.

Types of publications included in *SLNB* are books, pamphlets, periodicals (first issue or title change until 1973; currently, *SLNB* lists first issues), official and government publications, conference transactions, atlases, translations, standards, finding aids (guides, inventories, checklists, indexes, etc.) published by archival and manuscript repositories, manuals, handbooks and other publications of records management agencies.

Excluded from *SLNB* are reprints, audiovisual material, periodical articles, theses, musical scores, microforms, maps, general ephemera, works under four pages.

CONTENTS: Preface including information about coverage and arrangement, list of abbreviations, outline of the DDC, cataloguing information for *Sri Lanka National Bibliography*, bibliography, indexes for each of the three language sections, forthcoming publications.

CATALOGUING RULES AND CLASSIFICATION SCHEMES USED: AACR2 is used for cataloguing. Subject indexing method is based on the "Chain Procedure."

The classification scheme used is DDC (20th ed.). When the DDC number is not specific, verbal extensions have been added to render the subject more specific. Area notations are added only to specify countries other than Sri Lanka.

ENTRY INFORMATION: DDC number and heading, author, title, place of publication, publisher, date, pagination, size, series statement, notes including language, binding, price, accessions number and ISBN when known. In lower right corner is a number, letters and numbers, or letters in parentheses, e.g., 253882; NL 54270; ISBNP.

ARRANGEMENT: The bibliography is arranged in three parts: Sinhala, Tamil and English. Each part consists of a bibliography in a classified arrangement based on DDC subjects with an accompanying alphabetical index of authors, titles and subjects.

INDEXES: Author/title/series index and subject index is available in each of the three languages included in *SLNB*. Each index only includes entries in that language. Numbers refer the user to the DDC number.

Earlier issues (before 1990) included the author, title, series, subject index in one alphabetical sequence for each of the language sections.

Beginning in 1975, there are annual index cumulations.

NOTES AND COMMENTS: *SLNB* continues *The Ceylon national bibliography = Ilaṅkait tēcīya nūṟpattiyal = Laṅkā jātika grantha nāmavaliya-* Vol. 1, no. 1 (1963)-vol. 10, no. 4 (1972). Nugeboda, Department of National Archives and the Ceylon National Library Services Board, 1963-1972. Frequency varies (LCCN: sn80-74; OCLC:1749253; ISSN 0009-0883).

The *SLNB* has made several improvements since the 1980s: the outline of the DDC, the increase in frequency from a quarterly to a monthly, and the addition of forthcoming publications. It would be helpful to have a table of contents at the beginning of each issue, especially since there are three separate sections. It would also be useful to include an analyzed entry in the introduction. Although most information is standard, it is not clear what the numbers and letters in parentheses in the lower right corner are called. Also not included is a publishers' list which would be a nice enhancement.

Before *SLNB* was established, the *Register of Books Printed in Ceylon and Registered under Ordinance No. 1 of 1885*. - Colombo : Government Printing Works, 1889-1908 and *Catalogue of Books*. - Nugegoda : Office of the Registrar of Books and Newspapers helped to serve as a source for current titles based on legal deposit. Some numbers of the *Catalogue of Books* have been issued as a supplement to the country's *Government Gazette*.

Since the national bibliography does not include periodical articles, it is worth mentioning *Śri Laṅkā saṅgaṟā lipi suciya = Sri Lanka Periodicals Index: A Subject Guide to Current Periodical Literature Covering Articles in Sinhala and English Periodicals Published in Sri Lanka Received Through the Department of National Archives of Sri Lanka under Section 4 of the Printers and Publishers Ordinance*. - Colombo : National Museum Library, 19??-   . Three nos. a year. Text in English or Sinhalese. (LCCN: sn84-11916; OCLC: 8151619). This title continues *Ceylon periodicals index*. - Colombo, 1969-19?? (OCLC4485517).

SLNB does not participate in CIP.

AL,SA included Sri Lanka within its scope.

LATEST ISSUE EXAMINED/CURRENCY: The latest issue examined at the University Library, Cambridge in April 1995 was for no. 12, December 1994. It was received 10 April 1995.

In looking at several pages of entries, most have 1994 imprints, with some for 1993.

Delays in publishing, inadequate coverage of publications, and limited circulation are mentioned as problems experienced by *SLNB*.[1] If the above is any indication of timeliness, it appears as if the National Library of Sri Lanka is overcoming some of the problems.

AUTOMATION: not known.

FORMAT AND SERVICES AVAILABLE: printed.

CURRENT LEGAL DEPOSIT LAWS: Printers and Publishers Ordinance of 1 April 1885, with amendments from 1951, the latest listed being Chapter 175, Amendment Law No. 6 of 1976.[2]

AVAILABLE FROM: National Library of Sri Lanka, P.O. Box 1764, 14 Independence Avenue, Colombo 07.

SELECTED ARTICLES: Senadeera, Aryaratne. "A National Bibliography for Sri Lanka." In *Libraries and People: Colombo Public Library 1925-1975, a Commemorative Volume*. pp.107-111. Colombo: Municipal Council of Colombo, 1975.

VERIFIER: no reply received.

SUDAN

TITLE: *al-Fihris al-muṣannaf li-majmū'ar al-Sūdān. The classified catalogue of the Sudan collection in the University of Khartoum Library*. 1971- . Khartoum : Jamiat al-Khartum. al-Maktabah (University of Khartoum Library), 1971- .
Irregular.
DDC: not found; LC: Z3665.K48; LCCN: 72-980058; OCLC: 5212304
ISSN not found

---

1 Amarasiri, M. S. U. "The National Library of Sri Lanka. An Introduction." In *National Library of Sri Lanka. Commemorative volume*, p. 60.
2 *BSTW, 1975-1979*, p. 380.

COMPILER: University of Khartoum Library.

SCOPE AND COVERAGE: The *al-Fihris al-muṣannaf li-majmū'ar al-Sūdān. The Classified Catalogue of the Sudan Collection* (*CCSC*) lists titles in the Sudan Collection of the University of Khartoum Library, which includes legal deposit materials since 1966.

Types of publications listed within the scope are books, pamphlets, official and government publications, periodicals, newspapers, theses accepted for higher degrees from the University of Khartoum, and from foreign universities on studies relating to the Sudan or by Sudanese.

CONTENTS: Preface in Arabic and in English, Part 1: The classification scheme (in English); Part 2: The classified catalogue (in English); Part 3: author index (in English and in Arabic); Part 4: relative index (in English and in Arabic).

CATALOGUING RULES AND CLASSIFICATION SCHEMES USED: The cataloguing rules are not stated in the preface. Entries include the basic bibliographic elements.

The classification is by the "special scheme" used for classification of material in the Sudan library. ("Preface"in English.)

ENTRY INFORMATION: Entry number, author, title, edition, place of publication, publisher, date, pages, illustrations, occasional notes, internal number (e.g., [case 1801], [118275], [theses - microfilm]) in upper right corner.

ARRANGEMENT: The classified catalogue (part 2) is alphabetically arranged.

INDEXES: Author index, relative index. (This index gives the classification number under which the relevant literature on a subject is found.)

NOTES AND COMMENTS: A national bibliography for Sudan was not found. The *CCSC* has been analyzed as a substitute. According to the preface, the old Secretariat Library which once formed part of the Intelligence Department Library is the nucleus of the Sudan Collection in the University of Khartoum Library. Since 1966 it has been supplemented by legal deposit material.

"Although interrupted files of newspapers were kept in the collection it is only since 1966 that newspapers began to be kept regularly. Newspaper files are listed at the end of the catalogue." ("Preface.")

This listing is "perhaps for the first time a complete list of all Sudan Government publications—current and retrospective". ("Preface.")

This present *CCSC* could be considered the retrospective *Sudan National Bibliography*, with future supplements becoming the current national bibliography. ("Preface.")

Plans for future supplements of *CCSC* will include a catalogue of the Sudan maps in the collection and a catalogue of the Sudan Archives. ("Preface.")

The second supplement (1974) is the latest available for *CCSC*. The third and the fourth supplements have been at the printers for a while. Compilation is delayed by personnel shortage.[1]

CCSC has been produced by reproducing in reduced size the library card forms on the paper and then duplicating.

It would be helpful if the preface of *CCSC* could include an analyzed entry so that various parts of the entry could be properly labelled and understood by the user.

In searching the literature for additional information, various editions of *Theses on the Sudan* has been published by the Khartoum University Press from the mid-1960s to the beginning of the 1980s. The *National Register of Current Research* (is also a source for research done in or on the Sudan during the 1980s. The first reference found in OCLC was for the 1982/1983 volume. Subsequent supplements for 1983/84/85 and 1985/1986 have been published. (OCLC: 18203783, OCLC: 28377202).[2]

Another interesting source is *La République Démocratique du Soudan: bilan des recherches en France et en R.F.A.: bibliographie sélective 1900-1986* / Talaat El-Singaby. (Travaux et documents de l'I.R.E.M.A.M.; no. 4). (LCCN: 93-189399; OCLC: 22325108) It includes sources in France about Sudan.

AL,EA, vol.1, no.1(Jan. 1968)- vol. 25, no. 6 (Nov./Dec. 1992) included Sudan within its scope. (ISSN 0090-371X).

LATEST ISSUE EXAMINED/CURRENCY: Entries for the first issue were not intended to be current. Supplements will include more current entries.

The latest issue examined is the 1971 catalogue.

AUTOMATION: not automated.

FORMAT AND SERVICES AVAILABLE: printed.

CURRENT LEGAL DEPOSIT LAWS: Work Deposit Act of 1966 amended in 1971 and 1978, according to Beaudiquez, *BSTW, 1975-1979.*

AVAILABLE FROM: Inquiries addressed to the Sudan Collection, University of Khartoum Library, P.O. Box 321, Khartoum.

---

1 Information taken from a letter dated 11 September 1985 to the author by James Armstrong, Field Director, Library of Congress Office, Nairobi, Kenya. Libraries who have this title do not necessarily have the supplements; the University of Texas, Austin has the first supplement dated 1973.

2 The *National Register of Current Research* is cited in Cecile Wesley's article "National Information Policies and Networks in Morocco, Tunisia, Egypt and Sudan: A Comparative Study." *Alexandria* 2 (3 1990):31.

VERIFIER: no reply received.

SURINAME

No current national bibliography was traced for Suriname.
Two works record Suriname publications. Both are published in Leiden, The Netherlands by the Department of Caribbean Studies, Royal Institute of Linguistics and Anthropology. *Suriname, a bibliography, 1940-1980* / Gerard A. Nagelkerke. 1980 (LCCN: 82-140482; OCLC: 7355451). This 1980 work is a revised and updated edition of *Literatuur-overzicht van Suriname, 1940 tot 1970* (LCCN: 94-213851, OCLC: 31295600), and *Suriname, a bibliography, 1980-1989* / Jo Derkz & Irene Rolfes, published in 1990 (LCCN: 90-214342; OCLC: 22763968).

Caribbean Collection Quarterly Accession List (OCLC: 10857911) includes Suriname within its scope.

SWAZILAND

TITLE: *Swaziland national bibliography.* - 1973/1976-   . - Kwaluseni : University of Swaziland, 1977-   .
Irregular.
DDC: 015.681; LC: Z3560.S93; LCCN: 80-646437; OCLC: 3812657
ISSN 0378-7710

COMPILER: Professional staff members of the University Library, University of Swaziland are responsible for the compilation and editing of the national bibliography: D.R. Steinhauer, 1973/1976; Lynne Thorn and other professional staff of the University Library, University of Swaziland, 1978/1982; professional staff members of the University Library, University of Swaziland, 1983/1985; H. Dua-Agyemang, 1986/1987.

SCOPE AND COVERAGE: The scope of *Swaziland National Bibliography* (*SNB*) as stated in the 1978/1982 volume is to include all official and semi-official publications in Swaziland and abroad. However, recent issues appear to include titles published in Swaziland only.

Types of publications included in the 1986/1987 volume are monographs, monographic series, official and government publications, and serials not included in previous issues.

Omissions include certain ephemeral items and items regarded as confidential when permission has not been granted to be listed. With the 1986/1987 volume, the types of publications excluded in the national bibliography have increased. Dissertation and theses appendixes, periodical and newspaper articles on Swaziland, conference papers, and research in progress are not included as in earlier volumes. According to the Introduction, it is envisaged that these formats will be included in future University Library publications.[1]

CONTENTS: 1986/1987: Introduction, bibliography, annuals and other serial publications, appendix (comprising items inadvertently omitted from previous *SNB*s, 1978-1985), index, list of publishers.

Earlier editions included a DDC guide and appendices representing a broader coverage as follows: Preface; guide to DDC; text in systematic arrangement; appendix I: foreign publications on Swaziland; appendix II: research in progress and some future publications; appendix III: Swaziland legislation; appendix IV: copyright (amendment) order, 1978; appendix V: bibliographies of bibliographies; index; list of publishers.

CATALOGUING RULES AND CLASSIFICATION SCHEMES USED: Entries are compiled according to AACR2.

The DDC (19th ed.) is used to classify entries. The only deviation is use of the 18th edition area numbers for Swaziland.

ENTRY INFORMATION: Main bibliography: entry number, e.g., 92, in upper left corner, DDC in upper right corner, author, title, place of publication, publisher, date, pagination, illustration statement, series, notes, and brief annotation.

Annuals and other serial publications appendix: Entry number in upper left corner, responsible agency, title, place of publication, publisher, date, illustration statement, frequency.

Appendix: same as the main bibliography, but without DDC number.

ARRANGEMENT: The main bibliography is arranged by DDC, then alphabetically by main entry. The section Annuals and Other Serial Publications is arranged alphabetically; the Appendix is arranged chronologically.

Appendixes in earlier issues were arranged as follows. Appendix I is alphabetically arranged under types of publications, e.g., books, dissertations and theses, conference papers, etc., except the newspaper articles list which is chronologically arranged; Appendix II is alphabetically arranged; Appendix III is numerically arranged under the two forms of legislation, King's Orders-in-Council, and Legal Notices. Following the lists is a chronological table of the legislation cited; Appendix V is alphabetically arranged by main entry.

INDEXES: 1986/1987: Index includes authors and titles for entries in the main bibliography, annuals and other serial publications, and appendix. Government departments and ministries are listed under Swaziland, followed by the name of the department or ministry. Paratatal bodies are listed under their proper names.

---

[1] The next issue of *SNB* covering 1988-1994/95 will include dissertations, articles, and papers within its scope, according to Z.G. Ngcobo, Acting University Librarian.

In the 1978-1982 volume, the index includes authors and titles for entries in the main bibliography and appendix I, and includes only authors for appendix II. The number supplied refers the user to the entry number.

The 1977 index only included author/title entries for the main bibliography.

NOTES AND COMMENTS: *SNB* had a new look beginning with the 1978/1982 volume. It changed printing arrangements from the State Library, Pretoria, South Africa, to Swaziland printers. The "Bibliography of Bibliographies," a new feature in this issue but which does not appear in the 1986/1987 edition, includes bibliographies on and about Swaziland. Most of the material listed covers Botswana, Lesotho and Swaziland, Africa as a whole and the Commonwealth countries. This section should aid researchers in locating sources of information. There are some features from earlier volumes which are missing from the 1978/1982 one. According to the compiler, this is due to lack of time and space. Most notably missing is the Swaziland law reports section which is expected to appear in an independent volume in the future.

SNB has a problem with publishers not observing the legal deposit amendment legislation. A copy of the legal deposit law is included in Appendix VI of *SNB* 1977 and Appendix IV of the 1978/1982 volume, but does not appear in the 1986/1987 edition. Staff shortages are also a problem; this problem, combined with having to find published materials which have not been deposited, has been one reason for delay of the volumes which were intended to be annual.

Government publications are not marked by a special symbol. One is able to look in the index under Swaziland and then under the government bodies which are alphabetically listed under the Swaziland heading.

Each appendix has different guidelines for material included and the time period covered. Foreign imprints in all forms are listed together in Appendix I, 1977 and 1978/1982. The volume for 1973/76 included only books and dissertations; Appendix I, 1978/1982 includes books, dissertations and theses, articles in periodicals, articles in newspapers and conference papers. In 1986/1987, the appendix covers items omitted from previous *SNBs*.

As stated earlier, the scope of the *SNB* has narrowed beginning with the 1986/1987 volume. However, it may be useful to note the following about the previously included categories. The 1977 volume includes the first attempt to list articles on Swaziland found in periodicals and covers 1973-1977. The "Conference papers on Swaziland" section in the 1977 volume includes papers delivered at conferences between 1973-1977. The list for dissertations and theses in 1977 covers 1930-1977.

Although *SNB* has problems in its production, it can not be faulted for including many helpful bits of information that are elusive otherwise. This broad coverage is the result of the compilers feeling that *SNB* should "serve a greater purpose than a pure national bibliography."[1] It is also anticipated that each volume of *SNB* will introduce a new feature to enhance its value to users. In reality, however, the latest issue is more limited in scope and coverage than earlier issues. One hopes that the envisaged University Library publications materialize to give Swaziland wider bibliographic control of its publications. In future issues, if new publications are not

---

[1] D.R. Steinhauer, "Preface," *SNB* 1977: iii.

immediately forthcoming, it may be preferable to include a wider scope in *SNB* and eliminate time spent on the annotations recently added to the national bibliography.[1]

ISBNs are also being retrospectively assigned to books, thus an ISBN may not appear on a book, but will appear in the *SNB*. The 1986/1987 does not include ISBNs.

All SiSwati publications, whether published abroad or in the country are included in the main bibliography.

Serves in part to supplement the monograph *Swaziland Official Publications, 1880-1972: A Bibliography*, which was prepared by the State Library, Pretoria, 1975 (OCLC: 3145482).[2]

A helpful source of bibliographic information is the *Accessions List* of the Swaziland National Library (OCLC: 27428271).

The *AL,ESA* and *QIPL,ESA* include Swaziland within their scopes.

LATEST ISSUE EXAMINED/CURRENCY: The 1986/1987 volume was published in 1989. This is the latest volume examined.[3]

Because of the irregularity of serial publications in Swaziland and because of the ineffective legal deposit laws, many titles belonging in a previous volume are not discovered until later. When thought to be useful, these titles are included in the current volume.

Although the emphasis in the main bibliography section is on listing current years, entries from earlier years also appear; scopes of the appendices allow certain types of materials to range from 1930 to 1982.

AUTOMATION: not automated.

FORMATS AND SERVICES AVAILABLE: printed.

CURRENT LEGAL DEPOSIT LAWS: Copyright Act, No. 36 of 1912, as amended in the Copyright (Amendment) Act of 1978. The legal deposit legislation is not effective.

AVAILABLE FROM: The Librarian, University of Swaziland, Private Bag 4, Kwaluseni, Swaziland.

VERIFIER: M.R. Mavuso, University of Swaziland Library.

---

[1] In a letter to the author dated 10 July 1996, Z.G. Ngcobo stated that the next issue will not be annotated.

[2] Note included as part of OCLC number 3812657.

[3] Ngcobo stated that the next issue will cover 1988/1994-95; publication is planned in 1996.

SWEDEN

TITLE: *Svensk bokförteckning = The Swedish national bibliography.* - Jan. 1953-   . - Stockholm : Tidningsaktiebolaget Svensk bokhandel, 1953-   .
Frequency varies: six issues yearly 19<76>-   (Jan./Feb., Mar./Apr., May/July, Aug./Sept., Oct., Nov./Dec.), annual cumulation (*Årskatalog*), five or ten year cumulations (varies): *Svensk Bokkatalog.*
Cumulated from weekly entries in: *Svensk bokhandel.*
Supersedes an earlier publication with the same title, issued 1913-1952 (OCLC: 1777572), and *Årskatalog för Svenska bokhandeln* issued 1861-1952 (OCLC: 2010593, ISSN 0349-442X).
DDC: not found; UDC: 015(485); LC Z2625.S952; LCCN: 54-3266//r81; OCLC: 1642087
ISSN 0039-6443
COMPILER: Kungliga Biblioteket

SCOPE AND COVERAGE: *Svensk Bokförteckning = The Swedish National Bibliography* (*SB*) lists the material supplied to the Royal Library by publishers and other organizations, and supplemented with legal deposit copies sent to the Library by the country's printers. From and including 1984, *SB* will also include material that earlier had been listed only in the cumulated *Svensk bokkatalog.*

Types of publications included in *SB* are books, pamphlets, doctoral dissertations, maps (in book form) and atlases, selected yearbooks and special occasion periodical publications, teaching materials for schools, mimeographed and similarly produced works comparable with printed books, electronic publications, first volumes of new annuals, certain registers of people, and Swedish publications from regular publishers in Finland. Works of less than 16 pages are listed only when they are part of a series listed in full or are regular articles from publishers. Swedish Government public official reports, and Sveriges officiella statistik [Swedish official statistics] and matters published by administrative authorities for general dissemination are also included.

Periodicals, music scores, and Swedish fiction and children's literature in translation, plus works about Sweden in foreign languages are included in other national bibliography titles discussed in the Notes and Comments section below. Maps not in book form are included from 1986 onward in "Svensk kartförteckning" [Swedish printed maps], which is published as an appendix to the *Årskatalog.*

Excluded from *SB* are national and municipal administrative publications, such as parliamentary and committee minutes, authority statutes and circulars, military manuals, regulations and instructions; IGO publications, sheet maps, most offprints (exceptions mentioned in "Vägledning"), teaching materials for correspondence courses, ordinary Swedish translations of the Bible and hymn books, price lists, internal publications, original works by Swedish authors in foreign languages published abroad, translations from Swedish which were published abroad, works about Sweden in foreign languages published abroad, street directories, tourist information, music scores unless they include teaching materials in text form, ephemera.

CONTENTS: Bi-monthly: foreword, alphabetical bibliography, systematic bibliography (shortened entry information), information, outline of classification scheme (in Swedish and English), publishers' address list (supplement), publishers' ISBN prefixes.

Annual: introduction (with summary in English), abbreviations, publishers' addresses, publishers' ISBN prefixes, alphabetical bibliography, systematic bibliography (shortened entry information), information, outline of classification scheme (in Swedish and English), author/title index, alphabetical arrangement of subject headings with symbols used, book statistics for current year, Swedish printed maps.

CATALOGUING RULES AND CLASSIFICATION SCHEMES USED: Since 1986, cataloguing rules used are *Katalogiseringsregler för Svenska Bibliotek*, in agreement with ISBD(M), ISBD(S). The rules are based on AACR2.[1]

The classification scheme used is that of the national classification scheme *Klassifikationssystem för Svenska Bibliotek.*[2]

ENTRY INFORMATION: Author (with dates if known), title, edition statement, place of publication, publisher, date, pagination, illustrations, size, series statement; notes including ISBN, ISSN if part of a series, price (if included), original title. First letters of classification letters preceded by a bracket are given to the right of the imprint information, e.g., [Bf, [Oha). These indicate placement of the entry in the systematic section; sometimes more than one location is given.

A bullet (•) in the left margin indicates that the title is published abroad.

An asterisk (*) indicates that the title is part of a series. These titles are not listed in the systematic section. However, in the section for yearbooks the title of the series is stated.

A plus mark (+) indicates that the title is catalogued directly for the bi-monthly issue, and thus has not been recorded in any previous weekly list in *Svensk Bokhandel.*

ARRANGEMENT: Bi-monthly and annual: full bibliographic information is given in the alphabetical author/title listing; shortened entries are given in the systematic arrangement, arranged by subjects.

INDEXES: Bi-monthly: no index.

Annual: subject index, with subjects arranged alphabetically.

NOTES AND COMMENTS: *SB* is printed from entries in *Svensk Bokhandel*, a weekly alphabetical list of new publications voluntarily contributed by publishers and other organizations. *Svensk Bokhandel* is the official organ of Svenska Förläggareföreningen and Svenska Bokhandlareföreningen. (LCCN: 54-29478; LC: Z407.S84; OCLC: 1643023; ISSN 0039-6451). The bi-monthly list, *SB*, is a cumulation of the weekly lists supplemented with the legal deposit titles. *SB* is cumulated into the annual bibliography *Årskatalog. Svensk Bokkatalog* is the five or ten year cumulation.

---

[1] "Introduction," *SB Årskatalog* 1993; also mentioned in "UBC News: Sweden," *International Cataloguing* 13 (no. 2 Apr./June 1984):14.

[2] *BSTW, Supplement 1980*, p. 93.

The Swedish national bibliography consists of *Svensk Bokförteckning*, *Svensk Bokkatalog*, *Svensk Musikförteckning*, *Suecana extranea* and *Svensk Periodicaförteckning*. *Svensk Bokförteckning* is analyzed above. Below are the others.

Svensk Bokkatalog is the five or ten year edition cumulated from *Årskatalog*. The latest edition covers a ten year period (1976-1985).[1] All information is available from the LIBRIS database.

Svensk musikförteckning [Swedish printed music]/ [Edited by the Royal Library. - Stockholm : Kungl. biblioteket, 1956- includes complete register of printed music, literature on music, and song texts. Annual (ISSN 0347-8289). The five-year cumulation is *Svensk musikkatalog* which supersedes *Uppslagsbok för svenska musikhandeln*. (LCCN: 54-29580; OCLC: 29744450). The first volume covers 1889.

Suecana extranea. - . Stockholm : Royal Library, 1968- . - Annual (LCCN: 88-640746//r91; LC: Z2633.3.S84, PT9550; OCLC: 1766777; ISSN 0039-4599). Includes books in foreign languages concerning Sweden and Swedish fiction and children's literature in translation. Original works by Swedish authors in foreign languages published abroad are not included in this series.[2]

Svensk periodicaförteckning : tidskrifter, årsböcker, dagstidningar och rapportserier = Current Swedish periodicals. - 1993/94- . - Stockholm : Royal Library, 1994- . Triennial (LCCN: 96-652207; LC: Z2625.S97; OCLC: 32144836; ISSN 1104-1102). The scope includes periodicals, newspapers, series of research reports, and annuals (formerly in *SB*). This title continues *Svensk tidskriftsförteckning.* - 1967/68-1991. - Stockholm : Royal Library, 1968-1991. Publisher varies. Triennial (LCCN: sf86-91018; LC: Z2626.S953; OCLC: 1766891; ISSN 0586-0431). Alphabetical and systematic sections. The 1979/80 list was published by manual methods; subsequent lists use LIBRIS.

Other titles of interest are listed below.

Svenska diskografier [Swedish discographies] is published by Arkivet för ljud och bild [the National Archive of Recorded Sound and Moving Images]. - 1983- . It resumes *Nationalfonotekets diskografier* [National Recording Library's discography]. - Stockholm : Royal Library, 1967-1978. (LC: 78-644174/MN/r82; OCLC: 6566805). This title was not discussed in *SB*. According to *BSTW, 1975-1979* (p.386) "all audio-visual material is listed in *Nationalfonotekets diskografier*, which is one of the components of the national bibliography." It was published by the Royal Library, 1967-1978. Recorded sound is also listed in *Svensk fonogramforteckning*, published by the National Archive of Recorded Sound and Moving Images, available in printed form 1992-1995, and from 1996- is available only online alongside but not within LIBRIS.

In *SB*, government publications are not designated by any symbols. According to the "Introduction" *SB* includes public official reports, Swedish official statistics, and other matter published by administrative authorities for general dissemination. A complete list of state

---

[1] According to Ingrid Cantwell, this volume may be the last accumulated volume to come out in print. "The Swedish Bibliographic Scene," *ICBC* 19 (2 1990):19

[2] "Introduction," *SB*, Nov./Dec. 1994.

publications is given in *Statliga publikationer : årsbibliografi* [Swedish Government publications : Annual bibliography]. - 1985- 1994. - Stockholm : Riksdagsbiblioteket, [Library of the Swedish Parliament] 1987-1995. Annual (LCCN: 87-642584; OCLC: 16411647).[1] This title continues *Sveriges statliga publikationer. Bibliografi.* - Arg. 46/48 (1976-1978)- arg. 54 (1984). - Stockholm : Allmänna förl., 1984-1985. Annual (LCCN: 84-650026//r87; LC: Z2629.S94J406; OCLC: 10961484; ISSN 0281-6725). This title continues *Årsbibliografi över Sveriges offentliga publikationer* [Annual bibliography of Swedish official publications]. - 1931/1933-1974/1975. - Uppsala : Fritzes hovbokh., 1934-1980. Annual (LCCN: 85-19118; OCLC: 1695097; ISSN 0347-9005). The entries are arranged alphabetically by authorities and institutions, with author, title and subject indexing. Material from 1995- is only available online via Rixlex (the database of the Swedish parliament).

Two big changes were effected in the 1970s for *SB:* using new cataloguing rules (1974) and preparing for the automation of *SB.* The combination of these two changes caused some difficult times as adjustments and readjustments were made by the staff. Some spin-offs of these new procedures caused temporary problems, such as the number of entries in *Årskatalog* actually decreasing during that time period, which did not accurately reflect the publishing output. Publication dates are now back on schedule. According to the "Vägledning" (1983 annual volume) the five year cumulations include additional titles not in the annual cumulations. However, the 1976-1985 *Svensk Bokkatalog* does not state that this is still the current practice. Since 1984 *SB* includes all material.

ICNB recommendations 5 to 11 and 13 are carried out in *SB.* The "Förord" in the bi-monthly issues (in Swedish only) and the "Vägledning" (with a brief English summary included) in the annual includes information specific to the use of the title. An explanation of proper alphabetization of unique Swedish alphabet letters is given. An analyzed entry is included in both. In the bi-monthly and annual issues, there is a thorough explanation of the "Systematisk Avdelning" listing what is included or not included under various subject categories, something which is helpful to those users not familiar with the *Klassifikationssystem för Svenska Bibliotek.* If this explanation were in a second language (such as English) as is done in *Årskatalog* it would help those who are not fluent in Swedish. For instance, it is important to know that within a subject heading, general works about a subject and individual works are separated by a line. Those above the line are the general works, e.g., yearbooks. Also, all bibliographies, even in specific subject areas, are listed under Aa.

Since 1994, national bibliographic records have been included in CD-LIBRIS, published by the LIBRIS department, Royal Library, 1992- .[2]

The Swedish ISBN and ISSN centers are part of the Royal Library.

LATEST ISSUE EXAMINED/CURRENCY: The 1993 *Årskatalog* was published in 1994 and was the latest issue examined at the University of Minnesota in March 1995. The Nov./Dec. 1994 list, published in 1995, was the latest issue examined at the University of Minnesota in

---

[1] "Introduction," *SB. Årskatalog* 1993.
[2] Information received in a 14 March 1997 letter to the author by Ms. Gunilla Larsson, Royal Library, Stockholm.

March 1995. The *Svensk Bokkatalog* 1976-1985, published in 1994, is the latest cumulated edition examined.

AUTOMATION: *SB* is automated and is produced from LIBRIS (Library Information System, a computer based information system for Swedish research libraries).[1]

FORMAT AND SERVICES AVAILABLE: printed, magnetic tape, CD-ROM (CD-LIBRIS), Internet: http://www.libris.kb.se

CURRENT LEGAL DEPOSIT LAWS: Legal deposit law since 1661, with the current legal deposit law being the Legal Deposit Act 1993 (SFS 1993: 1392 with amendments 1995: 1375).[2]

AVAILABLE FROM: Seelig & Co., Box 1308, S-17125 Solna.

SELECTED ARTICLES: Antonsson, Birgit. "Kungliga biblioteket– Sveriges nationalbibliotek. Nu och i framtiden."[The Royal Library–Sweden's National Library. Now and in the Future] *DF– Revy* 14 (1 1991):3-5.

Antonsson, Birgit. "The Royal Library– National Library of Sweden." *Alexandria* 2 (2 1990): 39-49. See esp. pp. 41-43.

Cantwell, Ingrid. "The Swedish Bibliographic Scene." *ICBC* 19 (2 1990):19-22.

Guthartz, Catharina and Norman Guthartz. "The National Bibliography of Sweden." In *Guide to Nordic Bibliography*, pp. 37-42.

Larsson, Gunilla. *The Swedish National Bibliography: A Survey.* Stockholm : Royal Library, 1990.

Sandgren, Folke. "Den Svenska Nationalbibliografin." *Bok og Bibliotek* 47 (no. 3 1980):194-195, 216.

Selleck, Roberta G. "The Scandinavian National Bibliographies as Tools for Research and Book Selection." *Collection Management* 6 (Spring/Summer 1984):125-134.

Vokac, Libena. "Svensk Nasjonalbibliografi." *Synopsis* 15 (no. 1 1984):26-27.

VERIFIER: Gunilla Larsson, Royal Library, Sweden.

---

[1] "Sweden," International *Guide to MARC Databases and Services, National Magnetic Tape , On-line and CD-ROM Services,* 3rd rev. and enl. ed., München : K.G. Saur, 1993. pp. 128-133.
[2] Larsson letter.

SWITZERLAND

TITLE: *Das Schweizer Buch = Le livre suisse = Il libro svizzero* [The Swiss book]. - Vol. 43 (1943)- . - Bern : Schweizerischer Buchhändler-und Verleger-Verband, 1943- . Semimonthly, with semiannual and annual indexes.
Continues: *Bibliographisches Bulletin der Schweiz.*
DDC: 015.494; LC: Z2771.S4; LCCN: 50-32807//r94; OCLC: 4289116
ISSN 0036-732X

COMPILER: Schweizerische Landesbibliothek [Swiss National Library].

SCOPE AND COVERAGE: *Das Schweizer Buch* (*SB*) lists the new works published in Switzerland, works published abroad written by Swiss authors or about Switzerland. *SB* is not based on legal deposit, but on an agreement that the Swiss national library has with the publishers' and booksellers' associations. Current imprints and those for the immediate ten years which are newly received are included.

Types of publications in *SB* include books and pamphlets, annuals, periodicals (first numbers), official and government publications, theses and dissertations, geographical maps, musical scores, IGO publications based in Switzerland, calendars, and non-book materials.

Excluded are those non-book materials registered in the music issue.

CONTENTS: Introduction (in German, French), list of subject groups (in German and French), classified bibliography, errata, index.

CATALOGUING RULES AND CLASSIFICATION SCHEMES USED: Cataloguing rules followed are *Règles de Catalogage de l'Association des Bibliothécaires Suisses* and ISBD.

The classification scheme used is broad subject headings.

ENTRY INFORMATION: In upper right corner is the SLB or BN database number, e.g., SLB 0030-0590, BNS0030-05760, consecutive title number, author, title, place of publication, publisher, date, pagination, illustrations, size, series, notes including ISBN and price if known; in the lower left corner additional entries are introduced by E for secondary entries and R for cross references, number indicating shelf position in the National Library in lower right corner, e.g., KLq 2072 Res, Nq 139271.

From 1946-1993, the following symbols were used to distinguish certain types of publications: O indicates official publications, — indicates IGO titles published by IGO headquarters based in Switzerland, æ indicates books published abroad, ∞ following title number designates publications in series. Since 1994, only the ∞ sign is used to designate publications in series.

ARRANGEMENT: *SB* is arranged by 24 broad subject divisions, with errata being number 25.

INDEXES: Semimonthly issues have an alphabetical author, title index.[1] The indexes from the twenty four issues are cumulated into an annual index that is published separately in February. The number refers to the title number.

Bern. Schweizerische Landesbibliothek. *Katalog der Schweizerischen Landesbibliothek, Bern. Systematisches Verzeichnis der Schweizerischen oder die Schweiz betreffenden Veröffentlichungen.* Bern : H. Huber, 1901/29-1941/47 also served as a general index to the *SB*, with coverage from 1901. Although irregular, cumulations generally covered a ten year period. It has been replaced by *Schweizer Bücherverzeichnis = Répertoire du Livre Suisse* which cumulates the annual indexes of *SB*. Volumes from 1948- , are cumulated by this title in five year cumulations. However, it is stated in the introduction of the 1985/86 *SB* that the five year cumulations have been abandoned because of staff shortages, and it is necessary to rely on the annual volumes.

NOTES AND COMMENTS: *SB* continues *Bibliographisches Bulletin der Schweiz.*, 1, Jan./Feb. 1901-1942. Monthly. (OCLC: 4523596). This title continues *Bibliographie und literarische Chronik der Schweiz; Bibliographie et chronique litteraire de la Suisse.* - Basel, 1870-1901. (OCLC: 11653201).

Prefatory text in French and German.

SB was issued in two series, A (book-trade publications, bi-monthly) and B (non-book-trade publications, six issues a year), 1943-1975.

Number 16 is a special number concerning musical scores.

A bibliography listing all administrative publications is *Bibliographie der Schweizerischen Amtsdruckschriften = Bibliographie des Publications Officielles Suisses.* -vol. 1- . -Bern : Schweizerische Landesbibliothek, 1946- .

Since 1953, the author and title index of *SB* has been included in the monthly index of the *Deutsche Bibliographie* and the current title *Deutsche Nationalbibliographie und bibliographie der im Ausland erschienenen deutschsprachigen Veröffentlichungen.* From 1953-1975, only the Series A index was included.

It would be useful to have a publishers' list included in *SB*.

CIP is not practiced in Switzerland.

LATEST ISSUE EXAMINED/CURRENCY: *SB* includes entries for the period covered as well as those titles not listed in *SB* before for the ten preceding years.

Semimonthly issues are received by the University Library, Cambridge, England on an average of one month after date of coverage. Annual indexes, published in February of the following year, are also received approximately a month later. The latest issue of *SB* examined in

---

[1] The keyword and "titres et mots typiques" [significant titles and keywords] index is not included since 1993 per comments by Elena Balzardi, Head of Cataloguing and National Bibliography, Schweizerische Landesbibliothek.

September 1997 at the Bibliotekstjänst AB Library is 1997/14. The latest annual index examined at University of Minnesota in March 1995 was for 1993.

AUTOMATION: Since 1994 *SB* has used USMARC and a program (V-BIGR/3000) developed for the production of SB and other bibliographies of the Swiss National Library. The bibliography is produced with the data from the VTLS (Virginia Tech Library System) library catalogue.[1]

FORMAT AND SERVICES AVAILABLE: printed. The online catalogue is available via telnet (telnet helveticat.snl.ch and via www.wnl.ch/helveticat/english) and the data published in the national bibliography is a part of the online catalogue.

CURRENT LEGAL DEPOSIT LAWS: The loi fédérale de 1992 (Landesbibliotheksgesetz, SLBG, SR 432.21) does not include arrangements for legal deposit.[2] A legal deposit law does not exist on a national scale for Switzerland. The Swiss National Library works on a contract basis with publishers.

AVAILABLE FROM: Schweizerische Landesbibliothek, Hallwylstr. 15, CH-3003 Bern.

VERIFIER: Dr. J.-F. Jauslin, Director, Schweizerische Landesbibliothek, and Elena Balzardi, Head of Cataloguing and National Bibliography, Schweizerische Landesbibliothek.

SYRIA

TITLE: *al-Bibliyūgrāfiya al-waṭanīyah al-Sūrīyah.* [Syrian national bibliography] - 1984-   . - Dimashq [Damascus] : Maktabat al-Asad [Assad Library], 1985-   .
Annual.
Has supplement vol. for 1984.
DDC: not found; LC: Z3481.B54; LCCN: sn92-19000; OCLC: 25042952
ISSN not found.

COMPILER: Bibliographical Section, Assad Library.

SCOPE AND COVERAGE: *al-Bibliyūgrāfiya al-waṭanīyah al-Sūrīyah.* [*Syrian national bibliography*] (*SNB*) includes within its scope cultural and ideological titles published in Syria with the goal of distributing information from the local level to the international level. *SNB* is based on legal deposit. Publications written by Syrians outside of the country are within the scope of *SNB*; however, this coverage is not complete. Publications from the previous year which are received late are listed in the year they were received by the library.

Types of publications included are books, pamphlets, published theses, new periodical and newspaper titles.

---

[1] Information in a 7 July 1997 letter sent to the author from Dr. J.-F. Jauslin, Director, Schweizerische Landesbibliothek.
[2] Jauslin letter.

Excluded from *SNB* are special tourist information publications for other countries, unpublished university theses, maps, non-business advertisements, broad statistical tables, musical scores, drawings, microfiche and microfilm titles, cultural and other general films.[1]

CONTENTS: Table of contents, introduction, classification table, symbols, list of books, periodicals and pamphlets, indexes.

CATALOGUING RULES AND CLASSIFICATION SCHEMES USED: ISBD rules for cataloguing are used.

The classification scheme used in *SNB is* DDC, with Arabic adaptation for culture and sciences.

ENTRY INFORMATION: ISBD information is followed. Prices and notes are not included.

ARRANGEMENT: The bibliography is arranged by the DDC classification scheme.

The periodicals section is alphabetically arrianged.

INDEXES: Author and co-author index; title index; subject index; publisher index (no addresses given). Numbers refer user to the entry numbers in the bibliography.

NOTES AND COMMENTS: The Ministry of National Culture and Guidance published four issues of *al-Nashrah al-Maktabīyah bi-al-Kutub al-Ṣādirah fī al-Jumhūrīyah al-'Arabīyah al-Sūrīyah*. These issues covering the years 1970-1973 were published 1971-1974. According to the "National Bibliographies" article in the 1986 edition of the *ALA World Encyclopedia of Library and Information Services, SNB* continues this title.[2]

al-Bībliyūghrāfiya al-waṭanīyah al-Sūrīyah al-rāji'ah [*SNB*, retrospective] - 1985-   . - Dimashq : Maktabat al--Asad, 1987-   includes imprints published before 1984. Irregular (OCLC: 19460197). Titles published in Syria, or about Syria published elsewhere are included. ISBD is used to describe the publications. This title is arranged by a modified DDC. Indexes include alphabetical authors and co-authors, title, subject headings, and publishers.

The library publishes *al-Kashshāf al-taḥlīlī lil-ṣuḥuf wa-al-majalāt al-Sūrīyah* [*Analytical Index to Syrian Newspapers & Periodicals.*]. - 1985-   . - Dimashq : al-Mudiriyah, 1985-   . (LCCN 87-650131/NE; LC: AI19.A6K34; OCLC: 15160583). This is a separate quarterly index which analyzes the newspapers, periodical, and research articles, studies, statistics, and legislation. It is arranged by subjects. Information given is a summary and complete citation.

---

[1] Because the legal deposit system covers several of these categories, one copy is deposited at the national library but the titles are not included in the *SNB*.

[2] Seen in manuscript form while working at the Library of Congress, October 1985. The list was a revision of Ruth Freitag's article which appeared in *ALA World Encyclopedia of Library and Information Services*. The revision, done by Judith Farley, Reference Specialist, General Reading Rooms Division, Library of Congress appears in the second edition of the same title, published in 1986. This relationship is also mentioned in Van der Vate's *Books from the Arab World*, p. 30. The "Introduction" of the *SNB* mentions this publication but does not give the title.

A special list (irregular) is published by the library administration which gives an introduction of university theses by Syrian students in Syria as well as those Syrian students who study abroad. To date, one list has been compiled, and another is underway. The English title is *Syrian University Dissertations*. [1]

AL,ME (ISSN 0041-7789; ceased at the end of 1993) and *The Arab Bulletin of Publications* include Syria within their scopes.

LATEST ISSUE EXAMINED/CURRENCY: The latest issue examined is for 1989 at the Princeton University Library in April 1995.[2]

If the *SNB* could be more timely in its publication and distribution, it would be a good acquisitions source. It, however, is helpful in bibliographic control.

AUTOMATION: The *SNB* is not automated at present. There are plans to do this in the future.

FORMAT AND SERVICES AVAILABLE: printed.

CURRENT LEGAL DEPOSIT LAWS: Executive Decree established the national library in 1983. Presidential decree 17 of 26 July 1983 pertains to legal deposit.[3]

AVAILABLE FROM: Assad Library, Maliki Street, POB 3639, Damascus.

VERIFIER: Director General Dr. Ghassan Lahham, Assad National Library

TAIWAN (REPUBLIC OF CHINA)

TITLE: *Chung-hua min kuo ch'u pan t'u shu mu lu* . - Vol. 1- . - T'ai-pei : Kuo li chung yang t'u shu kuan [National Central Library], 1970- .
Quarterly (1992-); monthly (1970-1991), with annual and five yearly cumulations (cumulations published at infrequent intervals).
Cover title: *Chinese national bibliography*.
Continues *Hsin shu mu lu* [Monthly list of Chinese books].
DDC: not found; LC: Z3111.C59; LCCN: 75-838524/C/r862/V/r94; OCLC: 2245501
ISSN 0301-5165

---

[1] Mentioned in the *SNB* "Introduction." The title is supplied by Director General G. Lahham in his letter to the author dated 2 March 1997.

[2] In his letter, Director General Lahham indicates that the latest issue published is the volume for 1994.

[3] Information received in a meeting with Kathy Van der Vate, Curator, Arabic Section, Department of Oriental Manuscripts and Printed Books, The British Library on 7 June 1985, and as cited in her *Books from the Arab World*, p. 30. In his letter to the author, Director General Lahham confirms that this is the latest legal deposit law.

COMPILER: Bibliography Section, National Central Library.

SCOPE AND COVERAGE: The *Chung-hua min kuo ch'u pan t'u shu mu lu* or the *Chinese National Bibliography* (*CNB*) lists the publishing output of Taiwan during the time period covered which is deposited at the National Central Library according to the legal deposit legislation; gifts, exchanges, and newly published acquired books from overseas are also included. Older books, valuable for research and which have not been included in earlier issues, and foreign language publications are also listed in an appendix.

Types of publications included in *CNB* are books, Chinese periodicals published in free areas (first issues) including both free and purchased copies.

Excluded from the scope (temporarily) are pamphlets, musical scores, pictures, legends, cheap novelettes.

CONTENTS: Table of contents, outline of subjects with entry number location, introduction (which includes scope, exclusions, arrangement, analyzed entry, and rules followed), bibliography, title index, author index.

CATALOGUING RULES AND CLASSIFICATION SCHEMES USED: Materials are described using AACR2 with adaptations as needed.

The classification scheme used for the Chinese material is the National Central Library classification number which is based on the "New Classification Scheme for Chinese Libraries" by Yung-Hsiang Lai and the "First-Last Stroke Author System." The first number indicates the author's time period. The second element has up to three digits which represent the author's number determined by the strokes of the author's last name and first name. Research and dissertations are slightly different. The first three numbers represents the school's code, and the fourth digit indicates the Bachelors, Masters, or Doctorate degree represented by B, M, D respectively.

Foreign publications are classified by the LC classification system.

ENTRY INFORMATION: Consecutive sequence number in the upper left corner, title, author, editor or translator, edition statement, place of publication, publisher, date, pagination, illustration statement, size, series statement, Classification number is in the lower left corner, e.g., 948.4/8794; 005.1/002M 79; DS778.A1. The National Central Library (NCL) number in the lower right corner, e.g., NCL94008367. In the notes section, tracings are given for the books in Chinese; this is not done for the titles in English.

ARRANGEMENT: Arrangement is by the ten main classes based on "New Classification Scheme for Chinese Libraries" by Yung-Hsiang Lai. The ten classes are generalities, philosophy, religion, natural sciences, applied sciences, social sciences, history and geography, language and literature, and arts.

The 1970 volume was arranged in two sections: general publications arranged by the classification number, and government publications arranged by organization and then title. Entries are arranged with consecutive numbers.

INDEXES: Title index, author index. The indexes are organized by Chinese radical, the number of strokes, and the extension number. Index numbers refer to the consecutive sequence number.

NOTES AND COMMENTS: According to information in the introduction, this bibliography was first published in 1960. Before it received its present title in 1970, it was published from 1960 to 1970 under different titles. These titles include *Hsin shu chien pao* [The Monthly list of Chinese books]. (ISSN 0578-2007; OCLC: 1696965) which started in September 1960 and closed in June 1967, and *Kuo li chung yang t'u shu kuan hsin shu mu lu* which started in July 1968 and closed in November 1969. (LCCN: sn94-32241; OCLC: 1554639).[1]

LATEST ISSUE EXAMINED/CURRENCY: The latest issue examined in March 1997 is number 3, 1994, received by Indiana University Library 11 April 1995.

AUTOMATION: Since February 1984, *CNB* has been computerized. The URICA system based on NCR is used to produce the national bibliography.

FORMAT AND SERVICES AVAILABLE: printed, CD-ROM. Internet access is expected in March 1998.

CURRENT LEGAL DEPOSIT LAWS: Article 22 of the Publications Law, promulgated in 1930, and revised in 1937, 1952, 1958, and 1973. Article 14 covers magazines and newspapers.

AVAILABLE FROM: The National Central Library, 20 Chung-Shan S. Road, Taipei, 10040.

VERIFIER: Dr. Chi-Chun Tseng, Director of the National Central Library.

TAJIKISTAN

No current national bibliography has been traced for Tajikistan.[2]

The regional bibliography prior to 1991 was *Letopis' pechati Tadzhikskoĭ SSR = Gosudarstvennyĭ komitet Tadzhikskoĭ SSR po delam izdatel'stv, poligrafii i knizhnoĭ torgovli. = Gosudarstvennaіа knizhnaіа palata Tadzhikskoĭ SSR* (ISSN 0136-0892). The Tajik title is

---

[1] In a 14 July 1997 letter to the author Dr. Chi-Chun Tseng, Director of the National Central Library gave the 1968-1969 title as written here. The title in the OCLC record is cited as *Hsing shu mu lu*, with *Kuo li chung yang t'u shu kuan* given as part of the imprint information.

[2] In a 28 July 1997 e-mail message, Irina Egorova, head of the Moscow office on CIS publications for East-View Publications, informed Kirill Fessenko, periodicals, East View Publications, that the national bibliography or any substitute title is not available and is not published currently because of financial difficulties. No older issues were available for examination in libraries consulted or visited by the author. The author is grateful to Carl Horne, Indiana University Library, David Zmijewski, Harvard College Library, and to Mary Stevens, University of Toronto Library for their help.

Solnomai matbuoti RSS Tojikiston. Libraries who have this title only have holdings in the 1960s. It is not a widely distributed title.

When this bibliography was active, it was most recently published as a monthly, listing 12,000 entries yearly. Entries were presented in broad classification groups and listed in three language sections: Tajik, Russian, and Uzbek. Five individual sections made up the national bibliography: Knizhnaĩa letopis' = Solnomai kitobho [Bibliography of books], Letopis' gazetnykh stateĭ = Solnomai maqolahoi gazetaho [Bibliography of newspaper articles], Letopis' zhurnal'nykh stateĭ = Solomai maqolahoi zhurnaljo [Bibliography of journal articles], Letopis' retsenziĭ = Sonomai taqrizho [Bibliography of reviews], Tadzhikskaĩa SSR v pechati Sovetskogo Soĩuza = Adabietho dar borai RSS Tojikiston, ki dar matbuoti SSSR chop shudaast [Tajikistan in the press of the USSR].[1]

SELECTED ARTICLES: Leich, Harold M. "Bibliographic systems of the Soviet Republics: Moldavia and Tajikistan." *Government Information Quarterly* 2 (no. 3 1985):298.

TANZANIA

TITLE: *Tanzania national bibliography.* - 1974/75-   . - Dar es Salaam : Tanzania Library Services Board, 1975-   .
Annual (1989-   ); monthly, with annual cumulation (1983-Dec.1988); annual (1975-1982).
Continues *Printed in Tanzania*

DDC: 015.678; LC: Z3588.T37; Z3588.P74 [1975-1982]; LCCN: 83-980878//r902; 79-646650//r81 [1975-1982]; OCLC: 14169810, 4331972 [1975-1982]
ISSN 0856-003X

COMPILER: National Bibliographic Agency, Tanzania Library Service Board since 1983; from 1975-1982, Acquisitions Department, Central Reference Library. From 1969-1981, National Central Library.

SCOPE AND COVERAGE: *Tanzania National Bibliography* (*TNB*) includes publications produced in mainland Tanzania and deposited at the National Bibliographic Agency of Tanzania Library Services Board in compliance with the legal deposit law. Earlier volumes, e.g., 1974/75 and earlier, include publications deposited with the Tanzania Library Service and the University of Dar es Salaam Library in compliance with the legal deposit law.

Types of publications include books, reports, dissertations, mimeographed documents, first issues of new serial titles, local languages publications, official and government publications.

Omitted are ephemera, art prints, microfilms, audio-visual materials and debates.

---

[1] Harold M. Leich. "Bibliographic systems of the Soviet Republics: Moldavia and Tajikistan." *Government Information Quarterly* 2 (no. 3 1985): 298.

CONTENTS: Annual cumulation: contents, introduction, classified bibliography, fiction, author index, title index, statistics on book production; printers and publishers in Tanzania.

Monthly issues: Title page includes information about scope, coverage and frequency, arrangement and description, and indexes; classified bibliography, fiction, index.

CATALOGUING RULES AND CLASSIFICATION SCHEMES USED: Cataloguing and bibliographic description of materials follow AACR2 and ISBD since 1983.

Entries are classified and arranged according to DDC (19th ed.). Fiction materials are not classified.

ENTRY INFORMATION: Author, title, edition, place of publication, publisher, date, price, pagination, illustrations, size, series statement, ISBN or ISSN, notes, DDC number in lower right corner. *TNB* number is in lower right corner of entries.

ISBNs have been assigned by some publishers since 1982; ISSNs have been assigned since the beginning of 1983.

ARRANGEMENT: In the classified bibliography, entries are arranged according to DDC, and then alphabetically if there are multiple entries under the same number. Fiction material is arranged alphabetically in the fiction section following the classified sequence.

INDEXES: Each monthly list of *TNB* has one alphabetical index which includes author, editor, title and series. Entry numbers refer to the classified section's DDC number and the *TNB* number.

Since 1975, annual cumulations have a separate author and a title index.

NOTES AND COMMENTS: The Tanzania National Bibliographic Agency was established in February 1983 as a division of the Tanzania Library Services.

Most entries in *TNB* are in Swahili or in English.

Government publications are not designated with a symbol. However, by checking the index under Tanzania and then the various government departments, one is able to locate many titles, particularly in the 300 and 600 classification numbers.

In the annual volume the section on book production gives a good summary of book publishing in Tanzania.

Tanzania is included in the scopes of *AL,ESA* and *QIPL,ESA*.

Printed in Tanzania, compiled by the National Central Library, listed legal deposit items from 1969-1973. (DDC: 015/.678; LC: Z3588.P74; LCCN: 73-647643//r80; OCLC: 1789705; ISSN: not found).

Previous to *Printed in Tanzania*, legal deposit items were listed in the *University of Dar es Salaam Library Bulletin and Accessions List.* - 1962-   .

Zanzibar does not have a separate national bibliography and is not included in *TNB*.[1]

Once a year *Tanzania Notes and Records,* (ISSN 0039-9485) includes "Tanzania Bibliography" for the year covered. The 1976 list is in number 84 and 85 (1980), and is compiled by O.C. Mascarenhas. 566 entries are organized under broad subject headings which are further divided into more specific headings such as education of adults, livestock and pasture science, and maternal and child health. However, volumes for 1981 and 1982, the latest volumes checked, do not have a bibliography listed.

Up to 1995 the National Bibliographic Agency had registered 332 publishers for ISBN and 607 for ISSN.[2]

LATEST ISSUE EXAMINED/CURRENCY: The latest issue examined is for December 1988, received at the University Library, Cambridge, England, 28 January 1994. The first seven monthly issues of 1983 were received at the University Library, Cambridge, England, in one batched mailing, thirteen months after coverage of the most current number. The August issue was received fourteen months after the date covered. Annual cumulations received by the University Library were published an average of two years after the date covered and received on average a year after publication. The issues need to be distributed more quickly if one is to use the *TNB* for acquisitions purposes.

AUTOMATION: The National Bibliographic Agency is partly computerized since 1986. CDS/ISIS software is used.

FORMAT AND SERVICES AVAILABLE: printed.

CURRENT LEGAL DEPOSIT LAWS: The Libraries (Deposit of Books) Act of 1962; Section 5 (2) of Tanzania Library Services Board Act, 1975.[3]

AVAILABLE FROM: Tanzania Library Service Board, National Bibliographic Agency, P.O. Box 9283, Dar es Salaam.

SELECTED ARTICLES: Bankole, Beatrice S. "Current National Bibliographies of the English Speaking Countries of Africa." *International Cataloguing* 14 (Jan./Mar. 1985):5-10.

Mlaki, T.E. "Tanzania." *Afribiblios* 7 (no. 2 Dec. 1984):57-61.

Mlaki, Theophilus. "Tanzania." *Afribiblios* 9 (no. 1 June 1986):22-25.

VERIFIER: Irene B. Minja, Acting Head, National Bibliographic Agency.

---

[1] Information included in a letter to the author dated 1 July 1996 from Irene Minja, Acting Head, National Bibliographic Agency.

[2] Minja letter.

[3] J. N. Otike. "A Critical Analysis of the Legal Deposit Laws in East Africa." *ICBC* 17 (no. 1 Jan./Mar. 1988):13.

THAILAND

TITLE: *Bannānukrom hǣng Chāt = Thai national bibliography*. - 1975-   . - Bangkok : The National Library, [1978]-   .
Frequency varies: quarterly.
DDC: 015.593; LC: Z3236.B35; LCCN: sn97-47012; OCLC: 13730244
ISSN 0125-1899

COMPILER: Ministry of Education, Fine Arts Department, The National Library.

SCOPE AND COVERAGE: *Bannānukrom hǣng Chāt = Thai National Bibliography* (*TNB*) lists the publishing output of Thailand which is deposited at the National Library according to the legal deposit legislation. It also lists publications concerning Thailand published elsewhere.

Types of publications included in *TNB* are books, pamphlets, official and government publications, serials, theses and dissertations, standards, patents, conference proceedings, selected reports. All of the above are not always in each volume.

Prior to 1985, serials were included in *Periodicals and newspapers printed in Thailand between [   ]* which covered the periods 1935-1971, 1972-1973, 1974-1981 in three volumes. Since 1985, serials have been included in the *TNB* in a separate section after the books.

CONTENTS: The material is presented bilingually in Thai and in English: introduction (including an analyzed entry, cataloguing practices, DDC first level list), explanation, table of contents, main sequence, author index, title index, cremation index, serials index.

CATALOGUING RULES AND CLASSIFICATION SCHEMES USED: Cataloguing practices follow *Cataloging Rules for Thai Books*, by Sutthilak Amphanwong; AACR2 (North American text), ISBD(M), *Subject Headings for Thai Books*, *Subject Headings used in the Dictionary Catalogs of the Library of Congress*.

The classification scheme used is DDC.

ENTRY INFORMATION: Book section: DDC number in upper left corner, author, title, edition, imprint, collation, series statement, notes, tracings, ISBN, national bibliographic number.

Serial section: serial title, imprint year, date of first issue, place of publishing, publisher, address of publisher, first date of publication.

ARRANGEMENT: In the book section, the arrangement of entries is alphabetical within the DDC numbers. The serials section is alphabetically arranged by title.

INDEXES: Author index, title index, cremation index (not in each volume).

The author index is arranged alphabetically by the author's first name. Each entry includes the author (or translator, editor), title, and class number.

Entries in the title index are arranged alphabetically by titles, added entries and series titles and include title, author, and class number.

Entries in the cremation index include the name of person cremated in whose memory the work is done, author, title, and class number.

NOTES AND COMMENTS: The first attempt to compile a national bibliography for Thailand was done by the Thai Library Association in cooperation with the National Library in 1959, covering 1958. It was considered unsuccessful because of the ineffectiveness of the legal deposit laws and a decision was made to work on smaller projects rather than attempt another volume of the national bibliography.

A volume called the *TNB* was published in 1976 covering 1961/1967. The second issue which covered 1968-1970, was published in 1981.

From 1901-1967, the monthly *List of Books Published under the Copyright or the National Library Bibliography* was published.[1]

It is the custom to publish books for distribution at cremation ceremonies or other important ceremonies or anniversaries. This is reflected in the national bibliography, although the depositing of such works at the National Library is optional under the legal deposit regulations.[2]

The National Library is the ISSN for the five ASEAN countries in Southeast Asia, and publishes the *SEA Bulletin: International Standard Serial Number.* - Bangkok : ISSN Regional Centre for Southeast Asia, 1996-   . (ISSN 0859-6662; OCLC: 37104759). Since 1980, publishers have been using ISSNs on their publications. This number appears as part of the entry information in *TNB.*

Since the *TNB* does not include periodical articles within its scope, it is important to mention *Datchanī wārasān Thai = Index to Thai Periodical Literature.* -1960-   . - Bangkok : National Institute of Development Administration, 1964-   . Irregular (ISSN 0125-5827). It includes mostly academic journals.

AL,SEA (ISSN 0732-7374) included Thailand within its scope. One also may want to consult accessions lists from the libraries of Thammasat University and Chulalongkorn University.

LATEST ISSUE EXAMINED/CURRENCY: According to the introduction, only volumes published during the period covered are included.

In the libraries checked the latest volume located in May 1995 at the University of Wisconsin is the one covering Jan./March 1987. Currently there is a large gap between the last period

---

[1] Dayrit, Marina, "The Problems of Current National Bibliographies in Southeast Asian Countries: the Results of a Survey. Appendix IV," p. 203. *Proceedings of IFLA Worldwide Seminar 1976.* Seoul, Korea Library Association, 1976.

[2] Ambhanwong, Suthilak, "Bibliographical Control in Thailand," *International Library Review* 4 (1972):159.

covered and the current date. Because of this delay, the *TNB* can not be considered an effective acquisitions tool, but it is helpful in recording the historical publishing record.

AUTOMATION: *TNB* has been automated since 1982 with the publication of the national bibliography for 1975 consisting of four volumes.[1] Currently automated using an IBM RISC/6080 and DYNIX Automated Library System.

USMARC format is used.

FORMAT AND SERVICES AVAILABLE: printed. Future plans include issuing the national bibliography in CD-ROM.[2]

CURRENT LEGAL DEPOSIT LAWS: Thailand does not have a legal deposit law. Through the provision of Press Act B.E. 2484 (1941) the National Library receives two copies of each publication printed by commercial printers. The purpose of this law is to be able to exercise some control over publishers and printers. A revision of this Press Act relevant to the National Library is now with the Ministry of Interior who will submit this to the Parliament for enactment into law.[3]

According to the *Survey of Existing Legal Deposit Laws* (p. 74) this law is not as effective as it needs to be. It is estimated that sixty percent of the total number of printed material and ninety percent of periodicals and newspapers are deposited in the National Library. Books and newspapers published outside of Bangkok are not deposited. The law does not include government publications within its scope, but approximately eighty percent are included. Mr. William Tuchrello, formerly with the Asian Division, Library of Congress, feels that the above figures are a high estimate of titles included in *TNB*.

AVAILABLE FROM: The National Library, Samsen Road, Bangkok 3.

SELECTED ARTICLES: Phadungath, Suwakhon. "Bibliographical Standards: Evaluation of their Implementation in Thailand." In Congress of Southeast Asian Librarians (6th, 1983, Singapore). *The Library in the Information Revolution*, pp. 199-209. Singapore : Maruzen Asia, 1983.

VERIFIER: Mrs. Thara Kanakamani, Director, National Library of Thailand.

---

[1] "Thailand, Libraries and Librarianship in," *Encyclopedia of Library and Information Services*, suppl. 8 (1988):275. Khoo Siew Mun in the "Bibliographic Description in Southeast Asia, " p. 104 in *Standards for the International Exchange of Bibliographic Information* states that the *TNB* has been computer generated since 1978 with the assistance of the Data Procesing Centre of Thailand, National Statistical Office offering its facilities.... (*TNB*, 1985, Introduction).

[2] Information in a 24 September 1997 letter to the author from Mrs. Thara Kanakamani, Director, National Library of Thailand.

[3] Kanakamani letter.

TOGO

No current national bibliography has been traced for Togo.[1] Although some sources suggest that publication notices included in the *Journal Officiel de la République Togo.* - Lomé : l'Ecole professionelle de la Mission catholique, 1920-   could substitute for a national bibliography, the author was unable to find notices of publications mentioned in the years examined (1974, 1976 and 1982).

NOTES AND COMMENTS: The Bibliothèque Nationale has published *Bibliographie Retrospective du Togo: Periode 1950-1970.* This covers titles published in Togo and publications about Togo during the period covered. It includes monographs, serials and theses.[2] The bibliography is divided into three sections: monographs, serials and theses. The first two sections are subdivided by subject according to UDC. The bibliographic description follows ISBD. The index includes main entries. More information is available from Bibliothèque Nationale, B.P. 1002, Lomé, Togo.[3]

In 1995 the Bibliothèque Nationale published *Bibliographie nationale retrospective du Togo.* - Vol. 1- . - Lomé : Bibliothèque Nationale, 1995-   . (ISSN 1023-764X) which includes monographs and theses published in Togo and about Togo published elsewhere in an alphabetical main entry listing. A number of government publications are included under Togo and the Ministry responsible for the title. The largest concentration of publications included in volume one was published from 1979-1989, with 303 entries. Three publications are listed from the 1950s, 16 from the 1960s, and 64 from 1970-1978. The earliest publication listed is for 1929, and the latest are three from 1992 with a total of 420 entries. A keyword index follows the main entry listing. Information for entries include entry number, main entry, title, place of publication, publisher, date of publication, pagination, and location number.

CURRENT LEGAL DEPOSIT LAWS: Décret 72/160, 7 juillet 1972. The legal deposit law has been attached to the Ministère de l'Interieur and it is hoped that this will enable the legal deposit law to become more effective.[4]

SELECTED ARTICLES: Mamah, Zakari. "Coup d'oeil sur Bibliothèque nationale du Togo". *Documentation et Bibliotheques* 39 (no. 2 April-June 1993):75-77.

---

[1] The following hopeful sentence was taken from "Togo," *Afribiblios* 8 (no. 2 December 1985):99: "Toutefois le premier numéro de la bibliographie nationale vient de paraftre et nous pensons le parfaire à l'avenir." A further note on this: the ineffective legal deposit law has hindered the publication of the current national bibliography. In 1993 it was decided to produce a retrospective national bibliography covering the last ten years. See p. 76 of Z. Mamah, "Coup d'oeil sur Bibliothèque nationale du Togo" in Selected Articles section.

[2] "UBC News," *International Cataloguing* 13 (no. 3 July/Sept. 1984):27.

[3] "Togo," *African Research and Documentation* no. 36 (1984):60-61. Information also appeared in "Togo," *Afribiblios* 9 (no.1 June 1986):27

[4] Information is included in "Togo," *Afribiblios* 8 (no. 2 December 1985):98, and from a letter dated 12 March 1996 to the author from Balay Coulibaly, Chef, Département de la Bibliographie Nationale du Togo, Bibliothèque Nationale.

VERIFIER: Balaya Coulibaly, Le Chef du Département de la Bibliographie Nationale du Togo, Bibliothèque Nationale.

TOKELAU

TITLE: *Tokelau National Bibliography = Fakamaumauga o na Tuhituhiga o Tokelau.* - 1st ed. (Apr. 1992)- . - [Wellington, N.Z.] : National Library of New Zealand Te Puna Matauranga o Aotearoa, 1992 - .
Irregular.
DDC: 015.961/5; LC: Z4124.T65T65; LCCN: 94-641114; OCLC: 26738203
ISSN 1170-800X

COMPILER: 1st ed.: Lepeka Amato, Ofiha o no Matkupa Tokelau, Apia; Alyson Baker, Maria Heenan, Jenifer Moon, and Perine Renwick, New Zealand National Bibliography, Wellington.

SCOPE AND COVERAGE: *Tokelau National Bibliography = Fakamaumauga o na Tuhituhiga o Tokelau* (*TNB*) includes items published in Tokelau, about Tokelau, by Tokelau authors, and in the Tokelauan language. There is no restriction by date, size, or format of publication.

Types of publications include books, pamphlets, official and government publications, serials, unpublished typescripts, maps, posters, and Learning Media (New Zealand Ministry of Education) trial versions of children's material by Tokelau authors and in the Tokelauan language. Future issues will include theses by Tokelau authors or about Tokelau.

Omitted from *TNB* are articles published in journals, analytic entries of chapters from books, and general works that do not have at least one-fifth content by a Tokelau author or about Tokelau.

CONTENTS: [Preface to] Tokelau National Bibliography, acknowledgments, scope , Tokelau National Bibliography [introduction], analyzed sample entry, register of records, indexes.

CATALOGUING RULES AND CLASSIFICATION SCHEMES USED: AACR2 rules are followed. *LCSH* is used for subject headings. Simplified subject headings are used for children's books.

The classification scheme used is DDC.

ENTRY INFORMATION: Consecutive register number, author, title, place of publication, publisher, date, pagination, illustrations, size, series statement, notes including language information and ISBN, subject headings, DDC number, edition of Dewey used (in lower left corner) New Zealand Bibliographic Network number in lower right corner, e.g., [zbn91-044797]. Some entries have a simplified children's subject heading which is positioned below the DDC number and preceded by the letters AC:.

ARRANGEMENT: Arrangement of the register of records is numerically in the order that entries were entered in the NZBN database.

INDEXES: Author/title index, subject index, children's subject index. All indexes are arranged alphabetically in English language order. Numbers in the indexes refer the user to the consecutive register number in the register of records.

NOTES AND COMMENTS: It is always a treat to find a new national bibliography which follows many of the international guidelines suggested by the ICNB. The presentation of *TNB* is pleasing and its organization is clearly stated. The titles included in this first edition are extracted from the NZBN, and are not based on legal deposit since there are no legal deposit laws in Tokelau. The compilers included staff from Tokelau and New Zealand. A clear introduction includes the scope, coverage, arrangement of the publications, and an analyzed example of an entry. Entries in languages of Tokelauan, Samoan, and English are included and adhere to ICNB no. 6.

For future editions, the following considerations would allow the *TNB* to follow additional international guidelines. ICNB Recommendation no. 11 suggests that printed national bibliographies be arranged in a classified order in accordance with a stated internationally used classification scheme. Since DDC numbers are included for each entry, it seems that the DDC would be a suitable arrangement for the bibliographic entries.

ICNB no. 10 suggests that details of bibliographic and cataloguing tools used in the compilation of the bibliography be identified in the introductory remarks; this would be useful information. A list of special terms and abbreviations might be another useful addition.

The intention of the *TNB* is to be a cumulation of materials published in Tokelau or about Tokelau. For future editions it may be of use to consider adding a symbol which would help the user to easily identify the new entries in each issue.

Statements about frequency of publication, and the legal deposit laws followed would be additional information to add to the introductory remarks.

LATEST ISSUE EXAMINED/CURRENCY: The latest issue examined is the first edition (April 1992).[1]

Imprint dates cover from 1881 to 1992 (one each) with emphasis (63%) on the years 1985 to 1991. Sixty titles of the 228 listed were from years earlier than 1980.

AUTOMATION: Produced from the NZBN.

FORMAT AND SERVICES AVAILABLE: printed.

CURRENT LEGAL DEPOSIT LAWS: No legal deposit laws.[2]

---

[1] As of February 1997, this is the only edition published. The author received a copy from New Zealand for examination.

[2] *International Guide to Legal Deposit*, p. 98.

AVAILABLE FROM: The National Library Shop, P.O. Box 1467, Ground Floor, National Library Building, corner of Aitken & Molesworth Streets, Wellington. E-mail address: shop@natlib.govt.nz

VERIFIER: Karen Rollitt, Editor-in-Chief, New Zealand National Library, National Library of New Zealand, Wellington.

TRINIDAD and TOBAGO

TITLE: *Trinidad and Tobago national bibliography*. - vol. 1- . - Port-of-Spain, Trinidad : Central Library of Trinidad and Tobago; St. Augustine, Trinidad : University of the West Indies Library, 1975-   .
Frequency varies; from vol. 14/15- (1988/1989-   ), joint cumulative issue; vol. 1-12 (1978-1986), quarterly, the fourth issue being an annual cumulation.
DDC: 015.729/83; LC: Z1561.T7T74; LCCN: 76-649640; OCLC: 2791259
ISSN not found

COMPILER: Central Library of Trinidad and Tobago, Port-of-Spain, Trinidad; University of the West Indies Library, St. Augustine, Trinidad.

SCOPE AND COVERAGE: *Trinidad and Tobago National Bibliography* (*TTNB*) lists all works published and printed in Trinidad and Tobago and deposited at the Central Library of Trinidad and Tobago and the University of the West Indies Library in compliance with legal deposit legislation. Also included are titles acquired through purchase or donations.

Types of publications included in *TTNB* are books, pamphlets, official and government publications, first issues and title changes of periodicals, annual reports.

Omitted from *TTNB* are periodicals except as noted above, and certain government publications, e.g., acts, bills, gazettes; non-book materials, ephemera. Titles about the country or written by nationals and published abroad are not within the scope of *TTNB*.

CONTENTS: Preface, copyright law, list of terms, definitions and abbreviations, outline of the DDC, classified subject section, author/title/series index, list of publishers and printers and their addresses.

CATALOGUING RULES AND CLASSIFICATION SCHEMES USED: From vol. 7, *TTNB* uses AACR2.

For classification, DDC (19th ed.) scheme is used.

ENTRY INFORMATION: DDC number and DDC heading, author, title, edition, place of publication, publisher, date, pagination, illustrations, size, notes including price and binding information, LC classification number, accessions number.

ARRANGEMENT: The classified section is arranged by the DDC scheme and then alphabetically by main entry.

INDEXES: The alphabetical section is an author/title/series index. Entry information is given in brief form. Numbers given refer the user to the classification number in the main bibliography.

NOTES AND COMMENTS: *TTNB* supersedes *Trinidad and Tobago and West Indian Bibliography. Bi-monthly Accessions List* published by the West Indian Reference Section, Central Library of Trinidad and Tobago from 1965 - August 1974, and the *Recent Acquisitions of Trinidad and Tobago Imprints* published by the University of West Indies Library from 1973-1975, number 5.

The preface of *TTNB* for vol. 16/17 (published 1993) states that the frequency "hopes to return to an annual issue" beginning with the volume for 1992. However, in a letter to the author dated 1 Dec. 1995, the Director of Library Services stated that the library plans to publish *TTNB* in a cumulative issue covering the years 1992-1995, and then publish it annually from 1996.

TTNB is printed by the Government Printery, Victoria Ave., Port-of-Spain, Trinidad.

TTNB follows the pattern of most of the other national bibliographies of the Caribbean countries and territories. The format is presented in a pleasing manner, and ICNB recommendations 5, 8, 10, 11, 13 and most of 9 have been met.

The *CARICOM Bibliography* (1977-1986; OCLC: 3746719) and the *Bibliografía Actual del Caribe* (OCLC: 2241382) include Trinidad and Tobago within their scopes.

LATEST ISSUE EXAMINED/CURRENCY: Cumulative volumes for *TTNB* have been received by the libraries between one and two years after the period covered.

The latest volume examined by this author at the University of Minnesota in March 1995 was volume 16/17 covering 1990/91.

AUTOMATION: The acknowledgments in volume 16/17 give credit to the technical assistance of the librarians of the Ministry of Planning and Development Library who are gratefully acknowledged in the computerized production of this bibliography.

The Central Library of Trinidad and Tobago plans to be fully automated by the end of 1997; this includes the national bibliography.[1]

FORMAT AND SERVICES AVAILABLE: printed.

CURRENT LEGAL DEPOSIT LAWS: Copyright Law of 1966.

---

[1] Information in a letter from the Director of Library Services to the author dated 1 December 1995.

AVAILABLE FROM: Central Library of Trinidad and Tobago, P.O. Box 547, Port-of-Spain, Trinidad, and the University of the West Indies Library, St. Augustine, Trinidad.

VERIFIER: (Mrs.) Pamella Benson, Director of Library Services, Central Library of Trinidad and Tobago.

TUNISIA

TITLE: *Bibliographie nationale de Tunisie.* - 1977-   . - Tunis- : Bibliothèque nationale, 1978- .
Frequency varies; annual; quarterly, with last issue being the annual cumulation (1980-   );
quarterly, with annual cumulations (1978-1979); bimonthly (1977).
Publisher varies.
Added title page: *al-Bibliyūgrāfiyā al-qawmīyah al-Tunisīyah.*
Issued also on microfiche.
In French and Arabic.
DDC: 015.61; LC: Z3685.2.B52; LCCN: sn85-11434; OCLC: 5962478
ISSN 0330-1761

COMPILER: Bibliothèque Nationale.

SCOPE AND COVERAGE: *Bibliographie nationale de Tunisie* or *al-Bibliyūgrāfiyā al-qawmīyah al-Tunisīyah* (*BNT*) includes the publishing output of Tunisia, which is deposited at the national library according to legal deposit laws. Purchases, donations, and publications produced in Tunisia from organizations such as ALECSO are included also.

Types of publications included in *BNT* are books, pamphlets, official and government publications (since 1977), theses and dissertations, school textbooks, new periodical titles, maps and atlases.

Omitted from *BNT* are non-book materials.

CONTENTS: French and Arabic titles are listed in two distinct parts which are bound tête-bêche. The organization of the parts is as follows: table of contents, introduction, tabular subject breakdown by types of publications, language, and classes, UDC principal tables, classified bibliography: official publications, non-official publications, university works, author index, subject index, printer index, publisher index, recent periodicals.

Since 1993 the "university works" section is no longer included in the *BNT*. It is now included in the annual publication *Liste Bibliographique des Travauix Universitaires*. Information is in both French and Arabic.[1]

Earlier years were divided into official publications and non-official publications sections.

---

[1] Information is included in a 24 June 1997 letter to the author from General Director Djomâa Cheikha, Bibliothèque Nationale.

CATALOGUING RULES AND CLASSIFICATION SCHEMES USED: ISBD standards are followed.

The classification scheme used is UDC.

ENTRY INFORMATION: Official publications: consecutive entry number, author, title, place of publication, publisher, date, pagination, illustration statement, size, notes including bibliography, etc., legal deposit number, e.g., (Br) DL 924/91 (meaning brochure, legal deposit no. 924 in 1991), classification number, subjects.

Non-official publications: UDC number, entry number, author, title, place of publication, publisher, date, pagination, illustration statement, size, series statement, notes when needed, subjects.

University works: UDC number, entry number, author, title, director of thesis, place, department of university, date, pagination, size, subject.
In the new periodicals list: title, responsibility statement, place, date, first issue, frequency.

The same features are presented in the Arabic.

ARRANGEMENT: The official publications section is alphabetically arranged by the issuing agency, then by title. The non-official publications section is arranged by the UDC system, and then alphabetically by main entry.

The university works is arranged by UDC.

The new periodicals list is arranged alphabetically by title.

INDEXES: Author, translators, illustrators, etc. index, subject index, printer index, printer index.

In earlier years, official publications: title; non-official publications: author-collaborator index, title index, subject index, "index des collectivités," publisher-printer index.

The numbers used in the index refer a reader to the entry numbers in the bibliographies.

NOTES AND COMMENTS: Bibliographic coverage can be extended back to 1956 by *al-Bibliyūgrāfiyā al-qawmīyah al-Tunisīyah: al-manshūrāt ghayr al-ramīyah*. - 1956/68-1976. - Tūnis : al-Jumhūrīyah al-Tunisīyah, Wizārat al-Shuūn al-Thaqāfiyah, Dār al-Kutub al-Waṭanīyah, Maṣlaḥat al-Tawthīq [etc.], 1974-1977. (LCCN: 79-647913/NE/r82; LC: Z3685.2B54; DT245; OCLC: 3898706). These five volumes, 1956/68, 1969/73, 1974, 1975, and 1976, plus another retrospective compilation of Tunisian official publications covering 1881-1955, were issued by the Bibliothèque Nationale of Tunisia.[1]

Special supplements are issued periodically in *BNT*.

---

[1] "National bibliographies in Arab countries," *International Cataloguing* (Jan./Mar. 1984):4, (OCLC: 3898706).

Earlier issues of *BNT* include publications of interest to Tunisia that are published abroad. In checking through recent issues, there are very few non-Tunisian imprints.

Official and government publications have been listed in a separate section from 1978.

Tunisia is included in the scope of the Library of Congress' *AL,ME* (which ceased at the end of 1993; ISSN 0041-7769) and *Arab Bulletin of Publications* published by ALECSO.

The quarterly accessions list published by the Bibliothèque Nationale is *Informations Bibliographiques.* - no. 1-   . - Tunis : Ministère des affaires Culturelles, Bibliothèque Nationale 1965-   . (LCCN: sn87-18235; OCLC: 9439540; ISSN 0330-9282). The scope of this publication includes the new acquisitions of the Bibliothèque Nationale, and imprints from countries around the world which are received in the national library by purchase, legal deposit, and exchange.

Books for children are included in UDC class 8.

LATEST ISSUE EXAMINED/CURRENCY: The latest issue examined at Princeton University Library in April 1995 is the annual cumulation for 1991.[1]

Imprint dates cover from the period covered with few exceptions. If distribution to libraries overseas could be improved, this would be an excellent source for acquisitions and collection building.

AUTOMATION: The *BNT* has been automated since 1990. Software and hardware used are CDS/ISIS with Data Général and Hewlett Packard.

FORMAT AND SERVICES AVAILABLE: printed, microfiche.

CURRENT LEGAL DEPOSIT LAWS: Loi organique No. 93-85 du 2 Aout 1993 portant amendement du "Code de la Presse."[2]

AVAILABLE FROM: Service du Dépot Légal, Bibliothèque Nationale, BP 42, 20 Souk el Attarine, Tunis.

SELECTED ARTICLES: Attia, Ridha. "National Bibliographies in the Maghreb: A Survey of their Contents and Perspectives." Paper presented at the 50th IFLA General Conference, 19-24 August 1984, Kenya.

Van de Vate, Katherine. "Acquisition from Individual Countries: Tunisia." In *Books from the Arab World. A Guide to Selection and Acquisition.* Durham: Middle East Libraries Committee, 1988, pp. 23-25.

---

[1] The latest issue of *BNT* published is 1996, published in 1997. According to General Director Djomâa Cheikha, Bibliothèque National, *BNT* has not changed any features from the 1991 description provided in this entry.
[2] In the 24 June 1997 letter to the author from General Director Djomâa Cheikha.

VERIFIER: Djomâa Cheikha, General Director, Bibliothéque Nationale.

TURKEY

TITLE: *Türkiye bibliyografyası.* - 1928-   . - Ankara : Millî Kütüphane, Kultur Başkanliği [Turkish National Library, Ministry of Culture], 1928-   .
Frequency varies: monthly, some issues combined (no.1, 1981-   ); quarterly (1949- 1980) with cumulated annual index (1944-   ); monthly (1944-1948); quarterly (1939-1943); semiannual (1935-1938); annual (1934).
Publisher varies.
Irregular cumulations: decennial cumulations for 1928-1938 and 1939-1948; 1957-1964.
DDC: 015.561; LC: Z2835.T93; LCCN: 61-32528; OCLC: 1645271
ISSN 0041-4328

COMPILER: Prepared by Section Directorate, Preparation of Bibliography.
SCOPE AND COVERAGE: The *Türkiye bibliyografyası* (*TB*) includes printed and audio-visual materials published in Turkey, and deposited at the National Library according to the legal deposit law.

Types of publications listed in *TB* are books, pamphlets, government publications, theses, foreign language publications, minority group publications, periodicals, audio-visual materials, musical scores, maps, stamps, calendars, posters, advertisements, and bank notes.

Omitted are periodical articles.

CONTENTS: Introduction in Turkish, introduction in English, abbreviations, classified bibliography, indexes.

CATALOGUING RULES AND CLASSIFICATION SCHEMES USED: Materials are catalogued according to the AACR2 and 1988 revision.

Entries are classified according to DDC (20th).

ENTRY INFORMATION: Sequence number, author, dates if known, title, edition, place of publication, publisher, date of publication, place of printing, printing house, date of printing, pagination, size, illustration statement, price when known, series statement, notes including ISBN when known, added entries, DDC number in lower left, place number of the National Library in upper right.[1]

Before the mid-1980s, entries had a number assigned by the Directory of Collected Prints in the lower right, e.g., D.M. 356-82.

---

[1] Beginning in 1993, the primary DDC takes the place of the sequence number which is no longer used. An ALEPH system number, and a collected number are included in the entry information before the ISBN information. This information is included in a 21 October 1996 letter to the author by Sema Akinci, Section Director of the Preparation of Bibliography.

If more than one DDC number is assigned, reference to the entry will be listed under the subsequent number(s); complete bibliographic information is not repeated.

Information taken from the abbreviations list indicates that after the sequence number an asterisk (*) denotes a government publication, an equal sign (=) denotes a translation, and a zero (0) denotes a thesis.[1]

ARRANGEMENT: The arrangement of the classified bibliography is by the DDC scheme, then alphabetical within designated categories in the following order: books, magazines and newspapers, non-book materials.

Arrangement of some specific types of material are as follows. Periodicals on a specific subject are located at the end of the related subject under the heading "Periodicals"; periodicals of a general nature are under 050 (both magazines and reviews); newspapers under 070; a translation without the name of an author, or an author whose nationality is not known is found under "Literatures of other languages" (890); Musical scores are found under "Scores" at the end of "Music" (780); maps are located at the end of Geography" (910) under "Maps"; since 1971, stamps are at the end of "Commerce" (380) under "Stamps"; since 1972, bank notes are included at the end of the "Economics" section under "Moneys" (380); calendars are listed at the end of "Astronomy" (520) under "Calendars". Posters, declarations, and advertisements are listed in the annual index volume through 1992; beginning in 1993, these are included under their relevant subject and the heading of Audio-visual Materials.[2]

INDEXES: Monthly issues: personal author and corporate author index, title index, periodical title index. All are alphabetically arranged. The sequential number used in the indexes refers the user back to the bibliographic entry.[3]

The cumulated annual index includes personal author and corporate author, title; periodical title index, audio-visual materials index, ISBN index, and ISSN index. It also includes a list of publishers and printing presses that have appeared in *TB* during that year.

An additional listing that the annual index includes is the cumulated statistics of that year in both Turkish and in English in the following categories: books and pamphlets by class, periodical publications by frequency, newspapers listed by frequency.

Cumulated decennial indexes for 1928/38 and 1939/48 are available. 1928/38 is in two volumes: volume 1, Official publications; volume 2, Non-official publications. 1939/48 is in three volumes: volume 1 and volume 2 cover the UDC subject areas; volume 3 is the alphabetical index.

---

[1] Since 1993, the meaning of the asterisk, equal sign, and zero remains the same, but follow the primary DDC number. This information is included in Akinci's letter.
[2] Information about the treatment of posters, declarations, and advertisements is included in Akinci's letter.
[3] Since 1993, the DDC number included in the upper left-hand corner of the bibliographic entry appears in the index. This information is in Akinci's letter. The latest issue examined in July 1996 by the author is 1991.

NOTES AND COMMENTS: Although *TB* includes many of the ICNB recommendations it would be beneficial to its users to have complete prefatory material in each issue rather than to have to search for what an abbreviation means in another issue which incudes an abbreviations list or an introduction.

Although the publishers' and printing presses' list appears in the annual index, it would be useful to have it appear in each of the issues throughout the year. In this way, it is easier to keep up with changes in publishing houses and their addresses without waiting until the end of the year.[1]

The 1978 volume and earlier volumes included quarterly statistics of the publishing industry. Beginning in 1979, this is reported annually and is included in the cumulated annual index.

Türkiye Makalelerbibliyografyası =Bibliography of articles in Turkish periodicals.- v.1- . - Ankara : T.C. Kültür Bakanligi Millî Kütüphane Başkanliği, 1952-   is a monthly periodical index for Turkish periodicals. Periodicals articles and reviews, papers submitted to congresses, conferences and seminars which are acquired by the national library are treated in this title. Also included are laws, regulations, decrees, circulars and standards published in the *Official Gazette* since January 1992 (OCLC: 1481194; ISSN 0041-4344).[2]

T.C. Devlet Yayınlarıı Bibliyografyası Millî. Devlet Yayınları Dok Ümantasyon Merkezi. [Bibliography of the Turkish State Publications] published from 1971 - August 1989 (ceased) is a monthly listing of government publications. According to the *Survey on the Present State of Bibliographic Recording in Freely Available Printed Form of Government Publications and those of Intergovernment Organizations* it includes serials, monographs, internal documents, periodical articles, pamphlets, brochures, non-book materials, publications from Turkish branches of international organizations. (LCCN:85-651811/NE/r89; LC: Z2839.T2; OCLC: 12739042).

LATEST ISSUE EXAMINED/CURRENCY: Of 41 imprints in no. 10, 1991, 17 were from 1991, 16 were from 1990, 6 from 1989, and 2 from 1987. If distribution of *TB* could be more timely, this bibliography could be used for acquisitions and collection development purposes. Some delays have occurred with the publication of *TB* because of the transition to the automation of the library collection and how the computer works in relation to the bibliographies.

The latest issue examined was vol. 58, no. 12 for 1991 at the University of Wisconsin in July 1996, and at the Bibliotekstjänst AB Library in September 1997.

AUTOMATION: The *TB* has been published by computer since January 1989. After the publication of the January 1993 issue, it is being prepared by using new customized software. The transfer of the records from the ALEPH program (Automated Library Expandable Program of the Hebrew University) into the bibliographic program has been possible since 1996.

---

[1] A publishers' index will appear in each issue beginning with the publication of the *TB* for the 1995 year. This information is in Akinci's letter.

[2] "Publications of bibliographies," Millî Kütüphane = The Turkish National Library. Ankara, 1995, p. 29.

FORMAT AND SERVICES AVAILABLE: printed; accessible through the Internet at: http://www.mkutup.gov.tr

CURRENT LEGAL DEPOSIT LAWS: Legal Deposit Act, dated 1934, number 2527.[1]

AVAILABLE FROM: Subscription rate must be paid to account number 249, Ziraat Bankasi Mithatpasa Subesi (Ankara, Türkíye) in the name of Kültür Başkanliği Döner Sermaye Isletmeleri Merkez Müdurlügü Kuzilay-Ankara.

SELECTED ARTICLES: Atilgan, Doğan. *Türkiye Bibliyografyasi'nin Başlangicindan Bugüne Kataloglama ve Siniflama Açisindan Değerlendirilmesi. Evaluation of the Turkish National Bibliography from Start to Date for Cataloguing and Classifying of Viewpoint. 50. Kurulus Yilinda Ulusaldan Evrensele Türk Millî Kutuphanesi (1946-1996) Sempozyum Bildiri Özetleri. Summaries of Symposium Papers of 1946-1996. On its 50th Anniversary. TurkishNational Library from National to Universal.* Ankara, 1996. pp. 9-10. (Summary of papers given on 19-21 June 1996; complete publication forthcoming.)

Sefercioğlu, Necmeddin. "Türk Dünyasi'nda Bibliyografik Denetleme. Bibliographical Control in the Turkish World." *Türk Kütüphaneciliği. Turkish Librarianship* 9 (no. 1; March 1995):42-48.

VERIFIER: Ms. Sema Akinci, Section Director of the Preparation of Bibliography, Turkish National Library.

TURKMENISTAN

TITLE: *Türkmenistanyñg metbugat letopisi = Letopis' pechati Turkmenistana.* - no. 9 (1991)- . Ashgabat : Knizhnaîa palata Turkmenistana, 1991- .
Monthly.
Continues *Türkemenistan SSR-niñg metbugat letopisi.*
DDC: 015.585; LC: Z3413.T8; LCCN: not found; OCLC: 28606665
ISSN 0201-6788

COMPILER: Gosudarstvennyuĭ komitet po pechati Turkmeninstanai [i] Gosudarstvennaîa knizhnaîa palata Turkmenistana.

SCOPE AND COVERAGE: Types of publications included in *Türkmenistanyñg metbugat letopisi (TML)* are books, pamphlets, articles, reviews, government publications, dissertations, music and art publications. [2]

---

[1] Information in Akinci letter.
[2] The author appreciates the help of Helen Sullivan, Slavic Reference Center, University of Illinois, Urbana-Champaign.

CONTENTS: Classified bibliography, indexes, list of sources indexed for journal and newspaper articles, table summarizing by subject the number of publications in four areas: books, journal and newspaper articles, reviews, and Turkmen in CIS, colophon.

CATALOGUING RULES AND CLASSIFICATION SCHEMES USED: Cataloguing rules follow international standards.

Classification scheme used is a numbered subject arrangement similar but not exactly like the Russian system.

ENTRY INFORMATION: Consecutive entry number, title, author, place of publication, publisher, date, pagination, illustrations, size, place of printing, printer, series statement, ISBN, price and number of copies printed, legal deposit number in square brackets, e.g. [92-252], unidentified abbreviation, unidentified number in lower right corner.

ARRANGEMENT: Arrangement is by subject with the following categories included in each table of contents: psychology, atheism, religion, history, economics, statistics and demography, political science, youth and youth organizations, government and law, military science, semiotics, natural sciences, physical–mathematical sciences, earth science, biological sciences, technology, production, radio electronics and communications, automation, heavy industry, chemical industry and production, light industry, photography and cinema, transportation, construction, agriculture, horticulture, animal husbandry, public health and medicine, sports, culture, education, mass communications and propaganda, philogical sciences, national literature and folklore, children's literature and folklore, art and literature of universal interest.

INDEXES: Name index, geographical index, index of subject headings, and a list of sources indexed for journal and newspaper articles.

NOTES AND COMMENTS: The title and some additional information are in Turkmen and Russian.

It would be helpful to have in each issue a table of contents, and an introduction which explains the scope and coverage, the legal deposit law citation, standards that are adhered to in compiling the bibliographic information, abbreviations, the cataloguing rules and classification scheme used, and an analyzed entry which identifies the information given.

The children's literature is listed last.

TML's predecessor *Türkmenistan S.S.R.-ning metbugat letopisi* began in 1930 and ceased in 1991? (LCCN: 82-643125//r962; LC: Z3413.T8; OCLC: 8413922).

LATEST ISSUE EXAMINED/CURRENCY: The latest copy examined in June 1996 was for Dec. 1993, published 1994, and received by the University of Illinois, Urbana-Champaign in June 1996. Imprint dates included in no. 12 were for 1993, with some for 1992.

AUTOMATION: not known.

FORMAT AND SERVICES AVAILABLE: printed.

CURRENT LEGAL DEPOSIT LAWS: not known.

AVAILABLE FROM: National Library of Turkmenistan, Pl. Karla Marxa, 744000 Ashgabat.

VERIFIER: no reply received.

UGANDA

TITLE: *Uganda national bibliography.* Vol. 1, no. 1 (Mar. 1987)-   . - [Kampala, Uganda] :
Makerere University Library Services, 1987-   .
Frequency varies: bi-annual (vol. 3-   ); quarterly (vol. 1-2).
DDC: 016.96761; LC: Z3586.U37; DT433.222; LCCN: 88-980281; OCLC: 18346985
ISSN not found

COMPILER: Africana/Special Collections Section, Makerere University Library.

SCOPE AND COVERAGE: *Uganda national bibliography* (*UNB*) includes new books and other publications of Uganda, which are deposited at the Africana/Special Collections Section, Makerere University Library according to legal deposit laws.

Types of publications include books, pamphlets, reports, dissertations and other mimeographed documents, and first issue of new serial titles.

CONTENTS: [Preface] which includes the scope and coverage, arrangement and international standards followed, classified bibliography, index.

CATALOGUING RULES AND CLASSIFICATION SCHEMES USED: AACR2 is followed.

The classification scheme used is the DDC.

ENTRY INFORMATION: DDC number, author, title, place of publication, publisher, date, pagination, illustrations, size, series statement, frequency of serials, notes including bibliographic references, mimeographed, language, etc., consecutive entry number in lower right corner.

ARRANGEMENT: Arrangement is by DDC.

INDEXES: Author, editor and title index presented in alphabetical order. The index uses the DDC number to refer the user to the entry in the main section; consecutive entry number is also given.

NOTES AND COMMENTS: This is a new national bibliography since the 1986 *AGCNB*. It is good to see this commendable effort. Before the existence of the *UNB* the following two bibliographies, which were published in the 1960s and the 1970s, were helpful in filling the void.

"Uganda Bibliography." In *Library Bulletin and Accessions List*. - Jan./Feb. 1965-1976. - Kampala : Makerere University College Library, 1965-1976. This list includes titles published in Uganda and received on legal deposit by Makerere University Library and the East African Literature Bureau and other books about Uganda published abroad. Types of publications listed in "Uganda bibliography" are books, pamphlets, official and government publications, theses and dissertations, maps and atlases, and publications in the vernacular languages for Uganda. Entry information includes author, title, place of publication, publisher, date, notes. The *Library Bulletin* has been suspended since 1976.

"Uganda Bibliography." In *Uganda Journal*. 1961/62-1973. - Kampala : Uganda Society, 1962-1975. "Uganda Bibliography" includes current titles published in Uganda and elsewhere, most of which the compiler Bryan Langlands has seen. An asterisk (*) appears after the entry if the author has not seen the title. Types of publications included within the scope of "Uganda Bibliography" are books, pamphlets, annual reports, periodical articles, official and government publications, cyclostyled papers, book analytics, theses, and ephemeral materials. When this list was appearing, it was usually found in number 2 of *Uganda Journal*. "Uganda Bibliography" has a brief introductory paragraph giving the history of these bibliographies and the years that are covered in the current list, followed by the entries. Entry information given for monographs includes author, title, place of publication, publisher, size, pagination, illustrations, date, and notes as needed. Entry information for periodical articles includes author, title of article, journal title, place of publication, volume and number, date, and pagination. It is alphabetically arranged by broad subject divisions; within these divisions the entries are then alphabetical by the main entry. Examples of subject divisions are: general, agriculture (and its divisions), anthropology, archaeology, and botany. After Bryan Langlands left Uganda in 1976 or early 1977, this bibliography no longer appeared in *Uganda Journal*.[1]

A bibliography project compiled by the EASL, Makerere University is *Bibliography of Serial Publications of Uganda*. This is a list of current and retrospective serial pubications held by Makerere University. It also includes newspapers. Published in 1983, it is available from EASL, Makerere University, P.O. Box 7062, Kampala, Uganda.[2]

AL,ESA and *QIPL,ESA* include Uganda within their scopes.

Uganda does not participate in ISBN or ISSN.

The contents of *UNB* is mimeographed; the cover is printed.

LATEST ISSUE EXAMINED/CURRENCY: The latest issue examined is vol. 4, nos. 1-4, January - December 1990 which was examined at the University Library, Cambridge in November 1995.

In analyzing the imprint dates of this issue 17 were 1990, 16 were 1989, 6 were 1988, and 4

---

[1] Information supplied in a letter to the author by James Armstrong, Field Director, Library of Congress Office, Nairobi, Kenya dated 11 September 1985.

[2] "Uganda: Bibliography of Serials," *International Cataloguing* 13 (July/Sept. 1984):27. James Mugasha, University Librarian, verified in a 6 December 1996 e-mail correspondence that this is the latest edition available.

were earlier. It is good to see this bibliography produced. However, with this much of a gap between imprint date and distribution of the national bibliography the *UNB* will be used more as an historical record rather than as an acquisitions tool.[1]

AUTOMATION: The *UNB* is on a CDS/ISIS database; the hardware is an IBM PC 386.

FORMAT AND SERVICES AVAILABLE: printed.

CURRENT LEGAL DEPOSIT LAWS: Makerere University (Deposit Library) Act of 1958 (Revised edition, 1964); Deposit Library and Documentation Centre Act, 1969.[2]

AVAILABLE FROM: Makerere University Library, Africana/Special Collections Section, P.O. Box 16002, Kampala.

VERIFIER: Mrs. D. Kigozi, Senior Librarian, Makerere University Library Services, Makerere University

UKRAINE

TITLE: *Litopys knyh.* - Kyïv : Knyzhkova palata Ukraïny, 1924-   .
Frequency varies; monthly, 1994-   ; semi-monthly, 1924-1993.
On title page: *Derzhavnyi, bibliografichnyi, pokazhchyk, ukraïny.*
Publisher varies.
DDC: 016.89179; LC: Z2514.U5L5; LCCN: not found; OCLC: 5653543
ISSN 0130-9196

COMPILER: Knyzhkova Palata Ukraïny [Book Chamber of the Ukraine]

SCOPE AND COVERAGE: *Litopys knyh (LK)* includes the publishing output of Ukraine which is deposited at the national library according to legal deposit laws.

Types of publications include books, pamphlets, "autoreferati" dissertations, dissertations, preprints, conference theses, collections of scientific articles, abstracts, instructions, standards, textbooks, manuals, elections, dictionaries, guides, albums, atlases, anthologies, almanacs, catalogues, prospects, etc. [3]

Omitted from *LK* are periodicals and newspapers which are covered in other series.

[1] Uganda has started to produce *UNB* by computer, according to information in an email letter dated 6 December 1996 to the author by James Mugasha, University Librarian. It will be more regular than it has been in the past. A cumulative issue, v. 5, 1991-1994, should be ready by January 1997.
[2] Information from the preface of *UNB*, 1990, and from the *International Guide to Legal Deposit*, p. 99.
[3] The author is grateful for the help of Yuri Popov in the translation of the national bibliography text.

CONTENTS: Classified bibliography, indexes.

CATALOGUING RULES AND CLASSIFICATION SCHEMES USED: ISBD is followed. The Book Chamber is working on new national standards; currently the Soviet Union standards are still in use, e.g., Bibliographic description of document. General requirements and rules, GOST 7.1-84; Bibliographic record. Abbreviations in the Russian language. General requirements and rules, GOST 7.12-93.

The classification scheme used is UDC.

ENTRY INFORMATION: Consecutive entry number, author, title, place of publication, publisher, date, pagination, illustrations, size, series statement, notes including ISBN when known, various abbreviations giving information about price, no price given, free, numbers of copies printed, without number of copies printed, hard or soft cover, internal number, e.g., 94-3416, UDC number.

ARRANGEMENT: Arrangement is by UDC.

INDEXES: "Perelik mov" [books written in languages other than Ukrainian], name index, subject index, title index, geographical index, UDC heading index. The last issue in each year also has a series index.

NOTES AND COMMENTS: Before the breakup of the USSR, publications of the Ukraine were recorded in *Knizhnaĩa letopis'* and *Litopys' knyg*. Since the Ukraine established its independence, the primary record of its publishing output is recorded in *LK*.

Other titles of interest are as follows: [1]

Litopys hazetnykh stateĭ [Chronicle of newspaper articles]. - Kyïv : Knyẑhkova palata ukraïny, 1937- . Semimonthly (LCCN: 60-23901//r94; LC: AI15.L48; OCLC: 5652879; ISSN 0130-917X). This state bibliographic index includes citations to articles, documents, and fiction published in national and regional newspapers of the Ukraine.

Litopys kartografichnykh vydan' [Chronicle of cartographic editions]. - Kyïv : Knyẑhkova palata ukraïny, 1997- . Annual. This state bibliographic index includes information about cartographic editions (maps, plans, diagrams, atlases) published in the Ukraine. When the Ukraine was a part of the U.S.S.R., there was no need for this title since this material was listed in the Knizhnaĩa letopis'.

Litopys not [Chronicle of music]. - Kyïv : Knyẑhkova palata ukraïny, 1954- . Annual (ISSN 0130-0914). Title and frequency varies. This state bibliographic index includes information about separately published music, collections of musical works, training and methodological

---

[1] The author is indebted to the "Annotated Plan for Publication of Literature in 1997" / V.G. Volokh. - Kyïv : Book Chamber of Ukraine, 1997 for guidance in the brief annotations, and to the 23 March 1997 letter written to the author by Mykola Senchenko, Director, Knyẑhkova Palata. The help of Yuri Popov, Wooster, Ohio, with the translation of the material is very much appraciated.

music editions, text books integrally connected with music, and musical works published in literary, popular, and children's magazines and newspapers.

Litopys obrazotvorchykh vydan' [Chronicle of fine art editions]. - Divh./vhrt. 1978-   . - Kyïv : Knyžhkova palata ukraïny, 1978-   . Semiannual (LCCN: sn84-10736; OCLC: 7326582; ISSN 0136-0906). This title continues *Litopys drukovanykh. Tvoriv obrazotvorchoho mystetstva.* - Kharkiv : Knyžhkova palata Ukraïns'koï RSR, 1937-1977. The state bibliographic index includes information of fine art editions published in the Ukraine: posters, portraits, reproductions, prints, art postcards, albums, picture books, paint books, albums for painting, visual aids, and calendars.

Litopys periodichnih vydan' [Chronicle of periodical editions] Kyiv : Knyžhkova palata ukraïny, 1934-   . Annual. (ISSN 0201-6842). This state bibliographic index includes information about periodicals, bulletins, and bibliographical editions.

Litopys retsenziĭ [Chronicle of book reviews]. - Kyïv : Knyžhkova palata ukraïny, 1936-   . Annual (LCCN: 68-130612//r92; LC: Z1035.6A1L5; OCLC: 19481787; ISSN 0130-9250). This state bibliographic index includes information of reviews, critical reviews, articles and notices published in magazines, collections, and newspapers.

Litopys zhurnal'nykh stateĭ [Chronicle of magazine articles]. - Kyïv : Knyžhkova palata ukraïny, 1936-   . Semi-monthly. (OCLC: 5657387; ISSN 0130-9188). This state bibliographic index includes references to articles, documents, and fiction works from magazines, periodicals, serial editions, and bulletins published in the Ukraine.

Two titles which include books in print are:

Kataloh vydan' Ukraïny = Catalogue of editions (publications) *of the Ukraine.* - vyp. 1 (1996)-   . - Kyïv : Knyžhkova palata ukraïny, 1996-   . Semi-annual. (LCCN: 96-642096; LC: Z2519.6.K38; OCLC: 35634219; ISBN 966-7120-00-7 (for 1996 ed.)). This title includes bibliographic information concerning books of the Ukraine which are available. An index of the publishers is given at the end. Intended audience is the book distributor, library worker, and bibliophile.

Novi vydanniã Ukraïny [New editions of Ukraine]. - Kyïv : Knyžhkova palata ukraïny, 1958-   . Semimonthly (OCLC: 36384263, ISSN 0136-0922). This publishing bibliographic index includes information about books as well as music and fine art editions published by publishing houses and organizations of Ukraine. Annotations are included. This was not published from 1990-1996. In 1996, frequency is three times a month.

LATEST ISSUE EXAMINED/CURRENCY: The latest issue examined at the University of Illinois, Urbana-Champaign in June 1996 is no. 2, 1995. A sampling of entries showed 1993 and 1994 imprint dates.

AUTOMATION: The national bibliography is not automated, but the Book Chamber of the Ukraine anticipates automation at the end of 1997. In existence since the second half of 1996 is a local database of short bibliographic notes; it is based on the FOLIO system adjusted to the Cyrillic alphabet.

FORMAT AND SERVICES AVAILABLE: printed.

CURRENT LEGAL DEPOSIT LAWS: The current decree is 06.0.1992, No. 376. An update is 25.03.1996, No. 41 which has been sent for review to the highest legislation but is not yet approved by the Parliament. It has been approved by the Book Chamber.

AVAILABLE FROM: Knyžhkova Palata [Book Chamber of the Ukraine], prosp. Yuri Gagarina, no. 27, Kyïv 94, 253094.

Within the U.S.: East View Publications, 3020 Harbor Lane North, Minneapolis, MN 55447.

SELECTED ARTICLES: Jdanova, R. "She Raz Pro Ukrainskii Bibliographichnii Repertuar." *Visnyk Knyžhkovoï Palaty* (1996 no. 12):9-10.

Patoka, V. "Do Problem: Stvorenja Ukrainskogo Bibliographichogo Repertuaru: Iz Visturu na Drugomu Vseurkrainskogo Kongresa Bibliotekariv." *Visnyk Knyžhkovoï Palaty* (1997 no. 1):9-11.

Zagumenna, V. "Suchasni Problemi Theorii Natzionalnoi Bibliographii: Iz Vistupu na II Vseurkrainskogo Kongresa Bibliotekariv u Ramkah Vauch. Seminaru "Natzionalnii Bibliographii." *Visnyk Knyžhkovoï Palaty* (1997 no. 1):11-12.

VERIFIER: Mykola Senchenko, Director, Book Chamber of the Ukraine.

UNITED ARAB EMIRATES

TITLE: *al-Wirāqīyah al-waṭanīyah li-Dawlet al-Imārāt al-'Arabīyah al-Muttaḥidah* [The National bibliography of the United Arab Emirates]. - Abû-aaby : al-Dar, 1990-   .
Annual.
Chiefly Arabic; some English.
DDC: not found; LC: Z3028.U54W57; LCCN: 92-966132/NE; OCLC: 27731309
ISSN not found

COMPILER: al-Majma' al-Thaqāfī, Dār al-Kutub al-Waṭanīyah [National Library].

SCOPE AND COVERAGE: *al-Wirāqīyah al-waṭanīyah li-Dawlet al-Imārāt al-'Arabīyah al-Muttaḥidah* (*NBUAE*) includes the publishing output of the United Arab Emirates which is deposited at the national library according to legal deposit laws. Publications about the United Arab Emirates published elsewhere are also included.

Types of publications include books, pamphlets, dissertations, analyzed entries for books which include information about the United Arab Emirates, and video and sound cassettes (including lectures).

CONTENTS: English part: contents, abbreviations, bibliography, indexes. Arabic part: preface, contents, bibliography.

CATALOGUING RULES AND CLASSIFICATION SCHEMES USED: ISBD is followed.

Broad subject catagories are used to arrange the bibliographic entries. Although not stated, these categories follow the ten DDC subject headings. No classification numbering scheme is used.

ENTRY INFORMATION: Author (dates if known), title, place of publication, publisher, date, pagination, illustrations, size, series statement, notes including analyzed article bibliographic information, head of title information, consecutive entry number in lower right corner.

ARRANGEMENT: The entries are alphabetically arranged under broad subjects which follow the DDC subject headings.

INDEXES: Title index, author index. The consecutive entry numbers are used in the index to refer the user to the bibliographic information. No references are included in the English language index to entries in the Arabic language section.

NOTES AND COMMENTS: It is gratifying to see this new title which lists the publishing output of the UAE. It is very attractively presented. At present, the broad subject headings organize the books in a helpful manner. One ICNB recommendation which should be considered is the use of an international classification system to organize the bibliography.

The *NBUAE* is bound with the English and the Arabic bibliography tête bêche.

Another title worth mentioning is the *al-Intāj al-fikrī fī al-Imārāt : bibliyūgrāfiyā al-iṣdārāt al-waṭaniyah fī Dawlat al-Imārāt al-ʿArabīyah al-Muttahidah hāttá ʿam...* [Intellectual production of the United Arab Emirates] / iʿdād al-Maktabah al-Markaziyah, Shuʾūn al-Maktabāt wa-al-Wathāʾiq bi-Dāʾirat al-Thaqāfah wa-al-Iʿlām, al-Shāriqah [Prepared by the Administration of Libraries, Dept. of Media and Education]. - al-Shāriqah : al-Maktabah, 1991-   . Biennial. Contents are preface, table of volumes and number of entries from 1969 to the present, table showing DDC subjects, number of entries, and percentages in this volume, table by type of publisher, table of types of publications, list of people who worked on this volume, abbreviations, and the alphabetical bibliography. Types of publications listed are books, lectures, translations, investigations and research, official and government publications, reports and statistics, documents and laws. Publicatons in Bahrain and those by Bahraini living elsewhere are within the scope. The latest examined from the UCLA Library in July 1997 is for 1995. The 1997 issue will appear in December 1997. This title appears on a more regular basis than *NBUAE*. The *NBUAE* and this title are totally independent.[1] (LCCN: 95-648417/NE/r97; OCLC: 33092939).

The United Arab Emirates is included within the scopes of *The Arab Bulletin of Publications* (LCCN: 73-960585/NE/r902; LC: Z3013.N3; OCLC: 2239670) and *AL,ME.* - Vol. 1, 1963-Vol. 31, 1993. (LCCN: 75-644385//r843; OCLC: 2452246; ISSN 0041-7769).

---

[1] Information about *Al-intaj Al-fikri fī al-Imārāt* was included in a 24 August 1997 fax from Yousuf A. Aydabi, Director of Planning, Department of Culture and Information. This title was first called to the author's attention by David Hirsch, Middle East Studies Bibliographer, University Research Library, UCLA.

LATEST ISSUE EXAMINED/CURRENCY: The latest issue examined is for 1991/1992 (supplement) at the University Library, Cambridge in April 1995; as of December 1996, this is still the most current issue. As the procedures are established, it is anticipated that more current coverage for the period covered will be possible. Then it would be possible for libraries to use the national bibliography as an acquisitions source.

The English titles listed included imprint dates as follows: none for 1992, three for 1991, five for 1990, seven for 1989, eight for 1988, and 11 for earlier years or date unknown.

AUTOMATION: The national bibliography uses a local automated system.

FORMAT AND SERVICES AVAILABLE: printed.

CURRENT LEGAL DEPOSIT LAWS: no laws.

AVAILABLE FROM: National Library, POB 2380, Abu Dhabi.

VERIFIER: Jumaa al Qubaisa, Director of the National Library.

UNITED KINGDOM

TITLE: *British national bibliography*. - Boston Spa : The British Library, 1950-   .
Weekly, cumulating with interim cumulations January-April, May-August and January-December as annual cumulation.
Compiled from entries in the weekly lists.
Publisher varies: 1950-1973 issued by the Council of the British National Bibliography.
DDC: 015.42; LC: Z2001.B75; LCCN: 51-6468//r922; OCLC: 1028299
ISSN 0007-1544

COMPILER: National Bibliographic Service, British Library.

SCOPE AND COVERAGE: *British National Bibliography* (*BNB*) lists new and forthcoming titles published in the United Kingdom and the Republic of Ireland based upon, but not restricted to, materials deposited at the Legal Deposit Office of the British Library.

Types of publications listed in *BNB* are monographs and first issues of new serials.

Excluded from *BNB* are publications without a British imprint, except those published in the Republic of Ireland. Government publications, both British and Irish, are excluded. Also excluded are periodicals (except first issue of a new periodicals or first issue under a change of title), HM Inspectors' reports on individual institutions, local government publications, telephone directories, official town guides, non-book materials, books of camera ready illustrations, lettering, etc., large print books, calendars, diaries, knitting patterns, postcards, posters, promotional material, such as trade literature, house journals, publicity material, and prospectuses or syllabuses for educational courses, and ephemeral material, such as timetables, religious or political tracts, unbound material, and material on controlled distribution.[1]

Theses and dissertations, maps, musical scores, microforms, and audio-visual materials are included in supplementary titles included under the Notes and Comments section below.

CONTENTS: Weekly: brief introduction, classified bibliography, name/title index which also includes series and names as subjects. Records in the last category are marked with a dagger (†). The last week of the month includes a monthly cumulated name/title index and a subject index for that month's issues.

Interim cumulation: preface (including scope, contents, abbreviations list and an analyzed entry), classified bibliography, name/title index, subject index alphabetically arranged.

Annual: (Vol. 1) preface including an analyzed entry, outline of the DDC, classified bibliography, (Vol. 2) name and title index, subject index.

CATALOGUING RULES AND CLASSIFICATION SCHEMES USED: AACR2, ISBD(M) and ISBD(S) rules are followed. The *LCSH* is used from 1997 replacing COMPASS, a subject indexing system derived from the PRECIS system. For electronic data processing, UKMARC format is followed. Entries are in order according to the BLAISE [British Library Automated Information Service] Filing Rules.

All items are catalogued to AACR2 level 2.

The classification scheme used is the latest edition of DDC with verbal extensions in the classified sequence.

ENTRY INFORMATION: Monographs: DDC number and the edition of DDC used in parentheses, e.g. *(DC21)*, author, title, place of publication, publisher, date, pagination, illustrations, size, series, notes, ISBN, price, and tracings. The *BNB* number, e.g., B94-11453, in lower right corner.

Periodicals: DDC number and DDC edition used, title, beginning date, place of publication, publisher, date of publication, collation, frequency, notes, ISSN, price, tracings, and *BNB* number.

The address of a publisher is given in full as part of the entry information if it is not readily available elsewhere.

Since 1977, CIP information has been included in the weekly lists and is identified by "CIP entry." When titles are published and deposited at the British Library, entry information is verified. A new entry then appears in the *Weekly List* with the note "Formerly CIP." An asterisk (*) to the left of the main entry designates CIP entries.

ARRANGEMENT: The main bibliography is arranged by the DDC system.

---

[1] Neil Wilson. *"British National Bibliography*: exclusions policies 1993." *Select* 9 (spring 1993):4-5, and the "Preface" to *BNB* (Interim Cumulation May/ August 1994): iii.

INDEXES: Name/title index includes authors, titles, series, and names as subject, the latter designated by a dagger (†). The last weekly list, interim and annual cumulations include an alphabetical subject index. The classification number refers the reader to the more complete information listed in the classified bibliography.

NOTES AND COMMENTS: The scope of *BNB* is supplemented by the following titles.

British reports, translations, and theses. British Library, 1981- . Coverage is non-trade material, e.g. 'grey' literature. From January 1998 this will become *British National Bibliography for Report Literature.* Theses will be listed in a separate publications (details not yet available), and translations, the publication of which has declined greatly in recent years, will no longer be included. Also available on BLAISE.

British catalogue of audio-visual materials. - London : British Library Bibliographic Services Division, 1979- . (Supplements issued 1980 and 1983.) The bibliography is arranged by DDC. The scope does not include 16 mm. film, video recordings or musical sound recordings. Author, title, series and subject index. (LCCN: 80-498535; OCLC: 6863213). Also available on BLAISE.

The British catalogue of music. - Jan./Mar. 1957- . - London : British Library Bibliographic Services Division, 1957- . Published by the Council of the British National Bibliography, 1957-1961; by the British Library Bibliographic Services Division, 1974-1990. London : Bowker-Saur, 1991- . Quarterly, with annual cumulation. Contents include preface, outline of the classification, list of abbreviations, classified section, composer and title index and subject index. This bibliography, arranged according to the DDC, is based on printed material received at the British Library's Legal Deposit Office or purchased by the British Library's Music Library. The coverage includes new music printed in Great Britain, foreign music available in Great Britain through a sole agent, music acquired by the British Library Music Library from foreign publishers who do not have agents in Great Britain. This title does not include sound recordings and certain kinds of popular music. It is divided into three sections: classified section, composer and title index, subject index. AACR2, Name Authority List, "Proposed Revision of 780 Music" based on the DDC are used. An asterisk (*) indicates that the record has not previously appeared in an interim issue of the catalogue. (ISSN 0068-1407; OCLC: 1537143).

British national film and videoguide. - Vol. 1, no. 1 (spring 1995)- . - Boston Spa : British Library, 1995- . Quarterly, with annual cumulations. (ISSN 9664-4795; OCLC: 33346569). This title continues *The British national film & video catalogue.* - Vol. 22, no. 1 (spring 1984)- Vol. 29 (1991). - London : British Film Institute, 1984-1991. Quarterly, with annual cumulation (ISSN 0266-805X; OCLC: 11008973). This title continues, with its numbering, *The British national film catalogue.* - Vol. 1(1963)- vol. 21(1983). - London : British Film Institute, 1963-1983. This bibliography includes films, video cassettes, and video tapes made available for non-theatrical hire and for sale only in the UK, including non-fiction and short fiction items, feature films, television programmes, etc. Scope does not include products designed for home screening, foreign material available for sale only, filmstrips, slides or other non-film materials, newsreels. Production index and subject, title index.

Serials in the British Library. - 1981- . - London : British Library, 1981- . Quarterly, with annual cumulation (ISSN 0260-0005; OCLC: 7979766, 8264921). Includes newly acquired serials such as periodicals, newspapers, annuals, journals, monographic series, transactions. Excludes serials acquired primarily for loan or to support document supply services.

Index to theses accepted for higher degrees by the universities of Great Britain and Ireland and the Council for National Academic Awards - Vol. 1- , 1950/51-   . London : Aslib, 1953-   . Annual. Author and subject indexes. (ISSN 0073-6066). As of volume 27, this title is also published on magnetic tape.

The British Library General Catalogue of Printed Books in various cumulations is an alphabetical listing of authors and titles. The 1982-1985 volume is published by K.G. Saur, 1986 and is in microfiche. Cross references are used. Also available on BLAISE and on the British Library OPAC.

BNB on CD-ROM [computer file]. - 1950-   . - [London] : British Library, 1989-   . Monthly (1993-   ), quarterly (1989-1992) (ISSN 0968-3097; OCLC: 25836906). The scope of this title is the same as *BNB* from the present back to 1950. Searching is possible from over 20 indexes including authors, titles, ISBNs, keywords, DDC numbers, publication year, and subject headings. Boolean operators can be used to refine searches. The browsing option is possible from more than a dozen indexes. One disk includes the current bibliography from 1986 to the present, and one disk holds the backfile to 1950. (The DOS version of the backfile is issued on two disks.)

BNB on CD-ROM is available in the following versions:

Windows: hardware requirements – PC compatible with 386DX processor: 4Mb free RAM, 10 Mb free hard disk space; MS-DOS version 5.0 or higher, Microsoft Windows 3.1 or higher, CD-ROM drive, Microsoft CD-ROM extensions (MSCDEX) version 2.0 or higher.

Apple Macintosh: hardware requirements– Apple Macintosh running system 7.0 or higher, 4Mb free RAM, 10 Mb free hard disk space, CD-ROM drive.

DOS: hardware requirements– IBM PC XT or AT genuine compatible, MS-DOS 3.3 or above, 512k available RAM, 2Mb hard disk space, color (VGA or SVGA) or monochrome display, CD-ROM drive, Microsoft CD-ROM extensions (MSCDEX) version 2.0 or higher, optional mouse using an appropriate mouse driver.

A clearly written help manual accompanies the CD-ROM.

Official publications are not included in *BNB*. Beginning in August 1996, the *Stationery Office monthly catalogue* (LCCN: 97-648082; OCLC: 36102671), with annual cumulations is called Stationery Office (Great Britain). *Stationery Office annual catalogue*, and continues the listing of official and government publications found in *HMSO annual catalogue* covering 1985-1995. - [London] : HMSO, 1986-1996 (ISSN 0951-8584; OCLC: 14523756).   This continues *Government publications of [   ] Her Majesty's Stationery Office (HMSO) annual catalogue.* - 1976-1984. - London : HMSO, 1978-1985 (ISSN 0143-9499; OCLC: 14447803). This title continues Great Britain. Her Majesty's Stationery Office. *Government publications.* (LCCN: 36-13303; OCLC: 2882741). There are also daily lists and monthly lists. Includes publications for sale by HMSO. IGO publications available for sale are also listed.

The Catalogue of British official publications not published by HMSO and business and government. 1980- . - Cambridge : Chadwyck-Healey, 1981- includes official and government publications financed or controlled completely or partially by the British Government, which are published by sources other than HMSO. Quangos (quasi-autonomous non-governmental organizations), government departments, nationalized industries, research institutes are represented. Coverage includes periodicals, newspapers, serials, single-sheet updates and appendices, give-away leaflets and publicity material of value, atlases, selected maps, posters and audio-visual aids. Ephemeral material, ordnance survey maps, patents are excluded. Titles listed in this work are available on microfiche from the publisher. Over 400 organizations are included. (ISSN 0260-5619).

Bibliographic records for maps, atlases, charts, plans, and globes acquired since 1974 by the British Library Map Library are available on BLAISE.

Books in English combining UKMARC and LC/MARC records is available on microfiche issued every two months and cumulates on an annual basis.

Two multi-year cumulations of *BNB*, now issued in microfiche, are for 1950-1984 and 1981-1992.

With the use of CIP as an ordering and selection tool, it would seem to be appropriate to reinstate the publishers' list for easy access to addresses of publishers listed in *BNB*. This feature is included in the ICNB recommendations. Ways of accomplishing this are now being actively considered.

Titles in other languages were spotted in the national bibliography. In recent years it appears that more effort has been made to include titles published in other languages represented in the UK; this needs to continue.

Although the *BNB* includes all of the United Kingdom within its scope, both Scotland and Wales publish bibliographies which deserve to be mentioned. In each case, these titles, because of the very nature of their specificity, list titles not mentioned in *BNB*.

The Bibliography of Scotland. - 1976/77- . - Edinburgh : HMSO, 1978- . Annual (ISSN 0143-571X; OCLC: 26614315, 5655996). The National Library of Scotland compiles this list of books, pamphlets, serial publications, official and government publications, dissertations, musical scores, selected periodical articles, microforms from its accessions which are of major interest to the life and culture of the Scots at home and abroad. The scope also includes publications, including articles, published elsewhere but relating to Scotland. Excluded are maps, certain categories of official publications, (e.g., Parliamentary debates, circulars, planning appeal reports), periodicals (first issues and changes of title are listed), including annuals, and ephemera. Contents include introduction, list of journals indexed, topographical section, subject section, author/title index and list of publishers based in Scotland. Cataloguing is done according to AACR2 and ISBD(M). From 1976-1987, the *Bibliography of Scotland* was published in annual printed volumes. In 1988 an online bibliographic database linked to the National Library of Scotland's general catalogue of printed books, and is available to external users through international computer networks linked to the Internet. It is also available on microfiche produced by the National Library of Scotland covering 1990, published in 1991.

Both the database and microfiche edition contain records for 1988 or later, and items published between 1976 and 1987 which were processed 1988 or later.

Covering the period 1985/1986 onwards, the *Llyfryddiaeth Cymru / Llyfrgell Genedlaethol Cymru = A Bibliography of Wales* / The National Library of Wales. - Aberystwyth : The Library, 1992-   . Biennial (ISSN 0968-0748; OCLC: 28484424) continues in part *Bibliotheca celtica*. - 1901-1981/1984. - Aberystwyth : National Library of Wales, 1910-1990. Annual (ISSN 0067-7914; OCLC 2067361) and in part the *Subject index to Welsh periodicals*. - 1931-1981/84. - Swansea, 1931-1984 (OCLC: 1782624). The *Bibliography* includes works in Welsh or relating to Wales published during the period covered. Section 1 has records listed under subject headings using the scheme of the *Subject index to Welsh periodicals* which is in accordance with the Library of Congress list of *Subject headings used in the dictionary catalogue*. The *LCSH* provides for new subject headings. Section two gives full bibliographic records under the authors' name. Contents of *A Bibliography of Wales* include the foreword, list of periodicals and abbreviations, subject section, author section.

LATEST ISSUE EXAMINED/CURRENCY: The latest issue examined was a *BNB Weekly List* for May 1997 at the University Library, Cambridge in June 1997. The latest issue of *A Bibliography of Wales* is 1989/1990 published in 1994 at the National Library of Wales in November 1994. The latest issue examined of *Bibliography of Scotland* is 1994 when visiting the National Library of Scotland in November 1994.

AUTOMATION: The printed *BNB* is produced through the automated manipulation of UKMARC exchange records using the LOCAS software suite, an in-house product producing a photo-typesetting tape used to produce artwork for the printers.

The online version of *BNB* is available through BLAISE.

The CD-ROM version has a search interface developed by RTIS in the US.

FORMAT AND SERVICES AVAILABLE: *BNB*: printed, magnetic tape, microfiche, CD-ROM, Internet, direct file transfer, online file on BLAISE, floppy disk, OPAC.

Bibliography of Scotland: microfiche; *A Bibliography of Wales*: printed.

CURRENT LEGAL DEPOSIT LAWS: Copyright Act 1911. ("Preface," *Interim Cumulation BNB*, May-August 1994, iii.)

AVAILABLE FROM: Turpin Distribution, Blackhorse Road, Letchworth, Hertfordshire SG6 IHN. E-mail: turpin@rsc.org

BNB on CD-ROM: Overseas customers in northern and southern Europe, Latin America, the Caribbean and Japan should place orders via Chadwyck-Healey offices.

Other areas: Turpin Distribution, Blackhorse Road, Letchworth, Hertfordshire SG6 IHN.

Bibliography of Scotland: National Library of Scotland, George IV Bridge, Edinburgh EH1 1EW, Scotland

A Bibliography of Wales: National Library of Wales, Aberystwyth, Wales SY23 3BU.

SELECTED ARTICLES: Croucher, Margaret. "The British National Bibliography. An Historical Perspective." In *Standards for the International Exchange of Bibliographic Information. Papers presented at a course held at the School of Library, Archive and Information Studies, University College London, 3-18 August 1990.* Edited by I.C. McIlwaine. London : The Library Association, 1991.

The Future of the National Bibliography. Proceedings of a Seminar held by the British Library in June 1997. British Library, 1997.

"Scotland: National Bibliography." *International Cataloguing* 8 (July/Sept. 1979):27.

Stephens, Andy. *The history of the British National Bibliography, 1950-1973.* - Boston Spa : British Library, 1994. (book)

Wilson, Neil. "*British National Bibliography*: exclusions policies 1993." *Select* 9 (spring 1993):4-5

VERIFIER: Arthur Cunningham, Head of Publications, British Library.

UNITED STATES

TITLE: MARC Distribution Service. *Books U.S.* - Washington, D.C. : Library of Congress, Cataloging Distribution Service, 1983-   .
Weekly or daily for current year subscription.
DDC: not found; LC: not found; LCCN: not found; OCLC: not found
ISSN not found

COMPILER (PUBLISHER): Cataloging Distribution Service, Library of Congress.

SCOPE AND COVERAGE: *Books U.S.* lists all monographs published in the U.S., regardless of date, and in any language which has been catalogued by the Library of Congress.[1]

Types of publications include books, pamphlets, monographic official and government publications from all levels of government, monographic microform publications (both microform re-issues and items originally issued in microform), and librettos.

Excluded are music scores, sheet music, musical and non-musical recordings, motion pictures, filmstrips, kits, slide sets, video recordings, serials (monographs in series are included), maps, atlases, art objects, braille books, broadsides, art prints, posters and other single sheet graphic

---

[1] The possibility of including this title as a current national bibiliography for the U.S. was first brought to the author's attention by Mary Sauer Price, Director for Bibliographic Products and Services, The Library of Congress, when she presented her paper "The National Union Catalog Program" at the 51st IFLA Conference in Chicago, 1985.

materials. Many of these materials are included in other *NUC* series published by the Library of Congress.

CONTENTS: The machine-readable cataloging records in USMARC communications format are arranged in five sections: register, name index, title index, LC series index, and LC subject index.

CATALOGUING RULES AND CLASSIFICATION SCHEMES USED: AACR2 and pertinent *L.C. Rule Interpretations*, *Library of Congress Subject Headings*, *Name Authorities*, and *Library of Congress Classification* are all titles used in compiling *Books U.S.*

The classification scheme used is the Library of Congress classification system.

ENTRY INFORMATION: Register: register number in upper left corner, author, title, place of publication, publisher, date, pagination, illustrations, size, notes, ISBN, price, subjects and added entry tracings, classification number and the DLC (LC symbol) or the *NUC* symbol of the library which was responsible for the cataloguing appears in the lower left corner; DDC number, control number and cataloguing rules followed in the lower right corner.

Name index entry information: main entry, uniform title, title proper, place of publication, publisher, date, series statement, classification number (LC records only) in the lower left corner, LC or *NUC* control number in the lower middle, register number in lower right corner.
Title index entry information: main entry (when not the index entry element), uniform title, title proper (when not the index entry element), place of publication, publisher, date, series statement, classification number (LC records only) in the lower left corner, LC or *NUC* control (card) number in the lower middle, register number in lower right corner.

Series index entry information: main entry, uniform title, title proper, place of publication, publisher, date, classification number in the lower left corner, LC or *NUC* control (card) number in the lower middle, register number in lower right corner.

Subject index entry information: main entry, uniform title, title proper, date, classification number in the lower left corner, LC or *NUC* control number in the lower middle, register number in lower right corner.

ARRANGEMENT: Register: in record control number order, with new issues continuing the number order of the preceding issue. Entry information is complete, including information included on the LC cards. Access to the register is by the various indexes.

INDEXES: Name index, title index, LC series index, LC subject index. Shortened cataloguing information is given in each index. Records are content designated in USMARC communications format which enable extensive indexing by system developers.

The name index, arranged alphabetically, provides access to all names and name-title combinations used as main or added entry headings. It does not include names used in subject headings. Uniform titles are included within the scope of this index. The number refers to the register number.

The title index, arranged alphabetically, provides title access (whether as a title proper or as an added entry heading) to LC and contributed records. Titles were not fully developed access points in the printed format. Uniform titles and series titles are not included. The number refers to the register number.

The series index, arranged alphabetically, provides access to all series titles in LC records and contributed records that are given as added entries. Prior to 1986, only the series in LC records was included. The number refers to the register number.

The subject index provides access to subject headings in the LC records and the contributed records. Prior to 1986, only the subject headings to LC records were included. Names and titles appearing as subjects are also listed. The index does not include headings for children's literature, subject headings for the National Library of Medicine and the National Agricultural Library. The number refers to the register number.

NOTES AND COMMENTS: When the capability for extracting U.S. imprints from the *National Union Catalog* became possible with the change from a printed catalogue to microfiche, CD-ROM, and now only on tape, *Books U.S.* became the closest approximation to a current national bibliography that is available in the United States. There are a few ICNB recommendations that it does not meet. It is based on copyright, not on legal deposit legislation and it includes all U.S. imprints within its scope regardless of date that are held by LC or a contributing library. Titles for non-Roman languages are given in Romanized form only, and do not include the vernacular texts. Priority, however, is given to current titles (post-1955 imprints); earlier titles are catalogued as time permits. Complete information about the scope, contents, rules followed, and arrangement is found in an accompanying twenty-four page booklet by the same title.

The *National Union Catalog* (microfiche edition) is published in three parts: *National Union Catalog. Books* (*NUC. Books*), *National Union Catalog. Audiovisual Materials* (*NUC. AV*), and *National Union Catalog. Cartographic Materials* (*NUC. CM*).

All of the entries in *Books U.S.* appear in *NUC. Books*.

Books U.S. lists at least one location for each printed monograph.

Name authority records and cross references are included in *Name Authorities Cumulative Microform Edition* rather than in *Books U.S.* This list includes personal and corporate names, conference headings, uniform titles, geographical names of political and civil jurisdiction, and series. Quarterly, with the first three issues cumulative for the current year, and the fourth contributing to a multi-year cumulation.[1]

CIP and Minimal Level Cataloging (MLC) information is included in *Books U.S.*

A retrospective cumulation from 1968 of *Books U.S.* is available and can be purchased separately.

---

[1] Library of Congress Cataloging Distribution Service. *Catalog* 1997/98, p. 8. Multi-year Cumulations available are 1977-86 and 1987-96. 1997 begins a new multi-year cumulation.

The *Complete Service* from LC includes: *Books All* (including *Books English* and *Books U.S.*), *Maps*, *Music*, *Serials*, and *Visual Materials* services. Book tapes are shipped weekly, and non-book tapes are shipped every four weeks. Current as well as retrospective coverage from 1968 is available.[1]

In addition to the *NUC* titles, there are other sources that help to capture the vast publishing output in the U.S. Although the *NUC* includes selected government publications from all levels of government, the most comprehensive listing is found in *The Monthly Catalog of theUnited States Government Publications*. - Jan. 1895-   . - Washington, D.C. : Government Printing Office, 1895-   . Arrangement is by the Superintendent of Documents classification system. Access to the information is available through the author index, title index, subject index, series/report index, contract number index, bill number index, stock number index, classification number index, and title keyword index. Numbers in the index refer the user to the entry numbers in the issuing agency section. In recent years, this information is available on the Internet, in CD-ROM versions from Autographics, INFOTRAC, Marcive, SilverPlatter, and in MARC tapes from Library of Congress MARC Distribution Services.

American dissertations listed in *Dissertations Abstracts International*. - Ann Arbor : University Microfilms, 1938-   (title varies) are not catalogued and included in *Books U.S.* unless a reporting library includes an entry for a dissertation within its own collection. Therefore, the above title should be consulted for dissertations along with *American Doctoral Dissertations*. - 1955/56-   . - Ann Arbor : University Microfilms, 1957-   which lists "dissertations for which doctoral degrees were granted in the United States and Canada during the academic year covered, as well as those available on microfilm from University Microfilms."[2] (ISSN 0065-809X; OCLC: 1479778). Both titles are also available in machine-readable versions.

Serial titles are listed in *New Serials Titles*.

Other titles such as *Publishers' weekly*. - N.Y. : Publishers' Weekly, 1872-   , *Books in print*. - N.Y. : Bowker, 1948-   and *Cumulative book index*. - N.Y. : Wilson, 1898-   are commercial publications that list current titles published. The scope of *Cumulative Book Index* includes all books published in the English language for the period covered which is closer in scope to *Books English* (MARC records for monographs published in the English language anywhere in the world and catalogued by the Library of Congress) than to the*Books U.S.*

South Pacific Bibliography includes materials about the indigenous people of Hawaii.

LATEST ISSUE EXAMINED/CURRENCY: Entries include all U.S. imprints as they are catalogued regardless of date.

AUTOMATION: automated.

FORMAT AND SERVICES AVAILABLE: 1600 or 6250 bpi 9-track tape reel, 3280 tape cartridge, or Intenet FTP. Daily service available only via Internet FTP. The MARC tape and FTP distribution service is the predominant method for distributing the *Books U.S.* cataloguing

---

[1] Ibid, pp. 29-31.
[2] *GRB11*, entry AG11.

records. USMARC records are distributed in the MARC Distribution Service. *Books U.S.* records are also published by the Cataloging Distribution Service of the Library of Congress in microfiche as part of the *National Union Catalog. Books.* This product is published in a register/index format in 48X microfiche. The *Books U.S.* records were also published by the Cataloging Distribution Service in a CD-ROM product entitled CDMARC Bibliographic during the period 1991-96. This CD-ROM product was discontinued after 1996. The *Books U.S.* records are searchable over the Internet from the Library of Congress as part of its public online catalog at http://www.loc.gov/catalog.

CURRENT LEGAL DEPOSIT LAWS: The Copyright Law (Title 17, *U.S. Code*) defines copyright notice, deposit and registration.

AVAILABLE FROM: Library of Congress, Cataloging Distribution Service, Washington, D.C. 20541-4912. E-mail: cdsinfo@mail.loc.gov

SELECTED ARTICLES: Price, Mary Sauer. "The National Union Catalog Program." Paper presented at the 51st IFLA General Conference, Chicago, 18- 24 August 1985 (105-BIB-5-E).

VERIFIER: Kathryn Mendenhall, Product Development Supervisor, Cataloging Distribution Service, Library of Congress.

URUGUAY

TITLE: *Anuario bibliográfico uruguayo.* - 1946-   . - Montevideo : Biblioteca Nacional, 1947- .
Annual (suspended 1950-1967).
Supplements accompany some issues.
DDC: 015.895; LC: Z1881.A5, PQ8510; LCCN: 48-14586//r81; OCLC: 1481641
ISSN 0304-8861

COMPILER: Sección Bibliografia Nacional del Depto. Proceso Técnico, Biblioteca Nacional [National Bibliography Section, Department of Technical Processing, National Library].

SCOPE AND COVERAGE: *Anuario Bibliográfico Uruguayo (ABU)* lists titles published in Uruguay and deposited at the Biblioteca Nacional according to the legal deposit legislation. Works by Uruguayan authors published abroad, books about Uruguay by foreign authors published abroad, periodical publications published in Uruguay, Uruguayan periodical publications published by foreign institutions, and periodical publications of international organizations which are published in Uruguay are included. Works written by foreigners and published in Uruguay are also within the scope.

Types of publications included in *ABU* are books, pamphlets, serials (current issues), official and government publications, textbooks, children's books, art exhibition catalogues, braille books, international organizations publications, atlases, theses and dissertations if published.

Excluded are publications which have no literary or scientific text, e.g., catalogues, commercial, tourist, industrial materials; ephemeral publications, e.g., telephone guides, rules, calendars, almanacs, fair and exhibition programs; sound recordings, videos, periodical articles, publications that represent specific views of particular groups, e.g., political groups. Materials excluded from *ABU*, for the most part, are processed and in the library's catalogue.

CONTENTS: Table of contents, list of abbreviations, introduction, broad system of LC classification, national monographs and pamphlets, national periodical publications, publications of foreign authors and international organizations published in Uruguay (arranged by books and pamphlets, and periodical publications), indexes, list of publishers.

CATALOGUING RULES AND CLASSIFICATION SCHEMES USED: Follows AACR2 since the beginning of 1978, and ISBD rules.

The LC classification system is followed.

ENTRY INFORMATION: For monographs and pamphlets, information includes author (with dates of birth and/or death when known), title, place of publication, publisher, date, pagination, size, series statement, notes, *ABU* classification number in lower left corner, consecutive entry number in lower right corner.

The national periodicals section gives full bibliographic information including title, first volume, place of publication, publisher, date of first publication, size and frequency of publication, and entry number. No classification number is given.

The sections which include foreign authors and international organizations published in Uruguay, and periodical publications published in Uruguay give complete bibliographic information, but do not have a classification number assigned at the end of the entry.

ARRANGEMENT: Monographs, pamphlets, periodicals, foreign authors and international organizations published in Uruguay are arranged by broad classes of the LC classification system, then alphabetically by main entry.

INDEXES: Authors, co-authors, compilers, and illustrators index, title index (for books and pamphlets), periodicals index, general subject index, and publishers index (for books and pamphlets) are all alphabetically arranged. The number refers the user to the consecutive entry number in the main bibliography.

NOTES AND COMMENTS: "The country's first current bibliography was the *Anales de la Bibliografía Uruguaya* (1895), compiled by Pedro Mascaro, Director of the National Library at that time. This work appeared only once, in 1896."[1] Another effort to publish a current national bibliography was not attempted until 1946 when *ABU* was founded and continued until its publication schedule was interrupted from 1950-1967. After this period, *ABU* has assumed a regular publication schedule.

Beginning in 1982, an introduction was added which explains the scope, contents, and arrangement of the various sections. The index is now at the end of the volume rather than at

---

[1] *BSTW, 1975-1979*, p. 445.

the beginning as in 1978 volumes and earlier. A few additional features such as an analyzed entry in the introduction (which could explain the *ABU* classification number and entry number for new users) would add to the usefulness of this improved bibliography. It also seems that consolidation of similar sections would make this a more direct approach to the use of the material without detrimental effects. For instance, monographs, pamphlets and the foreign authors and international organizations publishing monographs and pamphlets in Uruguay could be consolidated, and the periodical publications could be consolidated into one list. The majority of the titles listed are published in Uruguay and are part of the national imprint regardless of the author's or issuing agency's nationality. For those Uruguayan authors whose works are published abroad, an asterisk (*) could be used to indicate foreign imprints. Periodicals are now arranged by broad subject category rather than alphabetically. It is obvious that changes are being made, such as the addition of an abbreviations list, in an effort to make *ABU* more useful and to meet international bibliographic standards.

The 1946 *ABU* had perforated pages with bibliographic information printed in a card format.

Supplements are issued periodically. For example, 1947 (published 1950) includes a supplement for 1946; 1978 "anexo" is a supplement issued for *ABU* 1978.

Government publications are not designated by any symbols. By checking the index, one may locate issuing agencies. By using the entry numbers given in the index, one is referred to the bibliographical information in the bibliography.

With the new legal deposit law in 1970, the Parliamentary Library was also designated a depository library. Even before then, during the interruption of *ABU*, the Parliamentary Library began publishing *Bibliografía Uruguaya*. - Vol. 1(enero/abr. 1962)-   . - Montevideo : Biblioteca del Poder Legislativo, 1962-   . (LCCN: 65-72510//r862; LC: Z1881.M76; OCLC: 1519755; ISSN 0523-1957). It was meant to appear three times a year with the third number being the annual cumulation. However, this has never appeared with any regularity and is now many years behind. According to information in *Survey of the Contents of Existing National Bibliographies* the arrangement of the volume for 1963 (in two volumes) is alphabetical with separate indexes for titles, subjects and classified (Dewey), authors and pseudonyms.[1] Contents include monographs, government publications and works published abroad (on topics of indigenous interest). According to I. Zimmerman, annotations were the rule. The second volume for 1963 was mostly bio-bibliographies.[2] Because of the slightly different scope from *ABU*, *Bibliografía Uruguaya* would be useful if it were kept current.

The *AL,BU,* (ISSN 1041-1763) and its *Annual List of Serials* (ISSN 1042-1734) include Uruguay within its scope from 1989 until 1992 when it ceased. Although not intended to include all titles published in Uruguay during a given year, these publications, listing acquisitions purchased by the Library of Congress, were timely publications and could be relied upon to list many titles currently published in Uruguay.

LATEST ISSUE EXAMINED/CURRENCY: Imprint dates for the 1990 volume are for the year covered.

---

[1] *Survey of the Contents of Existing National Bibliographies*, pp. 44-45.
[2] I. Zimmerman, *Current National Bibliographies of Latin America* (1971), p. 59.

After the interruption of 1950-1967, volumes were issued in combined form for a period, e.g., 1962-1968, published in 1971; 1969-1972, published in 1977. The volume for 1990 was published in December 1992 and received by University Library, Cambridge in 1994. This pattern of a two year lag from publication date and receipt, and between imprint dates and publication has been consistent for the last ten years, and even though this lag hinders the use of this current national bibliography, it is quite an improvement over earlier years when the publication was irregular. It is hoped that *ABU* may be able to continue to improve on the publication and distribution lags so that bibliographers, librarians and researchers may take advantage of the up-to-date imprint information which is found in *ABU*.

AUTOMATION: not known.

FORMAT AND SERVICES AVAILABLE: printed.

CURRENT LEGAL DEPOSIT LAWS: Ley No. 13.835, Arts. 191-193 de Depósito Legal (7 January 1970).[1]

AVAILABLE FROM: Sales Office: Instituto Nacional del Libro, San José 1118, Montevideo.

Departamento de Proceso Técnico, Biblioteca Nacional, 18 de Julio 1790, Casilla de Correo 452, Montevideo.

VERIFIER: no reply received.

UZBEKISTAN

TITLE: *Ŭzbekiston respublikasi matbuoti solnomasi = Letopis' pechati respubliki Uzbekistan.* - Toshkent : Ŭzbekiston Respublikasi Davlat Kitob palatasi, 199?-
Monthly.
Continues *Uzbekiston SSR matbuoti solnomasi.*
DDC: not found; LC: not found; LCCN: not found; OCLC: not found.
ISSN 0236-428X

COMPILER: Ŭzbekiston Respublikasi Davlat Kitob Palatasi

SCOPE AND COVERAGE: *Ŭzbekiston respublikasi matbuoti solnomasi* (*URMS*) includes the publishing output of Uzbekistan which is deposited at the Ŭzbekiston Respublikasi Davlat Kitob Palatasi according to the legal deposit laws.

Types of publications include books, pamphlets, journal articles, and newspaper articles.

Omitted from *URMS* are periodical articles from popular magazines, and periodical articles for children and teenagers.

---

[1] "Introduccion," *ABU* 1990, p. 11.

CONTENTS: Preface in Uzbek and in Russian; classified bibliography, journal articles [Zhurnal makolalari solnomasi], newspaper articles [Gazeta makolalari solnomasi], indexes.

CATALOGUING RULES AND CLASSIFICATION SCHEMES USED: Abbreviations follow the Abbreviation of Russian word groups of words in Bibliographical Descriptions (GOST 7.12-77), and the Bibliographic Description of Documents (GOST 7.1-84). General regulations and rules for compilations (1984) is followed for book descriptions.

The "United Classification of Literature for Book Publishing in the USSR," (2d ed., 1986) is used.

ENTRY INFORMATION: Books: general classification number given at the beginning of the section, consecutive entry number, author, title, place of publication, publisher, date, pagination, illustrations, size, series statement, ISBN, number of copies printed, price, government registration number, e.g., [94-1546].

Journal and newspaper articles: author, title of article, title of publication and other necessary bibliographic information for citations.

ARRANGEMENT: Arranged in three sections: books, journal articles, newspaper articles; within these sections, entries are arranged within the Uzbek, Russian, and Karakalpakski languages, then alphabetically arranged within the classification categories. One exception to this language grouping is that official articles and official documents written in Russian are included in the Uzbek section.

INDEXES: For books: names index (including author, co-author, editor, translator, artist), title index, subject index, series index; for journal articles: periodical title index, languages other than Uzbek and Russian index, author index; newspaper articles: newspaper title index, languages other than Uzbek and Russian index, author index.

Supplemental indexes for earlier numbers in previous issues are at the back. A general index at the back gives the order of the formats in the issue by their entry numbers. At the back of the issues, a subject listing of the classes is listed in tabular format and the page number for books, journals, and newspapers for each class is given.

NOTES AND COMMENTS: Before the breakup of the USSR, publications of Uzbekistan were recorded in *Knizhnaiā letopis* and *Ŭzbekiston SSR matbuoti solnomasi*. Since Uzbekistan established its independence, the primary record of Uzbekistan's publishing output is recorded in *URMS*.

As stated above, *URMS* continues *Ŭzbekiston SSR matbuoti solnomasi = Letopis' pechati Uzbekskoĭ SSR / Ŭzbekiston SSR matbuot davlat komiteti, Uzbekiston SSR davlat kitob palatasi = Gosudarstvennyi komitet Uzbekskoi SSR po pechati, Gosudarestvennaiā knizhnaiā palata Uzbekskoĭ SSR. - Toshkent : Uzbekiston SSR Davlat kitob palatasi, 1978-199?. Monthly (LCCN: 91-645275; LC: Z3413.U9U935; OCLC: 4886587; ISSN 0236-428X). This title was formed by the union of *Kitob solnomasi Ŭzbekiston sovet ittifoqi matbuotida, Zhurnal maqolalari solnomasi, Gazeta maqolalari solnomasi*, and *Ŭzbekiston SSR baqtli matbuot* *nashrlari solnomasi va notalar.* - Toshkent: Ŭzbekiston SSR davlat kitob palatasi, 1978-197? and *Ŭzbekiston SSR baqtli matbuot nashrlari solnomasi va notalar.*

Ŭzbekiston SSR matbuoti solnomasi / Ŭzbekiston SSR matbuot davlat komiteti, Ŭzbekiston SSR davlat kitob palatasi = Letopis' pechati Uzbekskoĭ SSR / Gosudarstvennyi komitet Uzbekskoi SSR po pechati, Gosudarstvennai͡a knizhnai͡a palata Uzbekskoĭ SSR. - Toshkent : Uzbekiston SSR Davlat kitob palatasi, 1978-   . (LCCN: 91-645275; LC: Z3413.U9U935; OCLC: 4886587; ISSN 0236-428X). These are publishers' catalogues. This title is formed by the union of: *Kitob solnomasi Ŭzbekiston sovet ittifoqi matbuotida; Źhurnal maqolalari solnomasi; Gazeta maqolalari solnomasi*; and *Ŭzbekiston SSR baqtli matabuot nashrlari solnomasi va notalar*. In Uzbek and Russian.

LATEST ISSUE EXAMINED/CURRENCY: The latest copy examined is no. 1, 1995 at the University of Illinois Urbana in June 1996. The imprints covered in this first issue of 1995 included 1994 and 1995 imprints.

AUTOMATION: not known.

FORMAT AND SERVICES AVAILABLE: printed

CURRENT LEGAL DEPOSIT LAWS: not known.

AVAILABLE FROM: Ŭzbekiston Respublikasi Millii kitob palatasi = Natsional'nai͡a knizhnai͡a palata Respubliki Uzbekitan, 700129 Toshkent, Navoii, 30.

Distributors for U.S.A.and the world except East Europe: East View Publications, 3020 Harbor Lane North, Minneapolis, MN 55447, USA.

VERIFIER: no reply received.

VENEZUELA

TITLE: *Bibliografía venezolana.* - vol.1 -   . - Caracas : Instituto Autónomo Biblioteca Nacional y de Servicios de Bibliotecas, 1982-   .
Semiannual (1992-   ); quarterly, with an annual cumulation (1982-1991).
Continues: *Anuario bibliográfico venezolano.*
DDC: 015.87; LC: Z1911.B52; LCCN: 83-645515; OCLC: 9642503
ISSN 0798-0086

COMPILER: Instituto Autónomo Biblioteca Nacional y de Servicios de Bibliotecas.

SCOPE AND COVERAGE: *Bibliografía Venezolana (BV)* includes titles by Venezuelan authors living in or out of the country, titles about the country, and titles about the country produced by foreign authors in other countries. Volumes published in Venezuela are required to be deposited according to legal deposit laws.

Types of publications included in *BV* are books, pamphlets, periodicals, official and government publications, annual reports, maps, audio-visual materials.

CONTENTS: Current edition: Explanation of entry elements are on verso of title page, table of contents, "La Bibliografía Venezolana" (explanation), guide to using *BV*. The bibliography is in two parts: the current and the retrospective (1513- [ ]), each with author index, title index, and subject index.

CATALOGUING RULES AND CLASSIFICATION SCHEMES USED: AACR2 is used; ISBD has been used since September 1979.[1] LCMARC format is used.

LCSH is used.[2]

Classification of entries are by the DDC (19th ed.), Library of Congress, and local Biblioteca Nacional schemes.[3]

ENTRY INFORMATION: National bibliography number (NBN) in upper left corner, e.g., 1991-0276, author, with dates when known; title, edition statement, place of publication, publisher, date, pagination, size, series, notes, including ISBN; tracings (added entries and subject), DDC number.

An asterisk (*) appearing to the side of some national bibliography numbers indicates that the work is printed outside of Venezuela.

ARRANGEMENT: The arrangement of the bibliography is chronological, beginning with the earliest dates catalogued during the period covered. Arrangement is in order by the national bibliography number.

INDEXES: Author index; title index; subject index. The author index includes personal, corporate, editor, and co-author entries. The number used in all indexes refers the user back to the national bibliography number in the entries.

A guide to the use of the index is given in the prefatory material.

NOTES AND COMMENTS: *BV* is an attempt to overcome the time lag that plagued *Anuario bibliográfico venezolano*. - 1942-1977. - Caracas : Centro Bibliográfico Venezolano, Biblioteca Nacional, 1945- 1979? Annual (ISSN 0378-1828). The title change also brought other changes, e.g., in arrangement. Following is an analysis of the former title.

Anuario Bibliográfico Venezolano (*ABV*) lists all separately published works published in Venezuela, and deposited at the Biblioteca Nacional. Types of publications included in *ABV* are

---

[1] "La Bibliografía Venezolana," in *BV, 1980-1981*(1982), p.XI.
[2] Information in a letter dated July 8, 1996 to the author from Ramon Parra Useche, Technical Coordinator for International Affairs, National Library, and information from Sara Da Rocha, editor, *BV*.
[3] Useche letter.

books, pamphlets, periodicals (current year), official and government publications, annual reports (first issue), theses and dissertations, musical scores, standards, inventories and lists.

Differing from *BV*, examples of the contents of the volumes for *ABV* are as follows. From the 1975 volume: Table of contents, introduction; I. Bibliographic Sources (arranged by main entry); II. Books, pamphlets, leaflets, etc. (arranged by main entry); III. Venezuelan periodicals (arranged by title); IV. Venezuelan authors who died during [ ] (arranged by name); V. Dictionary index of authors, titles and subjects (alphabetically arranged); Abbreviations.

From the *ABV* volumes for 1949-1952: Volume 1, I. Bibliographic sources; II. Books, pamphlets, leaflets, etc.; Volume 2, III. Foreign publications relating to Venezuela; IV. "Appéndice" 1942-1948; V. Authors, books, collaborators, "Censurados en el gobierno de Marcos Pérez Jímenez;" VI. Dictionary index; VII. Imprint index; VIII. Abbreviations.

Cataloguing rules used in *ABV* are ISBD(M) and ISBD(S). Entry information includes author, title, place of publication, publisher, date, pagination, series, size, notes. Entry number is in lower left corner and is a continuous sequence throughout the bibliography. No price information is given. Information given in section IV includes author, biographical note, bibliography, criticism and interpretation, obituary listings. This section is not included in the index.

Volumes for *ABV* have been published as follows: 1942 (1945), 1943 (1945), 1944 (1947), 1945 (1947), 1946 (1949), 1947-48 (1950), 1949-54 (1960, 2 vols.), 1967-68 (1976), 1969-1974, A-G (1979), 1975 (1977), 1976 (1977), 1977 (1978).

In *BV* government publications are not identified by any symbol, but they can be located by looking in the author index under Venezuela and the Ministry. The entry can be found by using the national bibliography number which is given in the index.

CIP is not practiced in Venezuela.

The *BV* database includes information about sound recordings, maps, video cassettes, and photographs.

LATEST ISSUE EXAMINED/CURRENCY: *BV* represents "catalogued materials" during the period of time covered. The cumulated volume for the first semester of 1992 includes all of the material from November 1991 to May 1992, and in the retrospective section (second part), titles from 1513-1991 which were catalogued during the period covered are also included. Less than a quarter of the over 600 pages in this volume is devoted to 1991-1992 titles.

Volume XIII, ler semestre no. 1 covers November 1991 to May 1992, was published in 1992. This is the latest volume examined.

AUTOMATION: *Bibliografía Venezolana* is automated using the NOTIS 6.0 version.

FORMAT AND SERVICES AVAILABLE: Printed, MARC tape, and CD-ROM. *BV* is also available on the Internet.

CURRENT LEGAL DEPOSIT LAWS: Several laws relate to legal deposit. Legal deposit law of 22 January 1945 (*Gaceta Oficial* no. 21618); Decree no. 2718 of 27 June 1978 is "responsible for the collection of non-print materials relating to the intellectual needs of the Venezuelan people."[1] Official publications are covered by Law of 22 July 1941. Current legislation dates from Legal deposit law 82-0028 (verso, title page of *BV* vol. XIII)

AVAILABLE FROM: Instituto Autónomo Biblioteca Nacional y de Servicios de Bibliotecas, Apartado 6525, Caracas 1010A.

VERIFIER: Sara Da Rocha, editor, *BV*; Ramon Parra Useche, Technical Coordinator for International Affairs, Biblioteca Nacional.

VIETNAM (SOCIALIST REPUBLIC)

TITLE: *Thư mục quốc gia.* - Hanoi : National Library, 1954-   .
Monthly (issues often combined), with annual index cumulations called *Thư mục quốc gia Việtnam.*
DDC: not found; LC: Z3226.T478, DS556.3 (monthly), Z3226.T48; DS556.3 (annual); LCCN: 89-644010 (monthly), 89-644009 (annual); OCLC: 20821409 (monthly), 20821470 (annual)
ISSN not found

COMPILER: Legal Deposit Department, National Library.

SCOPE AND COVERAGE: *Thư mục quốc gia (TMQG)* lists the publishing output of Vietnam which is deposited at the National Library according to the legal deposit legislation.

Types of publications included are books, pamphlets, periodicals (first issues), annual reports, newspapers, official and government publications, standards, microforms, photographs and drawings.

Excluded are theses and dissertations, maps and atlases, musical scores, phonorecords, internal documents, IGO publications. Films are deposited at the National Film Institute.[2]

The scope has varied over the years.

CONTENTS: Annual index volume for 1989: author index, "người dịch [translator index?]," title index, publishers index, "báng thống kẻ các xuất b?an ph?âm lưu chiếu nàm 1989," "báng thóng ke sách báo theo các thu tiéng," abbreviations.

Monthly: bibliography. (This issue has no preliminary pages or index.)

---

[1] Yola Medina McLeod, "The role of national libraries in Latin America: the example of the Biblioteca Nacional of Venezuela," *International Cataloguing* 11 (April/June 1982):22, *GIP-UNISIST Newsletter.*
[2] *BSTW, 1975-1979*, p.371.

CATALOGUING RULES AND CLASSIFICATION SCHEMES USED: The cataloguing rules followed are not stated. Full bibliographic information is given following the AACR2 format.
The classification scheme used is not stated. General subject groups are used, preceded by a letter. Examples are B: philosophy; R: biology, and L: art.

ENTRY INFORMATION: Entry number, author, title, statement of translator, illustrator, etc., place of publication, publisher, date, pagination, size, series statement, number of copies printed, price, location number, e.g., S49793, in lower right corner.

ARRANGEMENT: Alphabetical order by main entry within general subject headings.

INDEXES: The monthly number examined did not have an index. The annual index volume has author index, "người dịch [translator index?]," title index, publishers index.

NOTES AND COMMENTS: *TMQG* does not participate in UBC.

The National Library issues *Thư mục thông báo sách mỗingoai văn*, a bi-monthly list of current foreign language books.[1]

Periodicals articles are not treated in *TMQG* but are indexed in *Thư mục các bài đăng tap chí* (LCCN: 96-644244; LC: AI19.B53T48; OCLC: 36118049).

The national bibliography for 1976 was entitled *Mục Luc Xuất ban ph?am lưu* Chiếu [Catalogue of Deposited Publications]. (LCCN: 79-649876; LC: Z995.T48a; OCLC: 5105337).

TMQG is printed on newsprint, and in many places the text is difficult to read because of its uneven printing.

At the head of the annual title for 1981: Bộ van hóa và thông tin thu' viện quô´c gia Việt nam [Ministry of Culture and Information, National Library of Vietnam]; at the head of 1989 issue: Bộ van hóa thông tin thé thao và du lịch thư viện quô´c gia Việt nam.

It would be helpful to the user to have preliminary pages which included the scope and coverage of the bibliography, arrangement, and rules. This would be adhering to ICNB Recommendation no. 10.

Previously, South Vietnamese publications were listed in *Thư-tich quốc gia Việ´t-nam = National Bibliography of Vietnam. - Saigon : Directorate of National Archives and Libraries, 1967-197?* (LCCN: sn82-1311; OCLC: 1382619; ISSN 0300-4821). Since the unification, all Vietnam publications are included in *TMQG*.[2]

LATEST ISSUE EXAMINED/CURRENCY: The latest annual index volume examined was number 1989, published 1991, received at the University of London SOAS in April 1995. The

---

[1] Ibid.
[2] Judith Farley. "National Bibliographies." In *A.L.A. World Encyclopedia of Library and Information Services,* 2nd ed., p. 580, OCLC: 1382619.

latest monthly issue examined is no. 1, 1990, published 1990, and received at SOAS in March 1991. The lag from the period covered to date of publication and receipt at libraries around the world seems to have improved in the early years of the 1990s. However, the present lag between 1990 and 1997 makes it impossible to use this as an acquisitions tool, and for current research purposes. Other bibliographies and sources would need to be used to maintain a current collection of Vietnamese titles.

AUTOMATION: Automated since 1987, but no additional information is available.[1]

FORMAT AND SERVICES: printed.

CURRENT LEGAL DEPOSIT LAWS: Decree 18-SL of 31 January 1946, and Law of 22 July 1941 [for official publications].

Indications are that the legal deposit system is not working as it should. One reason is that publishers are reluctant to give free copies to the National Library, and the National Library is not able to purchase materials because of financial circumstances.[2]

AVAILABLE FROM: National Library, 31 Tràng thi, Hanoi.

SELECTED ARTICLES: Henchy, Judith A.N. "Extracts from a Field Trip Report to Vietnam, Laos, and Kampuchea by the Archivist of the William Joiner Center for the Study of War and Social Consequences, University of Massasschusetts at Boston." *South-east Asia Library Group Newsletter* 33 (1989):9-14.

Jarvis, Helen. "Restoring the Bibliographic Heritage of Vietnam and Cambodia" *ICBC* 22 (no. 3 July/Sept. 1993):42-45.

VERIFIER: No reply received. The author is grateful to Dr. Helen Jarvis, Head, School of Information, Library and Archive Studies, University of New South Wales, Sydney, Australia for reading the entry.

YEMEN

No current national bibliography has been traced for Yemen. George Selim, Near East Section, African and Middle East Division, Library of Congress assisted me in searching the Library of

---

[1] Information in a 24 July 1997 e-mail to the author from Dr. Helen Jarvis, Head, School of Information Library and Archive Studies, University of New South Wales, Sydney, Australia.
[2] Judith A. N. Henchy. "Extracts from a report of a trip to Vietnam, Laos and Kampuchea by the Archivist of the William Joiner Center for the Study of War and Social Consequences University of Massachusetts at Boston," *South-East Asia Library Group Newsletter* 33 (1989):10-11.

Congress holdings; no national bibliography was located.[1] *Theses Bi-monthly*, and *Theses Summaries and Abstracts* (semiannual) are published by the University of Aden. There are available in the literature a number of subject bibliographies on Yemen.

AL,ME. - Vol. 1-31 (1963-1993). - Cairo : Library of Congress Office, Cairo, 1963-1993. (ISSN 0041-7769) included Yemen within its scope. There is also an unnumbered volume for 1962.

al-Nashrat al-'Arabīyah lil-maṭbū'āt [The Arab Bulletin of Publications]. (LCCN: 73-960585/NE; LC: Z3013.N3) includes Yemen within its scope.

CURRENT LEGAL DEPOSIT LAWS: A law of 1968 (no. 24, Chap. 7) of the Ministry of Information.[2]

YUGOSLAVIA

TITLE: *Bibliografija Jugoslavije. Knjige, brošure i muzikalije.* - vol. 1 - . - Beograd : Bibliografiski institut FNRJ, 1950-   .
Publisher varies.
Continues *Jugoslovenska Bibliografija.*
Frequency varies: bi-monthly (1953-   ); monthly (1950-1952).
DDC: not found; UDC: 015 (497.1); LC: Z2951.B37; LCCN: 51-4056; OCLC: 1519761
ISSN 0523-2201

COMPILER: Yugoslav Institute for Bibliography and Information (YUBIN).

SCOPE AND COVERAGE: *Bibliografija Jugoslavije. Knjige, Brošure i Muzikalije.* (*BJ.K*) lists the publishing output of Yugoslavia which is deposited at the Jugoslovenski Bibliografsko-Informacijski Institut according to legal deposit legislation. *BJ.K* includes Serbian (Roman) and other languages.

Types of publications included are books, pamphlets, musical scores, official and government publications, maps and plans, theses and dissertations.

Omitted from *BJ.K* are statutes, plans, commercial catalogues, information about employment, drafts of law, rules of social/political organizations and clubs, local transportation timetables, picture books without text, telephone books of smaller towns, brochures, and "how to" information.

---

1 Since the first edition of *AGCNB*, Yemen (Arab Republic) and Yemen (People's Democratic Republic) reunited in 1990 to form the country of Yemen. According to S. Rehman, "National infrastructure of library and information services in Arab countries," *Library Review* 40 (1 1991):15-28, Yemen has no national bibliography.
2 *BSTW, 1975-1979*, pp. 452-453; no information was available in *International Guide to Legal Deposit.*

CONTENTS: Preface, abbreviations list, classified bibliography, indexes, subject headings list with page numbers.

CATALOGUING RULES AND CLASSIFICATION SCHEMES USED: Since 1975, bibliographic description follows ISBD(M), and *Pravilnik i prirucnik za izradu abecodnih kataloga*, I i II [Laws and rules for catalogue entries] by Eve Verone.[1]

The classification scheme used is UDC.

ENTRY INFORMATION: UDC general number and headings, author, title, edition, place of publication, publisher, date, place of printing, printers, pagination, illustrations, size, series statement, notes including the number of copies published, classification number, bibliographic registration number (0038058498), consecutive national bibliography number (YU 94-2074).

ARRANGEMENT: Alphabetically arranged within UDC subject groups.

INDEXES: Since 1950, an annual author index and subject index have been issued as a separate volume. An author, subject, title index, and a subject heading list appear in fortnightly issues. Numbers used refer readers to the consecutive national bibliography number in the entry. An abbreviated subject classification scheme guide including classification numbers, corresponding subject headings with appropriate page numbers appeared at the end of fortnightly issues.

Bibliografija Jugoslavije. Knjige, Brošure , Muzikalije, 1950-1980. - Beograd : Jugoslovenski Bibliografski Institut, 1981 cumulates the monthly and fortnightly issues for this period. In addition to author and subject indexes, it includes a geographical index according to republics and districts.

NOTES AND COMMENTS: The Yugoslav Bibliographic Institute was founded in 1950 with the main purpose to publicize the national bibliography. In 1990 the name was changed to Yugoslav Bibliographic Institute for Bibliography and Information and it is responsible for eight different editions of the national bibliography which are described in this entry: bibliography of books, bibliography of periodicals, bibliography of articles A, B, and C, bibliography of official publications, and bibliography of translations. After the bibliographic description is completed, the legal deposit materials are distributed to various libraries. No collection is maintained at YUBIN.[2]

BJ.K continues *Jugoslovenska Bibliografija*. 1945-1949. - Beograd : Izd. Direkcija za Informacije Vlade FNRJ, 1949-1951. Annual. (LCCN: 49-56212; OCLC: 8012957).

---

[1] *Survey on the Present State of Bibliographic Recording*, p. 101, and "Preface" of *BJ.K.*
[2] Tanja Ostojic, "Yugoslav Institute for Bibliography and Information." Unpublished. Manuscript sent to the author. The information about the legal deposit is from a letter dated 19 March 1997 to the author from Tahja Ostojic, Head of International Exchange Centre, Yugoslav Institute for Bibliography and Information (YUBIN).

From 1988, anthologies and compilations are treated as a monograph and listed in *BJ.K* without analytics. These are then analyzed in the national bibliography's clanci i prilozi [articles and contributions].

The 1990s have been a period of turmoil for Yugoslavia. The former Yugoslavian republics of Slovenia, Croatia, Macedonia, and Bosnia-Herzegovina are now independent. Yugoslavia currently consists of the republics of Serbia and Montenegro, including the formerly autonomous regions of Vojvodina and Kosovo. Some of the former republics, such as Slovenia, had a regional bibliography which has now become a national bibliography. These bibliographies are analyzed separately under the nation's name.

Government publications have been included from the beginning in *BJ.K*. An asterisk (*) distinguishes them from other items in earlier volumes of *BJ.K*. However, the asterisk is no longer used in current issues. There is also a government publications bibliography called *Bibliografija zvaničnih publikacija SRJ: knijege, serijske publikaije* [Bibliography of government publications of SRJ: books, serial publications] - 1992-   . - Beograd : Institut, 1993-   . (OCLC: 35589422; ISSN 0351-2843). This title continues *Bibliografija zvaničnih publikacija SFRJ = Bibliografija na oficijalnite publikacii na SFRJ*, 1971-1991. Beograd : Jugoslovenski Bibliografski Institut, 1974-1991. Annual. (LCCN: 81-641433; OCLC: 4284438; ISSN 0354-4761). This title is now compiled from the *BJ.K*.

The title *Bibliografija Jugoslavije. Članci i književni prilozi u časopisima* [Articles and book reviews in journals]. - Beograd : Jugoslovenski Bibliografski Institut, 1950. (LCCN: sn89-29643; OCLC: 19570897) lists periodical articles and newspapers. In 1951, the continuing title, *Bibliografija Jugoslavije. Članci i književni prilozi u časopisima i novinama* [Articles and book reviews in journals and newspapers] (LCCN: sn89-02945; OCLC: 1519795; ISSN 0006-114X) split into three sections; these are listed below from the most recent title to the earliest. All titles are published in Beograd by the Institut. Frequencies vary.

Bibliografiya Jugoslavije. Članci i prilozi u serijskim publikacijama. Serija A, Društvene nauke [Articles and contributions in serials. Series A. Social sciences] = *Bibliografija na Jugoslavija. Statii i prilozi vo seriskite publikacii. Serija A, Opshtestveni nauki*. - Beograd : Institut, 1977-   . Monthly (LCCN: 96-646867; LC: in process; OCLC: 1519762; ISSN 0373-6369) continues *Bibliografija Jugoslavije. Članci i prilozi u časopisima, listovima i zbornicima. Serija A. Društvene nauke* [Articles and contributions in journals, newspapers and miscellany. Series A. Social sciences] = *Bibliografija Jugoslavije. Čanki in prispevki v časopisju in zbornikih. Serija A. Družtvene vede*. - Beograd, Jugoslovenski Bibliografski Institut, 1972-1976 (LCCN: sn89-29662; OCLC: 19584054). This continues *Bibliografija Jugoslavije. Članci i prilozi u časopisima i listovima. Serija A. Društvene nauke* [Articles and contributions in journals and newspapers. Series A. Social sciences]. - Beograd : Institut, 1964-1971. Monthly (LCCN: sn89-29661; OCLC: 19584017) which continues *Bibliografija Jugoslavije. Članci i prilozi u časopisima, novinama i zbirnim delima. Serija A. Društvene nauke* [Articles and contributions in journals, newspapers and anthologies. Series A. Social sciences]. - Beograd, Institut, 1953-1963 (LCCN: sn89-29660; OCLC: 19583970). This continues *Bibliografija Jugoslavije. Članci i knjizevni prilozi u časopisima i novinama. Serija A. Društvene nauke* [Articles and book contributions in journals and newspapers. Series A. Social sciences], 1952 (ISSN 0352-5899). This continues in part *Bibliografija Jugoslavije. Članci i knjizevni prilozi u časopisima i novinama*. - Beograd : Institut, 1951 (LCCN: sn89-29645; OCLC: 1519765).

Continues *Bibliografija Jugoslavije. Članci i knjizevni prilozi u časopisima.* - Beograd : Institut, 1950. Quarterly (LCCN; sn89-29643; OCLC: 19570897).
    This series includes articles in the social sciences. The frequency has varied over the years, but it is mostly monthly. Bibliographic descriptions follow ISBD(S). The UDC scheme is used in arranging entries; if there is more than one entry under a UDC number, the entries are then alphabetically arranged. Each volume includes an author index and a subject index, as well as an index of periodicals with ISSN. Articles with more than three authors are listed under the title of the article. From 1991, bibliographic information includes the categories of an article if this is done in the primary source. All articles are placed in the following categories: scientific work (paper, study), introductory report, specialist work (paper, study), and congress report. From no. 3, 1989 this bibliography is supported by YUBIB.

Bibliografija Jugoslavije. Članci i prilozi u serijskim publikacijama, Serija B, Prirodne, primenjene, medicinske i tehničke nauke [Articles and contributions in serials. Series B. Natural, applied, medical, and technical sciences], Beograd : Institut, 1985- . Monthly (LCCN: 91-647998; LC: Z7409.B48l; Q158.5l; OCLC: 24480586; ISSN 0352-5945) continues *Bibliografija Jugoslavije. Serija B. Prirodne, primenjene, medicinske i tehničke nauke. Naučni i stručni radovi u serijskim publikacijama* [Series B. Natural, applied, medical, and technical sciences. Scientific and specialized contributions in serials]. - Beograd : Jugoslovenski Bibliografski Institut, 1977-1984 (LCCN: sn92-15300; OCLC: 4394940; ISSN 0352-2393). This title continues *Bibliografija Jugoslavije. Naučni i stručni radovi u serijskim publikacijama. Serija B. Prirodne, medicinske i tehničke nauke* [Scientific and specialized contribution in serials. Series B. Natural, medical, and technical sciences], Beograd : Jugoslovenski Bibliografski Institut, 1977. Monthly (LCCN: sn92-15299; OCLC: 24480586; ISSN 0523-218X) which continues *Bibliografija Jugoslavije. Članci i prilozi u časopisima, listovima i zbornicima. Serija B. Prirodne i primenjene nauke* [Articles and contributions in journals, newspapers and miscellany. Series B. Natural and applied sciences]. - Beograd : Institut, 1971-1976 (LCCN: sn80-1678; OCLC: 1361423; ISSN 0523-218X). This title continues *Bibliografija Jugoslavije. Članci i prilozi u časopisima i listovima. Serija B. Prirodne i primenjene nauke* [Articles and contributions in journals and newspapers. Series B. Natural and applied sciences]. - Beograd : Institut, 1964-1971. Monthly (LCCN: sn89-29659; OCLC: 19583011). This continues *Bibliografija Jugoslavije. Članci i prilozi u časopisima, novinama i zbirnim delima. Serija B. Prirodne i primenjene nauke* [Articles and contributions in journals, newspapers and anthologies. Series B. Natural and applied sciences]. - g. 4, br. 1 (Jan.-Mar. 1953) - g. 14, br. 11-12 (Nov.-Dec. 1963). - Beograd : Institut, 1953-1963. Frequency varies (LCCN: sn89-29658; OCLC: 19582888). This title continues *Bibliografija Jugoslavije. Članci i prilozi u časopisima i novinama. Serija B. Prirodne i primenjene nauke.* [Articles and book contributions in journals and newspapers. Series B. Natural and applied sciences]. - Beograd : Institut, 1952. Continues *Bibliografija Jugoslavije. Članci i književni prilozi u časopisima i novinama* [Articles and book contributions in journals and newspapers]. - Beograd : Institut, 1951. Quarterly (LCCN: sn89-29645; OCLC: 19750807; ISSN 0006-114X). Continues in part *Bibliografija Jugoslavije. Članci i knjizevni prilozi u časopisima* [Articles and book contributions in journals]. - Beograd : Institut, 1950 (LCCN: sn89-29643; OCLC: 19570897).
    This series includes articles in the natural, applied medical, and technical sciences. For further description, the information given above for *Serija A* also applies to *Serija B*. From no. 2, 1989, this bibliography is supported by YUBIB (Yugoslav bibliographic and catalogue data base).

Bibliografija Jugoslavije. Članci i prilozi u serijskim publikacijama. Serija C, Umetnost, sport, filologija, književost [Articles and contributions in serials. Fine arts, sports, philology, literature], 1985-   (LCCN:91-647999; LC: AI15.B465; OCLC: 24479964) continues *Bibliografija Jugoslavije. Članci i prilozi u serijskim publikacijama. Serija C. Umetnost, sport, filologija, književost i muzikalije* [Articles and contributions in serials. Fine arts, sports, philology, literature, and music], 1977-1984 (LCCN: sn87-36226; LC: AI15.B59 Ser. C; OCLC: 4395019; ISSN 0352-5996). This title continues *Bibliografija Jugoslavije. Članci i prilozi u časopisima, listovima i zbornicima. Serija C. Umetnost, sport, filolofija, književnost, i muzikalije* [Articles and contributions in journals, newspapers and miscellany. Series C. Fine arts, sports, philology, literature, and music], 1972-1976 (LCCN: sn89-29655; OCLC: 19578263) which continues *Bibliografija Jugoslavije. Članci i prilozi u časopisima i listovima. Serija C. Umetnost, sport, filolofija, književnost, muzikalije* [Articles and contributions in journals and newspapers. Series C. Fine arts, sports, philology, literature, music], 1967-1971. Monthly (LCCN: sn89-29654; OCLC: 19578216).   This title continues *Bibliografija Jugoslavije. Članci i prilozi u časopisima i listovima. Serija C. Književnost - umetnost* [Articles and contributions in journals and newspapers. Series C. Literature - fine arts], 1964-1967 (LCCN: sn89-29653; OCLC: 6406491) which continues *Bibliografija Jugoslavije. Članci i prilozi u časopisima, novinama i zbirnim delima. Serija C. Filologija, umetnost, sport, književnost, muzikalije* [Articles and contributions in journals, newspapers and anthologies. Series C. Philology, fine arts, sports, literature, music], 1953-1963 (LCCN: sn89-29652; OCLC: 1519794; ISSN 0523-2198).   This continues *Bibliografija Jugoslavije. Članci i književni prilozi u časopisima i novinama. Serija C. Filologija, umetnost, sport, književnost, muzikalije* [Articles and book contributions in journals, and newspapers. Series C. Philology, fine arts, sports, literature, music], 1952 (LCCN: sn89-29649; OCLC: 6406304). Continues in part *Bibliografiya Jugoslavije. Članci i književni prilozi u časopisima i novinama* [Articles and book contributions in journals, and newspapers], 1951 (LCCN: sn89-02945; OCLC: 1519765; ISSN 0006-114X). Continues in part *Bibliografija Jugoslavije. Članci i književni prilozi u časopisima* [Articles and book contributions in journals]. - Beograd : Institut, 1950 (LCCN: sn89-29643; OCLC: 19890419).

This includes articles in the literature and the arts from selected newspapers and periodicals. For further description, the information given above for Serija A also applies to Serija C. From no. 1, 1990, this bibliography is supported by YUBIN.

For serial publications see *Bibliografija Jugoslavije. Serijske publikacije.* - 1975-   . - Beograd : Jugoslovenski Bibliografski Institut, 1975-   . Title and frequency varies (LCCN: 76-647410//r88; LC: Z6956.Y9B58; PN5355.Y8; OCLC: 3346504; ISSN 0350-0349). Continues *Bibliografija Jugoslovenske periodike.* - 1959-1974, - Beograd, Jugoslovenski Bibliografski Institut [etc.], 1959-1974. (LCCN: sc80-1779; OCLC: 3347601; ISSN 0006-1158). Frequency and publisher varies. Continues *Spisak listova i časopisa štampanih na tritorije FNRJ.* - Beograd : Bibliografski Institut FNRJ. (OCLC: 2376837).

Bibliografija Jugoslavije. Bibliografija prevoda. - Beograd : Jugoslovenski Bibliografski Institut, 1992-   . Annual. This title continues *Bibliografija Jugoslavije. Bibligrafija prevoda u SRJ*, 1969-1991 (ISSN 0354-4710) Covers all books translated in Yugoslavia, including languages of minorities and translations of books from Serbian into foreign languages.[1]

---

[1] Information from 21 May 1997 letter to the author from Milena Durisic, Head of the Union Catalogue, YUBIN.

For collections and monographic series see *Bibliografija Jugoslavije : Zbirke i monografske serije*. 1984/1985-   . - Beograd : Institut, 1986-   (LCCN: 91-644923; LC: Z2951.B37; OCLC: 16208025; ISSN 0352-8847). Includes alphabetical listing of articles and monographic series titles.

A title which includes imprints from Serbia is *Bibliografija knjiga u Vojvodini*. - 1992-   . - Novi Sad : Biblioteka Matice srpske, 1995-   . In Serbo-Croatian (Cyrillic). (LCCN: 96-646794; LC: Z2957.V64B53; OCLC: 34100852; ISSN: 0354-6551). Continues *Bibliografija Vojvodine. Serija 1, Monografske publikacije*. - 198?-1991. - Novi Sad : Biblioteka Matice srpske, 1981-1992. Annual (LCCN: sn86-23223; LC: Z2951.B524; OCLC: 14259623; ISSN: 0352-3241). This regional bibliography records periodicals and books by authors from this region of Yugoslavia. Most of the listed publications should also be listed in *BJ.K*.

The indexing for *BJ.K* has improved in the last ten years. Also, the addition of a preface has also been useful. It would be helpful if an analyzed entry which would identify all of the information given were included in the preface.

LATEST ISSUE EXAMINED/CURRENCY: The latest issue examined was number 3/4, 1997 received at the Bibliotekstjänst AB Library, Lund, Sweden. Imprints of bibliographic entries in this issue were mostly from 1997.

AUTOMATION: From no. 7 for 1988, the *BJ.K* is automated. The computer processing and exchange of bibliographic data is developed according to UNIMARC format. Data transmission is by JUPAC network and compatible computer and communication equipment.[1]

FORMAT AND SERVICES AVAILABLE: printed.

CURRENT LEGAL DEPOSIT LAWS: The current legal deposit is "Zakon o kulturnim dobrima" (Službni glasnik republike Srbije, No. 71/1994). This is the Culture Property Law. The republics and autonomous regions have separate legal deposit laws: Montenegro – Zakon o obaveznom dostavljanju štampanih stvari (Službni list SRCG' br. 8/76), Serbia – Obaveze organizacije udruzenog rada koje stampaju publikacje, odnosno koje proizvode ili uvoze filmove za javno prikazivanje (Službni list SR Serbia' 34/1981), Voivodina – Zakon o obaveznom dostavljanju stampanih stvari (Službni list SAP Vojvodine' br. 16/75), and Kosovo – Zakon o obaveznom dostavljanju i nabavljanju štampanih stvari (Službni list SAP Kosovo' br. 24/78).[2]

AVAILABLE FROM: Jugoslovenski Bibliografsko-Informacijski Institut = Yugoslav Institute for Bibliography and Information (YUBIN), 11000 Beograd, Terazije 26.

SELECTED ARTICLES: Lazič, Ksenija B. "Jugoslovenska bibliotekarska bibliografija za 1982." *Bibliotekar* (Beograd)40 (no. 3/4 1988):85-163.

---

[1] Information from Ostojic's letter to the author.

[2] The 1994 law was cited in the Ostojic letter. Other information was taken from *International Guide to Legal Deposit*, p. 106.

Popovič-Boskovič, Gordana, and Milosavljevič, Ivana. "Delatnost Jugoslovenskog bibliografskog instituta (JBI) : tekuče nacionalne bibliografije u Jugoslaviji." *Bibliotekar* (Beograd)42 (nos. 1-2 1990/1991):56-64.

Skendizic, Nevenka. "Bibliografija Jugoslavije: Knijige, Brošure i Muzikalije; 1950-1980." *Bibliotekar* (Beograd)32 (nos. 1-6 1980):60-67.

Stojanovič, Miloš. "Sadržaj tekučih jugoslovenskih bibliotekarskih serijskih publikacija." *Bibliotekar* (Beograd)40 (nos. 1-2 1988):109-117.

VERIFIER: Tanja Ostojic, Head of International Exchange Department, YUBIN.

ZAMBIA

TITLE: *The National bibliography of Zambia.* - 1970/71-   . - Lusaka : The National Archives of Zambia, 1972-   .
Annual.
DDC: 015./689/4; LC: Z3573.Z3N37; LCCN: 75-640797; OCLC: 1798487
ISSN 0377-1636
COMPILER: National Archives of Zambia.

SCOPE AND COVERAGE: *The National Bibliography of Zambia* (*NBZ*) includes all works published in Zambia and received by the National Archives of Zambia under legal deposit legislation.

Types of publications included are books, pamphlets, first issues of new serials, e.g. periodicals, newspapers, magazines, etc., and subsequent title changes, publications of statutory bodies (parastatals), local authorities, and government publications, memoirs, proceedings and transactions of private societies, local language publications, theses.

Excluded from the *NBZ* are acts, bills, parliamentary debates, gazettes, periodical articles, audio-visual materials, and books on Zambia or by citizens of Zambia published outside of the country.

CONTENTS: Contents, introduction, list of abbreviations, outline of classification system, classified subject section, alphabetical author and title section, list of publishers.

CATALOGUING RULES AND CLASSIFICATION SCHEMES USED: *NBZ* uses AACR1 and AACR2 for cataloguing purposes. Entries are catalogued in their original language.

The classification scheme used is DDC (18th ed.).

ENTRY INFORMATION: DDC number in upper left corner, author, title, place of publication, publisher, date, pagination, illustrations, bibliography notes, series, price when known. Size, tracings and general notes are not given.

ARRANGEMENT: The classified subject section is arranged by the DDC scheme.

INDEXES: Alphabetical author, title, and series index. DDC numbers refer reader to the entry in the classified section.

NOTES AND COMMENTS: From 1961 to the dissolution of the Federation of Rhodesia and Nyasaland on 31 December 1963, publications of Northern Rhodesia (later Zambia) were included in *List of Publications Deposited in the Library of the National Archives.* (ISSN 0556-9168).

Government publications are not marked with any symbol. However, one may look under Zambia, and the government department desired to locate the documents listed.

AL,ESA, its *Serial Supplement*, and *QIPL,ESA* include Zambia within their scopes. This title could be used in addition to the *NBZ* since *AL,ESA* is received more currently by most libraries. It does not try to cover all titles published, but selects titles from the national imprint of interest to librarians and to those doing research.

The University of Zambia Library has published *A Subject Guide to Theses* held by the University of Zambia Library, Lusaka Campus / compiled by Augustine W.C. Msiska and Victoria B. Mukelabai, 1981. (Occasional publications. University of Zambia. Library, no. 2).[1]

In Zambia, bibliographic control has not moved forward as much as desired because of many problems which interfere with progress. Locating Zambian titles not deposited at The National Archives, lack of space and staff resignations are a few problems which have made it hard to make desired progress.[2]

It would be helpful to have an explanation of the entries included in information given in the introduction.

LATEST ISSUE EXAMINED/CURRENCY: Although *NBZ* has followed many of the recommendations of the ICNB, it is not a timely national bibliography. The latest volume examined at the University Library, Cambridge in November 1994 covered the year 1989 and was received in June 1994. It seems that the time from the period covered through distribution to libraries needs to be shortened before *NBZ* can be relied upon for acquisitions and collection development purposes.

Adding to this gap is the non-currency of many titles listed for a particular year. At least half of the entries are from earlier years than the period covered. An inadequate legal deposit observation by publishers, combined with inadequate publishing information on the title page of a book and overworked staff members creates a situation in which information is not current.

---

[1] James Armstrong, "An Abbreviated Report of a Trip to Lusaka, Zambia, April 12-17, 1982," *Africana Libraries Newsletter* no. 36 (Nov. 1983):6.
[2] Beatrice S. Bankole, "Current National Bibliographies of the English Speaking Countries of Africa," *International Cataloguing* 14 (Jan./Mar. 1985):8 as reported by H. K. Nyendwa, "Report on the Current Bibliographic Control Development in Zambia." (ASCOBIC, 1983). Also see related problems mentioned in C. Musonda, "Zambia," *Afribiblios* 9 (no. 1 June 1986):34-36.

However, in spite of these problems, it is positive to have the national bibliography appearing during these troubled times so that a bibliographic history of the year can be recorded.

AUTOMATION: not automated.

FORMATS AND SERVICES AVAILABLE: printed.

CURRENT LEGAL DEPOSIT LAWS: Printed Publications Act, Cap. 265 of the revised Laws of Zambia, 1972.

AVAILABLE FROM: The National Archives of Zambia, P.O. Box 50010, Lusaka.

SELECTED ARTICLES: Bankole, Beatrice S. "Current National Bibliographies of the English Speaking Countries of Africa." *International Cataloguing* 14 (Jan./Mar. 1985):5-10.

VERIFIER: no reply received.

ZIMBABWE

TITLE: *Zimbabwe national bibliography*. - 1979-   . - Harare : National Archives, 1980-   . Continues *Rhodesia national bibliography* (ISSN 0085-5677) which superseded *List of publications deposited in the library of the National Archives* (ISSN 0556-9168). Annual.
DDC: 015.6891; LC: Z3573. R5R54; LCCN: 80-647570//r852; OCLC: 6740584
ISSN 0085-5677

COMPILER: National Archives.

SCOPE AND COVERAGE: *Zimbabwe National Bibliography* (*ZNB*) lists all materials published in the country and received on legal deposit at the National Archives. Certain parliamentary papers, which are exempt from legal deposit, are also included.

Types of publications included are books, pamphlets, annual reports and publications of government, local authorities, statutory bodies, societies, schools and churches; maps, art prints, new and ceased periodicals as well as subsequent name changes of periodicals.

Excluded are reprints and ephemeral publications such as programs, brochures, and non-book materials. It is anticipated that non-book materials may be included in the future.[1]

CONTENTS: Introduction, table of contents, classified bibliography, author/title index, subject index, index to new periodicals, index to ceased periodicals, corrected ISBN list, list of publishers, publications of the National Archives.

---

[1] Rosemary Molem, "Zimbabwe: Country Report on Bibliographic Control Activities," *International Cataloguing* 13 (July/Sept. 1984):27. An examination of the 1991/92 volume, published in 1994, showed that the only non-book materials were maps.

CATALOGUING RULES AND CLASSIFICATION SCHEMES USED: Since 1981, cataloguing rules used by the *ZNB* are AACR2.

DDC (20th ed.) with minor adaptations is used for classification in the *ZNB*. The insertion of S and N after the main class number, followed by the subdivisions from relevant tables allows for subdividing the Shona and Ndebele languages and literatures. Another adaptation allows English literature by Zimbabwean authors to be prefixed by "Z" to distinguish these titles from locally published editions written by foreign authors.

Through 1974, the classified section was classified by the main headings of the DDC system; from 1975 to 1981, the entries are classified by the 100 main classes. Beginning with the 1982 volume, entries are fully classified.[1]

ENTRY INFORMATION: For books: DDC number, author, title, place of publication, publisher, pagination, illustration statement, size, series statement, notes, ISBN if known, price if known, entry number in lower right corner. For periodicals: DDC number, title, number, date, place of publication, publisher, pagination, size, series, frequency statement, ISSN if known, entry number in lower right corner.

ARRANGEMENT: The classified sequence of main entries in the bibliography is arranged according to the DDC system; ceased periodicals are alphabetically arranged by main entries.

INDEXES: Alphabetical listing of author, editors, title, series index; subject index. The number used refers the reader to the entry number in the classified section. The index to new periodicals, and the index to ceased serials are arranged alphabetically by title and follow the general index; numbers refer reader to entry numbers in the main classified section.

The subject index, first appearing in the volume covering 1986, uses the *LCSH* (10th ed.) and follows the American Library Association filing rules, 1980.

NOTES AND COMMENTS: From 1961-1966 publications were included in *List of Publications Deposited in the Library of the National Archives* (ISSN 0556-9168) issued in 1961 by the National Archives of Rhodesia, in 1962 by the National Archives of Southern Rhodesia and in 1963-1966 by the National Archives of Rhodesia. This title was superseded by the *Rhodesia National Bibliography* (ISSN 0085-5677) published by the National Archives from 1967-1978. ISBD format was adopted in 1974. Indexing of the national bibliography began in 1970. *The Rhodesia National Bibliography* was continued by the current title *Zimbabwe National Bibliography* in 1979-   .

Local language publications are included in *ZNB*; this follows ICNB 6.

In 1982, several Zimbabwean place names were changed. Names used in the index and the entries are those which appear on the publications.

---

[1] Ibid., p. 28.

The National Archives publication *Current Zimbabwean Periodicals* includes all serials current in September 1987. This title used in conjunction with the annual volumes of *ZNB* should give a current list of periodicals available. The previous title was *Current Rhodesian Periodicals.*[1]

CIP is not practiced in Zimbabwe.

Government publications are not marked by a symbol, nor are they separated in any way from other publications. By checking in the index under "Zimbabwe" and the name of the agency, one may find many of the government publications listed. In the 1970 volume of the *Rhodesia National Bibliography* there is a note which states that official publications are listed under "Rhodesia."

The 1976 volume states that government departments are alphabetical according to their function, e.g., Ministry of Education is indexed under Education. Bold type is used to make the proper order apparent. The listing by function is valid until 1982 when government departments are alphabetically listed.

The ISBN Agency was established in 1973. By 1982 there were eighteen publishers registered, and in 1995 there were 35 regular publishing houses and two dozen one-time or occasional publishers registered with the ISBN agency.[2]

The *Monthly Accessions List* of titles in the national bibliography, which is sent to selected libraries and booksellers, is in hiatus due to staff shortages.[3]

After the index to new periodicals, the section "Corrected International Standard Book Numbers" appears.

The publishers' list, which lists the addresses of publishers who have works listed in *ZNB*, started with the 1970 volume of the *Rhodesian National Bibliography.*

Rhodesia National Bibliography, 1890 to 1930, compiled by Anne Hartridge and published by the National Archives as number 2 of their Bibliographical Series in 1977 retrospectively covers Southern Rhodesia, Northern Rhodesia and Nyasaland (now Zimbabwe, Zambia and Malawi). A project to cover the gap of years 1931 - 1960, when coverage is assumed by the current national bibliography, is in abeyance until staffing improves.

The *List of Publications Deposited in the Library of the National Archives* included titles from Southern Rhodesia and Northern Rhodesia.

In 1993, the first issue of *Zimbabwe Books in Print* was published.

The 1962 foreword states that 1962 includes those items deposited in 1962 which were inherited by the new National Archives of Southern Rhodesia. It excludes Northern Rhodesia and

---

[1] Ibid., p. 28.

[2] Beatrice S. Bankole, "Current National Bibliographies of the English Speaking Countries of Africa," *International Cataloguing* 14 (Jan./Mar. 1985):8, and in the Douglas letter.

[3] Douglas letter.

Nyasaland. With the dissolution of the Federation of Rhodesia and Nyasaland at the end of 1963, each territory established their own national archives. Items received since 1947 and published in Northern Rhodesia or Nyasaland were returned to the proper national archive.

AL,ESA, its *Serial Supplement*, and *QIPL,ESA* include Zimbabwe within their scopes.

LATEST ISSUE EXAMINED/CURRENCY: The latest volume examined was the 1991/92 volume at the University of Wisconsin Library in May 1995.

In a sample of 35 entries analyzed from the 1991/92 volume, ten were from 1992, 15 were from 1991, and ten were from 1990.

AUTOMATION: not automated. The *ZNB* is compiled since 1990 using CDS-ISIS and PageMaker to produce camera-ready copy.[1]

FORMATS AND SERVICES AVAILABLE: printed.

CURRENT LEGAL DEPOSIT LAWS: Printed Publications Act, 1975.

AVAILABLE FROM: National Archives of Zimbabwe, Private Bag 7729, Causeway, Harare.

SELECTED ARTICLES: Bankole, Beatrice S. "Current National Bibliographies of the English Speaking Countries of Africa." *International Cataloguing* 14 (Jan./Mar. 1985):5-10.

VERIFIER: Gavin Douglas, Chief Librarian, National Archives of Zimbabwe.

---

[1] Information included in a letter to the author from R. G. S. Douglas for the director dated 27 June 1995.

Regional Bibliographies

NOTE: Regional bibliographies and The Library of Congress *Accessions Lists* have not fared as well over the past decade as have national bibliographies of individual countries. The majority of them have ceased. The most stable regional bibliography is *The South Pacific Bibliography*.

Included are some titles which may not be a regional bibliography in the true sense, but if the title covers a region bibliographically which is not otherwise covered by another source, it is included here.

According to the Overseas Operations Division of The Library of Congress, all *Accessions Lists* are being discontinued as current funding runs out. The United States Congress has ended appropriations for this program. Some had expanded, like *Accessions List, Eastern Africa* to *Accessions List, Eastern and Southern Africa,* but it too will cease publication immanently.

Because these regional bibliographies and accessions lists continued publication after the first *Annotated Guide*, they are included in this *New Annotated Guide*. All the information provided is current to the point of either their demise, the latest issue I have examined, or information received from the respective bibliographic agencies. References to these bibliographies and lists are mentioned in various entries.

ACCESSIONS LIST, BRAZIL AND URUGUAY

TITLE: *Accessions list, Brazil and Uruguay.* Vol. 15 no. 1 (Jan./Feb. 1989) - vol. 18, no. 6 (Nov./Dec. 1992). - Rio de Janeiro : Library of Congress Office, Brazil, 1989- 1992.
Bi-monthly.
Continues *Accessions list, Brazil.*
DDC: 015.81; LC: Z1671.U53a; LCCN: 88-641051//r90; OCLC: 18678777
ISSN 1041-1763

COMPILER: Library of Congress Office, Rio de Janeiro, Brazil.

SCOPE AND COVERAGE: *Accessions List, Brazil and Uruguay (AL,BU)* is a record of publications acquired by the U.S. Library of Congress Office, Rio de Janeiro, Brazil. It includes current materials from Brazil and Uruguay that are within the scope of the acquisitions program of the Library of Congress, and includes medical publications acquired for the National Library of Medicine.

Types of publications included are books, pamphlets, serials (new titles, changes and deletions), official and government publications, newspapers, atlases and maps, reports, music scores, sound recordings, sound cassettes, sound disks.

CONTENTS: Introduction, table of contents, bibliographic entries.

CATALOGUING RULES AND CLASSIFICATION SCHEMES USED: The preliminary cataloguing follows AACR2.

A classification scheme is not used.

ENTRY INFORMATION: For monographs, author, title, place of publication, publisher, date, pagination, size, series, ISBN or ISSN if known, price if known. For sound disks, rpms, mono or stereo, and size information given. For serials, title, beginning date, place of publication, publisher, publishing date, frequency, notes, including changes and cessations.

ARRANGEMENT: The bibliography is divided into three groups according to format. The monographs section is arranged alphabetically by main entry; the serials section lists new titles alphabetically by title, and then the changes and deletions for the period covered. Serial titles acquired for the "Brazil Popular Group Project" are included here. The non-book materials section is listed alphabetically by the main entry.

INDEXES: Bimonthly issues do not include an index. A cumulative author index is issued annually at the end of the year.

NOTES AND COMMENTS: Appropriations to support this acquisitions program are granted by the U.S. Congress. The cooperation of the governments of Brazil and Uruguay, and the book trades of Brazil and Uruguay have also helped make this program a success. The Library of Congress acquires titles only for its own collection. Unfortunately, the U.S. Congress did not renew the appropriations for this program to continue and the *AL,BU* ceased when funds ran out.

AL,BU continues, with its numbering, the *Accessions List, Brazil (AL,B)*. -Vol. 1, no. 1 (Jan. 1975)- vol. 14, no. 6 ((Nov./Dec. 1988). - Rio de Janeiro : Library of Congress Office, 1975-1988. Bi-monthly (1975, Nov./Dec. 1978-1988); monthly (1976-Oct. 1978). (ISSN 0095-795X; OCLC: 1559825).

A supplement to *AL,BU* includes *AL,BU. Annual List of Serials, 1989 through 1992*. (ISSN 1042-1734; OCLC: 18964222). This continues *AL,B. Annual List of Serials, 1975 through 1988*. (ISSN 0146-1060; OCLC: 2853623).

Publications in English, Spanish, and Portuguese languages are listed.

For the past several years, the Library of Congress Office has been collecting printed material related to Brazil's Popular Groups (Movimentos Populares). It is a selective collection of pamphlets, serials and posters gathered and organized in order to preserve and provide a first-hand analysis of the important role played by socio-political, religious, labor and minority grass-roots organizations. Starting with the *Annual list of serials* 1991 issue, serial titles that have been acquired for that collection are included in *AL,BU*.[1]

It would be extremely useful if this title had an index in each of the bimonthly issues; however, the addition of an annual cumulated author index has been helpful.

---

[1] "Introduction." *AL,BU* 18 (no. 6 Nov./Dec. 1992).

LATEST ISSUE EXAMINED/CURRENCY: The latest issue examined at The College of Wooster in August 1997 is Nov./Dec. 1992.

AUTOMATION: not known.

FORMAT AND SERVICES AVAILABLE: print, microfiche.

CURRENT LEGAL DEPOSIT LAWS: Not applicable.

AVAILABLE FROM: No longer published. Since 1985, microfiche copies of all issues of *AL,BU* are now available for purchase from Photoduplication Services, Library of Congress, Washington, D.C. 20540, U.S.A. For more information, contact the Photoduplication Services.

Correspondence about *AL,BU* from other than the U.S. should be directed to the Field Director, U.S. Consulate General, Av. Presidente Wilson 147, 20030 Rio de Janeiro.

Correspondence from the U.S. may be addressed to Field Director-LC, U.S. Consulate-Rio, Unit 3501, APO AA 34030, Brazil.

ACCESSIONS LIST, EASTERN AND SOUTHERN AFRICA

TITLE: *Accessions list, Eastern and Southern Africa.* - Vol. 26, no.1/2 (Jan./Feb.-Mar./Apr. 1993)- . - Nairobi : Library of Congress Office, 1993- .
Bi-monthly.
Continues, with its numbering, *Accessions List, Eastern Africa.*
Also available in microfiche from Photoduplication Service, Library of Congress.
Accessions List, Eastern and Southern Africa. Annual serial supplement (ISSN 0174-3820) issued biennially since 1995.
Accessions List, Eastern Africa. Annual publishers directory (ISSN 0145-8736) issued annually.
Nov./Dec. issue includes cumulative author index.
DDC: 016.9167; LC: Z3516.U52; LCCN: 93-642940; OCLC: 28310688.
ISSN 1070-2717

COMPILER: Library of Congress Office, Nairobi, Kenya.

SCOPE AND COVERAGE: *Accessions List, Eastern and Southern Africa (AL,ESA)* is a record of publications acquired by the U.S. Library of Congress Office, Nairobi from Botswana, Burundi, the Comoros, the Democratic Republic of the Congo, Djibouti, Eritrea, Ethiopia, Kenya, Lesotho, Madagascar, Malawi, Mauritius, Mayotte, Mozambique, Namibia, Réunion, Rwanda, the Seychelles, Somalia, Swaziland, Tanzania, Uganda, Zambia, and Zimbabwe with occasional acquisitions from other African countries.

Types of publications included are books, pamphlets, serials, official and government publications, reports, U.N. publications including speeches, non-book material such as maps, sound recordings, and sound cassettes.

CONTENTS: Table of contents, monographs, serials and non-book materials, annuals received, cumulated indexes, publishers' directory.

CATALOGUING RULES AND CLASSIFICATION SCHEMES USED: From January 1981, the preliminary cataloguing done by the Field Office conforms to AACR2. *Library of Congress Filing Rules* are applied in arranging the main entries and the indexes.

A classification scheme is not used.

ENTRY INFORMATION: Author, title, place of publication, publisher, date, pagination, illustrations, size, notes, LCCN in lower left corner.

ARRANGEMENT: Monographs, serials and non-book materials are arranged alphabetically by country, then arranged alphabetically by main entry under language. The annual issues received are arranged alphabetically by country, and then arranged alphabetically by main entry.

INDEXES: Entries for monographs, serials, and non-book materials are indexed by main entry heading, title, and added entry access points. Numbers refer back to the record number. Indexes are cumulated annually in number 6 (Nov./Dec.).

NOTES AND COMMENTS: Appropriations to support this acquisitions program are granted by the U.S. Congress. In addition to the acquisitions program for the U.S. Congress, the Nairobi office also acquires selected publications for over 30 U.S. institutions. Unfortunately, the U.S. Congress did not appropriate funds for the continuation of this program and *AL,ESA* will cease when funds run out.

This timely and reliable source is often the only place some titles and other additional information from these regions in Africa can be located and verified. It provides an invaluable service to the research community. The *AL,ESA* continues the *AL,ESA* (ISSN 0090-371X; OCLC: 2403577) which was published 1968-1992. This title is available for participating libraries through the U.S. government depository library program.

The *AL,ESA. Annual Publishers' Directory* includes the names and addresses of publishers of all monographs and serials listed in the individual issues of the *AL,ESA* except in the years when the *Serial Supplement* is published. In those years, all publishers of serials titles in the *Supplement* are included in the *Directory*. Publishers are not included whose addresses are not available, who are known not to exist any more, whose publications came out many years back and are believed to be out-of-print, and whose publications were acquired in photocopy format. Under an alphabetical listing of countries, publishers are listed alphabetically under the countries. "AL" refers to the monograph record number; "SS" refers the user to the serial record number (ISSN 1074-3839; OCLC: 29689265).

It is often difficult to verify and establish the beginning or cessation of African serial titles. The biennial *AL,ESA. Serial Supplement* lists all serial titles currently received by the Library of Congress Office, Nairobi in alphabetical order by country and then alphabetical by main entry under the country. The entry information given is entry number, the main entry (title or corporate author), beginning dates, place of publication, publisher, date, volume, illustration statement, size, frequency, notes, ISSN, LCCN, last issue received by the LC Field Office. The *Supplement* includes a main and added entry index, and a subject index. The index refers the user to the record number in the bibliography. Ceased serial titles are deleted from the *Supplement*, as are those titles not received for five years. Newspapers not received in three years are deleted (ISSN 1092-8421; OCLC:36441167).

Another valuable source is *Quarterly Index to Periodical Literature, Eastern and Southern Africa (QIPL,ESA)* which was initiated in 1991. This source is an index to over 250 selected periodicals which are acquired regularly from eastern and southern Africa. The emphasis is on scholarly journals, but selections are also made which include subject areas not found in widely-available literature, organizations which do not frequently circulate their publications, and to represent each of the countries. Articles in all languages are indexes, but not all selected journals are indexed exhaustively. Some cooperative indexing is done by persons in the country. The *QIPL,ESA* consists of a register of citations and an author index, geographic index, subject term index, title of article index, and title of journal index. The citation index is arranged by broad subject categories alphabetically arranged, and then alphabetical by author within each category. Each entry is numbered sequentially; this numbering continues through all subsequent issues. Index references refer to the sequential entry number. Approximately 30 subject terms are from the *United Nations Macrothesaurus for Information Processing in the Field of Economic and Social Development*, and from the *LCSH*. Requests for individual articles should be directed to the publishers (ISSN 1018-1555; OCLC: 24433891, OCLC: 26680120 (mf)).

LATEST ISSUE EXAMINED/CURRENCY: The latest issue examined is Sept./Oct. 1996. The imprints are mostly in the 1990s, with earlier imprints as they are available. The purpose is to be an effective acquisitions program rather than to list only current imprints.

AUTOMATION: Camera-ready copy is produced with the Minaret/Procite 2.1/WordPerfect 5.1 software packages on AT&T PC and the HP LaserJet printer.

FORMAT AND SERVICES AVAILABLE: printed, microfiche.

CURRENT LEGAL DEPOSIT LAWS: Not applicable.

AVAILABLE FROM: Correspondence regarding subscriptions and claims for missing issues from subscribers in the countries regularly included in the *AL, ESA* and from other parts of the world other than North America: Field Director, Library of Congress Office, PO Box 30598, Nairobi, Kenya.

From North America: Field Director-LOC, Unit 64100, Box 361, APO AE 09831-4100. The addresses are the same for the *Annual Publishers' Directory* and the *Serial Supplement*.

All correspondence for the *QIPL,ESA* shoul be addressed to the Field Director, Library of Congress Office.

Microfiche copies of all issues of *AL,ESA* are now available for purchase from Photoduplication Services, Library of Congress, Photoduplication Service, Washington, D.C. 20540, U.S.A.

ACCESSIONS LIST, MIDDLE EAST

TITLE: *Accessions list, Middle East.* - Vol. 1 (Jan. 1963) - vol. 31 (Nov./Dec. 1993) - Cairo : Library of Congress Office, Cairo. 1963-1993.
Bi-monthly (1982- 1993); monthly (1979-1981).
Serial supplement issued annually in July/August issue, 1982-   ; in July issue, 1979-1981.
Continues American Libraries Book Procurement Center, Cairo. *Accessions List, Middle East,* January 1963 - May/June 1974.
DDC: 015'.56; LC: Z3013 .U54; LCCN: 75-644385//r843; OCLC: 2452246
ISSN 0041-7769

COMPILER: Library of Congress Office, Cairo.

SCOPE AND COVERAGE: *Accessions List, Middle East (AL,ME)* is a record of publications acquired by the U.S. Library of Congress Office, Cairo from Algeria, Bahrain, Egypt, Iraq, Jordan, Kuwait, Lebanon, Libya, Morocco, Oman, Qatar, Saudia Arabia, Syria, Turkey, Tunisia, United Arab Emirates, Yemen. Countries outside of the scope of this list are Djibouti, Somalia, The Sudan, and Mauritania. The first three are included in *AL,ESA.* Publications of Iran are acquired and distributed by the Library Office in Karachi, Pakistan but listed in *AL,ME.*

Types of publications included are books, pamphlets, periodicals, official and government publications, reports, maps, sound cassettes.

CONTENTS: Introduction, participant selection table, Middle East program, participant selection table, Iran program, table of contents, bibliographic entries by country.
CATALOGUING RULES AND CLASSIFICATION SCHEMES USED: Since the autumn of 1980, AACR2 rules are used for cataloguing entries.

This list has been assembled from preliminary catalog cards prepared by the Cairo Office as a record of receipts and shipments, from Library of Congress printed cards whenever these are available, and in the case of Iranian publications from entries prepared in the Karachi Office.

A classification scheme is not used.

ENTRY INFORMATION: LC card number in upper right corner, author, title, place of publication, publisher, date, pagination, illustrations, size, series, notes, ISBN, tracings on occasion, price when known, translated titles, "acquired for" abbreviations used for participants in the Middle East Cooperative Acquisitions Program. A microfiche number is given at the upper left of the entry if applicable.

ARRANGEMENT: Beginning with volume 21 (1983), bibliographic entries are arranged by country and then are arranged alphabetically under monographs and serials in separate sections.

INDEXES: Bi-monthly issues do not include an index. Since 1979, a separate annual author/title index is issued at the end of the year (OCLC: 10035023). Prior to 1979 the annual index was included in the December issue of *AL,ME.*

NOTES AND COMMENTS: This title now has ceased since the first edition of *An Annotated Guide.* Helpful information can still be gleaned from the recent numbers, and it was thought important to offer this as a good bibliographic source from 1963 through 1993 and to record this cessation.

Appropriations to support this acquisitions program are granted by the U.S. Congress and it is conducted successively with the cooperation of the book trade of Egypt, the Government of the Arab Republic of Egypt, and the efforts of the citizens of the Arab Republic of Egypt working on the staff.

Beginning with the September/October 1982 issue, titles acquired by the Cairo office and microfiched by the Library of Congress are included in each issue of *AL,ME*. Beginning with the March/April 1984 issue, Iranian publications acquired by Karachi and microfiched by Library of Congress are also included in *AL,ME*. Entries that are microfiched are supplied with a microfiche order number, and may be acquired by using that number and sending orders to Photoduplication Services, Library of Congress, Washington, D.C. 20540, U.S.A.

Cross-references are used throughout the list which aids in easier access to the information.

Issues vary in the countries that are covered. Not every country is included in each issue.

It would be very useful to have an accompanying index with each bi-monthly issue. This would eliminate the necessity of looking through each issue for the country, and then for the title needed.

LATEST ISSUE EXAMINED/CURRENCY: Volume 31, no. 6 (Nov./Dec. 1993) was the latest examined at the Department of Information and Library Science, Aberyswyth, Wales in November 1994.

AUTOMATION: not known. Preliminary pages are typed.

FORMAT AND SERVICES AVAILABLE: no longer currently available. Since 1985, microfiche copies of all issues of *AL,ME* are now available for purchase from Photoduplication Services, Library of Congress, Washington, D.C. 20540, U.S.A. The microfiche number for ordering this title is (o)84/6. More information is available from Photoduplication Services.

CURRENT LEGAL DEPOSIT LAWS: Not applicable.

AVAILABLE FROM: Photoduplication Services, Library of Congress, Washington, D.C. 20540, U.S.A.

ACCESSIONS LIST, SOUTH ASIA

TITLE: *Accessions list, South Asia*. - Vol. 1 (1981) - vol. 16 (1996). - New Delhi : Printed and published by E. G. Smith for the U.S. Library of Congress Office, New Delhi on behalf of the American Embassy, New Delhi, 1981-1996.
Monthly.
DDC: 015.59 ; LC: Z3185.L52a; LCCN: ; OCLC:

ISSN 0271-6445

COMPILER: Library of Congress Offices in New Delhi, India and Karachi, Pakistan.

SCOPE AND COVERAGE: *Accessions List, South Asia (AL,SA)* is a record of publications acquired by the U.S. Library of Congress Offices in New Delhi, India and Islamabad, Pakistan (except for Iran) from the countries of Afghanistan, Bangladesh, Bhután, Burma, Cambodia, India, Laos, Malaysia (Chinese and Tamil only), Maldives, Mongolia, and Nepal, Pakistan, Singapore (Chinese and Tamil only), Sri Lanka, and Thailand, and Tibetan language publications from China (including the Tibetan Autonomous Region and other regions), Bhután, India, Mongolia, and Nepal.

Types of publications included are books, pamphlets, serials, official and government publications, newspapers, atlases and maps, reports, audio and visual recordings, international government organization publications, and other formats.

CONTENTS: Introduction, participating libraries and language coverage, outline of subject profile categories, table of contents, bibliographic entries arranged by country, special materials, Tibetan program, others, author/title index.

CATALOGUING RULES AND CLASSIFICATION SCHEMES USED: The cataloguing follows AACR2.

The Library of Congress Filing Rules are applied in arranging the main entries and the indexes.

A classification scheme is not used.

ENTRY INFORMATION: Sequence number in upper left corner, Library of Congress card number in upper right corner, subject entry codes with code number under LCCN, author, title, place of publication, publisher, date, illustrations, size, notes, price.

An asterisk (*) marks all new serial titles.

Subject entry codes are assigned to many titles. A key to the subject code is given on the pges following the Participating Libraries and Country/language coverage charts. Participants in the Cooperative Acquisitions Programs receive monographs only in the subject categories they have selected.

Material selected for minimal level cataloging uses MLC and the first letter of the LC class number in the call number at the left hand side of the entry.

A microfiche number is given in the left hand margin of the entry if applicable.

ARRANGEMENT: Bibliographic entries are arranged alphabetically by language and within language by main entry under each country. A second section lists other formats alphabetically by main entry by country without regard to language or format.

INDEXES: Author/title index. The numbers used in the author/title index refer to consecutive entry number. Symbols in parentheses indicate the language of the entry. Codes for the language symbols are given at the beginning of the index, covering over thirty languages and dialects.

Annual cumulations of the author/title index are issued as part two of the December issue.

NOTES AND COMMENTS: Appropriations to support this acquisitions program are granted by the U.S. Congress. Financial support from the American research libraries receiving the publications and the cooperation of the governments and book trades in each of the countries covered by *AL,SA* have also helped make this program a success. Unfortunately, the U.S. Congress did not renew these appropriations and *AL,SA* ceased at the end of 1996.

In addition to the acquisitions program for the U.S. Congress, the New Delhi and Karachi offices also acquire selected publications for the Library of Congress and other research libraries in the U.S. participating in one or more country programs, the National Library of Medicine, and the National Agricultural Library.

Since 1985, microfiche copies of all issues of *AL,SA* are now available for purchase from Photoduplication Services, Library of Congress, Washington, D.C. 20540, U.S.A. The microfiche number for ordering this title is (o)84/11. *AL,SA. Cumulative List of Serials* is available under microfiche number (o)84/12. Earlier lists, e.g., *Accessions List, Nepal*, are also available. For more information, contact Photoduplication Services, Library of Congress, Washington, D.C. 20540, U.S.A.

AL,SA is a merger of *Accessions List, India; Accessions List, Pakistan; Accessions List, Bangladesh; Accessions List, Sri Lanka; Accessions List, Nepal* and *Accessions List, Afghanistan.*

AL,SA. Serial Supplement will be published periodically cumulating all new titles, changes, and deletions listed in preceding monthly issues of *AL,SA*. It includes author/title and subject indexes (ISSN 0742-3586).

All entries are printed in Roman script regardless of the original script.

Beginning with the January 1982 issue, titles which have been microfiched (and thus have a microfiche number in the entry information) are available for purchase from Photoduplication Services, Library of Congress, Washington, D.C. 20540, U.S.A. Standing orders by country may be placed. For more information, contact Photoduplication Services.

LATEST ISSUE EXAMINED/CURRENCY: The latest issue examined at Princeton University in June 1997 is for November/December 1996.

AUTOMATION: Information not available.

FORMAT AND SERVICES AVAILABLE: printed, microfiche.

CURRENT LEGAL DEPOSIT LAWS: Not applicable.

AVAILABLE FROM: Correspondence originating from Pakistan: Field Director, Library of Congress Office, American Consulate General, Abdullah Haroon Road, Karachi, Pakistan.

Correspondence originating outside Pakistan should write to Field Director, Library of Congress Office, N-11, New Delhi South Extension, Part-1, New Delhi-110049, India.

ACCESSIONS LIST, SOUTHEAST ASIA

TITLE: *Accessions List, Southeast Asia.* - Vol. 1, no. 1/3, (Jan./Mar. 1975) - vol. 19, no. 6 (Nov./Dec. 1993). - Jakarta : Library of Congress Office, 1975-1993.
Bi-monthly (1982-1993), monthly (July 1975- Dec. 1981), quarterly (Jan./Mar. 1975-April/June 1975).
Continues: *Accessions list, Indonesia, Malaysia, Singapore, and Brunei.*
DDC: 016.956; LC: Z3221.U53a; LCCN: 75-940200//r842; OCLC: 2088682
ISSN 0096-2341

COMPILER: Library of Congress Office, Jakarta.

SCOPE AND COVERAGE: *Accessions List, Southeast Asia (AL,SEA)* is a record of publications acquired by the U.S. Library of Congress Offices in Jakarta and in New Delhi from the countries of Brunei, Burma (Myanmar), Cambodia, Indonesia, Laos, Malaysia, Philippines, Singapore, Thailand, and Vietnam for the Library of Congress and the Southeast Asia acquisitions program. Materials from Burma, Cambodia, Philippines, and Vietnam are purchased for Library of Congress only. Because of the shared cataloguing program begun in 1988 with some participating libraries, this list does not include entries for all materials acquired by the Jakarta field office since the material is shipped uncatalogued to the participant.

Types of publications included are books, pamphlets, serials, official and government publications, newspapers, atlases and maps, reports.

CONTENTS: Introduction, table of contents, bibliographic entries arranged by country, international government organizations, non-Southeast Asian imprints.

CATALOGUING RULES AND CLASSIFICATION SCHEMES USED: Cataloguing conforms to AACR2.

The 1980 *Library of Congress Filing Rules* is applied in arranging the main entries and the index.

A classification scheme is not used.

ENTRY INFORMATION: Library of Congress card number in upper right corner, author, title, place of publication, publisher, date, illustrations, size, notes. Two types of call numbers may appear to the left of the entry: a microfiche number, or a MLC (minimum level cataloguing) number for titles for which LC subject and classification work will not be available.

An asterisk (*) marks all new serial titles.

Each entry on a page has an alphabetical letter assigned to its position on the page; this letter is shown in the left hand margin.

ARRANGEMENT: The bibliographic entries are divided by country, and then arranged alphabetically under monographs, serials, and special materials in separate sections.

INDEXES: The bi-monthly issues do not include an index. An annual cumulated index is published in the November/December issue.

NOTES AND COMMENTS: Appropriations to support this acquisitions program are granted by the U.S. Congress. This program is conducted successfully with the cooperation of the governments and book trades in the countries, and the support of the participating libraries in the Cooperative Acquisitions Program. Unfortunately, the U.S. Congress did not renew appropriations to continue this program, and the *AL,SEA* ceased when funds ran out.

In addition to the acquisitions program for the U.S. Congress, the Jakarta and the New Delhi Offices also acquire selected publications from Brunei, Indonesia, Laos, Malaysia, Singapore and Thailand for the Library of Congress and for the Sourtheast Asia Cooperative Acquisitions Program. Publications from Burma, Cambodia, Philippines, and Vietnam are acquired for the Library of Congress only.

Three separate cumulative lists of serials are issued periodically for Burma, Laos and Thailand; Indonesia; and Malaysia, Singapore and Brunei. These lists periodically supersede previous issues for the respective countries unless otherwise stated.

This title continues *Accessions List, Indonesia, Malaysia, Singapore, and Brunei* (1970-1974) which in turn continues *Accessions List, Indonesia* (1964-1970).

Cross references which may be of help in using the *AL,SEA* are used in both the bibliographic entry section and in the index.

All entries are printed in Romanized script regardless of the original script of the publication.

Serial additions and changes are reported in each issue.

For easier use of this list, it would be helpful for each issue to include an index.

Beginning with the April 1978 issue, titles which have been microfiched by the Library of Congress and distributed on microfiche to participating libraries in the microfiche program are listed in *AL,SEA*. The microfiche numbering system since January 1982 has incorporated the LC shelf number, e.g., 85/51 001 (a monograph) or (o)85/51 001 (a serial). Prior to that date, the prefix SEI was used with the shelf number. The microfiche number may be used to order positive microfiche copies from Photoduplication Service, Library of Congress, Washington, D.C. 20540, U.S.A. Standing orders may be placed.

LATEST ISSUE EXAMINED/CURRENCY: The latest issue examined at The College of Wooster in August 1997 was November/December 1993.

AUTOMATION: automated.

FORMAT AND SERVICES AVAILABLE: printed, microfiche.

CURRENT LEGAL DEPOSIT LAWS: Not applicable.

AVAILABLE FROM: No longer published. Since 1985, microfiche copies of all issues of *AL,SEA* are now available for purchase from Photoduplication Services, Library of Congress, Washington, D.C. 20540, U.S.A. The microfiche number for ordering this title is (o)84/7. *AL,SEA. Cumulative List of Indonesian serials* (including *Accessions List, Indonesia. Cumulative List of Serials, and Accessions List, Indonesia, Malaysia, Singapore and Brunei. Cumulative List of Indonesia Serials*) is available on microfiche by ordering microfiche number (o)84/8.

Correspondence should be sent to the Field Director, Library of Congress Office, American Consulate General, Abdullah Haroon Road, Karachi, Pakistan. Correspondence from the United States should be sent to the Field Director, Karachi - Library of Congress, Department of State, Washington, D.C. 20520, USA.

All editorial comments should be addressed to the Field Director, Library of Congress Office, American Embassy, Box 1, APO San Francisco, 96356-0001. U.S.A.

Correspondence from Indonesia should be sent to the Field Director, Library of Congress Office, Tromol Pos 3502/JKT, Jakarta, Indonesia.

ANNUAIRE DES PAYS DE L'OCEAN INDIEN

TITLE: *Annuaire des pays de l'océan indien.* - 1(1974)-   . - Aix-en-Provence : Presses universitaires d'Aix-Marseille, 197 -   .
Annual.
Vols. for 1974- issued by the Centre d'étude et de recherches sur les sociétés de l'océan indien; 1976- with the Groupement de researches océan indien.
DDC: 969.005; LC : DT468.A54; LCCN: 78-645968//r83; OCLC: 4511432
ISSN 0247-400X

COMPILER: The Centre d'Etudes et de Recherches sur l'Océan Indien occidental (CERSOI) of l'INALCO is responsible for most of the bibliographic section, with individual compilers also mentioned.

SCOPE AND COVERAGE: Studies, background information on a specific topic, memoirs, and reports and bibliographic coverage from the Indian Ocean countries are covered. The bibliography section of this Indian Ocean periodical includes citations compiled mostly by CERSOI from the countries of Comoros, Madagascar, Mauritius, Réunion, Seychelles, and the general Indian Ocean area.

Types of publications include books, pamphlets, periodical articles, annual reports, proceedings, mémoires and theses.

CONTENTS: No. XII (1990/1991): Studies, background information on a specific topic, mémoires, reports, and bibliographic coverage ("informations bibliographiques") from the Indian Ocean countries.

CATALOGUING RULES AND CLASSIFICATION SCHEMES USED: The rules followed are not mentioned but complete bibliographic information is given.

No classification scheme is used.

ENTRY INFORMATION: Thèses and mémoires: author, date, title, thèse or mémoire, subject, place of degree; ouvrages et articles: author, date, article's title, periodical title, volume, number, pagination. Monographs include author, date, title, place of publication and publisher, pagination, illustration statement. Appropriate bibliographic information for analyzed titles in collected works and anonymous works are given.

ARRANGEMENT: Arrangement is by country, author's name, and date.

INDEXES: no index.

NOTES AND COMMENTS: Most years include a bibliographic section with different countries covered each year.

LATEST ISSUE EXAMINED/CURRENCY: The latest issue examined in May 1995 is XII (1990/1991) at the University of Wisconsin Library. XIII (1992-1994) was published in 1995.

Imprint dates cover 1984-1991.

AUTOMATION: not known.

FORMAT AND SERVICES AVAILABLE: printed.

CURRENT LEGAL DEPOSIT LAWS: not applicable.

AVAILABLE FROM: Centre National de la Recherche Scientifique, 20-22 rue St. Amand, 15, 75015 Paris, France.

THE ARAB BULLETIN OF PUBLICATIONS

TITLE: *al-Nashrah al-'Arabīyah lil-matbū'āt li'ām.* - 1970-   . Tunis : Arab League Educational Cultural and Scientific Organization (ALECSO), and National Library of Tunisia, 1972-   .
Annual.
Added title page: *The Arab Bulletin of Publications.*
DDC: not found; LC: Z3013.N3; LCCN: 73-960585/NE/902; OCLC: 2239670
ISSN not found

COMPILER: Department of Documentation and Information, ALECSO.

SCOPE AND COVERAGE: *al-Nashrah al-'Arabīyah lil-matbū'āt li'ām* or *The Arab Bulletin of Publications* (*ABP*) is compiled from current national bibliographies and typed or handwritten lists of current publications sent to ALECSO and the National Library of Tunisia from contributing Arab countries. Arab League states include: Algeria, Bahrain, Comoros, Djibouti, Egypt, Iraq, Jordan, Kuwait, Lebanon, Libya, Mauritania, Morocco, Oman, Qatar, Saudi Arabia, Somalia, Sudan, Syria, Tunisia, United Arab Emirates, Yemen, and Palestine. Not all countries are represented in each issue.

Types of publications included are books, pamphlets, official and government publications, theses and dissertations, new serials and periodical title changes.

Omitted from the bibliography are school and university publications, periodicals (except as new titles) and titles printed outside of the member countries.

CONTENTS: Table of contents, introduction, statistics on book production, abbreviations, general publications, government publications, author index, title index. Arabic and Western language entries are together in the 1992 issue, with separate indexes in Arabic and non-Arabic languages. Earlier issues had separate Arabic and non-Arabic language sections.

CATALOGUING RULES AND CLASSIFICATION SCHEMES USED: The Arabic version of the ISBD(M) rules are used in cataloguing entries for *ABP*.

The DDC scheme is used.

ENTRY INFORMATION: At top of entry: DDC number, contributing country's abbreviation and the consecutive entry number; author, title, place of publication, publisher, date, pagination, size, series statement, brief notes as needed.

ARRANGEMENT: As stated above, in the latest issue examined, the Arabic and non-Arabic entries are listed together. The classified bibliography is arranged by DDC scheme and has general publications. The classified bibliographies in the Arabic and the Western languages are arranged by DDC number, then alphabetically arranged by the main entry. Earlier volumes had an Arab and foreign languages section and were subdivided into general publications, government publications, and children's books.

Volumes preceding 1981 were organized in two sections: one section included all of the Arab League members plus the Palestine Liberation Organization; the second section included Egypt.

INDEXES: Author index, title index. A subject index was included in a few earlier volumes (1980) and was the DDC subject headings list in the Arabic section. Only author and title indexes exist in the Western languages section.

NOTES AND COMMENTS: At its inception, *ABP* was located in Cairo where is was published by ALECSO and the National Library and Archives of Egypt. It moved to its present location in 1981. Until the 1981 volume (covering 1979 publications), the title of this publication was *Bulletin of Arab Publications*.

The *ABP* functions both as a regional bibliography and as a union catalogue of titles for participating Arab countries. These functions necessitate a longer production period than that of a national bibliography. ALECSO relies on the efficiency of the relaying of publishing information from contributing libraries in the Arab world to ALECSO, a time- consuming step and one more step beyond that required of a national bibliography. It is also important to have the information presented in as consistent a format as possible following international standards. The desire to have cooperation in classification and cataloguing methods among participating countries is expressed in the introduction of *ABP*.

Book publishing statistics are included for Arab countries in the Arab section. Information covers the number of books published and a subject breakdown of titles.

LATEST ISSUE EXAMINED/CURRENCY: Each issue only includes titles for the year that it covers (except for school books). The latest issue examined at Princeton University in June 1997 is for no. 23, 1992 published in 1994.

Publication of the volumes are two years behind the year that is covered. Distribution time enlarges the gap even further. However, this is an historic bibliographic service to track publications from countries which do not have national bibliographies.

AUTOMATION: *ABP* is automated with MiniIsis, which is able to support both the Arabic and Roman character sets. The code used is CODAR-U/FD; ASMO standard 449 is followed.

FORMAT AND SERVICES AVAILABLE: print.

CURRENT LEGAL DEPOSIT LAWS: Not applicable.

AVAILABLE FROM: Arab League Educational Cultural and Scientific Organization, BP 1120, Tunis.

SELECTED ARTICLES: Attia, Ridha. "National Bibliographies in the Magreb: A Survey of their Contents and Perspectives." Paper presented at the 50th IFLA General Conference, Nairobi, Kenya, 19-24 August 1984.

BIBLIOGRAFIA ACTUAL DEL CARIBE

TITLE: *Bibliografía actual del Caribe = Current Caribbean bibliography = Bibliographie courante de la Caraïbe*. - Rio Piedras, Puerto Rico : Biblioteca Regional del Caribe, 1951- .
Irregular.
Title varies.
Place of publication and publisher varies.
DDC: 016.9729; LC: Z1595.C8; LCCN: 75-643729; OCLC: 2241382, 1565609
ISSN 0070-1866

COMPILER: Biblioteca Regional del Caribe.

SCOPE AND COVERAGE: *Bibliografía actual del Caribe/Current Caribbean bibliography/Bibliographie courante de la Caraïbe (BAC)* includes titles published in and relating to the Caribbean held by the Caribbean Regional Library or sent by twenty-one contributing libraries, including libraries from the Netherlands Antilles, Virgin Islands, Guyana, Haiti, Jamaica, St. Vincent, Dominican Republic, Puerto Rico, Barbados, Trinidad and Tobago. Other countries are listed from time to time as information is supplied (e.g., Belize).

Types of publications included are books, pamphlets, official and government publications, speeches, annual reports.

CONTENTS: Table of contents, introduction, list of contributing libraries and their librarians, localization codes, subject headings used in the arrangement of entries, list of books arranged under broad subject headings; author, subjects and titles index. Both the table of contents and the introduction are in Spanish and English.

CATALOGUING RULES AND CLASSIFICATION SCHEMES USED: The cataloguing rules are not given in the introduction. It is stated that bibliographic entries are reproduced from the participating libraries, including the subject entries and the classification number. Complete bibliographic information is given.

Subject headings taken from the Library of Congress and from the Spanish translation by Carmen Rovira's "Lista de Encabezamientos de Materia para Bibliotecas" are used in *BAC* with modifications using geographic subdivisions with the following subjects: social conditions, geography, description and travel, history, politics and government, and economic policy, which are normally used as abbreviations under the name of a country.

ENTRY INFORMATION: Classification number, author, title, edition, place of publication, publisher, date, pagination, acronym of the holding library, entry number in numerical order in lower right corner.

ARRANGEMENT: The main bibliography is arranged by broad subject headings which is alphabetically arranged.

INDEXES: Author/subject/title index. The number used refers back to the entry number in the bibliography.

NOTES AND COMMENTS: In 1971, I. Zimmerman mentions the *BAC* was then at a critical stage and had a precarious existence.[1] According to the introduction in volume 23, the director of the Caribbean Regional Library states that "We are making great efforts to bring this publication up-to-date; unfortunately we have not been able to do it, due to limitations of personnel." (p.vi)

Earlier issues had the English parallel title listed first.

The Caribbean Regional Library keeps a card for each title that it receives, adding the acronyms of all libraries that have sent cards for the same title. In this manner, the Caribbean Regional Library is creating a union catalogue of the region.

---

[1] For a discussion of the history and problems of *BAC*, see I. Zimmerman. *Current National Bibliographies of Latin America*. Gainesville, Fla. : Center for Latin American Studies, Univ. of Florida, 1971, pp.91-101.

"Volumes 1-7 were published in Port-of-Spain, Trinidad, volumes 8-15 and 17-23 were published in Puerto Rico, and volume 16, at the New York Public Library. Volumes 1-8 were issued by the Caribbean Commission and volumes 9-11, part 1, by the Caribbean Organization. Volumes 9-11, parts 2-14, and volume 16- have been issued by the Institute of Caribbean Studies, University Puerto Rico, and published by CODECA. Volume 15 was issued by the Caribbean Economic Development Corporation (Hayt Rey)" which was renamed the Biblioteca Regional del Caribe.[1]

Various cumulations have been issued.

LATEST ISSUE EXAMINED/CURRENCY: Timeliness is the biggest drawback of *BAC*. For several years, this title has been plagued with a lag in publication. The latest volume available, which is the latest issue examined, is volume 23, covering 1973, and published in 1976. The author could not verify that this title has ceased; it is certainly in hiatus.

Entries range over a period of years, with most entries 1970-1973. *BAC* has the characteristic time lag of regional bibliographies. It relies on the participating libraries to send the bibliographic information.

AUTOMATION: not known.

FORMAT AND SERVICES AVAILABLE: printed.

CURRENT LEGAL DEPOSIT LAWS: Not applicable.

AVAILABLE FROM: Biblioteca Regional del Caribe, Apdo. 21927, Estación de la Universidad, Rio Piedras, Puerto Rico 00931.

CARIBBEAN COLLECTION QUARTERLY ACCESSION LIST

TITLE: *Caribbean collection quarterly accession list.* - no.1- , Dec. 1973/Mar. 1974- . - Willestad : Curaçao Public Library, 1974- .
Quarterly.
Title varies slightly.
DDC: not found; LC (090): Z1595.W54; LCCN: not found; OCLC: 10857911
ISSN not found.

COMPILER: Curaçao Public Library.

SCOPE AND COVERAGE: *Caribbean Collection Quarterly Accession List* (*CCQA*) lists the accessions of the Curaçao Public Library for the period covered. Titles published in the Caribbean islands about the Caribbean area, focusing on the Netherlands Antilles (especially

---

[1] H. Woodbridge, with research assistance of Jane Larkin, "Latin American National Bibliography," *Encylopedia of Library and Information Science*, vol. 36, supp. 1 (1983).

Curaçao and Aruba) and titles about the Caribbean area, especially on the Netherlands Antilles, published elsewhere (e.g., Rotterdam, New York). Suriname is also within the scope.

Types of publications included are books, pamphlets, official and government publications, periodicals, periodical articles, theses and dissertations, university publications, IGO publications.

CONTENTS: Bibliographic entries.

CATALOGUING RULES AND CLASSIFICATION SCHEMES USED: AACR2 is followed.

The classification scheme used is DDC.

ENTRY INFORMATION: Monographs: DDC number in the left margin, author, title and subtitles, place of publication, publisher, date, pagination, illustrations, size, series statement, brief notes including ISBN when known.

Periodicals: DDC number in the left margin, title, beginning volume and date. When a periodical article is cited, complete bibliographic information is given.

ARRANGEMENT: Entries are alphabetically arranged within DDC subject groups.

INDEXES: No indexes.

NOTES AND COMMENTS: Entries in Dutch, Spanish, English and Papiamento are found in this duplicated list. *CCQA* is helpful to identify and verify titles that are not within the scope of other regional bibliographies and are otherwise difficult to locate.

Although it is not expected that this accession list have an introduction as in a current national bibliography, it would be useful to have a short symbol and abbreviations list which would explain the use of an asterisk (*) marking some entries in front of the classification number.

LATEST ISSUE EXAMINED/CURRENCY: Entries reflect the acquisitions of Curaçao Public Library during the period covered. The latest issue examined is vol. 13, no. 1 (Jan./Mar. 1986) received by the Library of Congress. The University of Florida Latin American library has received volume 13, no. 3. No later copy was located. This may be ceased?

AUTOMATION: not known.

FORMAT AND SERVICES AVAILABLE: printed.

CURRENT LEGAL DEPOSIT LAWS: Not applicable.

AVAILABLE FROM: Curaçao Public Library, Johan Van Walbeeckplein 13, Curaçao.

THE CARICOM BIBLIOGRAPHY

TITLE: *The CARICOM bibliography.* - vol. 1(1977)-vol. 10, nos. 1 & 2 (Jan.-Dec. 1986). - Georgetown, Guyana : Caribbean Community Secretariat, Information and Documentation Section, 1977-1986.
Semiannual, with the second issue being an annual cumulation (vol. 6-10, 1982-1986); semiannual (vol. 3-5; 1979-1981); annual (vol. 1-2; 1977-1978).
DDC: 015.729; LC: Z1501.C36; LCCN: 78-646856//R842; OCLC: 3746719
ISSN 0254-9646

COMPILER: Caribbean Community Secretariat, Information and Documentation Section.

SCOPE AND COVERAGE: *The CARICOM Bibliography* lists all material currently published in the Caribbean Community (CARICOM) member states: Antigua and Barbuda, The Bahamas, Barbados, Belize, Christopher, Dominica, Grenada, Guyana, Jamaica, Montserrat, St. Kitts/Nevis, Saint Lucia, St. Vincent and the Grenadines, Trinidad and Tobago. Information has been compiled from the national bibliographies of those countries producing one, along with bibliographic information from member states which do not yet produce a national bibliography.

Types of publications included are books, pamphlets, first issue and change of title in periodicals, official and government publications, maps and plans, audio-visual materials, annual reports, ephemera, e.g., flashcards.

Omitted from *The CARICOM Bibliography* are periodicals (except first issues and new titles), certain government publications—e.g., acts, bills, subsidiary legislation, gazettes and parliamentary debates.

CONTENTS: Table of contents, preface, abbreviations and terms used, ISO country codes used, outline of the DDC, classified subject section, alphabetical section [index], index to LDC material, non-book material, list of publishers and their addresses.

CATALOGUING RULES AND CLASSIFICATION SCHEMES USED: The subtitle to volume 10, nos. 1 & 2, 1986 states the following: "A subject list of current national imprints of the CARIBBEAN COMMUNITY MEMBER COUNTRIES, arranged according to the Dewey Decimal Classification, 19th edition, and catalogued according to the *Anglo-American Cataloguing Rules*, 2nd edition, 1978." ISBD(M) and ISBD(S) has been used since the beginning.

ENTRY INFORMATION: DDC number and subject heading, author, title, edition, place of publication, date, pagination, size, series, notes including binding information, price when known. In lower right corner is the ISO country code and the accession number (e.g., JM81-70).

Information for periodicals include DDC number and subject heading, title, issuing agency, date of first issue, place of publication, publisher, date, size, frequency, notes, including change of title, price, format, binding, etc., ISO country code and accession number.

ARRANGEMENT: The main bibliographic section is arranged by the DDC scheme.

INDEXES: Author/title/series index, alphabetically arranged. Information given includes the DDC number, which refers the user to complete bibliographic information in the classified bibliography. The LDC (less developed countries) index is arranged by subject, and then alphabetically arranged, giving page, classification and accession numbers.

NOTES AND COMMENTS: As with any regional bibliography, there is a time lag from the date of coverage to the time of receipt. The value is not so much in the current acquisitions as in the indentification and coverage of titles and countries not otherwise listed in other bibliographical sources. Because of the valuable list of publishers and their addresses, one is able to correspond directly with the publisher to determine if a title is still available. The problem remains one of timeliness since so many of these titles are probably out-of-print by the time a library receives *CARICOM Bibliography*.

A regional bibliography is only as strong as the connections with the states and territories of the region. If the participants cooperate, then there is good regional coverage. When countries, especially those not having a national bibliography, have trouble gathering bibliographic information, that is reflected in inadequate coverage for that country in the regional bibliography. Not covered by *CARICOM Bibliography* are the Turks and Caicos, British Virgin Islands, Bermuda, U.S. Virgin Islands and Cayman Islands.[1]

Issued by the Caribbean Community Secretariat's Library, 1977-[1978], and by the Caribbean Community Secretariat's Information and Documentation, [1980]-1989.

The "LDC list" began in volume 5, 1981. However, nowhere was the author able to determine what the initials mean. The author assumes that "LDC" refers to "less developed countries" as often cited in other sources. It would be helpful to include this abbreviation in the abbreviations list.

In looking at volumes from the beginning to the present, it is obvious that the editors want to meet international bibliographic standards. Additions have been made to improve the quality and use of this bibliography. An example is the addition of the publishers' list. *The CARICOM Bibliography* is presented in a pleasing, easy-to-use format.

Another regional bibliography in the Caribbean is *Current Caribbean Bibliography* (ISSN 0070-1866). At present, this bibliography is quite far behind in publication.

LATEST ISSUE EXAMINED/CURRENCY: Generally, the current volume covers two to three previous years (usually stated in the preface), published a year later, and received a year later still. It is not unusual to have a four year delay in listing imprints. *The CARICOM Bibliography* will include materials published within the previous two years, provided that the contributing country's bibliographic centre acquired them within the year of the publication of its national bibliography. Although regional bibliographies cannot be expected to be as timely as a national bibliography, it would be more useful if it were not so far behind. As stated earlier, the usefulness is in the identification of titles published in countries covered, especially those with no national bibliography.

---

[1] As stated by Mr. Bloomfield in "Working Paper No. B-7", 1979 SALALM Meeting, p.3 and quoted by H. Woodbridge. "Latin American National Bibliography," *Encyclopedia of Library and Information Science*, vol. 36, supplement 1 (1983):275.

The latest volume examined at the University Library, Cambridge in June 1997 was volume 10, nos. 1 & 2, 1982, published in 1989.

AUTOMATION: *The CARICOM Bibliography* is mimeographed.

FORMAT AND SERVICES AVAILABLE: print.

CURRENT LEGAL DEPOSIT LAWS: Not applicable.

AVAILABLE FROM: No longer published. Correspondence may be directed to CARICOM Secretariat, Bank of Guyana Building, PO Box 10827, Georgetown, Guyana.

NOTES BIBLIOGRAPHIQUES CARAÏBES

TITLE: *Notes bibliographiques caraïbes.* - No. 1 (Oct. 1977)-   . - Basse-Terre, Guadeloupe : l' Association des Archivistes, Bibliothécaires et Documentalistes francophones de la Caraïbe, 1977-   .
Monthly.
Publisher varies.
DDC: not found; LC: Z1595.N67; LCCN: 82-645903; OCLC: 5179489
ISSN 0180-4103

COMPILER: Members of the Commission N.B.C. of l'Association des bibliothèques universitaires de recherche et institutionnelles de la Caraïbe.

SCOPE AND COVERAGE: *Notes Bibliographiques Caraïbes* (*NBC*) is a periodical for members which includes a list of titles published in the French Caribbean islands or about the islands published elsewhere which are acquired by participating libraries. Publications from the islands of Dominique, Guadeloupe, Guyane, French Antilles (Aruba, Bonaire, Caracao, St. Martin, Saba et Saint-Eustache), French West Indies, Haiti, Martinique, and St. Barthelemy are included.

Types of publications include books, pamphlets, and periodicals.

CONTENTS: Number 64: Table of contents, editorial, periodical articles, UDC table, bibliographic entries.

Contents vary. Number 43: Table of contents, abbreviations list, list of deposited periodicals; Part I: Articles; Part 2: Bibliographical notices; Part 3: Announcements.

CATALOGUING RULES AND CLASSIFICATION SCHEMES USED: An adaptation of the AACR2 format is used for the bibliographic entries.

The classification scheme used is UDC.

ENTRY INFORMATION: Number 41 (special periodicals supplement): title, sub-title or parallel title, place of publication, publisher, beginning date, frequency (when known), symbol for participating libraries owning the title and the holdings of that library.
Number 43: UDC number, author, title, sub-title or parallel title, place of publication, publisher, date, illustrations, size, notes, symbol for participating libraries owning the title.

Number 64: Title of periodical article, responsibility statement, title of periodical, place of publication, date, issue, pagination. Periodical articles are in UDC subject groups.

ARRANGEMENT: In "Notices Bibliographiques" the entries are arranged alphabetically within UDC subject groups.

The periodical supplement listed titles alphabetically.

INDEXES: No index observed.

NOTES AND COMMENTS: This title is a helpful source for verification and acquisition of materials that are hard to locate and identify. Number 64 lists only periodical articles.

An editorial announced that number 64 is the last issue in the present form. The author has not been able to find issues beyond this to describe changes.

NBC serves as a "periodical" to members as well as a conduit for listing bibliographic information.

Participating libraries listed in number 41 are Archives départementales de la Guadeloupe, Bibliothèque départementale de la Guadeloupe, Bibliothèque universitaire Antilles-Guyane (Guadeloupe), C.D.I. Collège Solitude de Capesterre, Conseil régional du patronat guadeloupéen and Centre de documentation INSEE de Pointe-à-Pitre.

Number 43 is the "Catalogue collectif regional des periodiques."

In the introduction of number 41, the first number after "a long interruption," the history and reason for this title's existence are stated briefly and an explanation of an entry is given. Later issues do not include this.

LATEST ISSUE EXAMINED/CURRENCY: The latest copy examined from the University of Florida in September 1997 is for June 1993, no. 64.

AUTOMATION: not known.

FORMAT AND SERVICES AVAILABLE: printed.

CURRENT LEGAL DEPOSIT LAWS: not applicable.

AVAILABLE FROM: Documentation et Lecture en Guadeloupe (DLG), BP 148, 97190 Le Gossier, Guadaloupe.

SOUTH PACIFIC BIBLIOGRAPHY

TITLE: *South Pacific bibliography.* 1981-   . Suva : University of the South Pacific Library, Pacific Information Centre, 1982-   .
Biennial (1989/1990, 1992/1993-   ); annual (1981-1985, 1988, 1991).
Supersedes *Pacific collection accessions list* .
DDC number: 011.5099; LC: Z4001.S65; LCCN: 84-641270; OCLC: 9921005
ISSN not found

COMPILER: University of the South Pacific Library, Pacific Information Centre.

SCOPE AND COVERAGE: *South Pacific Bibliography* (*SPB*) lists works published in the region as well as works published overseas relating wholly or in part to American Samoa, Cook Islands, Easter Islands, Federated States of Micronesia (Kosrae, Pohnpei, Truk, Yap), Fiji, French Polynesia (Austral Islands, Marquesas Islands, Society Islands, Tuamotu Archipelago), Guam, Irian Jaya, Kiribati, Nauru, New Caledonia, Niue, Norfolk Island, Northern Mariana Islands, Palau, Papua New Guinea, Pitcairn Island, Solomon Islands, Tokelau, Tonga, Tuvalu, Vanuatu, Wallis and Futuna Islands, and Western Samoa. It also includes materials on Pacific and indigenous peoples in Australia, Hawaii and New Zealand.

Types of publications included in *SPB* are published and unpublished books, pamphlets, official and government publications, current serials on first appearance, maps, local language publications, and any other material that is related to the social, cultural and other aspects of the countries. Programmes, trade catalogues and art catalogues are selectively included.

CONTENTS: Contents, preface (including scope and coverage, frequency, and arrangement), abbreviations, outline of DDC, monographs, author/title/series index, subject index, periodicals, legal notices, maps.

CATALOGUING RULES AND CLASSIFICATION SCHEMES USED: *SPB* uses AACR2R, with some modifications. LC tracings and subject headings are followed.

The DDC (20th ed.) is the scheme used in the bibliographical sequence.

ENTRY INFORMATION: DDC number, author, title, place of publication, publisher, date, pagination, size, series statement, notes including ISBN for foreign publications if known, tracings, LC classification number.

Periodicals: Title, place of publication, publisher, frequency, date and/or number (holdings), notes, tracings, LC classification number.

ARRANGEMENT: Monographs: by classification number; periodicals: alphabetical by title; maps: alphabetical by geographical area; legal notices, statutes, etc.: alphabetical by country. Within each country the notices are listed alphabetically by the main entry and then by the legal notice number.

INDEXES: Author/title/series index; subject index (arranged according to the *LCSH*). The DDC numbers refer the user to the main bibliography.

The indexes include entries for monographs only. Maps, periodicals, and legal notices are not listed.

The series was added to the author/title index with the 1991 volume.

A list of printers and publishers and their addresses is given at the end of the volume. This is a helpful resource since it includes some otherwise hard-to-locate addresses from the region. The 1992/1993 volume did not include this list in its contents.

NOTES AND COMMENTS: The first issue of *SPB* lists publications received and registered in the University of the South Pacific Library, Suva in 1981 irrespective of the date and place of publication of the material. It also includes titles published after 1975 not previously listed and other items that are received but not catalogued or processed such as maps, legal notices, statutes.

Entries in earlier volumes include the holdings of the participating libraries. One of the specific reasons for the existence of a regional bibliography is to aid in the identification and cataloguing of titles, and to aid in bibliographic control of the region. Entries of this cooperative bibliography have been received from Cook Islands Library, Kiribati National Library and Archives, Nelson Memorial Public Library, Solomon Islands National Library, South Pacific Commission Library, Tuvalu National Library and Archives, and University of the South Pacific Library. Location symbols of contributing libraries are given in the prefatory material. With later issues of *SPB*, however, the preface states that all entries are now catalogued and classified by members of the Cataloguing Department of USP Library. This is a big contribution to the region and gives guidance and uniformity of names, etc., and eliminates duplication of cataloguing efforts for the libraries of the region.

The volume for 1986/1987 was not published.

SPB is an attractively presented regional bibliography which follows recommendations of the ICNB.

SPB continues *The Pacific Collection Accession List*, vols. 1-8; 1975-1982 (LCCN:76-649267//r84; OCLC: 4162147) supersedes the *University of the South Pacific Library's Legal Deposit Accessions* (1972-1974; LCCN: 73-643679//r81; OCLC: 1786815).

South Pacific Periodicals Index. - vol. 6/8 - , 1979/81-   . - Suva : Pacific Information Centre in association with the University of the South Pacific Library, 1984-   , (LCCN: 85-641342; OCLC: 11434038) is an index to the periodical literature of the region. Since periodical articles are not included within the scope of *SPB*, this title may be used to supplement the regional bibliography for a more complete listing of the literature of the South Pacific. The *South Pacific Periodicals Index* continues *Bibliography of Periodical Articles Relating to the South Pacific.* - vol. 1-4/5. - Suva : University of the South Pacific Library, 1974-1977/78 (LCCN: 77-151147//r85; OCLC: 3725669).

PROMPTNESS RECEIVED/CURRENCY: The latest issue examined of *SPB* is for 1992/1993 which was the latest available at SOAS in April 1995. It was received by SOAS 13 May 1994.

The Preface states that the *SPB* includes publications catalogued by the USP Library in 1992 and 1993 irrespective of date and place of publication of the material. It also includes items published after 1975 not previously listed. In an analysis of the imprints included in the 1992/1993 issue, 1 was published in 1993, 6 in 1992, 2 in 1991, 5 in 1990, 15 were published before 1990, and 2 had no date.

AUTOMATION: not known.

FORMAT AND SERVICES AVAILABLE: printed.

CURRENT LEGAL DEPOSIT LAWS: Not applicable.

AVAILABLE FROM: The Editor, South Pacific Bibliography, Pacific Information Centre, University of the South Pacific Library, P.O. Box 1168, Suva, Fiji.

SELECTED ARTICLES: "South Pacific: Regional Bibliography." *International Cataloguing* 12 (no. 3 July/Sept. 1983):27.

VERIFIER: Jayshree Mamtora, Librarian, Pacific Information Centre.

SELECTED BIBLIOGRAPHY ON
CURRENT NATIONAL BIBLIOGRAPHIES

WESTERN EUROPE   478
General Sources
Countries: Austria, Belgium, Denmark, Finland, France, Germany, Greece, Iceland,
   Ireland, Italy, Malta, Netherlands, Norway, Portugal, Sweden, United
   Kingdom.

PART ONE: GENERAL GUIDES AND SOURCE MATERIALS

Aguolu, C.C. "National Bibliography: Its Evolving Conceptions, Utility, and International
Dimensions." *International Library Movement* 6 (no. 2 1984):92-96.

Anderson, Dorothy P. "IFLA's Programme for Universal Bibliographical Control: The
Background and the Basis." *IFLA Journal* 1 (no. 1 1975):4-8.

Anderson, Dorothy P. "An International Framework for National Bibliographic Development:
Achievement and Challenge." *Library Resources & Technical Services* 30 (January/March
1986):13-22.

Anderson, Dorothy P.   "National Bibliographies in Third World Countries: National
Developments in an International Environment." In Gorman, G.E., and Mahoney, M., *Guide to
Current National Bibliographies in the Third World*, 2d rev. ed., pp. 1-20. Munich, New York,
London, Paris: Hans Zell, an imprint of K.G. Saur, 1987.

Anderson, Dorothy P. "Recent Contributions to National Bibliographic Control." In Conference
on the Acquisition and Bibliography of Commonwealth and Third World Literatures in English
(1982. London). *Proceedings of the Conference on the Acquisition and Bibliography of
Commonwealth and Third World Literatures in English, Commonwealth Institute, London, 21-
22 October 1982*, pp. 145-158. London: Commonwealth Institute Working Party on Library
Holdings of Commonwealth Literature, 1983.

Anderson, Dorothy P. "Role of the National Bibliographic Centre." *Library Trends* 25 (January
1977):645-663.

Anderson, Dorothy P. "Universal Bibliographical Control." In Conference on Universal
Bibliographical Control in Southeast Asia (1975. Singapore). *Conference on Universal
Bibliographical Control in Southeast Asia, held at the Regional English Language Centre,
Singapore, 21-23 February 1975: Papers and Proceedings*, pp. 15-27. Edited by Hedwig Anuar,
Yolanda Beh, Lim Hong Too, Quah Swee Lan. Singapore: Library Association of Singapore,
1975.

Anderson, Dorothy P. "Universal Bibliographic Control." In *Encyclopedia of Library and
Information Science*, vol. 37, suppl. 2, pp. 366-401. Edited by Allen Kent. New York and
Basel: Marcel Dekker, Inc., 1984. Also published by the IFLA International Office for UBC,
London, as *Occasional Paper No. 10*, 1982. (ISBN 0-903043-38-6).

Anderson, Dorothy P. *Universal Bibliographic Control: A Long Term Policy, a Plan for Action.* Pullach/Munich: Verlag Dokumentation, 1974.

Anderson, Dorothy P. "Universal Bibliographic Control and the National Bibliography." In *IFLA Worldwide Seminar (1976. Seoul, Korea). Proceedings of IFLA Worldwide Seminar, May 31 - June 5, 1976,* pp. 179-188. Seoul, Korea: Korean Library Association, 1976.

Anderson, Dorothy P. *Universal Bibliographic Control (UBC): What It Is.* London: IFLA International Office for UBC, Reference Division, British Library, 1979.

Anderson, Dorothy P. "Waiting for Technology: An Overview of Bibliographic Services in the Third World." *IFLA Journal* 9 (no. 4 1983):285-295.

Avicenne, P. *Bibliographical Services Throughout the World, 1965-1969. Documentation, Libraries, and Archives. Bibliographies and Reference Works*, vol. 1. Paris: Unesco, 1972.

Beaudiquez, Marcelle. *Bibliographical Services Throughout the World, 1970-1974.* Documentation, Libraries, and Archives. Bibliographies and Reference Works, vol. 3. Paris: Unesco, 1977.

Beaudiquez, Marcelle. *Bibliographical Services Throughout the World, 1975-1979.* Documentation, Libraries, and Archives. Bibliographies and Reference Works, vol. 7. Paris: Unesco, 1984.

Beaudiquez, Marcelle. *Bibliographical Services Throughout the World. Supplement 1980. Les Services Bibliographiques dans le Monde. Supplement 1980.* Paris: Unesco, 1982. Also available as supplement to *General Information Programme - UNISIST Newsletter* 10 (no. 1 1982).

Beaudiquez, Marcelle. *Bibliographic Services Throughout the World. Supplement 1981/1982. Les Services Bibliographiques dans le Monde. Supplement 1981/1982.* Paris: Unesco, 1985.

Beaudiquez, Marcelle. *Bibliographic Services Throughout the World. Supplement 1983-1984.* Paris: Unesco, 1987. (PGI-87/WS/4)

Beaudiquez, Marcelle. "Current National Developments 1970-1974." Paper presented at the 42d IFLA General Conference, Lausanne, 1976. (42/A/BI/1B).

Beaudiquez, Marcelle. "National Bibliography as Witness of National Memory." (Paper given at the 1991 IFLA Conference, Moscow). *IFLA Journal* 18 (no. 2 1992):119-123.

Beaudiquez, Marcelle. "Quelques Réflexions sur les Travaux de la Section de Bibliographie de l'IFLA et le Congrès International sur les Bibliographies Nationales." *IFLA Journal* 4 (no. 1 1978):17-20.

Bell, Barbara. *An Annotated Guide to Current National Bibliographies.* Cambridge, England and Alexandria, VA.: Chadwyck-Healey, 1986.

Bell, Barbara. "An Annotated Guide to Current National Bibliographies, 2d edition." Paper given at 63rd IFLA General Conference, Copenhagen, 3 Sept. 1997 (100-BIBL-2-E)

Bell, Barbara L. "The Dewey Decimal Classification System in National Bibliographies." *Dewey Decimal Classification Edition 21 and International Perspectives. Papers from a workshop held at the IFLA Conference, Beijing, China, August 29, 1996.* Ed. by Lois Mai Chan and Joan S. Mitchell. Sponsored by the IFLA Section on Classification and Indexing and OCLC Forest Press. Albany: Forest Press, 1997. pp. 43-58.

Bell, Barbara L. "The Future of National Bibliographies: An International Perspective." In *The Future of the National Bibliography / Proceedings of a Seminar held by the British Library in June 1997.* British Library, 1997. (forthcoming)

Bell, Barbara L. "National Bibliography Today as National Memory Tomorrow: Problems and Proposals." *International Cataloguing & Bibliographic Control* 21 (no. 1 Jan./Mar. 1992):10-12.

Bell, Barbara L. "Progress, Problems and Prospects in Current National Bibliographies: Implementations of the ICNB Recommendations." International Federation of Library Associations and Institutions. *Proceedings of the National Bibliographies Seminar, Brighton, England, 18 August 1987.* Held under the auspices of the IFLA Division of Bibliographic Control.. Ed. by Winston D. Roberts. London: IFLA Universal Bibliographic Control and International MARC Programme, 1988. pp. 29-37.

Bell, Barbara L. "Reviewing Recommendations from the International Congress on National Bibliographies, Paris, 1977." *International Cataloguing & Bibliographic Control* 22 (no. 1 Jan./Mar. 1993):29-33.

Bourne, Ross. "Bridging the Gap: Technological Differences in the Production of Current National Bibliographies." *International Cataloguing & Bibliographic Control* 23 (no. 1 Jan./Mar. 1994):13-14.

Bourne, Ross. "National Bibliographies–Do They Have a Future?" *Alexandria* 5 (No. 2 1993): 99-109.

Cheffins, Richard H.A. "Current General Bibliographies." In *Printed Reference Material*, pp. 423-453. Edited by Gavin Higgens. 2d ed. Handbooks on Library Practice. London: The Library Association, 1984.

Cheffins, Richard H.A. "Current National Bibliographies Under the Aspect of UBC." Paper presented at the 42d IFLA General Conference, Lausanne, 1976. (69/A/BI).

Cheffins, Richard H.A. "Developments in National Bibliographies Since the Paris Congress of 1977." Paper presented at the 49th IFLA General Conference, Munich, 1983. (129/BIB/6/E).

Cheffins, Richard H.A. "Recent Developments in National Bibliography." Paper presented at the 49th IFLA General Conference. *International Cataloguing* 13 (April 1984):20-22.

Cheffins, Richard H.A. *A Survey of the Contents of Existing National Bibliographies.* Paris: Unesco, 1977. (PGI-77/UBC/Ref.1).

Cheffins, Richard H.A. "Universal Bibliographic Control and the Work of the IFLA International Office for UBC." *Leads* 23 (Winter 1981):6-9; *IFLA Journal* 8 (no. 2 1982):213-217.

Clarke, T.C. "National Bibliographic Control in Developing Countries." In *Meeting on National and Regional Bibliography (1978. Suva). Meeting on National and Regional Bibliography. Record of Proceedings [3-8 July 1978]*, pp. 97-102. Sponsored by the International Development Research Centre and the University of the South Pacific. Suva: Meeting on National and Regional Bibliography, 1978.

Commonwealth National Bibliographies: an Annotated Directory. Compiled by the IFLA International Office for UBC. 2d ed., rev. London: Commonwealth Secretariat, 1982, c1983.

"Commonwealth National Bibliographies: Classification Practices." *International Cataloguing* 11 (July/September 1982):26-27.

"Le Contrôle Bibliographique Universel dans les Pays en Développement." In *Table Ronde sur le Contrôle Bibliographique Universel dans les Pays en Développement, Grenoble, 22-25 Aôut 1973.* Compte-rendu édité par Marie-Louise Bossuat, G. Feuillebois, M. Pelletier. Munich: Verlag Dokumentation, 1975.

"Coverage of Documents in Current National Bibliographies." *International Cataloguing* 11 (January/March 1982):4-7.

Current National Bibliographies. Compiled by Helen F. Conover. Washington, D.C.: Library of Congress, 1955.

Current Research in Library & Information Science. Vol. 1, no. 1 March 1983-. London: The Library Association, 1983-. (ISSN 0263-9254). Continues *RADIALS Bulletin.* No. 1 1974-no. 2 1982. (ISSN 0302-2706).

Cybulski, Radoslaw, and Zotova, Kremera. *The Dynamic Model of a Coverage of the Current National Bibliography.* Arlington, Virginia: ERIC, 1979. (ED 186 011).

Farley, Judith. "Current National Bibliography." In *ALA World Encyclopedia of Library and Information Services.* Edited by Robert Wedgeworth. 2d ed. Chicago: American Library Association, 1986. pp. 575-580.

Fartunin, Y.I. "Implementation of the Recommendations of the International Congress on National Bibliographies, 1977, by the National Bibliographic Service of the USSR." *International Cataloguing* 9 (April/June 1980):23-24.

General Information Programme - UNISIST Newsletter. Vol. 7-. Paris: Unesco, 1979-. Quarterly. (ISSN 0379-2218). Continues *Bibliography, Documentation, Terminology, UNISIST Newsletter.*

Gorman, G.E., and Mahoney, M. "Current National Bibliographies in Developing Countries of the Commonwealth." Paper presented at the Conference on the Acquisition and Bibliography of Commonwealth and Third World Literatures in English, 1982, London, England. *Libri* 33 (September 1983):177-189.

Gorman, G.E., and Mahoney, M. *Guide to Current National Bibliographies in the Third World,* 2d rev. ed., London, Munich: Hans Zell, an imprint of K.G. Saur, 1987.

Greer, Roger. "National Bibliography." *Library Trends* 15 (no. 3 1967):350-377. Also in: Downs, Robert B., and Jenkins, Francis B., eds. *Bibliography: Current State and Future Trends.* Urbana: University of Illinois, 1967.

Guide to Reference Books. Compiled by Robert Balay 11th ed. Chicago: American Library Association, 1996. See "General Reference Works/Bibliography/National and Trade" section.

Guidelines for the National Bibliographic Agency and the National Bibliography. Prepared by IFLA International Office for UBC. Paris: Unesco, [1979]. (PGI/79/WS/18).

Heyl, Lawrence, comp. *Current National Bibliographies. A List of Sources of Information Concerning Current Books of all Countries.* rev. ed. Chicago: American Library Association, 1942.

IFLA. International Office for UBC. The National Bibliography: Present Role and Future Developments. Organized by Unesco within the framework of its General Information Programme in collaboration with IFLA. Paris: Unesco, 1977. (PGI/77/UBC/2).

IFLA. International Office for UBC. Standardization Activities of Concern to Libraries and National Bibliographies: An Outline of Current Practices, Projects and Publications. Compiled by IFLA International Office for UBC. London: IFLA Committee on Cataloguing, 1976. (PGI/77/UBC/Ref.5).

IFLA Journal. International Federation of Library Associations. Vol. 1, no. 1-. Munich: Verlag Dokumentation, 1975-. Quarterly. (ISSN 0340-0352). With Vol. 3-, International Federation of Library Associations and Institutions.

Information Sources in Official Publications." Ed. by Valerie J. Nurcombe. London, New Providence, NJ: Bowker/Saur, 1997. Under each country, national bibliographies are discussed.

International Cataloguing and Bibliographic Control. 1988-. Vol. 17, no. 1 (Jan./Mar. 1988) - . Munich: IFLA Programme for UBCIM. Quarterly. (ISSN 1011-8829). From 1972-1976, issued by London: IFLA Committee on Cataloguing. Continues *International Cataloguing,* Vol. 1-16 (1972-1987).

International Committee for Social Sciences Documentation. *Étude des Bibliographies Courantes des Publications Officielles Nationales: Guide Sommaire et Inventaire. A Study of Current Bibliographies of National Official Publications; Short Guide and Inventory.* Compiled by Jean Meyriat. Unesco Bibliographical Handbooks, 7. Paris: Unesco, 1958.

International Congress on National Bibliographies (Paris. 1977). *Final Report*. Organized by Unesco within the framework of its General Information Programme in collaboration with IFLA. Paris: Unesco, 1978. (PGI 77/UBC/Ref. 3).

"The International Congress on National Bibliographies, Paris, 12-15 September 1977: Report." *International Cataloguing* 6 (October/December 1977):42-44.

International Guide to MARC Databases and Services. 3d rev., enl. ed. Ed. by the IFLA UBCIM Programme with the assistance of Kathleen McBride and Paula Jones - Fuller. Munich: K.G. Saur, 1993.

"International Symposium on Automation of National Bibliographies, Prague, 14-16 October 1980." *IFLA Journal* 7 (no. 2 1981):211-212.

"ISBD(M) Checklists." *International Cataloguing* 2 (July/September 1973):6-8.

Jaison, Jan T. *International Guide to Legal Deposit*. Aldershot, Eng.: Ashgate, 1991.

Jover, Barbara. "Survey on the Implementations of the Recommendations of the International Congress on National Bibliographies, Paris, 1977." *International Cataloguing* 9 (October 1980):41-42.

Kaltwasser, Franz George. "The Quest for Universal Bibliographic Control." *Wilson Library Bulletin* 46 (June 1972):894-907.

Kilton, Tom D. "National Bibliographies — Their Treatment of Periodicals and Monographic Series." *The Serials Librarian* 2 (Summer 1978):351-370.

Lewis, Peter. "The Future of the National Bibliography." *Library Association Review* 89 (Oct. 1987):510+.

Line, Maurice B. "Inclusion of Materials in Current National Bibliographies." *Libri* 24 (no. 1 1974):78-86.

Line, Maurice B. "Universal Availability of Publications." *Unesco Bulletin for Libraries* 31 (May/June 1977):142-151.

Lunn, Jean. *Guidelines for Legal Deposit Legislation*. Paris: General Information Programme and UNISIST, 1981. (PGI-81/WS/23).

Lunn, Jean. "National Bibliographies and UBC." Paper presented at the 39th IFLA General Conference, Grenoble, 1973. (15/E/BIB/2).

McGowan, Frank M. "National Bibliography." In *Encyclopedia of Library and Information Science*, vol. 19, pp. 50-60. Edited by Allen Kent. New York and Basel: Marcel Dekker, Inc., 1976.

Manual on Bibliographic Control. Compiled by the IFLA International Office for UBC [for the] General Information Programme and UNISIST. Paris: Unesco, 1983. (PGI-83/WS/8).

Massil, S. *Resource Sharing for National Bibliographic Services*. Prepared for the International Congress on National Bibliographies, Paris, 12-15 September 1977. Organized by Unesco in collaboration with IFLA. Paris: Unesco, 1977. (PGI 77/UBC/Ref.3).

Names of States: An Authority List of Language Forms for Catalogue Entries. Compiled by IFLA International Office for UBC. London: IFLA International Office for UBC, 1981.

"National Bibliographies." In Kumar, G., and Kumar, K. *Bibliography*, pp. 30-45. New Delhi: Vikas Publishing House, 1976.

"National Bibliographies." In *Walford's Guide to Reference Material*, vol. 3, ed. by J. Walford, with assistance of Anthony Harvey and H. Drubba. pp. 17-51. 7th ed. London: Library Association, 1996.

Nowak, Kurt. "Machine-Readable National Bibliographies in the Framework of the International MARC Network." Paper presented at the 48th IFLA General Conference, Montreal, 22-28 August 1982. (134/BIB/4-E).

Ochola, Francis W. "The National Bibliography and Universal Bibliographic Control." *Maktaba* 7 (no. 2 1980):8-21. Published February 1983.

Pomassl, Gerhard. *Survey of Existing Legal Deposit Laws: International Congress on National Bibliographies, Paris, 12-15 September 1977*. Organized by Unesco in collaboration with IFLA. Paris: Unesco, 1977.

Pomassl, Gerhard. "Unesco-Experten-Treffen zur Beratung eines Aktionsplanes für Universal Bibliographic Control (UBC) vom 14 bis 16 Mai 1975, Paris." *Zentralblatt für Bibliothekswesen* 89 (September 1975):414-416.

Sapienza, A.F. "UBC: The Benefits for Developing Countries." *International Cataloguing* 3 (April 1974):7.

Sciberras, Lillian. "Some Problems Facing the Current National Bibliographies in Mediterranean Countries." *Libri* 37 (no. 4 1987):279-293.

Shaw, Thomas Shuler. "Legal Depository Libraries." In *Encyclopedia of Library and Information Science*, vol. 14, pp. 140-181. Edited by Allen Kent. New York and Basel: Marcel Dekker, Inc., 1975.

Smith, Robert. "National Bibliographies on CD-ROM. Development of a Common Approach." *International Cataloguing & Bibliographic Control* 23 (no. 1 Jan./Mar. 1994):15-18.

Soosai, J.S. "Universal Availability of Publications: A Third World Perspective." *IFLA Journal* 4 (no. 2 1978):146-150.

Survey on the Present State of Bibliographic Recording in Freely Available Printed Form of Government Publications and Those of Intergovernmental Organizations. Prepared by Françoise Sinnassamy. Paris: Unesco, 1977. (PGI/77/Ref.4).

Synoptic Tables Concerning the Current National Bibliographies. Compiled by Gerhard Pomassl and a working group of the Deutsche Bucherei. Berlin: Bibliotheksverband d. DDR; Leipzig: Deutsche Bucherei, 1975.

Tate, Elizabeth L. "International Standards: The Road to Universal Bibliographic Control." *Library Resources & Technical Services* 20 (Winter 1976):16-24.

Unesco. *General Information Programme. UNISIST newsletter.* Paris : Unesco, 1979- . (0379-2218).

Walford, Albert John, ed. *Walford's Concise Guide to Reference Material.*, 2d ed. London: Library Association, 1992.

Walford's Guide to Reference Material, 7th ed. London: Library Association, 1996 See vol. 3, pp. 17-51.

Wanjohi, G. "The Function of the National Bibliography and the National Bibliographic Agency." *Maktaba* 5 (no. 1 1978):7-14.

Williams, Sheila. "National Bibliographies: The Paris Congress." *New Zealand Libraries* 41 (October 1978):79-82.

Wise, D.A. "List of National Bibliographies and References Containing Citations on Atlases and Maps." Special Libraries Association. Geography and Map Division. *Bulletin,* no. 128 (June 1982):39-41.

Woodbridge, Hensley C. *Guide to Reference Works for the Study of the Spanish Language and Literature and Spanish American Literature.* 2nd ed. New York: Modern Language Association of America, 1997. For national bibliographies, see pages 192-196.

Zotova, Kremena. "Serials in the Current National Bibliography." *The Serials Librarian* 22 (nos. 3/4 1992):319-333.

PART TWO: GEOGRAPHIC AREAS

AFRICA

General Sources

Africana Libraries Newsletter. No. 1-33 July 1975-November 1982. Boston: African Studies Library, Boston University, 1975-1982. Bi-monthly. (ISSN 0148-7868). No. 34-44 July 1983-1985. Urbana-Champaign, Illinois: African Studies Program, University of Illinois, 1983-1985. Quarterly. No. 45-66 March 1986-July 1991. Bloomington, Indiana: Indiana University Library, 1986-. No. 67- Aug. 1991- . East Lansing, Michigan : Michigan State University Library, 1991- .

Anderson, Dorothy P. "Second Unesco Seminar on Bibliographic Control in African Countries, Dakar, Senegal, 19-23 March 1979." *IFLA Journal* 5 (no. 3 1979):255-256.

Attia, Ridha. "National Bibliographies in the Maghreb: A Survey of Their Contents and Perspectives." Paper presented at the 50th IFLA General Conference, Nairobi, Kenya, 19-24 August 1984. (55-BIB-1-E).

Bankole, Beatrice. "Current National Bibliographies of the English Speaking Countries of Africa." *International Cataloguing* 14 (January/March 1985):5-10.

"Bibliographies." *Africana Libraries Newsletter*, no. 42 (June 1985):4.

Boadi, B.Y., and Havard-Williams, P. "Legislation for Library and Information Services in Anglophone West Africa." *Libri* 33 (no. 1 1983):9-21.

Boy, Joachim. *Nationalbibliographien Schwarzafrikas: Entwicklungen und Heutiger Stand.* Cologne: Greven, 1981.

Ifidon, Sam E. "Special Problems Facing African Librarians: The West African Experience." *Libri* 24 (no. 4 1974):310-318.

Joint Acquisitions List of Africana. Vol. 1- 1962-. Evanston, Illinois: African Department, Northwestern University Library, 1962-. Bi-monthly. (ISSN 0021-731X). Compiled by the African Department of the Northwestern University Library. 1962-1972; Melville J. Herskovits Library of African Studies, Northwestern University, 1972-1978/1988. Annual cumulations 1978-1980. Boston: G.K. Hall, 1980-1982.

Kotei, S.I.A. "Some Notes on the Present State of National Bibliography in English-Speaking Africa." *Africana Library Journal* 2 (Winter 1971):13-18.

M'baye, S. *ASCOBIC Manual on Bibliographical Control in Africa.* Paris: Unesco, 1981. (PGI-81/WS/29).

"National Bibliographies of Africa." *International Cataloguing* 1 (January/March 1972):5; (April/June 1972):6.

Panofsky, Hans E. "National Libraries and Bibliographies in Africa." In Jackson, Miles M., ed. *Comparative and International Librarianship: Essays on Themes and Problems*, pp. 229-255. London: Clive Bingley, 1970.

"Second Unesco Seminar on Bibliographic Control in African Countries, Dakar, Senegal, 19-23 March 1979." *International Cataloguing* 8 (April/June 1979):15-16.

"Serials." *Africana Libraries Newsletter* 41 (March 1985):9.

Witherell, Julian W. "Abbreviated Report of a Trip to Africa, March-June 1984." Parts 1-3. *Africana Libraries Newsletter*, no. 40 (1984):10-15; no. 41 (1985):10-12; no. 42a (1985):2-15.

Algeria

Attia, Ridha. "National Bibliographies in the Maghreb: A Survey of their Contents and Perspective." Paper presented at the 50th IFLA General Conference, Nairobi, Kenya, 19-24 August 1984. (55-BIB-1-E).

Cameroon

Njikam, Martin. "Quelques Sources Bibliographiques du Cameroun." In *International Conference on African Bibliography (1967. Nairobi). The Bibliography of Africa. Proceedings and Papers of the International Conference on African Bibliography, Nairobi, 4-8 December 1967*, pp. 113-119. Edited by J.D. Pearson and Ruth Jones. London: Frank Cass & Co., 1970.

Congo (Democratic Republic of)

Isofa Bomolo' oka Nkanga. "Experiences Zaïroises Concernant le Contrôle Bibliographique." *Afribiblios* 7 (no. 1 1984):32-36.

Côte d'Ivoire

Gueye. "Côte d'Ivoire." *Afribiblios* 7 (no. 1 1984):19-21.

Ethiopia

Belay, Arefine. "Department of National Library and Archives." Addis Ababa, s.n., 1983. Typescript.

Gabon

Bouscarle, Marie Elizabeth. "Gabon Libraries." In *Encyclopedia of Library and Information Science*, vol. 37, suppl. 2, pp. 156-177. Edited by Allen Kent. New York and Basel: Marcel Dekker, Inc., 1984.

The Gambia

Bankole, Beatrice S. "Current National Bibliographies of the English Speaking Countries of Africa." *International Cataloguing* 14 (Jan./Mar. 1985):5-10.

Ghana

Bankole, Beatrice S. "Current National Bibliographies of the English Speaking Countries of Africa." *International Cataloguing* 14 (Jan./Mar. 1985):5-10.

Kisiedu, Christine O. "Ghana and the Knowledge Explosion — The Problems of Bibliography." *African Research and Documentation*, no. 8/9 (1975):34-41.

Kwei, Christina. "Ghana," *Afribiblios* 8 (no. 2 Dec. 1985):51-52.

Kenya

Njugana, J.R. "Acquisition of Library Material in Kenya: Problems and Prospects." Paper presented at the 50th IFLA General Conference, Nairobi, Kenya, 19-24 August 1984. (38/ACQU/1-E).

Ochola, Francis W. "The Kenya National Bibliography." *International Cataloguing* 13 (July/September 1984):29-31.

Otike, J.N. "Bibliographic Control in Kenya." *Information Development* 5 (No. 1 Jan. 1989):23-28.
Wanyama, Patrick G. "Legal Deposit Law and Bibliographic Control in Kenya." *International Cataloguing* 13 (July/September 1984):31-32.

Lesotho

Ambrose, David. "The Collection and Bibliographic Control of Grey Literature of Lesotho." *African Research and Documentation*, no. 36 (1984):11-17.

Libya

Attia, Ridha. "National Bibliographies in the Maghreb: A Survey of their Contents and Perspectives." Paper presented at the 50th IFLA General Conference, Nairobi, Kenya, 19-24 August 1984.

Schlüter, H. "Nationale Bibliographie Libyens." *Zeitschrift für Bibliothekswesen und Bibliographie* 22 (January 1975):47-49.

Van de Vate, Katherine. *Books from the Arab World: a Guide to Selection and Acquisition.* Durham: Middle East Libraries Committee, 1988. See pp. 28-29.

Madagascar

Lyutova, K.V. "Stanovlenie Natsional'noi Bibliografii v Demokraticheskoi Respublike Madagaskar." ["The Establishment of a National Bibliography in the Democratic Republic of Madagascar."] *Sovetskaya Bibliografiya* no. 2 (1976):109-114.

Nucé, M.S. de. "La *Bibliographie Nationale à Madagascar.*" In International Conference on African Bibliography (1967. Nairobi). *The Bibliography of Africa. Proceedings and Papers of the International Conference on African Bibliography, Nairobi, 4-8 December 1967*, pp. 120-125. Edited by J.D. Pearson and Ruth Jones. London: Frank Cass & Co., 1970.

Rahary, Espree. "Madagascar. " *Afribiblios* 9 (no. 1 June 1986):7.

Rakoto Rzafindrakotohasina Rabakonirina. "Rapport Présenté à Dar-es-Salaam par le Représentant de Madagascar." *Afribiblios* 7 (no. 1 1984):22-24.

Malawi

Bankole, Beatrice S. "Current National Bibliographies of the English Speaking Countries of Africa." *International Cataloguing* 14 (Jan./Mar. 1985):5-10.
Najira, Dick D. "Malawi." *Afribiblios* 7 (no. 1 1984):25-26.

Morocco

Auerbach, W. "The National Bibliography of Morocco." *Africana Library Journal* 3 (Spring 1972):7-13.

Namibia

Bell, Barbara L. "The Making of the *Namibia National Bibliography*." *International Cataloguing and Bibliographical Control* 25 (no. 2, April/June 1996):31-33.

Nigeria

Abimbola, S.O. "National Bibliography of Nigeria, Past, Present and Future." *Nigerbiblios* 1 (October 1976):10-12, 16, 18-19, 22.

Aguolu, C.C. "National Bibliography in Nigeria: Its Growth, Development and International Dimensions." *African Research and Documentation*, no. 28 (1982):2-9.

Aje, S.B. "Bibliographical Developments: West Africa — Nigeria, Ghana, Sierra Leone." In Standing Conference on Library Materials on Africa. *Progress in African Bibliography: Proceedings [of the] SCOLMA Conference*, Commonwealth Institute, London, 17-18 March 1977. London: SCOLMA, 1977.

Alabi, G.A. "Nigerian Legal Deposit Publications." *International Library Review* 13 (July 1981):301-310.

Anyanwu, Virginia. "The Bibliographic Control of Nigerian Government Publications." *Government Publications Review* 19 (no. 5 Sept./Oct. 1992):505-512.

Bankole, Beatrice S. "Current National Bibliographies of the English Speaking Countries of Africa." *International Cataloguing* 14 (Jan./Mar. 1985):5-10.

Bankole, Beatrice S. "National Bibliographies: The Nigerian Experience." Paper presented at the ISBD/ISDS Seminar, Lagos, 30 January - 3 February 1978. 1978.

Bankole, Beatrice S. "Nigeria." *Afribiblios* 9 (no. 1 June 1986):11-17.

Bankole, Beatrice S. "Nigeria. Report of the Bibliographic Activities of the National Library of Nigeria since the Last ASCOBIC Meeting in December, 1981." *Afribiblios* 7 (no. 1 1984):27-31.

Ita, N.O. "Problems of bibliographic control in Nigeria." *Libri* 36 (Dec. 1986):320-328. See especially pp. 327-328 on national bibliography.

"Nigeria: National Bibliography." *International Cataloguing* 6 (April/June 1977):17.

Nweke, Ken M.C. "Legal Deposit Laws in Nigeria and Bibliographic Control of Nigeriana since 1950." *Government Publications Review* 18 (no. 4 July/Aug. 1991):339-345.
Obasi, John U. "Bibliographical Control of Nigerian Publications: Social Science Primary Materials." *Journal of Documentation* 38 (June 1982):107-124.

Oderinde, Sam O. "Cataloguing of National Materials: Problems of Compiling Nigeria's National Bibliography." *International Cataloguing* 5 (July/September 1976):7-8.
Shoyinka, Patricia H. "Bibliographic Control in Nigeria." *International Library Review* 11 (January 1979):77-91; *Libri* 28 (December 1978):294-308.

Ukoh, R.A. "Cataloguing and Bibliographic Control Problems: Nigeria." *International Library Review* 9 (July 1977):269-277.

Rwanda

Lévesque, Albert. *Contribution to the National Bibliography of Rwanda 1965-1970.* London: G.K. Hall and Co., [1979].

Senegal

"Senegal." *Afribiblios* 7 (no. 2 1984):51-53.

Sierra Leone

"Sierra Leone Publications." *International Cataloguing* 13 (no. 3 1984):27.

South Africa

Behrens, Shirley, "National Bibliographic Control in South Africa," *Mousaion* 9:1 (1991):42-54.

Musiker, Reuben. *South African Bibliography. A Survey of Bibliographies and Bibliographical Work.* 2d ed. Cape Town: D. Philips, 1980.

Westra, P.E., Zaaiman, R.B. "The Two National Libraries of South Africa." *Alexandria* 3: 2 (Aug. 1991), pp. 101-119.

Tanzania

Armstrong, James C. "Abbreviated Report of a Trip to Dar-es-Salaam and Zanibar [sic], Tanzania, October 16-30, 1982." *Africana Libraries Newsletter*, no. 38 (May 1984):15-21.

Bankole, Beatrice S. "Current National Bibliographies of the English Speaking Countries of Africa." *International Cataloguing* 14 (Jan./Mar. 1985):5-10.

Langlands, B.W. "The Amateur Status of National Bibliographies: Some Problems Facing Bibliographical Work, Based on Uganda and Tanzania Experience." In International

Conference on African Bibliography (1967. Nairobi). *The Bibliography of Africa. Proceedings and Papers of the International Conference on African Bibliography, Nairobi, 4-8 December 1967*, pp. 66-74. Edited by J.D. Pearson and Ruth Jones. London: Frank Cass & Co., 1970.

Mlaki, T.E. "Tanzania." *Afribiblios* 7 (no. 2 1984):56-61.

Mlaki, Theophilus. "Tanzania." *Afribiblios* 9 (no. 1 June 1986):22-25.

Togo

Mamah, Zakari. "Coup d'oeil sur Bibliothèque nationale du Togo". *Documentation et Bibliotheques* 39 (no. 2 April-June 1993):75-77.

"Togo." *Afribiblios* 7 (no. 2 1984):62.

Tunisia

Attia, Ridha. "National Bibliographies in the Maghreb: A Survey of their Contents and Perspectives." Paper presented at the 50th IFLA General Conference, 19-24 August 1984, Kenya.

Attia, Ridha. "La Bibliothèque Nationale de Tunisie." *Documentation et Bibliothèques* 39 (no. 2 Apr./June 1993):79-82.

Van de Vate, Katherine. "Acquisition from Individual Countries: Tunisia." In *Books from the Arab World. A Guide to Selection and Acquisition*. Durham: Middle East Libraries Committee, 1988, pp. 23-25.

Uganda

Abidi, S.A.H. "Bibliographical Activities in Uganda." *Afribiblios* 7 (no. 2 1984):78-81.

Kasajja, Jane. "Uganda." *Afribiblios* 7 (no. 2 1984):63.

Langlands, B.W. "The Amateur Status of National Bibliographies: Some Problems Facing Bibliographical Work, Based on Uganda and Tanzania Experience." In International Conference on African Bibliography (1967. Nairobi). *The Bibliography of Africa. Proceedings and Papers of the International Conference on African Bibliography, Nairobi, 4-8 December 1967*, pp. 66-74. Edited by J.D. Pearson and Ruth Jones. London: Frank Cass & Co., 1970.

Langlands, B.W. "On Problems of Compiling a National Bibliography." *Ugandan Libraries*, Special issue (March 1975):1-19.

Zambia

Nyendwa, H.K. "Zambia." *Afribiblios* 7 (no. 2 1984):64-67.

Bankole, Beatrice S. "Current National Bibliographies of the English Speaking Countries of Africa." *International Cataloguing* 14 (Jan./Mar. 1985):5-10.

Zimbabwe

Molem, Rosemary. "Zimbabwe: Country Report on Bibliographic Control Activities. An ASCOBIC Report. 4th Unesco Regional Seminar, Dar-es-Salaam, 1-8 August 1983." *International Cataloguing* 13 (July/September 1984):27-28.

Bankole, Beatrice S. "Current National Bibliographies of the English Speaking Countries of Africa." *International Cataloguing* 14 (Jan./Mar. 1985):5-10.

CENTRAL ASIA

General

Beynen, G. Koolemans. "The National Bibliographies of the Turkic Republics of the Soviet Union." *Government Information Quarterly* 3 (no. 2 1986):141-152.

Kazakhstan

Zarema, S. "La Bibliothèque Nationale de la République du Kazakhstan." *Bulletin d'Informations de l'Association des Bibliothècaires Française* 162 (no. 1 1994):441-448.

Kyrgyzstan

Beynen, G. Koolemans. "The National Bibliographies of the Turkic Republics of the Soviet Union." *Government Information Quarterly* 3 (No. 2 1986):141-152. See esp. pp. 147-148.

Tajikistan

Leich, Harold M. "Bibliographic Systems of the Soviet Republics : Moldavia and Tajikistan." *Government Information Quarterly* 2 (no. 3 1985):291-298.

EAST ASIA

General Sources

Khurshid, Anis. "The Far East, Libraries In." In *Encyclopedia of Library and Information Science*, vol. 37, suppl. 2, pp. 107-138. Edited by Allen Kent. New York and Basel: Marcel Dekker, Inc., 1984.

Wijasuriya, D.E.K. "ISBD Application to Asian National Bibliographies." *Unesco Bulletin for Libraries* 31 (July 1977):223-232.

Wong, William Sheh. "Oriental Literature and Bibliography: Introduction"; "Chinese Literature and Bibliography." In *Encyclopedia of Library and Information Science*, vol. 21, pp. 35-131. Edited by Allen Kent. New York and Basel: Marcel Dekker, Inc., 1977.

China

Anderson, Dorothy P. "IFLA's Visit to the People's Republic of China: Notes on Bibliographic and Cataloguing Activities." *IFLA Journal* 8 (no. 2 1982):184-187.

Huang Jungui. "Bibliographic Control in the People's Republic of China." Trans. by Charles Aylmer. *BEASL Bulletin of the European Association of Sinological Librarians* no. 4 (1990):1-15.

Koo, Ja Young. "The Problems and Solutions of National Bibliographies in the East Asian Countries: Current Bibliographic Controls in China, Japan and Korea." In IFLA Worldwide Seminar (1976. Seoul, Korea). *Proceedings of IFLA Worldwide Seminar, May 31-June 5, 1976*, pp. 210-227. Seoul, Korea: Korean Library Association, 1976.

National Bibliography Section, National Library of China, Beijing. "National Bibliography of China--Retrospect and Prospect." *International Cataloguing* 15 (no. 1 Jan./Mar. 1986):5-8.

Japan

Koo, Ja Young. "The Problems and Solutions of National Bibliographies in the East Asian Countries: Current Bibliographic Controls in China, Japan and Korea." In IFLA Worldwide Seminar (1976. Seoul, Korea). *Proceedings of IFLA Worldwide Seminar, May 31-June 5, 1976*, pp. 210-227. Seoul, Korea: Korean Library Association, 1976.

Maruyama, Shojiro. "National Bibliographic Control in Japan: Past and Present, an Approaching Effort to UBC." In IFLA Worldwide Seminar (1976. Seoul, Korea). *Proceedings of IFLA Worldwide Seminar, May 31-June 5, 1976*, pp. 427-433. Seoul, Korea: Korean Library Association, 1976.

Miyasaka, Itsuro. "From the National Diet Library, Tokyo: Recent Developments of the Japanese National Bibliography." *International Cataloguing* 10 (January/March 1981):5-7.

Niki, K. "National bibliographic control of Current Publications in Japan." *Bulletin - Association for Asian Studies Committee on East Asian Libraries*, no. 90 (June 90):9-18.

Oda, Yasumasa. "Japanese National Bibliography." In *Encyclopedia of Library and Information Science,* vol. 12, pp. 248-249. Edited by Allen Kent. New York and Basel: Marcel Dekker, Inc., 1975.

Korea (Republic)

Choo, Yong Kyu. "National Bibliographic Control of Current Publications in South Korea." *Bulletin – Association for Asian Studies, Inc. Committee on East Asian Libraries.* No. 90 (June 1990):19-23.

Kim, Young Kuy. "A Study on the Script and Pronunciation of Japanese Person's Name in Library Cataloguing: About Index of "Korean National Bibliography." *Do-seo-gwan-hak Non-jip* [Journal of the Korean Library and Information Science Society] 20 (1993):285-315.

Koo, Ja Young. "The Problems and Solutions of National Bibliographies in the East Asian Countries: Current Bibliographic Controls in China, Japan and Korea." In *IFLA Worldwide Seminar (1976. Seoul, Korea). Proceedings of IFLA Worldwide Seminar, May 31-June 5, 1976*, pp. 210-227. Seoul, Korea: Korean Library Association, 1976.

Lee, Pongsoon and Young Ai Um. "The State of Bibliographic Control and Services." pp. 105-115. In *Libraries and Librarianship in Korea.* Westport, CT: Greenwood Press, 1994.

Lee, Seong Duk. "A Study on Korean National Bibliography." Seoul : Sook Myung University, 1993. (Master of Library and Information Science)

Park, Ke Hong. "Libraries and Librarianship in the Republic of Korea." In *IFLA Worldwide Seminar (1976. Seoul, Korea). Proceedings of IFLA Worldwide Seminar, May 31-June 5, 1976*, pp. 407-419. Seoul, Korea: Korean Library Association, 1976.

Taiwan

Li, Tze-Chung. "Taiwan: Library Services." In *Encyclopedia of Library and Information Science*, vol. 30, pp. 1-70. Edited by Allen Kent. New York and Basel: Marcel Dekker, Inc., 1980.

EASTERN EUROPE AND RUSSIAN FEDERATION

General Sources

Gosudarstvennye (Natsional'nye) Bibliograficheskie Ukazateli Sotsialisticheskikh Stran. [National Bibliographical Indexes of the Socialist Countries]. Compiled by T.R. Kusnetsova. Edited by N.V. Gavrilenko. Moscow: The V.I. Lenin State Library of the USSR, 1984.

Official Publications of the Soviet Union and Eastern Europe, 1945-1980: A Selected Annotated Bibliography. Edited by Gregory Walker. London: Mansell, 1982.

Scrivens, Ray. "Selection Aids for Soviet and East European Publications." Paper presented as a contribution to a seminar held at University Library, Cambridge, England, January 1983.

"Socialist Countries: Annotated Directory of National Bibliographies." *International Cataloguing* 14 (April/June 1985):13.

Whitby, Thomas J., and Lorkovic, Tanja. *Introduction to Soviet National Bibliography.* Littleton, Colorado: Libraries Unlimited, Inc., 1979.

Bosnia and Hercegovina

Kujundzic, Enes. *Prilog bibliografiji bibliografija Bosne i Herzegovine* / Prepared by Dr. E. Kujundzic, et al. – Sarajevo : NUB BiH, 1994.

Bulgaria

Maichel, Karol. "Bulgarian National Bibliography: An Historical Review." *Library Quarterly* 29 (January 1959):43-47.

Zotova, Kremena. "Novyi Zakon ob Obiazatel'nom Ekzempliare v Narodnoi Respublike Bolgarii." *Sovetskaya Bibliografiya*, no. 1 (1978):108-113.

Zotova, Kremena. "Problemi na Avtomatizatsiyata na Tekushtata Natsionalna Bibliografiya." *Bibliotekar* (Sofia) 27 (no. 10 1980):13-16.

Zotova, Kremena. "Sovremennoe Sostoianie Tekushchei Natsional'noi Bibliografii v Bolgarii." *Sovetskaya Bibliografiya*, no. 3 (1978):74-81.

Zotova, Kremena. "Sucasna Narodna Bibliografia Bulharska: Stav a Problemy." *Kniznice a Vedecke Informacie* 8 (no. 1 1976):35-43.

Czech Republic

"Czech Bibliography: the 20th Century." In Ryznar, Eliska and Croucher, Murlin. *Books in Czechoslovakia: Past and Present.* Wiesbaden: Otto Harrassowitz, 1989. pp. 70-74.

Estonia

Eenmaa, Ivi. "The National Library of Estonia," *Alexandria* 3 (3, 1991):169-177

Riuitel, A. "Zakon Estonskoi Respublici o Natsional noi Biblioteke Estonii." [Law of the Estonia Republic Concerning the National Library of Estonia] *Bibliotekar* 1991 (no. 9):31-32.

Hungary

Benyei, M. "A Kurrens Magyar Nemzeti Bibliografia Otven Eve" [Fifty Years of the Hungarian Current National Bibliography]. *Könyvtari Figyelö* 42 (3 1996):391-402.

Berke, Barnabásné. *A Kurrens Magyars Nemzeti Bibliográfiai Rendszer Mai Probléméi* [Current Issues of the Hungarian National Bibliography System]. In *Könyvtári Figyelö* 41 (5 1995):585-590.

Berke, Susanne. "Hungarian National Bibliography." Paper delivered at the International Conference on Library Automation in Central & Eastern Europe, April 11-13, 1996, Budapest, Hungary. (publication forthcoming)

"Hungary: Mechanization of the National Bibliography." *International Cataloguing* 6 (January 1977):4-5.

Moldova

Leich, Harold M. "Bibliographic Systems of the Soviet Republics : Moldavia and Tajikistan." *Government Information Quarterly* 2 (no. 3 1985):291-298.
Poland

Karamac, Barbara. "Bibliographic Control in Poland," *International Cataloguing and Bibliographic Control* 20 (no. 1, Jan./March 1991):3-7.

Romania

Banciu, Doina. "Automation of the Romanian National Library." *General Information Programme. Unisist Newsletter.* Special edition: Romania [n.d.]: p. 13-14.

Ciorcan, Marcela. "National Bibliographies: Automation of the Bibliographical Work." *Probleme de Informare si Documentare* 28 (nos. 3/4 Jul./Dec. 1994):114-116. Article also in Romanian, pp. 111-113.

"Romania: National Bibliography." *International Cataloguing* 10 (Jan./Mar. 1981):4.

Stefancu, Mircea. "Bibliografia Nationala Româna Curenta." *Revista Bibliotecii Nastionale* 1 (no. 1 1995):23-24.

Russian Federation

Babkina, O.I. "Soviet Experiences: Recent Developments in Classification, Cataloguing and the National Bibliography. 3. The Present State of Standardization of Bibliographic Description in the USSR: the Work of the USSR Joint Cataloguing Committee." *International Cataloguing* 9 (October/December 1980):43-45.

Dzhigo, A. "Gosudarstvennaîa Bibliografiîa Strany - Kul'turnoe Bogatstvo Obshchestva." *Kniga: Issledovaniîa i Materialy* no. 65 (1993):22-26.

Dzhigo, A., Lenskii, B. "Novye Tekhnologii v Natsional'noĭ Bibligrafii." *Kniga: Issledovaniîa i materialy* no. 69 (1994):58-72.

Dzhigo, A. "Osnovnye Funktsii Natsional'nykh Bibliograficheskikh Tsentrov." *Kniga: Issledovaniîa i materialy* no. 62 (1991):47-59.

Dzhigo, A. "Primenenie UDK v Natsional'noĭ Bibliografii Rossii." *Nauchnye i Tekhnicheskie Biblioteki* no. 4 (1994):32-37.

Dzhigo, A. "Sistema Obîazatel'nogo Ekzemplîara i Sozdanie Edinogo Informatsionnogo Prostranstva." *Informatsionnyĭ Biulleten' Bibliotechnoĭ Assotsiatsii Evrazii* no. 1 (1993):54-56.

Dzhigo, A. "Zakon "Ob Obzîatel'nom Ekzemplîare Dokumentov." *Bibliography* no. 5(1995):3-10.

Dzhigo, A. "Zakon "Ob Obĭâzatel'nom Ekzemplĭâre Dokumentov - v Deĭstvii." *Bibliotekovedenie* no. 2 (1995):3-10.

Dzhigo, A., Sukhorukov, K. "Obĭâzatel'nyĭ Ekzemplĭâr i Natsional'naĭâ Bibliografiĭâ." *Bibliografiiĭâ* no. 6 (1993):126-133.

Gruzinskaĭâ, N., Dzhigo, A. "Kniga Slov." *Sovetskaĭâ Bibliografiĭâ* no. 2 (1991):37-42. *Voprosy National'noĭ Bibliografii* . Sost. A. Dzhigo, N. Gruzinskaĭâ. Moskva: Knizhnaĭâ Palata, 1991.

Slovakia

Celkova, Lúdmila. "Zakladne Slovenske Narodne Bibliografie." *Citadel'* 30 (nos. 77-8 1981):suppl. I-VIII.

Katuscák, Dusan. "Narodna Bibliografia." *Kniznice a Informacie* 29 (1 1997):27-29.

Durovcik, Stefan. "Projekt Automatizovaneho Systemu Slovenskej Narodnej Bibliografie." *Citadel'* 27 (no. 9 1978):318-320.

Katuscák, Dusan. "New Developments in Librarianship and Bibliographic Control in Slovakia." *International Cataloguing and Bibliographic Control* 25:1 (Jan./Mar. 1996):16-19.

"Slovak Bibliography from 1918 to the Present," In Ryznar, Eliska and Croucher, Murlin. *Books in Czechoslovakia: Past and Present.* Wiesbaden: Otto Harrassowitz, 1989. pp. 94-97.

Ukraine

Jdanova, R. "She Raz Pro Ukrainskii Bibliographichnii Repertuar." *Visn. Knijnoi Palati* (1996 no. 12):9-10.

Patoka, V. "Do Problem: Stvorenja Ukrainskogo Bibliographichogo Repertuaru: Iz Visturu na Drugomu Vseurkrainskogo Kongresa Bibliotekariv." *Visn. Knijnoi Palati* (1997 no. 1):9-11.

Zagumenna, V. "Suchasni Problemi Theorii Natzionalnoi Bibliographii: Iz Vistupu na II Vseurkainskogo Kongresa Bibliotekariv u Ramkah Vauch. Seminaru "Natzionalnii Bibliographii." *Visn. Knijnoi Palati* (1997 no. 1):11-12.

Yugoslavia

Lazic, Ksenija B. "Jugoslovenska Bibliotekarska Bibliografija za 1982." *Bibliotekar* (Beograd)40 (no. 3-4 1988):85-163.

Popovic-Boskovic, Gordana, and Milosavljevic, Ivana. "Delatnost Jugoslovenskog Bibliografskog Instituta (JBI) : Tekuce Nacionalne Bibliografije u Jugoslaviji." *Bibliotekar* (Beograd)42 (nos. 1-2 1990/1991):56-64.

Skendezic, Nevenka. "Bibliografija Jugoslavije: Knjige, Brosure i Muzikalije, 1950-1980." *Bibliotekar* (Belgrade) 32 (nos.1-6 1980):60-67.

Stojanovic, Milos. "Sadrzaj Tekucih Jugoslovenskih Bibliotekarskih Serijskih Publikacija." *Bibliotekar* (Beograd)40 (nos. 1-2 1988):109-117.

LATIN AMERICA AND THE CARIBBEAN

General Sources

"Bibliographies: National and Trade." In *Latin America and the Caribbean. A Critical Guide to Research Sources.* Ed. by Paula J. Covington. (Bibliographies and Indexes in Latin America and Caribbean Studies, no. 2). NY: Greenwood Press, 1992.

"Bibliography and General Works." In *Handbook of Latin American Studies.* Prepared by a number of scholars for the Hispanic Division of the Library of Congress. Austin: University of Texas Press, 1935-. Various publishers.

"Bibliography–National." *Bibliography of Latin American and Caribbean Bibliographies.* SALALM Secretariat, University of Texas, Austin, 1992- Annual. Formerly published by University of Wisconsin, Madison, 1986-1991. 1984 Title: *Bibliography of Latin American Bibliographies.* "Formerly published as a working paper in the *Papers* (earlier, *Final Report and Working Papers*) of the Annual Seminar."

Cordeiro, Daniel Raposo. *A Bibliography of Latin American Bibliographies: Social Sciences & Humanities, Supplementing the Original Works by Arthur E. Gropp.* Daniel Raposo Cordeiro, editor. Solena V. Bryant, Haydée N. Piedracueva, and Barbara Hadely Stein, associate editors. Metuchen, New Jersey: Scarecrow Press, 1979-.

Foster, David W., and Foster, Virginia R. *Manual of Hispanic Bibliography.* 2d ed., rev. New York: Garland, 1977.

Freudenthal, Juan R. "Advances in Latin American Bibliography and Librarianship: Papers of the Eighteenth SALALM Conference." *International Library Review* 6 (1974):293-298.

Garlant, Julia, et al. *Latin America Bibliography: A Guide to Sources of Information & Research.* Edited by Laurence Hallewell. London: Published for the SCONUL Latin American Group by the Institute of Latin American Studies, 1978.

Gropp, Arthur E. *A Bibliography of Latin American Bibliographies.* Compiled by Arthur E. Gropp. Metuchen, New Jersey: Scarecrow Press, 1971.

Gropp, Arthur E. "The National Library in Latin America." In *Comparative and International Librarianship: Essays on Themes and Problems*, pp. 199-228. Edited by Miles M. Jackson, Jr. London: Clive Bingley, 1970.

Latin America: A Guide to the Historical Literature. Edited by Charles Carrol Griffin. Conference on Latin American History, Publication 4. Austin and London: University of Texas Press, 1971.

Monte-Mór, Jannice. "ISBD Application to Latin American National Bibliographies." *Unesco Bulletin for Libraries* 31 (July/August 1977):233-239, 254.

"National Bibliographies." In *A Bibliography of Latin American Bibliographies, 1975-1979: Social Sciences and Humanities*. Edited by Haydée Piedracueva. Metuchen, New Jersey: Scarecrow Press, 1982.

"National Bibliographies." *Latin American Studies. A Basic Guide to Sources.* 2d ed., rev. and enl. Ed. by Robert A. McNeil and Barbara G. Valk. Metuchen, NJ: Scarecrow Press, 1990. pp. 118-139.

Nilges, Annemarie. *Nationalbibliographien Lateinamerikas.* Cologne: Greven, 1983.

O'Connell, John Brian. "Some Recent Bibliographic Aids in the Field of Latin Americana." *International Library Review* 16 (1984):429-436.

Piedracueva, Haydée. *A Bibliography of Latin American Bibliographies, 1975-1979: Humanities and Social Sciences.* Metuchen, New Jersey: Scarecrow Press, 1982.

Woodbridge, Hensley C. *Guide to Reference Works for the Study of the Spanish Language and Literature and Spanish American Literature.* 2nd ed. New York: Modern Language Association of America, 1997. For national bibliographies, see pages 192-196.

Woodbridge, Hensley C. "Latin American National Bibliography." In *Encyclopedia of Library and Information Science*, vol. 36, suppl. 1, pp. 271-343. Edited by Allen Kent. New York and Basel: Marcel Dekker, Inc., 1983.

Zimmerman, Irene. *Current National Bibliographies of Latin America: A State of the Art Study.* Gainesville, Florida: Center for Latin American Studies, University of Florida, 1971.

Argentina

Sabor, Josefa E. "La Bibliografía General Argentina en Curso de Publicación." *Handbook of Latin American Studies* 25 (1963):374-381.

Brazil

Caldeira, Paulo da Terra. "A Situação do Brasil em relação ao Controle Bibliográfico Universal." *Revista da Escola de Biblioteconomia de Universidade Federal de Minas Gerais* 13 (Sept. 1984):260-283.

Caldeira, Paulo da Terra, and Carvalho, Maria de Lourdes Borges de. "O Problema Editorial da Bibliografia Brasileira Corrente." *Revista de Biblioteconomia de Brasileira* 13 (July/December 1980):210-216.

Hallewell, Laurence. "The Development of National Bibliography in Brazil." *Libri* 23 (no. 4 1973):291-297.

Zimmerman, Irene. "Brazil." *Current National Bibliographies of Latin America.* Gainesville, University of Florida Center for Latin American Studies, 1971. pp. 29-35.

Caribbean

Avafia, Kwami. "Legal Deposit Problems in the West Indies." *Unesco Bulletin for Libraries* 30 (May 1976):147-151, 161.

Collins, Carol. "The Production of Current National Bibliographies in the Commonwealth Caribbean." *International Cataloguing* 6 (April/June 1977):21-23.

Jordan, Alma, and Commissiong, Barbara. *The English-Speaking Caribbean. A Bibliography of Bibliographies*. Boston: G.K. Hall, 1984.

McMurdoch, Agnes E. "Regional Workshop on National Bibliographies of the English-Speaking Caribbean, Georgetown, Guyana, 25-29 November 1974." *Unesco Bulletin for Libraries* 29 (May/June 1975):148-150.

Nilsen, Kirsti. "Commonwealth Caribbean Government Publications: Bibliography and Acquisition Aids." *Government Publications Review* 7A (no. 6 1980):489-503.

Chile

Freudenthal, Juan R. "Chile, Libraries and Information Centers In." In *Encyclopedia of Library and Information Science*, vol. 38, suppl. 3, pp. 72-129. Edited by Allen Kent. New York and Basel: Marcel Dekker, Inc., 1985.

Freudenthal, Juan R. "Chilean National Bibliography: Origins and Progress." *Libri* 22 (no. 4 1972):273-280.

Villalobos R., Sergio. "La Bibliografia en Chile. Desarrolo de las Investigaciones Bibliograficas." *Cuadernos de Historia* 5 (jul. 1985):69-70, 73.

Woodbridge, Hensley C. "Latin American National Bibliography." *Encyclopedia of Library and Information Science* 36, suppl. 1 (1983):271-343.

Cuba

Garcia Carranza, Araceli and Jiménez Lopez, Xonia. "Contribucion de la Biblioteca Nacional de Cuba a la Bibliografia Corriente y Retrospectiva," *International Cataloguing and Bibliographic Control* 23 (Apr./June 1994):23-26. This article is based on a paper given at IFLA General Conference Havana 1994. English translation: "The Contribution of the National Library of Cuba to Current and Retrospective Bibliography." (096-BIBL-3-E).

Jamaica

Bandara, S.B. "Jamaican National Bibliography." *International Library Review* 13 (July 1981):311-321.

Ferguson, S. "Acquisitions in Developing Countries: Problems and Possible Solutions - The Jamaica Experience." Paper presented at the 50th IFLA General Conference, Nairobi, Kenya, 19-24 August 1984. (39/ACQU/2-E).
Nicaragua

Elmsdorf, George F. "Nicaraguan National Bibliography: Historical Aspects." In Seminar on the Acquisition of Latin American Library Materials (28th. 1983. San José, Costa Rica). *The Central American Connection: Library Resources and Access: Papers of the Twenty-eighth Annual Meeting of the Seminar on the Acquisition of Latin American Library Materials, University of Kansas, Universidad de Costa Rica, San José, Costa Rica, June 30- July 4, 1983.* Edited by Jane Garnet. Madison, Wisconsin: SALALM Secretariat, University of Wisconsin-Madison, 1985.

Krentz-Viana, Janice Lee. "Nicaraguan National Bibliography: Technical Aspects." In Seminar on the Acquisition of Latin American Library Materials (28th. 1983. San José, Costa Rica). *The Central American Connection: Library Resources and Access: Papers of the Twenty-eighth Annual Meeting of the Seminar on the Acquisition of Latin American Library Materials, University of Kansas, Universidad de Costa Rica, San José, Costa Rica, June 30- July 4, 1983.* Edited by Jane Garnet. Madison, Wisconsin: SALALM Secretariat, University of Wisconsin-Madison, 1985.

Venezuela

McLeod, Yola M. "Role of National Libraries in Latin America: The Example of the Biblioteca Nacional of Venezuela." *International Cataloguing* 11 (April 1982):22-23.

THE NEAR AND MIDDLE EAST

General Sources

Churukian, Araxie P. "Current National Bibliographies from the Near East as Collection Development Tools." *Library Resources & Technical Services* 23 (Spring 1979):156-162.

"Current National Bibliographies for Arab Publications." *Unesco Journal of Information Science, Librarianship and Archives Administration* 4 (July/September 1982):221-222.

Hopwood, Derek. "Book Acquisition from the Middle East." In Ligue des Bibliothèques Européennes de Recherche. *Acquisitions from the Third World: Papers of the Ligue des Bibliothèques Européennes de Recherche Seminar, 17-19 September 1973*, pp. 79-84. Edited by D.A. Clarke. London: Mansell, 1975.

Husam al Din, Mustapha. *National Bibliographic Control of Arab Imprints: An Analytical Study.* Publications de l'Institut Supérieur de Documentation No. 6. Tunis: Institut Supérieur de Documentation, 1984.

"National Bibliographies in Arab Countries." *International Cataloguing* 3 (January 1974):3-4.
Partington, David H. "National Bibliographies from the Middle East." Parts 1 and 2. *Foreign Acquisitions Newsletter* no. 45 (Spring 1977):1-9; no. 46 (Fall 1977):8-10, 84-87.

Samarkandi, Abdullatif Abdulhakeem. "National Bibliography in Saudi Arabia, Egypt and Tunisia : Analytical and Comparative Study with a View to Planning a Saudi Arabian National Bibliography." Diss. Loughborough University of Technology, 1990.

Van der Vate, Katherine. *Books from the Arab World. A Guide to Selection and Acquisition.* Durham: Middle East Libraries Committee, 1988. Under each country the national bibliography is discussed.

Iran

"National Bibliographies, Iran." *Current Research in Library & Information Science* 2 (September 1984):103.

Sultani, Poori . "Iranian National Bibliography: An Approach to New Standards," *International Cataloguing and Bibliographic Control* 18 (April/June 1989):30-32.

Soltani, Poori. "National Library of Iran in Action." *International Cataloguing* 14 (April/June 1985):18.

Iraq

Ali Hashmi, Syed. "Iraq and its National Library." *Libri* 33 (no. 3 1983):236-243.

Jordan

Van de Vate, Katherine. "Jordan." In *Books from the Arab World. A Guide to Selection and Acquisition.* Durham: Middle East Libraries Committee, 1988, pp. 31-32.

Qatar

Aman, Mohammed M., and Khalifa, Sha'ban A. "Libraries and Librarianship in Qatar." *International Library Review* 15 (July 1983):263-272.

Turkey

Atilgan, Dogan. *Türkiye Bibliyografyasi'nin Baslangicindan Bugüne Kataloglama ve Siniflama Acisindan Degerlendirilmesi. Evaluation of the Turkish National Bibliography from Start to Date for Cataloguing and Classifying of Viewpoint. 50. Kurulus Yilinda Ulusaldan Evrensele Türk Millî Kutuphanesi (1946-1996) Sempozyum Bildiri Özetleri. Summaries of Symposium Papers of 1946-1996. On its 50th Anniversary. Turkish National Library from National to Universal.* Ankara, 1996. pp. 9-10. Summary of papers given on 19-21 June 1996; complete publication forthcoming.

Sefercioglu, Necmeddin. "Türk Dünyasi'nda Bibliyografik Denetleme. Bibliographical Control in the Turkish World." *Türk Kütüphaneciligi. Turkish Librarianship* 9 (no. 1; March 1995):42-48.

NORTH AMERICA

Bermuda

"UBC News." *International Cataloguing* 13 (no. 4, 1984):38-39.

Canada

"Canada: National Bibliography." *International Cataloguing* 6 (April/June 1977):15; also 11 (April/June 1982):15.

"Canada: National Bibliography in Microfiche." *International Cataloguing* 10 (January/March 1981):4.

Shindryaeva, N.M. "Tekushchaya Natsional'naya Bibliografiya Kanady." *Bibliotekovedenie i Bibliografia za Rubezhom* 94 (1983):32-42.

Wilson, Marion C. "Canadiana: Changes in the National Bibliography." *Canadian Library Journal* 34 (December 1977):417-419, 421.

United States

Price, Mary Sauer. "The National Union Catalog Program." Paper presented at the 51st IFLA General Conference, Chicago, Illinois, 18-24 August 1985. (105-BIB-5-E).

OCEANIA

General Sources

Baker, Leigh R. "National and Regional Bibliography in the South Pacific: A Development Appraisal." In Meeting on National and Regional Bibliography (1978. Suva). *Meeting on National and Regional Bibliography. Record of Proceedings [3-8 July 1978]*, pp. 103-116. Sponsored by the International Development Research Centre and the University of the South Pacific. Suva: Meeting on National and Regional Bibliography, 1978.

"South Pacific: Regional Bibliography." *International Cataloguing* 12 (no. 3 July/Sept. 1983):27.

Australia

"Australian National Bibliography." *Acquisitions, Bibliography, Cataloguing News* 12 (March 1984):13-17.

Ellis, A. "Australian National Bibliography (ANB)." *International Library Review* 7 (April 1975):235-244.

Gatenby, Pam, Still, Graham, and Witsenhuysen, Mary. "The Australian Scene 3. Current and Retrospective National Bibliography." *International Cataloguing and Bibliographic Control* 17 (no. 3 July/Sept. 1988):35-38.

Kenny, January. "Australian National Library; Australian Bibliographic Services." *International Library Review* 7 (April 1975):227-233.

New Zealand

Fields, Alison. "The National Bibliography in New Zealand. Part I: Development and Description." *New Zealand Libraries* 48 (no. 3 Sept. 1995):46-51.

"The National Bibliography in New Zealand. Part II." *New Zealand Libraries* 48 (no. 6, June 1996):107-110.

Papua New Guinea

Butler, A.C. "National Bibliography in Papua New Guinea." In Meeting on National and Regional Bibliography (1978. Suva). *Meeting on National and Regional Bibliography. Record of Proceedings [3-8 July 1978]*, pp. 151-156. Sponsored by the International Development Research Centre and the University of the South Pacific. Suva: Meeting on National and Regional Bibliography, 1978.

"Papua New Guinea: National Bibliographic Services." *International Cataloguing* 11 (Apr./June 1982):15.

SOUTH ASIA AND SOUTHEAST ASIA

General Sources

Dayrit, Marina G. "Major Problems in the Improvement of National Bibliographies in Southeast Asia." In Conference on Universal Bibliographical Control in Southeast Asia (1975. Singapore). *Conference on Universal Bibliographical Control in Southeast Asia, held at the Regional English Language Centre, Singapore, 21-23 February 1975: Papers and Proceedings,* pp. 133-141. Edited by Hedwig Anuar, Yolanda Beh, Lim Hong Too, Quah Swee Lan. Singapore: Library Association of Singapore, 1975.

Dayrit, Marina G. "The Problems of Current National Bibliographies in Southeast Asian Countries." In IFLA Worldwide Seminar (1976. Seoul, Korea). *Proceedings of IFLA Worldwide Seminar, May 31-June 5, 1976,* pp. 189-209. Seoul, Korea: Korean Library Association, 1976.

Dayrit, Marina G. "The Problems of Current National Bibliographies in Southeast Asian Countries: The Results of a Survey." Appendixes. In IFLA Worldwide Seminar (1976. Seoul, Korea). *Proceedings of IFLA Worldwide Seminar, May 31-June 5, 1976,* pp. 197-209. Seoul, Korea: Korean Library Association, 1976.

Khoo Siew Mun. "Bibliographic Description in Southeast Asia." In *Standards for the International Exchange of Bibliographic Information. Papers presented at a course held at the School of Library, Archive and Information Studies, University College London, 3-18 August 1990*. Edited by I.C. McIlwaine. London: The Library Association, 1991. pp. 97-110.

Khurshid, Anis. "The Far East, Libraries In." In *Encyclopedia of Library and Information Science*, vol. 37, suppl. 2, pp. 107-138. Edited by Allen Kent. New York and Basel: Marcel Dekker, Inc., 1984.

Khurshid, Anis. "Problems of Bibliographical Accessibility of South Asian Collections." *International Library Review* 15 (January 1983):61-93.

Lim Huck Tee, Edward. "SEAPRINT: A Computerized Regional Bibliography Project." In *Congress of Southeast Asian Libraries (6th, 1983. Singapore). The Library in the Information Revolution: Proceedings of the Sixth Conference of Southeast Asian Librarians, Singapore, 30 May-3 June 1983*, pp. 244-258. Singapore: Maruzen Asia, 1983.

Lim Huck Tee, Edward. "The SEAPRINT Pilot Project." *IFLA Journal* 12 (no. 4 1986):347-349.

Cambodia

Henchy, Judith A.N. "Extracts from a Field Trip Report to Vietnam, Laos, and Kampuchea by the Archivist of the William Joiner Center for the Study of War and Social Consequences. University of Massachusetts at Boston." *South-east Asia Library Group Newsletter* 33 (1989):9-14.

Jarvis, Helen. "Restoring the Bibliographic Heritage of Vietnam and Cambodia." *International Cataloguing and Bibliographic Control* 22 (no. 3 July/Sept. 1993):42-45.

India

Downing, Joel. "The Indian National Bibliography - Its Present State and Future Prospects." *Library Resources & Technical Services* 28 (January/March 1984):20-24.

Downing, Joel. "Reorganization of the Indian National Bibliography." *SALG Newsletter* 22 (June 1983):1-4.

Govi, K.M. "The Genesis and Growth of India's National Bibliography." *Libri* 27 (no. 2 1977):165-174.

The Indian National Bibliography, 1958-1992. Calcutta: Granthalaya Pvt. Ltd. for Govt. of India, 1992. [pamphlet]

Nagaraj, M.N. "Indian National Bibliography." In IFLA Worldwide Seminar (1976. Seoul, Korea). *Proceedings of IFLA Worldwide Seminar, May 31-June 5, 1976*, pp. 441-442. Seoul, Korea: Korean Library Association, 1976.

Viswanathan, C.G. "What Ails the Indian National Bibliography?" *Library Association Record* 81 (July 1979):333.

Indonesia

Prakoso, M. Hardjo. "The Development of National Bibliographies in Indonesia." *International Cataloguing* 10 (July 1981):35-36.

Rachmananta, Dady P. "Bibliographic Standards of Indonesia: Implementation and Progress." In Congress of Southeast Asian Librarians (6th, 1983. Singapore). *The Library in the Information Revolution: Proceedings of the Sixth Conference of Southeast Asian Librarians, Singapore, 30 May-3 June 1983*, pp. 171-178. Singapore: Maruzen Asia, 1983.

Tairas, J.N.B., and Kertosedono, S. "National Bibliographic Control in Indonesia." *International Cataloguing* 6 (October 1977):47-48.

Laos

Henchy, Judith A.N. "Extracts from a Field Trip Report to Vietnam, Laos, and Kampuchea by the Archivist of the William Joiner Center for the Study of War and Social Consequences. University of Massachusetts at Boston." *South-east Asia Library Group Newsletter* 33 (1989):9-14.

Khamsing Sundara. "The Present State of National Bibliographical Control in Laos." In Conference on Universal Bibliographical Control in Southeast Asia (1975. Singapore). *Conference on Universal Bibliographical Control in Southeast Asia, held at the Regional English Language Centre, Singapore, 21-23 February 1975: Papers and Proceedings,* pp. 43-45. Edited by Hedwig Anuar, Yolanda Beh, Lim Hong Too, Quah Swee Lan. Singapore: Library Association of Singapore, 1975.

Phonthipasa, B. ["Prerequisites of creation, contemporary state and perspectives of development of the National Bibliography of Laos People's Democratic Republic."] In [National bibliography, Publishing activity and Librarianship in the countries of Asia and Africa.] St. Petersburg : Library of Russian Academy of Sciences, 1992. pp. 89-103. In Russian.

Thammachak, Bounleuth. "Reports on Implementing the National Bibliography Project 1975-1990." *IFLA/RSAO Newsletter* 8 (no. 2 Dec. 1996):11-13.

Malaysia

Kadir, Mariam Abdul. "ISBD: A Review of its Application in the Malaysian National Bibliography." *International Cataloguing* 10 (April/June 1981):22-24.

Kadir, Mariam Abdul. "National Bibliography of Malaysia: Problems and Prospects." In Conference on National and Academic Libraries in Malaysia and Singapore (1974. Universiti Sains Malaysia). *National and Academic Libraries in Malaysia and Singapore: Proceedings of a PPM and LAS Conference held at Universiti Sains Malaysia, Penang, 1-3 March 1974*, pp. 77-82. Edited by Lim Huck Tee and Rashidah Begum. Penang: Persatuan Perpustakaan Malaysia, 1975.

Khoo Cheng Yee. "Bibliographical Control of Government Publications in Malaysia." In Conference on National and Academic Libraries in Malaysia and Singapore (1974. Universiti

Sains Malaysia). *National and Academic Libraries in Malaysia and Singapore: Proceedings of a PPM and LAS Conference Held at Universiti Sains Malaysia, Penang, 1-3 March 1974*, pp. 69-76. Edited by Lim Huck Tee and Rashidah Begum. Penang: Persatuan Perpustakaan Malaysia, 1975.

Noor, Norpishah Mohd. "Bibliographical Standards: Evaluation of their Implementation in Malaysia." In Congress of Southeast Asian Librarians (6th, 1983. Singapore). *The Library in the Information Revolution: Proceedings of the Sixth Conference of Southeast Asian Librarians, Singapore, 30 May-3 June 1983*, pp. 179-185. Singapore: Maruzen Asia, 1983.

Wijasuriya, D.E.K. "National Bibliographic Systems: A Review of Arrangement in Relation to Malaysia." In Conference on Universal Bibliographical Control in Southeast Asia (1975. Singapore). *Conference on Universal Bibliographical Control in Southeast Asia, held at the Regional English Language Centre, Singapore, 21-23 February 1975: Papers and Proceedings*, pp. 47-52. Edited by Hedwig Anuar, Yolanda Beh, Lim Hong Too, Quah Swee Lan. Singapore: Library Association of Singapore, 1975.

Wijasuriya, D.E.K. "Resource Sharing: Existing Arrangements and Future Developments: Malaysia." *International Library Review* 12 (April 1980):137-149.

Nepal

Jacob, Louis A. "Nepalese Bibliography Now Available." *Library of Congress Information Bulletin* 42 (October 3, 1983):340.

Pakistan

Mohammadally, R. "Bibliographical Control in Pakistan." *International Library Review* 18 (January 1986):33-56.

Philippines

Dayrit, Marina G. "Philippine Bibliographical Control: Present State and Prospects for UBC." In Conference on Universal Bibliographical Control in Southeast Asia (1975. Singapore). *Conference on Universal Bibliographical Control in Southeast Asia, held at the Regional English Language Centre, Singapore, 21-23 February 1975: Papers and Proceedings*, pp. 53-74. Edited by Hedwig Anuar, Yolanda Beh, Lim Hong Too, Quah Swee Lan. Singapore: Library Association of Singapore, 1975.

Orbase, Lily O. "Implementation of Bibliographical Standards in the Philippines." In Congress of Southeast Asian Librarians (6th, 1983. Singapore). *The Library in the Information Revolution: Proceedings of the Sixth Conference of Southeast Asian Librarians, Singapore, 30 May-3 June 1983*, pp. 186-190. Singapore: Maruzen Asia, 1983.

Singapore

Chan, Luck. "The Implementation of Bibliographical Standards in Singapore Libraries: A Country Report." In Congress of Southeast Asian Librarians (6th, 1983. Singapore). *The*

Library in the Information Revolution: Proceedings of the Sixth Congress of Southeast Asian Librarians, Singapore, 30 May-3 June 1983, pp. 191-197. Singapore: Maruzen Asia, 1983.

Khoo, George. "The Singapore National Bibliography." *Singapore Libraries* 1 (1971):55-57.

Kularatne, E.D.T. "Producing a National Bibliography for Multi-Language Multi-Script Publications: An Analysis of Existing Practices." In *I*FLA Worldwide Seminar (1976. Seoul, Korea). *Proceedings of IFLA Worldwide Seminar, May 31-June 5, 1976*, pp. 228-233. Seoul, Korea: Korean Library Association, 1976.

Lee, Judy. "The Singapore National Bibliography and Universal Bibliographic Control." In Conference on Universal Bibliographical Control in Southeast Asia (1975. Singapore). *Conference on Universal Bibliographical Control in Southeast Asia, held at the Regional English Language Centre, Singapore, 21-23 February 1975: Papers and Proceedings*, pp. 115-126. Edited by Hedwig Anuar, Yolanda Beh, Lim Hong Too, Quah Swee Lan. Singapore: Library Association of Singapore, 1975.

Lee, Judy. "The Singapore National Bibliography: Problems and Prospects." In Conference on National and Academic Libraries in Malaysia and Singapore (1974. Universiti Sains Malaysia). *National and Academic Libraries in Malaysia and Singapore: Proceedings of a PPM and LAS Conference Held at Universiti Sains Malaysia, Penang, 1-3 March 1974*, pp. 83-93. Edited by Lim Huck Tee and Rashidah Begum. Penang: Persatuan Perpustakaan Malaysia, 1975.

Wicks, Yoke-Lan. "Official Publications in Singapore." *Singapore Libraries* 10 (1980):25-29.

Sri Lanka

Senadeera, Aryaratne. "A National Bibliography for Sri Lanka." In *Libraries and People: Colombo Public Library 1925-1975, a Commemorative Volume*, pp. 107-111. Edited by I. Corea. Columbo: Municipal Council of Columbo, 1975.

Thailand

Kaesri, Songuit. "Bibliographical Services and Control in Thailand." In Conference on Universal Bibliographical Control in Southeast Asia (1975. Singapore). *Conference on Universal Bibliographical Control in Southeast Asia, held at the Regional English Language Centre, Singapore, 21-23 February 1975: Papers and Proceedings*, pp. 95-113. Edited by Hedwig Anuar, Yolanda Beh, Lim Hong Too, Quah Swee Lan. Singapore: Library Association of Singapore, 1975.

Phadungath, Suwakhon. "Bibliographical Standards: Evaluation of their Implementation in Thailand." In Congress of Southeast Asian Librarians (6th, 1983. Singapore). *The Library in the Information Revolution: Proceedings of the Sixth Congress of Southeast Asian Librarians, Singapore, 30 May-3 June 1983*, pp. 199-209. Singapore: Maruzen Asia, 1983.

Vietnam

Henchy, Judith A.N. "Extracts from a Field Trip Report to Vietnam, Laos, and Kampuchea by the Archivist of the William Joiner Center for the Study of War and Social Consequences.

University of Massachusetts at Boston." *South-east Asia Library Group Newsletter* 33 (1989):9-14.

Jarvis, Helen. "Restoring the Bibliographic Heritage of Vietnam and Cambodia." *International Cataloguing and Bibliographic Control* 22 (no. 3 July/Sept. 1993):42-45.

WESTERN EUROPE

General

Jefcoate, Graham. "Gabriel. Gateway to Europe's National Libraries." *Program* 30 (no. 3 July 1996):229-238.

Guide to Nordic Bibliography. / Erland Munch-Petersen, General Editor. Kobenhavn : Nord, 1984.

Guide to Nordic Bibliography. Suppl. 1, 1983-1986 / Erland Munch-Petersen, General Editor. Ballerup: Dansk BiblioteksCenter, 1988.

Guide to Nordic Bibliography. Suppl. 2, 1987-1990 / Erland Munch-Petersen, General Editor. Ballerup: Dansk BiblioteksCenter, 1992.

Sciberras, Lillian. "Some Problems Facing the Current National Bibliography in Mediterranean Countries." *Libri* 37 (No. 4 1987):279-293.

Smith, Robert. "National Libraries Project on CD-ROM." *Select 11* (winter 1993):7-9.

Austria

Schonberger, V. "50 Jahre Österreichische Bibliographie." *Biblios* 45(1 1996):159-169.

Belgium

Goedemé, G., and Vanderpijpen, W. "De Geautomatiseerde Belgische Bibliografie op Weg Naar Meer Volwassenheid." *Bibliotheekgids* 57 (July/December 1981):181-187.

Lefevre, Marc. "La Bibliographie de Belgique." *IFLA Journal* 3 (no. 1 1977):56-61.

Denmark

Clausen, H. "The Business of National Bibliography: An Example of Co-operation between Public and Private Institutions." *Business Information Review* 14 (1 Mar. 1997):27-35.

Madsen, Mona. *Nationalbibliografi, Formål og Funktion--Med en Oversigt over Dansk National Bibliografi.* Kongelige Danmarks Biblioteksskole, 1994.

Optagelseskriterier for Dansk Bogfortegnelse og Dansk Periodicafortegnelse. 4 udg. Ballerup : Dansk BiblioteksCenter, 1995.

Waneck, Kirsten. *The Danish National Bibliography* (May 28, 1996). Translation of the Danish BiblioteksCenter's annual report to the Danish National Library Authority.

Waneck, Kirsten. "Public/Private Sector Relationships in the Production of National Bibliographies: The Danish Model." Paper given at 63rd IFLA General Conference, Copenhagen, 3 Sept. 1997 (100-BIBL-1-E).

Waneck, Kirsten. "The Role of the National Bibliographic Agency." In *ISBN Review* 15 (1994).

Finland

Forsman, Maria. "The Finnish National Bibliography." In *Guide to Nordic Bibliography. Suppl. 1 (1983-1986)*, pp. 23-27.

Häkli, Esko. "A Finn Koenyvtari-informacios Rendszer es Informacios Politika. Tervezes, Iranyitas, Finanszirozas." [The Finnish Library and Information System and Information Policy: Planning, Administration and Financing] *Tuudomanyos es Mueszaki Tajekoztatas* 38 (7 July 1991):263-266.

Häkli, Esko. "Das Finnische Nationalbibliographische System." *Informationsmittel für Bibliotheken (IFB)* 1994:492-500. (Besprechungsdienst und Berichte 2). This is an article in a Festschrift for Professor Häkli.

Häkli, Esko. "Helsinki University Library- The National Library of Finland." *Alexandria* 2 (1 1990):29-39. See especially "Bibliographic Activities" and "Automation."

Karstu, Eeva-Marjatta. "The National Bibliography of Finland." In *Guide to Nordic Bibliography*, pp. 43-45.

Murtomaa, Eeva. "Fennica CD-ROM." *Kirjastolehti* 83 (no. 5 1990):205-207.

Schauman, Henrik, and Puttonen, Kaarina. "Finland." In *Official Publications of Western Europe, vol. 1,* pp. 27-43. Edited by Eve Johansson. London: Mansell, 1984.

Selleck, Roberta. "The Scandinavian National Bibliographies as Tools for Research and Book Selection." *Collection Management* 6 (spring/summer 1984):125-134.

Soini, Antti. "Den Finländska Nationalbibliografin och dess Automatisering." *Nordisk Tidskrift för Bok-och Biblioteksväsen* 66 (no. 3 1979):73-77.

Suhonen, Irja-Leena. "Kansallisbibliografian Kansalliset ja Kansainvaliset Tehtavat. National and International Duties of a National Bibliography." *Signum* 27(2 1994):36-39.

France

"Automation of the Official Part of *Bibliographie de la France.*" *Unesco Bulletin for Libraries* 29 (July 1975):231.

Bernard, Annick. "Le Point sur la Bibliographie Nationale Française." *Bulletin d' informations de l'Association des bibliothècaires Française* 148 (1990):54-56.

Chauveinc, Marc. "Library Automation in France." *Libri* 25 (no. 1 1975):48-74.

Seckel, Raymond Josué. "French National Bibliography." Translated from French by Mildred S. Myers. In *Encyclopedia of Library and Information Science*, vol. 37, suppl. 2, pp. 138-156. Edited by Allen Kent. New York and Basel: Marcel Dekker, Inc., 1984.
Germany

"Deutsche Bibliographie." *Börsenblatt für den Deutschen Buchhandel* 40 (6 July 1984):1627-1630.

Die Deutsche Bibliotek. *Deutsche Nationalbibliographie = German National Bibliography*. Frankfurt : Buchhändler-Vereinigung [1997].

"Die Neukonzeption der Deutschen Bibliographie in Gedruckter Form." *Bibliotheksdienst* 18 (no. 5 1984):528-534.

Lehmann, K-D. "Die Deutche Bibliothek : Germany's National Library and National Bibliographic Agency." *Alexandria* 5 (3 1993), pp. 161-174.

Wolf, Dieter. "Different Outputs and Possible By-products of Automated National Bibliographies, as illustrated by the Deutsche Bibliothek." *International Cataloguing* 14 (April/June 1985):22-24.

Wolf, Dieter. "3. The National Bibliography: Deutsche Bibliographie." In "Cataloguing and Bibliographic Development in the Federal Republic of Germany." *International Cataloguing* 12 (July/September 1983):30-31.

Greece

Bokos, George. "National Library of Greece: Automation and Choice of Format." *International Cataloguing and Bibliographic Control* 21:2 (April/June 1992):24-28.

Iceland

Hannesdóttir, Sigrún Klara. "The National Bibliography of Iceland." In *Guide to Nordic Bibliography*, pp. 34-36.

Ireland

Peare, J.D. Trevor; McKenna, Brian; Cullen, Clara, "Producing the *Irish Publishing Record* at the National Library of Ireland," *Program* 26 (no. 3 July 1992):271-278.

Italy

Alberani, Vima. "Italy." In *Official Publications of Western Europe*, vol. 1, pp. 107-149. Edited by Eve Johansson. London: Mansell, 1984.

Borghetti Marzulli, L. "L'ISBD e la Normalizzazione della Descrizione Bibliografica." *Associazione Italiana Biblioteche Bollettino d'Informazioni* 22 (July/December 1982):25-53.
Farfara, Fulvia. "L'Automazione della Bibliografia Nazionale Italiana." *Associazione Italiana Biblioteche Bollettino d'Informazioni* 15 (April 1975):157-158.

Martinucci, Andrea. "La Nuova BNI." *Bollettino AIB* 34 (no. 4 Dic. 1994):449-452.

Peruginelli, S. "Il Controllo Bibliografico Universale: Situazione a Livello Internazionale e Prospettive nella Costituzione del Sistema Bibliografico Nazionale Italiano." *Associazione Italiana Biblioteche Bollettino d'Informazioni* 22 (July/December 1982):13-24.

Peruginelli, Susanna. "Role and Function of the National Bibliography in the Italian System (SNB: Servizio Bibliotecario Nazionale)." In *Bibliographic Access in Europe: first International Conference: The Proceedings of a Conference Organised by the Centre for Bibliographic Management and held at the University of Bath 14-17 September 1989.* Lorcan Dempsey, ed. Aldershot, England: Gower, 1990. pp. 125-127.

Malta

Bibliography '84: Papers and Proceedings of a COMLA Regional Workshop, Msida, Malta, 13-16 November 1984. Edited by Paul Xuereb. Valletta, Malta: Ghaqda Bibljotekarji, 1985.

Sciberras, Lillian. "The *Malta National Bibliography*: Headings and Descriptive Cataloguing, Problems and Solutions." *International Cataloguing* 14 (January/March 1985):11-12.

Sciberras, Lillian. "The *Malta National Bibliography*" In *A Marketing Tool for the Information Industry.* London : University of London, 1986.

Netherlands

Heijligers, A., and Owen, J. Mackenzie. "Bibliographic Control in the Netherlands." Based on a paper by A.L. van Wesemael. In Western European Seminar on the Interchange of Bibliographic Information in Machine Readable Form (1974. Banbury, England). *The Interchange of Bibliographic Information in Machine Readable Form. Papers given at the Western European Seminar on the Interchange of Bibliographic Information in Machine Readable Form held at Banbury, England, 12-16 May 1974.* Sponsored by the British Council, the British Library and the Library Association. Edited by R.E. Coward and M. Yelland. London: The Library Association, 1975.

Maanen, A. van and Willemsen, A.W. "Cataloguing-in-Publication in the Netherlands." Background paper number 8. In International Cataloguing- n -Publication Meeting (1982. Ottawa, Ontario). *Proceedings of the International Cataloguing-in-Publication Meeting Ottawa, 16-19 August 1982.* Organized by IFLA in association with Unesco. Edited by the IFLA International Office for UBC. London: IFLA International Office for UBC, 1983.

Schiltman, Maria J., Schwarz-Blokhuis, T.H.H., and Voogt, L. "Netherlands." In *Official Publications of Western Europe*, vol. 1, pp. 163-182. Edited by Eve Johansson. London: Mansell, 1984.

Norway

Engelstad, Kirsten. "Frå Informasjon til Kulturarv." *Synopsis* 15 (February 1984):5-7.

Holm-Olsen, Anne Grete. "Den Nasjonalbibliografiske Situasjon: Fremtidsplan og Prioritering for det Nasjonalbibliografiske Arbeid." *Bok og Bibliotek* 47 (no. 2 1980):104-106.

Langballe, Anne M.H. "Nytt om de nasjonalbibliografiske produktene." *Bok og bibliotek* 1994, no. 2:23.

"Legal Deposit in Norway." *International Cataloguing* 13 (July/September 1984):26.

MARCposten : informasjon fra Bibliografisk avdeling, Universitetsbiblioteket i Oslo (1984, no. 1- , ISSN 0800-9767, usually two numbers a year) regularly gives information on the national bibliography.

Rugaas, Bendik. "Developing a New National Library in Norway." *Alexandria* 2 (1 1990):41-49.

Portugal

Cabral, Maria Luísa. "The modernization of Portuguese libraries: five decisive years." *Program* (Belfast, Northern Ireland) 26 (no. 3, 1992):249-258.

Campos, Fernanda Maria Guedes de ; Lopes, Maria Inês. "Biblioteca National: automation activities: progress report 1992." In Library Systems Seminar (17, 1993, Graz, Austria). *Library Systems Seminar: the virtual library*, pp. 98-101. Graz: Universitatsbibliothek der Karl-Franzens Universita, 1993.

Campos, Fernanda Maria Guedes de ; Lopes, Maria Inês. "Biblioteca Nacional: automation activities: progress report 1993. In Library Systems Seminar (18, 1993, Budapest). *Library Systems Seminar: library services in an electronic environment*, pp. 105-107. Budapest: National Széchényi Library, 1994.

Lopes, Maria Inês. "Base Nacional de Dados Bibliográficos- PORBASE." *Revista da Biblioteca Nacional* (S. 2) 9 (no. 2, Jul.-Dez. 1994):165-184.

Lopes, Maria Inês. "Base Nacional de Dados Bibliográficos- PORBASE." *Revista da Biblioteca Nacional* (S. 2) 10 (no. 1-2, Jan.-Dez. 1995):266-271.

Sweden

Antonsson, Birgit. "Kungliga Biblioteket – Sveriges Nationalbibliotek. Nu och i Framtiden."[The Royal Library–Sweden's National Library. Now and in the Future] *DF– Revy* 14 (1 1991):3-5.

Antonsson, Birgit. "The Royal Library – National Library of Sweden." *Alexandria* 2 (2 1990): 39-49. See especially pp. 41-43.

Cantwell, Ingrid. "The Swedish Bibliographic Scene." *International Cataloguing andBibliographic Control* 19 (2 1990):19-22.

Guthartz, Catharina and Norman Guthartz. "The National Bibliography of Sweden." In *Guide to Nordic Bibliography*, pp. 37-42.

Larsson, Gunilla. *The Swedish National Bibliography: A Survey*. Stockholm : Royal Library, 1990.
Sandgren, Folke. "Den Svenska National Bibliografin." *Bok og Bibliotek* 47 (no. 3 1980):194-195, 216.

Selleck, Roberta G. "The Scandinavian National Bibliographies as Tools for Research and Book Selection." *Collection Management* 6 (Spring/Summer 1984):125-134.

Vokac, Libena. "Svensk Nasjonalbibliografi." *Synopsis* 15 (February 1984):26-27.

United Kingdom

Cameron, Sheila H.M. "Compiling a National Bibliography." *Scottish Library Association News* 156 (March/April 1980):53-56.

Croucher, Margaret. "The British National Bibliography. An Historical Perspective." In *Standards for the International Exchange of Bibliographic Information. Papers presented at a course held at the School of Library, Archive and Information Studies, University College London, 3-18 August 1990.* Edited by I.C. McIlwaine. London: The Library Association, 1991.

The Future of the National Bibliography. Proceedings of a Seminar held by the British Library in June 1997. London : British Library, 1997. (forthcoming).

Mowat, Ian R.M. "Regional or National? The Aims of the Bibliography of Scotland." *Catalogue & Index* 49 (Summer 1978):5, 8.

Stephens, Andy. *The History of the British National Bibliography, 1950-1973. A Catalogue of achievement.* Boston Spa, Wetherby, West Yorkshire : 1994.

APPENDIX

International Congress on National Bibliographies
Unesco
September 1977

Recommendations[1]

The International Congress on National Bibliographies, held at Unesco from 12 to 15 September 1977,

Endorsing the concept of Universal Bibliographic Control (UBC) as a long-term programme for the development of a world-wide system for the control and exchange of bibliographic information,

Emphasizing the need to strengthen national bibliographic control as a prerequisite for universal bibliographic control,

Recognizing the importance of the national bibliography as a major instrument in ensuring national bibliographic control,

Makes the following recommendations:

Legal deposit

1. Member States should examine existing deposit legislation and consider their provisions in relation to present and future requirements in order to develop and maintain national bibliographic control; and, where necessary, existing legislation should be revised;

2. Member States currently without legal deposit should examine the possibilities of its introduction as a means of strengthening national bibliographic control;

3. New deposit laws, or regulations pursuant to such laws, should state the objective of legal deposit in relation to the national bibliography; should ensure that the deposit of copies is relevant to the requirements of the national library system; should be comprehensive in terminology and wording to include existing types of materials with information content and others which may be developed; and should include measures for enforcement of the laws;

4. Unesco should draft model legislation which would serve as a basis for Member States in attaining national bibliographic control, and which would take into account the relationship between copyright and legal deposit;

---

[1] Permission to include the International Congress on National Bibliographies "Recommendations" as they appear in the ICNB. *Final Report* was kindly given by Mr. Philippe Queau, Director of the Information and Informatics Division, Unesco.

The selection of materials for the national bibliography

5. National bibliographies, as a minimum, should include the records for monographs and first issues and title changes of serials, including official publications, of the national imprint; and other categories of materials should be included as rapidly as possible to meet the requirements of the national library community and the resources of the national bibliographic agency. When national bibliographic agencies for linguistic, cultural or other reasons include records for publications clearly not part of the national imprint, such records should be identified as not belonging to the national imprint;

6. The national bibliography should include records for materials in all the languages and/or scripts in which publications are produced within a country; and wherever possible these records should be in the languages and/or scripts in which the publications originally appeared;

7. Further study should be undertaken to define additional categories of materials and to suggest priorities for their inclusion in the national bibliography;

The presentation and frequency of the printed national bibliography

8. The printed national bibliography should appear as a minimum quarterly with at least annual cumulations;

9. Each printed issue should conform to the following:

use of an international paper size (recommended A 4);

clear and unambiguous layout and typography of cover and/or title page to include:

title of the bibliography;

the period which the issue covers;

place of publication;

name of publisher;

date of publication;

ISSN in top right-hand corner

verso of title page to include:

copyright information;

cataloguing-in-publication entry;

details of availability, price, details of printing;

introduction (in each quarterly issue at least);

main body of text;

indices (cumulated annually) covering complementary arrangements to that of main text;

10. In the introduction should be included details stating:

the basis for the records, for example, records made from copies deposited in the national library in accordance with legal deposit stipulations;

coverage, including exceptions;

frequency;

arrangement;

bibliographic and cataloguing tools used;

list of special terms used, with definitions and abbreviations;

outline of classified arrangement (if used);

outline of transliteration schemes (if used);

description of filing system;

11. The current issues of the printed national bibliography should be arranged in a classified order in accordance with a stated internationally-used classification scheme and the arrangement of cumulations should be decided at the discretion of the national bibliographic agency;

Catalogue cards

12. A study should be undertaken of the extent of production of catalogue cards by national bibliographic agencies and their use internationally; and an examination should be made of the desirability of establishing an international standard for the physical form of the card;

Contents of the bibliographic record

13. The national bibliographic agency should undertake responsibility for preparing the comprehensive bibliographic records of its national imprint and in so doing follow international cataloguing principles and adopt international bibliographic standards, specifically the ISBDs; and international numbering systems such as ISBN or ISSN; should maintain an authority control system for national names, personal and corporate, and uniform titles, in accordance with international guidelines; and should consider the adoption of an internationally-used classification scheme for the records;

14. The national bibliographic agency, in anticipation of the introduction of new cataloguing rules, descriptive practices, or subject approaches, should ensure that training courses are

provided within the country to familiarize the national library community with the new practices;

15. Specific projects to promote international bibliographic standards and guidelines should be undertaken for authority control applicable to both manual and mechanized systems; abbreviated and minimum records as required, e.g. for CIP;

Publications of intergovernmental and international non-governmental organizations

16. Intergovernmental and international non-governmental organizations should introduce cataloguing-in-publication schemes in accordance with international bibliographic standards;

17. Intergovernmental organizations should co-operate in a joint effort to produce a current bibliography of all their publications;

Information systems

18. Studies should be made of the utilization of records produced for national bibliographies as national input to information systems, and vice versa;

19. Greater efforts at national and international levels should be made to ensure compatibility between the bibliographic exchange formats of the library and information communities;

The International Serials Data System (ISDS)

20. Member States should establish national and/or regional centres for ISDS, if possible within the national bibliographic agency;

21. A study should be made of the interrelationship of the ISDS register and the serial records of national bibliographies and the results should be taken into account in the revision of the *ISDS Guidelines*;

Resource sharing

22. Studies should be made into issuing multinational bibliographies in areas where for any reason it is not feasible at present to publish national bibliographies and/or where there are some geographical, linguistic or cultural links;

23. Unesco and other appropriate institutions should be asked to assist in the establishment of pilot schemes for national bibliographic agencies, or in the production of national bibliographies, and in the organization of national, regional or international seminars and training workshops for these.